D1564414

LORE

LORE

An Introduction
to the Science of Folklore
and Literature

MUNRO S. EDMONSON
Tulane University

HOLT, RINEHART AND WINSTON, INC.
New York   Chicago   San Francisco   Atlanta
Dallas   Montreal   Toronto   London   Sydney

Acknowledgments

The author wishes to thank the following copyright holders for permission to reprint extracts from their listed works:

American Anthropological Association and the author for "The Autobiography of a Papago Woman," by Ruth Underhill. *Memoirs of the American Anthropological Association*, 46.

American Folklore Society and the authors for "Playing the Dozens," by Roger D. Abrahams; "Meter in Eastern Carolinian Oral Literature," by J. L. Fischer; "The Vseslav Epos," by Roman Jacobson and Marc Szeftel; "Myths of the Toba and Pilagá Indians of the Gran Chaco," by Alfred Métraux; "Seeking Life," by Vera Laski; "New Evidence of American Indian Riddles," by Charles T. Scott; "Albanian and South Slavic Oral Epic Poetry," by Stavro Skendi; "The Ossetian Tale of Iry Dada," by George Vernadsky and Dzambulat Dzanty.

Anthropos-Institut and the authors for "La Fête National du Fandroana en Imerina (Madagascar)," by Soury-Laverge and De la Devèze, Anthropos, 8.

Asia Sociey and the author for *The Burman, His Life and Notions*, by Shway Yoe. Published by W. W. Norton and Co., Inc.

Ernest Benn Limited and the author for *The Lango: A Nilotic Tribe of Uganda*, by J. H. Driberg.

William Blackwood and Sons, Ltd. and Mentor Books for *The Dark Ages*, by W. P. Ker.

Bishop Museum Press for "Songs of Uvea and Futuna" by Edwin Grant Burrows; for "Tales and Poems of Tonga" by E. E. V. Collocott.

Clarendon Press, Oxford, and the authors for *Aboriginal Siberia: A Study in Social Anthropology*, by M. A. Czaplicka; *Dictionary of Modern English Usage*, by H. W. Fowler; *Babylonian Wisdom Literature*, by W. G. Lambert; *The Lore and Language of Children*, by Iona and Peter Opie.

Commonwealth Press and the author for *Fitzgerald's Omar Khayyam with Persian Text*, by Eben F. Thompson.

Condominas, Georges, for *Nous avons mangé la Forêt*.

Doubleday & Company for *An Introduction to Haiku*, by Harold G. Henderson. Copyright © 1958 by Harold G. Henderson. Reprinted by permission of Doubleday & Company, Inc.

Dublin Institute for Advanced Studies for *Lectures on Early Welsh Poetry*, by Ifor Williams.

Duke University Press for *The Oral Art and Literature of the Kazakhs of Russian Central Asia* by Thomas G. Winner.

E. P. Dutton and Company for *Everyman and Other Interludes*; *History of the Kings of Britain* by Geoffrey of Monmouth; *Kalevala*, translated by William F. Kirby; *The Manners and Customs of the Modern Egyptians*, by E. W. Lane.

Ediciones Siglo Veinte and the author for *Folklore y Psicoanalysis*, by Paulo de Carvalho Neto.

Editions Gallimard for *Trésor de la Poésie Universelle* by Roger Caillois and Jean-Clarence Lambert. © Editions Gallimard 1959.

Editorial Sucre and the author for *Warao Oral Literature* by Johannes Wilbert.

The John Das Company, Inc., for *The Winged Serpent* edited by Margot Astrov. Copyright © 1946 by Margot Astrov.

Ethnohistory and the author for "Butterfly's Mandan Winter Count," by James H. Howard.

Ethnology and the authors for "Mossi Joking," by Peter B. Hammond. *Ethology*, 3. "Cultural Anthropology and the Cuneiform Documents," by S. N. Kramer. *Ethnology*, 1.

Exposition Press Inc., and the author for *Tales of Mullah Nasir-ud-Din*, by Eric Daenecke.

Faber and Faber Limited for *The Sacred State of the Akan* and *The Akan of Ghana: Their Ancient Beliefs*, both by Eva L. R. Meyerowitz. Reprinted by permission of Faber and Faber Ltd.

Grove Press, Inc., and the authors for *Japanese Literature: An Introduction for Western Readers*, by Donald Keene. Copyright © 1955 by Donald Keene; *The Nō Plays of Japan*, by Arthur Waley. Published by Grove Press, Inc.

Harper and Row, Publishers, for *A Black Civilization* (passage adapted), by W. Lloyd Warner. Poem "The Beginnings of Civilization" by Sir Leonard Wooley in *History of Mankind*, Vol. I, by Jacquetta Hawkes and Sir Leonard Wooley. By permission of Harper & Row, Publishers, and George Allen & Unwin, Ltd.

George C. Harrap and Company, Ltd., and the author for *The Heath Anthology of Spanish Poetry*, by Janet H. Perry.

John F. Goins, for *Huaxculi: The Quichua of the Cochabamba Valley, Bolivia*.

Harvard University Press and the authors for *Mandarin Primer*, by Yuen Ren Chao; *The Bhagavad Gītā: Part I: Text and Translation*, by Franklin Edgerton; *Music in Primitive Culture*, by Bruno Nettl.

Hill and Wang, Inc. and the authors for *The Origin of the Theatre*, by Benjamin Hunningher. Introduction to Jean Giraudoux *Four Plays*, by Maurice Valency.

Hooykaas, C. for *The Lay of Jaya Prana: The Balinese Uriah.*

Houghton Mifflin Company and the authors for *The Navajo Indians,* by Dane and Mary R. Coolidge.

Humanities Press, Routledge and Kegan Paul, and the author, for "Traditional Literature," by G. P. Lestrade. In J. Schapera, ed., *Bantu Tribes of South Africa.* Copyright Routledge and Kegan Paul.

Institut d'Ethnologie and the author for "Récits Bara," by Jacques Faublée. *Travaux et Mémoires de l'Institut d'Ethnologie.*

International African Institute and the author for "!Kung Bushman Religious Beliefs," by Lorna Marshall. *Africa,* 32.

Librairie Bloud & Gay for *Les Pygmées de la Forêt Équatoriale* by R. P. Trilles

Librairie Orientaliste Paul Guenthner and the author for *Religions, Moeurs et Coutumes des Agnis de la Côte d'Ivoire,* by L. Tauxier.

Librairie Plon for *Le Cru et le Cuit.* by Claude Lévi-Strauss.

Little, Brown and Company for "Oh, Please Don't Get Up," by Ogden Nash. *Verses from 1929 On.* Copyright 1935 by Ogden Nash.

Macmillan and Co. Ltd. for *Al-Akida and Fort Jesus,* by Mbarak Ali Hinawy.

The M.I.T. Press and the author for *Style in Language,* by Thomas A. Sebeok.

Melbourne University Press for *Aranda Traditions,* by T. G. H. Strehlow.

Mentor Press for *The Papal Encyclicals in their Historical Context,* edited by Anne Fremantle; *The Sayings of Chuang Chou,* translated by James R. Ware.

Mouton & Co. n.v., for Yuen Ren Chao's "Tone, Intonation, Singsong, Chanting, Recitative, Tonal Composition and Atonal Composition in Chinese," in *For Roman Jacobson* by Morris Halle *et al.*

John Murray, Publishers, and the author for *The Message of Milarepa,* by Humphrey Clarke in the series *Wisdom of the East.*

Museum of the American Indian, Heye Foundation, for "Medicine Ceremony of the Menominee, Iowa and Wahpeton," by Alanson B. Skinner. *Indian Notes and Monographs.*

New American Library of World Literature, Inc. and the estate of Dudley Fitts for "Eight Poems by Martial," translated by Dudley Fitts. *New World Writing.* Copyright © 1956 by New American Library of World Literature, Inc.

New Directions Publishing Corporation for "Blood Wedding" by Federico García Lorca, *Three Tragedies.* Translated by James Graham-Luján and Richard L. O'Connell. Copyright 1941 by Charles Scribner's Sons, Copyright 1947 by New Directions Publishing Corporation.

Oxford University Press and the author for *Burmese Drama,* by Muang Htin Aung.

Penguin Books, Ltd. for *The Penguin Book of Chinese Verse,* by Robert Kotewall and Norman L. Smith. Copyright © 1962; *The Hittites,* by O. R. Gurney; *Buddist Scriptures,* by Edward Conze; *Sacred Books of the World,* by A. C. Bouquet; *The Epic of Gilgamesh,* by K. N. Sandars.

Philosophical Library, Inc., for *Djanggauwul,* by R. M. Berndt; *Encyclopedia of Literature,* by Joseph T. Shipley.

Routledge & Kegan Paul Ltd. for *The Malays: A Cultural History* by Richard Winstedt.

St. Gabriel Verlag and the author for *Die Negrito Asiens,* by Paul Schebesta.

Shimkin, Dmitri for "Wind River Shoshone Literary Forms." *Journal of the Washington Academy of Sciences.*

Smithsonian Institution Press and the authors for "The Alacaluf," by Junius Bird. *Handbook of South American Indians;* "Nootka and Quileute Music," by Frances Densmore. *Bureau of American Ethnology Bulletin,* 124; "Songs and Stories of the Ch'uan Miao," by David Crockett Graham. *Smithsonian Miscellaneous Collection,* 123.

Southern Methodist University Press and the authors for *Walk in Your Soul: Love Incantations of the Oklahoma Cherokees*, by J. F. and A. G. Kilpatrick.

Franz Steiner Verlag and the author for *Mongolische Volksdichtung*, by Nikolaus Poppe.

Syracuse University Press and the author for *Riddles in Filipino Folklore: An Anthropological Analysis*, by Donn V. Hart.

The University of Chicago Press and the authors for *The Kumulipo: a Hawaiian Creation Chant*, by M. W. Beckwith; *Chinese Thought from Confucius to Mao Tse-tung*, by H. G. Creel (and permission of Curtis Brown, Ltd.); *The Peoples of Siberia*, by M. G. Levin and L. P. Potapor; *Wax and Gold: Tradition and Innovation in Ethiopian Culture*, by Donald N. Levine; *History of the Persian Empire*, by A. T. Olmsted.

The University of Nebraska Press and the author for *A Hundred Merry Tales*, edited by P. M. Zall.

University of Tennessee Press for *The Ballad of Heer Halewijn*, by Holger Olaf Nygard.

University of Washington Press for *Flower in My Ear: Arts and Ethos of Ifaluk Atoll*, by Edwin Grant Burrows.

P. L. Villanueva, S. A. for *Canciones y Cuentos del Pueblo Quechua*, published by Editorial Huascarán.

Wassén, S. Henry for Contributions to Cuna Ethnography. *Ethnologiska Studier*, 16.

Wayne State University Press and the author. Reprinted from *The Song of the Nibelungs*, by Frank G. Ryder. By permission of the Wayne State University Presss. Copyright © 1962 by Wayne State University Press.

Wenner-Gren Foundation and the author for "Ethiopic Documents: Gurage," by Wolf Leslau. *Viking Fund Publications in Anthropology, 14*.

Witwatersrand University Press and the author for *Korana Folktales*, by L. F. Maingard.

*for Evelyn, Ann,
and Sallie*

Preface

The intent of this book is to provide two kinds of perspective on the scientific study of literary materials. On the one hand, I have tried through sampling and selection to depict with clarity the enormous scope of "world literature" in space and time and to correct the narrow and myopic impression often created by the pretensions of modern Europeans to represent the ecumene. On the other hand, I have tried through analysis of a broad range of contexts and styles to attain a measure of synthesis of the somewhat disparate scientific theories bearing on literary structure.

My interest in this area of study springs from the conviction that the central problem blocking our progress in dealing scientifically with human culture is the problem presented by what I have here called "lore." I am persuaded that only a considerable reorientation of scientific method will enable us to deal adequately with this problem, and I would hope that this work may make some modest contribution to that end.

I must also confess to another motive, in a sense humanistic. It is my belief that our capacity as a species to solve our increasingly pressing problems of adaptation on this crowded planet is ultimately controlled by our capacity for understanding each other. And the point at which such understanding becomes most vital but also most problematic is not, in my view, in the area of science but in the area of lore. It is our metaphors that have divided us, and it is through sharing them that we have begun to come together again. Our age has no more pressing business.

The book is designed to serve as a textbook in the field of folklore and comparative literature. To this end it includes extensive materials for analysis drawn from literary traditions all over the world and representing primitive and folk as well as sophisticated forms. It also includes an outline guide to the world's literatures and a special index to help the student find his way into them quickly and easily for reference or research purposes.

No attempt has been made to summarize the extensive technical research now going on in this field. Instead my object has been to draw together a panorama of the relevant materials and to present it in a form facilitating its further interpretation and analysis along diverse lines, historical and critical as well as analytical. The work is in this sense an introduction to the field rather than a summary of it, and may therefore be of interest to general readers curious about the broader framework and more exotic byways of human self-expression.

My debts are many. I am grateful to colleagues at Tulane University and elsewhere who have read and offered thoughtful comments on all or parts of the manuscript: Drs. John L. Fischer, Marshall E. Durbin, Edward B. Patridge, Alan Dundes and Dell Hymes. I am grateful to my students and to many friends and acquaintances who have assisted me in finding out about a wide range of things from African pig Latin and Russian nicknames to Chinese versification, medieval Hebrew bibliography and Bolivian drama. My special thanks are owing to Drs. Elizabeth Colson, John J. Bodine, Samuel J. Fomon, Paul Bohannan, Colin N. Edmonson, George Zollschan and Stephen A. Tyler. The librarians of the Latin American Library at Tulane (Edith B. Rickettson and Marjorie E. LeDoux), and at the Peabody Museum Library at Harvard (Margaret Currier) have been creatively helpful at drawing my attention to materials I might easily have overlooked. For the final preparation of the manuscript I am grateful to Elizabeth Wauchope, whose painstaking work and dedication saved me from many a mistake. I am truly grateful also to the editors at Holt, Rinehart and Winston, and particularly to David Boynton and Ruth Stark, who have reduced the final preparation of a complex book to a feasible and even pleasant task. Finally I am grateful to my wife, Barbara Edmonson, for her patience and willingness to act as sounding board for ideas, and to my daughters, who are now persuaded that they too should write stories, since it is all so easy. The work is dedicated to them.

M. S. E.

Contents

LORE

Chapter 1

Science and Lore

Science is a differentiable mode of acquiring and transmitting knowledge. In contrast to lore, it rests on a narrow base. Science attempts to come to grips with the world through a strict preoccupation with denotative meaning and logical relational statements. Lore does not reject either of these modalities but is willing to include connotation and analogy as well. We may describe lore as the primitive field from which literary patterns are derived. And what is distinctive to lore and literature is their preoccupation with connotative semantics and analogic systems of thought.

A lore (Saxon *lar*, "teaching") is a special dimension or aspect of cultural tradition, marked by a high degree of particularity. Logic and observation bind science to modes of knowledge and communication that different men may yet perceive alike in total independence of each other. Similarity of lore is restricted to people with a common communicative background—who share the same connotations and have been taught the same analogies. The statement *Hier wohnt Bertie* may be scientifically translated "Bertie lives here" and declared true or false. Or we may make the analogic and connotative translation "Kilroy was here" and understand much more of the meaning of the sentence and why German soldiers scrawled *Bertie* across the walls of wartime Europe. There is in a sense no "reason" for such a translation, for the equation could not possibly be divined by a disinterested intelligence. But the particularity of an item of lore does not mean that it is not subject to causation—only that it is subject to somewhat distinctive causation. There is no reason that we cannot have a science of lore, just as there is no impediment to a lore of science, and both exist.

This book is an introduction to the science of lore, a somewhat loosely delineated field of study commonly described by such terms as *folklore* or *comparative literature,* here defined as the study of connotative meaning. We will survey the scope and problems of this field and the modest but significant achievements it has so far attained. I should perhaps state at the outset that I do not intend to trespass on the proper and necessary spheres of literary history or literary criticism, nor do I conceive it to be the proper function of science to do so. I shall, however, be concerned with much the same range of material. I will discuss the aspect of literary phenomena that aids our scientific understanding of the processes of human culture. I need hardly say that this does not exhaust the phenomena.

It is in something of the same spirit that Temple has offered us a literary analysis of applied mathematics:

> . . . it is in the realm of aeronautical science that the romantic spirit of modern applied mathematics finds its most vivid expression. Here all that is best in abstract analysis, in fluid dynamics, in engineering and in the spirit of the fighting services of the Crown unite and issue in some of the finest text-books and treatises which mathematicians have been privileged to study. To avoid an invidious choice among contemporary writers on fluid dynamics, let me be content to cite a treatise produced by a committee of experts—the famous volumes entitled *Modern Advances in Fluid Dynamics*—firmly moulded in one splendid and coherent whole by the literary and scientific genius of the editor.
>
> The reader who opens these volumes is immediately aware of an atmosphere of calm, lucid exposition which becomes steadily more and more transfused with a sense of gay adventure and mounting excitement. Unexpected achievements and unexpected difficulties enliven the romantic quest for the key to the problems of fluid flow, while the practical requirements of the aeronautical industry and civil and military operators infuse a stimulating sense of urgency and responsibility (Temple 1955:16).

And a more extended analysis of Darwin, Marx, Frazer, and Freud from the literary point of view makes the same point with some elegance and completeness (Hyman 1962).

There is no doubt that the specialization of modern science is often a severe barrier to comprehension by any but the trained specialist and that this barrier has been the locus of considerable debate and opposition between science and the arts, as has been argued at length by C. P. Snow (1960). But if science and lore are to be considered two cultures, we must nonetheless acknowledge that they are deeply interpenetrating cultures. The necessity for drawing firm lines between their practitioners is an aspect of current society and of academic and intellectual organization. The manifestations of these contemporary preoccupations in literature, whether scientific or artistic, involve no such cleavage. There is a vast zone of intellectual ambiguity in which the differentiation must be made, if at all, with subtlety and sensitivity.

The problems and possibilities of a scientific approach to lore may be illustrated. Consider this list of English nouns:

ape	dog	parrot
bat	eagle	ram
beetle	fox	rat
buffalo	goose	skylark
bug	gopher	snake
bull	hog	turtle
chicken	horse	weasel
clam	louse	wolf
crane	monkey	worm

Denotatively the list presents few problems. If you have a fairly fluent command of a foreign language, for example, you can readily find the equivalent translational terms with a good dictionary. Now go back and consider the same words as verbs. You will at once confront a basic fact about connotative meaning. There is in fact no guarantee that exactly the right connotation can be found at all in another language. "He bulled his way through and then chickened out." "Don't monkey with that." "She foxed me." "I'm buffaloed." Something of the meaning of these expressions may be captured in comparably subtle idioms in another language, but it is likely that most of them will be no more than distant analogies if we go beyond the European languages whose history we have in large measure shared. Wolves have been eating (or seducing) little girls since early Germanic tribal times in northwestern Europe, but wolves elsewhere are often sly, base, brave, or protective.

The connotative meanings that constitute a lore grow up in patterns held in common by populations with an intensively shared history. Sometimes they are found in only one language group; often they are found among groups of related or adjacent languages; just as often they may be peculiar to a single tribe, class, region, city, or even family. They may become characteristic of only a single individual. Under somewhat special circumstances we can trace the spread of lore over very broad geographic areas or even the whole of mankind.

Most of the world's lores have thus the quality of being at least in part incomprehensible to one another, translatable only when we possess the experiential key. Connotative significance cannot be inferred except from the actual coincidence or association of elements in the particular case. The wartime poem of Konstantin Simenov to his wife pleads:

> Wait for me and I'll return,
> Wait and wait again.
> Wait though sorrow starts to burn
> Through the yellow rain.
> (Fastenberg 1945:124; tr. mine)

To us "yellow rain" connotes either bright sunlight or some bilious condition. We must be told that *yellow* connotes mourning in Russia, just as it connotes sanctity in Thailand, maturity in Yucatan, or cowardice in England. The meanings are not intrinsic to the nature of the images.

Often such meanings are intentionally obscure or even secret. The young knights of the high Middle Ages elaborated an almost codelike slang for describing the ritualized hunting that was the prerogative of their class, establishing in English the tradition of differentiated animal names like buck, doe, and fawn and animal parts like the "brush" of a fox or the "scut" of a deer. Directly or indirectly derivative from the language of venery are also the collectives: a "pride" of lions, a "gam" of whales, and special verbs (to "dismember" a duck, but to "fruch" a chicken). German hunting tradition has analogous usages. A deer has *Lichter* ("lights") rather than eyes; his tail is the *Fahne* ("flag"); if he has antlers *er hat auf*, he has "something up"; when he leaps, it is *übersetzen* ("to transit"); to skin him is *aus der Decke schlagen* ("to strike off the cover"); to butcher him is *aufbrechen* ("to break up"). A similar elite language was found in heraldry: "On a field quarterly gules and argent two lions rampant guardant or armed of the first and in dexter chief on a fess or a roundel sable" describes a shield divided into red and white quarters, the shield containing prancing gold lions on the red quarters facing the viewer with red claws and tongues and containing a black dot to the right on a gold band across the top of the shield.

Papago songs refer to the coyote as "the bushy tailed one" or "our shining eyed comrade." West African bush schools used a secret vocabulary to confuse the uninitiated. Apache warriors had a special war language with circumlocutions for weapons, tracking, water holes, and everything else relating to the warpath. Jakun Malays speak a special language (*pantang kapur*) while they are working in the forest. Specialized patterns of meaning are of a staggering diversity.

It should not be supposed that quaint and strange meanings are found only in remote times and places. The gremlin, the goon, the finfinella, the pixie, little green men, and the schmoo are native to the United States, where they coexist with all manner of immigrant zombies, vampires, poltergeists, leprechauns, fairies, and trolls, and with the "bugs" in new machinery and the "bats" in people's belfries. All American children know that "good guys" and "bads guys" wear different colored Stetsons, just as all Thais know that people from the "ko-ka-la-su" provinces are mendacious and all Guatemalans know that people from the innocuous and undistinguished little town of Huité are hilariously rustic. Our cats have "nine lives"; Persian dogs have "seven." Some people kill flies because they carry germs, and other people kill them because they bite; still other people leave them alone because they are the reincarnate souls of ancestors. Among Utah Mormons, dancing connotes a solidarity with the general community; among Latin Americans it connotes eroticism and seduction; to the Hopi rain dancer pounding his prayer into the thirsty dust, dancing is a form of worship; to the European ballerina it is a narrative and lyric language; to the American teenager it is a competitive symbol of skill and popularity; while to the Ashanti priest it is a means to trance and possession by a god. Even a casual examination of these meanings demonstrates their remarkable specificity: it is a basic feature of lore that it is not easily communicated.

The ready elaboration of these subtle meanings and their rapid redevelopment under appropriate circumstances are sufficient indications of their vitality. Although we may note how difficult it has sometimes been for them to cross the invisible boundaries between one culture and another, we must also observe that their growth and communication within groups is often spectacular. The slang vocabulary of American teenagers suffers an almost complete metamorphosis about every ten years but remains general to the country at large. Here are some of the changes of the last few decades, with approximate dates:

1920	1930	1940	1950	1960
keen	swell	neat	cool	way out
kid	guy	mac	hey	man
boob	drip	jerk	slob	square
boot	thrill	kick	charge	thing
stinky	lousy	crummy	hairy	nowhere
fag	smoke	weed	cig	fix
sissy	pansy	fairy	queer	gay

Precisely because they rest on analogy, items of lore are not bound to the orderly and progressive laws governing the development of science. Lore does not "evolve." And although it is not easily communicated, it can on occasion leap across ethnic and other boundaries with remarkable facility. "Davy Crockett" and the Hula Hoop rounded the globe in less than two years. Under conditions of less adequate communication, the Ghost Dance of 1890 spread to most of the tribes of the North American plains in the same period, ignoring tribal and subtribal jealousies and linguistic differences. The zoot suit, associated with Negro jazz fans in

Harlem in the early 1940s had been transposed into rebellious Pachuco Spanish in Los Angeles by 1943 and by 1944 it had reached wartime Bucharest, where it was also associated with jazz and with opposition to authority—in that context, Hitler.

COMMUNICATION OF LORE

It is apparent that lore can be easily communicated where channels exist to convey it, but it is extraordinarily resistant to diffusion where the channels are lacking. Because the relevant channels are of varying stability, it follows that lore traced through time may diverge into separate paths of development or flow back together into a single tradition: it can undergo both differentiation and synthesis. The process of differentiation is easily documented by a simple experiment. Arrange two chains of communication composed of individuals 1, 2, 3 . . . n. To the first individual of each chain tell some story; then allow him to repeat it privately to the next person in his chain. When the story has traveled the length of the chain, the results may be something like mine (see also Bartlett in Dundes 1965:243–258):

Initial Story

On the day before Mardi Gras there was an incident during the parade on Canal Street at Bourbon involving two revelers and a visiting couple. All were said to have been drinking. Bystanders reported that the revelers, one of whom was Negro, were accosted without provocation and insulted and struck by one of the visitors, but managed to escape from the scene. Witnesses intervened in the struggle, which spread to near-riot proportions. Police are holding ten persons for questioning.

Fifteenth Person

CHAIN A	CHAIN B
There was a riot in the French Quarter. Everybody got dressed up. A Negro was killed.	On the last day of Mardi Gras at the corner of Canal and Bourbon two men started a riot. Two more men came over and accused the second man of starting the riot.

The materials used in this experiment are not particularly folkloristic or literary, but they indicate something of the divergence that is to be expected under these communicative conditions.

The operation of this process in real literary history is illustrated in Figure 1, which shows a partial family tree of the *Five Books* or *Pañca*

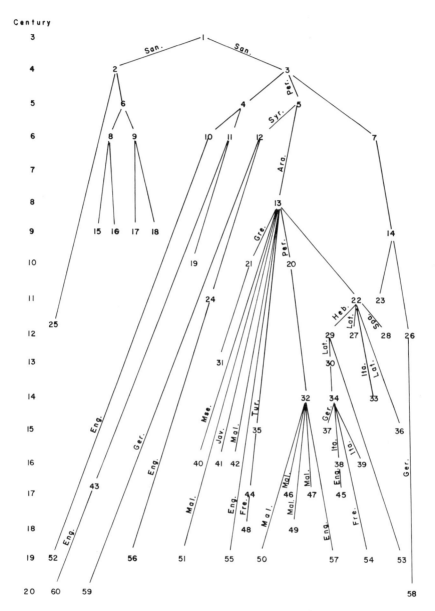

Figure 1 Divergences of the Five Books

Tantra, also called "The Fables of Bidpai," a Sanskrit tale collection with a most ramifying body of descendants. There are probably many hundreds of extant works revealing the influence of this early Indian collection. Sixty of them are depicted in Figure 1. Some are merely modern translations of the older texts. Others involve very partial borrowings—of particular tales. Still others may be considered variant recensions closely similar to the original work. Careful scholarship and textual comparison enable us to trace the recent works back to their literary sources and even to reconstruct sources that no longer exist. The works listed, and the numbers by which they are identified in Figure 1, are listed below. (Abbreviations and dating notation are explained at the beginning of the Appendix. Extant works are italicized; lost or hypothetical ones are in roman type in parentheses.)

1. (Pañca Tantra: original lost)
2. (Tantra Akhyaayika: original lost)
3. (Pañca Tantra: K Text, partially reconstructed)
4. (Pañca Tantra: hypothetical)
5. (Pañca Tantra [Per. 4] Burzoe: lost)
6. (Tantra Akhyaayika: Simplicior Text, reconstructed)
7. (Pañca Tantra: hypothetical northwestern recension)
8. (Tantra Akhyaayika: hypothetical Kashmir recension)
9. (Tantra Akhyaayika: hypothetical Jain recension)
10. *Pañca Tantra* (San. 6)
11. (Pañca Tantra: hypothetical)
12. *Kalila and Dimna* (Syr. 6), Bodh
13. *Kalila and Dimna* (Ara. 8), Ibn Muqaffa
14. (Bṛhat Kathaa [San.] Guna Adhya: lost)
15. *Tantra Akhyaayika* (San.) (Extant Kashmir recension)
16. *Tantra Akhyaayika* (San.) (Extant Kashmir recension)
17. *Tantra Akhyaayika* (San.) (Extant Jain recension)
18. *Tantra Akhyaayika* (San.) (Extant Jain recension)
19. *Pañca Tantra* (San.) (Southern recension)
20. *Kalila and Dimna* (Per. 10), Ruudagi
21. *Stephanites kai Ikhnelates* (Gre. 11)
22. *Thousand and One Nights* (Ara. 11)
23. *Bṛhat Kathaa Mañjarii* (San. 11), Ksmendra
24. *Kalila and Dimna* (Syr. 11)
25. *Tantra Akhyaanaka* (San. 12), Puurna Bhadra
26. *Kathaa Saritsa Agara* (San. 12), Soma Deva
27. *Kalila and Dimna* (Lat. 12), Baldo
28. *Kalila and Dimna* (Spa. 12)
29. *Kalila and Dimna* (Heb. 12), Joel
30. *Directorium Vitae Humanae* (Lat. 13), Capua
31. *Aesop's Fables* (Gre. 13), Planudes
32. *Anvaar i Suheylii* (Per. 14), Husayn Va'iz
33. *Decamerone* (Ita. 14), Boccaccio
34. *Liber de Dina et Kalila* (Lat. 14), Béziers

35. *History of the Forty Viziers* (Tur. 15), Zaada
36. *Gesta Romanorum* (Lat. 15)
37. *Buch der Beispiele der alten Weisen* (Ger. 15), Pforr
38. *Kalila and Dimna* (Ita. 16), Doni
39. *Kalila and Dimna* (Ita. 16), Firenzuola
40. *Kalila and Dimna* (Madurese 16)
41. *Kalila and Dimna* (Jav. 16)
42. *Kalila and Dimna* (Mal. 16)
43. *Hito Padeśa* (San. 17), Naara Ayana
44. *Humaayan Naama* (Tur. 17), Chelebi
45. *The Morall Philosophie of Doni* (Eng. 16), North
46. *Hikayat Golam* (Mal. 17)
47. *Hikayat Puspa Wiraja* (Mal. 17)
48. *The Imperial Book of Chelebi* (Fre. 18), Galland
49. *Hikayat Kalila dan Damina* (Mal. 18)
50. *Kalila and Dimna* (Mal. 19)
51. *Kalila and Dimna* (Mal. 19). Munshi 'Abdu'lla
52. *Panchatantra* (Eng. 19), Ryder
53. *The Kalila and Dimna of Joel* (Fre. 19), Derembourg
54. *The Dimna and Kalila of Raimund* (Fre. 19), Hervieux
55. *The Kalila and Dimna of Ibn Muqaffa* (Eng. 19), Knatchbull
56. *The Syrian Kalila and Dimna* (Eng. 19), Keith-Falconer
57. *The Lights of Canopus of Husayn Wa'iz* (Eng. 19), Eastwick
58. *The Kalila and Dimna of Bodh* (Ger. 20), Schultess
59. *The Ocean of Rivers of Soma Deva* (Ger. 20), Panzer
60. *The Book of Wholesome Counsel* (Eng. 20), Johnson and Barnett

One group of extant versions is made up of the *Book of Narratives* or *Tantra Akhyaayika*, which exists in two Kashmir recensions and two Jain ones (Nos. 15–18) and which is related to the twelfth-century *Book of Narration* or *Tantra Akhyaanaka* of Puurna Bhadra (No. 25). A second group is made up of the best-known *Five Books* (*Pañca Tantra*), translated into English by Ryder in the last century (Nos. 10, 52), and a less-familiar southern recension (No. 19) related to the book of *Wholesome Counsel* (*Hito Padeśa*: Nos. 43, 60). A third group goes back to a Syrian version of the sixth century, the *Kalila and Dimna* of Bodh, and includes a later Syrian version and translations of both (Nos. 12, 24, 56, 58). A fourth group springs from the Arabic *Kalila and Dimna* of Ibn Muqaffa in the eighth century (No. 13) and includes the extremely ramified descendants of the *Thousand and One Nights*, the *Deeds of the Romans*, and other important collections in Turkish, Greek, Italian, Spanish, Hebrew, and other languages (Nos. 13, 20–22, 27–29, 30–42, 44–51, 53–55). The fifth and final group includes the *Ocean of Rivers* of Soma Deva and the *Digest of the Brihat*

Romance of Ksmendra, both drawn from a Sanskrit work now lost, the *Brihat Romance* of Guna Adhya (Nos. 14, 23, 26, 58).

The earlier relationships among these five groups have been carefully studied. The common ancestor of Nos. 15–18 has been reconstructed and published (No. 6), and we can confidently assume an earlier text (No. 2), ancestral to all of the first group. An ancestral version for Group 2 may also be safely inferred (No. 4). The common ancestor of the Syrian and Arabic versions (the third and fourth groups) is supposed to have been the Persian translation by Burzoe, unfortunately lost (No. 5). The ancestor of the fifth group is supposed to have been a lost northwest Indian recension (No. 7), though this geographical identification has been questioned. There is general agreement that the four earliest versions thus traced (Nos. 2, 4, 5, 7) are derived from a common original, and one scholar has prepared a partial reconstruction of a hypothetical original for the last three of them, known as the K Text (No. 3). Thus the existence of an original work (No. 1), probably called the Pañca Tantra and compiled no later than the third century A.D., may be considered certain, and we can have a fairly good idea of what it said. This reconstruction of its history is largely based on Keith (1956).

The divergence of versions of the *Five Books* is typical of the literary process. But it is not merely a matter of literary "drift." At each point in the chain there is the possibility of more than one "ancestor," and at many points in this particular example such multiple origins are certain. Thus the book of *Wholesome Counsel* certainly drew on some version of the *Five Books*, but it certainly also drew on other sources as well. The *Five Books* itself almost certainly derived in part from some text known also to Kautilya, author of the *Doctrine of Politics* (*Artha Śaastra*), but it appears to have obtained some things from a reservoir (perhaps oral) that also served as a source for Aesop. Literary process is thus convergent as well as divergent.

This sketchy outline of the history of one tale collection does not begin to exhaust its influence. For example, some specific tales from the *Five Books* found their way into the tales of *Buddha's Former Births* (*Jatakas*), whence they proliferated into most or all of the literatures of eastern Asia. Some of the medieval derivatives of the *Five Books* were drawn upon for the books of *exempla* or canned sermons of the later Middle Ages, and themes from the same sources are traceable to the tales of Chaucer, the plays of Shakespeare, and many comparable bodies of work that have had the most extensive influence upon modern literature.

The plural ancestry of literary works is as notable a feature of them as their plural progeny. A particularly clear example is the complex of Dances of the Conquest among the Indians of Middle America, which are almost invariably syncretisms of the tradition of the Spanish mystery plays (*autos*) and that of the Indian ritual dances (*xahoh*). One such is the *White Demon* (*Zaqi Q'axol*), a Quiche Maya play, in which the Aztecs speak Quiche and the Spanish speak Indianized Spanish—all within the traditional chant form of Mayan poetic style. Thus Montezuma, lapsing into broken Spanish but unbroken Mayan couplets, rejects the Spanish ultimatum:

> Consider my power,
>> The multitude of my people.
> These people have come to me
>> With arms to kill my vassals.
> I, from my power,
>> Will see you leave, fallen.
> And as for places,
>> The kingdoms
> And provinces,
>> Subject to my crown,
> Number
>> Five hundred,
> From my empire at this count,
>> And I hold them subject
> By power
>> And will,
> By force,
>> And privilege,
> Compelled
>> To fear the priests.
> Therefore I do not promise you my jewels.
>> I shall fight breast to breast.
>> (Anon., 1726; tr. mine)

Syncretisms of this sort are common in literature.

A striking example of the synthetic nature of literary composition is afforded by T. S. Eliot's footnotes to *The Wasteland* (1958), diagrammed in Figure 2. The predominance of native (in this case, English) sources is doubtless characteristic of most literary works, underplayed if anything by Eliot's scholarly habits. But this single work has been directly influenced from firsthand contact with at least six foreign literatures, and if we were to trace the secondary and tertiary ancestry of the works cited, we would no doubt come close to sampling from most of the historical literatures of the world. The sources Eliot himself cites (and the number key to Figure 2) are as follows:

1. *Poems* (Gre. −6), Sappho
2. *Upanishads* (San. −6)

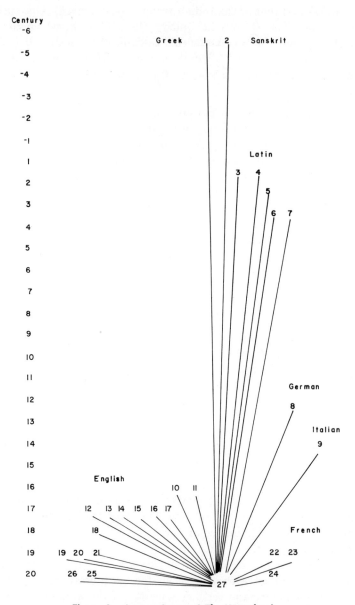

Figure 2 Antecedents of *The Wasteland*

3. *Aeneid* (Lat. 1), Virgil
4. *Metamorphoses* (Lat. 1), Ovid
5. *Pervigilium Veneris* (Lat. 2)
6. *Bible* (Lat. 4)
7. *Confessions* (Lat. 4), Augustine

8. *Nibelungenlied* (Ger. 12)
9. *Divine Comedy* (Ita. 14), Dante
10. *Spanish Tragedy* (Eng. 16), Kyd
11. *Prothalamion* (Eng. 16), Spenser
12. *Parliament of Bees* (Eng. 17), Day
13. *To His Coy Mistress* (Eng. 17), Marvell
14. *Women Beware Women* (Eng. 17), Middleton
15. *Paradise Lost* (Eng. 17), Milton
16. *The Tempest* (Eng. 17), Shakespeare
17. *White Devil* (Eng. 17), Webster
18. *The Vicar of Wakefield* (Eng. 18), Goldsmith
19. *Fleurs du Mal* (Fre. 19), Baudelaire
20. *The Golden Bough* (Eng. 19), Frazer
21. *Elizabeth* (Eng. 19), Froude
22. *Les Chimères* (Fre. 19), Nerval
23. *Parsifal* (Fre. 19), Verlaine
24. *Blick ins Chaos* (Ger. 20), Hesse
25. *Buddhism in Translation* (Eng. 20), Warren
26. *From Ritual to Romance* (Eng. 20), Weston
27. *The Waste Land* (Eng. 20), Eliot

From diverse examples of literary process so far presented we may conclude that the study of patterns of connotative meaning poses some special problems. Generally speaking, these problems can be phrased as a matter of communication. The patterns range from simple and clear to general and vague; they are subject to change and transmission both rapidly and slowly. With the passage of time they both diverge and merge. A general explanation of these facts must be at once precise and flexible. It will be my argument that the specific behavior of lore in concrete cases is best understood as a problem in communication and that no hard distinction is necessary between primitive and sophisticated or written and oral literary canons. The relevant communicative processes are the same throughout, and cultural complexity or the use of writing necessitate only relatively mechanical and circumstantial qualifications.

A clearer idea of the contextual association responsible for connotation can be gained by considering the relation of social interaction to cultural communication. In the simplest case, we can trace the phenomenon of the perpetuation of an idea by transmission from person to person and from generation to generation. Here we may talk of a simple linear linkage between individuals of the type pictured in Figure 3. Under certain condi-

Figure 3

tions any cultural message introduced at one point in such a linear chain will be communicated to the end (or ends). To a first approximation, the certain conditions required are that the interaction at each link be sufficiently intensive to transmit the message in question. Any of the traditional motifs or elements of lore is an adequate example. The diffusion of the motif will take place lineally as long as the contacts between adjacent individuals in the chain are sufficiently intense. When they are not, the chain will be broken and the items will diffuse no farther. The sequence of derivation of North's *The Morall Philosophie of Doni* from the *Five Books* illustrates an unusually long linear chain of this type (Figure 1, Nos. 1, 3, 5, 13, 22, 29, 30, 34, 38, 45). Even longer chains occur commonly in oral folklore, albeit often without documentation.

Many communicative contexts have a very different structure. In the case of a nuclear family, for example, the interaction pattern may approximate a certain kind of saturation at some level of intensity. This is diagrammed in Figure 4. Here every individual has direct communicative access to every other many times a day. Particular messages may still flow lineally within such a context (for examples, from A to D to C to E to B), but the communicative fate of the message is emphatically conditioned by the previous and simultaneous transmission of other messages within the same complex circuit, and any element introduced may potentially diffuse to the whole system in only one step. Whenever the intensity of the system is adequate for the purpose, it will do so. If the intensity level of interaction in a saturated group is too low, the element may not diffuse at all. If it is too high, the element will be transmitted in the company of other elements: it will undergo elaboration. Saturated groups of high interactive intensity are thus likely to share complex patterns of lore, as can be seen in certain tribal, occupational, or other traditions.

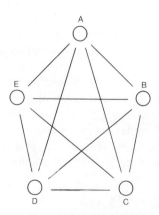

Figure 4

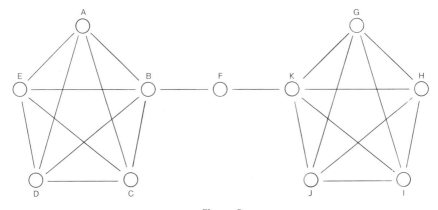

Figure 5

Lineal communication chains are often made up of linked saturated systems. They may be singly linked or multiply linked, through inter-communication of single individuals or of many from each saturated system. What can be communicated along such chains is, of course, determined by their weakest links. An element cannot leap a gap in such a chain any more than in the simple linear chain. Chains of this complex type have, however, another interesting property. The saturated systems operate as reservoirs of communicative redundancy, with a higher communicative and creative potential than linear chains (Figure 5). This creates a strong probability of the genesis of different patterns within these reservoirs, the simpler elements of which can be transmitted back and forth between them. The more complex elements cannot be so communicated, thus leading to diversity. The differentiation of partly overlapping tribal traditions depends on conditions similar to those of this model.

The communicative potential of the chains linking saturated systems is subject to variation. Hence the patterns they produce may, as we have already noted, both merge and diverge. This may be pictured as an intersecting double linear system, illustrated by Figure 6. Communicative chains of this general type, whether simple or complex, are clearly the basis for the convergence and divergence illustrated in the history of *The Waste Land* and the *Five Books*.

The complex history of literary ideas may be viewed as a natural laboratory, displaying a wide variety of cultural (and hence communicative) circumstances. We may assume that each element has been transmitted from individual to individual separately or as part of a complex in strict dependence upon the communicative state of the circuits in which it flowed. Often, circuits of a high degree of communicative potential have been maintained over wide areas and long periods of time, with conse-

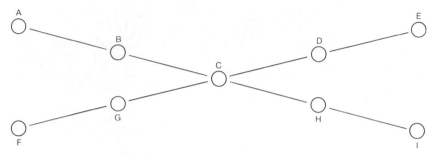

Figure 6

quently broad and extensive transmission of quite complex patterns. Sometimes these circuits lose these properties and the patterns break up or disappear. Generally speaking, such communicative or cultural events can be identified with the history of social institutions—of the interaction matrix upon which interindividual communication depends. The history of the Christian church in the Western world or of Buddhist monasticism in Asia are striking examples of the broadest type.

The communicative assumptions that have been proposed can also furnish us with a model for intraindividual communicative processes. In the individual and in society, the creation of structures (that is, of complex patterns of associated elements) results from a nonrandom loading of communication. The uniqueness of individual patterns of this sort follows from the uniqueness of the communicative history of the individual. Consider, for example, the situation of an individual who is the sole common member of two saturated and intensively organized groups, a situation occupied by all individuals some of the time. An individual so placed would necessarily be in a position to share some ideas with each group, but because the two groups could not possibly be communicatively identical, he would inevitably come to possess some ideas from each group that could not be communicated to the other. Such a convergence of ideas, furthermore, would, by the intensiveness of their impingement upon him, create in the individual, additional associations of ideas unique to him, some of them likewise incommunicable.

The basic character of connotation relates precisely to this kind of communicative association. The models would predict what appears in fact to be the case, that some connotations are idiosyncratic while others are general in various degrees and that these results are predictable from past communicative history. The models would also suggest that we can gain a more precise grasp of connotative phenomena by describing them in terms of communication: that is, in terms of varying degrees of structural complexity in relation to particular types of circuits and to different levels of intensity or redundancy.

This is, in fact, only a slightly tighter way of describing what we are already doing with these problems. The description of literary forms in both oral and written literature has long involved us in attempts to delineate patterns and structures. We have long been aware of the problem of context—the position of literary elements in social and cultural history— which is another way of describing the circuits in which communication has historically flowed. We have known for some time that the success or failure of cultural communication is strongly dependent upon the intensity of contact. We are beginning to be able to be somewhat more precise about these matters. In a favorable case, we can even quantify them.

It will be obvious that none of these remarks on the general structure of human communication (of culture) is inapplicable to the communication of denotative or logico-empirical propositions. It remains, therefore, for us to clarify the peculiar quality of connotation in this connection. Denotation differs communicatively from connotation in that it involves an additional input (sensory experience) and a particular type of association among elements (logic). We may view these distinctive attributes as a special case of the general communicative process—a case in which the communicative loading involves an intense redundancy of sensory messages and a highly redundant and generally shared system of stating relationships among them. Thus, denotative meanings, whether idiosyncratic or cultural, may be said to share an empirical basis and a characteristic logical pattern, whereas connotative meanings are conventional rather than empirical and are freely associative or analogical rather than logical. These defining criteria are also diagnostic of differential communicability.

Other things being equal, it requires a higher intensity of contact to communicate lore than to communicate science. If we observe the distributions of hypotheses and metaphors, it is the hypotheses that prove to be the more contagious. This is true because the relatively tenuous communicative channels necessary for the communication of hypotheses are more widely available than the more intensive channels needed for the communication of metaphor. Furthermore, the relevance of denotation to sensory experience lends it an a priori redundancy that connotation cannot possess; hence, two persons or cultures linked by any given degree of communicative intensity are far more likely to share denotative than connotative meanings and are correspondingly more likely to share complex denotations.

It is striking that despite the difficulty of communicating matters of mood, of nuance, of feeling, it is nonetheless true that the poetic language of lore may often surmount the objective barriers of language, space, and time and may speak to us with a directness that is surely one of the great charms of literature. A lonesome Welsh captain of thirty generations ago makes contact with this sort of force as he broods with wistful dignity:

> I shall not talk even for one hour tonight.
>> My retinue is not very large,
> I and my Frank, around our cauldron.

> I shall not sing, I shall not laugh, I shall not jest tonight,
>> Though we drank clear mead,
> I and my Frank, round my bowl.

> Let no one ask me for merriment tonight,
>> Mean is my company.
> Two lords can talk: one speaks.
>> (Williams 1944:29)

It is obvious that successful contact across a thousand years is dependent upon literacy. The preservation of even very good Welsh *englynion* through thirty generations of lineal oral transmission is impossible. Even with a text, we are in this case greatly indebted to sound scholarship and a felicitous translation. (The poem inevitably suffers in translation from the terser, rhymed, and versified original.) The cultural distance between modern English and ancient Welsh can, then, be annihilated by proper information, conveyed in this case by careful selection of English words. A good translation into, say, Chinese would certainly have to be very different and might well require more footnotes and explanations to succeed at all.

The intercultural transmission of literature is an ancient and omnipresent process. It has been studied intensively not only by folklorists but also by students of written literature. The latter usually choose to describe their task as the tracing of literary influences, and although the critic or the literary historian often restricts himself to a particular tradition, there is a lively interest in comparative literature as a field explicitly devoted to intercultural literary influences. The folklorist almost inevitably becomes involved in both internal and external aspects of the transmission of lore, and surely any broad view of literary influences must consider written and unwritten, direct and indirect, spatial and temporal, and form and content aspects of the process. How these matters may be studied in a specific case can be illustrated from a particularly well-documented examination of the variants of one ballad, the Dutch *Heer Halewijn* (Nygard 1958).

This ballad tells the story of a Bluebeard-type knight who is tricked and killed by a maiden whom he attempts to add to his grisly conquests. The Dutch version is probably the earliest and may go back in its original form to the fifteenth century. Nygard has assembled 235 variants of the ballad, in English (19), French (64), German (83), Danish (27), Norwegian (19), Icelandic (12), Swedish (5), and Dutch (6), and additional versions are known to exist in Polish, Magyar, Italian, Spanish, and Portuguese. In the great collection of English ballads by Child (1857–1859; 1882–1898), this is listed as No. 4, *Lady Isabel and the Elf-Knight*. The common French form is *Renaud le Tueur de Femmes*; in Scandinavia it is called *Kvindemorderen*, and in German it takes several forms, including *Nicolai, Ulrich,* and *Uliger*.

The approximate relationships among the variants are indicated in Figure 7. There are several features of interest. The relative autonomy of each national tradition is striking. The processes of both differentiation and recombination are much in evidence. Note, for example, the northern Irish version, combining both major British traditions with the Scottish one. The presence of two major traditions in France and Canada, three in Germany, and two in England attests to the subdivision of the national social media in which the ballad was transmitted. The lines on Figure 7 may be assumed to indicate channels of particularly intensive communication, but even this network does not exhaust the contacts that must have taken place. The actual history of the ballad involves innovation of various sorts, differential preservation of details, and reworking of the materials for artistic or ideological reasons. Discontinuities appear particularly between languages.

The earliest Dutch ballad was heavily supernatural. The evil knight's severed head, for example, continued to plead with the maiden for a magical restoration. In later and more realistic versions, this is omitted, and the maiden's retort is displaced to precede the knight's death. The major episodes of the ballad in the various national traditions are indicated in Figure 8. Only the thirteenth and twenty-third episodes are common to some versions in each major national tradition studied. Although the investigation is concerned only with one song and its variants, its documentation of the nature of literary creativity is eloquent and detailed.

No one has yet attempted to reconstruct the original form of the ballad. The following excerpts from various versions may, however, given an impression of the whole work and its variations. They are identified by numbers and letters corresponding to those in Figure 8. The page references in Nygard (1958) are given after each quotation:

> 1a. Lord Halewijn sang a little song
> And all who heard it would near him be. (Dut., 40)
> 2. False Sir John a wooing came
> To a maiden of beauty fair;
> May Colven was this lady's name,
> Her father's only heir. (Eng., 261)
> 3a. And he was heard by a king's daughter
> Who was her parents' dearest joy. (Dut., 40)

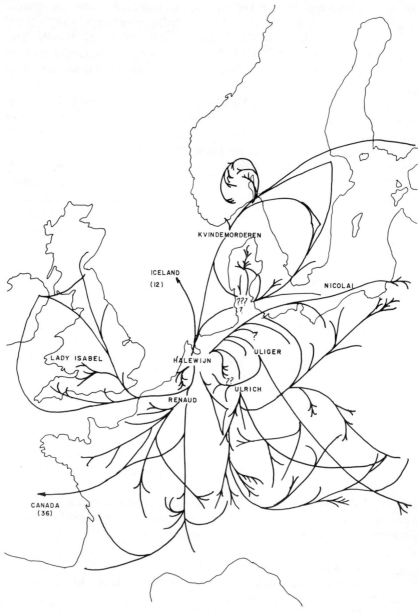

Figure 7

4a. She went and stood before her father,
    "Oh, father, may I go with Halewijn?" (Dut., 42)
 5. "Why I'll come along as guard with you,
    First of all as a watch and to hold you for me." (Dan., 101)

	DUT.-GER.	DAN.	ENG.	FRE.
1.	a. Knight's song	///	b. Expository opening	
2.	///	Courtship		///
3.	a. Captivation	b. Solicitation		
4.	a. Maid questions family	b. Maid's reply		c. Maid's hunger and thirst
5.	///	Maid's protection	///	///
6.	Preparations			///
7.	Journey			///
8.	Meeting with Knight	///		
9.	a. Journey with Halewijn	b. Wish to rest	///	
10.	a. Gallows	b. Grave	///	
11.	a. Choice of deaths	b. The villain announces his intentions		
12.	///		Order to undress	
13.	The maid's ruse			
14.	///	Success of the ruse		
15.	///	Sword	///	
16.	///	Waking the villain	///	
17.	a. Decapitation	b. The maid's taunt		
18.	///	///		Cutting the branch
19.	Villain's pleas	///		Villain's pleas
20.	a. Maid's retort	b. Villain's death	///	
21.	a. Depart for home	b. Reversal of fortune	///	
22.	Meeting with villain's family		///	
23.	Return home			
24.	///	a. Other closes	b. Parrot and father	///

Figure 8   *Heer Halewijn:* **Structure of the Ballad**

6. Put on a dress of white satin
   To be as beautiful as a goddess. (Dut., 44)

7. So sat she sideways on the steed
   And rode singing loudly toward the wood. (Dut., 46)

8a. When she to the middle of the wood had come,
   There found her Milord Halewijn. (Dut., 47)

9a. They rode up hill, they rode down dale,
   'Til they came at last to a mountainside. (Ger., 48)

10a. They came all by a gallows field
   Whereon hung many a woman's form. (Dut., 50)

11a. And so he turned and said to her:
   "Since you are the fairest of them all,
   It's time now to kill you off." (Dut., 50)

12. "Undress yourself, my bonnie Jean,
   Undress yourself, I beg of you." (Fre., 209)

13. "But first bring forth your supreme lament
   For maiden's blood that spreads so far." (Dut., 52)

14. He laid his head upon her lap.
   He slept a sleep that was not sweet. (Dan., 18)

15. Then went she to the little knoll
   Beneath which lay eight maidens' gold,
   Then went she to the little stream
   Beneath which ran eight maidens' blood. (Dan., 120)

16. She then put on her mantle blue.
   So went she to where his scabbard lay. (Dan., 122)

17. She took his sword right by the hilt
   And brought it down on his false head.
   He fell into the green grass. (Ger., 52)

18. The beauty drew his sword.
   The branch of laurel then she cut. (Fre., 217)

19. "Go yonder to that corn
   And blow upon my horn
   That all my friends may hear it!" (Dut., 53)

20a. "Into the corn there go I not,
   Upon your horn there blow I not." (Dut., 54)

21a. She seized the horse well by the reins
   And swung herself upon his back. (Ger., 55)

22. And when she was halfway down the road
   Came Halewijn's father out to meet her.
   "Fair maid, saw you not my son go by?" (Dut., 56)

23. Then rode she forth as Judith did
   And reached her father's palace.
   There she was received with honor and glory.

She blew the horn with glad intent
In victory as a heroine
And all the court received her badly. (Dut., 59)

24b. Ye ladies a', wherever you be
That read this mournful song,
I pray you mind on May Colvin
And think on fausse Sir John.

Aff they've taken his jewels fine,
To keep in memory;
And sae I end my moanful song
And fatal tragedy. (Eng., 286)

Nygard's careful reconstruction of a partial history of this one ballad illustrates many of the general features of literary communication—of the creation and transmission of metaphorical structure. It does not, of course, exhaust the structure of this ballad, even for the range of variants considered; and indeed the analysis remains very close to the texts of the corpus. Broader historical relationships and a subtler grasp of the peculiarly pluralistic character of metaphor may be illustrated by another example drawn from Lévi-Strauss' interpretation of South American Indian mythology.

STRUCTURE OF LORE

Like Nygard, Lévi-Strauss starts from a consideration of a range of variants. His procedure, however, is to reduce the mythical narrative to a series of universalistic dichotomies: he retells the myth "logically." This method reveals with peculiar clarity the analogic character of metaphor, as in the following schematic outline juxtaposing a Carib-Arekuna myth on the origin of sickness and fish poison with a Toba-Mataco myth on the color of birds.

TOBA-MATACO

1. A deceptive spirit, male, is traveling near a river, not far from which there is a hut.

2. The owner of the hut is a grandmother who is caring for a baby.

3. The owner of the hut reveals and generously offers to share her reserves of water.

4. The spirit asks for a drink (although he is hungry).

5. The spirit visitor makes the drink offered him too hot.

CARIB-AREKUNA

1. A faithful spirit, female, visits a hut, not far from which there is a river.

2. The visitor to the hut is a mother nursing a baby.

3. The owner of the hut hides and selfishly refuses to share her reserves of water.

4. The spirit accepts food (but will be thirsty).

5. The human host makes the food he proffers too hot.

6. The hostess goes to the river to find cool water for her visitor, abandoning her baby.

7. The spirit eats the hostess' baby roasted (or in the Toba version gulps it down raw).

8. The cannibal monster is stopped up.

9. The rescuing birds reopen his orifices.

10. Centrifugal action (body substance flows out).

11. Origin of (colors of birds and) fish poison.

6. The visitor goes to the river to find cool water for herself, abandoning her baby.

7. The hostess boils the spirit's baby (without eating it).

8. (In the Arekuna myth) the cannibal monster is skinned.

9. The hostile birds divide his skin.

10. Centripetal action (colors put on).

11. Origin of the colors of birds (and fish poisons).

(Lévi-Strauss 1964:313–314)

The relation of this outline to the original myths as told may be indicated by Lévi-Strauss' summary of the Mataco myth, which he draws from the works of Métraux and Palavecino:

> The demiurge and trickster Tawkxwax was traveling beside a river. He spent the night on the bank. When he woke up, he was hungry, went on and about noon came to a hut surrounded by innumerable jars full of water. An old woman lived in it. Tawkxwax came up and asked for a drink. The old woman showed him the jars and told him to drink as much as he wanted.
>
> But Tawkxwax arranged for the water to get hot and asked the old woman to go get him cool water from the river. Since she was worried about her granddaughter, whom she was caring for, Tawkxwax advised her to put her down in the hammock, and he murmured some magic words so that the old woman's jar wouldn't fill up until he had finished eating the child. Reaching the river, the old woman tried in vain to draw the water. Meanwhile, Tawkxwax took the child, roasted it and ate it, putting a stone in its place. [Toba version: Fox put his mouth on the baby's anus and inhaled all its substance, leaving nothing but the skin.] Then he lifted the spell, the jar filled and the old woman returned.
>
> Seeing the stone, she wept and got angry. This old woman was a wild bee of the kind called moro-moro [another version: a mud-dauber wasp]. She made the trickster fall into a deep sleep and while he was asleep she filled his body openings with wax or earth: mouth, nose, eyes, armpits, penis, anus; and she plastered up all the spaces between his fingers.
>
> When the demiurge woke he found he was swelling up dangerously. The birds [who were then men] came to his rescue and tried to unplug him with their axes, that is their beaks, but the wax was too

hard. Only a very small woodpecker was able to pierce it. The demi-urge's blood poured through the hole and covered the birds with red splashes, except for the crow, who got dirty from the filth that came from his anus (Lévi-Strauss 1964:311–312).

It is characteristic of Lévi-Strauss' treatment of the Indian myths that Entries 8–10 in the contrasting outline, which are missing in the Carib version, are supplied from an Arekuna myth concerned with the origin of both fish poisons and bird colors.

The correspondence between the Toba and Carib myths is, on balance, remarkable. When we remember that the two groups belong to totally different linguistic phyla and are separated by more than 2000 miles of difficult terrain, it becomes startling. What Lévi-Strauss has demonstrated is the astonishing persistence of certain metaphorical structures over very long periods of time, and he has described these structures with a precision largely lacking in previous studies of myth.

A range of relations appears in the comparison of the Toba and Carib myths. There are identities, there are inversions, and there are all manners of analogies in between. What Lévi-Strauss has discovered is the relation between these poles: that a structure is mythic (in my terms, metaphorical) only when it escapes logic (in the limiting case, when it is susceptible to inversion). The descriptive dichotomies in these myths (false-true, male-female, host-visitor, generosity-selfishness, food-drink, spirit-human, other-self, raw-cooked, close-open, friendly-hostile) have no intrinsic relationships among them. They are related only within the arbitrary framework of a particular myth context. The legitimacy of these constructs as a structural description is validated by Lévi-Strauss' repeated demonstration that A:B::C:D. That is, *in context* particular structural relationships are stable, and at least temporarily A is to B as C is to D. These structures are conventional, arbitrary, and culturally (that is, contextually) specific. Although they may include many kinds of relationships, their arbitrariness is demonstrated by the frequent occurrence of inversion.

It is the peculiar property of a metaphor to be capable of linking elements that are both logically and empirically opposite. And it is the peculiar property of such linkages that they may be inverted. Thus in the myths cited, eating may be cognate with not eating, self with nonself. In the very first element, truth is cognate with falsehood. Furthermore, the inversion of structures may be multiple: the structure may be doubly or triply inverted or partially inverted, or it may not be inverted at all.

We may view Lévi-Strauss' myth outlines as a sequence of narrative metaphors. But the most remarkable thing about them is not the fact that they are structured; it is, rather, the persistence of their structural specificity. Spirits are not in nature raw, nor are humans cooked. Nor are they consistently so in South American Indian belief. Indeed, the inverse assertion is frequently explicit and is part of the metaphorical structure of "raw and cooked" in South America. But the pervasiveness and endurance of such an idea, although it may tell us nothing about the landscape of South America, may reveal a great deal about the nature of human communication—of human culture.

Transformational inversion is not restricted to myth. It is likely, in fact, that it is quite general to all of lore—to the whole range of metaphor. The significance of this discovery would be difficult to exaggerate, because it tells us in more precise terms what we suspected at the outset: the nature of lore is fundamentally distinct from the nature of science because it is not bound by the laws of logic or the limitations of experiment. If we would understand the nature of human culture, we must recognize that an important half of it is metaphorical and is organized and communicated analogically and traditionally. Furthermore, communication of this sort is specialized, and is largely confined to the more intensive and intimate of the channels made available by human social life.

METAPHOR AND HYPOTHESIS

From the standpoint that has been outlined metaphors may be contrasted with hypotheses. In the broadest sense both metaphors and hypotheses are relational statements, and both undergo transformational manipulation. But whereas metaphor is connotative and undergoes analogical transformation (including inversion), hypothesis is denotative and undergoes logical transformation (certainly precluding inversion). A considerable proportion of our primitive metaphors or analogies have been taken over by the peculiarly elaborated system we call science, for scientific naming cannot escape metaphor, but the operations of science tend progressively to eliminate from primitive images the personally or communally incidental meanings and to preserve an ever more denotative and universal residue. The allegoric features of scientific thought thus tend to be progressively displaced as logic replaces analogy and metaphor gives way to disciplined hypothesis. The nonscientific reaches of our experience remain untouched by this process, and we continue to view them metaphorically.

Scientific methods for the study of hypothetical systems are fairly well advanced. In recent years, particularly, there has been increasing attention to the formal analysis of how different cultures classify plants (ethnobotany), animals (ethnozoology), kinship relationships, colors, and a wide range of other phenomena. The broad enthusiasm for a more "cognitive" approach to culture has given rise to important new departures in what has come to be called ethnoscience, in ethnopsychology, and in transformational linguistics, and has greatly illuminated a number of traditional problems in the analysis of culture. The semantic problems of analyzing hypothetical or denotative systems are enormously facilitated by the fact that they are denotative and by the additional fact that men everywhere apply to the classification of such phenomena the rules of universal human logic. The discovery of the universal in the particular is, after all, the primary goal of science.

Vastly less attention is being paid by anthropologists to the metaphoric side of culture, the semantic problems of which are far less tractable. We cannot usefully compare the denotative references in a form of statement that is intrinsically connotative. And we cannot usefully apply the laws of logic to structures that specifically refuse to obey them. The linkage in a metaphorical transformation, like that in a hypothetical one, is real and experiential. But whereas hypotheses are tested and accepted or rejected by their "fit" with universal extracultural experience, metaphors are selected by their communicability—by their "fit" with cultural experience in a specific context. The natural taxonomy of metaphors is a matter of structure and context. In theory, the latter is the cause of the former: the context explains which structures will be communicated and which will not.

We are at present much farther along in developing a methodology for the study of structure than in describing and analyzing context. Much of contemporary behavioral science, indeed, is dedicated to structural description. In the present connection, therefore, it is necessary to specify that the study of connotative structure rests on the same assumptions and may usefully employ the same techniques but requires the special operation of eliminating denotation. A folk classification or ethnoscientific taxonomy that recognizes the differences between black and white birds is hypothetical, not metaphoric. A classification that differentiates people as "upper" and "lower" or "raw" and "cooked" rests on metaphor.

The study of context is appreciably more problematic. Location of cultural events in space and time requires a description of cultural space and cultural time, and our existing systems of description and classification are often too imprecise for the purpose. Cultural position is perhaps best defined in terms of role structures. The location of an event may be specified in terms of the roles represented in it—the social positions of the participants and the behavior triggered by their juxtaposition. It is not difficult to identify the social positions (the statuses) represented in most social situations. It is much more difficult to be sure which of them the situation will activate. The reason would seem to be that we can locate persons in cultural space in a general way, using a somewhat static methodology and hoping they will stay put, but the precise identification of roles requires more than coordinates in space—even cultural space. It requires time as well.

A man in conversation with his wife and child may act as a husband

and father, male, playmate, or even small child, either simultaneously or successively, but which he will be doing at a given moment depends on the location of that moment in a larger sequence of events. We cannot predict what he will be doing at the moment of observation until we can identify the pattern in the events that lead up to it. The crucial relevance of this problem to the study of metaphor may be illustrated with an example. Consider the shifting significance of the word *dear* in the following usages:

a dear	dear, dear	dear John	dear heart
dear me	dear sir	dearest	dearie
my dear	oh dear	yes, dear	dearie-o

Each expression implies a context. A novelist wishing to manipulate or describe such contexts can readily paint the scene for us through careful selection of such metaphors. We immediately know a great deal about the role structure depicted (the age, sex, class, and relationship of the in-dividuals) and about their past and present interaction. For the scientist, the problem is to identify how we know these things—how to generalize the case of which this is but an isolated set of examples. We can do this only by placing the events within the communicative context that pro-duces them—in time as well as space. We need to know who says what to whom, but we also need to know when he will say it. The archaism of *dear heart*, the initial position of *dear sir*, or the vocative use of *my dear* are patterned in time as well as social setting.

Full identification of context in time and space is thus essential to the scientific study of the metaphor. There is, however, no generally accepted method for such identification. Careful collection of texts can give us the microsequences necessary for relating utterances to their immediate en-vironment. Often we need more: a description of setting in something like the dramatist's sense of scene. Winter tales or winter rituals may be struc-tured by their position within the year. Day and night evoke different roles from the same persons. A historic moment may sharply condition particular metaphoric structures. We need a much more adequate con-ceptualization of these problems than we have so far developed.

As a means to this end, the present work is designed to explore the relationships between the contexts and communication of lore. My guiding hypothesis about *metaphor* is that it is less communicable at any given level of intensity of contact than *hypothesis*. A number of well-established facts make this a far from self-evident assertion, but it is not readily brought to decisive test. I remain persuaded that it is true. We know, for example, that folktales (like those of the *Panca Tantra*), ballads (like *Heer Halewijn*), and myths (like that of *Tawkxwax*) have spread widely, and sometimes rapidly, over whole continents and beyond. But, to choose an accessible example, it took Lévi-Strauss to diffuse Tawkxwax to me, and I doubt that very many North Americans got it much sooner. I have read Lévi-Strauss' analysis of the myth with close attention, but although I can reproduce the scientific argument with fair accuracy, I doubt that I could retell the myth with anything like the same precision. In contrast, the equally South American potato reached both Lévi-Strauss' ancestors and mine several generations back. If Paraguay invents a better mouse-trap, I would predict that it will beat *Tawkxwax* to Omaha even now.

Sheer geographic diffusion is, of course, not the point. *Heer Halewijn* spread in the days and at the hands of specialized ballad singers in each country. If it were to be diffused today, both its path and the results would certainly be different. But it is my argument that it or any other metaphorical structure requires more intense contact and a more specialized context to be diffused at all than would a hypothetical structure of comparable complexity. What is distinctive about the formation of lore is its context—the communicative arrangements that give it structure by permitting it to survive and to be perpetuated when the context is right for it.

In considering lore a laboratory for bringing such a theory to test, we must be more precise about describing its contexts in communicative terms. We must seek out favorable test cases for applying general theoretical principles, cases approximating the linear transmission of our classic model or the more elaborate networks of institutional social life. While much of our knowledge of such matters is at present describable only in qualitative terms, we need ultimately to quantify the communicative loading and structural complexity that appear to be our most promising leads to explaining why the complex lore of mankind behaves as it does. And we need to expand our view of lore to include the whole phenomenon, accepting no traditional distinctions that impede free and precise comparison and analysis of how metaphors are created and transmitted.

Chapter 2

Preliterature

There is a sense in which the modern mind can be traced more surely to the convergence of the world's lore upon post-Renaissance Europe than to the parallel convergence and elaboration of scientific and technological ideas. Gradually but cumulatively modern Europe has been brought into ever more intimate contact with the ideas of mankind. Once breached by the Crusades and the rediscovery of the Greek and Roman classics, Europe's isolation has given way at an accelerating pace before the broadening literary and scientific horizons of the age of exploration and discovery, colonialization and colonialism, world trade and world politics, and self-analysis. In a relatively brief span Europe has come abruptly face to face with the great and exotic civilizations of the present and the past and with its own history and prehistory. Our own generation may be the first in several centuries that has not discovered a new civilization.

In a broader sense, of course, the "discovery" of a civilization is not a momentary event—it is a gradually unfolding process. Even in our own day we continually "discover" important parts of the lore of mankind as new translations or better scholarship make available to us the scrolls of Qumran, the Egyptian papyri, the oral traditions of little known peoples of New Guinea, Buddhist texts, Chinese poetry, and Central American, Cretan, or Etruscan inscriptions. Our generation is clearly heir to a continuing Renaissance, a vast and still growing treasurehouse of the lore of the past to which we have access on a scale unparalleled in history.

Europe's discovery of the rest of the world was simultaneous with the world's discovery of Europe, but in several significant respects the process was far from mutual. The confluence of the ideas of Hellenism, Islam, the Orient, and the Americas did not take place on the African coast or the Yang-tze, but in the great cities and universities of Western Europe. And while Europe began to have increasing access to Latin or vernacular translations of other literatures, the flow of information in the reverse direction was almost negligible. Chinese, Arabic, Bengali, Malay, or Persian translations of Europe's (or one another's) works suffer even now from an almost insurmountable lag. Even in Japanese and Russian the problem is serious. The question here is not whether Japanese or Russian translate as much of Western European literature as we do of theirs. It is whether Japanese or English is in the better position to confront simultaneously the lore of Latin, Zulu, Mongolian, Polish, and Quechua. Needless to say, if Japanese comes off second best in such a comparison, the situation of Malay or Swahili is still more isolated. It is apparent that in a significant sense Europe has fallen heir to the world's ideas in a relatively unilateral and exclusive degree.

Almost from the first, European awareness of these new and foreign ideas has been phrased in terms of distance in time and space. Things have seemed "ours" or "theirs" or prosaic or exotic in proportion to remoteness in geography or history. And the exotic, the quaint, the fantastically different, or the incredibly ancient have exercised a powerful fascination in the European imagination. The dichotomy has precedents, for example, in Herodotus' fascination with the antiquities of Egypt or in Tacitus' admiration for his German contemporaries. By the early nineteenth century this sense of wonder had found its way into the nascent science of "folklore."

PREHISTORY OF FOLKLORE

Men were obviously interested in lore long before the nineteenth century. Greek and Roman intellectuals even had theories about it: that popular lore was the decadent representation of a former golden age that the poets felt bound to restore, or the related (and much debated) view attributed to Euhemerus that myths and legends represented allegories of the real historical events of former times, distorted by memory and confused by substituted elements. Not only in Greek and Latin but also in most other written languages of ancient times, we are indebted to the curiosity and interest of our ancestors in the lore of their forebears for the recording and preservation of a huge corpus of folkloristic materials: Aesop's *Fables*, the *Vedas, Brahmanas, Upanishads, Jatakas*, the *Mahabharata* and *Panchatantra*, the *Thousand and One Nights*, the *Avesta*, the *Old Testament*, the sagas and *Eddas*, the romances, exempla, fabliaux, the *Gesta Romanorum*, the *Shih Ching, Tripitaka*, and the *Pert em Hru* or "book of the dead"—thousands of pages of ancient literature that would otherwise be lost to us.

By the sixteenth century, European travelers, missionaries, and explorers were able to give relatively accurate accounts of the cultures they encountered, including fragments of their literatures, as in Sahagún's *Relación* of the culture of ancient Mexico. By the seventeenth century Europeans were taking an active interest in seeking out foreign oral literature, as is attested to by such works as Joseph Justus Scaliger and Thomas Erpinius' *Proverbiorum Arabicorum Centuriae Duae* ("Two Centuries of Arabic Proverbs"), written in 1614. There was also a continuing tradition of literary exploitation of Europe's own folklore, of which the *Pentamerone* of Giambattista Basile (1634–1636) may be taken as characteristic. By the eighteenth century it began to seem less necessary to rework folklore materials to suit established literary canons; the materials became interesting in themselves. The transition may be seen in such works as Charles Perrault's *Contes de ma Mère l'Oye* (1697), Thomas Percy's *Reliques of Ancient English Poetry* (1765), Johann Gottfried von Herder's *Stimmen der Völker* (1778–1779), and Sir Walter Scott's *Minstrelsy of the Scottish Border Ballads* (1802). Even in the eighteenth century leading figures of the Romantic movement had begun to take a real interest in folklore materials. Goethe, for example, was such a "folklorist." Something of the same interest drove Hans Christian Andersen to the composition of his enormously popular *Eventyr* ("Fairy Tales"; 1835–1872).

Increasingly accurate recording of folk literature caused scholars to recognize a difference between oral and written expression. The controlling hypothesis of the science of folklore has been that oral literature is conservative and therefore constitutes a strategic datum for the understanding of whatever is primitive, exotic, ancient, and childish. There can be little question of the debt that folklorists owe to Rousseau's conceptions of the nobility of the unspoiled barbarian, just as there seems little question of Rousseau's debt to the wistful pastoralism of the Roman poets or to Caesar's high regard for the sturdy Belgians. With its passion for history and origins and for science and first causes, the nineteenth century saw in folklore a direct representation of ancient traditions, the scientific study of which would lead to the reconstruction of the primeval origins of literature.

Almost from its inception, the serious comparative study of folklore has been importantly subject to schism. Three basic attitudes may be broadly distinguished, which have also come to be organized as schools of thought and even as separate traditions of comparative literature: (1) belletristic, (2) philological, and (3) culturological. Roughly speaking, these approaches correspond respectively to the opinions of (1) writers, critics, and teachers of "language and literature," (2) linguists, historical folklorists, historians, and folk artists, and (3) anthropologists and other social scientists. We hardly need to insist that this classification is at best a clumsy description of a complex reality.

The literati tend on the whole to suspicion, mistrust, or outright hostility toward scientism in literature. Accustomed to the intricacy and subtlety of connotative problems in sophisticated genres of written literature, they incline to believe that only intuition, insight, judgment, taste, and style are reliable guides in any literary problem. And although they may accept the disciplines of historical and textual criticism, they doubt the efficacy of broad comparative theories and extol the importance of uniqueness and creativity. This attitude does not preclude the study of folklore, and many folklorists have always been influenced by it. But the implied assumptions are crippling to scientific folklore. Francis James Child (1825–1896), the Harvard Chaucerian scholar whose *English and Scottish Ballads* (8 vols., 1857–1859) is one of the great monuments of folklore study, exemplifies this stance.

The philologists and others who accept a broader range of generalization tend to see folklore as at least a possible science. They tend to be historical taxonomists, classifiers, and reconstructers, working by painstaking comparison from variant to type to archetype. If the center of interest of folklore in literature proper is *Geist*, among folklorists of this type it is history. And, accordingly, methods have been elaborated for applying to unwritten materials the evaluative, comparative, and critical sense of the historian, always with an eye to illuminating in this way reaches of history not otherwise accessible to us. The Finnish school of folklore is one major focus of this attitude to folklore study.

Social scientists have approached folklore problems eclectically and sporadically, often with a scientistic bias against the analogic and connotative complexity they imply. Methods have been comparative, interpretative, analytic, and, occasionally, experimental; and problems have tended to be derived from regnant psychological, sociological, ethnological, or philosophic issues rather than from the character of literature as such. Franz Boas (1858–1942), whose contribution to the establishment of folklore as a field of study in the United States was enormous, exemplifies this approach.

It may readily be seen that such consensus as we have had on the nature of lore rests on the widely shared suspicion that it is historically conservative, that its simplicity and primitivism result from an unusual degree of resistance to change. This is an axiom difficult to assess, but it has found very widespread acceptance, and it has been fundamental to folklore studies for more than a century. Most of the characteristic uses of folklore have been closely related to this fact, and it is the primary intellectual basis for the continuing segregation of oral from written literature.

POLITICS OF FOLKLORE

The maturation of modern nationalistic sentiments in Western Europe toward the end of the eighteenth century brought about a new political myth. If right and truth could no longer be sought in the divinity of the king's person and the mystique of the imperial tradition, they could be traced to the sublime will of the people of the nation. It was stirring at such a moment to find (or imagine) the integrity of the untutored *folk* still intact and resistant to all manner of sophisticated (and corrupting) influences. Revindicative movements for social justice and the glorification of the citizenry came into being almost spontaneously as nation after nation came under the influence of the new romantic ideology. The exaltation of whatever was national became a major part of the European way of life, and in this process folklore was often important. The secondary states particularly sought in folklore a substitute for the literary traditions they largely lacked. Finland founded the first folklore society in the world, and the Baltic and Balkan states entered the field with a vigor they have marshaled for few other enterprises. Like nationalism itself, the interest in folklore has since spread to most of the world and has everywhere proved to have an astonishing immunity to ideology. The *folk* have been courted almost equally by dictators and democrats, royalists, republicans, fascists, and communists.

If the seeds of folklore studies lie in antiquarian curiosity, the growth of the young plant was fertilized by politics. In Europe particularly, it became vital to have a careful and precise identification of popular culture and its role in history. Strangely, this identification crystallized around the term *folklore*. Coined around 1846 by William John Thoms (1803–1885), the founder and long time editor of *Notes and Queries*, the English word has come to be adopted across Europe from Portuguese to Russian. It is even occasionally used in German, in which the commoner expression is the cognate *Volkskunde* ("lore of [a] people"), as distinguished from *Völkerkunde* ("lore or science of peoples" and hence "ethnology").

A representative modern definition of *folklore* is that of Ralph Steele Boggs (1901–):

> As a body of materials, folklore is the lore, erudition, knowledge, or teachings, of a folk, large social unit, kindred group, tribe, race, or nation, primitive or civilized, throughout its history. It is the whole body of traditional culture, or conventional modes of human thought and action (Leach, 1949–1950:690).

Everywhere the concept tends to focus on the cultural conservatism and ambivalent political importance of the traditions of the "folk"—in Europe the illiterate peasant class. In addition to circling the globe and exploring the past, Europe began to discover itself in its folklore.

LINGUISTICS OF FOLKLORE

Attention of the earliest folklorists was naturally drawn to the peculiarly linguistic character of their materials and especially to the parallel value of folklore and language for purposes of historical reconstruction.

The period was passionate in its search for origins, and it was spectacularly rewarded by the successful reconstruction of the relationships among the Indo-European languages and the discovery of the laws of phonetic correspondence among them. Both the folklore and linguistics of the time are dominated by the figure of Jakob Ludwig Karl Grimm (1785–1863). His principal works are:

> *Über den altdeutschen Meistergesang,* 1811.
> (with Wilhelm Karl Grimm) *Kinder- und Hausmärchen,* 2 vols., 1812–1815.
> *Deutschen Sagen,* 1816–1818.
> *Deutsche Grammatik,* 1819.
> *Deutsche Mythologie,* 1835.
> *Deutsches Wörterbuch,* 1854.
> *Deutsche Rechtsaltertümer,* 1899 (4th ed.).

Given the context of their work, the Grimm brothers were naturally inclined to relate Indo-European folklore to Indo-European linguistics, and the resulting emphasis upon India introduced a distortion into folklore from which it has not yet entirely recovered. This was one of the most important roots of the Aryan myth that confused the folklore of the nineteenth century and devastated the politics of the twentieth century, for the Grimms were inclined to credit the Indo-Europeans with the invention of tales even when they knew the tales to occur in Southern Bantu, and they were willing to trace tales from place to place on fragmentary evidence. The latter foible came about because of a conviction that folktales were originally myths and that the reconstruction of their original forms could only be achieved by the piecing together of extant fragments. The linkage that justified the piecing was philology: the etymological relationships of words and meanings. Although later scholarship has pointed up the weaknesses in the Indo-European and mythological theories with heated ridicule and satire, there can be no question that they are in part correct. Neither the linguistic affiliation of a people nor its traditional mythology is irrelevant to its folk literature. But it is inaccurate to reduce all of oral literature to these two components alone, and to do so leads to erroneous reconstructions.

The philological and linguistic methods of the Grimms were eagerly taken up and run into the ground by a colorful and controversial Sanskrit scholar, Friedrich Max Müller (1823–1900), in his works:

> *The Rig Veda,* 1848.
> *Lectures on Comparative Morphology,* 1856.
> *History of Ancient Sanskrit Literature,* 1859.
> *Lectures on the Science of Language,* 1863.
> *Chips from a German Workshop,* 4 vols., 1872.

> *Introduction to the Science of Religion*, 1873.
> *The Gifford Lectures*, 4 vols., 1892.
> *Contributions to the Science of Mythology*, 1897.

Müller was not alone. He was seconded in his speculations by George Cox, Angelo de Gubernatis, John Fiske, Adalbert Kuhn, Daniel G. Brinton, and Paul Ehrenreich, with whom he shared the view that mythology was the fundamental source of folklore and that the modern tales therefore had hidden meanings that could be unearthed by philology. In large part these hidden meanings were revealed as cosmological: they related to ancient and hypothetical ideas about the heavenly bodies or recurrent circumstances of primitive life. Motifs of folklore were felt to be adequately explained when they had been associatively linked to such phenomena. Some of the associations were certainly ingenious; many were downright fanciful; but while it is legitimate to comment that the mythologists never found a compelling validation of the correctness of their reconstructions, it is equally difficult to prove that associations of this sort have no bearing on folk literature. The errors implicit in etymologizing folklore appear to result more from an exclusive reliance on one aspect of the phenomenon than from any intrinsic illegitimacy of the procedure.

SOCIOLOGY OF FOLKLORE

The later nineteenth century was variously caught up in the socialism, positivism, and evolutionism with which Marx, Comte, and Darwin had stamped the period. The romantic idealism of philology in the person of Müller collided with sociological realism in folklore in the person of Andrew Lang (1844–1912) and in his works:

> *Ballads and Lyrics of Old France*, 1872.
> *Custom and Myth*, 1884–1885.
> *Myth, Ritual and Religion*, 1887.
> *Perrault's Popular Tales*, 1888.
> *The Blue Fairy Book*, 1889.
> *The Red Fairy Book*, 1890.
> *Magic and Religion*, 1901.
> *The Mystery of Mary Stuart*, 1901.
> *History of Scotland*, 4 vols, 1900–1907.

The result was a long and often polemical dispute that greatly enlivened the literature of folklore without generating much light. Müller appears to have been particularly prone to attract this form of argument. A critical parody of the time, for example, used Müller's methods to prove that Müller himself was a myth.

In his positive views Lang shows a broadened grasp of the social bases of literature, suggesting that an ancient tale could be preserved by the peasantry and secondarily re-elaborated by ancient epic poets or modern writers. He was willing to see more diffusion from "race" to "race" than previous writers had admitted, while simultaneously admitting the possibility of autonomous evolution:

> I have frequently shown the many ways in which a tale, once conceived, might be diffused or transmitted. . . . On the other hand, I have frequently said that, given a similar state of taste and fancy, similar beliefs, similar circumstances, a *similar* tale might conceivably be independently evolved in regions remote from each other (Introduction to Cox, *Cinderella*, xi ff., quoted in Thompson 1951: 381–382).

In these views Lang reflected the anthropology of his time, which had begun to wrestle with the intricate problems of historical and evolutionary theory that have dominated the field from the period of Adolf Bastian and Edward B. Tyler.

The new evolutionary and sociologistic context of folklore in the later nineteenth century was never fully stated by Lang, but it found monumental expression in the works of James George Frazer (1854–1941):

> *Totemism*, 1887.
> *The Golden Bough*, 12 vols., 1890.
> *Pausanias' Description of Greece*, 6 vols., 1898.
> *Lectures on the Early History of Kingship*, 1905.
> *Adonis, Attis, Osiris*, 1906.
> *Psyche's Task*, 1909.
> *Totemism and Exogamy*, 4 vols., 1910.
> *The Belief in Immortality and the Worship of the Dead*, 3 vols., 1913–1924.
> *Folklore in the Old Testament*, 3 vols., 1918.
> *Man, God and Immortality*, 1927.
> *Myths of the Origin of Fire*, 1930.
> *Garnered Sheaves*, 1931.
> *The Fear of the Dead in Primitive Religion*, 3 vols., 1933–1936.
> *Aftermath*, 1936.
> *Totemica*, 1937.
> *Anthologia Anthropologica*, 4 vols., 1938–1940.
> *Magic and Religion*, 1944.

Like several of his distinguished contemporaries, Frazer was too good a scholar to be a doctrinaire evolutionist, but the *Zeitgeist* expressed itself in his conviction that what is childish, simple, or primitive must also be atavistic, and his total view of the history of literature shared much with the subtly differentiated simplicity of Darwin's insight in biology. Isolated scraps of lore from here and there could be seen as parts of a grand and orderly process. Customs of the Caribs and Eskimos illuminated those of the Greeks and Hebrews. Frazer was a scholar of enormous industry and great good sense. Despite the often unreliable sources of world ethnography during most of the period of his work, his facts remain by and large sound. He raised important questions. Sometimes, as in his careful analysis of magic, he also contributed mightily to answering them. But his general view of folklore as responsive to a unilinear law of progress ultimately proved unsatisfying and has been largely abandoned. He did as much as any man has ever done to extend the general awareness of folklore materials and folklore problems. *The Golden Bough* has probably been read or consulted by more people than any other work of folklore except perhaps the Grimms' and Andersen's collections of fairy tales. Its principal scientific value may well lie in its ecumenical scope and its careful, detailed documentation of literary and folkloristic regularities around the world.

Just as Lang had seen folk literature as a social fact, to be related to customs, ritual, and law, so Frazer saw clearly the dilemmas of literary context in a world where traditional religious values were attacked on all sides. Even the earliest collectors of folklore had recognized the intimacy of its relation to religion and mythology. Bernardo de Sahagún had sensed this challenge in sixteenth-century Mexico, although he was unable to answer to it. Frazer went farther. He dedicated much of his lifetime to the relation between folklore and folk belief and the basic social institutions of marriage and the state. Although his view of these matters was very far from that of the sociology of his time and his own historical interests kept it that way, Frazer nonetheless achieved an importantly sociological theory of folklore. It is no accident that Durkheim and Lévi-Strauss as well as Freud followed him into the serious study of totemism.

Frazer's sociologism was carried farther by Arnold van Gennep (1873–1957), in his works:

> *Mythes et légendes d'Australie,* 1906.
> *Les rites de passage,* 1909.
> *Légendes populaires et chansons de geste en Savoie,* 1910.
> *La formation des légendes,* 1910.
> *Religion, moeurs et légendes,* 5 vols., 1911–1933.
> *Le folklore.* 1924.
> *Manuel de folklore français contemporain,* 5 vols., 1949–1953.

In van Gennep's work the social context of folklore becomes an explicit and causal feature of it. Rites, customs, beliefs, and legends are seen to have a close and necessary relationship to the makeup of societies, to be in fact specific to the social development of particular societies. Although sharing Frazer's interest in totemism, van Gennep treats the subject much more flexibly and is perfectly willing to consider the same item of lore as myth, legend, or tale in different places or at different times. He sees clearly the functional utility of folklore in furthering the efficacy of rites (myths), teaching proper behavior (animal tales and fables), and explaining duties (legend), and he acknowledges the cosmological significance of complex mythologies for complex cultures. It is characteristic that he pointed out the functions of life crisis rituals in signalizing and ritualizing important changes in social status. Van Gennep's ideas are parallel to those of Hans Naumann and Bronislaw Malinowski, who were also inclined to look for the explanation of lore in the complexities of social (and sometimes psychological) experience.

PSYCHOLOGY OF FOLKLORE

The radically sociological view of folklore was challenged by alternative psychological interpretations. Perhaps the most popular and certainly the most wrong-headed of these was proposed at length by Lucien Lévy-Bruhl (1857–1939) in his works:

> *Les fonctions mentales dans les sociétés inférieures*, 1910.
> *La mentalité primitive*, 1922.
> *L'âme primitive*, 1927.
> *Le surnaturel et la nature dans la mentalité primitive*, 1931.
> *La mythologie primitive*, 1935. (4th ed.)
> *Les carnets de Lucien Lévy-Bruhl*, 1949.

Lévy-Bruhl's thesis was that the primitive mind was "prelogical," and functioned differently from that of civilized mankind. This argument has been attacked in detail by Franz Boas (*The Mind of Primitive Man*, 1911), Richard Thurnwald (*Psychologie des primitiven Denkens*, 1918), Bronislaw Malinowski (*Myth in Primitive Psychology*, 1926), R. R. Marett (*Psychology and Folk-Lore*, 1920), and Paul Radin (*Primitive Man as Philosopher*, 1927), as well as more briefly by many other scholars. Lévy-Bruhl himself, in fact, eventually took much of it back, but the idea has died hard both inside and outside of folklore studies. His phrasing of the proposition was both awkward and erroneous. Had he chosen to defend the prelogical (or analogical) character of connotative thought in all men, we might have been spared a great and noisy controversy and have been farther along.

A quite different psychology of peculiar relevance to folklore was proposed by Wilhelm Max Wundt (1832–1920) in his works:

> *Lehre von den Muskelbewegungen*, 1858.
> *Beiträge zur Theorie der Sinneswahrnehmung*, 1858–1862.

Vorlesungen über die Menschen- und Thierseele, 1863.
Grundzüge der physiologischen Psychologie, 2 vols., 1872-1874.
Logik, 1880.
Ethik, 1886.
System der Philosophie, 1889.
Grundriss der Psychologie, 1896.
Völkerpsychologie, 10 vols., 1900-1920.
Einleitung in die Philosophie, 1901.
Einführung in die Psychologie, 1911.
Elemente der Völkerpsychologie, 1912.

Wundt's ethnopsychology emphasized the psychological differences among different peoples while recognizing the occurrence of pan-human themes as well. Its strength was the careful description of the distribution of particular themes in different groups of mankind. Its weakness lay in its failure to explain these distributions. A vague biologism clings to the concept of ethnic psychology, as it does to the other psychologies of the period. Descriptively, Wundt's was a social psychology, but it failed to explain how particular elements became social in a particular group and why other elements did not. Wundt's ideas were very influential, particularly in Germany and the United States, but modern social psychology has set them aside in favor of conceptions more closely linked to specific contexts of interindividual communication.

The psychology that has had the widest impact on twentieth-century literature as well as on folklore theory is unquestionably that of Sigmund Freud (1856–1939). His major works are:

(with Josef Breuer) *Studien über Hysterie*, 1895.
Die Traumdeutung, 1900.
Über den Traum, 1901.
Zur Psychopathologie des Alltagslebens, 1904.
Der Witz und seine Beziehungen zum Unbewussten, 1905.
Drei Abhandlungen zur Sexualtheorie, 1905.
Der Wahn und die Träume in W. Jensens 'Gradiva,' 1907.
Über Psychoanalyse, 1910.
Eine Kindheitserrinerung des Leonardo da Vinci, 1910.
Totem und Tabu, 1913.
Vorlesungen zur Einführung in die Psychoanalyse, 1917.
Jenseits des Lustprinzips, 1920.
Massenpsychologie und Ich-analyse, 1921.
Das Ich und das Es, 1923.
Selbstbiographische Studie, 1925.
Civilization and Its Discontents, 1930.
Neue Folge der Vorlesungen zur Einführung in die Psychoanalyse, 1933.

Moses and Monotheism, 1939.
Abriss der Psycho-analyse, 1940.
(with D. E. Oppenheim) *Dreams in Folklore*, 1958.

Freud shared with other psychologists of his time the conviction that the causes of psychological phenomena were often hidden and that they were ultimately traceable to biology. But his interest in specific pathologies led Freud to devise methods for exploring the psychic history of the individual in a manner that placed great weight upon interpersonal relationships and communication. His successors have rejected his conceptions of instincts, but his ideas about the interrelationships of learning experiences have had a profound impact on our time. In many areas, Freud's studies led him into the subtlest problems of meaning—in dreams, in humor, in totemism, errors, and religion.

Even if we discount for the breadth of his definitions, Freud's involvement in evolutionary biologism led him to an unwarranted overemphasis on the erotic, an overemphasis deriving from his conviction that psychic processes were energized and directed by the frustration of powerful instincts. Nonetheless, Freud's great achievement was to bring these problems within the scope of scientific discussion and observation, to the enormous enrichment of subsequent theorizing. We may reject the instinctual basis of the Freudian libido, but we shall not again suppose that sexuality is irrelevant to human psychology.

If sex is not simply an instinct, it is nonetheless a central feature of human experience. It is important not because it is physiologically intense, but because it is intimate and private—in Freud's terms, because it is controlled and repressed. Freud demonstrated at length that we cannot understand the associations among ideas unless we are prepared to trace private and disavowed connections. Often the connections are sexual.

Freud also demonstrated that meanings generated in individual experience, including sexual experience, are widely represented in literature. The enormous importance of this finding has led to excesses sometimes comparable to those of the earlier euhemerists and mythologists—some theorists have talked as though the "real" meaning of myths were sexual and as though the other planes of meaning that are undeniably also "there" were purely epiphenomenal. In a particular myth, the marriage of the Sun and Moon may be interpreted as a sexual metaphor or as a cosmological metaphor, but neither interpretation exhausts the motif. Why Sun? Why Moon? Why marriage? Freud has sensitized us to the fact that highly organized sexual conceptions are ubiquitous in lore. We must not forget this fact, but we must not confuse it with the whole of wisdom.

The confrontation of individual psychology (which is Freud's principal preoccupation) and social psychology (which is Wundt's) poses problems that greatly transcend the boundaries of folklore. They are, however, critically relevant to folklore and cannot be sidestepped. Even the earliest folklorists wrestled with the problem of the independence of literary inventions in different times and places. An instinct psychology like Freud's would make true independence unthinkable. On the other hand, the alternatives have not always been clear, hard-headed science. Maurice Halbwachs (*La mémoire collective*, 1948), for example, derived from social analysis as Carl Gustav Jung (with C. Kerenyi, *Essays on a Science of Mythology*, 1949) did from psychoanalysis, a conception of shared psychological traditions that may be widespread without in fact being universal. These efforts suffer, however, from a crippling vagueness on the crucial matter of how these psychological configurations are created and maintained. The concepts of "collective memory" and the "collective unconscious" seem to imply little more in the last analysis than that some kinds of psychological attitudes are socially shared.

HISTORICO-GEOGRAPHICAL SCHOOL

In considerable independence of these psychological developments, a separate tradition of folklore developed along predominantly historical lines. Traceable to the very cradle of European folklore in Finland, this development involved a kind of apostolic succession from Elias Lönnrot (1802–1884), the compiler-editor of the *Kalevala*, and the founding of the Finnish Literary Society in 1831. Lönnrot's works are:

> *Kalevala*, 1835.
> *Kanteletar* ("Lyric Songs"), 1840.
> *The Proverbs of the Finns*, 1842.
> *The Riddles of the Finns*, 1844.
> *The Magic Runes of the Finnish People*, 1880.

It was Lönnrot's good fortune to mine a vein of folklore definitionally beyond the range of Indo-European and hence immune to "Aryanism" from the first. When Aryanism gave way in the rest of Europe to the pan-Indianism of Loiseleur Deslongchamps, Theodor Benfey and Emmanuel Cosquin and to the pan-Egyptianism of Grafton Elliot Smith, Finnish scholarship was again immune. The Finnish folklorists were simply forced to have a more realistic view of how tales vary in passing back and forth between unrelated languages. Lönnrot spent his life on the study of the song cycles that form the *Kalevala*. He also passed the problem on to his student, Julius Krohn (1835–1888), who wrote:

> *The Genetic Explanation of the Kalevala*, 2 vols., 1884–1885.
> *Kalevalan toisinnot* ("The Variants of the Kalevala"), 1888.

The History of Finnish Literature, 1897.
Investigations Concerning the Kanteletar, 1900–1902.

Krohn's achievement was the development of the "historico-geographic method," a carefully reasoned system for deriving reconstructive results from the examination of numbers of variants of a single tale. His final works were edited by his son, Kaarle Krohn (1863–1933), who continued his father's work in his books:

Volkssagen, 1886–1893.
Bär (Wolf) und Fuchs, 1888.
Mann und Fuchs, 1891.
Skandinavisk Mytologi, 1922.
Magische Ursprungsrunen der Finnen, 1924.
Die folkloristische Arbeitsmethode, 1926.
Übersicht über einige Resultate der Märchenforschung, 1931.
Zur finnischen Mythologie, 1932.

Kaarle Krohn was the founder (with Axel Olrik) of the Folklore Fellows (1907) and edited the *FF Communications* until his death. His book on method codified his father's historico-geographic approach, which was also taken up and given still fuller expression by Antti Aarne (1867–1925) in:

Vergleichende Märchenforschungen, 1907.
Verzeichnis der Märchentypen, 1910.
Die Zaubergaben, 1911.
Leitfaden der vergleichenden Märchenforschung, 1913.
Übersicht der Märchenliteratur, 1913.
Die Tiere auf der Wanderschaft, 1913.
Der Tiersprachkundige Mann und seine neugierige Frau, 1914.
Schwänke über schwerhörige Menschen, 1914.
Der Mann aus dem Paradiese, 1915.
Der reiche Mann und sein Schwiegersohn, 1916.
Vergleichende Rätselforschungen, 1918–1920.
Das estnisch-ingermanländische Maie-Lied,
Das Lied von Angeln der Jungfrau Vallamos,
Die magische Flucht, 1930.

Aarne's methods of folklore reconstruction are a careful blending of the principles of historical criticism and historical linguistics. He insisted on beginning from the particular—carefully recorded texts of many closely related *variants* of a similar tale. Where the resemblances among the variants could be documented fully, they were then assumed to be derivative of a common original, which he called a *type.* If enough different recensions could be amassed over a broad enough area, one could then move backward from contemporary lore to relatively remote origins and reconstruct the *archetype* in much the same fashion that linguists reconstruct the lexicon of proto-Indo-European. The method implies, however, full documentation and explanation of the similarities and differences among the variants by explicit and geographically plausible hypotheses of contact of the traditions represented at each stage of the work.

This method is, of course, slow and costly. It also inevitably places a great emphasis on historical particularity. It has been widely recognized that there are many other resemblances among literary products that elude Aarne's careful seining operations, some of them of the widespread character of *Elementargedanken*, the fundamental ideas that Bastian attributed to human nature and that Frazer documented in such overwhelming volume. Subsequent folklore studies have pursued both these leads, as seems right and proper, for they are not truly contradictory. Lore has both particularity and generality, and it seems inevitable that we should study both. Aarne's method of painstaking reconstruction from a substantial corpus of variants remains today the most rigorous and useful approach to the historical reconstruction of particular tales.

In addition to clarifying, codifying, and demonstrating the historico-geographic method of the Finnish school, Aarne made a major contribution to comparative folklore in his catalogue of European folktale types. This classification has been widely used and has later been modified and expanded into a worldwide classification system by Stith Thompson.

Closely related to the Finnish school in spirit, albeit not in close historical contact with it, were the German and American ethnological traditions, both of which developed specific techniques for relating cultural history to geography. Both agreed on the "age area principle": that the oldest culture traits should be the most widely distributed. This assumption is also material to Aarne's method in folklore. Beyond this point, the Americans became pragmatic historians, while the Germans became theoreticians. The result was the theory of "culture areas" in the United States and of "culture areas and strata" (*Kulturkreise und Schichten*) in Germany and Austria.

The central theoretical concern of all of these scholars was the problem of invention and diffusion: how much inventiveness and how much dependency upon their neighbors must we attribute to the "folk"? On this point, Aarne was conservative: each tale had to be considered a completely separate entity for purposes of reconstruction, and its diffusion from a given origin could be proved only by the fullest possible documentation of detailed correspondences accompanied by the explanation of variations. Clark Wissler (1870–1947) was a moderate. He advocated that continuous distribution of elements of even moderate complexity could be considered evidence of historical contact. Wilhelm Schmidt (1868–1954) was more radical. He advocated that diffusion was considered demonstrated even when the distribution of elements was discontinuous if there were a sufficient number of sufficiently detailed resemblances between two areas. Alfred Louis Kroeber (1876–1960) added the suggestion that "stimulus diffusion" might link two cultural phenomena showing discontinuous distribution. He advocated that the general idea might have been diffused and the details independently invented.

In the fields of technology and ecology (or, more broadly, of science) the evolutionists or "parallelists" have generally had the better of the argument. Parallel invention of similar scientific ideas has been documented very extensively. It is otherwise in fields of cultural experience less intimately related to environment. Indeed, we may say that the broad range of the materials of folklore generally support the assumption that in this aspect of culture the recurrence of even very simple elements can never be satisfactorily traced to independent invention but is invariably a consequence of communicative contact on some historical level. Here the "diffusionists" seem justified in their assumption of limited human creativity.

A large number of apparent exceptions to this conclusion continue to plague folklore studies. Very commonly these prove on closer inspection to be hypothetical rather than metaphoric. The association of seasonal phenomena with the agricultural cycle (light : spring : fertility), for example, is empirical, not poetic, and is easily independently invented. The association of stars with rabbits and alcoholic drinks (Aztec) would appear to be thoroughly metaphorical and wildly unlikely to occur similarly to two separated minds. Folklorists have learned only slowly to concentrate on truly folkloristic problems, and many traditional themes and motifs are not literary problems at all, but scientific ones.

REVISED FOLK

The twentieth century has greatly expanded and developed our understanding of the social groups that were formerly called the "folk." Drawing on the traditions of German sociology, and particularly on Ferdinand Tönnies' distinction between community (*Gemeinschaft*) and society (*Gesellschaft*), rural sociologists and social anthropologists have dedicated considerable attention to the study of "folk communities." The leading figure in this field was Robert Redfield (1897–1958), whose conception of the folk showed a continuous growth and development over the length of his distinguished and influential career. His major works are:

Tepoztlan, a Mexican Village, 1930.
(with Alfonso Villa Rojas) *Chan Kom, a Maya Village,* 1934.

The Folk Culture of Yucatan, 1941.
Chan Kom: A Village That Chose Progress, 1950.
The Primitive World and Its Transformations, 1954.
The Institutions of Primitive Society, 1954.
The Little Community, 1955.
Peasant Society and Culture, 1956.

Redfield saw folk culture as a "type," differentiated from nonfolk or sophisticated culture by the degree of its isolation and localism. All of culture was seen as developing away from this folk type by virtue of the increasing integration of society and the increasing cultural communication among peoples. Redfield's achievement was the gradual conversion of the concept of folk society from a stage or category into a range of points on a communicative continuum. The term became relative rather than absolute, and dynamic rather than taxonomic.

Redfield's students have documented the utility of this approach in "little communities" all over the world. In effect, these studies demonstrate that no categorization of cultures into "folk" and "sophisticate" can be anything but arbitrary and relative. The cultural process as Redfield described it is unitary and dynamic. Cultural isolation is never total, and it is relevantly present even in the most complex societies. It is apparent that the lore of the folk can be set apart from that of the sophisticates only in a relative sense. An adequate theory of the processes that shape it must therefore span the whole of the "folk-urban continuum."

STRUCTURE AND FUNCTION IN LORE

Modern folklore has been enriched by all of the insights and ideas of the history that has been briefly sketched. Its scope and richness are nowhere better represented than in the works of Stith Thompson (1885–):

European Tales among North American Indians, 1919.
The Types of the Folk-Tale, 1928.
Tales of the North American Indians, 1929.
(with Curtis H. Page) *British Poets of the Nineteenth Century,* 1929.
Motif-Index of Folk-Literature, 6 vols., 1936.
Our Heritage of World Literature, 1938
(with B. D. N. Grebanier) *English Literature and Its Backgrounds,* 1939.
The Folktale, 1946.
(with Jonas Balys) *The Oral Tales of India,* 1958.

Thompson's work is lineally related to the tradition of the Finnish school of folklore studies, but it has involved a considerable expansion of scope and method. Thompson early translated and expanded Aarne's classification of folktale types, the somewhat rigid taxonomy of carefully reconstructed families of tales resulting from rigorous application of the historico-geographic method to Europe. But Thompson's later classification of *motifs* is in some respects a new departure—an essay in thematic analysis applicable more or less directly to any item of lore, whether or not rigorous comparative reconstruction can be achieved.

No system of universal classification solves all of the relevant problems. Thompson's motif index is, however, an important modernization of folklore technique. The basic unit of the system is a pattern concept consonant with the structural ideas that have characterized general culture studies in recent decades. Motifs in folklore are like the phonetic dimensions of linguistics or like patterns, themes, configurations, and values in general culture theory. They are, to a first approximation, structural units.

Probably the first significant progress in the strictly structural analysis of folklore occurs in the works of Vladimir Iakovlevich Propp:

Morfologiia Skazki ("Morphology of Tales"), 1928.
Istoricheskie Korni Volshebnoi Skazki ("Historical Roots of the Fairy
    Tale"), 1946.
Russkii Geroicheskii Epos ("The Russian Heroic Epic"), 1955.
Narodnye Liricheskie Pesni ("Lyric Popular Songs"), 1961.
Severnorusskie Skazki v Zapisiakh A. I. Nikoforova ("North Russian
    Tales in the Writings of A. I. Nikoforov"), 1961.
Russkie Agrarnye Prazdniki ("Russian Agricultural Festivals"),
    1963.

Propp saw that fairy tales share as a genre a limited number of constant and stable elements that he called the *functions* of the actors, occurring in the same sequence, regardless of how and by whom they are executed in a particular tale. In a sense Propp's phrasing is indeed analogous to functionalist theory in other areas of science at the same time: he was concerned with the invariance of the relationship between certain structural units and the whole (in this case, the tale) in which they are embedded. He himself calls the schematic coding of the anatomy of tales a *structure*, and it is as an analyst of structure that he has lately begun to have an important impact on Western folklore studies.

The most coherent and comprehensive spokesman for the structuralist point of view is Claude Lévi-Strauss (1908–). His major works are:

La vie familiale et sociale des indiens Nambikwara, 1948.
Les systèmes élémentaires de la parenté, 1949.
Race et Histoire, 1952.
Tristes Tropiques, 1955.

Anthropologie structurale, 1958.
Le totémisme aujourd'hui, 1962.
La pensée sauvage, 1962.
Le cru et le cuit, 1964.
Du miel aux cendres, 1966.

In common with other contemporary anthropologists, Lévi-Strauss sees folk literature as a reflection of folk culture, but unlike many theorists in this field he does not see this "reflection" as a functional transformation of folk psychology. Literary structure is interpreted as a cultural phenomenon to be related directly to other dimensions of cultural structure. The method of description and analysis he proposes is cognate with componential analysis of linguistic features, and the result is the depiction of pure structure. The one functional postulate he retains is that of coherency or integration. Hence, the nearest thing to a "cause" of the structure of literature is the structure of the rest of the culture from which the literature springs. The association of two metaphors in a particular relationship is presumed to correspond to other parallel relationships in and out of literature. If in literature older brother is to younger brother as the sun is to the moon, we are led to expect a comparable complementarity of roles and concepts elsewhere, as, say, between generations, between the sexes, or between social groups (and, of course, between other dichotomous terms of metaphor).

Although Lévi-Strauss has given us the clearest exposition of these postulates so far, the most extensive structural analysis of a literary genre known to me is Rassers' (1959) careful dissection of the Javanese folk theater. Rassers analyzes the dramatic structure not only in relation to the semantic content of the plays and the social system in which they are performed but also in relation to the physical organization of the household, the village, and the stage itself. He is not indebted to Lévi-Strauss for this mode of analysis, but arrived at it through independent consideration of the body of theory from which other modern structuralists also draw. The result is in any case a brilliant and thoroughly detailed application of the structural method. For an introduction to other notable halls in the museum of folklore, modern as well as historical, the reader may be referred to Alan Dundes' admirable book *The Study of Folklore* (1965) and its excellent selected bibliography.

In recent decades the sciences of culture have tended to move away from the question of origins toward a kind of dynamic theory—a theory of structure and process. Concepts like "structure," "pattern," and "configuration" have come to be central, and historical problems have tended to be pushed aside in favor of close examination of the synchronic interrelatedness of cultural phenomena. The modern period has greatly altered our perspective on culture, broadening as well as deepening our understanding of it in numbers of ways that bear on lore. It is now possible to see that the "functionalist" themes represented in various fields of science in the earlier part of this century have a logical place in this development but are no longer the frontier.

It does not seem altogether premature to speculate that we are now witnessing a kind of synthesis of the ahistorical theories of the first half of the century with the abiding historical sense of the preceding period. Structural and functional theories (of personality, of society, of culture, of organism) have always declared dynamics to be their goal. They now appear to be approaching that goal. The integrity and sharp boundaries of these organismic concepts have grown blurred and probabilistic. We are ready to put them back into the context from which they were ripped by Darwin, Freud, Durkheim, and Malinowski—the ebb and flow of real history. But we are in a position to do so with a new sophistication and precision.

It is my personal conviction that the key concept in this emerging synthesis is communication. I am further persuaded that we can single out one particular contribution to the theory of communication as being of very nearly decisive relevance: Claude E. Shannon's proof (1949) of the mathematical characteristics of "noisy" circuits. There are several other mathematical models for the communicative process. Shannon's appears to me to come closest to conceptualizing what a minimal theory of cultural structure might involve: the differentiation of structure from randomness or of news from noise. Shannon's proof states that the amount of information that can flow in any noisy circuit (that is, in the presence of random interference) is proportional to redundancy, and, conversely, that the information value of any one message is proportional to nonredundancy or to uncertainty (the surprise value of the item). Although communications engineers disclaim any very broad applicability of these principles, it is my belief that they come very close at least to providing us with a model for how structures of the type found in lore may be generated.

The structures of lore do not come from nowhere. They emerge from randomness (that is, from nonstructure) only as they are forced to do so in the presence of antecedent structure. Because the structure of lore cannot be ascribed to the environment, it can only derive from the communicative properties of the circuits that create it. It is my belief that we do not create lore because we need it. We don't. We create it because our social and cultural arrangements as men give us too much redundancy not to. We have simply developed as a species more communicative potential than we "need" for environmental purposes and hence we transmit in culture an overload of highly consequential but entirely metaphorical structure. From the standpoint of our groping efforts toward science and rationality, we are prisoners of our lore.

It follows from these assumptions that there is only one way in which an identical metaphor can occur in two human minds: they must be, directly or indirectly, in contact. Despite its continued importance in many modern theories, instinct appears to me to be an untenable alternative. This is not to say that the experiential residue of common environment may not look very much like "instinct" over most of the range we are called upon to examine. Our experience of the "internal environment" of our own bodies, for example, must surely condition in us many similar reactions. I shall argue that such reactions (the universal Freudian symbols, for example) are learned: they are hypotheses rather than metaphors (see Chapter 7). For present purposes, it is enough to note that a similar pattern of true lore can be theoretically attributed to independent invention only on the basis of some type of instinct theory. Modern psychology does not encourage this inference.

Chapter 3

Speech

"In the beginning was the Word." In a literal and scientific sense the origin of culture (of the uniquely human capacity for highly intensive communication) is coincident with and dependent upon speech. It is my contention that the original "word" was a metaphor, and that it had to be so in the nature of things.

Communication is not in nature restricted to man. On the contrary, it is an intrinsic feature of energy transformations in inorganic matter and lies at the heart of the genetic mechanism that links all life. Many other animals communicate by touch, smell, gesture, or sound, and some animal systems of communication are sufficiently similar to human language to suggest that they may even be *strictu sensu* protocultural. Many animals have been shown to be far more dependent upon experience and learning than we formerly believed. They signal, they express themselves, they even symbolize. But no animal except man attains the intensity, complexity, and flexibility of speech. In a sense what the other animals lack is connotation. And connotation is intrinsic to human speech.

A minimally effective communication system could theoretically be derived for a species like ours, which would eliminate unnecessary redundancies and concentrate on the efficient transmission of necessary information. Such a system might be somewhat like a computer language but one that carries with it the necessary duplication of information to guarantee successful transmission under conditions of random interference. It would be somewhat like a mathematical system, in that it would be programmed in an orderly and self-consistent fashion, but it would have to be an applied mathematics, since it would receive "inputs" of information relevant to the species. It would have to be a biologically adaptive system, managing its environmental information to the advantage of the species.

Such a system could in theory be purely denotative, operating at a redundancy level capable of communicating only about relevant environing events (including those of the internal environment as well as those of the world outside). Such a system might have advantages, but it would be totally different from any known human language.

Natural selection, with its marked preference for efficiency, might well have created such a system for us, had it been possible to produce one under the conditions of our evolution. What natural selection did, on the other hand, was to evolve the systems we have. Prodigal in experiment, nature has given us a communicative potential that greatly exceeds our adaptive needs. Not only do we communicate all manner of environing facts (pain and pleasure, sights and sounds, emotion and cognition) but also we communicate volubly about things we can share with no other species because they do not exist "out there." Aztec dogs were not fearful that the world would be destroyed at the end of the year. Navaho horses are not afraid of witches. We talk of things like honor, guilt, ghosts, and utopia, not because we must in order to adapt to the world we live in, but because we can. And loquaciously we create another and mythical world not given us by nature but designed, often unaware, by ourselves. Having done so, we must live in both worlds, simultaneously and ambiguously. Since the invention of speech, man's fate has been to live uncertainly between connotation and denotation. It is worth examining why this is so.

PALEOLITHIC LORE

It is paradoxical that we cannot adequately define our species except in terms of language, but we cannot account for our biological evolution without invoking language as a cause. Did man create culture or did culture create man?

We know that the human species emerged gradually both biologically and culturally. No theory of the origin of the species can be predicated on sudden or eventful change. The last great movement toward our modern condition may be said to be the slow increase in the size of the brain and in the efficiency of manufacture of stone tools covering the first half of the Pleistocene, from about 1 million or more to 500,000 years ago. Although the same period involved major climatic changes, including glacial advances and retreats, there is no reason to suppose those might have led to larger brains or better fist axes. Such developments must be explained by natural selection, but the climate does not appear to be the relevant factor.

The changes involved in man's increased brain size are extraordinarily complex. A larger-headed baby means a larger birth canal, a longer infancy, greater dependency, more restriction on the mother's food quest; in short, a whole complex of factors must be altered coordinately, each in a particular direction. No known combination of environmental factors that may have been operating in the early Pleistocene appears to account for these humanizing trends. But one set of conditions has long been felt to explain most of them. If we can just set up a truly human family organization, providing care and protection of wives by husbands and of children by mothers, a new kind of environment is produced. And in this new social environment the mutations prolonging infancy, providing for longer suckling, increasing the disability of pregnancy and increasing head size, may be favorably selected. Otherwise they would be deleterious.

But if the species had to be human to become human, the riddle remains. I believe it can be answered by the assumption that what occurred to set this chain of events in motion was a nongenetic mutation: the invention of language. And we may further assume that this began among the protocultural Australopithecine "man apes" of Africa and Asia early in the Pleistocene and was far along among their *Homo erectus* descendants of the middle Pleistocene. It all goes back to the first Australopithecines to say no—at the right time.

The conversion of wandering bands of man apes into human families is primarily a matter of redundancy. Even modern apes can generate sounds of speechlike complexity, and some of them have the capacity to organize them into systems. In the wild, however, ape bands shift and dissolve and individuals leave and join at intervals, so that even a modest signal system tends to dissolve after a while and remains to be re-invented by a newly constituted group or the next generation. What is required, then, is to stabilize the vocalizing activities of the band so as to guarantee their perpetuation as a system from one generation to the next. Many groups of Australopithecines could well have generated systems of moderate complexity but could have failed to perpetuate them reliably. Binary distinctions of the yes-no type could certainly have been made in such systems. They occur in more primitive forms of animal communication.

A natural selection advantage accrued to the Australopithecine group that first learned to say no about sex. This is true not because their sex life needed regulation but because sex is the behavioral link between the generations, and by controlling sex they created a new communicative situation. An animal capable of saying yes and no, with a million years more or less in which to experiment, could apply the distinction at random to a very large number of contexts. But whereas a food taboo or a grooming taboo might be interesting, it would be devoid of important communicative consequences. An incest taboo is a special and uniquely privileged case.

A specific reorganization of interindividual relationships is required to convert an animal band into a human society. In technical terms, what is required is the simultaneous introduction of endogamy and exogamy.

This could be achieved through a simple yes-no regulation of mating to de-fine the group within which one should mate and the group within which one should not mate. Even if this were done by accident, the nature of the society that did it would be permanently communicatively altered: it would become cultural. Regulated mating, whatever its "functions," has the effect of greatly structuring communications, rendering more intensive the in-group interaction while correspondingly reducing communication with "outsiders." This modest Australopithecine Revolution probably occurred many times, and may even have failed many times over a long period, given the small groups and possible exigencies of Australopithecine life, but its eventual survival was assured by the adaptive advantages of a system thus organized. Such a system guaranteed its proprietors a new order of cumulative evolution enormously more rapid than genetic selection. As has been noted, it even altered their biological nature. But it involved a price: cultural communication made connotation not only possible but in-evitable. Metaphor is intrinsic to human speech because in the last analysis man was created by a metaphor.

The introduction at the dawn of human culture of the polarization of in-group and out-group relationships means that all of subsequent man-kind is condemned to operate on two communicative planes. Some kinds of information (Help! Fire! Watch out!) readily transcend the communica-tive barrier thus erected. Scientific (environmentally relevant) information demonstrably does so. Other kinds (for example, the in-group joke) cannot transcend it at all. Despite strenuous efforts on the part of national security forces of the United States, the Russians had the basic facts of the atomic bomb only a few years after the Americans developed it. Despite equally strenuous efforts of United States propaganda, American democracy re-mains one of our state secrets, vaguely comprehended (but disapproved) in Canada, Australia, and the British Isles, and quite mysterious elsewhere. We are emphatically the victims of endogamy and exogamy.

What the "Southern Apes" invented was ego. Man has no monopoly on individuality, as any observer of animals knows. And if anything other animals are communicatively more isolated than we. But the evolution of human culture imposes on man a consciousness of isolation, exacerbated by the structure of human society itself. With a brain capable of communi-cating with itself far more than with anything else, our extra input of communicative redundancy (implied by in-group loquacity from two structurally differentiated directions: marriageable and nonmarriageable) inevitably strengthens the distinction between self and other. We may therefore hazard the guess that the original expression of truly human awareness was the metaphor *I:you.*

It may be supposed that the differentiation of one's self from others is an evidential matter, a scientific fact. And so it might be under the hypothetical condition of a minimal communication system. In actuality, however, all men learn the distinction and furthermore, learn it in the intense and parochial microenvironment of a specific family or surrogate family. What is learned therefore greatly transcends the minimal truth that I am not you. *I am like you* (*I:you*) is a personification of myself and of you, and a statement of social (and moral) relationship that does not preclude my being like something (or someone) else. Under the rule of transformation by inversion, it can and often does become *I am not like you*. This susceptibility to inversion proves the pattern a metaphor rather than a hypothesis, and the same feature explains the peculiarly human ambiguity ordained by endogamy and exogamy. The human ego is shaped in an Oedipal environment.

In another perspective, the invention of ego is the invention of ego- and ethno-centrism. It converts the loose communicative organization of the protohuman horde into a system guaranteed to create highly structured meanings, share them within the group, and transmit them to the next generation. Revolutionary as such a system must necessarily be, there is every reason to suppose that there were many false starts before a formula was found that would have the effects I have outlined. And many thousands, or even hundreds of thousands, of years were required to establish a fully cultural pattern throughout the species. Many more hundreds of thousands of years have passed since, implying the creation and disappearance of a huge range of human variation of which the modern world leaves only pale reflections. In the later Palaeolithic we find incontrovertible evidence of the cumulative technical evolution and the parochial cultural practices that were the inevitable fruits of this development. The practices are already complex and fully human. Of the earlier period, we can say only that in the beginning was the word, and the word was a pronoun, probably the "pronoun" *no*.

The earliest clear evidence of prehistoric metaphors may well be the burial practices of the Neanderthals of Europe and Western Asia. First perhaps at Wadi el Mughara in Israel and later at many other sites, burials were found in which the body was accompanied by food and weapons. Such a denial of the permanency or finality of death may be taken as evidence of a compounded metaphor something like *life:death::breath:spirit*. The implication seems clear that the individual will have a use for food and weapons after death on a plane unmistakably different from life, yet analogous to it. This in germ is the myth of animism, universal among modern cultures and probably already in existence before 50,000 B.C.

We may be sure that whatever animism may have been shared by the widespread groups of Neanderthals, there must also have been a marked parochialism to their myths as well. Although the elements of this are impossible to reconstruct, it is suggested by such items as the use of red ocher at Chapelle-aux-Saints and elsewhere, the occurrence of a roofed grave at La Ferrassie, and the mountain sheep horns in the burial at Teshik Tash. It has been proposed that certain occasional geometric designs may be spirit journey maps analogous to those drawn by the modern Australian aborigines. Such a metaphor is on the face of it very close to basic animism.

Some scholars believe that the famous *batons de commandement* that make their appearance by about 25,000 B.C. in the Aurignacian culture of Europe may be ritual objects used for shamanistic curing. There seems to be no clear way of deciding the point, but it is possible. It is only later, in Magdalenian times, that these objects are customarily decorated with animal drawings (bison, horse, boar, reindeer, bird, mammoth), and even then the possibility that these are curing spirits remains speculative. The fact that curing beliefs of a generally shamanistic or animatistic type appear to be universal in the cultural traditions of modern man makes it at least credible that they should be found in the Upper Palaeolithic cultures.

By around 13,000 B.C. in the European Gravettian culture there is evidence of a fertility cult, represented in phallic carvings and the widespread execution of small figurines of pregnant women like the famous "Venus" of Willendorf. The underlying metaphor may be something like *man:woman::hunting:pregnancy*. Sexualization of mythology may well be substantially earlier than this. Even in the Mousterian culture, grave offerings seem to be somewhat structured by a kind of sexual dualism— the womblike tomb and the nurturing food versus projectile points and horns. But by Gravettian times this idea clearly became explicit, and while it remains obscure or even ambivalent (as in the Laussel goddess holding bison horns), the evidence is so widespread as to underline the importance of the idea for a large area of ancient Europe.

Western Europe at about the same time shows an overwhelming preoccupation with animals. Speculation that the purpose of the famous cave paintings may have been to assure the game supply seems plausible in view of the Gravettian fertility ideas, and the possible development of animal spirit belief out of an older Aurignacian shamanism has also been suggested. However, the Magdalenians went farther. They danced, played music, and almost certainly sang, and they personified imaginary animals, as in the famous Sorcerer of Trois Frères. Here the metaphor may be *man:spirit::animal:god*. The man is masked and dressed in a reindeer skin but with a tail suggesting a horse: the animal represented must be imaginary. A similar juxtaposition of man and animal occurs in the frieze at Lascaux depicting a dead man and a wounded bison. The ubiquitous animals of Magdalenian cave art may well relate, as has been argued, to an early form of totemism, although any very specifically totemistic structure remains to be demonstrated.

MESOLITHIC CREATION MYTH

It is probable that metaphorical ideas invented any later than the early Mesolithic period would not have had time to spread to all of mankind by the present date. A set of motifs can be identified, however, that is so widely distributed that it strongly suggests that the species had had time enough to share its ideas about creation to a very considerable extent. On the basis of the present (highly incomplete) distributional evidence, it is likely that the men of Mesolithic times already had a creation story somewhat like the sketch that follows, all the elements of which probably occur on every continent today.

In the beginning the God of heaven, supreme and all-wise, created the world. Some say God was neither a man nor a woman, but both. Some say God was born from an egg; others that He sprang from a tree; and still others that He was made by magic or that God was a woman who fell from the sky or even that God was twins. But God was lonely, and so He created the world and all the gods and goddesses. It was not easy, because the Devil was opposed to God's creation and tried to spoil it. When He had made the world, God went to live in the sky.

Many gods and goddesses were created: the Sun God, the Moon God, the Star Gods, the Wind God, the Thunder God, the Rain God, the Storm Goddess and the Thunderbird, the God and Goddess of the Underworld and the dead, the Gods of War, Death, Fire, Drunkenness, Water, and Vegetation, and the Gods and Goddesses of Earth and Love. Some of the gods were part animals. Some were good and some were bad, and they were opposed to each other. They often had banquets and committed incest. Often they were in love with mortals. It is said that the gods lived inside of a hill. The gods are the ancestors of men.

God's son was a great hero, who was conceived miraculously and snatched from his mother's side. God tried to eat him when he was born, and he had to be hidden to escape his enemies. His growth to maturity was miraculous. Some say the hero was twins and that one was good and the other bad. Some say he was a trickster; others that he was a dupe. He overcame monsters and taught people their arts and crafts and customs, and he died to teach men how to die. But he is still alive and will some day return to men.

Before God created the universe there was only chaos and darkness, and only God existed. Then the Sky Father descended to the Earth Mother and begat the universe. After that the sky was raised, and it is held up by pillars or by the four gods of the quarters. Some say that there were several different creations and that the world of the gods above existed before the world of men. There are many worlds. There are three heavens (some say nine) and three lower worlds, and there is a great world tree that has its roots in the lowest world and reaches all the way to the highest heaven. Heaven is a happy world, but the lower world of Hell is a place of torment. To get to Hell you have to cross a river and the way is barred by the Hound of Hell.

There are many stories about the creation of the Sun and the Moon and the Stars. The Sun was once a man born to the First Parents, who had to leave the earth and live in the sky, where he travels around the earth, pursued by the Moon. Some say that the Moon is the sister of the Sun, and others that the Sun is the sister and the Moon is the brother. They are supposed to have been lovers and got married. But some say that Moon and Sun are older and younger brothers or that the Moon was a person who was transformed into the Moon for some reason. One time the Sun and Moon were stolen, and sometimes a monster comes and eats them, causing an eclipse. At one time the Moon was kept in a box. There is a figure on the Moon said to be a man sent there as a punishment, or possibly a rabbit or some other animal. Moon is a great lover and often sleeps with women. Once the Moon married a woman. Once a month the moon wanes because she is sick. The Stars are children of the Moon, but they are also people or things that have been thrown into the sky. Once a mortal man married a Star Girl. That is where all the stars come from: the Great Bear, Orion, the Pleiades and Hyades, Scorpio, Venus, Jupiter and the comets and the Milky Way. The Milky Way is a path of spirits or birds. Some call it a river, or ashes, or smoke. Shooting stars are star dung. Other things were created in the sky, like the rainbow snake and the northern lights.

Originally there was no Earth. Everything was covered with water. God created the earth by making it rise from the sea. He is said to have scattered his cuticle on the waters in the four directions. The earth rests on posts or columns which hold it up, though some people say it is Atlas or a turtle. Under the earth there is a monstrous fettered serpent who causes earthquakes. At the first the earth was small and soft, but it was made larger until it was big enough, and hardened in the sun. Most of the things on the earth were created at the same time—the tides, lakes, springs, and mountains—though some of them came out of the adventures of gods and heroes. Many cliffs resulted from the suicide of despairing lovers, and many rocks are people turned to stone. Often you can find the footprints of ancient men or beasts or gods or saints in the rocks.

After it was created, the world was destroyed and had to be re-created or renewed. In fact, it has been destroyed several times, and will be again. Each time, the earth has been repopulated from the few living things that survived, usually by a single couple. Once there was a great Flood caused by the gods as a punishment or revenge for immorality or injury. Some say it was caused by a fight between the Sea God and the Rain God, so that the waters welled up from the belly of the earth. The survivors escaped in a boat or wooden cask or on a mountain or a tree or in a cave. With them were two of every animal. Once there was a great Fire that destroyed the world, but men hid from the Fire and again survived. Once there was a great Freeze that destroyed the world. And once it was a great Eclipse and earthquakes.

All the things on the earth had to be created—clouds, lightning, thunder, and the seasons. At one time water was kept from men and they had to get it back. Rain came from the Rain God, or, some say, from the sea in the upper world. Wind came from God's breathing or from the Hero, who made great wings to flap and cause wind. Once, all the winds were kept in a cave, and different ones were let out to cause different weather. Night and day were divided after a discussion. Sometimes the sky turns red with blood.

And God made man. They say man was made from God's own body, from eggs, from animals or worms, from a human-animal mating, from stone or a tree or food. The Devil tried to make a man, too, but he couldn't bring him to life. Even God did not succeed on the first attempt, but he made an image of clay or wood and finally made it live. The first man is said to have come down from the sky or out of a tree or up from the ground or from under the earth or from a cave. He was not perfect because man and woman were not separated, and his genitals were misplaced. So man and woman were distinguished and given a penis and breasts, and women got teeth in their vaginas. Later they all lost their tails.

In the beginning there was a Golden Age and there was no pain or sadness or death, but man ate the forbidden fruit and learned pain. This was the origin of sexual intercourse and of death, which came about after a false message, and of disease and war, childbirth and labor, of the confusion of tongues and the subservience of women to men. Everything men know they were taught by the gods and the ancestors. Light and fire had to be stolen. Light was swallowed and reborn when the thief got home. Fire was originally the property of one being who found it in his own body. It was a gift of God, and was stolen in a hollow reed by animals or a bird. This led to the fire drill. All the game was hoarded up, but the gods had it released to man. So people learned about vegetables, seeds, drink, medicine, spinning, cooking, hunting, fishing and making fishhooks, and burial.

All the different tribes began and spread over the earth, wandering from place to place. Those who are our enemies had a meaner origin than ours. So all places and things were created and given names.

And all the animals were created and came out of the tree. Sometimes they were made from things and sometimes from people, being magically transformed: dogs, birds, insects (who come from the body of a slain monster), mosquitoes, fish, snakes, turtles, and frogs. Each one got his own color, like raven or crow, by being painted or having color spilled on him, or from something that happened during the Flood. Plants grew from the graves of people or animals who had been killed, but some of them were made directly by God, or were transformed from parts of the bodies of people or animals.

Animals often go on journeys or act as messengers, or they may become friends and be helpful to men. Sometimes this is because a man has befriended them, giving them food or performing some service for them. A lion once became a friend to a man who removed a thorn from his paw. Other animals have been grateful for having bones removed from their throats. Dogs, foxes, rodents, and fish have become friends to men in this way. Birds offer advice, but it is often ignored. Frequently the animal gives his human friend a part of his body as a talisman for summoning his aid, and he may come and destroy the man's enemy, although in some cases it is the enemy who kills the animal. Animals often feed men; even bees and frogs have nursed and fed abandoned infants. They may perform various tasks, guard people or houses, serve as bridges, teach people medicine or restore their sight. Swans or geese have been known to draw boats. Animals and men also mate and marry. Tigers and owls are suitors. Bears, dogs, and snakes are known as lovers, and marriage is common with tigers, foxes, birds, fish, and snakes. Sometimes the offspring of these unions are human, sometimes animal; often they are mixed. Sometimes the "animal" turns out to be a person in disguise. Sometimes a human spouse turns out to be really an animal, especially a fox or serpent.

If you break a taboo you will be severely punished. Never call upon a spirit in vain. If you wish for an animal husband, you're likely to get one. It is dangerous to offend a supernatural spouse, particularly by mentioning his or her origin. It is dangerous to steal from a god or saint or otherwise attack a deity or sacred person. It is dangerous to have sexual contact with spirits. A loss of chastity is a loss of power. You should be chaste for a certain time after marriage. Menstruation and mothers-in-law are dangerous. You must not eat in the other world, nor certain meat, such as the flesh of a totem animal or animal helper, nor certain fruit. You must not drink from certain fountains, nor look at certain things, such as the rainbow or the Secret Box. You must not look back. It was curiosity that let the winds and other troubles out of the bag. Do not tell secrets, such as the real identity of a transformed person, nor boast. Do not speak certain names nor touch certain things. Do not enter certain rooms nor open certain doors. Avoid a certain tree. Do not rest on a journey nor sleep at certain times nor build too high a tower. Death or other punishments follow certainly upon the breaking of these taboos, often instant death or death by drowning or burning. Or you may suffer the disappearance of your animal helper, the collapse of the building, a loss of fortune, a sore mouth or other sickness or weakness, an inability to return from the other world, a flood, transformation into stone, wood, or an animal, or damage to your unborn child. (After Thompson 1955)

Although it is unlikely that this tradition ever existed anyplace in this form, the sketch may well suggest the content of a set of beliefs widely current by the ninth millennium B.C. Some variants have been included in order to suggest further the transformations to which the basic fabric has been subject. No particular tradition has maintained even a large proportion of these beliefs without considerable reworking. Substitutions, elimination of elements, and elaboration of subthemes make the creation myths of contemporary peoples quite distinct despite their sharing of many of these motifs.

It must not be thought that ancient man was concerned only with creation. A list of the motifs of folklore that appear to have near-universal distributions can go on almost indefinitely. The basic motifs of the following familiar stories, for example, are known to occur in both the Old and New Worlds. Motif numbers refer to Thompson 1955: Achilles' Heel (Z311), Amazons (F565.1), Androcles and the Lion (B381), Atalanta (D672), Atlantis (F133, F725), Banquo's Ghost (E231), La Belle Dame Sans Merci (G264), Brigadoon (F377), Cerberus (F150.2), Dracula (D113.1.1, E251), Fountain of Youth (D1338.1.1), Jack and the Beanstalk (D482.1), Janus (F511.1.1), Jonah (F911.4, F913), Lot's Wife (C331), Magic Flight (D2135), Magic Flute (D1224), Man in the Moon (A751), Medusa (D2061.2.1), Mowgli (B535), Orpheus (F81.1), Pandora's Box (C321), Paul Bunyan (A901), Penelope (H400), Pygmalion (D435.1.1), Rip Van Winkle (D1960.1), River Styx (F141.1.1), Rumpelstiltskin (H1091), Samson (D1831, F610), The Weeping Willow (E631).

NEOLITHIC AND LATER LORE

Even by the ninth millennium B.C. we can begin to discern the emergence of regional specificities in the scattered archeological evidences of mythology and lore. The emergence of the neolithic cultures, first in the

Near East and later in India, Europe, China, and America, had the effect of fixing and codifying this regionalism in the areas affected. The rapid increase in population, and the growth in the intensity of internal communication within the region led to elaboration of the themes locally available and a corresponding swamping of influences from elsewhere. By the fourth millennium B.C. the cultures of northern Europe had developed an axe cult probably associated with a sky god and storm god, and this apparently merged with the agricultural mother goddess cults to create the basic mythology and pantheon widely shared by the earliest historic peoples. A concordance of some of these divinities among the ancient Near Eastern peoples is given in Table 1. The cosmological associations are variable and

TABLE 1 Divinities of Ancient Near Eastern Peoples

	SUM.	EGY.	BAB.	HIT.	SYR.
Sky, sun	Anu	Aton	Shamash	Arinna	El
Storm	En Lil	Shu	Addu	Teshub	Hadad
Earth	Nin Tu	Nut	Ti'amat	Hebat	Anat
Water, earth	En Ki	Geb	Gilgamesh	Kessis	Ba'al
Rebirth	Marduk	Osiris	Tammuz	Telepinus	Dagan
Mother	Inanna	Isis	Ishtar	Kubaba	Asherat
Moon	Nan Nar	Thoth	Nana?	(?)	(?)

approximate. The quite similar configuration presented by the earliest Indo-European pantheons is outlined in Table 2.

TABLE 2 Divinities of Early Indo-European Peoples

	GRE.	LAT.	PER.	SAN.	ICE.
Sky, sun	Apollo	Jove	Dyaosh	Dyaus	Woden
Storm	Zeus	Jupiter	Mithra	Indra	Thor
Earth	Cybele	Ceres	Anahita	Prithivi	Freya
Water, earth	Poseidon	Neptune	Apam Napat	(?)	Frey
Rebirth	Adonis	Eros	Tishtrya	Krishna	Balder
Mother	Aphrodite	Venus	(?)	Shakti	Frigg
Moon	Artemis	Diana	Mah	(?)	(?)

For most areas of the world we lack even the scattered hints afforded by European archeology into the prehistory of lore. It is clear all the same that the differentiation of traditions was not restricted to the precociously literate peoples. Although we have documented the widespread sharing of some basic literary motifs, it would be erroneous to conclude that the folk literature of primitive peoples is entirely derivative. In each continent, in each culture area, and in each particular culture there are literary ideas not found in the rest of mankind (see Thompson 1955).

In Oceania, for example, the creator is often a bird or a snake; ghosts wander around carrying their own bodies; men are transformed into waves or thunder; and bananas are taboo. There are gods of suicide and of the seat braces of canoes, and night is generally considered to be the time of the gods. The winds are said to be controlled by a leper; there is a mythological giant clam and a giant shark. There are three worlds of the dead. The creator is said to have made the clouds from his own vitals, and men may recover their youth by riding the surf. None of these ideas appears to occur elsewhere.

Apparently peculiar to Africa are such motifs as lending one's stomach to an animal, soothsayer ants, singing dogs and elephants, and becoming invisible by scarification. The sun, moon, and stars are held to have been forged by a smith, and the creation of the moon preceded that of the sun. The creation of the world is believed to have occurred from below. People are reincarnated as whirlwinds, and storms are caused by the singing of birds.

Among the peculiarities of European folklore are six-legged horses and headless horsemen, the olive branch of peace, and the king of the cats. Europeans get transformed into smoke and dragons, and people with a missing limb cannot rest in their graves. There are wild hunts and Wandering Jews on land and Flying Dutchmen at sea. There is a taboo on apples. Animals are attracted by music, and bees are God's spies. European tales also feature a god for frost, for the slain and for the hanged, and the creation of the world by a cow.

Middle Eastern stories include man-eating cattle, a female snake seven years pregnant, the phoenix and the chimera (part lion, part dragon, part goat). Men are transformed into roses. One drop of blood when licked satisfies hunger. The sun and moon are said to have come from the belly of a fish, and women are known to have killed dragons. Souls sometimes appear in the form of grasshoppers, and there are different sun gods for night and day. Also originally Middle Eastern is the idea that God cannot be comprehended.

In Oriental folklore there are giants so big they have to bend to keep from bumping the sky. There are weeping toads, flying apes, and devastating shellfish. There are nine-tailed foxes, and men are sometimes transformed into snails or peaches. Men suffer from the danger of having their genitals retract magically into the abdomen. Souls appear as wasps; women marry dragons; and there is a goddess of the North Star.

To the North American Indians, the sun is sometimes a father-in-law figure. Turkeys talk, and falling stars are the ashes of the gods' cigars. Bears and fish have ghosts. One can fly magically after a bite on the ear, and it is taboo to hunt at the time of the solstice. There is dancing in the afterworld, and there is a mythological dog so old he has no skin on his head. Corpses can be resuscitated by being pricked in the anus or by using a mummified dog or a magic feather. Magpies have a reputation for wisdom, and only sorcerers are supposed to be able to see ghosts.

In South America, people are apt to be reincarnated as meteors or peanut plants or to be transformed into iguanas. There is a mythical two-headed tiger and a horned water monster, as well as a horned armadillo who lives underground. The creator, who is sometimes a beetle or a worm, and sometimes a grandfather (or even two brothers), has a pet armadillo, and occasionally gets drunk and beats his wife. Corpses can be brought back to life by being stepped on, and rivers can be magically widened.

ONOMASTICS

We may illustrate the problems presented by the enormous range and variety of metaphorical ideas by selecting one particular and fundamental domain: the naming of persons, or onomastics. Naming confronts us with the metaphor in perhaps its simplest guise: a proposition of resemblance between two elements that are not in nature the same. Such analogies may be esoteric or obscure, but at least in simple names they are not greatly compounded, and we may thus explore them without the elaborate analysis necessary to the more highly structured literary forms.

A peculiar feature of usages relating to persons is that they are often relative. Absolute names exist, of course, in the naming of persons for places, animals, or personal attributes, but the most frequent mode of alluding to a person is in relative terms. The basic pronouns, the terms of kinship, vocative usages implying relative age, relative sex, relative rank or kinship all share a common cognitive geometry that is rare in other domains of usage. They are intrinsically relational.

Probably the most fundamental of personal metaphors is the "I:you" reciprocal. An argument could perhaps be made that this expression is a hypothesis rather than a metaphor. I believe the underlying structure, however, is a statement of analogy—$I:you::you:I$, which is roughly translatable as "I refer to as 'I' what you call 'you' and you refer to as 'I' what I call 'you.' " This analogically assumes that I am *like* you and will therefore speak and understand as though I were you. Modern English is trivially ambiguous on the point, because *you*, which may be plural and accusative as well as singular and nominative, is not perfectly reciprocal with *I*. Most languages have forms implying the clearer structure of the older English *I* and *thou*. The differentiation of the two pronouns may well be universal, but is not actually necessary, for the same analogy may be presented in a single inclusive dual. Something of the sort is implied by the maternal or nursing *we* in "Shall we have our bath?"

The reciprocity of the first and second person pronouns is, of course, generic. A more specific reciprocal frequently occurs among the terms of kinship as in the archaic English *coz* as a vocative for cousin. You may call *coz* all persons who may also call you *coz* and only such persons. Similarly in Navaho a person calls his mother's father *chái* and a man calls his daughter's child *chái*. In either case the analogy is a metaphor of identification, just as in the pronominal examples already cited, but in these cases the metaphor is restricted to particular relationships.

There are a number of borderline cases in which pronominal or quasi-pronominal vocative usages retain something of this relativistic structure. These include the metaphorical treatment of the first or second person by synechdoche, in which the whole person is invoked by reference to some partial attribute or character, as in "your humble servant." In Quiche, *utz nu vach*, literally "good my face," is the normal way of saying, "I am fine, sober, or in good health." A similar case is reflected in the honorific pronouns as in the "polite form" apocopation of Spanish *vuestra merced* ("your mercy") into *usted*, of Russian *vashe vysokoprevoskhoditel'stvo* ("your excellency") into *vashestvo*, or of Quiche *ahavalal* ("lordship") into *lal*. The first person may be represented by the third, as in the French use of *on* or the Spanish impersonal *se rompió* ("it broke itself"). It may be arbitrarily pluralized as in the royal or editorial *we*, or objectified as in the American slang "sez me." Plural pronouns may have similar resonances, as in the pseudoplurals of the Southernism "y'all" or the Spanish *voseo*. Duals and plurals also become complicated by including or excluding the speaker, the listener, or others, as in the French *nous autres*. It is clear that even the pronouns have extensive connotations.

Vocative kinship terms remain sufficiently relative to be considered quasipronouns. They are marked by the frequent use of hypocorisma, apocopation, and diminutive affixes. Hypocorisma is illustrated in the reduplicative forms *papa*, *mamma*, *dada*, and many others in many languages. Apocopation occurs in the German *Oma* (*Grossmama*), the English *dad*, or the Quiche *chu* (from *chuch* "mother"). Diminutive affixes may be illustrated by *daddy* or *auntie* in English, *mamale* in Yiddish, or *nantzin* (from *nantli* "mother") in Aztec. Although these forms may be subtly differentiated (as in the English forms cited for father), the common metaphoric basis is "you:small" (and, hence, harmless, dear, honored, and so forth, as implied by various other metaphoric meanings of small size). Vocative kinship terms have not usually been carefully collected by folklorists and anthropologists, and their connotative meanings are not well explored.

All these usages are permutations of the basic metaphor "I:you." Several of them, however, are subject to a measure of displacement to the third person. In normal referential kinship terms this displacement is built in, and the naming of kinship persons may be either relative or absolute in different contexts. Some common connotations of the terms of nuclear kinship are summarized in this list:

KINSHIP TERMS	EXAMPLES
father:ruler	Attila ["little father"]
mother:origin	mother lode
brother:loyal	fraternity, *germania*
sister:weak	sissy
son:follower	infantry
daughter:subordinate	daughter organization
husband:producer	to husband
wife:lady	Mrs.

Many of the connotations of kinship terms in other cultures suggest meanings less familiar than these. *Older brother* in Quiche means also "traitor, specter." *Mother* in Pachuco Spanish is significantly a "chieftainess" (*jefa*), and *daughter* in French has become a "prostitute" (*fille*). *Aunt* has conveniently become a "midwife" in German and a "matchmaker" in Yiddish (*muhme*), while Navaho mothers-in-law are "unviewable" and are so named.

The structural or "componential" analysis of kinship terms has lately become the primary technique for clarifying and describing their denotative meanings—always in terms of the categories of biological reproduction: mating and descent, age and sex. Connotative meanings have been very largely ignored and require other techniques. As the previous examples suggest, connotations may be inferred from the "extension" of kinship terms to nonkinship usages and from the extension of nonkinship terms to kinship usages. Much of traditional anthropology has assumed that such extensions are always from kinship outward, but the assumption is unwarranted. In Maya, for example, a child is *al* ("something carried") as is also implied by the Germanic *born* ("bairn"). In various Mayan languages, the principal word for son also means "semen." It is not difficult to document the wealth of connotations of kin terms, but we know very little about their structure. The analysis of this structure requires a broader field of observation than the componential analysis of denotations, but it may be doubted that its essential intellectual geometry need be different.

The fundamental pattern of naming in relative (or first and second person) contexts is neither separate nor notably different from the pattern of absolute names. The latter, however, emphasize a different range of metaphoric associations. Denotatively, of course, the effect of absolute naming systems is to provide an unambiguous mode of reference to a particular individual. This could be done with nonce words. But it never is.

Names have (and continually acquire from the contexts of their usage) connotative meanings as well. Broadly speaking, these connotations equate persons with their statuses, with their attributes, or with things.

Among the components of status, age connotations enter into naming in a variety of ways. Many and perhaps most societies differentiate baby names from those relevant to other phases of the life cycle—baptismal or ceremonial names, school names, initiation names, adult names, praise names, honorifics, and even post-mortem names. Our own implicit assumption of the continuity of social identity is by no means universal, and in many parts of the world a major change in status is marked both by acquisition of a new name and by abandonment of the old one. Often the age implications of names are expressed in a metaphor of size, as in the kinship terms *grandpa* or *petit-fils* or in the common European pattern of diminutive nicknames. Table 3 gives some of the commoner Russian diminutives.

TABLE 3   Common Russian Nicknames*

NICKNAME	NAME	NICKNAME	NAME
Afonia	Afanasii	Osia	Iosif
Agafosha	Agafon	Pasha (Pavlusha)	Pavel
(A)liosha	Aleksei	Piotia	Piotr
Andriusha	Andrei	Platosha	Platon
Arkasha	Arkadii	Prosha	Prokofich
Boria	Boris	Sasha (Shura)	Aleksandr
Dima	Dmitrii	Seriozha	Sergei
Edik	Eduard	Seva	Vsevolod
Filia	Filip	Sidorka	Sidor
Fiodia	Fiodor	Sima	Serafim
Grisha	Grigorii	Siomia	Semion
Iemelia	Iemel'ian	Slava	Sviatoslav
Ierosha	Ierofei	Stiopa	Stepan
Ignasha	Ignat	Teka	Tekkadii
Igoriok	Igor'	Tima (Timosha)	Timofei
Ilia	Il'ia	Trosha	Trofim
Iura	Iurii	Vadik	Vadim
Klimka	Klim	Valerik	Valerii
Kolia	Nikolai	Valia	Valentin
Kostia	Konstantin	Vania	Ivan
Kuzia	Kuz'ma	Vasia	Vasilii
Lavrusha	Lavrentii	Vitia	Viktor, Vitalii
Lionia	Leonid	Vova (Volodia)	Vladimir
Misha	Mikhail	Zhenia	Ievgenii
Nik	Nikita	Zhora	Georgii

* After informants from Smolensk and Orel.

It is notable that Russian shares with other European societies the conception of nominal continuity. The forms cited are only one of several sets of Russian diminutives through which various connotations of age, familiarity, respect, and endearment are connoted, always expressed, however, by root modification rather than by substitution of totally new names. The limited number of such nicknames is also noteworthy: around 100 such names suffice for the huge populations of each of the European languages.

Age and time implications are also expressed in number names, as in the widespread East Asian birth order nomenclature, or the Latin Quintus, Sextus, Septimus, and so on. Sometimes the distinction is purely relative, as in Junior and Senior; sometimes it goes well beyond ontogenetic time, as in the numbering of kings and popes. Age set and dynasty names may take on similar temporal implications whether or not they are explicitly numerical (as in the naming of reigns in China and Japan); and calendrical names may reflect time cycles much smaller than the life cycle. Although they measure time, such names may or may not have age connotations.

Sex connotations in naming are ubiquitous, and most systems of onomastics appear to involve a broad and imperfect distinction between male and female names. Our own equation of girls with flowers is a widespread conceit in both the Old and New Worlds, perhaps an ancient one.

In most societies the most important way of identifying an individual is to relate him to his kin group. This may be done in a variety of ways—through teknonymy, identifying his children; through patronymy (or, rarely, matronymy), identifying his parents; or through stating his relationship to other relatives (siblings, or grandparents, or affinals). The proto-Indochinese Mnong Gar of South Vietnam illustrate several of the possibilities in a single system:

> Married men are customarily called by their own name followed by their wife's: Kröng-Jôong (Kröng is married to Jôong, who would conversely be called Jôong-Krong), Bbaang-Aang, Tôong-Biing, Chaar-Rieng, Tôong-Jieng . . . ; or very often, when they have children, by the name of the eldest preceded by *Baap*, "Father of . . .": thus Baap Can, "Father of Can,". . . When two brothers are known as supporting each other on all occasions, or as forming a bloc, or for some other common event in their lives, their names are joined together to make a single entity, a kind of dual: Taang Truu (this is the case of Baap Can and his brother the canton chief), Ngkoi Bbaang (the latter two are however only first cousins from our point of view), etc. Others, women as well as men, are known rather by their names followed by a nickname with which they have been tagged in childhood: Kroong-the-Big-Navel and his wife Aang-of-the-Drooping-Eyelid (they are sometimes called Kroong-Aang and

Aang-Kroong), Jôong-the-Hernia, Bbaang the Stag, etc. (Condominas 1957:26).

In most primitive societies kinship terms themselves may be an unambiguous way of designating or addressing persons in many or most contexts; and in most societies, complex as well as simple, such usages remain common at least within the nuclear family. For broader identification, an individual's kinship group may be specified: his family, clan, caste, lineage, marriage section. In the present millennium, patronymic surnames have come to be the predominant pattern throughout most of the literate world. They derive from a variety of sources: old clan, lineage, or tribal names; geographic, religious, or occupational designations; or older patronymics, as in the Norse Anders*son*, the Spanish González, the Irish *Mac*Diarmid, or the Hebrew *Ben* Maimon. This older patronymic pattern appears to have involved generally naming each generation afresh by compounding the father's name with a special linguistic element to indicate its derivative character, as in the Greek Arist*ides*, the Latin Juli*anus*, the Russian Nikola*evich*, or the Arabic *Ibn* Sina.

Specification of persons by kinship status may involve any corporate kinship unit as well. Usually such names carry a heavy freight of connotative meanings, and often they have religious as well as kinship significance. The special totemic or other functions of a particular kinship unit, its size and importance, wealth, habits, and traditions inevitably become a part of the "meaning" of its name in something of the sense that *Clancy* means "policeman" in the United States. The calendar names of aboriginal Mexico and Guatemala, like the saints' names of Christendom or the clan and sib names of many North American Indians, imply a supernatural patron or protector, a linked or guardian spirit; and with varying degrees of ambiguity the name is felt to be diagnostic of the fate and character of him who bears it. (See, for example, the Burmese mnemonic rhyme for the character types of different names, p. 206.) Typical of the pattern of naming by kin group are the Ossetian "Nado, of the Burgalty clan" or the Hebrew "Kohath the Levite."

Although kin group affiliations may have religious overtones, specifically religious names and titles are also widely used, as in the Sikh *Singh* ("lion"), the Arabic *Hajji* ("pilgrim") or the Armenian *Kashishian* ("priest"). Sometimes the name identifies an individual as a devotee of a particular sect or cult, as in the Egyptian *Ptah Hotep* ("Ptah is content"). Commonly, a cult name, far from being an aid in identifying or designating the individual, is carefully kept secret and may be used only in esoteric ritual. The sanctity of some religious statuses may demand a new and specific name for those who assume them, whether or not they are esoteric, as in the case of popes, kings, nuns, lamas, and others; and such names

TABLE 4 *Ashanti Personal Names**

	BOYS	GIRLS
Sunday	Kwame	Amoriba
Monday	Kwassi	Akwassiba
Tuesday	Kodio	Adiula
Wednesday	Kwamina	Aminaba
Thursday	Kwaku	Akuba
Friday	Yao	Ayaba
Saturday	Kofi	Afuba

* Bastide 1967:61.

shade taxonomically into titles as did the name Caesar in the early principate at Rome. Not infrequently a person's name pledges him to the service of a god, as in the Indic *Chandi Das* ("slave of Chandi," the goddess of love) or the Persian *Artakhshathra* ("Arta's kingdom"—the Greek Artaxerxes). In ancient Mexico and Guatemala as in Catholic Europe, dedicatory religious names were linked to the ceremonial calendar. Children were named (with advice from a diviner) for one of the 260 days of the ritual calendar, with a numeral prefix from 1 to 13 and with 1 of the 20 day names: 12 Flint, 6 Dog, 1 Lord, 7 Rain, and so on. In actual usage the numbers were commonly omitted, and the recurrence of day names even within a family necessitated further specification by status: Little Wind, or Jaguar the Captain. A similarly calendrical pattern occurs in Ashanti, where children are named for the day of the week (see Table 4).

The surname system of Europe abounds in occupation-derived names. Such a supplement to naming is very old and widespread, for in any complex society such designations may eliminate the ambiguity created by a limited number of personal names. Some European examples are assembled in Table 5. It would be interesting to know more about the distribution of such names in modern society, but although some work along these lines has been done in Poland, I am unaware of the results.

Politics is no less involved in naming than is economics, providing an ample range of titles that may be used for identification of political status, many of which have also become surnames, for example, King and its congeners (LeRoy, Korol, König, Shah, Raja, Rajendra, Kaiser, Vasileos, Malik, and many others). Honorific titles closely associated with naming but not in themselves names are also widespread (*sir, pan, mynheer, san, sri, don, tat, tovarisch*) and often differentiate age and sex as well as rank and other aspects of status. The denial of these titles to slaves and peasants is often associated with specific treatment of different social ranks, just as grander titles delimit the status of the nobility with precision.

TABLE 5 European Occupational Surnames

ENGLISH	FRENCH	GERMAN	RUSSIAN
Baker	Boulanger	Bäcker	Pekarsky
Brewer	Brasseur	Brauer	Pivnik
Butcher	Boucher	Schlächter	Reznik
Carpenter	Charpentier	Zimmermann	Plotnikov
Chandler	Chandelier	Krämer	Svetkey
Mason	Masson	Maurer	Kamensky
Master	Le Maître	Lehrer	Uchitel
Merchant	Marchand	Kaufmann	Kupchik
Miller	Molinier	Müller	Melnik
Potter	Potier	Töpfer	Goncharov
Shepherd	Berger	Schäfer	Ovcharov
Shoemaker	Soulier	Schuhmacher	Sapolsky
Smith	Taillefer	Schmidt	Kuznetsov
Taylor	Tailleur	Schneider	Portnoy
Weaver	Tisserand	Weber	Tkachuk

Purely political names shade into rank or prestige titles and rank-connected names, and it is not always possible to make the distinction. Sometimes such names are collectives, like the caste nomenclature of India. Or again they may be individualized, or even relative. The ranking implications of some pronoun systems have been mentioned. In particular systems of nomenclature, there may be considerable overlap between the taxonomies of power and prestige and those of other lineal or serial hierarchies, such as age or kinship order. Often the connotative play in these terms reveals outmoded meanings now largely forgotten, as in these European examples:

bourgeois:urban (*Burger*; cf. citizen, police)
captain:headman (*capitanus*)
chancellor:usher (*cancellarius*)
duke:leader (*dux*)
emperor:commander (*imperator*)
footman:horseless (cf. *peón*)
governor:helmsman (*gobernator*)
knight:rider (*caballero, Ritter*)
lieutenant:place holder (*lieu-tenant*)
lord:breadkeeper (*hlaef-weard*; cf. *dominus*)
marquis:frontiersman (*Mark-Graf*)
mayor:judge (cf. *al-calde*)
minister:room service (cf. chamberlain)
peasant:countryman (*paysan*; cf. *khrest'ianin*)

prince:first man (*princeps*)
serf:slave (*servus*)
sergeant:attendant (*serjeant*; cf. *servientem*)
sheriff:county official (shire reeve)

It would appear that only a limited number of metaphors lend themselves to political use.

Personal names have also commonly been derived from residential groups, and hence from place names. This may be indirect, as in the localized names of the Navaho clans; it may be casual enough that it has no strong naming implication and is, rather, an occasional method of identification, as in the New Testament. In some cases, however, it becames a developed pattern. The formal titles of the British peerage are a well-known example. Status naming from places shades into status naming for ethnic groups, and the two are often indistinguishable. Inevitably such names are at least implicitly collectives, and all manners of social group affiliations may be involved.

It may be significant that ethnic groups often do not name themselves. It is the name given by the opposition that frequently sticks. The Apache, like many primitive groups, call themselves *dénè* ("the people"), but they are known to the world as some kind of *aabachu*, the Zuñi word for "enemy." *Deutsch* means "German" only to the Germans; the rest of the world calls them *Germani*, like Tacitus, or *nemetski* (Russian), *tedeschi* (Italian), *allemands* (French), or *djaman* (Pidgin English). The Japanese do not use the word *Japan* but *Nihon*; the Eskimos do not use the word *Eskimo* but *Inuk*; the Greeks do not call themselves Greeks but *Hellenikes*; the Egyptians call their country *Misr*. The Finns call themselves *Suomi*, the Armenians *Hay*, and the Chinese *Han*. France was named by the Germanic Franks, England by the Angles, Turkey by the invading Turks, and Russia by the Swedes. The Pima are said to have been named from their expression for "I don't know." The Bushmen were named by the Afrikaners and the Pygmy Negritos of the Philippines by the Spanish. The Sioux call themselves *nakota* ("allies"). African "tribal" names are often nothing but the name of some lineage prominent in the region, and the origins of such identifications as the South American *Comechingón* ("filth eaters"), the Russian *Samoyed* ("cannibals"), or the North American *Flathead* obviously have little to do with local pride. To the Turks or Afghans all Europeans are still Franks, just as to the Europeans the "tribes" of the Amazon basin are "Indians," whether they know it or not. Many ethnic groups do succeed in naming themselves (for example, so far as we know, the Britons, Gauls, Choctaw, Maya, Chukchi, Maori, Zulu, or Icelanders), but it is an interesting feature of ethnic names that the self-name is so seldom accepted by others and so frequently replaced by some more ethnocentric label.

A special type of collective naming is the "folk heraldry" or *blason populaire* in which Russia is always a mother, Germany a father, France beautiful, Italy sunny, Japan great, England merry, and Spain eternal. More local usages make it perfectly clear to Argentines and Americans that Boston and Córdoba are stuffy or to Colombians and Mexicans that Antioquia and Monterrey are stingy. *Blason populaire* may be further elaborated by letting an individual stand for the collectivity: Uncle Tom, G.I. Joe, John Bull, Don Fulano de Tal, Louis Blanc, or Tommy Atkins. These types appear to be a relatively modern development, and their relation to older group figures is by no means clear.

In addition to the complex modalities of naming people by status, there are various ways of naming persons for other people without any necessary status implications. Such names may be directly commemorative or honorific, as in the widespread bestowal of Presidents' names in the United States. Even a fortuitous identity of name was felt by the Aztecs to establish a special relationship between namesakes (*tocaitl*). This pattern also has its negative expression in the taboos often placed on the names of the recently dead, sometimes carried to the point of necessitating circumlocutions for common nouns that are elements in such names. The metaphor underlying these diverse usages is animistic—reuse of a person's name implies linkage with his spirit, which may be viewed positively or negatively. Something of the same sort is involved in pseudonyms, which may be imaginary or even nonce names but which invariably deny the individual's "true" identity, for secrecy (as in the *noms de guerre* of the Bolshevik revolutionaries or the *noms de plume* of Chinese literati writing trashy novels), glamor (as among actors), or innuendo (in *romans à clef*). The formula here is *Person A : Person B*, where *Person B* may be a hero, relative, acquaintaince, "someone," or no one at all.

Personification is also reflected in the naming of persons for things (*person : thing*), or of things for persons, metaphorically attributing personality to nonpersons or denying it in people. The changes that can be rung through personification give an almost indefinite extension to naming usages. Table 6 shows the scope of this extension by illustrating naming of individual people and groups of people for things and individual things and groups of things for people in fourteen different semantic domains.

It is clear that personal names are deeply involved in and readily lend themselves to the process of metaphor formation in many dimensions of meaning and experience. They may become or be derived from any part of speech (except perhaps prepositions). We are forced to the conclusion that in naming nothing is impossible. A person may be analogized to anyone,

TABLE 6 *Naming and Personification*

| | PERSON:THING | | THING:PERSON | |
	SPECIFIC	GENERIC	SPECIFIC	GENERIC
Anatomy	Red	Flathead	Sam*	Adam's apple
Animal	Black Hawk	Zotzil*	Peter Rabbit	Thompson's gazelle
Clothes	Old Man Hat*	Yellow Hats*	St. Stephen's crown	Prince Albert
Cosmology	Morgenstern	Eastern Star	Haley's comet	Heaviside layer
Houses	Javier*	Pentagon	Blair House	Georgian
Ideas	Irene*	Stoics	Boyle's law	Arianism
Institutions	Church	Confederate	Harvard	Potemkin's village
Minerals	Eisenhower	Golden Horde	Cullinan diamond	Wolframite
Places	Guadalupe*	Indian	Pike's Peak	Levittown
Plants	Rosen	Dogwood Clan*	Ygdrasil*	Bougainvillea
Ships	Schiff	Mayflower descendants	Scharnhorst	Higgins boat
Sounds	Cantor	Philharmonic	Roland's horn	Doppler effect
Time	Goodyear	Winter People	Valentine's day	Wednesday
Weapons	Lance	Long Knives*	Excalibur	Bowie knife

* The less obvious of the examples may be explained as follows.
  Dogwood Clan. The leading clan of the Zuñi.
  Guadalupe. From Ara. *wadi al lub* ("river of black gravel").
  Irene. Greek for peace.
  Javier. From Bas. *etxe a varri a* ("new house").
  Long Knives. The Sioux term for White soldiers.
  Old Man Hat. A Navaho chanter.
  Sam. I had given up on this category when my attention was drawn to a comic usage in which a well-endowed actress facing breast surgery apostrophized her left breast with the words, "So long, Sam." The experience convinces me that it would be extraordinarily difficult to establish a null category in this table, even were it to be considerably extended.
  Yellow Hats. Tibetan lamas.
  Ygdrasil. Norse name of the World Tree.
  Zotzil. A Mayan tribe; literally, "bat people."

anything, or nothing; and although there may be some combinations that have not been tried, none seems to be ruled out. This does not, however, preclude a marked specificity of pattern in particular naming systems. Each culture tends to have a limited fund of names and a sharp enough pattern of them to make it clear that they are names. Even in polyethnic America we can say, "What kind of a name do you call that?"

A binomial system of personal names was developed by the ancient Germanic peoples and was spread by them during the Germanic invasions of pagan and Christian times from Visigothic Spain to Kievan Russia.

Typical elements of this system are the common roots of Anglo-Saxon names in eighth-century England (after Ström, 1939).

ald:old	fled:beauty	sex:dagger
alh:refuge	frid:peace	sig:victory
badu:battle	gils:hostage	suid:strong
bald:bold	hard:hard	tat:glad
behrt:bright	helm:helmet	thruid:power
ceol:ship	here:army	trum:firm
ecg:edge	hild:war	ualch:foreigner
ed:wealth	man:man	uald:rule
edil:noble	mund:hand	uil:will
elf:elf	os:god	uini:friend
ercon:holy	ric:strong	uulf:wolf
	sa:sea	

Sometimes, but not always, children's names are combinations of elements taken from their parents' names, so that three brothers might have names beginning with *Edil-* because their father's or mother's name had begun so. By the end of the first millennium of the Christian era most Europeans went by names like Albert ("All-Bright"), Godfrey ("Good-Lord"), Edwin ("Wealth-Joy"), Oswald ("God-Rule"), Sexbald ("Dagger-Bold"), Vladimir ("Rule-Fame"), or Gonzalvo ("Battle-Elf").

The naming system of the Sioux of the northern Great Plains is in some ways strikingly similar. It is also predominantly binomial, although a few names are actually trinomial. The elements in a Sioux name include (a) actions and attributes, (2) animals, and (3) body parts. Most Sioux names are composed of one element from the first class and one from the second or third (for example, Black Hawk, Sitting Bull, Hairy Chin, and Flying Cloud). A few are single elements (for example, Gall), and some contain all three categories (for example, Black Eagle Feather).

Binomials are not everywhere the predominant pattern, but they may well be the commonest naming system around the world, and examples may be found from Chinese (Lao Tzǔ "old master") and Hawaiian (Ha Loa "long stick") to Nahuatl (Cuauhtemoc "falling eagle") and Cherokee (Wahhya Gigagéei "red wolf"). Other usages are, however, common. Roman custom required three names: one personal, one patrilineal, and one a sobriquet. Russian uses a personal name, a patronymic, and a patronymic surname. Spanish employs one or more personal names with both a paternal and a maternal patronymic (and formerly retained the surnames of all four grandparents). English uses a trinomial in which the first two are usually personal names and the last a surname, but permits variations (double surnames, two "middle names," or no "middle name" at all). Chinese uses a trinomial composed of a surname and a two-element

personal name. Arabic traditionally allows for a flexible polynomial including a personal name, one or more patronymics, and one or more so-
briquets.

Despite the enormous variety and scope of the metaphors of onomastics, they retain a fundamental simplicity. They ring the changes on the
simple analogies that *person:person*, *person:status*, or *person:thing*. The
controlling contexts that produce these usages are similarly global and
simple. Any repetitive relationship between persons or between persons
and things not only may but also will give rise to a name. The salient feature of this kind of structure formation is perhaps its brevity, and the
imagery of names can afford to be eclectic precisely because it can be
shaped by any brief, repetitive experience. It is clear that there are limits
to the process. We have bothered to give individuating names, for example,
to a large number of stars, as we frequently individuate large or important
animals, but our interaction with them does not permit us to give personal
names to the potatoes on a dinner plate, the leaves on a tree, or the bacteria
in a test tube. We can identify hundreds of individual humans but only a
score or so of individual dogs, and perhaps only one or two gnus. We name
battleships, number landing craft, and give up altogether on canoes.

FORMULAS

Even in naming, there are some usages that are contextually specific.
The use of nicknames or honorifics, of slang or formality, is context bound
for both personal and place names. Frequently recurrent contexts not only
affect naming but also give rise to more organized metaphorical structures,
the compounded and standardized metaphors of formulaic discourse. Greetings and farewells, toasts and curses, formulas of politeness and insult,
spells, proverbs, riddles, and the like exemplify these structures. Such expressions have a considerable range of context, from battle cries (Spanish
"St. James and at them!") and telephone greetings (Japanese "Maybe,
maybe") to bathroom graffiti ("Until further notice, tomorrow is can-
celled"), curses (Arabic "Son of a pig") and clichés ("the nose on your
face").

Usages of this type tend to be so often repeated as to lose much of
their semantic value. It is difficult to get an answer to the English question,
"How are you?" Such expressions are not in fact devoid of meaning, but
their true function in discourse is often remote from their denotative content. Malinowski has described their communicative significance as "phatic." That is to say that they are more or less pure signs of contact and
solidarity, supporting and sustaining speech by the affirmation of continued
attention. Actually, most of the metaphors in any language are tired ones.
They are, however, vitally necessary, for it is only through continual repeti-

tion of redundancies of this type that we can succeed in communicating the occasional novelties that human beings find tolerable.

The formulaic (or ritualistic) redundancy of metaphors is characteristic of contexts involving heterogeneous social contacts. It is consequently maximal, for example, in the formulas of polite greeting suitable for any occasion or in the platitudes of a religion intended for use by society at large. For similar reasons mass poetry is more hackneyed than esoteric poetry—it must be communicable to a more heterogeneous population. In a society no longer dominated by witchcraft, a formalistic interest in a man's health is a safe way of expressing vague good will; the Navaho prefer a guarded and contentless observation (and perhaps hope) about the universe, "It is good" (*yá'át'èh*).

Closely related to the stereotyped phrases of phatic communication are a number of types of brief statements or "sayings" of a more or less formal sort, recurrent in the speech of many cultures. Typical of these is the *proverb*, defined by Taylor (Leach 1950:902) as "a terse didactic statement that is current in tradition." Proverbs are usually formulaic: they are recited verbatim and preserved without textual alteration. Like fables, with which they have some historical association, they are instructive but not necessarily moralistic—their burden is common sense rather than righteousness. Some examples are:

> *Ashanti*: When you are a child, you do not laugh at a short man.
> *American*: You can't fight City Hall.
> *Chaha*: Who gives advice to a stupid man cooks in a broken pot.
> *Latin*: There are as many opinions as there are people (*quot homines, tot sententiae*).
> *Moroccan*: What is bitter does not become sweet even in a bee's ass.
> *Nahuatl*: Wolf and fox don't stop to cook.

A number of subvarieties of proverbs may be distinguished by form, context, and meaning. Broadly, we may differentiate (1) *maxims* (proverbs with specifically moral content), (2) *idioms* (expressions similar to or related to proverbs but looser in form), and (3) *epigrams* (proverbs expressed in some particularly structured form, often poetic).

Maxims (which are more or less indistinguishable cross-culturally from precepts, aphorisms, and apothegms) are moral proverbs:

> *American*: God helps those who help themselves.
> *Chinese*: You can't clap hands with one palm.
> *Latin*: Speak nothing but good of the dead (*de mortuis nihil nisi bonum*).
> *Sanskrit*: Immortal becomes he whose Self is death.
> *Spanish*: None before the king (*ante el Rey ninguno*).
> *Sulu*: A sleeping crab will be carried away by the current.

Sometimes a maxim may be adopted as the formal expression of aims of a social group. Usually it expresses a moral aspiration and is considered the motto or slogan of the group:

> *Communist Party*: Workers of the world, unite (*proletarii vsekh stran soiediniaites'*).
> *Kaiser Corporation*: I am ready (*je suis prêt*).
> *Order of the Garter*: Evil to him who thinks ill of it (*honi soit qui mal y pense*).
> *United States*: One from many (*e pluribus unum*).
> *University of Mexico*: The spirit will speak through my race (*por mi raza hablará el espíritu*).

A special case of the maxim is the *brocard*, a traditional principle of law, usually stated in Latin:

> *Caveat emptor* ("let the buyer beware").
> *De minimis non curat lex* ("the law is not concerned with trifles").
> *Primum non nocere* ("first do no harm").
> *Qui tacet, consentire videtur* ("silence gives assent").
> *Ultra posse nemo obligatur* ("no one is obligated beyond his power").

Proverbs of all types shade off into the proverbial phrases and other idioms that give folk speech much of its color. They are generally avoided as hackneyed by self-conscious literary stylists. In this case, the proverb is evoked but not formally stated; either by paraphrase or by ellipsis the original saying is brought to mind. Proverbial phrases may also be complete metaphors. The Burmese "dig for turtle eggs (while worshipping) at the pagoda" when we would "kill two birds with one stone." Many similar phrases become part of the stock of daily speech so familiarly as to lose any specific connection with their sources, which may or may not be proverbs: "the memory of living man," "creeping like snail," "ship of state," "the cat's pajamas." When such a phrase is applied in a context where a simple and more natural phrasing would do just as well, it is said to be a *cliché* (for example, "Let me consult my *better half*").

Idioms of this sort are only loosely distinguishable from the general body of metaphor that suffuses speech. They differ from proverbs in their lack of specific structure and in the flexibility with which they may be rephrased or truncated. We may suppose that these differences correspond to variations in detailed communicative patterns and that a careful study matching context to content might prove very rewarding.

Other proverbial expressions tend to be even more highly structured than are proverbs. These may be called *epigrams*, although this word is also employed in reference to some sayings of a strictly proverbial type. Classically, an epigram was a particularly polished brief thought, complete in itself. Often it was in verse, or it attained its effect through a play on words or exaggerated brevity. Frequently it was witty. Thus Martial wrote:

> *Miraris quarè dormitum non eat Afer?*
> *accumbat cum quâ, Caeciliane, vides.*

Dudley Fitts has translated it:

> Cecil, you find it strange that our friend Coons
> Sits up so late at night?
> Take another (and more thoughtful) look, dear Cecil,
> At Mrs. Coons.
> (Fitts 1956:132)

A Chinese poem of epigrammatic quality was said to have been composed by Yang Chi Sheng (1516–1555) on his way to execution:

> This infinite spirit I restore to the mighty void,
> But a loyal heart will shine for whatever time.
> All that in this life I have left undone
> I bequeath to posterity to make good.
> (Kotewall and Smith 1962:59)

Epigrammatic statements of a cumulative sequential type united in some unexpected way are called *priamels*:

> *Burmese*: Monks and hermits are beautiful when they are lean; four-footed animals when they are fat; men when they are learned; and women when they are married.
> *Moroccan*: Honey is not fat, and *beshna* sorghum is not food, and Berber is not a language.
> *Norse*: Praise the day when it is ended, the ale when it is drunk, ice when it is crossed, a woman after the funeral fire.
> *Spanish*: *Italia para nacer, Francia para vivir, España para morir* (be born in Italy, live in France, die in Spain).

Proverbs and epigrams are often attributed to particular people, but when the attribution becomes part of the saying, they become Wellerisms:

> *American*: As the monkey said when he cut off his tail, "It won't be long now."
> *Moroccan*: As the lion said when he lost his prey in the river, "People should be eaten dry."

Sometimes the point is that there is no point, as in the mock Wellerism:

> In the words of Chekhov, "On the contrary."

Wellerisms rapidly go in and out of fashion. A subvariety is the *Swiftly*, which shuddered through American society in 1962–1963. Here the form is a quotation, but attention is focused on an adverbial pun:

"What are you doing for Easter?" asked Judas crossly.
"Isn't that Notre Dame?" she asked archly.
"We lost," he said winningly.
"It's up to the Senate," he said incongruously.

Puns and word play are a common feature of proverbs and epigrams, as of metaphor in general. A metaphor that is formally proposed as a puzzle in which a hidden meaning is to be guessed is a *riddle* (enigma, conundrum). Riddles are both ancient and widespread. One of the best known is the Greek:

What we caught we left behind;
What we brought we didn't find.
(*Answer*: Fleas)

Actually, there are much older riddles. A Sumerian example of around 2100 B.C. runs:

A house which like heaven has a plow,
Which like a copper kettle is cloth covered,
Which like a goose stands on a base;
He whose eyes are not open enters it,
He whose eyes are open comes out of it.
(*Answer*: The school)
(Kramer 1962:311)

The plow is a reference to a constellation; the study of the stars was of course a major preoccupation of Sumerian schooling.

Probably the most famous riddle in history is that of the Sphinx:

What walks with four legs in the morning, two at noon and three in the evening? (*Answer*: Man)

Riddles are not common among the Indians of the New World, but they do occur. An Aztec example goes:

What goes through a valley clapping like a woman making tortillas? (*Answer*: A butterfly) (Sahagún 1956:II:235)

And the South American Chipaya say:

There is . . . a person, who is small and real fat, and who has a black face. He has the habit of eating a lot of bread. (*Answer*: An oven) (Scott 1963:238)

The firm establishment of a riddle tradition leads naturally to the pointless riddle. A mock riddle of this sort from Yiddish runs:

> What is it that is red, hangs on the wall, and whistles? (*Answer*: A herring. You could paint it red and hang it on the wall. All right, so it doesn't whistle.)

A special category of brief sayings is the *mnemonic rule*, specifically designed to aid memory. Thus, in Navy lore "True virgins make dull company" gets you from the true direction through the variation, magnetic heading and deviation to the reading on the (magnetic) compass, and "St. Wapniacl" gave schoolchildren the order of succession of U. S. Cabinet officials from 1913–1947: State, Treasury, War, Attorney-General, Post-master-General, Navy, Interior, Agriculture, Commerce, and Labor. A Burmese children's mnemonic rule for the meanings of last names is given on p. 206.

Often the brief rhetorical forms are ritualized and verge on the proto-dramatic character of all ritual. Some such forms, however, have a minimal specification of role—they are not the exclusive property of ritually de-fined persons. Some brief prayers, blessings, oaths, and incantations fall into this category. The European expressions for warding off soul loss through sneezing are of this type (*Salud! Gesundheit! Za vashe zdorove!*). Mention of catastrophes, disasters, or misfortunes formerly called forth similar spells: "May God protect us." "May he rest in peace" following the name of a dead person was felt to avert the similar danger of calling up his ghost. One might run this sort of magical risk willfully, in order to impress the listener with one's certainty and truthfulness: "So help me God." Or one may swear by God, by His wounds, by His blood, by His heart. The possible frustration of one's desires by evil spirits was warded off by a disclaimer: "God willing." Analogous formulas are used around the world in similar contexts and so are others for blessing food before eating it, for pledging drink (especially when it contains spirits), for undertaking arduous or hazardous tasks, and for dedicating the labor once completed.

Magical formulas include spells and incantations, curses, charms, and countercharms. Some of these, of course, attain a considerable complexity and may become full-length rituals in prose, poetry, or drama. We are here concerned only with the simpler varieties. Words themselves are magical to primitive men, and merely to pronounce them in certain contexts is fraught with power and danger. The power is greater if they are repeated, and this ancient sentiment may well be responsible for the primitive poetic devices. Sometimes the word is too powerful to be safely repeated except under special safeguards; hence, ellipsis and circumlocution may also have a magical basis. Sometimes the prosaic word is felt to have little power, so a more powerful secret word must be employed, usually one that is archaic, metaphorical, or meaningless (*abracadabra, alakazam*). Many expressions derive from magical gestures ("cross my heart," "King's X," "knock on wood").

RHETORIC

Brief forms of speech (naming, formulas, sayings, and the like) comprise a large proportion of all lore. Longer and more complicated forms are, nonetheless, important in all societies, and may be patterned in highly distinctive styles for various degrees of formality or for different contexts. Prayers, debates, prophecies, proclamations, lectures, sermons, and orations and a variety of other forms exemplify these styles.

Some of the characteristics of formal oratory can be at once appreciated in the following example from the seventeenth century B.C., the "Political Testament" of the Hittite king Hattusilis I:

Behold,
I have fallen sick.
The young Labarnas I had proclaimed to you
Saying, "He shall sit upon the throne."
   I, the king, called him my son,
   Embraced him,
   Exalted him
   And cared for him continually.
But he showed himself a youth not fit to be seen:
He shed no tears;
He showed no pity;
He was cold and heartless.
   I, the king, summoned him to my couch
   And said, "Well, no one will in future bring up the child of his sister as
     his foster son!"
   The word of the king he has not laid to heart,
   But the word of his mother the serpent he has laid to heart.
Enough! He is my son no more!
Then his mother bellowed like an ox,
"They have torn asunder the womb in my living body!
They have ruined him and you will kill him!"
   But have I, the king, done him any evil?
   Behold, I have given my son Labarnas a house;
   I have given him arable land in plenty;
   Sheep in plenty have I given him.
Let him now eat and drink.
So long as he is good he may come up to the city;

But if he come forward as a trouble maker,
Then he shall not come up, but shall remain in his house.
  Behold,
  Mursilis is now my son.
  In place of the lion
  The god will set up another lion.
And in the hour when a call to arms goes forth
You, my servants and leading citizens, must be at hand to help my son.
When three years have elapsed he shall go on a campaign.
If you take him while still a child with you on a campaign, bring him back
  safely.
  Till now no one of my family has obeyed my will;
  But thou, my son Mursilis, thou must obey it.
  Keep thy father's word!
  If thou keepest thy father's word, thou wilt eat bread and drink water.
When maturity is within thee, then eat two or three times a day
And do thyself well!
And when old age is within thee, then drink to satiety!
And then thou mayest set aside thy father's word.
  Now you who are my chief servants, you too must keep my, the king's
    words.
  You shall only eat bread and drink water.
  So the kingdom of Hattusas will stand high and my land will be at peace.
  But if you do not keep the king's word you will not remain alive: you will
    perish.
My grandfather had proclaimed his son Labarnas as heir to the throne in
  Sanahuitta,
But afterwards his servants and the leading citizens spurned his words and
  set Papadilmah on the throne.
Now how many years have elapsed and how many of them have escaped
  their fate?
The houses of the leading citizens, where are they—have they not perished?
  And thou Mursilis shalt not delay nor relax.
  If thou delayest it will mean the same old mischief.
  What has been laid on thy heart, my son,
  Act thereupon always!
(Gurney 1952:171–172)

A large proportion of the rhetorical figures of classical Greek and Roman oratory are to be found in this address of a millennium earlier. Note, for example, the effective use of hyperbole (exaggeration: "his mother bellowed like an ox"), the rhetorical question (posed for effect: "but have I, the king, done him any evil?"), chiasmus (cross parallelism of two successive phrases: "I have given him arable land in plenty;/Sheep in plenty have I given him"), antithesis (emphatic contrast: the son's misdeeds, the king's generosity), metonymy (substituting attribute or other thing for what is intended, as "lion" for "prince"), personification ("Hattusas will stand high") and apostrophe (interruption to address someone: "but thou, my son Mursilis"). The speech also illustrates anaphora (emphatic repetition: "I, the king"), and a balanced and stanzaic poetic form based on parallelism.

Court oratory is commonly ritual in character. The varying stringency of European court manners has attracted some considerable attention. The following example is an exchange at the court of Dahomey in the nineteenth century. A leader of the "Amazons," the Dahomean women soldiers, addresses the king:

As the blacksmith takes an iron bar
  And by fire changes its fashion,
    So we have changed our nature.
We are no longer women,
  We are men.
    By fire we will change Abeahkeutah.
The king gives us cloth,
  But without thread it cannot be fashioned:
    We are the thread.
If corn is put in the sun to dry
  And not looked after,
    Will not the goats eat it?
If Abeahkeutah
  Be left too long,
    Some other nation will spoil it.
A case of rum cannot roll itself.
  A table in a house becomes useful when anything is placed thereon.
    The Dahomean army without the Amazons are as both unassisted.
Spitting makes the belly more comfortable,
  And the outstretched hand will be the receiving one:
    So we ask you for war that our bellies may have their desire and our
    hands be filled.

The king replies equally ceremoniously:

    The hunter buys a dog,
      And, having trained him,
        He takes him out a-hunting,
    Without telling him the game he expects to meet.
      When in the bush he sees a beast,
        And, by his teaching the dog pursues it.

If the dog returns without the game,
  The huntsman, in his anger, kills him
    And leaves his carcass a prey to the wolves and vultures.
If I order you to clear the bush,
  And you do not do it,
    Will I not punish you?
If I tell my people
  To put their hands in the fire,
    They must do it.
When you go to war, if you are taken prisoners,
  You will be sacrificed,
    And your bodies become food for wolves and vultures.
          (Forbes, quoted in Herskovits, 1938:II:90)

In this example there is the repeated use of the explicit simile (Stanzas 1, 3, 6, and 7) elaborated almost into allegory (especially in the parable that begins the king's speech). Note also the use of such "sophisticated" devices as antithesis (Stanza 2) and the rhetorical question (Stanza 4). The stately poetry of ceremonial discourse seems to be generally resorted to for occasions of solemnity and importance. The triadic form is characteristically African.

The following example in dyadic form is the formal announcement of the great communal ritual of the *Fandroana* among the Imerina of Madagascar:

Here is what I say to you,
  You who are under heaven,
And it is an order
  Which I give you.
The Fandroana is coming,
  And the days when living beings may be killed
Will be the fifth day before
  And the fifth day after.
If anyone exceed these limits,
  I shall cause him to lose wife and children.
(Soury-Lavergne and De la Devèze 1913:310)

Even in a prose form, a similar poetic enrichment is commonly employed for elegance, force, dignity, and solemnity. Compare the examples already cited, for instance, with the following passage from the papal bull *Ineffabilis Deus* ("Ineffable God") of December 8, 1854, which promulgated the doctrine of the Immaculate Conception of Mary:

We declare, pronounce, and define that the doctrine which holds that the most blessed Virgin Mary, in the first instant of her conception, by a singular grace and privilege granted by almighty God, in view of the merits of Jesus Christ, the Saviour of the human race, was preserved free from all stain of original sin, is a doctrine revealed by God and therefore to be believed firmly and constantly by all the faithful. (Fremantle 1956:134)

The rhetoric of persuasion, exhortation, and command exemplified in these selections appears to use everywhere a similar range of emphatic devices. This need not surprise us, because the problem presented by such communications has at least a general similarity wherever it occurs. A different context of discourse produces not only different content but also different form. Thus, in the distinctive situation of joking relationships between relatives whose contacts with each other are subject to cultural and psychological tension and restraint, a pattern of mandatory discourse is developed quite distinct from political or ritual colloquy. The following example is from the African Mossi. A man is greeting his wife's sister:

> Eh! Here come women more worthless than my wife! What do you want here? Are you looking for a millet cake? Who eats well here? Do you want an old groundnut? No one here has tasted millet cakes with sauce since your sister came to my house! (Hammond 1964:265)

Levity of this sort would be equally unthinkable in a papal bull or at the Dahomean court. Nor is hortatory power and dignity attained by such a combination of bald assertions and rhetorical questions.

The forms of discourse we have examined, from simple naming to highly formalized oratory, illustrate both the range and the power of metaphor. They also violate in some measure our purely European literary expectations. We tend to draw a sharp line between poetry and prose, fiction and nonfiction, narrative and drama. In many cultures these lines are blurred or nonexistent. What a man will say (both in form and in content) when he rises to speak is conditioned by the tradition that prompts him. If the motives of the moment are dominant, he may make a "speech." If the confrontations of social position are more salient, he may participate in a more or less ritualized play. If it is the action itself that prompts him, he may tell a story. If the urgency is expression, he may turn to song. Obviously, he may do more than one of these at once. If the moment or his message be sacred, he may speak in traditional and immutable poetry used only by defined personages on special occasions and chant the holy mystery of creation, as in this Hawaiian story of the creation:

> O ke au i ka huli wela ka honua.
> O ke au i ka huli lole ka lani.
> O ke au i kuka'iaka ka la
>   E ho'o malamalama i ka malama.

O ke au o makali'i ka po
 O ka walewale ho'okumu honua ia.
O ke kumu o ka lipo, i lipo ai.
 O ke kumu o ka po, i po ai.
O ka lipolipo, o ka lipolipo.
 O ka lipo o ka la, o ka lipo o ka po,
Po wale ho 'i.
 Hanau ka po.
Hanau Kumulipo i ka po, he kane.
 Hanau Po'ele i ka po, he wahine.

(It was that time when the earth warmed in passion.
 It was that time when the sky writhed in passion.
It was that time when the sun swelled and subsided
 And made bright moonlight on the moon.
It was the time when the weak-eyed night
 All by itself gave rise to the earth there.
That was the source of darkness, in the darkness then.
 That was the source of night, in the night then.
The utter darkness was utter darkness.
 The sun was dark and the night was dark,
And there was nothing at all but night.
 And the night gave birth.
Born was Source of Darkness in the night, a man.
 Born was Embrace of Night in the night, a woman..)
 (Beckwith 1951:58, 187; translation mine)

Obviously, we can read such discourse in many ways. While recognizing the dangers of our own categories, let us first read it as poetry.

Chapter 4

Song

All men sing and are aware of doing so. The distinction between song and various forms of speech is made everywhere, even though the elements emphasized may not be the same. In a crude way, this resembles the distinction between poetry and prose, and like the latter it cannot usefully be made absolute. In general, of course, the focus of interest in songs is on the esthetics of sound—musicality. In most speech, the center of attention lies in meaning. Yet there are borderline cases. In many primitive traditions, songs are often composed of meaningless syllables, traditional perhaps to particular settings but devoid of semantic value. In all traditions the muscality of speech is manipulated for euphonious effects in oratory and conversation, and in all traditions it is customary to play with the sounds of language and their often ambiguous relationship to meaning. All peoples pun.

WORD PLAY

Puns, or playing with words generally, may well be a primitive manifestation of the impulse that tends everywhere toward poetry. They are a delight to children: "Why did the coal scuttle? Because it saw the kitchen sink." Sometimes the emphasis is on meaning, sometimes on sound. Often it is the sheer dexterity of pronunciation that is at issue, as in such tongue twisters as the French: "*Dis-moi, gros gras grain d'orge, quand te dé-gro-gra-graindorgeras-tu?*" "*Je me dé-gro-gra-graindorgerais quand tous les gros gras grains d'orge se dé-gro-gra-graindorgeront.*" Or the Chinese: ssu^4 $shih^2$ ssu^4 ssu^3 $shih^2$ $shih^1$ ("forty-four dead stone lions"). A sixth-century Sanskrit example from an epic by Bhaaravi runs:

Na nonanunno nunnono naanaa naanaananaa nanu
Nunno 'nunno nanunneno naanenaa nunnanunnanut.

(No man is he who is wounded by a low man; no man is the man who
wounds a low man, o ye of diverse aspect;
The wounded is not wounded if his master is unwounded; not guiltless is
he who wounds one sore wounded.)

(Keith 1956:114)

A similar schoolboy spoof on the word agglutination in German is the story
of the Hottentot's stuttering grandmother and her kangaroo:

> In Afrika lebte mal eine alte Frau, die stotterte und war auch
> sonst geistig nicht mehr ganz auf der Höhe. Deswegen nannte man
> sie die Hottentottenstottertrottelmutter. Sie hatte eine Beutelratte.
> Damit nun das Tier nicht ausriss und auch während der Regenzeit
> Schutz hatte, liess sie ein Lattengitterwetterkotter bauen. Aber wie
> es so geht, jemand hatte es auf diese Beutelratte abgesehen. Eines
> Tages, als die Hottentottenstottertrottelmutter ihr Tierchen in seinem
> Lattengitterwetterkotter fütterte, wurde sie überfallen und zu Boden
> geworfen. Der Attentäter raubte die Beutelratte und riss aus. Und
> nun wurde für das Wiederbringen der Lattengitterwetterkotterbeutel-
> ratte eine Prämie ausgesetzt, das war die Hottentottenstottertrottel-
> mutterattentäterlattengitterwetterkotterbeutelrattenfangprämie. Wer
> nicht verspricht, bekommt sie! (traditional)

A favorite tongue twister of the Crow Indians is *Basakapupétsdets akapu-
papá'patdetk* ("My people who went to the Nez Percé are not wearing
Nez Percé belts") (Lowie 1935:170). And an African example is the Am-
bede: *Kusa le podi kudi; kudi le podi kusa* ("The morning glory twines up
the post; the post twines up the morning glory") (Adam 1941:133). In
other cases, the word play is less of sound than of grammar or meaning, as
in the Dutch: *Amsterdam die groote stad. Mes hoeveel lettres spel je das?*
("Amsterdam is a big city, but how many letters does it take to spell *it*?")
Particularly comic effects are gained by controlled mispronunciation or
inversion, as in spoonerisms: "The rout of the Spanish Loyalists shows what
comes of putting all your Basques in one exit." A similar mechanism is
commonly employed in Turkish poetry. It is called *tejnis*, a pithy pun
rhyme of the epigrammatic type like the English "Travel is travail," or
the Italian *Traduttore traditore* ("The translator is a traitor"). Punning for
fun is not uncommonly part of the license of traditional clowning in ceremonial contexts, as in this example from a modern Maya play:

SCRIBE: That's just it, man. You haven't caught a thing. Just once or
twice you might look for a meaning (*naoh*) that's right in front of you
(*ch u va a va*).

OLD MAN: Praise be to Christ the Father! Is there anybody with his reason
(*naoh*) hanging down the front? Isn't that the business (*pena*)! (Mace
1954; tr. mine)

The Old Man willfully misinterprets *ch u va a va* ("before your face") to be *ch u va av a* ("before your legs"); *pena* ("sorrow, matter") is played against *pene* ("penis"); the play on *naoh* is not a true pun but probably contributes to the effect. Interlingual puns such as are implied here in Maya and Spanish are a commonplace among groups in intimate contact with each other but speaking different languages. Much is made among the African Tonga of the expression *ndâkutanda,* which means "I chase you" in Tonga but "I love you" in Zulu. The Siberian Tungus delight in pun stories somewhat like the American stories about Little Audrey:

> Ivul has a clever elder brother. The brother sends Ivul to fetch some willow roots (*ngingtel*) to build a boat. Instead of this, Ivul kills some children and brings their heels (*ngingtyl*). The brother asks him to bring a clamp for the boat (*ninakir*); but Ivul brings some dogs (*nginakir*). He is sent for ribs for the boat, but he brings the ribs of his mother whom he has killed. The brother asks him to go away on a trip and set up the tent on a sloping bank (*ngeku*), but Ivul sets it up on a scaffolding (*neku*); and so on (Levin and Potapov 1964:650).

A similarly playful use of puns is attested for many other groups.

But the significance of punning is not always playful. Religion and magic often place considerable emphasis on the similarities of sound among various words. Ancient Egyptian catechism, for example, asserted solemnly that the male Cat (*mau*) is Raa because "he is like (*mau*) unto that which he hath made." It is apparent that recurrent patterns of sound capture the human imagination and that we tend to endow them with special force and meaning even when they are but isolated examples. All communities, however, build them into songs with real words, and inevitably these compositions come to represent some synthesis of the considerations of sound and meaning. In the poetic spectrum thus defined, we encounter a large number of specific devices that have become traditional to this form of expression, sometimes combining in highly formalized ways, but at other times only very loosely arranged.

CHANT

The simplest, most fundamental, and most widespread feature of poetry is rhythmic structure, and we may conveniently distinguish the songs that rely primarily upon simple repetition as *chants*. Repetition is not only a poetic device, of course. It is a common mode of emphasis in "prose" as well, and in many languages it may become structured as an element of grammar itself. When this happens, the repetition of an element usually has a meaning related to plurality, augmentation, repetitive action, intensification, and the like. Even grammatically, repetition appears to convey urgency and emphasis. We may note in English that things look very, very bad. Many another language would declare with equal gravity that they are bad, bad, bad.

A formulaic use of repetition is characteristic of magical spells. To say something twice or three, four, or seven times is felt to have specific power. It also has, of course, specific rhythm. In the compelling, if monotonous, repetition of spells, prayers, and charms, we may in fact be close to one origin of simple chanting. The use of the "Hail Mary" in the Catholic liturgy of penance is one contemporary example. A poetically more sophisticated example is the rhyme:

> Three blind mice—
> Three blind mice—
> See how they run?
> See how they run?
> They all ran after the farmer's wife.
> She cut off their tails with a carving knife.
> Did you ever see such a sight in your life
> As three blind mice?
> (traditional)

Here the repetition is augmented by a number of other poetic devices in a form that is not a chant at all, but a *verse*. Disregarding for the moment the verse features (balanced use of lines of particular length, of stress meter, and of rhyme), we may note the gain in poetic significance that is involved in controlled repetition. This can readily be tested by rereading the poem, omitting Lines 2, 4, and 8.

Most poetry is embellished by metaphors. In a particular tradition, the standardization of metaphors and stock phrases can make possible even a secondary and tertiary substitution of meanings without damage to the intelligibility of the poetry—at least to those familiar with it. In Norse poetry, for example, certain metaphors called *kennings* are regularly substituted for the more prosaic expressions, and with time there come to be many kennings for the commoner elements: "whale path" or "fishes' way" for *sea*, "ring giver" or "dispenser of the candles of the fishes' way" for *king*. The last expression may be explained by the fact that the sea god was rich, hence the light of the sea was gold: the giver of gold is the king. Norse kennings get much more complex than this, but then so do the ritual riddles of the Maya or the catechistic mysteries of the Egyptians. A kind of diphrastic kenning is common in the poetry of Middle America. In Nahuatl poetry, for example, the coupling of *water* and *hill* means "city"; *water* and *hearth* or *dart* and *shield* means "war"; *tail* and *wing* means "lower class"; *cloud* and *smoke* means "fame"; and *mat* and *chair* means "authority" (Garibay 1940:112–113). Many traditions have standardized their metaphors in analogous ways.

Consider the wild beauty of the "War God's Horse Song" of the Navaho, with its extensive use of startling simile and unexpected kennings, its delicate structure of interlocking repetitions, and its surprise ending of inverted personification:

> I am the Turquoise Woman's son.
>> On top of Belted Mountain (are)
>>> Beautiful horses—slim like a weasel!
>
> My horse has a hoof like striped agate;
>> His fetlock is like a fine eagle plume;
>>> His legs are like quick lightning.
>
> My horse's body is like an eagle-plumed arrow;
>> My horse has a tail like a trailing black cloud.
>
> I put flexible goods on my horse's back;
>> The little Holy Wind blows through his hair.
>>> His mane is made of short rainbows.
>
> My horse's ears are made of round corn.
>> My horse's eyes are made of big stars.
>>> My horse's head is made of mixed waters
>>>> (From the holy waters—he never knows thirst).
>
> My horse's teeth are made of white shell.
>> The long rainbow is in his mouth for a bridle,
>>> And with it I guide him.
>
> When my horse neighs, different colored horses follow.
>> When my horse neighs, different colored sheep follow.
>>> I am wealthy because of him.
>
> Before me peaceful,
>> Behind me peaceful,
>>> Under me peaceful,
>>>> Over me peaceful,
>>>>> All around me peaceful—
> Peaceful voice when he neighs.
>> I am everlasting and peaceful.
>>> I stand for my horse.
>>>> (Coolidge 1930:2)

Here the pattern of repetition is irregular but forceful. The modalities are at once flexible and intricate, and both the form and the imagery are quite unlike the poetry of the modern neighbors of the Navaho. It may, in fact, be suggested that the affiliations of Athabaskan poetry may lie outside America altogether, among the aboriginal peoples of Siberia. The following chant, in which a Yakut shaman invokes his spirit, expresses a quite different ideology, but its poetry is strikingly similar to the Navaho chant in form as well as metaphor:

> Mighty bull of the earth!
> Horse of the steppes!
> I, the mighty bull, bellow!
> I, the horse of the steppes, neigh!
> I, the man set above all other beings!
> I, the man most gifted of all!
> I, the man created by the master all powerful!
> Horse of the steppes, appear!
> Teach me!
> Enchanted bull of the earth, appear!
> Speak to me!
> Powerful master,
> Command me!
> All of you who will go with me,
> Give heed with your ears!
> Those whom I command not,
> Follow me not!
> Approach not nearer than is permitted!
> Look intently!
> Give heed!
> Have a care!
> Look heedfully!
> Do this,
> All of you,
> All together,
> All,
> However many you may be!
> Thou of the left side,
> O lady with thy staff,
> If anything be done amiss,
> If I take not the right way,
> I entreat you, correct me!
> Command!
> My errors and my path show to me!
> O mother of mine!
> Wing thy free flight!
> Pave my wide roadway!
> Souls of the sun,
> Mothers of the sun,
> Living in the south

In the nine wooded hills,
Ye who shall be jealous,
I adjure you all,
   Let them stay.
   Let your three shadows stand high!
    In the east
    On your mountains,
    Lord,
    Grandsire of mine,
    Great of power
    And thick of neck—be thou with me!
    And thou, grey bearded wizard Fire,
    I ask thee:
      With all my dreams,
      With all comply!
      To all my desires
      Consent!
    Heed all! Fulfill all!
    All heed! All fulfill!
(Quoted by Czaplicka 1912:235–236)

The general structure of this chant may perhaps be read as follows: Lines 1 and 2 are given contrastive repetition in Lines 3 and 4; this is then underlined in Lines 5, 6, and 7, a tightly repetitive triad, loosely recapitulating Lines 3 and 4; Lines 8, 10, and 12 are another similar triad that repeat the preceding structure in inverted order; Lines 12–13 climax and summarize the invocation. There is then a break in structure, signalized by a change in pace, subject, and form, as the shaman addresses the onlookers in the second stanza. The triadic structure of the stanza provides continuity with what has gone before. A further triad in the third stanza is addressed to the female ceremonial assistant and the spirits she stands for. The remainder of the poem apostrophizes the spirit who is to possess the shaman, presumably the same spirit addressed in the beginning; and the final couplet summarizes the poem dramatically and simply with an inverted repetition (chiasmus). The complexity of structure is fully matched by the complexity of the imagery. Redundancy, periphrasis, personification, synechdoche, and especially hyperbole are all employed. Every effort is made to invoke and exaggerate symbols of power and strength. Primitive chants may often be richly decorated with such figures.

    Even simple patterns of repetition can attain quite musical effects, and primitive poetry is capable of producing very complex rhythms. North American Indians commonly employ for this purpose a limited range of meaningless syllables, as in this Arapaho song, which means nothing in

Arapaho:

> Ye no wi chi hay
> Yo wi hay
> Wi chi hay
> Yo wi chi no
> Wi chi ni. (*Repeat from beginning.*)
> Wi ni wi chi hay
> Yo wi hay
> Wi chi hay
> Yo wi chi ni hay
> Yo wi chi ni hay
> Yo wi how
> Wi chi hay
> Yo wi chi no
> Wi ni no wa.
> (Nettl 1956:23)

The poetic scansion here is intricate. Only 9 syllables fill out the 53 syllables of the song, scanning *abcde, fce, cde, fcdb, cdg* (repeat), *cgcde, fce, cde, fcdge, fcdge, fch, cde, fcdb, cgbi.* The initial and final syllables (and one other) are not repeated. The cadence is thoroughly characteristic of Plains Indian music, and carries over into the poetry of the region in meaningful as well as purely musical texts.

A poetry of simple repetition would be crude indeed, and even the most primitive peoples go far beyond such a pattern. Much can be done, in fact, with repetition itself. Consider, for example, the poetic value of contrast, in which the urgency of repetition adds force to a strategic variation in only one element, as in the *Kyrie Eleison*:

> Lord, have mercy upon us.
> Christ, have mercy upon us.
> Lord, have mercy upon us.

This kind of repetition and contrast is a widespread feature of primitive rhetoric and of primitive poetry. Whether it is complex, as in the preceding Arapaho song, or simple, as here, it usually attains a kind of poetic balance. In effect, the lines are divided by a caesura or break into two elements, thus presenting a structure of *abcbab*.

The following Nutka couplet on "Fog" is structurally almost as simple. Its subtle use of restrained progressive repetition, contrast, balance, and climax in a minimal compass give it both force and depth:

> Don't you ever, you up in the sky,
> Don't you ever get tired of having the clouds between you and us?
> (Densmore 1939:284)

Unlike the liturgical Greek example, involving synonymic contrast, the figure here is close to paradox, the *abab* structure being divided by caesura with the first term synonymic and the second contrastive.

In the love charms of the Cherokee there is an insistent use of repetition by fours and sevens. The following example from the Oklahoma Cherokee is characteristic:

Anagaliisgi gigagéei iyúusdi . . .
Uughvhada iyúusdi . . .
Dhlvvdatsi iyúusdi . . .
Wahhya gigagéei iyúusdi . . .
Hidaaweehi iyúusdi tsinanugóotsiigá.
Tsadaanvdhoogi ayv ayeehliyu gaiiseesdi.
Gha?! Hnaagwo tsoola unéegv tsughasv́vsdi tsaayalv́tsiigá tsughasv́vsdi!

(Like the Red Lightning . . .
Like the Fog . . .
Like the Panther . . .
Like the Red Wolf . . .
Like You, You Wizard, I have just come to make my appearance.
I will be walking in the very middle of your soul.
Now! Now the Smoke of the White Tobacco has just come to wing down
   upon you!)

(Kilpatrick 1965:42–43)

Although the translation of this poem is clear and literal, it is necessary to add that it contains certain standard metaphors obvious in Cherokee but not in English. Lightning, Fog, Panther, and Wolf are the spirits who give the charm its power. The Wizard is a person or spirit of boundless power. Red is a symbol of the east, of power and victory; white represents the south, happiness, and peace. The charm is intended to "remake" tobacco, investing it with the power to attract women. Not only do four and seven appear in the structure of the poem as it stands, but the whole charm is to be repeated four times under proper ceremonial circumstances. Formal use of number is a widely distributed poetic device, and is particularly characteristic of spells.

As several of the poems already cited illustrate, patterns of repetition may be semantic as well as phonological. The repetition of a particular image in other words is called parallelism. It is illustrated in the following introduction to the long narrative poem of *Djanggauwul* from northern Australia. As in this example, the repetition of parallelism has many modes. It may be synonymic, antonymic, partial, or progressive:

Although I leave Bralgu
   I am close to it.

I, Djanggauwul, am paddling . . .
   Paddling with all the paddles
With their flattened tapering ends.
   Close I am coming with my older sister,
Coming along from Bralgu.
   We splash the water as we paddle,
Paddling wearily with my younger sister,
   Undulating our buttocks as we paddle.

We paddle along through the roaring tide,
   Paddle a long way.
I am paddling along fast through the rough sea . . .
   Beside me is foam from our paddling, and large waves follow us.
With Bralbral we move our wrists as we paddle,
   Making noise as we go through the sea.
We, Djanggauwul, are paddling along,
   Lifting our paddles, slowly going along . . .
All the way we have paddled.
   I rest my paddles now, as we glide.

On the sea's surface the light from the Morning Star
   Shines as we move, shining on the calmness of the sea.
Looking back I see its shine,
   An arc of light from the Morning Star.
The shine falls on our paddles,
   Lighting our way.
We look back to the Morning Star and see its shine,
   Looking back as we paddle.
Star moving along, shining! We saw its disc quite close,
   Skimming the sea's surface and mounting again above Bralgu.
                       (Berndt 1953:63–64)

The structure of this chant is notably complex, but it is elaborated from simple patterns of repetition—in stanzas of five couplets each. The passage is unified by the aperiodic repetition of the key word, to make us increasingly aware of the effort involved ("paddling" occurs 16 times in 30 lines). The figure verges on onomatopoeia. On the whole, this poem seems to me couched in a poetic language at once soberly realistic and impressionistically evocative. We are told point blank that we are paddling the canoe Bralbral at sea near the island of Bralgu with the brother and sister Djanggauwul who are the culture heroes, but what finally convinces us is a nice use of simple poetic devices.

     The most widespread form of parallelism is the couplet form represented in the Australian example. This was also the commonest form in the ancient Near East, as in the "Epitaph of Taba" in Syrian:

> Blessed be Taba, daughter of Ta Hapi,
> The devoted worshiper of Osiris the God;
> Naught of evil have you done,
> Slander of no man have you spoken;
> There before Osiris be blessed,
> From before Osiris take water.
> (Olmstead 1948:463)

Couplet parallelism was equally common in aboriginal America. This is a passage from the "Creation" poem in the *Popol Vuh* of the Quiche Maya:

> So then the earth was created by them.
> Only their word was the creation of it.
> To create the earth, "Earth," they said.
> Immediately it was created.
> It was just like a cloud,
> Like a mist then,
> The creation,
> The whirlwind.
> (Edmonson 1970)

Aboriginal American poetry is overwhelmingly composed in parallelistic couplets. Examples may be found in this volume from Eskimo, Nutka, Nahuatl, Mayan Spanish, Yucatec, Cakchiquel, Warrau, Quechua, Araucanian, and Alacaluf. On the other hand, the poetry of much of North America (the Woodlands, the Plains, and the Canadian interior) appears to use other patterns of polynomial repetition. The invocation to an Iroquois oration is a forceful illustration:

> I come again to greet and thank the League;
> I come again to greet and thank the kindred;
> I come again to greet and thank the warriors;
> I come again to greet and thank the women.
> My forefathers—what they established!
> My forefathers—harken to them!
> (Hale 1883:123)

The contrasting repetition of the first four lines sets the stage in this example for a contrastive use of the same device in the next two. Monotony is avoided by using different numbers of lines for the two purposes. Actually, the whole effect is heightened here by a further device: the deliberate use of sequence. The whole passage is thereby given a definite climax structure by proceeding in descending order of emphasis for the first four lines and returning strongly on the last two. Finally, the exact number of repetitions may also have formal poetic meaning. In the Iroquois case, the number *four* is completive in something of the sense that the number *three* would be in a comparable European context. (Third time's a charm; compare the structure of "Three Blind Mice.") The Iroquois ear is therefore particularly prepared for the shift of pace in Line 5, which leads swiftly and economically to the climax.

The structural resemblance between this poem and the Cherokee love charm previously cited suggests a family relationship, perhaps one characteristic of Iroquoian poetry. There is even a distant kinship of form with the Siberian-Athabaskan pattern already discussed. It is all the more striking that Eskimo poetry makes extensive use of the couplet form so widespread in the Old World and in Middle and South America:

> Pa ma ya
>> Pa ma ya
> A ya ya
>> A ya ya
> A ya ya ya
>> Ya ye ya
> I ya ya ya
>> I ye a ya.
> I call to mind the first coming of spring,
>> That it was really I who came slowly, slowly in to land.
> (*Repeat refrain.*)
> And all this I love best to think of,
>> For on land I was never lucky in stalking.
>> (Rasmussen 1929:69)

The introductory syllables in this chant have no specific meaning, a device characteristic of American Indian song in somewhat the same spirit that "fa la la" or "waly o" may be used in English folk songs to eke out a meter. Ulivfak, the Eskimo poet, is allusive and delicate. In old age he thinks of spring, remembering his success at sea hunting, but then he reflects philosophically that, of course, one remembers what he did well. Now he is old and landbound, a poignant circumstance in a culture where suicide is expected of those who can no longer hunt.

From a general survey, it would appear that native American poetry uses couplets or variable numbers of semantic repetitions, possibly in different areas. It is my belief that it never attained true versification in aboriginal times. A possible exception to this assertion is the following Shoshone poem recorded by Shimkin. It is a flyting song composed by Black Faces (warriors) to shame the "Pretty Boys" who stay home and enjoy the women while the warriors are away:

> Ën nggánhi túiwich i
> Mak në huúawaini.

> Ke ën óar ndóiwaixw̲
> Mak në huúawaini̲. (*Repeat.*)
>
> Áya hanzh, dichir gwëkant!
> Nan mawiíyahant.
> Döyawant noómia'yu̲.
> Keha nëëcidëi̲?
> Enggwëgwëpaini̲ në wizha wën.
> Dúkobi̲ utuwék.
>
> (You're at home, Pretty Boy,
> While I go off to the forest.
> You didn't go out anywhere,
> While I go off to the forest.
>
> Oh Friend! Bad Husband!
> You had better keep her tied!
> Keep on moving through the mountains.
> Maybe you'll be ill.
> I will stay with your wife for a wife.
> Let a Black Face provide.)
> (Shimkin 1947:37:329–352, quoted in Hymes 1964:349–350)

The poem consists of a repeated stanza of four lines followed by one of six. Shimkin interprets the structure as an alternating six- and seven-mora line, the latter accented on the third mora, which is double. This interpretation appears to me to exaggerate the regularity of the scansion. Syllabically it should scan 6-6-6-6/7-5-6-5-9-5, and assuming two long vowels to one short vowel, with vowels followed by consonant clusters counted as long, yields a semimora count of approximately 9-9-9-9/10-8-9-7-11-6. (This is only approximate because of difficulties in interpreting the status of triphthongs and unstressed vowels, and there are some other textual problems. The unstressed vowels are underlined. Alternative scansions would be even more irregular.) Nor is the accent quite as regular as described, falling wrong on the last line. I remain unconvinced that this Shoshone song is metric.

Characteristically American is the following passage from the Yucatecan *X 'Okoot Kay H 'Ppum t Huul*, the sacrificial "Song of the Dance of the Bowman," although it is transcribed in pseudoverse form:

> Tz'aa u yaax, ti ca sutil
> Ch'a a p'um tz'a uhul ch ei i,
> Toh tant u tzem; ma kabeilt
> A tz'iic tu lacal a muuk tiyal
> A huul lomtci tio; lalma u

Kilic tu tamil u bakel u
Tial ca paatac u muk yaatic
Hu hum p'iiltil ley u yota
Ciliich celem yum ku.

(Make the first turn, Then on the second
Seize your bow And set your arrow;
Point it at his breast; It is not necessary
that you put all your strength into it
To shoot him, So that you don't
wound him To the marrow And the
quick; Thus he will suffer
Little by little, For thus it is desired
By the beautiful lord god.)
(Marti 1961:60)

The text of this poem is from an eighteenth-century document from Campeche discovered in Merida, Yucatan in 1952. There is probably little reason to treat the strophe and line divisions too seriously, but it is worth noting that the song has been transcribed as an apparently unversified and unrhymed chant in six- to nine-syllable (seven- to ten-vowel) lines. Actually, it scans in parallelistic couplets, as I have indicated in the translation by capitalization.

Verse does occur in American Indian languages as a consequence of European contact. The Quechuan play *Ollantay*, for example, is composed in a Spanish verse form. The following Nahuatl poem illustrates some of the problems of interpretation:

Nonantzin ihcuac nimiquiz
Motlecuilpan xinechtoca.
Ihcuac tiaz titlaxcalchihuaz
Ompa nopampa xichoca.
Ihuan tla acah mitztlatlaniz:
"Nonantzin, tleca tichoca?"
Xiquilhuiz: "Ca xoxohui in cuahuitl
Ihuan in nechochoctia
Ica cecenca popoca."

(My mother, when I have perished,
Have me buried at your hearth stone.
When you come to put your bread on,
Stop for a moment and mourn me.
Someone may drop in then to ask you,
"Why, mother, why are you crying?"

> Just tell him, "Well, the wood is still green
> And always makes my eyes water—
> All of this smoke from the fireplace.")
> (original source u.n.; variant in Taggart 1957:319, 351)

Vowel and consonant length are not significant in Nahuatl, and the stress accent is always on the penultimate syllable. The orthography can be read as in Spanish without important error (*x* having the value of *sh* in English). The syllabic scansion is 8-8-9-8-9-8-10-8-8, and the stress scansion is:

/ $-\prime-\prime--\prime-$ / $--\prime---\prime-$ / $\prime-\prime----\prime-$ / $\prime--\prime--\prime-$ /
$\prime--\prime---\prime-$ / $-\prime-\prime--\prime-$ / $-\prime---\prime--\prime-$ / $\prime-----\prime-$ /
$\prime--\prime--\prime-$ /. Finally, the rhyme is *abcbdbefb*. It seems impossible, despite some irregularities, to avoid the conclusion that a specific pattern of rhymed and metered verse is being approximated. No such pattern is attested in native Nahuatl poetry, nor is this poem thematically consistent with Nahuatl tradition. I believe we may consider it a product of Spanish influence.

Even without versification, the poetic use of sequence can be intensively exploited more or less for its own sake, as in the familiar type of "The House That Jack Built." This is a widespread motif in stories and children's games as well as in poetry. The following example is from a cumulative *cante fable* of the Ugandan Lango about "The Girl Who Went to Pick Cherries." As the story unfolds, the song is sung repeatedly, first consisting only of the final quatrain, and adding the next preceding line on each repetition. The final verse is:

> Behold ye, these men kill my cow:
> My cow I got from the man who broke my razor:
> My razor I got from those children who upset my milk:
> My milk I got from that man who broke my stick:
> My stick I got from that boy who broke my feather:
> My feather I got from the kite that snatched my fish:
> My fish I got from that river that upset my cherries:
> My cherries I got on the rocks where the girls left me.
> I went with those girls: they left me at the cherries:
> They made me stay on the dung and on the rocks;
> The dung cried fa - la - la - la (*alurukok*),
> Fa - la - la - la was cried on the rocks.
> (Driberg 1923:452)

Cumulative repetition of this sort may take a variety of forms. English ballads frequently use the "climax of relatives: her mother said . . ., her father said . . ., her brother said . . ., etc. Counting songs (*comptines*) of several types are also widespread. The following Cheremis "sonnet" is a polished example of what can be done with the controlled use of sequence and climax:

> Sky's cuckoo, my father, remains.
> Cuckoo wing, my mother, remains.
> Sky's swallow, my elder brother, remains.
> Swallow wing, my elder brother's wife, remains.
> Summer butterfly, my younger brother, remains.
> Butterfly wing, my younger sister, remains.
> Summer flower, myself, I depart.
> Flower blossom of mine remains.
>   (Sebeok 1960)

The structural basis of this poem is clearly an octet of semantically parallel lines of approximately equal syllabic length, subdivided into two quatrains and four couplets, the lines being arranged in descending order of super-ordination within and between couplets. The lines end in a refrain word (rather than a rhyme) and the fourth couplet has a contrastive refrain word (Line 7). The structure of the metaphors is:

1. I:mine::depart:remain
2. I:male::mine:female
3. Male:female::whole:part
4. Self:juniors::flower:butterfly
5. Senior:junior::sky:summer
6. Blossom:flower::wing:flying thing
7. Cuckoo:parent::swallow:older sibling
8. Cuckoo:swallow::butterfly:flower

From this analysis (which is based upon but differs somewhat from Sebeok's) the poetic structure appears to have a primary implication that "I" am transitory but what is "mine" remains; that what is mine is my beloved and is part of me, just as I am beloved of my immediate relatives and the flower is beloved of the butterfly; that what is immediate is partial and ephemeral like the summer blossom (or the butterfly's wing), but what is older is as whole, complete, and immutable as my father the sky, in strict proportion as it is senior and superordinate. The poetic effect is attained through highly economic repetition, ellipsis, and ambiguity, and the last line poises all these metaphors in a delicate suspension of mortality and suggested self-extension toward which all the remainder of the poem has built. This analysis does not, of course, exhaust the structure of the poem, which in fact contains several obscurities. My younger brother and sister cannot stand to me in the relation of my parents to my older brother. The term translated as "older brother" has, however, the additional meaning "father's brother," and should perhaps be so rendered. The fifth metaphor could probably be further analyzed, as it is compound, apparently asserting both the summer-like passage of youth and an earth-sky expression of (possibly sexual) superordination. The precise meanings of the cuckoo and the swallow are not clear, and may involve the mating as well as flight habits of those birds, and perhaps other associations as well (song?). The metaphors for sex (wing, blossom:female; self, whole:male) are also ambiguous. It is probably impossible to exhaust the metaphoric resonances of even a very simple poem.

Even irregular repetitions can produce poetic emphasis. Keying, for example, or aperiodic repetition of key words and phrases, is a common feature of ancient Hebrew poetry, as in this psalm:

God is our refuge and strength,
    A very present help in trouble.
Therefore will we not fear, though the earth be removed,
    And though the mountains be carried into the midst of the sea;
Though the waters thereof roar and be troubled,
    Though the mountains shake with the swelling thereof.
                        Selah.
There is a river, the streams whereof shall make glad the city of God,
    The holy place of the tabernacles of the most High.
God is in the midst of her; she shall not be moved;
    God shall help her, and that right early.
The heathen raged, the kingdoms were moved;
    He uttered his voice, the earth melted.
The Lord of hosts is with us;
    The God of Jacob is our refuge.
                        Selah.
Come, behold the works of the Lord,
    What desolations he hath made in the earth.
He maketh wars to cease unto the end of the earth;
    He breaketh the bow,
And cutteth the spear in sunder;
    He burneth the chariot in the fire.
Be still and know that I am God:
    I will be exalted in the earth.
The Lord of hosts is with us;
    The God of Jacob is our refuge.
                        Selah.
              (Psalm 46)

The modalities of repetition in this poem are multiple. There is paraphrase, or synonymic repetition, as in Lines 1 and 2 and repeatedly throughout the poem, which is in parallelistic couplets. There is the double parallelism of

Line 6 to Lines 5 and 4. There is the partial parallelism of Lines 8 and 9 and the progressive parallelism of Lines 10 and 11. And, finally, there is the refrain word *selah*, and the refrain couplet of the second and third stanzas, which combine with the aperiodic repetition of key words ("God," "refuge," "earth") to give both semantic and phonetic unity to the poem. (Note also the cumulative addition of one couplet to each successive stanza.) Nor is the poetic structure entirely captured by these mechanisms, for as in all poetry some part of the impact depends on a parallelism of meaning and repetition of form familiar to the poet and the hearer from other parts of the same tradition. Key phrases ("tabernacles of the most High," "the Lord of hosts," "the God of Jacob"), the couplet form, and the unity of the stanza gain most of their significance from this order of repetition, which lies beyond the structure of a particular poem. In a similar way, for example, the formal poetry of the Japanese *haiku* has little meaning for us until we have heard several poems with five-, seven-, and five-syllable lines.

Keying may be made regular in the refrain. This may be a single word, as in the Hebrew example; it may be a phrase or complete line; it may be a stanza. Even very isolated cultures like those of the Andaman Islanders or the African Pygmies make full use of the poetic refrain. The following example, "The Man Weary of Life," a twelfth-dynasty Egyptian lament, illustrates the effectiveness of the device:

> Death is in my eyes today
> > As when a sick man becomes whole,
> > > As when one walketh abroad after sickness.
> Death is in my eyes today
> > Like the scent of myrrh;
> > > As when one sitteth under the boat's sail on a windy day.
> Death is in my eyes today
> > Like the smell of water-lilies;
> > > As when one sitteth on the bank of drunkenness.
> Death is in my eyes today
> > Like a well-trodden road,
> > > As when one returneth from the war unto his home.
> Death is in my eyes today
> > Like the unveiling of heaven,
> > > As when one attaineth to that which he knew not.
> Death is in my eyes today
> > As when one longeth to see his house again
> > > After he hath spent many years in captivity.
> > > > (Hawkes and Woolley 1963:807)

Although markedly less common than the couplet in ancient Egyptian poetry, the triplet form of this poem is noteworthy. Relatively rare elsewhere, the triplet is so common in African poetry that it may be considered characteristic. Thus the Sotho, at the opposite end of Africa from Egypt, compose in triplets with progressive repetition or linking:

> E sa lemile le bo ea, khomahali,
>> Khomahali ea bo Setebane,
>>> Ea bo Setebane, ea bo Rapolile.

> (It has ploughed with hair on its body, the big beast,
>> The big beast of the Setebanes,
>>> Of the Setebanes, of the Rapoliles.)
>>>> (Lestrade 1937:307)

Linking is highly characteristic of Sotho poetry, and is, in fact, its principal structural device. A similar but looser structure of incremental repetition is characteristic of English folk ballads after about the twelfth century.

Parallelistic triplets do not, of course, require either the Egyptian refrain or the Sotho linking. A simpler example is this Bushman ritual poem:

> You must sing well.
>> We are happy now.
>>> Our hearts are shining.
> I shall put on my rattles,
>> And put on my headband,
>>> And put a feather in my hair,
> To explain to // Gauwa how happy we are that he has helped us
>> And that we have eaten.
>>> My heart is awake.
> When we do not have meat
>> My heart is sad from hunger
>>> Like an old man, sick and slow.
> When we have meat my heart is lively.
>> (Marshall 1962:247)

In the Americas, the couplet form is so deeply rooted that it is used for everything from prayers to swearing. Folk tales, history, and drama may all be composed in couplets. In parts of Africa the same thing appears to be true of triplets. The following example is a Hottentot folk tale of "The Moon and the Hare":

> //xãs kiekie he ti mi
>> kwen keni tir na //'o kamma //'o
>>> ekie !kõas ti mi //'o tsẽ //'o !kũ
> ikie //nati //xãs xa !kõas ≠noa kx'am !nãe

≠noa ≠kx'ari kx'am he
//nati ekie !kõas //nap
sats kenī ho o //nakx'op //garasi
!kaba, ats tsi /hummi aisi ≠nū
ats ≠nūã !kup !na !na

(The moon spoke thus:
"Men must die as I die."
    But the hare said, "They must die and die altogether."
So the moon struck the hare in the mouth.
Its mouth was struck and split.
    So the hare said,
"You must become the shoulderblade of a bushpig.
Ascend and sit in heaven.
    You must sit and light up the world.")
    (Maingard 1962:47)

The poetry of East Africa has been deeply influenced by contacts
with the Near East. It thus employs true verse and rhyme in patterns
clearly linked to the forms of Arabic verse. Such forms are found among
various Ethiopian peoples, in Swahili, and perhaps in Malagasy. Here we
may cite an Ethiopian praise song in which the Chaha (who call themselves
"Mogemene") celebrate their own excellence:

Mogämänä yäsäb mächi.
Yäwyä zëso yäbchäbwächi;
Yägër dëngwä yägwraghäghi.
Yänëbrät shanda wänäghi.
Bäshandä ṭeṭä tirachi,
Arisa täfwäm täbwächi.
Akwänäm därar agwäghi.

Yaris mosa mwan akärä?
Yorq atam mwan wäthärä?
Yägäsh samër mwan gyäbärä?
Gunär yarshi aqäpwärä.
Yäwŭrghä awändäm känä
Yarisa agoghnäm donä.

(The Mogemene are the best part of mankind.
They are fresh honey one has diluted;
They are the sliced red meat of the haunch.
They went down to Shanda to work.

While picking cotton in Shanda
They caught the rhino.
They brought it up and tied it behind the house.

Who has raised the rhino's young?
Who has pulled the knot tight?
Who has given the eighth calf in tribute?
Their women have put on the festive hair style.
It confers the right of boasting
To have put the bell on the rhino.)
(Leslau 1950:122–123)

The poem scans as eight-syllable verse in six- to seven-line stanzas, with every line of each stanza syllabically rhymed. The broken scansion in the ninth line is probably due to textual corruption: the translation is also uncertain at that point. (The *th* in the ninth line is an aspirated *t*.)

Final syllabic rhyme occurs also in Swahili poetry. The *utenzi* or epic form employs it in eight-syllable quatrains with *aaab* syllabic rhyme in a line virtually identical with that of early Turkish epics, as in this stanza from the *Utenzi wa Al Akida* ("Ballad of Al Akida") by Mazrui:

Nilisema haidiri
Sitatoka Zinjibari
Hayoneya khatari
Kuikosa Mombasiya.

(I said to myself
I shall never leave Zanzibar,
And I saw that I was in danger
Of losing Mombasa.)
(Hinawy 1950:82)

The use of the quatrain in Swahili poetry is particularly notable. The quatrain form is basic to literate verse from Iceland to China; it is very rare in the poetry of preliterate peoples. Even in North America, where the sacred number *four* is reflected in poetry in various ways, sequences of fours are rare.

Northern Africa has, of course, been more or less completely Arabicized, although the southern boundary of this influence would be hard to draw on present evidence. West Africa is a problem, as may be seen in the following Ashanti praise poem linking a deceased priestess, Afua Amaa Nyame, to the Creator (Nyame), the "settler" of the primeval waters:

Afua Amaa Nyame,
Agyene Kwaku
Agyengyensua bi.

Agyene Kwaku se
Òreagyene nsuo
Onnim se òrèpuka nsuo,
Tema Agyene Kwaku Amo.

(Afua Amaa Nyame,
Settler [of water] born on Wednesday,
He settled the water.
The settler born on Wednesday,
Settler of Water,
Let us thank him,
The settler of Mud.)
(Meyerowitz, 1951:131)

The syllabic scansion of these lines would appear to be 6-5-5-6-5-8-9, although elision of vowels would reduce it to 5-5-5-6-5-7-7. Whether it should be so read, and whether Ashanti poetry is in fact versified, I am unable to determine.

The Nigerian Efik are reported to versify their riddles in octosyllabic couplets (question-and-answer) with caesura and a high-low tone scansion of the form *lhhl/hhhl*. As in some other tonal forms, it seems rather arbitrary whether we consider this as tonal verse, tonal metrics, or tonal rhyme, although in Efik, as in Chinese poetry, in which it is superimposed upon a regular syllabification (verse), it seems best to call it either meter or rhyme in order to distinguish the mechanisms.

Characteristically, West African poetry appears to be less regular than the Efik riddle form. It is syllabically uneven, and although it uses tone for poetic effects, it does not always pattern it rhythmically. The following example is a Yoruba *arofo* or abstract poem on "Variety," which displays a stanza structure of typical African triads. The translation is described as "free":

Igi gbun n'igbo, a nsò (Ototo enia k'ó gbun larin ilú)?
Osupa le a ni o le re.
Nwon l'eni t'owo re ba to o.

K'o yara mura k'o lo tún u se. (Eyi ti o l'ogbe kô ni 'rèré),
Eyi t'o n'irèré ko l'ogàn l'esè.
Eyi t'o l'ogan l'ese kò le ko bi akuko.

Eni t'o l'ori ô ni fila, eni t'o ni fila ô l'orí,
Eni t'o l'ejika ô l'ewu, éni t'o l'ewu o l'ejiká.
Owa l'ohun pe, ko n'iwô esin.

Eni t'o mo 'fá ko m'ona ofà, (Eni t'o m'ona Ofà, ko mo 'fá).
Iyan è wa 'le marinaje, (Oti ô wa 'le marumanu).
Oro abaso màlàmàlà!

(Why do we grumble because a tree is bent (When in our streets there are
even men who are bent)?
Why must we complain that the new moon is slanting?
Can anyone reach the sky to straighten it?

Can't we see that some cocks have combs on their heads but no plumes in
their tails?
And some have plumes in their tails but no claws on their toes,
And others have claws on their toes but no power to crow?

He who has a head has no cap to wear and he who has a cap has no head
to wear it on.
He who has good shoulders has no gown to wear on them, and he who has
a gown has no good shoulders to wear it on.
The Owa has everything but a horse's stable.

Some great scholars of Ifa cannot tell the way to Ofa. (Others know the
way to Ofa but not one line of Ifa.)
Great eaters have no food to eat, and great drinkers no wine to drink.
Wealth has a coat of many colors!)
(Lasebikan 1956:49–50)

The original text makes separate lines of the segments in parentheses. The
author comments that the tonal effects of the poem, like its subject, are
characterized by variety. If the triadic scansion is correct, it is notable
that the first line of each stanza ends on a high tone, while the last is
middle or low. The tonal scansion would be *hmm/hlm/hhm/hml*; the syllabic
scansion may be 18-9-9/20-11-14/17-17-10/20-9-9. The pattern is suggestive
of a use of tone somewhat analogous to the use of stress in early Germanic
verse.

African poetry must be differentiated into at least three zones. The
North and East are within the orbit of influence of the Semitic tradition of
the Near East. West Africa presents a number of complexities not yet well
described but which may include tonal verse. Southern and Central Africa
appear to compose chants, particularly favoring a triplet form.

RHYME

Exploitation of the sound values of words tends to be somewhat irregular in primitive poetry. The more organized use of word sounds appears, in
fact, to be a gradual and evolutionary development—a process of slow
and cumulative discovery of the nature and potentialities of the sound
systems of particular languages and language families. Languages differ
considerably in their susceptibility to consonantal, vocalic, stress, tone,
juncture, syllabic, or phrase structuring, and even the modes of singing or

writing may have a drastic effect on the patterns of poetry. Of the areas of the world that lack writing, Oceania is the only one in which there is an appreciable elaboration of rhyme and verse, and even within Oceania there is considerable variation.

The Malay verse form called *pantun* is similar to Japanese *haiku* or to some Chinese forms in its elliptical quality and use of contrast and balance. It is somewhat irregular syllabically, but is commonly rhymed. Quite often there is a cryptic connection between the first and second couplets in the quatrain, as in this case:

> Kerengga di dalam buloh
> Serahi berisi ayer mawar:
> Sampai hasrat di dalam tuboh
> Tuan sa orang jadi penawar.

> (Large ants in the bamboo cane,
> A flasket filled with rose water:
> When the passion of love seizes my frame,
> From you alone I can expect the cure.)
>   (Winstedt 1950:158)

The implication is that fire ants are to rose water as passion is to its satisfaction. The *abab* rhyme is typical, as is the irregularity of the 8-10-9-9 syllabic scansion. The *pantun* thus represents the relatively rare phenomenon of a poem that is rhymed but not versified.

True syllabic verse also occurs in Malay and in Balinese, as well as in Ponapean and Trukese, where the commonest line is seven syllables (sometimes five). In Ponapean verse, long vowels (and perhaps doubled consonants) count as two syllables, and the resulting pattern is remarkably similar to Japanese poetry, although it may antedate the modern Japanese influence in the central Pacific. The weighting of long vowels may be considered a simple type of poetic meter. The following poem is a *sapei* or women's seated dance song from Ponape on the *Origin of Kava*:

Luuk koosangi leng,	(Luuk came from heaven
Koola Pesiiko.	And went to Fiji.
A'pwala diaridi	He went and discovered
Kedini Kasaunok,	Kedin Kasaunok,
A e mwarekiieng	And she gave him a love gift
Aa likini pwake.	Of her bracelet,
A e dipungkiida	So he responded with
Kilin peikin nee.	The skin of the back of his heel.
A'pwala pòdokedi;	She then went and planted it;

Ii me wiaada	And that is what started
Sekewen Pesiiko.	The kava of Fiji.
Make mwedengeier,	The rat got to it quickly,
Sakaukilaar.	And became drunk on it.
Aapwala keedi	It then went and nibbled on
Neira seun eir,	Their southern sugarcane,
Kenei sakauki.	And made a relish for the kava.
Sukusuk Eirilap,	Great South pounding,
Ra pa engeengerek.	They suddenly made a commotion.
Likiliked pwuupwu	The kava pounding rhythm
A pa sansareki leng.	Was heard in heaven.
Li Teme Li Tepwira	Li Teme and Li Tepwira
Ira koosangi leng.	Came from heaven.
Koodi, pirapa	Came down, and stole
Karaini mes uwen.	That kava cutting.
Ira samwekidaar	They departed with it
Pòd duwienleng;	And planted it in the Kava Plot of heaven;
Pwuredi pòdokedi	They came back and planted it
Pohn Saladak uwet.	Here in Saladak.
Ii me wiaada	That is what formed
Mwoodeni aramas.	A sitting person.
I' ede Li Saladak;	This is her name, Saladak Woman;
Ii me i rongimet,	This is what I hear,
Eei!	Yes!)

(Fischer 1959:50)

The scansion in this poem is regularly seven syllables except for Lines 13, 23, 28, and 30, which have six syllables, and Line 26, which has five. If we count consonant clusters as a syllable (except the digraph *ng*) we can scan seven syllables in Lines 26 and 28, but strict application of such rules would create eight lines of eight syllables. The apostrophe in this transcription indicates poetic shortening of long vowels.

Final assonance or vowel rhymes of the single- or double-vowel type occurs in Polynesian poetry, as in the Tongan *cante fable* of the lovers *Tongamaulu'au and Kulakehahau*, the terminal verse of which finds their child pleading with her mother to return to her father:

E Tongamaulu'au,
Ke ke ha'u;
Kuo hela 'a Kulakehahau
Pea ne fekau
Keu tangi atu,
Ke ke 'ofa mai na'aku manatu.

(Ah, Tongamaulu'au,
Do thou come;
Aweary is Kulakehahau
And he orders
That I plead
That thou love us lest I pine remembering.)
                                        (Collocott 1928:63)

Here there is double assonance (*a-u*) even though Tongan poetry does not appear to use either syllabification or meter. Appearances may be deceptive, because vowel length is phonemic in the Polynesian languages and is omitted in this recording as in most others. Double-vowel assonance in *a-u* and *a-a* are preferred forms in Fijian poetry also (Quain 1942:15).

The scansion of poetry in particular traditions is almost always complicated by tacit rules of "poetic license." We may recall the English poet's freedom to employ archaisms and abbreviations like *o'er*, *'twas*, *upon 't* or *markèd*. The French poet counts the silent final *e* and similar syllables as sounded for versification purposes (and reads poetry accordingly). The Spanish poet counts the last two syllables of words with antepenultimate accent as a single poetic syllable, so that *pálida* counts as a two-syllable word at the end of a line (this is called *esdrújula*). The Tibetan poet counts a final *i* or a diphthongal *u* as syllables or not, ad libitum, to make his verses scan. The Zuñi poet may drop a final consonant or reduplicate a penultimate vowel to make his strophe end in a vowel. Cambodian poetry counts syllables as assonant if they would be so in Pali, whether or not they are in Cambodian. Arabic poetic license permits omission of a short syllable at the beginning of any line or substitution of one long for two short syllables. The Swahili poet counts each vowel (and vocalic *m*, *n*, or *l*) as a separate syllable. The Balinese poet using the *ginada* form is allowed to use *o* in place of the customary *a* in the third line rhyme, as in this stanza from the ballad of *Jaya Prana*:

> Kukunei pañjang kumrèdap;
> Tayunganei mèmbat miring,
> Tan pêndaḥ padapa layon;
> Alisei tajèp ñalikur;
> Paliyat manis agalak;
> Keñung manis;
> Isitei ngembang rijasa.

> (Her nails were long and pointed too,
> Her step was slow and quivering,
> Supple, like a sapling swaying;

> Brows drawn sharp, far as her temple,
> Her eyes were kind but yet afire;
> Her smile was sweet,
> Her gums as a rijasa flower.)
> (Hooykaas 1958)

The syllabic scansion is 8-8-8-8-8-4-8; the rhyme is supposed to be *a-i-a-u-a-i-a*. The *n* is pronounced *ny* as in Spanish. Another peculiarity of Balinese verse is what might be called elision of nouns. If a noun beginning a line has ended the preceding one, it is simply omitted.

The poetry of Melanesia and Australia stands in sharp contrast to that of the other Pacific peoples. It is also somewhat different in the two areas. Melanesian ritual poetry is in chant form, partly couplets and partly polynomial. Australia, on the other hand, appears to have a marked preference for the couplet form, as in the *Djanggauwul* chant already quoted. There is a suggestion (see p. 226) that Australia may have had true verse, but the sole example of it is equivocal and does not appear to have resulted in any extensive use of the form.

VERSE

Outside of Oceania (and possibly West Africa), the use of rhyme and versification is confined to the areas of the Old World that are now literate. This is not to say, of course, that some of the more elaborate poetic techniques may not have preceded literacy in at least some parts of this area. Possibly the simplest (and conceivably the earliest) form of pure verse is that of the Chinese, which developed early forms of five- and seven-syllable lines (and, later, four-syllable lines and others). This T'ang dynasty quatrain in five-syllable lines points up clearly the susceptibility of Chinese to this treatment:

> Ch'un mien pu chueh hsiao;
> Ch'ü ch'ü wen t'i niao;
> Yeh lai feng yü sheng;
> Hwa luo chih tue shao?

> (Spring sleep is so deep that one fails to realize it is dawn;
> Everywhere one hears crying birds;
> Last night I heard the sounds of wind and rain;
> How many flowers have fallen as a result?)
> (Hsu, Francis L. K., text and trans.)

The old style or *ku shih* poetic tradition in China is marked by the use of vocalic rhyme or assonance: *ywet* ("moon") was considered to rhyme with *sek* ("beauty") because the vowels are identical. The previous poem is assonated *aaba*.

After the sixth century, the new style or *lü shih* developed in China, involving an increasingly specific and precise use of tone in poetry. For this purpose the level or "flat" tone (*p'ing*) was contrasted with the three "deflected" tones (*tsê*), and the vocalic rhyme now had to correspond in tone as well as vowel quality (or if the strophe demanded contrast, it had to be dissonant in tone as well as vowel).

Li Po's "Night Thought" illustrates the scansion of Chinese tonal verse. It is given here in English, Mandarin, and Wu:

> In front of my bed is the moon's light.
> I thought it was frost on the ground.
> Lifting up my head, I gaze at the moon,
> Lowering my head, I think of home.

> Chwang^2 chyan^2 ming^1 yueh^4 guang^1,
> Yi^2 sh dih^4 shanq^4 shuang^1.
> Jeu^3 tour^2 wanq^4 ming^1 yueh^4,
> Di^1 tour^2 sy^1 guh^4 shiang^1.

> Zwang zĩ ming yüe kwang.
> Nyi zy di zang swang.
> Kü dei vang ming yüe,
> Ti dei sy ku xyang.
> (Chao 1956:55; 1957:276–277)

I have simplified somewhat Chao's orthography for Wu and omitted the tones. The Wu reading, however, scans like the Mandarin: *aaba* (the Wu tones being upper even, lower even, lower going, upper even on the final syllables of the four lines of the poem). Although such a notation is actually redundant with his orthography, I have supplied numerical indicators of the Mandarin tones where Chao's indication of them is too complex to be readily scanned. In later Chinese poetry, tones also came to be patterned in pairs within the line, triples being avoided unless separated by a caesura. Contrasting tone patterns in the two lines of a couplet, particularly in the last part of the lines, were another common feature.

A similar poetic use of tone is found elsewhere in the Orient where tone is phonemic, as in Burmese and Thai verse. Long Thai love ballads called *nirat* are written in the tonal *klong* and *kap* meters with rhyme. Shorter love lyrics or "thumbnail love songs" called *klon'pet ton* are written in eight lines of eight syllables, using the *klon* tonal meter and dividing into two stanzas. The earliest surviving example of Thai poetry comes from the thirteenth-century works of Ram Kamhaeng. A popular passage often quoted in Thailand is:

> Muang Suko Thai ni di.
> Nai nam mi pla
> Nai naa mi kao . . .
> Krai chag krai kaa chang, kaa;
> Krai chag krai kaa maa, kaa . . .
> Krai chag mug len, len;
> Krai chag mug hua, hua . . .
>
> (Good is the land of Thai.
> Fish in the sea,
> Rice in the field . . .
> Who wants to trade elephants, trades;
> Who wants to trade horses, trades . . .
> Who wants to play, plays;
> Who wants to laugh, laughs . . .)
>   (Shipley 1946:II:843)

The syllabic scansion is 6-4-4-6-6-5-5, and there may be tone rhymes involved, but the transcription does not record them. Cambodian and Burmese verse also shows a preference for four- and six-syllable schemes.

Burmese poetry is written in a variety of verse forms, principally in four-syllable lines. A number of modes are distinguished, including the English (*kayaathan*), Siamese (*yodaya*), Chinese (*pyigyithan*), divorcées' laments in musical prose (*lôngyin, ngogyin*), love plaints (*sangbasa*), and others (*dobatthun, nabethan, nanthein*). Rhyme is extensively employed, successive lines sometimes being completely assonated, as:

> Ta ko dè pa
> Ma so bè hma
> A ngo thè hla.

An unusual rhyme pattern that may be called retrocessive is among the complex devices in Burmese, Thai, and Cambodian. It is illustrated in the following stanza from a modern Burmese poem, "Whither?" by Min Thu Wun:

> Kar la nauk *naung*
> Law ka *baung* wè
> Lay *saung* tain *thar*:
> Ho thi *yar*: tho
> Lar *thwar*: ma *ti*
> Char char *li* cin
> Sait *kyi* shwin *gyaung*
> *Mye* thu *chaung* yway

Pyaw *pyaung* cho thar
. . . Phaw mya nee.

(Later in this life
When I am wandering
Like a wind driven cloud,
Unsettled,
Then who will look after me
And make me happy
With a soft, sweet voice?)
(Min Thu Wun 1947:19)

The rhyme words are italicized; the translation is very loose. Even more complicated rhyme schemes are sometimes employed.

Such elaborate use of rhyme and tone does not appear in the less literary traditions of southeastern Asia. There appears to be no pattern, for example, to the use of tone in the Kxa^5 Gey^3 ("Open the Road"), a part of the funeral ritual of the Miao, the closing lines of which are:

Gao^2 mho^5 ja^6 $nxën^5$ $nttuw^5$.
$Ngga^2$ $lxuw^9$ $ntsay^2$ $nggxay^2$ $ntsëw^5$ $nchhang^3$;
$Nchhang^3$ $lxuw^9$ $ntsay^2$ $nggxay^2$ $ntsëw^5$ la^2.
Gla^5 $tsë^1$ $nggxay^2$ nao^2 $ngga^5$?
$Nchëw^4$ $gang^6$ $dzuw^5$ $nggxay^2$ nao^2 $ngga^5$.
Gla^5 $tsë^1$ $nggxay^2$ $ntsay^5$ $nchhang^3$?
$Nchëw^4$ $gang^6$ $dzuw^5$ $nggxay^2$ $ntsay^2$ $nchhang^3$.
Gla^5 $tsë^1$ $nttow^5$ gao^2 $ttiy^5$ $nën^6$?
$Nchëw^4$ $gang^6$ $dzuw^5$ $ndzo^9$ gao^5
Tti^5 $nën^6$ tti^5 ti^5 $chang^3$.
$Jong^5$ $nyxang^2$ i^3 ji^5 tuw^1 ji^2 na^5.

(You go among the many living.
Your flesh is rotten gore and blood;
The blood and gore mix with earth.
What comes down to eat your flesh?
Ants come down to eat your flesh.
What comes down to suck your blood?
Ants come down to suck your blood.
What is intimate with your people?
Ants are intimate with your people
And love intimately.
It is all over; it is entirely finished.)
(Graham 1954:71, 73)

Miao reportedly has nine tones: 1 (high), 2 (low), 3 (high-low), 4 (low-high), 5 (mid), 6 (mid-low), 7 (half high), 8 (mid-high) and 9 (half low). The syllabic scansion of this passage should be 5-6-6-5-6-5-6-6-5-5-7. In terms of flat (*a*) and deflected (*b*) tones the pattern of the poem is: / *babaa* / *bbbbab* / *bbbbab* / *abbba* / *bbabba* / *abbab* / *bbabbb* / *ababab* / *bbaba* / *abaab* / *abbabba* /. The question-and-answer form creates a certain pattern of couplets, but there are no true rhymes, and the tendency toward assonance in *a* appears to be fortuitous. Neither in tone nor in vowel rhymes does the Miao text follow the Chinese poetic canon. Whether it has a pattern of its own is uncertain.

Syllabic verse is probable in Tibetan, although I have been unable to find a text illustrating it. The following passage from a longer poem by Tibet's great poet-saint Mila illustrates Tibet's participation in the world of sophisticated verse by the twelfth century. The full poem has a series of triplet verses with a refrain quatrain:

> This slender arrow grasped in my right hand,
> Adorned with four feathers and a vermilion tip,
> If I loose it, will pierce whatever it strikes.

> This which I the mortal need not, I offer, O teacher.
> I pray thee lead this black stag into the place of great bliss,
> This bitch red lightning into the place of enlightenment;
> And Gonpodorje into the place of liberation.
>
> (Clarke 1958:37)

Despite the depth of Indian influence on the literature and religion of Tibet and Southeast Asia, the predominant influence on poetic form is probably Chinese throughout—a consequence perhaps primarily of the common linguistic structure of the region.

Syllabic verse similar to the Chinese forms is also employed in Korean. The earliest collection of Korean poetry, *Saenaennorae*, has unfortunately been lost, but the *Silla Songs* that have survived from the ninth century use five- and six-syllable lines in stanzas of four, eight, or ten lines (the *hyangga* form). Later verse forms in Korean include *kasa* (eight-line stanzas of eight syllables per line), and after the fourteenth century the overwhelmingly popular *sijo*, a verse of 45 syllables or less in three lines of 14 to 16 syllables each, divided by caesura into syllabic groups in the pattern: 3-4-3(4)-4(3)/3-4-3(4)-4(3)/3-5-4-3. This example is a fourteenth-century *sijo* by Chŏng To-chŏn. The scansion is slightly irregular (3-4-4-3/3-3-4-4/3-5-4-3):

> Sŏnin-kyo narin mur-i Chaha tong-e hŭrŭni
> Panch'ŏn nyŏn wangŏp-i mulsorŭi ppun-i roda
> Ahŭiya kogukhŭng mang-ul muri mŭsam hario.

(The water that passes Sonin bridge flows to the Chaha grotto.
For five hundred years royal works were merely the sound of water.
Ah, why in the world inquire after the fortunes of past kingdoms!)
(Ristaino 1964:36)

Korean verse is also traditionally assonated, although I have not found a description of its rhyme patterns.

Japanese verse forms are modeled on the Chinese pattern, but adapting the form to the language has involved modifications, including a versification that is truly metric. The *tanka*, for example, is a verse of five lines of 5-7-5-7-7 syllables; the *haiku* is identical except that it omits the last two lines. The following poem is in the developed *tanka* form called *renga* or "linked verse," because it involved a break at the end of the third line and was sometimes given to someone else to finish at that point. This one was written by the Emperor Gotoba:

Miwataseba	(When I look far out
Yamamoto kasumu.	The mountain slopes are hazy.
Minase gawa—	Minase River—
Yuube wa akito	Why did I think that only in autumn
Nani omoikemu?	The evenings could be lovely?)

(Keene 1955:36)

Eventually the "caesura" in the *renga* form became complete; the last two lines were dropped and the truncated *tanka* became a *haiku*. This, however, resulted in the introduction of a caesura and dynamic balance within the briefer poem as well, so that the typical *haiku* often balances a general condition against a momentary perception, as in Buson's poem:

Nashi no hana—	(Blossoms on the pear—
Tsuki ni fumi yomu	And a woman in the moonlight
Onna ari.	Reads a letter there.)

(Henderson 1958:105)

The caesura may fall at the end of either line. The scansion of this poem and the preceding one is dependent on the fact that both consonantal and vocalic length are phonemic in Japanese, and long sounds count as double syllables for poetic purposes: thus *yuube* and *onna* are read as three syllables each.

The Ural-Altaic, Indo-European, and Afro-Asian languages of western Eurasia and north Africa often do not lend themselves to the simple pattern of syllabic verse that fits so neatly the structure of Chinese and its relatives. It seems likely that parallelism may have been the basic poetic technique throughout this area in very ancient times, and all of its earliest poetry (Sumerian and Semitic) is in parallelistic couplets. As late as the

sixteenth century B.C. the couplet form is still predominant, as in the
Akkado-Babylonian creation poem "When Above":

> When above the heaven was not yet named,
>> And the land beneath bare no name,
> And the primeval Abyss, their begetter,
>> And Chaos, the mother of them both—
> Their waters
>> Were mingled together,
> And no field was formed,
>> No marsh was to be seen;
> When of the gods still none
>> Had been produced,
> No name had yet been named,
>> No destiny yet fixed;
> Then were created the gods
>> In the midst of heaven . . .
>>> (Bouquet 1954:47)

Among the western languages, the Semitic group would seem to be particularly hospitable to syllabic verse, given their general structure of alternating consonants and vowels and their syllabically analytic writing systems. The existence of phonemic vowel length, however, would require
that a strict syllabic verse form solve the problem of metrics, as Japanese
seems to have done independently. When the ancient Semites achieved
metric verse does not appear to be established, but a late Babylonian poem
of the eleventh century B.C. possesses sufficient syllabic regularity to suggest versification. This poem, known as the "Theodicy," is of interest on
several counts. It is an acrostic made up of 27 stanzas of approximately
syllabic verse, each containing 11 lines of around 12 syllables beginning
with the same initial syllable. The 27 initial syllables together spell out
the message, "I, Saggil Kiinam Ubbib the incantation priest, am adorant
of the god and the king." Acrostic poems are later found in such diverse
literatures as Arabic, Tibetan, and Swahili, as well as in European tradition.
The Babylonian instance is the earliest I have found. The poem takes the
form of a dialogue between a despondent pessimist and his optimistic
friend. The gloomy man answers his friend's advice to trust the gods:

Iltanu ṭèenga manit nishimesh ṭaabu.
  Illu nuussuqu milikka damqu.
Ilteen zikra muttaka luttiir.

Illaku úruukh dumqí la mushte'u ìlí,
  Iltapni iteenshu mushtemiqu shá ìlti.

Illigimiiaama tèem ili askhuur;
  Illabaan appi u temiqi eshe'e ishtarti.
Ilku sha la némeli asháat apshánu.
  Iltakan ilu kii mashree katuta.
Ilannu kuussudu panaanni lilli.
  Iltaquú kharkharuu anaku altashpil.

(Your mind is a north wind, a pleasant breeze for the peoples.
  Choice friend, your advice is fine.
Just one word would I put before you.

Those who neglect the god go the way of prosperity,
  While those who pray to the goddess are impoverished and dispossessed.
In my youth I sought the will of my god;
  With prostration and prayer I followed my goddess.
But I was bearing a profitless corvée as a yoke.
My god decreed, instead of wealth, destitution.
The cripple is my superior, a lunatic outstrips me.
The rogue has been promoted, but I have been brought low.)
(Lambert 1960)

Initial syllabic rhyme does not appear to be otherwise represented in Babylonian, and it is rare elsewhere. There appears to be a tendency toward having equal numbers of long and short syllables in each line of this poem, but this may be a linguistic rather than a poetic fact. Note the couplet parallelism, with the third line standing alone at the point of semantic break in the stanza. Late Babylonian lyric poetry is reported to be metered in one-line sentences paired in couplets with caesura and a fixed number of stress accents in each line.

Although the date at which Semitic poetry began to employ metric scansion remains obscure, by about the sixteenth century B.C. the earliest metric Indo-European poetry, the Sanskritic hymns of the *Rig Veda*, were already extant. Indo-European metrics must usually (as in Sanskrit) accommodate consonant and vowel clusters as well as (sometimes) vowel length.

Classical Sanskrit employs quantity meters in a scansion closely similar to that of Greek and Latin, at least in some of its verse forms; in others it is more exacting, requiring both syllabic and metric regularity. Thus the *aaryaa* and related meters (*udgiiti, upagiiti, vaitaaliiya, aaryaagiiti,* and *aupacchandasika*) may vary slightly in the number of syllables per line but scan rigorously in the number of *morae* (long syllables or equivalent, two short syllables equaling one long). Other Sanskrit meters specify a precise number of syllables and morae and may further demand long and short syllables in a particular exceptionless pattern. The *bhu-*

jaṅgavijṛmbhita meter, for example, is made up of lines of 26 syllables and 19 morae in the pattern: – – – – – – – – / ◡ ◡ ◡ ◡ ◡ ◡ ◡ ◡ ◡ – / ◡ – ◡ ◡ – ◡ –. One of the commonest of the Sanskrit meters is the *śloka*, which is slightly less exigent, albeit still more demanding than most Latin and Greek verse. The *śloka* quatrain is made up of eight-syllable lines of two four-syllable feet each. The fourth foot of the quatrain must be diambic. Other feet are relatively free, but certain combinations are precluded. For example, if the second foot is ◡ – – ≍, then the first may not be ≍ ◡ ◡ ≍ and the third may not be ≍ ≍ ◡ ≍, and if the second foot takes any other form, there are other restrictions on the first to avoid monotony (*vipulaa* meters). The following quatrain from the *Bhagavad Giita* illustrates the *śloka* meter:

> Doṣair etaiḥ kulaghnaanaam,
> Varṇasaṃkarakaarakaiḥ,
> Utsaadyante jaatidharmaaḥ,
> Kuladharmaaś ca śaaśvataḥ.

> (By these sins of family-destroyers,
> Which produce caste mixture,
> The caste laws are destroyed,
> And the eternal family laws.)
>   (Edgerton 1952:11)

In Sanskrit scansion, *aa, ii, uu, o, e,* all diphthongs, and vowels followed by more than one consonant (other than *h*) are long. Syllables based upon other vowels (and apparently the vocalic ṛ) are short. Thus the scansion of the above verse is – – – – – ◡ – – – – / – ◡ – ◡ ◡ – ◡ – / – – – – – – – – / ◡ ◡ – – ◡ – ◡ ◡. Note the diambic fourth foot and the pattern of the first and third in relation to the second.

The rise of the Indic vernaculars during the first millennium of the Christian era gave rise to new poetic forms (the *doha* meters), many of which are notably freer than the ancient Sanskritic versification. There was later, especially in western India, a strong influence from Islam, which brought Persian and Arabic meters into Kashmiri, Punjabi, and other western Indic languages. One of the innovations was final syllabic rhyme, illustrated here by the famous "book of verses" quatrain from the twelfth century *Rubaiyat* of Omar Khayyam in Persian:

> Tangii maĩe l'ul kh'aaham u diivaanii.
> Saddi ramakii baayad u nasafi naanii,
> Waangah man u tuu nishasta dar wairaanii
> Khushtar buud az mamlukati Sultaanii.

(A skin of red wine I wish and book of poetry.
A bare subsistence is necessary and a half loaf,
And then that I and thou sitting in the solitude
Were sweeter than the empire of the Sultan.)
(Thompson 1907:19)

Rhyme of this type is, of course, general in modern Europe, but it was lacking in Sanskrit, Latin, and Greek and in ancient Europe generally, as well as in northern Asia, most of Africa, and all of Oceania and America.

The scansion of classical Greek verse depended upon syllabic length. Long vowels, diphthongs, and vowels followed by consonant clusters (except sometimes those ending in *l*, and in the present transcription *h*) were poetically long. Here are the opening lines of Homer's *Iliad*:

Meenin a'eide, the'aa, Peelee'i'adeo Akhilee'os
Oulomenoon, hee muuri Akhai'ois alge 'etheeke
Pollaas d ifthiimous psukhaas A'idi pro'i'apsen
Heeroo'oon, autous de heloori'a teukhe kunessin
Oi'oonoisi te paasi, Di'os d etelei'eto boulee,
Eks ou dee ta proota di'asteeteen erisante
Atre'idees te 'anaks androon kai dii'os Akhilleus.

(Sing, goddess, the wrath of Achilles, Peleus' son,
The ruinous wrath that brought on the Achaians woes innumerable
And hurled down into Hades many strong souls
Of heroes and gave their bodies to be a prey to dogs
And all winged fowls; and so the counsel of Zeus
Wrought out its accomplishment from the day when strife first parted
Atreides king of men and noble Achilles.)
(Lang, Leaf and Myers, n.d.)

The scansion is dactyllic hexameter, with occasional substitution of spondees for dactyls and a spondaic or trochaic final foot: – ⏑ ⏑ – ⏑ ⏑ – – –
⏑ ⏑ – ⏑ ⏑ – ⏑ / – ⏑ ⏑ – – – ⏑ ⏑ – – – ⏑ ⏑ – ⏑ / – – – – – – – ⏑ ⏑
– ⏑ ⏑ – ⏑ / – – – – – ⏑ ⏑ – ⏑ ⏑ – ⏑ ⏑ – ⏑ / – – – ⏑ ⏑ – ⏑ ⏑ – ⏑ ⏑
– ⏑ ⏑ – – / – – – – – ⏑ ⏑ – – – ⏑ ⏑ – ⏑ / – ⏑ ⏑ – ⏑ ⏑ – – – – –
⏑ ⏑ – –. There is a regular caesura in the third foot of each line. The interpretation of Greek diphthongs is complicated by the occurrence of non-diphthongal vowel clusters, indicated in this transcription by apostrophes. Note the syllabic irregularity.

A similar use of poetic conventions is found in Latin, as exemplified by the opening lines of Virgil's *Aeneid*:

Arma virumque canoo, Troojae quii priimus ab ooriis
Iitali'am faatoo profugus Laaviinjaque veenit

Liitora, multum-ille-et terriis jactaatus et altoo
Vii superum saevae memorem Juunoonis ob iiram,
Multa quoque-et belloo passus, dum conderet urbem
Iinferretque de'oos Lati'oo, genus unde Latiinum
Albaaniique patrees atque-altae moeni'a Roomae.

(Of arms and the hero I sing who first from the shores
Of Italy was driven by fate and came to the Lavinian
Coasts; much was he tossed about both on land and sea
By the higher forces of the remembered wrath of angry Juno;
Many things, too, he underwent in war 'til he should found the city
And bring the gods into Latium where there are the Latin tribes
And the Alban fathers and the walls of high Rome.)

(tr. mine)

The Latin canon is like the Greek in contrasting long and short syllables by quantity and in reading long vowels, vowels followed by consonant clusters, and diphthongs as long. In Latin poetry, however, terminal short vowels and short syllables ending in *m* are elided before a vowel, as indicated by hyphenation in Lines 3, 5 and 7. Separately articulated vowels are again set off by apostrophes. This gives a scansion of: $-\;\cup\;\cup\;-\;\cup\;\cup$
$-\;-\;-\;-\;-\;\cup\cup\;-\;-\;/\;-\cup\cup\;-\;-\;-\;\cup\cup\;-\;-\;-\cup\cup\;-\cup\;/\;-\cup\cup\;-\;-\;-\;-$
$-\;-\;-\;\cup\cup\;-\;-\;/\;-\cup\cup\;-\;-\;-\;\cup\cup\;-\;-\;-\;\cup\cup\;-\cup\;/\;-\cup\cup\;-\;-\;-\;-\;-$
$-\;-\cup\cup\;-\cup\;/\;-\;-\;-\cup\cup\;-\cup\cup\;-\cup\cup\;-\cup\cup\;-\cup\;/\;-\;-\;-\cup\cup\;-\;-\;-\;-\;-$
$\cup\cup\;-\;-.$

The temporal and geographic distribution of poetic forms strongly suggests that the elaborate metrics of classical verse from India to Italy (perhaps including the Semitic traditions of the last millennium B.C.) were local adaptations of particular languages to the ideal of syllabic verse, an ideal difficult to attain in the ancient Indo-European languages. This suggestion is rendered more likely by the extensive occurrence of purely syllabic verse forms over a wider area that includes parts of southern Europe as well as central Asia. Metric verse may thus have been an historical alloform of a fundamentally syllabic idea of versification employed by a series of cultures in more or less continuous distribution from Spain to Japan and Polynesia.

The transition to syllabic versification among the Ural-Altaic peoples is reflected in the Ostiak and Vogulic chant tradition, which manifests a marked preference (61 percent) for seven- and eight-syllable lines. The frequency distribution of lines of various length in 2500 lines of Ostiak-Vogulic poetry is as follows (Austerlitz 1958:86):

Syllables	3	4	5	6	7	8	9	10	11	12
Percent	.9	2.6	2.8	14.8	32.6	28.6	13.2	3.4	.9	.2

Central Asian Turkish epics of the eleventh century were also composed in syllabic verse of seven- and eight-syllable lines but employ final rhyme *aaab* in four-line stanzas and maintain the *b* rhyme throughout the poem. The earliest Turkic epic (the Orkhon inscriptions in Uighur from Mongolia) has a similar but somewhat looser structure:

> Tabghach budunqa bäglik ury oghlin qul bolty
> Silik qyz oghlin kün bolty.
> Türk bäglär Türk atin ytty
> Tabghachghy bäglär Tabghach atin tutupan
> Tabghach qaghanqa körmüsh
> Alig jyl äshig küchüg bärmish.
> Ilgärü kün toghsuq da
> Bökli qaghan qa tägi süläjü bärmish.

> (Your manly sons became slaves of the Chinese people,
> Your pure maidens became slaves.
> The Turkish beys abandoned their Turkic titles
> And after receiving Chinese titles, like Chinese beys
> They looked into the eye of the Chinese Khan.
> For fifty years they gave their work and strength,
> Forward towards sunrise they went to Bökli Khan.)
> (Winner 1958:55)

The rhyme here seems to be *aaabccdc*, and the syllabic scansion 14-8-8-12-7-8-7-12. The translation of the last three lines is loose.

A preference for syllabic verse of seven- and eight-syllable lines is also characteristic of traditional and modern Mongolian folk songs. Usually these are initial rhymed in stanzas of three, four, or five lines, as in the following picturesque example:

> Ulaang Baatar xotondaa
> Olong surguul'iing bagatshuud
> Ulaang odoniig toirodzh
> Uidxar jugaang sergeejää.
> Sergeejää.

> (In Ulan Bator schools
> What all we children want today
> Is to gather round the Red Star
> And pass the time away.
> Time away.)
> (Poppe 1955:46–47)

The poetic pattern here is identical with that of humorous and other non-political verse from modern Mongolia and may therefore be presumed characteristic. The Buryat Mongol *uliger* involves similar initial rhyming or alliteration.

Syllabic verse is also the form used in the Finnish *Kalevala*, which is composed in couplets of eight-syllable lines, decorated here and thereby rhyme within the line:

> Tuo oli kaunis Pohjan neiti
> Maan kuulu, ve'en valio
> Istui ilman wempelellä,
> Taivon kaarella kajotti
> Pukehissa, puhtaissa,
> Walkeissa vaattehissa;
> Kultakangasta kutovi,
> Hopeista huolittavi
> Kultaisesta sukkulasta
> Pirralla hopeisella.

> (Lovely was the maid of Pohja
> Famed on land, on water peerless,
> On the arch of air high-seated,
> Brightly shining on the rainbow,
> Clad in robes of dazzling luster,
> Clad in raiment white and shining.
> There she wove a golden fabric,
> Interwoven all with silver,
> And her shuttle was all golden
> And her comb was all of silver.)
> (Kirby 1907:xiv, 71)

Although length of vowels and consonants is phonemic in Finnish, no specific poetic use is made of them, nor are they counted differently in verse. The syllabification (but not necessarily the meter) of the translation is representative of that in the original. Its resemblance to Longfellow's *Hiawatha* is not accidental: Longfellow consciously imitated the Finnish epic.

The pattern of what may be called aboriginal European poetry appears to have been based on stress rhythms rather than on syllabic regularity, although syllabic verse was introduced into southern Europe no later than the tenth century and was eventually incorporated into all the European poetic traditions. Stress meters are well known in early Germanic poetry; they were probably fundamental to Celtic and Slavic verse as well. In the following passage from the Russian *Epic of Vseslav* describing the miraculous birth of Volkh Vseslavich, the eleventh-century werewolf prince, the versification is irregular, scanning syllabically 10-11-11-13-11-7-10-10-9-12-12. The stress accent pattern, however, is regular enough to border on meter. The accents marked are phrase accents rather than those of individual words:

> Pó sadu, sádu po zeléznomu,
> Khodíla-guliála molodá kniazhná,
> Molodá kniazhna Márfa Vsesláv'ievna.
> Ona s kámeniu skochíla na liutá zmeia,
> Na liútogo na zméia na Gorýnicha:
> Liútoi zméi obviváetsia
> Ókolo chébota—zelén saf'ián,
> Okolo chulóchika shélkova,
> Khóbotom b'ét po belú stegnu.
> A vtápory kniagínia ponós poneslá,
> A ponós poneslá i ditiá rodilá.

> (Through the garden, garden green,
> Walked-meandered the young princess,
> The young princess, Marfa Vseslavevna;
> She leaped off a stone on a serpent fierce,
> On the fierce serpent Gorynich.
> The fierce serpent now winds himself
> Round the boot—Morocco green,
> Round the stocking made of silk;
> With his tail he strikes her white thigh;
> Thereupon the princess conceived.
> She conceived and bore a child.)
> (Jakobson and Szeftel 1949:21, 81)

Ancient Welsh poetry was commonly written in a triplet called *englyn*, with final syllabic rhyme. An interesting embellishment often added to the form was the catchword (*gair cyrch*), which followed the rhyme at the end of the first line. An example from a ninth-century manuscript goes:

> Gur dicones remedaut—elbid
> Anguorit anguoraut
> Nigaru gnim molim trintaut.

> (He who made the wonder of the world—
> He who saved us—will save us:
> No hard work to praise the Trinity.)
> (Ker 1958:213)

Often the catchword is made to rhyme with an internal syllable in the second line (-*id* and -*it*). Old Irish poetry appears to have preferred quatrains, but commonly employed final syllabic rhyme at least in the court verse. The older Celtic form was probably a syllabically irregular line with internal alliteration, as in Germanic verse.

A peculiar feature of Irish poetry that also suggests this conclusion is the final-initial chain rhyme called *conaclon*. It is illustrated in the following translation of Amergin's "Incantation," in which the sage stills the winds for the Scottish (Milesian) invasion of Ireland:

> Erin shall longer,
> Stronger, show honor
> On our Milesians.
> Wishing in trouble
> Noble isle's wooing,
> Suing, we stay her;
> Pray her to sail in,
> Wailing maids royal!
> Loyal chief leaders,
> Pleaders, blend prayer in.
> So we seek Erin.
> (Hawthorne 1903:5:307)

Rhyming effects are combined with stress pattern in the alliterated meters of early Germanic poetry. Consonantal (alliterated) and vocalic (assonant) rhyme are both common poetic devices, but in *Beowulf* and the poetic *Edda* the former is brought under stringent rules. Thus the *fornyrthislag* or "old verse" of Icelandic poetry is made up of stanzas of four lines, each divided by sharp caesura into balanced halves, and each half being composed of two accented and two (or three) unaccented syllables. Thus there were four accented syllables to each line, and the rhyme consisted in the consonantal alliteration of three (or sometimes two) of them. The *malahattr* or "speech verse" was identical except that it added an extra unstressed syllable to each half line. The following example is in "old verse" from the younger or poetic *Edda*. Stress is indicated by italics:

> V*rei*thr vas V*i*ngthorr, es v*a*knathi
> Ok s*í*ns h*a*mars of s*a*knathi;
> Sk*e*gg nam hr*i*sta, sk*ŏ*r nam d*ý*ja,
> R*é*th J*a*rthar burr *u*mb at thr*ei*fosk.

> (Wild was Vingthor when he awoke
> And when his mighty hammer he missed;
> He shook his beard, his hair was bristling,
> To groping set the son of Jorth.)
> (Bellows 1936:xxv, xxvii)

The verse follows the preferred pattern perfectly. The alliteration is triple in Lines 1 and 4 (the *th* in the latter line, although *r* is also alliterated) and double in Lines 2 and 3. Later Norse poetry developed a syllabically regular "court meter" (*dróttkvaett*) of 12-syllable lines with caesura at the sixth line and with alliterative rhyme on three stressed syllables. The form also required a final trochee in each half line. Full syllabic and even di- and trisyllabic rhymes were added in the *Kürenberger* meter of the *Nibelungenlied*, the first stanza of which runs:

> Uns íst in álten máerèn wúnders víl giséit
> Von hélden lóbebáerèn, von grózer árebéit,
> Von fröúden, hochgezíten, von wéinen únd von klágen
> Von küéner récken stríten muget ír nu wúnder hóeren ságen.

> (Wondrous things are told in ancient tales
> Of famous men and bold, of great travails,
> Of joy and festive life, of woe and tears,
> Of warriors met in strife—the wonder shall fill your ears!)
> (Ryder 1962: vii, 43)

Here the pattern is again a quatrain. In the first three lines, there are four stressed syllables before and three after the caesura; in the fourth line there is a fourth stressed syllable at the end. The rhyme is *abab* and is normally terminal: the caesural rhyme of this particular stanza is rare.

Early Spanish poetry was commonly composed in syllabic verse and vocalic rather than syllabic rhyme. The final consonant might be different, but the vowel was the same. Sometimes this vocalic rhyme, or assonance, was double. In the following example alternating *i-o* double assonance is maintained (*abcbdb*), although true syllabic rhyme is (accidentally?) achieved in Lines 4 and 6:

> Nunca fuera caballero
> De damas tan bien servido,
> Como fuera Lanzarote
> Cuando de Bretaña vino,
> Que dueñas curaban dél,
> Doncellas de su recino.

> (Never was knight
> Of ladies so well served
> As Launcelot
> When he from Britain came;
> Ladies took care of him—
> Damsels of his horse.)
> (Perry n.d.: 27)

The scansion is octosyllabic and regular.

Serbian epic poetry is decasyllabic and is similar to the *lahuta* form in Albanian and to a common epic form in Mordvinian and elsewhere. The following example is taken from *The Daughter of Ljubović Beg*:

> U struku je tanka i visoka,
> U obrazu b'jela i rumena,
> Kao da je do podne uzrasla
> Prema tihom suncu proljetnome;
> Oči su joj dva draga kamena,
> A obrve morske pijavice,
> Trepavice krila lastavice
> Rusa kosa kita ibrišima;
> Usta su joj kutija šećera,
> B'jeli zubi dva niza bisera;
> Ruke su joj drila ladubova,
> B'jeli dojke dva siva goluba;
> Kad govori, kanda golub guče,
> Kad se smije, kanda sunce grije;—
>
> (She is slim and tall in stature,
> White and rosy in face,
> As if she had grown in the morning
> Facing the soft spring sun;
> Her eyes are like two precious stones,
> And the eyebrows like sea leeches,
> The eyelashes are like the wings of a swallow,
> And the reddish hair is like a silk tassel;
> Her mouth is like a candy box,
> The white teeth as two rows of pearls;
> Her hands are like the wings of a swan,
> The white breasts like two grey doves;
> When she speaks it is as if the pigeon coos,
> When she laughs, as if the sun shines;—)
> (Skendi 1954:162–163)

The scansion is completely regular, but depends upon a vocalic *r* in Line 6. The *j* is pronounced like *y* and *c* like *ts* in English.

Some modern European poetry has remained strongly syllabic. In Portuguese, Spanish, Italian, and Czech verse, for example, the strong stress accent is subordinated to the syllable count in poetic scansion. The lack of phonemic stress in modern French makes syllabic pattern the fundamental element in French poetry. The following example is a Louisiana Negro folk song in the local dialect of Haitian Creole. Although it is rhymed as well (*aabbccdede*), it is composed in eight-syllable lines. The reference is to the Battle of New Orleans:

> Fiziz ãgle ye fe bĩ! bĩ!
> Karabĩ kèntòk ye fe zĩ! zĩ!
> Mo di mo, "Sove to la po."
> Mo zete kor o bor do l o.
> Kã mo rive li te fe klèr.
> Madam li prã ã kou d kolèr.
> Li fe don' mo ã kat wiki
> Paska mo pa sive miche.
> Me mo, mo vo mye kat wiki
> Pase ã kou d fizi ãgle.

> (English rifles go bang! bang!
> Kaintuck carbines go zing! zing!
> I say to myself, "Save your skin."
> I throw myself down on the riverbank.
> When I got back it was already light.
> Missy, she had a fit.
> She had me given a whipping
> Because I didn't follow Massa.
> But me, I'd rather have a whipping
> Than catch a hit from an English rifle.)
> (Traditional; translation mine.)

Unlike French, most modern European languages combine syllabic with stress patterning in their verse. The combination is very effective, for example, in Italian *terza rima*, a hendecasyllabic iambic stress meter ($- \prime - \prime - \prime - \prime - \prime -$), as in this verse from the *Divine Comedy*:

> E canterò di quel secondo regno
> Dove l'umano spiritu si purga
> E di salire al ciel diventa degno.

> (And I shall sing about that second kingdom
> Wherein the human spirit gets its purging
> And to depart for heaven is made worthy.)
> (translation mine)

Stress meter established (or re-established) its hold over Greek poetry as early as the fourth century A.D., and asserted itself in medieval Latin shortly afterward. Its modern incorporation into syllabic verse is beautifully exemplified in the perfection of Pushkin's quatrains, like this one from "Winter Road":

> Ni orá, ni chiórnoi kháty . . .
> Gluch' i snieg . . . Navstriéchu mnie
> Tól'ko viórsty polosáty
> Popadáiutsia odnié.

> (Not a fire, no blackened peat hut
> Through this wild and snowy zone.
> Only mileposts stand and greet, but
> Drop behind, each one alone.)
> (translation mine)

The syllabic scansion is 8-7-8-7; the stress scansion is perfectly trochaic; the rhyme is *abab*. (The apostrophe in Russian transliteration indicates palatalization.)

Arabic verse also combines syllabification with stress meter, although the scansion depends importantly upon elision of adjoining vowels. The following example is a Moorish (Maghrebi Arabic) poem by Argote de Molino called "Granada":

> Al Hambra hanina, walko sor tafki,
> Alamoyarali-ia Mulei-Abu-Abdali.
> Ati nii farasi-ii-adarga ti-al bayda,
> Vish nansi nikatar ana hod 'l Hambra.
> Ati nii farasi-ii-adarga ti didi,
> Vish nansi nikatar ana hod 'l idi.
> 'l idi f' Wadish, vamarati f' Jul-'l Fata.
> Ha hata di novi-ia seti-o Malfata.
> 'l idi fi Wadish, ana fi Jul-'l Fata.
> Ha hata di novi-ia seti-o Malfata.

> (Oh, aching Alhambra, weeping, your castles,
> Oh, Moulay Abdullah, see themselves fallen.
> So bring me my horse and spear, yes, the white one,
> For I must go on and fight for Alhambra.
> So bring me my horse and spear, yes, the blue one,
> For I must go on and rescue my children.
> My sons are in Guadix, wife in Gibraltar.
> Oh, Lady Malfata—you've made me wander.
> My sons are in Guadix, wife in Gibraltar.
> Oh, Lady Malfata—you've made me wander.)
> (my translation from Spanish)

The vowel complexes connected by hyphenization are elided in each case into single syllables. This is called *synalepha*. The scansion is regularly hendecasyllabic with weak caesura after the sixth syllable and double final assonance in the pattern *aabbaabbbb*. The general scheme is close to that of the Spanish *décima*. The stress scansion is $- ' - - ' - / ' - - ' -$, and is reproduced in the translation.

POETRY

To the degree that poetry involves musicality, it confronts a technical and not a literary problem. The makeup of particular languages may facilitate or impede particular forms of musicality, and we have seen that there are many different solutions to the problem of how speech can be rendered regular, rhythmic, and euphonious. In a sense, however, these patterns lie outside of the main concern of this book, for the discovery of techniques of sound manipulation that fit particular languages is a scientific and not a literary enterprise. It is, in fact, properly the concern of linguistics, and is closely linked to it. This is particularly obvious, for example, in the close relationship between the poetics and the linguistics of ancient India, but it is also more generally true. We have seen that the achievement of strict versification is a mark of linguistic virtuosity of sufficient technical difficulty that, like alphabetic writing, it may have been invented only once. There would seem to be no inherent reason, however, that it could not be independently achieved, because the environmental elements required, the sounds of language, are everywhere available.

Even primitive poetry is in no sense confined to the search for musicality. It is also a matter of the manipulation of meaning. And it is the semantics of poetry that link it to the broader literary process. The metaphors of poetry do not appear to differ from the metaphors of speech itself. They are, however, more elaborately organized. To build metaphors into a song inevitably involves a measure of redundancy, and it is this quality that gives to poetry its sense of emphasis and urgency. Quite apart from considerations of sound, an idea becomes poetic only when it becomes insistent. The poetic form is a kind of cultural italics, exacting of us more than ordinary attention.

Poetry requires poets. Precisely because of the technical requirements of formulating resonant ideas euphoniously in a given canon, the creation of a song is characteristically an act of individual expression. The apparent exceptions to this rule, such as parody, or the elaboration of an already extant song through adding verses or producing variants, seem to me only to confirm it. Even folk songs are not composed by committees. Even choruses do not spring spontaneously from the throat of the group. The impulse to poetry, then, is the impulse of the poet, a need to communicate more urgently than prose permits.

The poet, even the "folk poet," is a prophet, precisely because the urge to create imagery does not arise when what we have to say can be readily encoded in less redundant language. Poetry grapples with the hard problems of capturing nuance, of sharing meanings not readily shared. It manipulates second- and third-order overtones of meaning not reducible to explicit statement, and it does so because the communication of these overtones is important. This urgency is felt first by the poet, but if he is successful, the aptness of his imagery and its intelligibility in its tradition will transmit the feeling to his audience. Once created, the song may gradually or quickly become communal, but it does not begin so.

Because of its personalization, poetry does not necessarily represent the most important communal values of a culture. Indeed, its range is extraordinary and certainly covers the triviality of jingles as well as the sacredness of hymns. Cultural importance will find expression in song when it becomes a matter of urgency to individuals. Communally shared ideas may be weightily expressed in other ways—for example, in the more explicitly social and ritual form of drama or in the action-oriented matter of narrative. These forms have their own relation to the cultural redundancies that order metaphor. But the ordering principle of poetry is the redundant experience of an individual, communicating with intensity in the language his culture gives him the mysteries that only rhythmic metaphors can communicate.

Chapter 5

Story

Persons, things, time, and space coalesce in human experience in action and events, and we, as a species, have an enormous curiosity about them. The basic interrogatives of all languages reflect this passion for the "who-ness," "what-ness," "when-ness," and "where-ness" of things. Specific traditions may crave other details (means, motives, certainty, sentiments, status, agency, frequency) but the simplest narratives satisfy our curiosity in the simplest ways. They tell us what happened, and where and when. Most of the narration of all the ages has taken place on this simple and anecdotal plane. It is still the fragmented form in which suburban wives hear the chronicles of the "office" and the prophecies of "friends who know" and the actualities of gossip. But although narrative discourse is both necessary and satisfying, it is only when our interest in the event causes us to detach it from the matrix of conversation that it becomes a story.

The simplest and most ephemeral of the forms that stories take is anecdotal. But primitive anecdotes are not to be confused with the sophisticated and humorous brief stories now codified under that name. They are usually less structured and less demanding; they may have very little "point." By modern tastes they are usually dull. Anecdotes of this general type are the prime source of most of the rest of narrative lore, and they continually replenish it. They preserve much of the naïveté and confusion of real experience, little touched by the clarifying distortions of theory, style, and interpretation.

The following transcribed conversation exemplifies the informal pattern of such communications in our own culture:

"Who did you tell first?"
"I told my mother."
"Did you tell her alone, or were other people present?"

"No. She was alone. I told her, I says, 'I got to talk to you.' And between she and I—You see, whenever I went up there I took a pack of this literature that we had here at the hospital. I took that up there with me. I had the feeling that if they didn't believe me, then I'd show it to them in black and white—"

"You took the literature when you went up there to tell her?"

"That's right."

"Do you remember what you said to her?"

"Well, I told her, I said, 'Mother, I've got to talk to you. This is something that concerns you, and I'm sure that you'd be interested in it.' She wanted to know what it was, and I says, 'Well, sit tight and just wait until I finish before you have anything to say.' So she set down on the couch and I started talking to her. I told her that, uh, first thing I did I apologized for fibbing to her because that's something I wouldn't like to do, you know, to fib to her. But in my case I felt like I needed to and, uh, so she forgive me for that. So I explained it all to her. I told her, I said, 'Now I have some literature here that I would like for you to read and find out a little more about it.' So it would wipe out any ideas that she might have. So she accepted this, and since then, well, I mean, I'm sure she's told people up there that I'm in the hospital here. And I've told practically all my friends. In fact, I think this is the way I think that we should educate the public. For them to see firsthanded cases of it."

The context of this narrative is an interview: a man is explaining to an anthropologist how he broke the news to his mother that he had leprosy. But despite the relatively dramatic content of his account and the likelihood that he has not told the story before, he casts it in a characteristic form, warming to his subject with direct discourse ("I told her, I said"), making extensive use of elliptical references contingent upon the interviewer's familiarity with the subject matter, occasionally recasting the story to straighten our narrative sequence. A conversation between two close friends might be even more elliptical, but even in such a context we could identify narrative form and techniques. The interpolation of "flashbacks" out of chronological order is characteristic of the unstandardized story.

In the following example, Igjugarjuk, an Eskimo shaman, recounts to another anthropologist his recollection of his novitiate. The account is somewhat more formal and organized, in part perhaps because it is a story that has been told before:

When I was to be a shaman, I chose suffering through the two things that are most dangerous to us humans, suffering through hunger and suffering through cold . . . . My instructor was my wife's father, Perqanaq. When I was to be exhibited to the gods Pinga and Hila, he dragged me on a little sledge that was no bigger than I just could sit on. He dragged me far over on the other side of Hikoligjuaq . . . . It was in wintertime and took place at night with the new moon. One could just see the very first streak of the moon; it had just appeared in the sky. I was not fetched again until the next moon was of the same size. Perqanaq built a small snow hut no bigger than I could just get into and sit down. I was given no sleeping skin to protect me against the cold, only a little piece of caribou skin to sit upon. There I was shut in. The entrance was closed with a block, but no soft snow was thrown over the hut to make it warm. When I sat there five days, Perqanaq came with water, tepid, wrapped in caribou skin, a watertight caribou-skin bag. Not until fifteen days afterwards did he come again and hand me the same, just giving himself time to hand it to me, and then he was gone again, for even the old shaman must not interrupt my solitude . . . . As soon as I had become alone, Perqanaq enjoined me to think of only one thing all the time I was to be there, to want only one single thing, and that was to draw Pinga's attention to the fact that there I sat and wished to be a shaman. Pinga should own me. My novitiate took place in the coldest winter, and I, who never got anything to warm me and must not move, was very cold, and it was so tiring having to sit without daring to lie down, that sometimes it was as if I died a little. Only towards the end of the thirty days did a helping spirit come to me, a lovely and beautiful helping spirit whom I had never thought of. It was a white woman. She came to me while I had collapsed, exhausted, and was sleeping. But still I saw her lifelike, hovering over me, and from that day I could not close my eyes or dream without seeing her. There is this remarkable thing about my helping spirit, that I have never seen her while awake, but only in dreams. She came to me from Pinga and was a sign that Pinga had noticed me and would give me powers that would make me a shaman (Astrov 1946:297–298).

As in the preceding example, the episode is closed with a suitable summation.

Even brief anecdotes have characteristic features and a measure of elaboration. "One time when I was little I . . ." is a classic beginning for an English anecdote, which might well end, ". . . and I never did find out." Formal Hausa tales begin with, "A story, a story," to which the listeners reply, "Let it go, let it come." Then at the end is the stock phrase, "Off with the rat's head," and the tale is over. Comparable patterns occur in all languages. The canons of narration are usually quite specific. Different kinds of tales are reserved for particular contexts and related in character-istic styles. "Did you hear the one about ...?" "Once upon a time ...." "In the name of Allah, the Compassionate, the Merciful ...." "Where-as ...." "A certain man ...." A Polynesian narrator may indicate the passage of time by a long drawn out "e-e-e-e"; he identifies direct discourse by raising the pitch of his voice. The variation is one of content as well as of form and technique, but regardless of content we can say that an anec-dote that has become standardized and traditional has become a tale.

Almost everyone dominates at least some of the narrative styles of his culture, but an important feature of folktales is that some people tell them better than others. Much of the traditional character of narrative lore results from the designation of special times for recounting it and gifted individuals as narrators. A Papago woman recalls her childhood:

> On winter nights, when we had finished our gruel or rabbit stew and lay back on our mats, my brothers would say to my father, "My father, tell us something." My father would lie quietly upon his mat with my mother beside him and the baby between them. At last he would start slowly to tell us about how the world began. This is a story that can be told only in winter when there are no snakes about, for if the snakes heard they would crawl in and bite you. But in winter when snakes are asleep, we tell these things. Our story about the world is full of songs, and when the neighbors heard my father singing they would open our door and step in over the high threshold. Family by family they came, and we made a big fire and kept the door shut against the cold night. When my father finished a sentence we would all say the last word after him. If anyone went to sleep he would stop. He would not speak any more. But we did not go to sleep ... (Underhill 1936:22).

In other cultures, too, the traditional tales pass into the keeping of story-tellers. Russian *skazki* are told by *skaziteli*. The preservation of Irish lore is largely due to the tenacity of the *seancaidë* ("shanachie"), who remem-bered and preserved it despite the general decline of Celtic tradition.

ANIMAL TALES

Formalization and standardization of tales often centers on the device of animal characters, a technique most familiar to us in the fables of Aesop, Krylov, La Fontaine, Thurber, "Uncle Remus," or the *Pañca Tantra*. But not all animal tales are fables. Some are tales of horror, origins, or humor. Some are anthropomorphic nature tales. In each tradition, how-ever, there is a marked tendency for the character of each animal to be-come fixed and hence for the situations in which they find themselves to become stock. Inevitably, the story begins to focus on a didactic "moral." In general, the animal protagonists of these stories are not moral beings. They do not confront moral choice. Entrapped in their several natures, they behave as they inevitably must, and somewhat mechanically they suffer the consequences. The lesson of the more primitive of these animal stories is often more realistic than moralistic; their teaching is sophistication rather than virtue. As Gummere (1959:340) has remarked of the English ballads, "they echo without comment the clash of man and fate." An example from the Murngin of northern Australia runs:

> Red-breasted Parrot and Whistle Duck, in Wongar times, decided to change their feathers. Duck said,
> "Younger brother, you give me those feathers that belong to you, because I am going to live in the ponds and water places, and you are going to live on dry land and in the trees."
> Parrot said, "All right, older brother."
> Parrot got the nice feathers that he has today, and Duck has only the brown ones which aren't very fine in their appearance. Duck was happy, however, and went off singing and swam in the water. Parrot went up into the trees and built a nest.
> Duck gave up his pretty feathers because he liked fresh water and swimming, which seems a little bit silly (adapted from Warner 1958:532–533).

Although overlaid with the virtue of patience in affliction, Aesop's story of the fox and the hedgehog preserves something of the same air:

> A Fox swimming across a rapid river was carried by the force of the current into a very deep ravine, where he lay for a long time very much bruised and sick, and unable to move. A swarm of hungry blood-sucking flies settled upon him. A Hedgehog passing by compassionated his sufferings, and inquired if he should drive away the flies that were tormenting him.
> "By no means," replied the Fox, "Pray do not molest them."
> "How is this?" said the Hedgehog, "Do you not want to be rid of them?"
> "No," returned the Fox, "for these flies which you see are full of blood and sting me but little, and if you rid me of these which are already satiated, others more hungry will come in their place, and will drink up all the blood I have left" (Townsend n.d.: 90).

No "morals" are stated in these tales, although they are strongly implied. It takes very little further development to establish a moral, usually in proverbial form, as an intrinsic part of the story, as in this example from the African Mbundu:

> "Squirrel," the people said, "directly we will give him the king-ship."
> He said, "It shall be today."
> The people said, "We are looking for the insignia of the kingship."
> Squirrel said, "I, it shall be today, at once."
> The people said, "We only told him, 'we are going to get the in-signia'; and he says 'it shall be today.' Why we won't give it to him then. If we gave it to him, he could not govern the people."
> Squirrel, they talked of giving him the kingship. He said, "It must be today." It remained among the people: "Today, at once" de-prived Squirrel of the kingship.
> I have told the little story. Finished.

A Chinese fable may serve as an example of the form at its most sophisticated and without reference to animal characters. It is cognate with the Biblical parables and "edifying stories" from Hindu and Buddhist tradition:

> Southern ocean's emperor is Immediately, northern ocean's is Suddenly, and the center's is Undifferentiation. Whenever the first two met in the domain of the last, he treated them very well. So, wishing to repay his kindness, they reasoned thus:
> "Everybody has seven orifices for seeing, hearing, eating, and breathing. Undifferentiation alone is without them, so let's try to bore them for him."
> Then they bored one orifice per day, and on the seventh day, Undifferentiation died (Ware 1963:58).

TRICKSTER CYCLES

The interest generated by certain types of characters often results in their becoming protagonists for many varied tales. The characters main-tain their identity and characterological consistency from tale to tale in a fashion in which the animals of fable do not. The result is a tale cycle. Such a character is the Fox of the South American Toba, a trickster too clever for his own good, whose every adventure ends in disaster and destruc-tion. Each Fox story must thus begin with his resurrection:

> A little rain fell. Fox returned to life and said,
> "I had better get to work instead of sleeping here."
> He set out. He arrived at another village deserted by its inhabi-tants. Nobody was there, and he found only an old sandal which had been left behind. He asked,

"Where did the people of this village go?"

The sandal answered, "I don't know."

"Why not?" asked Fox.

"How can I know, since I have been discarded and thrown away?"

"Listen," ordered Fox, "tell me the truth or I'll toss you into the air."

"You may throw me into the air, but I don't know anything."

"Speak or you'll see!" Fox took the sandal and tossed it into the air. The sandal fell and hit him on the head. Fox died (Métraux 1946:121).

Fox has relatives all over the world. Among the North American Indians it is often Coyote who gets into this kind of trouble. In France it is Renard; among Southern Negroes it is Brer Rabbit; in Central and South America it is often the hero Twins, and in Polynesia the culture hero Maui. Tricksters are reported from Australia as well.

The West African trickster is commonly identified with Spider, and is called Anansi in Ashanti and related languages. Imported to America, she becomes the heroine of 'Nansi stories, which have been collected from all over the Caribbean area. Here is an Anansi story from the Anyi of the Ivory Coast:

One day Spider went to visit God in heaven, and He offered her such a fine meal that He went to sleep afterwards. Spider, misbehaving as usual, took advantage of this to kill God's mother, and bringing the body down from heaven, took it and hid it in the forest after a hasty embalming. But God was beside Himself, and had it proclaimed throughout heaven and earth that he would give numberless treasures to whoever could recover his mother, or at least return her body to him! Spider told one of her friends where the body was and told him, "Go dig it up!"

When this was done, the friend was going to take the body to God, but Spider said, "Leave it alone! It was I who killed the old lady!"

So she took over the body, surrounded it with silken threads and thus hoisted it up to heaven, where she presented it to God. God was very happy, and counted out priceless treasures for Spider. Then, stopping to think, He finally said, "But who killed my mother?"

"Why, I did," said Spider. "I killed her but I am returning her to you."

Then God turned red with anger and threw himself on Spider. But she made a leap towards the earth, and falling at last into her web and knitting with her feet, she got away. God was never able to catch her (Tauxier 1932:232).

A partial list of tricksters like Fox and Anansi is given in Table 1.

The distinguishing features of tricksters in folk literature are characterological. Not all of them are animals, but all of them figure in cycles of tales in which they habitually engage in some sort of battle of wits and are "out-foxed." They tangle with tar babies or get left holding the bag, or are tricked into juggling their eyes and then dropping them. Sometimes they fall into their own traps. They are not bad types, and we feel no glow of moral satisfaction at their fall, for we know they will rise to fight again. As characters they are simple and schematic, and it is the contest nature of their relations with the world that makes them appealing. Fox always loses, but there will always be a Fox.

TABLE 1 Tricksters

TRICKSTER	TRADITION
Anansi (Spider)	Ashanti
Bamapama	Murngin
Bluejay	Salish
Cinanev (Wolf)	Ute
Coyote	Southwestern North America, Plains
Dyayku	Nganasan
Fox	Toba
Jackal	Hottentot
Kulu (Turtle)	Fang
Kurkyl	Chukchi
Legba	Dahomey
Loki	Germanic
Maui	Polynesian
Mink	Kwakiutl
Mouse Deer	Java
Nanabozho	Ojibwa
Nihansan	Arapaho
Rabbit	U.S. Negro
Raven	Tsimshian, Tlingit
Reynard	Flemish
Sendeh	Kiowa
Sitconski (Inktonmi)	Assiniboine
Ti Malice	Haitian
Unktomi	Santee
Wadjunkaga	Winnebago
Wisakedjak	Salteaux
Yo	Dahomey

The development of narrative cycles dealing with related but not necessarily sequential events is one of the simplest and most flexible ways in which folk literature expands. Another, more mechanical procedure is the codification of tales in series in which each story leads into the next.

No doubt this, too, began as a flexible arrangement, in which the connection could be very loose, but eventually it was standardized in the device of the *framing story*, or story within a story. In the Sanskrit *Five Books* the tales are neatly bound together by multiple use of framing. Strongly reminiscent of Aesop, the tales are introduced by a "moral" in verse, a quatrain citing a proverb that relates to the tale and leads into it. This alternation of prose and poetry is a frequent device of storytelling known from Uganda to the Arizona desert. A tale of this type is called a *cante fable*. Here is the beginning of the story of the plover who fought the ocean:

"My dear fellow," said Victor the Jackal, "this is not a good plan because

> He loses fights who fights before
> His foeman's power is reckoned;
> The ocean and the plover fought,
> And ocean came out second."

"How was that?" asked Lively the Bull. And Victor told the story of

The Plover Who Fought the Ocean

A plover and his wife lived by the shore of the sea, the mighty sea that swarms with fish, crocodiles, turtles, sharks, porpoises, pearl oysters, shellfish and other teeming life. The plover was called Sprawl, and his wife's name was Constance.

In due time she became pregnant and was ready to lay her eggs. So she said to her husband, "Please find a spot where I may lay my eggs."

"Why," said he, "this home of ours, inherited from our ancestors, promises progress. Lay your eggs here."

"Oh," said she, "don't mention this dreadful place. Here is the Ocean near at hand. His tide might some day make a long reach and lick away my babies...."

"My dear," said the plover, "feel no anxiety. Who can bring humiliation upon you while my arms protect you?..."

The next day, when the two plovers had gone foraging, Ocean made a long reach with his wave-hands and eagerly seized the eggs. Then when the hen plover returned and found the nursery empty, she said to her husband, "See what has happened to poor me. The Ocean seized my eggs today. I told you more than once we should move.... Now I am so sad at the loss of my children that I have decided to burn myself."

"My dear," said the plover, "wait until you witness my power, until I dry up that rascally Ocean with my bill...."

"Well," said his wife, "if you feel that you must make war on the Ocean, at least call other birds to your aid before you begin. For the proverb says:

> Woodpecker and sparrow
> With froggy and gnat,
> Attacking en masse, laid
> The elephant flat."

"How was that?" asked Sprawl. And Constance told the story of

The Duel between Elephant and Sparrow

(Ryder 1949:125–132, with omissions).

It is several stories later before the plover gets the eggs back—with a considerable assist from Vishnu—for the *Pañca Tantra* inserts stories within stories within stories. Framing has remained a vital technique in literature. It is the main structural device in the *Thousand and One Nights* (all the stories being framed by the tale of Scheherezade) and the *Canterbury Tales* (in which the pilgrimage is the frame), and is in constant use in the flashbacks and dream sequences of modern novels and plays.

FAIRY TALES

In Europe one of the most characteristic forms of popular narrative is the *fairy tale*. It has been defined by Krappe (1964:1) as "a continued narrative . . . centering on one hero or heroine, usually poor and destitute at the start, who, after a series of adventures in which the supernatural element plays a conspicuous part, attains his goal and lives happy ever after." Fairy tales (*Märchen, skazki*) in this sense have been collected all over the literate world—in Europe, northern and eastern Africa, southern and southeastern Asia, and the Far East. Motifs, plots, and particular tales (types) can be shown to have spread back and forth across this range from various points of origin, and in some cases they can be traced to older strata of narrative in myths. As a kind of "success story" however, they seem particularly linked to the agrarian class system of the feudal and postfeudal world; and although elements of them may have spread to primitive peoples, the fairy tale as such is associated with peasants.

On the basis of an analysis of a large body of Russian fairy tales, Propp identifies the structure of a typical one as involving a sequence of *functions* of the actors in the tale. The result is a narrative of the following form:

> One member of the family is forced to leave home. The hero is exposed to a taboo and breaks it. The transgressor then attempts to

achieve a quest, is liberated by his victim, whom he then attempts to conquer or rob by trickery. The victim yields to the trick, unwillingly aiding his enemy. The transgressor does some harm or damage to a member of the family. Misfortune or unhappiness is conveyed, which turns back on the hero as a request or order which he discharges or permits, the transgressor consenting or refusing. The hero then leaves home and investigates, questions, submits to attack, etc., being prepared to win out by magical means or aid. He reacts in turn and resorts to magic. He is then conveyed to the place where he finds the object of his quest. He enters into direct battle with the villain, pulls his trick and conquers him, eliminating the original misfortune or unhappiness. The hero is then restored, but he is pursued, escapes and then arrives home (or elsewhere) unrecognized to confront a false hero. The hero proposes a task, which is decided upon. The hero is recognized and the imposter exposed. The hero then takes on a new appearance; the villain is punished, and the hero marries and is crowned (Propp 1958: *passim*).

No single formula of this sort can capture all of the stories that might be relevant nor eliminate a degree of overlap between this and other types of traditional narrative. Propp's structure, however, does define a frequent and widespread genre, and although its historical relationships to other forms are complex, it is clearly a primary product of the peculiar circumstances of peasant life.

CREATION CYCLES

Most animal tales and fairy tales take place in a vague narrative past, but some stories have a broader chronological significance. They portend; they explain; they teach. Eventually they may memorialize events of real history or traditions of folk philosophy. Particular tales may thus take on etiological functions: "Ducks have dull plumage because they were silly enough to trade with parrots—once upon a time."

Etiological tales are often suspended in ancient mythical time—the *alcheringa* or dream time of the native Australians—and they may be isolated stories or they may be organized into general cycles, explaining everything. All peoples possess a cycle of stories that together constitute the myth of creation or the origin of things. Implicit in such myths is the archaic placement of these formative events in time, even though the sequence of the constituent motifs and tales may remain indefinite. This is the story of the origin of night told by the Tupi Indians of Brazil:

In the beginning there was no night. There was only day all the time. Night was asleep at the bottom of the water. There were no animals, and everything could talk. The daughter of the Great Serpent, they say, married a boy who had three faithful servants. One day he called the three servants and said to them,

"Go out for a walk, because my wife doesn't want to sleep with me."

The servants went out, and then he called his wife to sleep with him. The daughter of the Great Serpent replied,

"But it isn't night." The boy said to her,

"There isn't any night; there is just day." The girl said,

"My father has night. If you want to sleep with me, send them over to the big river to get some."

The boy called the three servants, and the girl sent them to her father's house to bring back a tucuman fruit. The three servants went, and came to the house of the Great Serpent, who gave them a tucuman fruit and said to them,

"Here it is. Take it. But careful! Don't open it or everything will be lost."

The servants went, and they began to hear noises inside the shell of the tucuman like this: ten! ten! ten! It was the sound of crickets and frogs who sing at night. When they were far away, one of the servants said to his companions,

"Let's see what this noise is."

The pilot said,

"No, no. We'll be lost. Come on, then, row there!"

So they went on, and still they heard that noise inside the tucuman shell and they didn't know what the noise was. When they were very far away, they got together in the middle of the canoe, lit a fire, tore off the husk that covered the shell, and opened it. Immediately everything became dark. Then the pilot said,

"We are lost, and the girl in her house knows that we opened the tucuman shell."

They continued their journey. The girl at her house said then to her husband,

"They let night out; let's wait for morning."

Then everything that was scattered around in the forest was transformed into animals and birds. The things that were scattered around in the river were changed into ducks and fishes. From the *paneiro* there sprang the jaguar; the fisherman and his canoe were changed into a duck; from his head emerged the head and bill of a duck, from the canoe its body, and from the oars the duck's feet. The daughter of the Great Serpent, when she saw the morning star, said to her husband,

"Dawn is breaking. It's going to separate day from night."

Then she rolled up a thread and said to it,
"You will be a parrot." So she made a parrot. She painted the parrot's head white with *tabatinga*; she painted his feet crimson with *urucú*, and then she said to him,
"You will always sing whenever you see dawn breaking."
She rolled up a thread and shook ashes over it and said,
"You will be an *inambú* bird, to sing at different times at night and in the morning." Ever since that time the birds sing at their own times at night and in the morning, to enliven the beginning of the day. When the three servants got back, the boy told them,
"You were not faithful. You opened the tucuman shell and let night out and everything was lost, so you too have now been transformed into monkeys, and will always travel along the branches of trees." The black mouth and the yellow stripe that they have on their arms is still, they say, the mark of the sap contained in the tucuman shell which spilled on them when they opened it (Carvalho Neto 1956:263–265).

Etiological tales and myths account for an extraordinary range of things from the most general to the most specific. They attest to the wide-ranging curiosity of even primitive men, and they satisfy it with explanations of the origin of the universe itself, the elements (water, fire), the heavenly bodies, animals, wild and cultivated plants, people and the parts of their bodies and their inventions and their customs. There are tales of the origin of illness and death, of rain, of language, and of the colors of birds—in short, of almost everything that fixes the human attention. Myths occur that account for things that do not exist, and often they imply depth and subtlety. It has even occurred to primitive people to account for the origin of emotional states, like anger (see p. 224). However unsystematic and analogical these accounts may be, they constitute cycles of extraordinary comprehensiveness.

PROPHECY

Human curiosity about the future is at least as great as is our interest in the past, and all human traditions have their prophecies as well as their explanations of origins. Sometimes the prophet speaks for the gods, as in this outburst from an outraged sheepherder, the prophet Amos:

Thus saith the Lord:
"For three transgressions of Damascus and for four, I will not turn away the punishment thereof, because they have threshed Gilead with threshing instruments of iron, but I will send a fire into the house of Hazael, which shall devour the palaces of Ben Hadad.

I will break also the bar of Damascus, and cut off the inhabitant from the plain of Aven, and him that holdeth the sceptre from the house of Eden, and the people of Syria shall go into captivity unto Kir," saith the Lord (Amos 1:3–5).

Amos' predictions of destruction are based on a relatively simple system: God will punish wickedness. Like most sheepherders, Amos is convinced that wickedness is an urban phenomenon.

Other prophetic works are often more technical, and frequently they are intentionally vague—bizarre in diction and imagery, archaic, obscurantist, or ambiguous. Sometimes the system is numerological, as in the Chinese *I Ching*. Sometimes it is calendric, as in zodiacal astrology. Although based on astrology, the prophecies of Merlin quoted (or invented) by Geoffrey of Monmouth attain much the same apocalyptic tone as those of Amos:

The shining of the sun shall be dimmed by the amber of Mercury, and shall be a dread unto them that behold it. Stilbon of Arcady shall change his shield, and the helmet of Mars shall call unto Venus. The helmet of Mars shall cast a shadow, and the rage of Mercury shall overpass all bounds. Iron Orion shall bare his sword. Phoebus of the ocean shall torment his clouds. Jupiter shall trespass beyond his appointed bounds, and Venus forsake the way that hath been ordained unto her. The malignity of Saturn the star shall fall upon earth with the rain of heaven, and shall slay mankind as it were with a crooked sickle. The twice six houses of the stars shall mourn over the wayward wandering of their guests. The Twins shall surcease from their wonted embrace, and shall call the Urn unto the fountains. The scales of the Balance shall hang awry until the Ram shall set his crooked horns beneath them. The tail of the Scorpion shall breed lightnings, and the Crab fall at strife with the Sun. The Virgin shall forget her maiden shame, and climb up on the back of the Sagittary. The chariot of the Moon shall disturb the Zodiac, and the Pleiades shall burst into tears and lamentation. None hereafter shall return unto his wonted duty, but Ariadne shall lie hidden within the closed gateways of her sea-beaten headland. In the twinkling of an eye shall the seas lift them up, and the dust of them of old again begin to live. With a baleful blast shall the winds do battle together, and the sound thereof shall be heard among the stars (Monmouth 1958:151–152).

Prophecy may also be ritualistic, as in the Egyptian *Pert em Hru* or "book of the dead," or be mystical and theological, as in the *Atharva Veda*. Sometimes it is visionary, as in the tales of saintly miracles, or is enigmatic, like the Greek oracle traditions of puns and riddles in verse.

The prophecies of the Maya are often of a Delphic opacity, and commonly express the same dismal view of the future as the prophecies already quoted. (Indeed, prophets are generally inclined to pessimism, and even those who foresee utopia often predict dire portents and catastrophes before the happy ending.) Mayan prophets are clear enough, however, about predicting the Spanish conquest, foreseen as follows by the prophet Balam for 2 Ahau (a twenty-year period or *katun* ending in 1520):

> This is the katun
> In which will come
> Those of light color,
> The bearded men.
> So he said;
> So he knew,
> The Sun Priest
> And Prophet:
> "This is the time
> When there will arrive
> Your fathers,
> Your brothers."
> Thus they were told,
> The Great Water Witches:
> "You shall feed them;
> You shall wear their clothes;
> You shall use their hats;
> You shall speak their language;
> But their ways
> Shall be ways of discord."
> (Barrera Vásquez 1948:120–121; tr. mine)

The broad cosmological questions framed by the literature of origins and prophecy are inherent in the cultural philosophy of every tradition and are expressed in the most diverse fashion throughout every literature. It is an enduring part of the lore of mankind that our most treasured stories, songs, and dramas have been those that most profoundly touch us in our confrontation with the unsolved riddles—that speak most to us about the human condition and human destiny. The language in which such discourse is achieved has undergone great historical changes, and it is difficult for us to recapture the satisfaction of a previous age or a more isolated culture with the simplicity and indirection of primitive myths, dogmas, or humor.

It is otherwise with the early genres that trend in the direction of biography. For it must be admitted that our modern interest is at once aroused when we encounter something like a real person emerging from the flat, impersonal narratives so far considered. The emergence of a literature concerned with the scope and span of the life of one man was certainly a very gradual development. We find it foreshadowed in the characterological consistency of the animals of fable, and greatly extended in the cycles of stories dealing with a single character. The trickster cycles are a special case of this. The next step finds the story focused on a hero.

HERO CYCLES

Most, perhaps all, cultures have more than one hero. There may be major and minor heroes or ancient and modern ones, for heroic traditions result from the gradual accretion of legends around a particular real or imaginary figure, and there may be both gradual and sudden changes in their popularity, or the partial or total (but usually syncretistic) replacement of an older by a newer idol. In classical Greek literature, heroes of varying stature abounded, some clearly older than others. We have only to think of Jason, Hercules, Theseus, or Orpheus as early protagonists in a long line leading to Achilles, Odysseus, and the later tragic heroes like Oedipus. Not infrequently, a change in heroes may be closely connected to a nativistic religious movement, but secular heroes are just as plausible, and we continue to manufacture them in our own century. Cycles of hero tales may occur in relatively primitive and disjointed form and in no necessary sequence, as in the Paul Bunyan, Quetzalcoatl, Robin Hood, Pedro de Urdemales, or Tyl Eulenspiegel traditions. They may wane to brief ballads, like Joe Hill, Casey Jones, Valentín Mancera, or Stenka Razin. Or they may wax to become codified in narrative prose or epic poetry.

In the perspective of literary history, heroes are made, not born. They are men who have so captured the imagination of their peers that they become legends even before they die. They are recognized as heroes because their contemporaries have come to have standards of heroic action. A long tradition of primitive literature leads gradually to the characterological definition of the heroic role. When a particular figure represents the heroic virtues for a whole people, we may call him a culture hero.

Culture heroes differ from real men in a number of important respects. They are born miraculously, most often by parthenogenesis, being spiritually fathered by a god. They mature amazingly (sometimes incredibly) rapidly. They are virtuous (brave, strong, intelligent) beyond belief. They confront and overcome enemies of fabulous malevolence and power, and obstacles of insurmountable difficulty. They teach their peers all manner of practical and moral wisdom, and they usually die young, promising to return. To illustrate the range and problematics of heroic literature, a list of some of the more celebrated culture heroes is given in Table 2.

TABLE 2 Heroes

HERO	CULTURE, DATE, AND WORK
Achilles	(Greek, −9; *Iliad*)
Aeneas	(Latin, 1; *Aeneid*)
Alexis	(Greek, 12; *Alexiad*)
Amadis	(Portuguese, 14; *Amadis de Gaula*)
Arjuna	(Sanskrit, −2; *Mahaabhaarata*)
Arthur	(English, 15; *La Morte d'Arthur*)
Asin	(Toba, 19)
Beowulf	(English, 8; *Beowulf*)
Blood-Clot	(Blackfoot, 19)
Buddha	(Sanskrit, −3; *Tripitaka*)
Caragabi	(Chocó, 19)
Child of the Water	(Apachean, 19)
Cuchulain	(Irish, 7; *Táin Bó Cuáilnge*)
Da Gama	(Portuguese, 16; *As Lusiadas*)
Damsan	(Moi, 17)
Datu Sumakwel	(Panay, 19)
Dede Korkut	(Turkish, 14; *Dede Korkut*)
Dzangar	(Kalmuck, 19)
Fingal	(Irish, 18)
Gilgamesh	(Sumerian, −28; *Gilgamesh*)
Gluskabe	(Abnaki, 18)
Grandfather	(Cariri, 19)
Haitsi-aibab	(Hottentot, 19)
Hayk	(Armenian, 4)
Hiawatha	(English, 19; *Hiawatha*)
Hisagita-misi ("Breathmaker")	(Seminole, 19)
Hrolf Kraki	(Danish, 16; *Hrolfssaga*)
Ibeorgun	(Cuna, 19)
Iry Dada	(Ossetian, 19)
Italapas ("Coyote")	(Chinook, 19)
I'wai ("Crocodile")	(Koko Ya'o, 19)
Jaya Prana	(Balinese, 19; *Jaya Prana*)
Jesus	(Greek, 1; *New Testament*)
Jonayaíyin	(Jicarilla, 19)
Keresaspa	(Persian, 11; *Shah Nama*)
Kesar	(Tibetan, 19; *Kesar*)
Kresnik	(Slovenian, 6)
Kuksu	(Maidu, 19)
K'ung	(Chinese, −5; *Lun Yü*)
Lam Ang	(Ilocano, 19)
Lao	(Chinese, −3; *Tao Tê Ching*)
Liyongo	(Swahili, 18)
Mohammed	(Arabic, 7; *Al Qur'an*)
Moses	(Hebrew, −6; *Old Testament*)
Nanak	(Punjabi, 17; *Granth*)
Orlando	(Italian, 15; *Orlando Furioso*)
Osiris	(Egyptian, −21)

TABLE 2 *(continued)*

HERO	CULTURE, DATE, AND WORK
Pañji	(Javanese, 18)
Quetzalcoatl	(Nahuatl, 15)
Rama	(Sanskrit, 3; *Raamaayaṇa*)
Ratuvuañtani	(Sakalava, 19)
Rinaldo	(Italian, 16)
Rodrigo	(Spanish, 12; *El Poema del Mio Cid*)
Rustam	(Persian, 11)
Siegfried	(German, 13; *Nibelungenlied*)
Sigurd	(Norse, 13; *Völsunga Saga*)
Tahmurath	(Persian, 5; *Avesta*)
Tchué	(Bushman, 19)
Tcikapis	(Montagnais, 18)
Theodoric	(German, 13; *Eckelied*)
Tumua	(E. Madagascar, 19)
Uazale	(Paressí, 19)
Väinamöinnen	(Finnish, 19; *Kalevala*)
Xelas	(Lummi, 19)
Zarathustra	(Persian, 5; *Avesta*)
Zatuvu	(Bara, 19)

Typical of the lore of heroes is this version of the birth of Buddha from the *Buddha Carita* ("Acts of the Buddha") of Aśva Ghosa:

> There lived once upon a time a king of the Shakyas, a scion of the solar race, whose name was Shuddhodana. He was pure in conduct, and beloved of the Shakyas like the autumn moon. He had a wife, splendid, beautiful and steadfast, who was called the Great Maya, from her resemblance to Maya the goddess. These two tasted of love's delights, and one day she conceived the fruit of her womb, but without any defilement, in the same way in which knowledge joined to trance bears fruit. Just before her conception she had a dream. A white king elephant seemed to enter her body, but without causing her any pain. So Maya, queen of that god-like king, bore in her womb the glory of his dynasty. But she remained free from the fatigues, depressions and fancies which usually accompany pregnancies. Pure herself, she longed to withdraw into the pure forest, in the loneliness of which she could practice trance. She set her heart on going to Lumbini, a delightful grove, with trees of every kind, like the grove of Citraratha in Indra's Paradise. She asked the king to accompany her, and so they left the city, and went to that glorious grove.
>
> When the queen noticed that the time for her delivery was approaching, she went to a couch overspread with an awning, thousands

of waiting women looking on with joy in their hearts. The propitious constellation Pushya shone brightly when a son was born to the queen, for the weal of the world. He came out of his mother's side, without causing her pain or injury. His birth was as miraculous as that of Aurva, Prithu, Mandhatri, and Kakshivat, heroes of old who were born respectively from the thigh, from the hand, the head or the armpit. So he issued from the womb as befits a Buddha. He did not enter the world in the usual manner, and he appeared like one descended from the sky. And since he had for many aeons been engaged in the practice of meditation, he was born in full awareness, and not thoughtless and bewildered as other people are. When born, he was so lustrous and steadfast that it appeared as if the young sun had come down to earth. And yet, when people gazed at his dazzling brilliance, he held their eyes like the moon. His limbs shone with the radiant hue of precious gold, and lit up all the space around. Instantly he walked seven steps, firmly and with long strides. In that he was like the constellation of the Seven Seers. With the bearing of a lion he surveyed the four quarters, and spoke these words full of meaning for the future: "For enlightenment I was born, for the good of all that lives. This is the last time that I have been born into this world of becoming" (Conze 1959:35–36).

Heroes are a central problem to literature and one with the broadest and subtlest ramifications. Lord Raglan has argued persuasively, in fact, that heroes are the key problem to all folklore, that the whole body of our traditional lore is a more or less attenuated reflection of the typical hero myth, formalized in ritual. The argument seems weakened by his gratuitous assertion that the "folk" never compose anything and his consequent derivation of all lore from an elitist source. To parody his view only slightly, we can consider this variant of a minor poem:

> Born on a roof top in Battersea,
> Joined the Teds when he was only three,
> Coshed a cop when he was only four
> And now he's in Dartmoor for evermore.
>   Davy, Davy Crockett,
>   King of the Teddy boys.
> (Opie and Opie 1959:119)

The miraculous birth and precocious development of the hero, his overcoming of monsters, and his apotheosis and immortality summarize in a minimal space the general configuration of Raglan's heroes. Moreover, there is no reason to question the elitist origin of the modern Davy Crockett song, nor its conceivable derivation from older and more ritualistic epics.

But it seems impossible to maintain that this specific variant was elaborated by the elite rather than the folk.

Lord Raglan also holds that heroic lore never has an historical base; that is, he resolutely opposes the euhemeristic view of folklore (originally proposed by Euhemerus in the fourth century B.C.) that myth is always or often a disguised retelling of history. The total rejection of this view again seems excessive. We can very well accept the evidence of the frequent occurrence of purely fictional or ritual heroes without arguing that no real man has ever been fictionalized. We can hardly doubt the historicity of Caesar or Christ, yet the life histories of both have been extensively assimilated to the pattern that holds for culture heroes generally.

Despite his excessive dogmatism, Raglan is surely right to draw our attention to the close linkage of ritual, myth, and epic in the heroic pattern: the calendrical associations of many folklore heroes, the dramatistic treatment of them in certain epics, and the mythical and ritual elements in narrative tales about them. To extend this configuration to include, say, proverbs, seems strained and even provincial. How can we relate this to the African proverb, which is known to have a primarily legalistic function in many areas?

The Ossetian (Nartian, Alanic, or Sarmatian) epic of *Iry Dada*, for example, has a generally heroic structure, but it has the ring of history to it, and it seems altogether credible that it may record some real details of a lineage feud between the Sarmatians and the Kievan Russians. There appears to be no ritualistic warrant for such an episode as:

The hero Alamat's head swam because of the Russian drinks.
He cannot restrain himself any more. Opposite him at the table sat a young prince, son of Mstislav's sister.
By his dissolute manners he offends the guests. But lo! Has he not unsheathed his sword? Is he not going to strike Alamat?
When the hero Alamat saw this, he by one stroke knocked the prince's sword from his hand to the side. By Alamat's second stroke the Russian prince is killed on the spot. To the enemy—the deserved fate!
(Vernadsky and Dzanty 1956:229)

This may be ritual, but it sounds to me like a drunken quarrel between mistrustful in-laws.

EPICS

Heroes are variously treated in literature. Some are embodied in myth and commemorated in ritual. Some are the focus of cycles of heroic tales. Some become incorporated into epic poems. The epic is a form apparently restricted to Africa, Europe, and South Asia. It is not confined to literate peoples. Such familiar epics as *Beowulf*, the *Kalevala*, the early Icelandic sagas, and perhaps even the *Iliad* may have been largely shaped before literacy. The Rundi of Central Africa have an epic poem on the *Nyoro Invasion*. The Ossetian epic just quoted was preserved into the present century in oral form. There are epics or near-epics in Southeast Asia, Indonesia, and the Phillippines.

In a sense, the epic is a matter of degree, for heroic tale cycles more or less in verse merge by degrees into fully organized and unified epic poems. The Turks distinguish clearly between a story (*hikâye*) and an epic (*hamasiyat*), but the Turkish national epic has been lost and is represented only by the surviving *Dede Korkut Stories*. More or less organized and more or less versified epics exist in Irish, Russian, and Tadjik. It is all the more astonishing that there is nothing even close to an epic from the Far East. The omission is particularly startling because the heroic concept was clearly present in Chou (and perhaps Shang) China.

One Chinese epic hero was Hou Chi ("Millet Ruler"), an ancestor of the Chou dynasty, who was conceived when his mother stepped in the footprint of Heaven. He survived exposure and grew up to teach the people the cultivation of grain—in the classic manner of culture heroes. The *Classic of Poetry* says of him:

> He was laid in a narrow lane,
> But sheep and oxen protected him tenderly.
> He was placed in a large forest,
> But woodcutters found him there.
> He was laid on cold ice,
> But birds covered him with their wings.
> (Creel 1953:18)

Clearly, Oriental tradition included the right sort of heroes, but it did not produce epics.

The earliest extant epic is the Sumerian *Gilgamesh*, but it is extremely fragmentary. From the more complete Babylonian version of later date we can derive the basic narrative, which exemplifies the sweep and scope of epic poetry as a form of storytelling. The whole was supposed to have been comprised of 12 poems and around 3600 lines. We can reconstruct perhaps 80 or 90 percent of the story. The Babylonian version begins:

> Two thirds of him is god;
>   One third of him is man.
> There's none can match
>   The form of his body . . .
> All things he saw,
>   Even to the ends of the earth.

He underwent all,
  Learned to know all;
He peered through all secrets,
  Through wisdom's mantle that veileth all.
What was hidden he saw;
  What was covered he undid.
Of times before the stormflood he brought report.
  He went on a long far way,
Giving himself toil and distress;
  Wrote then on a stone tablet the whole of his labor.

(Leonard 1934:3)

The general narrative may be outlined as follows (in paraphrase from Sandars 1962:30–43):

> Gilgamesh, king of Uruk, was a man two-thirds god—of unequalled strength and beauty and a driving energy that wore his subjects out. They appealed to the gods, who provided him with a companion, Enkidu, a wild man raised by animals but seduced by a harlot and induced to come to the city where, after a wrestling bout, he becomes the hero's dearest friend, and tells him of the mysterious cedar forest they must win together. In the forest they are protected by the sun god Shamash but are met by the giant Humbaba. Enkidu's hand becomes paralyzed in opening the magic gate; Gilgamesh is put to sleep upon felling the great cedar, and is almost overcome by the giant's "eye of death," but with the help of Shamash and the eight winds the giant is overcome.
>
> Gilgamesh is then glorified, robed, and crowned, and attracts the attention of the goddess Ishtar, who tries to woo him. Rejected, Ishtar sends the Bull of Heaven to punish him, but Gilgamesh kills this monster. The gods then take counsel and decide that one of the two friends must die. Enkidu goes to the underworld and is tricked into remaining. Gilgamesh is inconsolable.
>
> In his grief he decides to seek out Utnapishtim the Faraway, his ancestor who survived the flood. Seeking wisdom, he crosses the wilderness, kills the lions playing in the moonlight at the mountain passes, and reaches the mountains of the sun, guarded by man-scorpions. Eventually, he comes to the garden of the gods, beside the sea, where he finds the seductive woman Siduri, who instructs him how to cross the waters of death. The boatman Urshanabi takes him across to the earthly paradise in a boat with a serpent prow.
>
> Utnapishtim the Faraway then tells Gilgamesh the (somewhat pessimistic) secrets of life and the story of the flood. Reluctant to conclude that his quest is futile, Gilgamesh must be further tested.

Challenged, he fails to stay awake. At the Spring of Youth he learns that possessions outlive the body. He briefly brings the Plant of Youth Regained from the bottom of the sea but loses it again. The snake of Self Renewal appears, but returns to its pool.

His disillusionment is complete and his "searching for the wind" is over. Gilgamesh returns summarily to Uruk "weary, worn out with labor," and dies, greatly mourned. He has lost everything but has learned the secret of the destiny of man.

Later epics carry the secularization that is already discernible in *Gilgamesh* very much further. They are characteristically the literature of the martial courts of the heroic age, and although they are often marvelous and magical, they are not sacred. As the courts became more refined, the heroic epic became transmuted into the medieval romance. But secularization of mythology leads even in primitive literature to the composition of real history.

HISTORY

A great deal of argument has been expended on the question of the historical value of primitive and folk traditions. No simple conclusion seems possible. Certainly we must read differently texts that are patently assimilated to a ritual pattern and those which attempt to chronicle real history. Certainly the availability of writing or of mnemonic devices may affect the accuracy of traditional history. Even written history must be critically evaluated before it can be related to real events, and unwritten history requires the same treatment. But people without writing often maintain some kinds of traditional history, and such records may tell us something of value about actual conditions if they are carefully interpreted.

Many North American Indian tribes kept oral annals, often using carved sticks or other mnemonic aids. Such chronicles are often accurate when they can be precisely checked against known storms, eclipses, volcanic eruptions, or other events. The following example comes from Butterfly's *Winter Count*, a Mandan chronicle which was written down around 1911 but begins with 1833:

> 1851–2. The next winter our people wintered at Smellbad Lodge.
>
> 1852–3. The next winter our people wintered at the same place. They dug mud out of their lodges because the overflow of the river the previous summer had filled their lodges with mud.
>
> 1853–4. The next winter our people wintered near Smellbad Lodge, at the place where Four Bears was afterwards killed. Their chief was Snot. This winter Black Shield went hunting and Blackfoot Indians came and stole his horse. The summer following, seven Blackfoot

Indians came to our village to visit us. They were out on a war party
and had to pass our village. Black Shield knew that his pony had
been stolen by members of the Blackfoot tribe; and he asked the
visitors to bring him back his horse, a black one. They promised to do
so the next time they came; and afterwards they kept their promise
and returned the horse (Howard 1960:34).

The motive for remembering history is just as important in evaluating
primitive as in evaluating written history, and often just as obvious.
The Plains Indian absorption in raiding and horse stealing is well known.

An authentic chronicle of pre-Columbian Maya history is preserved
in the *Annals of the Cakchiquels*, begun by a man of the Dancer (Xahila)
lineage about the middle of the sixteenth century and continued into the
seventeenth century by his son. Here is the tradition for the year 1516,
committed to writing half a century later:

> On 3 Corn
> > It made one cycle
> Since the death of the Woodpeckers,
> > Since they made their revolt.
> And with the day 13 Corn
> > It made another year [1516].
> During this year
> > They took up shields again
> Against the Red House
> > Because of the lord 10 Smoke.
> On 8 Blood they occupied the fort
> > And they really made a great fire again,
> The lords there.
> > All seven tribes came.
> 1 Wind
> > And 10 Smoke
> Made the fire.
> > They fought the war, your grandfathers,
> The captain counsellor Jaguar,
> > The captain counsellor Wind,
> And the head captain Net.
> > And it made the second year
> In the second cycle
> > On the day 10 corn
> Since the revolt [1517].
> (Villacorta 1934:256–257; tr. mine)

The deeds of 10 Smoke or Black Shield are of sufficient interest to be
sketchily remembered by their people in somewhat historical form for

periods of less than a century, a period rarely exceeded in oral annals. In the Cakchiquel record there appears to be a mnemonic use of poetic form, and there may have been traditional histories among the Cakchiquel literally or schematically recorded in hieroglyphic writing. Doubtless the Peruvian quipu was similarly used, although none of the chronicles that have come down to us appear to be in aboriginal form.

Traditions more than a century long tend to be reworked and schematized, losing their immediacy of detail and becoming reorganized by the abstract or fictional attributes of the protagonists' roles—as heroes, kings, seers, or gods. It is in this borderland between epic and myth, chronicle and legend that biography is born. Perhaps the earliest form of historical biography is genealogy, and it is particularly likely to be remembered if it is coupled with political and religious history, as in the ancient king lists of Egypt and Sumer. Polynesian genealogical history is much elaborated, and although it cannot be used for absolute chronology, it establishes valid sequences of population movements that can be documented in other ways. Biblical genealogies are similar, and there are comparable traditions in many parts of the world.

Typically genealogical is the migration legend of the Delaware Indians called the *Red Score*, a curious historical relic transcribed in both pictographs and Delaware prose by C. S. Rafinesque in 1835. In the following text each line is the textual commentary on one pictograph:

When Clever One was chief on the road toward Islands,
He taught all to be destructive by killing Strong Stone.
When Hands Over Everything was chief, he destroyed things belonging to
  the Snake people.
When Strength In Goodness was chief, he destroyed things belonging to
  those who traveled in the north.
When Lean One was chief, he destroyed things belonging to the Snake
  clan of the Ottawa.
When Opossum Face was chief, he worried about the destruction of things
  belonging to others.
Now when daylight came, he spoke three times: "Let those going east be
  many."
They separated at Fish River; and the ones who were lazy returned to
  Snow Mountain.

(Black *et al.* 1954:124–131)

It is possible that Fish River is the Mississippi and that Snow Mountain may lie in the Rockies. If so, this section of the legend records a tradition of events several hundred years earlier in the late Hopewell period of eastern North American archeology. Whether there ever was a Delaware chief called Opossum Face we have no way of knowing.

It is certainly minimal biography to remember only the name and office of a chief, but even primitive cultures may have interest in other details. The following Cuna Indian account from Panama sketches the *Life of Tulikana* with what may be reasonable historicity. It is from a document written in Spanish in the present century to help bolster a request for reservation status for the Cuna. The implication that Tulikana lived before the arrival of the Spanish may not be literally false, because it may refer to a relatively recent "first contact."

> The first Indian shamans lived in the mountains of Takarkunyala. They were named Tulikana and Kwittar, and they encountered half-human tribes along the Kakirwala which now belongs to Darien. The shaman Tulikana travelled among all the tribes of the mountains and Kwittar along the coast and on the islands. The first village that Tulikana entered was Tukkes River, where he met the Tukkestulakan Indians. Then he passed on to the Tupkanti River, where the Tuppu Indians lived. He stayed one year among them to teach them how to live. Later on he came to the Flame River where the Candle Indians lived. He gave it the name Flame River because he saw flames on the river. . . .
>
> Afterwards he was followed by others to the Mamoni River. Upon arriving at Chepo, he joined a chief named Tatsippu. Here they had much trouble fighting against the Spaniards. Because of severe epidemics in the mountains they had to settle on the coasts of Mandinga, where the Cuna increased in numbers through the generations. The shaman Tulikana, having finished his long travels, settled permanently with his brother in the region of Nurtarkana. He had many children and grandchildren and died in Mandinga when nearly 100 years old (Wassén 1949:62–63).

It is apparent that primitive biography does not strive for individuality. On the contrary the whole point is to cast the person in a role of recognizable importance and provide him with the proper attributes. In a sense, this is intrinsically fictionalizing, but an encounter with spirits will necessarily be recorded as a real event by someone who believes in the spirits in question. This would not necessarily mean that the man did not have the experience he has thus interpreted.

The end of the trail for American Indian literature of the historical or any other type is represented by the complete acculturation exemplified in this passage from the famous *Cherokee Phoenix* for February 19, 1831, published as the movement to force the migration of the Cherokee to Oklahoma gained momentum:

> This week we present to our readers but half a sheet. The reason is, one of our printers has left us; and we expect another, who is a white

man to quit us very soon, either to be dragged to the Georgia Penitentiary for a term of not less than four years, or for his personal safety to leave the Nation, to let us shift for ourselves as well as we can. Thus is the liberty of the press guaranteed by the constitution of Georgia (Foster 1885:141).

We have come a long way from Smellbad Lodge.

HUMOR

Specifically narrative humor is not well documented in primitive lore, and the examples we have do not usually tickle the modern mind. There is, for example, an old Navaho chestnut about a man whose wife got even with him for chasing around by tricking him into making love to a bundle of sheepskins wrapped in her blanket. Many stories of the trickster type are basically humorous in this same vein, and making a fool of some one is certain to be successful everywhere. The Moroccans shake their heads over the Gnawa, who built a town without any gates and then asked where the gate was.

It is often difficult to determine whether humor is intended. In a tale of the Bara of Madagascar accounting for the origin of women, God makes a statue of a woman. One man finds it but leaves it in the care of another, who turns it over. They quarrel about possession of the woman and go to God with their argument:

> "I found her," said the first man.
> But God didn't give her to him.
> "Even if he found her," said the other man, "it is I who turned her over."
> "Whoever it was who turned her over," said God, "is her master."
> That is the origin of marriage because he had turned her over (Faublée 1947:354–355; my translation from French).

The whole story hinges on a pun on "woman" (*vali*) and "turn over" (*valiki*). Ancient as well as primitive literature confronts us with relatively rare and equivocal instances of humor. Clowns and joking relationships were almost certainly very ancient, but they have left little trace in literature before the advent of Attic comedy.

In the Europe of the Middle Ages there were extensive collections of "merry tales." This story from the *Fables* of Alfonce and Poge (1484) is characteristic:

> There was in a certain town a widower wooed a widow for to have and wed her to his wife. And at last, they were agreed and sured together. And when a young woman, being servant with the widow,

heard thereof, she came to her mistress and said to her: "Alas, mistress, what have ye to do?"

"Why?" said she.

"I have heard say," said the maid, "that ye be assured and shall wed such-a-man."

"And what then?" said the widow.

"Alas," said the maid, "I am sorry for you because I have heard say that he is a perilous man. For he lay so oft and knew so much his other wife that she died thereof. And I am sorry thereof that if ye should fall in like case."

To which the widow answered and said: "Forsooth, I would be dead—for there is but sorrow and care in this world."

This was a courteous excuse of a widow (Zall 1963:54–55).

In later times, humor is abundant in fables, trickster stories, and jokes as well as merry tales. The following example is from the lore of modern Iran, but doubtless has a respectable antiquity. Mullah is the protagonist of hundreds of Persian stories of this sort:

Once Mullah went to a Turkish bath. The attendants ignored him.

Upon leaving the bath, Mullah gave each of the servants two derhams as tip.

Next time the attendants gave Mullah special attention, hoping to get much more in tips than on the previous occasion.

Upon coming out of the bath, Mullah paid only one derham as a tip.

"Why is it that you paid us much more in tips last time but so little this time?"

"Well," said Mullah, "last time's tip was for today and today's tip is for last time," as the attendants looked at Mullah in astonishment (Daenecke 1960:29).

Many of the Mullah stories are satirical.

A more developed satire is illustrated in the fifteenth-century Telegu commentary on Yogis:

The dog loves to wander among the trees,
The crane to stand still;
Monotonously the donkey brays,
The frog croaks.
What does the yogi know about this,
And about all the desires for which our hearts beat?
            (Caillois and Lambert 1958:693)

Satire covers a very broad spectrum of literary expression, and may sometimes be serious rather than humorous, but most commonly it is mocking and witty. There is little clarity in the classification of the various forms of developed humor, but the Table 3, from Fowler's *Modern English Usage*, may be helpful in clarifying the customary distinctions. The following Turkish poem by Yunus Emre may serve to illustrate the problems of

TABLE 3   Forms of Humor*

	MOTIVE OR AIM	PROVINCE	METHOD OR MEANS	AUDIENCE
Humor	Discovery	Human nature	Observation	The sympathetic
Wit	Throwing light	Words and ideas	Surprise	The intelligent
Satire	Amendment	Morals and manners	Accentuation	The self-satisfied
Sarcasm	Inflicting pain	Faults and foibles	Inversion	Victim and bystander
Invective	Discredit	Misconduct	Direct statement	The public
Irony	Exclusiveness	Statement of facts	Mystification	An inner circle
Cynicism	Self-justification	Morals	Exposure of nakedness	The respectable
The sardonic	Self-relief	Adversity	Pessimism	Self

* Fowler 1965:253.

classification in this area. It has as a whole a certain detached humor, and the play of metaphors is witty. Its general tone is satirical, but it makes explicit use of invective ("wretch") and cynicism (about death), and the figure in the fourth line from the end verges on but does not quite become sarcasm. The final couplet is elegantly ironic, or perhaps sardonic, because the poet apostrophizes himself. It is clear that an exclusive categorization of the forms of humor would be of the utmost difficulty, but the range is well illustrated here in a single poem:

Supposing you had conquered all the world from Caucasus to Caucasus,
Or that you'd won in gambling everything in play;
Consider yourself as king mounted on Solomon's throne;
Let's grant you powers over giants and fairies—
Supposing you have added to your wealth all Pharaoh's treasure,
The riches of Chosroes and of Croesus.
You well know that this world is but a mouthful chewed;
And what is it to swallow a thing chewed? Let's say it's swallowed.
Supposing that your life is like an arrow poised upon your bow;
And what is staying for such an arrow? Let's suppose it's shot.
With each breath taken, life in your strongbox lessens,

And when the box is halfway empty, suppose that's all.
Since you are in the sea with water at your throat,
Don't fight it like a fool, wretch; say you're drowned.
Death is, you know, so why should you ignore it?
Far from it all, you are already in your tomb at rest.
O Yunus, live happy for a hundred years:
The final end is but a gasp; give up and grant you have forgotten it.
(Caillois and Lambert 1958:266–267)

The more sophisticated forms of humor appear to be a consequence of the civility of urban life. Even the joke as a form does not appear to occur in primitive and peasant cultures. To be sure, there are funny stories—the tall tales of Texas or the witty embellishment of folk tales—but most such humor is thoroughly contextual and hard to reproduce. The packaging of humor in brief, self-contained stories creating their own structure and resolving it seems to be even now a pattern of the "sophisticates" rather than the folk. A traditional Polish example runs:

A man caught a thief in his vegetable garden and demanded, "How did you get into my garden?"
"Why a tremendous wind came along and blew me in."
"Well, then, how did my vegetables get uprooted?"
"Oh, this wind was so strong it must certainly have uprooted them."
"In that case, how did the vegetables wind up in your bag?"
"You know, that's just what I was wondering."

Chapter 6

Plays

The essential features of dramatic literature constitute a configuration of roles, rules, action, and symbols also present in rudimentary form in ritual, in games, and in children's play. In fully developed drama, these elements may be further elaborated by compounding with other forms of expression: masking, costuming, and setting, the dance, vocal and orchestral music, prose and poetic dialogue. But these elements are of variable occurrence, while the more nuclear focus of the dramatic (the seemingly essential core) is a pattern of roles.

Drama shares with ritual and games a structure of differentiated roles in contrast. The actors may vary greatly in their positions in the drama, but they never coalesce. The shaman or priest always stands apart from the spirit or god, and from the onlookers or other officiants in a ceremony. The players in a game are only interchangeable under strict rules. In these cases, the possible action is governed by artificial regulations, guaranteeing the expression of a particular conflict within a framework narrower than that of life. The actors don't use real bullets; the skeptic does not interrupt the mass; the fighter does not hit below the belt. Dramatic conflict is conventional and symbolic in that some part of its structure is expressly different from what "really" happens—that is to say, what happens outside the framework of dramatic conventions. As Eberle says (1955:18), "the elements of the theater are the representation and experience of roles . . . of the 'other ego.' "

APPLE CORE

Role playing among children is commonplace, universal, and specific. All children, for example, "play house." But even among children, play may become ritualized and formally dramatic, as in the common American game "Apple Core":

(*Scene: Any street.* AGGRESSOR has just eaten an apple.)

AGGRESSOR: Apple core!

ALLY: Baltimore!

AGGRESSOR: Who's your friend?

(NERVOUS *runs.*)

ALLY: Uh... (*hesitating*) Victim!

(VICTIM *runs.* AGGRESSOR *throws the apple core at him.*)

This rather elaborate little drama (note, for example, the rhymed dialogue) displays a four-part structure; it has a speaking cast of two, but the dramatic turning point at the end of the third line may be conducive to evasive action by any number of bystanders. The four implied roles are completely distinct: Aggressor, Ally, Nervous, and Victim can never possibly be merged. The treachery of Ally is the pivotal point of the drama, for his allegiance to Aggressor is ritual and self-protective, but his choice between Nervous and Victim is poignantly indeterminate. Nervous must play his part gracefully; he avoids the choice only through cowardice, which makes him unworthy to be Ally's "friend"; he is consequently the fool of the piece. Victim is too courageous, like all sacrificial heroes.

Riddling games, too, have a simple dramatic structure, and often alternate by formal rules. A Filipino example goes:

> A wonder for Juan.
> Plenty of vines in its belly,
> It will talk to the people immediately
> When you twist its ear.
> (*Answer:* Radio)
> (Hart 1964:185)

Such riddles may come to have contest and flyting implications similar to those of the Apple Core game and many other children's pastimes.

DOZENS

Children's play is not always so formalized, nor is the dialogue usually so traditional. Sometimes a similar formality of structure can be achieved entirely in action, as in the "Chinese Finger Game" or "Scissors, Paper, and Rock," which can attain a certain mathematical complexity of role and anticipatory role definitions. More often perhaps, there is at least some modicum of dialogue. Most children have any number of contest games, sometimes demonstrating physical skill and prowess, sometimes testing verbal agility. A particularly structured form is the insult game called "The Dozens" played by American Negro boys. Taunting games are a staple of children's lore, but "sounding" or "playing The Dozens" is an especially violent form in which sexual slang figures very largely in a manner at once ritual and initiatory:

> ONE: I hear your mother plays third base for the Phillies.

> TWO: I can tell by your knees
> Your mother climbs trees.

> ONE: I saw your mother flying through the air;
> I hit her in the ass with a rotten pear.

> TWO: Roses are red,
> Violets are blue.
> I fucked your mamma
> And now it's for you.

> ONE: At least my mother ain't no cake—everybody get a piece.
> (Abrahams 1962: *passim*)

The contest may be short or long, ending in a fight or distraction or ennui. The obscenity is essential.

The Dozens can be paralleled in contest games from various cultures. In Anglo-Saxon tradition there were flyting songs of boasting and challenge to ridicule one's enemies or opponents and assert oneself. The Eskimos often settled arguments with *nith* songs of a similar character, and the Plains Indians had boasting songs in which successful warriors tried to best each other in bragging of their exploits. Brazilian Negroes have a highly developed form of verbal battle, and in West Africa insulting songs are sung by the principals in lawsuits or by their representatives before the tribal courts.

WAX AND GOLD

A very distinctive kind of contest punning and riddling called *sam ennaa warq* ("Wax and Gold," referring to the outer and inner meaning of the verse) is highly developed in Ethiopian Amharic. A famous example is an exchange between Asfaa Wassan, the Duke of Shoa, and Tedu, the

Governor of Morat, in which the latter, fearing conquest, quipped:

> Asfaa Wassan Yefaat ṭankeraw yerrasu
> Morat ṭeduaal belaw kamamalaalasu.

> (O Asfaa Wassan, stoutly plough Yefat
> Rather than eye what's baking [or "Rather than think
>   about Tedu"] in Morat.)

The Duke replied:

> La mofar la qanbar yamihonaññen
> Saalquarṭaw alqerem zandro ṭedun.

> (To get me yokes and plowbeams in this year
> I will not fail to cut the juniper [Tedu also means "juniper"].)
> (Levine 1965:34–35)

The *double entendre* of Wax and Gold is frequently encountered in invective and in games of verbal contest throughout the world.

BATTLE OF THE SEXES

In many cases an informal drama can be built out of the lore of courtship. The traditional *piropos* or *coplas* of Spanish, for example, may serve as flyting songs or courtship games with equal ease. They are thoroughly formalized, and some individuals can bandy them back and forth almost indefinitely without repetition. There are established verses for accepting as well as for rejecting a sally, and new verses may be tailored to the occasion to express any desired nuance of coqueterie. The following verses are a sample of the form from Vietnamese, in which it is also highly developed and traditional:

> GIRL: If that river weren't but one measure wide,
>   I would make a bridge, my friend,
>   Of the ribbon from my blouse.

> BOY: Girl carrying water on a rattan frame,
>   Give me a little pail to sprinkle on the plane tree;
>   On the finest and greenest tree the phoenix will light.

> GIRL: I am like a piece of rose silk.
>   It floats around the market.
>   I don't know whose hand it will fall to.
>   (Caillois and Lambert 1958:487–488)

The overtones of these verses, like those of Spanish, are often intentionally ambiguous or elliptical, which heightens the flexibility of the game, however opaque it may make it for the uninitiated observer. Nor are such songs restricted to courtship: the Araucanian Indians have a kind of flyting song adapted for arguments between husband and wife.

TLACHTLI

Adult games often involve a very elaborate ritual-dramatic structure. Sometimes the element of contest predominates, as in chess, poker, bridge, or football. At other times, it is the ritual element, as in bullfighting in Spain or professional wrestling in the United States. In many games, both factors are blended together, as in the Middle American ritual ball game, Tlachtli. Tlachtli was played in a special I-shaped court with a dividing line midway along the waist of the I. Two players defended each half of the court, dressed in special leather aprons from waist to knee (and sometimes face masks and gloves as well). A hard, heavy rubber ball about the size of a man's head was knocked across the court under soccer rules: it could be touched only by the leather apron (that is, with hips, thighs, and buttocks). Points were scored by hitting the opponents' back wall with the ball, and lost by failing to return the ball beyond the center line after once bounce and in two hits (one per player). High on the side walls at the center line were two stone rings; to knock the ball through either of these was an automatic victory, but was very difficult and rare. Heavy bets were laid on the outcome of the game, which was witnessed by fairly large crowds, and probably followed by even larger ones.

The ritual elements in Tlachtli are less precisely known, but can be approximately reconstructed as follows. The ball was thought of as blood (rubber sap:blood); it was also equated with the head of a sacrificial victim (through mythology) and with the sun (by shape). The players were identified with mythological figures of calendrical significance. They were probably schematically costumed in accordance with these personifications. The game was played on particular occasions in the ceremonial calendar, and the personification of the players may have varied correspondingly. The general significance of the game may thus be seen as a complex allegory, at once commemorative and prophetic. It memorialized a mythical ball game among the gods, but it also symbolized the calendrical cycles, and by its outcome foretold the divinatory content of the cycle yet to come. At times, further meaning was introduced by direct participation of politico-religious leaders (such as Montezuma), with corresponding factionalism in the audience. Tlachtli was high sport, high ritual, and high drama at once.

REINDEER DANCE

One of the most ancient indications of ritual of any type is the famous representation of a masked dancer on a cave wall at Trois Frères in southern France. The figure is that of an otherwise naked man wearing a reindeer headdress and decorated in a manner suggestive of body painting. He is staring solemnly if enigmatically at the viewer and he is obviously dancing. The date of the painting may be around 20,000 B.C. Comparable human figures are found over a large part of Europe and Africa at something like the same level of antiquity, although none is as interesting, as readable, or as artistically impressive as this one. The suggestion of a hunting ritual is inescapable in this mural. Masked dancing for such a purpose is widespread among primitive peoples, where it is accompanied by instrumental music, singing, poetry, and ritual prose. Musical instruments (whistles and perhaps drums), although not found in association with the dancing shaman, have been discovered in other deposits of the same general time level and cultural character. Thus, an archaic ritual drama may plausibly be supposed to have existed among the Cro-Magnon hunters of very early times—a Reindeer Dance involving the ancient use of such later dramatic techniques as costume, music, masks, dancing, and perhaps poetry and dramatization of the relationships among the shaman, the hunters, and the animals hunted. Later ritual and drama are everywhere commonly at least this dramatic and complex.

WHALE

The ritual with which the Alacaluf of southernmost South America prepare for sealing and whaling expeditions involves a preliminary vigil, the donning of a thong braid (*chepana*), a ceremony in the conical ritual hut (Big House) in which shellfish poles were painted for the women to use while the men were away, and a further vigil inside the Big House. The program is outlined in an initial hymn, the "Whale Song":

> We sing upon the mountain.
>   We put the *chepana*
> Over our heads
>   And bodies.
> We enter the Big House
>   To paint the little poles.
> The buzzard is flying
>   At the top of the sky.
> Today we will not go out.
>   Tomorrow we will not go out.
> This we command all.
>   (Bird 1946:75)

Schematically, this ceremony represents at a primitive level the dramatization intrinsic to ritual, and even the marginal Indians of Tierra del Fuego have an extensive repertoire of different presentations with masks, music, and poetic elements.

THE PILLAR OF HEAVEN

The Semang, a Negrito people of the mountains of Malaya, have a well-developed ritual drama for approaching the gods and spirits of the mountain called the "Pillar of Heaven." A part of the dialogue goes:

FEMALE SPIRIT: Peak of the Pillar,
> Greetings, oh head!
> I hold fast,
> Suddenly springing up
> To hold fast
> To the breast of the Pillar of Heaven.
> We are going up to the Lord God,
> Dizzily in the cleft of the Lady of Trees.
> Where is the star string,
> The wreath of flowers?

MALE SPIRIT: Greetings, oh head,
> Father of mine!
> I am climbing up.
> I'm coming!
> Father, come forth
> From the center of the earth!

SHAMAN: I am the tiger Liwon,
> Straight from Lanka; out of my way!

FEMALE SPIRIT: What song is this?
> Where is the star string?
> Spin!
> I'm climbing on
> To the peak of the Pillar,
> The top of the bridgeway.
> Spin!
> I'm climbing on!
> Shaman, throw high!
> Greetings, oh head!

MALE SPIRIT: With handclapping
> Climb on!
> Greetings, oh head!
> Father, I climb on!

SHAMAN: I spin!
　I spin!
　The color of the tunic
　On the bank of Sengo River!

A GOD: Father!
　Father!
　He climbs the sunset path!
　He is before the folding doors!
　There!
　There!

SHAMAN: Of course!
　I am spinning!
　I spin!
　I spin!
　It is I indeed!
　I am spinning!
　I spin!
　I spin!

FEMALE SPIRIT: What does the teacher say?
　Maiden Spirit, pant up the hill!

PHEASANT SPIRIT: We maidens of the moon
　Fly directly upwards!
　　　(Schebesta 1957:2:144–145; my translation from German)

In this passage the shaman, possessed by a tiger spirit, is spinning the threads that link the gods and spirits at the top of the sacred mountain with the human actors who are attempting to reach them through impersonation, dancing, and song, and with the onlookers who participate in the ritual.

YUNCA

Many rituals reflect and dramatize the roles of real life. This is particularly true of life crisis rituals (Van Gennep's *rites de passage*), which emphasize the importance and meaning of particularly critical changes in the individual's social position. They may celebrate birth, naming, weaning, the first haircut, initiation and coming of age, marriage, childbirth and recovery from childbirth, promotions, anniversaries, installations and inductions into offices, retirement, death, and burial. The following example is a *yunca* or funeral song of the Peruvian Quechua:

SON: Where are you going,
　Father of mine?

FATHER: I am going to the Great Forest;
I am going travelling.

SON: Why are you going?
Who's taking you?

FATHER: I shall harvest the sweet coca;
I'm going alone.

SON: Come back soon!
Come back soon!
I shall wait for you weeping;
I shall wait for you groaning.
On the mountain you must pass
Flames a black flag.
In the pass you must cross
The departed grass blooms in blankets.
Oh bitter, bitter heart
On taking leave of the beloved dove.

FATHER: Little bell of Paucartambo,
Play the farewell for me.
I am going to the Great Forest!
I shall never return.
(Arguedas 1949:46)

FERTILITY

Agricultural peoples commonly possess a developed ritual drama
expressing in mystical form and through the oblique personification of
natural forces their need for fertility, in the fields, in the annual cycle of
nature, and in humans. The earliest extant drama of any kind is a fragment
of one scene from such a drama dating to the very dawn of history (about
3500 B.C.) in Egypt. We do not know how this ritual was performed, but
even the very earliest of Egyptian paintings suggest the use of elaborate
masks to identify the gods, and there is every likelihood that poetry,
music, and the dance may have been involved.

Scene 19

(*Enter two milkmaids and two butchers.*)
HORUS (*to the milkmaids*): Ye shall fill my house upon earth with
my eye. (*To Thoth, referring to the butchers.*) They must bring
it themselves. (*Referring to the offspring of the king.*) I have protected you. ... lay on the ground ... (Bouquet 1959:57).

Horus is the son of Osiris, and succeeds his father as god of fertility and life by avenging himself on his father's brother (and murderer), Seth. He is usually represented as a hawk. Thoth is the author of creation, god of words and intelligence, and is commonly allied with Horus against Seth. He is usually represented as an ibis or baboon. This particular scene may be related to a myth concerning Horus' inspection of his estate and house, apparently also alluded to in the eighty-ninth chapter of the Book of the Dead.

TANO THE HYENA

The New Year's ceremony in the village of Kuntunso in north-central Ghana is dedicated to the death and rebirth of the god Tano the Hyena, who is personified by a high priest in trance in a dramatic ritual, part of which is:

HIGH PRIEST (*staggering under the weight of the large brass fetish bowl*):
Praise, praise, oh Oyee,
We listen trembling.
If we were beasts,
We should be freed.

PRIESTESSES: Our ancestors said
That we should come, ee,
And we have come to say:

HIGH PRIEST: We have come from Amovi Cave, oh,
We have come from Amovi Cave, oh,
Creator, from Amovi Cave, oh, ee.
We have come from Amovi Cave, oh, ee, Creator.

PRIESTESSES: Tano, do not mind our conduct.
We serve you.
Ally, forgive us our conduct.

HIGH PRIEST (*now in trance, personifying the god*):
I am unhappy; during the smallpox epidemic you prayed to me,
During the war you prayed to me,
And now I am abused.
There was war and I was in the middle of it [unhurt].
Who can do this?
There was death and I was there unhurt.
Who can do this?
Moon goddess
Be silent!

Let somebody do the same for me to see.
Who can do this?
I am no more than a basket made of palm leaves
That has been thrown away when it has served.

PRIESTESSES AND PEOPLE: Cat Tano

Does not serve only one person, but all.
(Meyerowitz 1958:70–71)

Trance possession is characteristic of West African ritual and has been carried over into many Negro cults in the New World as well.

RAINGODS

The Pueblo Indians of the Southwestern United States are not given to trances and possession states. But the ceremonies in which their gods are welcomed back into the village for the winter are intensely dramatic. They are actually close to being primitive operas, embodying instrumental and vocal music, poetry, dance, and costumed performers, both serious and comic. Like several of the rituals already cited, these ceremonies center upon fertility, giving thanks for the harvest just past and expressing welcome to the gods who will spend six months in the village and leave again at midsummer to send the rains. They are also mythologically commemorative, for the gods represented are the figures of myth. They are not ancestors but are associated with the ancestral spirits; they are not creators but are associated with the Creation. Their arrival in the village is portrayed in the following scene:

FIRST CLOWN: You said that they are right at the foot of the ladder, didn't you?

SECOND CLOWN: Yes.

FIRST CLOWN: Well, from the foot of the ladder
They start climbing the steps;
They keep climbing,
Keep climbing,
Climbing,
Climbing,
Until they are right here
At the mouth of the kiva.

SECOND CLOWN: And here they are with their thunder,
Their wind,
Their lightning,
Their bird songs,
Their cricket chirpings!

FIRST CLOWN: Here they are with their power of corn raising,
    Of squash raising.
    Of watermelon raising;
    With their deer killing power,
    Their buffalo killing power,
    Their fox killing power;
    Their power to bring rain, and thunder, and lightning;
    Their power to bring fertility, and growth, and abundance,
    Right here
    At the MOUTH OF THE KIVA!

(*There is a deafening roar, breaking up into the distinctive cries of the several Raingods. A spirit hand reaches into the kiva, distributing blessed corn and pinyon nuts. The clowns cower in fright, fastening on their sheepskins, then rush towards the entrance.*)

CLOWNS: Yes, yes, may it be so!
    Our Great Ones,
    Ye wise gods and revered goddesses,
    Come hither
    And warm yourselves
    In our hearts.
    Ye have come to see us;
    Ye are bestowing honor upon us
    By coming to see your Children.
    We rejoice seeing you.
    Yes, yes, our Great Ones,
    Come hither and feel welcome!

(*The Chief Raingod enters and advances toward the* TOWN CHIEFS, *preceded by the* FIRST CLOWN.)

FIRST CLOWN: This way, Great One, this way.

PEOPLE (*breathing on their cornmeal and scattering it to feed the gods*):
    Ye Great Ones,
    Ye have come to see us.
    We are rejoicing
    And we welcome you.

(*The First Clown accepts a watermelon from the Chief Raingod and presents it to the Town Chiefs. Each of the other Raingods enters in turn until all ten are present, dancing.*)

FIRST CLOWN (*approaching with outstretched arms*):

    Yes, Great Ones! Let us be friends!

(The Chief Raingod strikes him with his yucca whip.)

Ouch, goddam, that hurts!

(He jumps aside, but then approaches again.)

Come on! Let's make friends!

(The Chief Raingod extends his arms alternately to right and left in a gesture of welcome. Each of the clowns repeats this rejection and acceptance with each god. The Chief Raingod then approaches the Town Chiefs.)

SECOND CLOWN: Yes, yes, Oh Great One.
I think you have something on your mind,
Something you want to say, don't you?

(The God nods with his whole body, then pantomimes "we" "have come" "here" "to talk to the Town Chiefs.")

FIRST CLOWN: *(pointing to a young man)*: Here he is.

(The God shakes his head violently and the Town Chiefs stand up. The Winter Chief interprets the God's gestures.)

WINTER CHIEF: We have come from far, as we are concerned about you,
And we wanted to see how our children are getting along.
It has reached my ear
That you people have not listened to your gods,
And we came to punish you.

(Then he speaks for the people.)

No, ye Great Ones,
We have not been bad;
We have tried to get along with one another;
We have lived in peace;
We have lived in harmony with one another.
We have been good people,
Haven't we, Children of the Great Ones?

PEOPLE: Yes, yes, yes!
(Laski, 1959:46–51)

The total ritual of which this is a part reflects a wealth of dramatic techniques beyond the elements of conflict, climax, and poetry here represented, but the drama remains nonetheless disjointed. The ballet is only loosely joined to the chorale; both are loosely related to the role structure; the play of comedy and seriousness seems erratic rather than controlled. Impressive as primitive drama, the *kachina* or Raingod ceremony is perhaps closer to a choral tableau than to a fully developed play. It has all the elements of opera, but they are not organized.

THRESHING CEREMONY

Even after considerable acculturation, the Indians of Latin America often preserve native forms of ritual and literature. The following text records the threshing ceremony and payoff on a Chilean farm in the last century. It has been translated from the Picunche dialect of Araucanian.

MEN: Let's go, let's go, honey;
　　　What are you stepping on, honey?
　　Is it the rye you are treading, honey?
　　　Treading rye is something I have done before, honey mine.
　　Keep in step, honey, go on;
　　　There, there, honey.
　　There, there, go on, honey.
　　　If this touches your horn
　　It will take you, honey.
　　　Go on!

WOMEN: Let's go honey; let's go honey.
　　　There, there, so some shell will be yours.

MEN (*shouting*): I'm going to have this girl.

OTHER MEN (*murmuring*): Take her by the snatch; have her.

PEOPLE (*to the Corporal*): How are you?
　　　Better have one [i.e., drink], Corporal.

CORPORAL (*to the Chief*): Isn't there enough liquor for a drink?
　　　My people are so tired;
　　They worked so hard.
　　　"Liquor," they beg me.

OWNER: Sure there is. How goes it?
　　Is my field threshed?

CORPORAL: Almost done.
　　　This is being separated already.
OWNER (*offering liquor*): Here then, Corporal,
　　　Dedicate it to your people.

CORPORAL: Your work is done then, the duty of the Corporal.
　　　Your field is threshed.

OWNER: Very well, then. Thanks be to you.
  Very good, then. Thank you for my work.
My work is done, then.
  Here's liquor then;
Offer it
So your people can drink, then.

CORPORAL: When it's finished, when it's almost finished,
  "It's finished," they'll say to me.
That's why these lads of mine,
  My people,
Ask me for so much,
  Er, liquor.
When it's finished then,
  "It's finished," they'll say to me.

OWNER: Well, then, they'll drink.
  I'll give you all of it.
I'll give you all of it, then.
So that your people can drink, then.

CORPORAL: Very well. It's good that I gave it,
  That I have come out of the shame.
[I've finished up?] with my boys.
  This work is done then.
That's why they're asking me for liquor.
  I'm very grateful to you, then.

(The liquor is distributed.)

ALL *(singing)*: Let us drink then,
  Our hearts being alive.
Let us drink well then,
  Our day has really come
For us to toast,
  For us truly to toast,
For us to drink then.
  I'm drunk, my friend, from the liquor.
    (Lenz 1895–1897:116–118; my translation from Spanish)

Whether the sex play, haggling, and drinking have any aboriginal analogues in Araucanian tradition is uncertain, but the whole is cast in standard American Indian poetic form. Comparable ritualization of bargaining and drinking occurs elsewhere in the Americas.

LOST SON

In the kachina cult of the Pueblo Indians the children are instructed in the lore of the gods through the use of carefully painted and embellished dolls. Dolls of this type have been found in the Southwest of the United Stated dating back to the seventeenth century B.C. The use of dolls and figurines for what are usually described as ceremonial purposes is widespread in prehistory, and may well antedate even the obese "Venuses" of Aurignacian Europe (nearly 30,000 B.C.). Whether adult doll play ever had in ancient times the dramatic structure that inheres in children's doll games seems dubious, but eventually some form of puppetry seems a natural and expectable development. In Mexico as early as the fifteenth century B.C. there were figurines with articulated joints suggestive of such use. This is not, however, confirmed by later development of puppets among American Indians. The clacking beak of the Zuni Shalako, moving parts on Northwest Coast masks, or the *deus ex machina* of Roman theater are also suggestive of puppetry, as are some of the techniques of Siberian shamans. But the hand puppets and string-manipulating marionettes familiar to Europe from *Punch and Judy* appear to be relatively late. Indecent puppet plays like *Kara Gyuz* were introduced to the Arabs by the Turks as late as the eighteenth century.

In southern and eastern Asia the use of puppetry in drama is very highly developed, particularly in shadow plays, in which two-dimensional puppets are maneuvered behind a screen to cast their shadows for the audience, while actors provide the voices of the characters. Long traditional narratives, both heroic and mythological, are commonly represented. An example of a leather puppet (*wayang kulit*) play from Malaya is the story of the *Lost Son:*

> An old man appears, weeping for a long lost son, and moves to and fro for some time, bewailing his loss; the showman speaks each figure's part, and alters the tone of his voice to suit the age of the speaker; a second figure comes on, representing a young man armed with a kris, who endeavors to pick a quarrel with the first comer, and the conversation is witty and characteristic, eliciting roars of laughter from the lookers-on; a fight ensues, and the old man is wounded; he falls and cries out that were he a young man, or if his lost son were present, his adversary should not thus triumph over him. In his conversation he happens to mention his son's name; the young man intimates that his name is the same, an explanation ensues, and it ends by the old man discovering in his late adversary his long lost son. The old fellow weeps and laughs alternately, caresses his son frequently, and declares they shall never part again; the scene ends by the youth shedding tears over his late inhuman conduct, and he finally walks off with the old gentleman on his back (Skeat 1967:515).

The motif of the story is familar from *Sohrab and Rustam*. Themes from the epic of the *Ramayana* or from the Jataka tales of the life of Buddha are very popular in Southeast Asia. Other folklore is also richly represented: witches, giants, ogres, the pagan gods, and legendary heroes are embodied in plays, many of them never written down. Battle plays may hold the attention of the crowd for hours at a time, much as *The Raingods* holds the Pueblo imagination. But whereas the mythological background is important to the comprehension of both types of drama, the narrative in shadow plays is explicit and is joined to dialogue and action. Often the shadow drama is accompanied by a native orchestra, and frequently it includes songs. It cannot, of course, do more than simulate dancing. But it is no longer ritual: it is drama.

KNIGHT OF RABINAL

The finest example of the developed drama of the Maya that has come down to us was transcribed in Quiche from the dictation of Bartolo Ziz in the nineteenth century: *The Knight of Rabinal*. It is a masked dance drama with poetic dialogue and instrumental accompaniment. Although there is some faint suggestion that one of the characters was intended to be comic, it is fundamentally a tragedy, describing the capture and sacrifice of the Knight of Quiche by his enemy, the Knight of Rabinal. The former is the true hero of the piece.

The narrative moves slowly through the heavily ritualized dialogue in archaic poetry, interrupted at intervals for a wordless dance. The musical theme is varied for these dance interludes, and the dance steps and music of the play may involve Spanish influences, as does the marimba-drum-shawm orchestra. The dance is stately and formal rather than active or athletic, and the dialogue is muffled by the masks of the characters. It is well known anyway, and, like ritual, can be followed by the spectators without actually hearing the words. The theme of the play is ostensibly a historical event of the fifteenth century, but it has been assimilated to ritual traditions and poetic forms already well established. The text is archaic and obscure, and is unquestionably indigenous.

The first act deals with the capture of the hero; the second with his presentation to the father of his captor, 5 Rain; the third takes him through the ritual preparatory to sacrifice. In the final climactic scene the Knight of Quiche demonstrates that he has the magical power to escape his captors. However, like all tragic heroes, he is doomed by his own character and musing poignantly he accepts his fate:

QUICHE: Ah, would to heaven!
Ah, would to earth!
If I am indeed to die here
And be lost

> Between heaven
>   And earth,
> Would then that I could change places with that squirrel
>   Or that bird,
> Who die on the tree branch
>   Or the tree limb
> Which was their hunting place for food
>   And sustenance
> Here between heaven
>   And earth.
> Indeed ye Eagles,
>   And ye Jaguars,
> Come then and so perform what is your duty,
>   So perform your office,
> So use your teeth
>   And claws
> That in a single instant
>   Ye have me surely flayed.
> For truly I am unafraid
>   At returning
> To my mountains,
>   My valleys.
> Thus heaven
>   And earth be with you,
> Ye Eagles
>   And ye Jaguars!
> (*The Eagles and Jaguars surround him, bend him across the stone, and
>   sacrifice him.*)
>
> (Brasseur 1862:114–9; my translation from Quiche)

The Knight of Quiche is a great magician. Having demonstrated his ability to escape death by magical disappearance, he nonetheless accepts it voluntarily, wistfully but stoically accepting the death of the tragic hero implacably condemned by his own excellence: his courage. There is no tragic flaw, no hubris, for the Mayan tradition is far more fatalistic than the Greek, but we are not very far from classic tragedy here.

The transition from ritual to secular drama has probably taken place many times, but in every case it manages to achieve historical obscurity. It is the view of Gilbert Murray that such a transition directly underlies the great age of Attic drama. The argument is summarized neatly by Hunningher:

> It now appears that at Delphi so-called *dromena* (things done) were
> executed—in other words, rites—corresponding to the rites for the

year and tribal god. Of that ritual year-drama, exactly the same in nature as the Egyptian Osiris-drama, the struggle, or *agon*, was a relic; so was the suffering and downfall connected with it, which formed the *pathos*, the tale of the messenger, the mourning or *threnos*, the recognition of new life or *anagnorisis;* [there] finally appeared, as an incarnation of renewed life in a young daemon or god, the *epiphany.* . . .

As soon as the participants in the rites no longer believed in the practical purpose of these rites, the greater part of the community which had originally danced the rites lost the enthusiasm that had once inspired them to take part; they became spectators, and the *dromenon* performed for them became drama (Hunningher 1963:37).

Mayan drama of the present day is in just this stage of skepticism. It is no longer understood as ritual even by ritual experts, yet it remains linked to the ritual dates and contexts that once gave it its only meaning.

MARY MAGDALENE

Didactic religious drama, perpetuating the traditional lore in dramatic narrative, is European Christian as well as Mayan or Malayan. The following example is the beginning of a Cornish mystery play of the seventeenth century (but certainly earlier in origin) taken from the cycle of the Resurrection. I have slightly altered the line divisions in the first three speeches to bring them into conformity with the triadic scansion of the remainder of the play. The poetic form is suggestive of Welsh *englynion:*

MARY MAGDALENE:
> Now, O apostles, I will tell you news:
>> Jesus is risen from the tomb;
>>> I saw Him lately; I spoke to Him also.
> I looked on His wounds;
>> Pitiful it was to see them.
>>> To the world they bring healing.

THOMAS:
> Silence, woman, with thy tales,
>> And speak truth, as I pray thee;
>>> Christ who was cruelly slain to be alive I will not believe.
> Waste no more words,
>> For lies I do not love;
>>> Our Lord is dead; alas! I tell the truth.

MARY MAGDALENE:
> I speak true, Thomas,
>> And I, though poor, will prove it.

Lately I saw Him—the Lord (none equal to Him).
And by me He sent, I swear to ye, as ye may know,
    Like as He promised;
        He named to me none but Peter.

THOMAS:
    Silence, and speak not, woman!
        I pray thee, mockery with us
            Now do not make.
    Stout though Castle Maudlen be,
        If thou mock, I will break thy head
            About thee from above.

MARY MAGDALENE:
    I will not be silent from fear;
        I will prove it true what I say
            Before we separate.
    Like as He is King of heaven,
        He is with God the Father,
            On his right side.

The remainder of this brief play continues to express the skepticism of
Thomas the Doubter as each of the apostles in turn acknowledges his belief in the Resurrection. It closes with the Pentecostal appearance of Christ,
although Thomas exits unmoved. James the Greater concludes

    That Jesus Christ is risen again—
        A day is coming that shall tell
            All them that do believe it not!
                (Anon. 1948:129–136)

LORD OF KANATA

A syncretistic religious drama is widely established among the Indians
of Latin America, often involving an account of the Spanish conquest in
which the Indians end by being happily converted to Christianity. A very
unusual case is a drama performed by the Bolivian Quechua for the festival
of the *Lord of Kanata* in the village of Toco (Department of Cochabamba).
The play recounts the death of Atahuallpa and Indian feelings about it,
but remains unregenerately pagan. The play opens with a portent of the
disaster:

INCA: Huaylla Huisa,
        My brother,
    You have lived a long time alone in our mountains
    So that you might be nearer to our Father the Sun.

You who know what those mountains speak,
  Who have heard out of the dry mouths of the sacred mummies
Things which no other man could hear,
  Come close.

HUAYLLA HUISA (*prostrating himself*) : Our Inca,
  Atahuallpa,
Our Father,
  The Sun,
Who illuminates the universe
  And shines upon all, I await you.

INCA : Huaylla Huisa,
  Inca,
I wish you to explain to me what I have dreamed,
  Because that dream still troubles me.
I awakened from it crying
  Like the baby punished by his father.
I dreamed that men of iron,
  Going about the land,
Destroyed our houses
  And robbed our temples.
The sky
  And the hills
Were red
  Like the breast of the bluebird.
Though you should have to run faster than the wind,
  I command you to discover what this may mean.

HUAYLLA HUISA : Our Inca,
  You who command,
I shall fly like the dove;
  I shall sleep in my palace of gold,
And perhaps I can make out
  What you have dreamed.
(*He goes to sleep, then awakens, exclaiming:*)
  Ay! Ay! My beloved Inca,
  My heart is clouded
Because something of great sorrow is sure to happen.
  Your dream will be fulfilled.
    (Goins 1954:269–278)

The interpretation of the diviner is proved correct, and the play ends with
maidens and princesses mourning the death of Atahuallpa.

PEASANT'S DEBT

Despite its involvement in ritual, drama lends itself to unorthodox as well as orthodox uses. In a complex society it comes to express explicit social criticism. The present example is one of the farces (*moḥabbaẓiin*) traditional in Islamic society for private celebrations, in this case a circumcision party in early nineteenth-century Cairo. The genre is commonly vulgar and comic. This particular play was performed before the Pasha, partly as a criticism of the tax collectors.

> (*The farce opens with a dance by two dancers accompanied by two drummers and a piper; they then become the* PEASANTS. *The* GOVERNOR *than asks the other players to enter.*)

GOVERNOR: How much does 'Awad the son of Regeb owe?

PEASANTS: Desire the Christian to look in the register.

GOVERNOR: How much is written against 'Awad the son of Regeb?

COPT: A thousand piasters.

SHEIKH: How much has he paid?

COPT: Five piasters.

SHEIKH: Man, why don't you bring the money?

PEASANT: I haven't any.

SHEIKH: You haven't any! Throw him down!

(*The* PEASANT *is beaten with an inflated piece of intestine.*)

PEASANT: By the honor of thy horse's tail, O Bey! By the honor of thy wife's trousers, O Bey! (*Etc.*)

(*His beating finished, he is imprisoned.*)

WIFE: How art thou?

PEASANT: Do me a kindness, my wife. Take a little wheat cake and some eggs and noodles and go with them to the house of the Christian clerk and appeal to his generosity to get me set at liberty.

(*She goes to the* COPT'*s house with the three baskets.*)

WIFE: Where is the M'allim Hanna the clerk?

PEASANTS: There he sits.

WIFE: O M'allim Hanna, do me the favor to receive these and obtain the liberation of my husband.

COPT: Who is thy husband?

WIFE: The peasant who owes a thousand piasters.

COPT: Bring twenty or thirty piasters to bribe the Sheikh.

(*She goes, returning with the money, giving it to the* SHEIKH.)

SHEIKH: What is this?

WIFE: Take it as a bribe and liberate my husband.

SHEIKH: Very well; go the Governor.

(*She retires to put kohl on her eyes and henna on her hands and feet, then goes to the* GOVERNOR.)

WIFE: Good evening, my master.

GOVERNOR: What dost thou want?

WIFE: I am the wife of 'Awad, who owes a thousand piasters.

GOVERNOR: But what dost thou want?

WIFE: My husband is imprisoned, and I appeal to thy generosity (*she smiles to show that such generosity will be rewarded*) to liberate him.

(*The* GOVERNOR *claims the reward, taking the husband's part, and then liberates the* PEASANT.)
(Lane 1944:394–397)

WAYTHANDAYA

The *Peasant's Debt* is of course a very particular reflection of the tastes and purposes of a highly complex society. Its structure is simple and its general character crude. At another extreme we encounter court dramas of considerable refinement and subtlety. In this Burmese example, the *Waythandaya* of U Pon Nya, the playwright is free to assume that his audience is totally familiar with the plot (taken from one of the Buddhist birth stories) and even with the dramatic treatment of it by other writers. He may therefore address himself to more sophisticated tastes, as in this scene in which the guardian hunter of the exiled hero becomes a vehicle for burlesquing the heroic style of some of the author's dramatic contemporaries.

Scene 3

(*The forest in which* Waythandaya *is living in exile. Enter* SAYTA, *the guardian-hunter, with his dogs.*)

SAYTA: Hark! I hear a strange noise from that hillock on my right. A faint sound, but a strange sound, an ugly noise. What can it be? It is the cry of an elephant in pain? Oh, no. It sounds as if some children are crying in terror. But how can that be? I must go and investigate at once. I will go in haste with my bow and arrow. No, stay! I must be careful, for I do not know what strange enemy I may meet. I must take my hounds with me.... O you enemy over there, you are in for it! Know you not that this is Master Sayta, possessor of a valiant temperament, Master of the gold bow? And this is my domain, this forest is my domain in which I dwell and spend my days in jasmine-happiness. O enemy over there, even if you are the king of elephants come with his army, I am not afraid. My arrow will pierce all mine enemies. Listen, my faithful hounds, hearken, my valiant dog-officers, Cunning-red, Striped-red, Solitary-survivor-of-the-litter, Bitch-leader; your master, this mighty hunter Sayta, this possessor of the big bow, your beloved Generalissimo, thinks that we shall soon find some business for our mighty army this day. So we must form ourselves into battle-array and march on to attack the enemy.

Lieutenant Beautiful-brave and Lieutenant Victor-black, the son-in-law of Bitch-leader, will lead the vanguard. Ensign Dark-raincloud will act as scout and see that the hounds do not march too close together. White-forepaws, son of a wild-dog and nephew of the famous Mistress Yellow, is appointed, because of his ability and bravery, to be the orderly officer for the whole army. Flighty, flirtatious bitches, who have been divorced from their lawful husbands, must march together in the center of the main body, and you, gallant Female-Lieutenant Shoulder-stripes, I promote to be Captainess, and I hold you responsible for the discipline of those divorced bitches. Dogs over there, youths who are wild and still fiery-tempered and who are always showing their ivory teeth, you are placed under the uncle of the hairless Bitch-leader, an importation from Lower Burma, the Pegu-hound, Captain Victor-red, who is now granted letters-patent appointing him to be Commander. You will run swiftly to that hill on our left, usually occupied by eagles. You will hold the hill at all costs, for it will be the base of our operations, and the whole army will retreat to it if things should go against us. Widows, old maids, diseased dogs, mothers with suckling babes, lame, rheumatic, anaemic dogs must not accompany the army. You must remain behind here. Your duty is to guard our huts, and watch the entrances to our kitchen and our dining rooms. See that no stranger breaks in here to steal our treasures, to wit, our cooking utensils, our cooked rice, that half-baked rabbit's leg, and half-consumed wing of chicken. Dog Sapphire, Dog Like-a-cat, though old, do not forget your past glories and past experience in wars. You will please see that discipline and ordered life remain unimpaired in my absence, and guard you well my hut. March on, dogs, to battle and to victory.

(*Exeunt.*) (Aung 1956:253–254)

Although the passage involves something close to parody, U Pon Nya manages to convert the image into one not only elegantly comic but also highly and broadly satirical.

ATSUMORI

The formal *noo* dramas of Japan developed out of temple drama. Characteristically, they feature a priest and an apparition brought together in a place of some significance. In the *Atsumori* of Seami, one of the fifteenth-century founders of *noo*, the priest is on a journey of penance to Ichi no Tani where he had killed in battle the young warrior Atsumori. Naturally, he encounters the spirit of Atsumori, and together, with the help of the Chorus, they relive the battle. The end of the play illustrates very well the structure of *noo*:

ATSUMORI: But on the night of the sixth day of the second month
　　　My father Tsunemori gathered us together.
　　　"Tomorrow," he said, "we shall fight our last fight.
　　　Tonight is all that is left us."
　　　We sang songs together, and danced.

PRIEST: Yes, I remember; we in our siege camp
　　　Heard the sound of music
　　　Echoing from your tents that night;
　　　There was the music of a flute...

ATSUMORI: The bamboo flute! I wore it when I died.

PRIEST: We hear the singing...

ATSUMORI: Songs and ballads...

PRIEST: Many voices...

ATSUMORI: Singing to one measure. (*He dances.*)
　　　First comes the Royal Boat.

CHORUS (*as the* PRIEST RENSEI *and* ATSUMORI *mime the action*):
The whole clan has put its boats to sea.
Atsumori will not be left behind;
He runs to the shore.
But the Royal Boat and the soldiers' boats
Have sailed far away.

ATSUMORI: What can he do?
He spurs his horse into the waves.
He is full of perplexity
And then...

CHORUS: He looks behind him and sees
That Kumagai [that is, the PRIEST RENSEI] pursues him;
He cannot escape.
Then Atsumori turns his horse
Knee deep in the lashing waves,
And draws his sword.
Twice, three times he strikes; then, still saddled,
In close fight they twine; roll headlong together
Amid the surf of the shore.
So Atsumori fell and was slain, but now the Wheel of Fate
Has turned and brought him back.

ATSUMORI *rises from the ground and advances towards the* PRIEST *with uplifted sword.*)

"There is my enemy," he cries, and would strike,
But the other is grown gentle
And calling on Buddha's name
Has obtained salvation for his foe;
So that they shall be reborn together
On one lotus seat.
"No, Rensei is not my enemy.
Pray for me again, oh pray for me again."
                    (Waley 1920:71–73)

The *noo* plays became popular in Japan but remained under the patronage of the court and were mostly performed for the elite. Puppet theater and *kabuki* were more widely disseminated.

BLOOD WEDDING

Court drama remains leisurely and ritualistic, often with very parochial conventions and arbitrary and mechanical techniques. Its object is often the evocation of traditional themes and plots already thoroughly familiar;

and although it aims at beauty, elegance, and subtlety, it does not necessarily seek novelty or surprise. Modern drama differs from it in several respects, but one which is immediately striking is its pace. In the following example, Federico García Lorca's *Blood Wedding*, we are plunged into the situation, apprised of the characters, and drawn forward into the drama with an economy as artful and subtle as it appears simple and realistic:

Act 1

Scene 1

(*A room painted yellow.*)

BRIDEGROOM: (*entering*): Mother.

MOTHER: What?

BRIDEGROOM: I'm going.

MOTHER: Where?

BRIDEGROOM: To the vineyard. (*He starts to go.*)

MOTHER: Wait.

BRIDEGROOM: You want something?

MOTHER: Your breakfast, son.

BRIDEGROOM: Forget it. I'll eat grapes. Give me the knife.

MOTHER: What for?

BRIDEGROOM: (*laughing*): To cut grapes with.

MOTHER (*muttering as she looks for the knife*): Knives. Knives. Cursed be all knives, and the scoundrel who invented them.

BRIDEGROOM: Let's talk about something else.

MOTHER: And guns and pistols and the smallest little knife—even hoes and pitchforks.

BRIDEGROOM: All right.

MOTHER: Everything that can slice a man's body. A handsome man, full of young life, who goes out to the vineyards or to his own olive groves—his own because he's inherited them . . . .

(Graham-Lujan 1941:34)

CHU YUAN

Kuo Mo Jo's five-act drama *Chu Yuan* is a political play. Written in 1942, it expresses in reference to the warring kingdoms of the fourth century B.C. the themes of national unity, official iniquity and popular virtue, and the regenerative power of the (Communist) North over the (Kuomintang) South. To judge from the translation, it is effective drama and subtle propaganda. Chu Yuan is a scholar and sage with an unexplained affinity for the cause of national unity and the sufferings of the common people. He is the victim of a frame-up by the wicked queen and her feudal henchmen, is stripped of his honors and offices, and is abandoned by his students and friends. Only Chan Chuan, his faithful maidservant, proves staunch. They are helped by a Fisherman, but are nonetheless imprisoned and are both to be executed. Chu Yuan echoes the abandoned Lear:

> CHU YUAN (*addressing the wind, thunder and lightning*): Wind! Roar, roar! Roar with all your might! In this pitchy darkness without the light of day everything is asleep, wrapped in deep slumber or dead; it is time for you to roar, for you to roar with all your might! Yet, however you roar, you cannot awake them from their dreams, you cannot bring to life what is dead, you cannot blow away the darkness which weighs heavier than iron upon our eyes.
>
> ...Burst, my body! Burst, universe! Let the red flames leap forth like this wind, like the plunging sea, until all material things, all filth, are consumed in your flames, and let this darkness be consumed, the cloak of all evil! ...

Chan Chuan is rescued by a Guard, but dies from drinking a cup of poisoned wine intended for the hero. The play ends:

> CHU YUAN: Now all is over, what is your name?
>
> GUARD: Master, you do not need to ask my name; I want to follow you forever. Just call me your follower.
>
> CHU YUAN: What do you want me to do now?
>
> GUARD: Master, why do you ask me?
>
> CHU YUAN: Because my life is given me by you and Chan Chuan. Since Chan Chuan is dead I ask you.
>
> GUARD: Master, our country needs you, and China needs you. It is too dangerous here, you must not stay. I come from north of the Han River. If you please, I would like to take you there. We northerners all admire you and have come under your influence.

We love truth and goodness, and resist aggression in defence of our country. Master, we northerners will protect you as we would protect our own eyes, you who are the soul of our country.

CHU YUAN: Very well, I shall do as you say. I am resolved to defend our motherland and our freedom side by side with the people north of the Han River. Quickly change your dress, there is the costume ready. (*Pointing to the watchman's cap and coat.*)

GUARD: That's right, I have been foolish. I never thought of it. It is lucky we have it. (*Changing his dress.*)

(*Fire and smoke become more apparent.*)

CHU YUAN: (*holding high the scroll in his hand*): Ah, Chan Chuan, my daughter, Chan Chuan, my dear pupil, Chan Chuan, my benefactor, you have set the place on fire, you have conquered darkness, you are forever and ever the angel of light! (*Holding the scroll by one end he throws it toward* CHAN CHUAN, *and the scroll unfolds itself over the corpse.*)

(*The curtain descends slowly, and behind it* "The Last Sacrifice" *is heard*):

The rites performed, the wizards strike the urn,
Pass round the sacred herbs, and dance in turn;
With grace the lovely damsels dance and sing:
"Asters for autumn, orchids for the spring,
Through endless years this sacrifice we bring."
(Kuo 1953:109, 111, 122–123)

The development of the character of the hero in this play has many elements of interest. He is a classical scholar who insists on violating the classical norms and writing "vulgar" poetry; he is in the nobility but not of it. His impatience with ideological blindness is thoroughgoing and perhaps in Marxist terms "correct," but he also praises authority and the ancients. And while his value to the nation is stressed, it is he who is saved by the People rather than vice versa. Ideologically the message appears to be that of complex accommodation and the continuity of Chinese tradition rather than doctrinaire Communism.

The range of the dramas quoted in this chapter is considerable, yet they focus upon only a few kinds of role structures. Although these roles by no means represent the full gamut of dramatic forms, it is notable how variably they are treated in this limited sampling. A recurrent theme, for example, is "the enemy," but note the vividness with which each dramatic fragment attains its full measure of specificity of flavor and treatment: the haughty punning of an Ethiopian duke, the refined moralizing of a

Japanese monk, the divinatory fatalism of a Peruvian emperor, the satirical bravado of a Burmese huntsman, the stoic surrender of a Mayan warrior, the ideological conversion of a Chinese scholar, the embattled taunting of a Negro boy. A number of the selections exemplify ritual drama, emphasizing the shaman or priest and the gods or spirits, but, again, with a pronounced specificity. Recall the Malayan tiger shaman spinning his way up the sacred mountain, the Ashanti hyena priest in trance for the good of the community, the Alacaluf seal shaman keeping vigil in his hut over his prayer poles, the Egyptian hawk priest inspecting his estate, the Palaeolithic reindeer shaman dancing the success of the hunt, the Aztec ballplayer jousting with the sun, the Pueblo clown cowering under the whip of the Raingods, the Cornish Magdalen preoccupied with doubt and faith.

Even the recurrent family roles underlying so much of drama—primitive or sophisticated—are exemplified here with an individuality that draws our attention to the real subtlety of role: the nuanced and allusive courtship of the Vietnamese, the resignation of the Quechua son mourning his father, the fatalistic protectiveness of the Spanish mother toward her son, the complete subjection of the Arabic wife to her husband's need, the solicitousness of the Malay son who has found his father, the heavy-handed coquetry of Araucanian peasants at threshing time.

We have now completed the journey we began four chapters ago, through the speech, song, story, and play that make up literature. If the reader is left with some feeling for the enormous range and extreme variations to which the human susceptibility to the metaphor exposes us, he will have arrived at his destination. It remains for us to return to our starting point and to reexamine the questions of causation with which we set out. How can we classify this huge array of seeming spontaneity and inventiveness? How can we understand it? The answer to these questions can be summed up as a matter of style.

Chapter 7

Style

A relationship between two ideas is likely to become established in proportion as the ideas are contextually associated. If they are denotative ideas, the probability of such association is conditioned by the structure of the real world, our perceptual apparatus, and our slow accretion of the conceptual traditions of science. If they are connotative ideas, they have no such anchor. Connotative ideas are associated not because their objective manifestations can be perceived to coexist and overlap, but only because they recur conjointly in speech and thought. Denotative relationships state what is communicable about our perceptions of the world; they are hypotheses. Connotative relationships add the rest of what is communicable—presumed contingencies of one idea upon another springing from the nature of communication itself; they are metaphors.

Sometimes a denotative proposition continues to be asserted long after there is sufficient evidence to reject it. Although such a proposition may have have every appearance of a "scientific" statement, it is in fact only a pseudohypothesis. It is really a metaphor—a "belief," which may be widely shared but which springs from a common tradition rather than from perception. Modern racism, for example, is largely made up of such metaphors. Conversely, it may happen that a metaphorical expression may take the form of a hypothesis merely as one means of expressing a thought, and with no intention whatever of subjecting the relationship implied to scientific validation. An example is Lewis Carroll's "why the sea is boiling hot, and whether pigs have wings."

Despite the complexity and sometime subtlety of the distinction, it can usually be drawn clearly. And once drawn, it has consequences. Two human minds placed in contact with the same denotative relationship are quite likely to conceptualize it in similar ways, provided only that they have a somewhat comparable conceptual background. They are quite unlikely to come up with the same metaphor. Parallel but independent invention of hypotheses is a commonplace of cultural history. Independent invention of metaphors does not appear to occur at all. Metaphors are intrinsically conventional and traditional; they cannot spring from a general similarity of background, but are, rather, dependent upon actual identity—upon real cultural contact. For in the cultural world as in the physical one of which culture is a part, two objects cannot occupy the same space at the same time. The conjunction of ideas responsible for producing a metaphor is a determinate result of a particular location in cultural space. It follows that each location in cultural space is unique.

Let us consider, for example, what is surely one of the most evocative of English poems, "Kublai Khan" by Coleridge. Coleridge reports that he dreamed this poem in visual images while under the influence of an opiate. He did not, however, create it out of whole cloth. J. L. Lowes (1927) has plausibly or certainly identified the following sources among the poet's own notes and readings of the period:

In Xanadu did Kublai Khan
A stately pleasure dome decree

> "In Xamdu (Xandu) did Cublai Can build a stately palace ... and in the midst thereof a sumptuous house of pleasure ..." (Samuel Purchas *Purchas His Pilgrimage.* London, 1617:472.)
> "... an house of pleasure of the ancient kings of Kachemire ..." "These cabinets, which are in a manner made like domes ..." (Churchill *A Collection of Voyages and Travels.* London, 1747:VII:238; VIII:229.)

Where Alph the sacred river, ran
Through caverns measureless to man

> "... there is a rumor that Alpheus bears his stream hither from Elis by hidden ways under the sea; and that he now at your mouth, Arethusa, is mingled in the Sicilian waves." (Virgil *Aeneid.* III:694–696.)
> "... as well as her immediate utility in swelling the waters of that sacred river [the Nile] ..." (Thomas Maurice *The History of Hindostan.* London, 1795:I:102.)
> "... subterraneous rivers, which wander in darkness beneath the surface of the earth, by innumerable doublings, windings and secret labyrinths ..." (William Bartram *Travels through*

North and South Carolina, Georgia, East and West Florida, etc.
Philadelphia, 1791:226.)
"... fountains of the Nile, fountains which it is impossible
to fathom ..." (Herodotus *History.* II:28, 31.)

Down to a sunless sea.

"I do not, indeed, suppose that you will long hesitate to believe
that there are underground rivers and a hidden sea.... And
what are you to say when you see the Alphaeus ... sink in
Achaia and having crossed the sea, pour forth in Sicily ..."
"the depths of the earth contain a vast sea with winding shores.
I see nothing to prevent or oppose the existence of a beach down
there in the obscurity...." (Seneca *Quaestiones Naturales.* VI:
vii, 1–3; VI:vii, 5.)

Metaphors are conditioned by experience, but the predominant influence
is the experience of other metaphors.

The fundamental task of the student of lore is thus the description
and analysis of its very complex structure, which is the structure of all
culture itself in its connotative aspects. There are many facets to this
structure, but perhaps the most general term descriptive of their range and
scope is *style*. We can study style as the pattern of elements in a particular
language or culture area, or in a particular period of time; we can analyze
it into elements and examine their provenience and distribution; we can
differentiate styles by context, by content or by form, and relate them to
various of the dimensions of culture history or (without contradiction)
individual experience. In a commentary on the personal style of Giraudoux,
Valency remarks somewhat lyrically:

No man can establish title to an idea—at the most he can only
claim possession. The stream of thought that irrigates the mind of
each of us is a confluent of the intellectual river that drains the whole
of the living universe. But a man's style is intrinsic and private with
him like his voice or his gesture, partly a matter of inheritance,
partly of cultivation. It is more than a pattern of expression. It is
the pattern of the soul (Valency 1958:ix).

The point is well taken. There is every reason why a particular individual should have a recognizable style, for every individual occupies a
unique position in the web of culture, and the patterned character of his
experience by virtue of that fact is thoroughly likely to impose upon his
personality and his mode of expression a systematically distinctive quality.

Any literate American can identify by author, for example, the following particularly individual style:

There is one form of life to which I unconditionally surrender,
Which is the feminine gender. . . .
Because the proportions of feminine social chitchat are constant always;
One part of sitting down in the sitting room to four parts standing up
    saying good-by in foyers and hallways,
Which is why I think that when it comes to physical prowess,
Why woman is a wow, or should I say a wowess.
                    (Nash 1944:111–112)

The distinctive elements in Nash's poems are few and simple, and none of them—not the outrageous pun-rhymes nor the wild variations in length of line nor the curious blend of literate and slang vocabulary—is in fact unique. The effect of these mechanisms, together with other features (choice of theme, psychological attitudes) is nonetheless a highly identifiable pattern, analogous to the literary "signature" of other individual writers. There is nothing ineffable about such a style; it can, in fact, be described with some precision and completeness.

    Style of this sort is not restricted to writers. We can readily recognize kindred features in the characteristic modes of expression of anyone we know well. Individual style is certainly a general reality, and it can be identified and recognized by more or less detailed study. Where the facts are known, it can also be related successfully to known influences on the individual—literary and psychological. Although we possess a considerable fund of information on this point for many major writers of modern times—particularly in the "life and times" biography—we have very little comparable material on the composers of ancient literature and folklore. It is safe to surmise that the mechanisms of the formation of personal style have operated also in ancient times and among primitive people, but our control of the facts is unlikely ever to permit us to examine the process in that field.

    Perhaps the most direct information we can acquire on the formation of personal style and the influences that bear on it can be obtained from the study of dreams. If anywhere, in the pattern of dreams we may find purely personal metaphors. The study of dreams is somewhat similar to the study of a foreign literature in a language one does not understand. We require an interpreter (the dreamer) and a denotative translation (his associations to the dream symbols). Any account of a dream is, of course, a verbal description of an experience that may or may not have been importantly verbal, and some distortion is inevitable on this account. In a favorable case, however, dream metaphors can be reliably reported and translated, and we can then specify their meaning even when they are personal, as in the following series of metaphors from one of Freud's dreams. The translations are Freud's:

    great hall:Bellevue (country house)
    number of guests:wife's friends
    Irma (a patient):wife's friend
    your own fault:my fault
    I am startled:I hope
    she is choked:somebody else is choked
    she is pale and puffy:somebody else (my wife) is pale and puffy
    like a woman who has false teeth:is a woman who has false teeth
    mouth opens readily:would talk easily
    diphtheria:daughter's illness
    Matilda (daughter):Matilda (patient)
    scabby turbinal bones:danger to my own health
    quickly call Dr. M.:I am medically incompetent
    Dr. M. looks quite unlike his usual self:he is somebody else
    Dr. M. is shaven and limps:Dr. M. is his brother
    on the (patient's) left shoulder:on my left shoulder
    I can feel in spite of the dress:I can feel on my own body
    Dr. M. talks nonsense:Dr. M. is a fool
    it doesn't matter:you are not at fault
    injections given rashly:your (and my) incompetence
    dirty syringe:medical incompetence (Freud 1938:*passim*)

There are only a fraction of the associative meanings in a single dream, but they may be considered representative of the metaphors springing from individual experience. Not all these images are completely idiosyncratic (e.g., he/she:somebody else), nor is there any reason to suppose that dream metaphors should be so restricted.

Personal styles have doubtless existed always and everywhere, but they are nowhere the only stylistic systematization. Just as the communicative uniqueness and isolation of the individual lead to a characteristic structuring of his expression, just so the social differentiation of mankind into communicatively isolated or partly isolated groups conduces to a wide variety of cultural styles. Much of our information on these is and must be folkloristic. For purposes of cultural analysis, individual styles may be viewed as variations on culturally given themes. Ogden Nash could not have used rhyme had he been an American Indian bard of the fourteenth century.

This construal should not be taken to imply that the individual never innovates—never adds creatively to the store of cultural ideas. On the contrary, he is the only possible source of innovation. But as a matter of quantity or probability he successfully communicates novelty very little and very rarely. He reproduces tradition very much and very often. Most of what gives form to individual styles is a result of selection among pre-existing cultural ideas. Our view of creativity in modern times is unduly distorted by the enormous wealth of past lore to which the modern writer has direct access. The mere juxtaposition of two old themes may (and frequently does) pass for creativity. We can study the process more safely and in some respects more accurately in the reaches of history not yet confused by world-wide colonization and literacy.

New metaphors constantly arise—not perhaps as often as the worshippers of the "creative artist" would have us believe, but they do occur. Sprung first from individuals, they may then, under favorable conditions, come to be characteristic of social groups. Some folklorists have tended to pay particular attention to the bodies of lore that have come to be characteristic of the familistic "tribes" of mankind, the ethnic groups or communities *sensu strictu* that tend to share a tightly organized network of communication by virtue of intermarriage, a common religion and political organization, a localized economic life, and a common language. Such a group tends to share as a group a store of metaphorical ideas different from those of even adjacent peoples.

Something of the history of some ideas of this sort has already been traced. In theory, the history of metaphor is virtually infinitely complex, for every element or pattern of elements must necessarily have a partially unique history. A complete description of such complexity can, of course, never be written. Every particular idea must of necessity have its own origin and its own communicability, but our grasp of these particulars can hardly be more than partial even in a favorable case.

In tracing the stylistic features of literature, then, historians, anthropologists, and folklorists have legitimately undertaken studies of the most diverse kinds. The fundamental process that underlies and unifies them is that of culture—of communication itself. The specification of the history of lore inherently requires description of distributions of elements not only in space and time but also in relation to one another. A morphology of structure (that is, a taxonomy of style) must achieve just such a description. Enough has been said to indicate that such a taxonomy must be both individual and social. There is such a thing as Shakespearean style, just as there is an Italian style, and both types of usage are well established. Equally familiar are the generic terms descriptive of historical periods. Archaic, classical, humanist, romantic, bardic, neoclassical, revolutionary, *fin-de-siècle*, heroic, Victorian, Dadaist, Vedic, Republican, Renaissance, scholastic, and like terms reflect, often with some precision, the degree of stylistic distinctiveness of particular periods and the degree of haziness of our knowledge about them. Such terms have a considerable utility for well-documented and well-digested periods of history. They are notably less illuminating in relation to ancient or prehistoric times, where they are likely to be merely suggestive of true history or merely fanciful.

Very broad stylistic distinctions of this type have rarely been used with consistency or precision. Indeed, they are not often defined, but tend to grow up rather by general agreement (with consequently general disagreement). Philosophers of history have been fond of using (and fonder of coining) such terms to define historical epochs typifying particular turning points or configurations in history, and very often they have leaned especially on literary history for their interpretations. Style terms like Dionysiac (Nietzsche), Faustian (Spengler), Undifferentiated (Northrup), Hellenic (Toynbee), or Sensate (Sorokin) are at least metaphors easily adapted to literary criticism. We cannot but be grateful for any enrichment of our sensitivity and taxonomic vocabulary in this enormously complex area. It may be noted that work at this very general level has yielded little or no consensus as yet, but it is emphatically worthwhile to have a vocabulary descriptive of general configurations, whether or not we are prepared to be precise about them.

Style is a communicative phenomenon. A stylistic similarity can be attained only by people who are in contact with each other. Literary critics and others frequently use the same style terms to compare trends and authors who are not in any significant sense in contact, but I believe it is fair to say that the sense of such comparisons is usually metaphorical. When they are not so intended, I believe them to be in error. Such a usage is the description of an American Indian style as "classical" or of an Oriental one as "Gothic."

It may plausibly be argued that similarity in social or psychological circumstances could give rise to stylistic similarity. It could indeed. But does it in fact do so? The cultural development of the New World appears in many ways to duplicate the development of the Old (with some lag); but despite the many parallelisms, there is no similarity in their lore that cannot be plausibly attributed to their archaic contact before the Americas were peopled, or to their rare and limited contacts since. It is in fact important that such widespread Old World ideas as syllabic verse or the epic (*pace* Radin) appear to be entirely lacking in the Americas, many parts of which are surely sophisticated enough by any criterion to have exploited such ideas, had they but run across them. The principle of limited possibilities can hardly be invoked in a theory of metaphor, because the possibilities of metaphor have no known limitations. Societies of a generally similar degree of complexity may bear many resemblances to each other (in social differentiation, general technology, political centralization) but they are not noticeably alike in their lore. Similarly, individuals with similar psychiatric problems and similar experiences express themselves in symptomatic and sometimes colorful language, but can we document that they ever independently have identical dreams?

Parallel but independent developments in different individuals or in different cultures can and do occur, but they result from circumstances more constraining than the metaphor. These circumstances are environmental and sensory; and whether they are ecological or physiological, they constitute an essential part of all experience. Two cultures may discover independently the utility of crop rotation, just as two men may dream they have a headache, and the discoveries or the dreams may be very similar, because the environing background is similar and similarly perceived: they are limited by real possibilities. But two cultures will not discover the same gods, and two men will not dream the same paradise, because the only limits to the attributes of these are those of the extant symbols available in each case. An occasional chance identity could conceivably occur, but it should be astronomically rare. It appears in fact to be so.

Stylistic similarities then differ from social similarities (insofar as these are ecologically conditioned) and from psychological similarities (insofar as these are physiologically conditioned). They are not, as has often been argued, intrinsically subjective, nor are they confined to some mystical plane of untouchable esthetics. They can be quite rigorously examined in terms of their thoroughly real and material manifestations in words and actions. They are simply similarities in patterns of symbols, particularly pure indicators of the communicative process.

In a general sense styles are established through the structure creating cultural process within the individual, and among individuals with a socially shared background. It follows that in the complete literature of a people there will be individual styles but there will also be styles characteristic of each social group, distinctive in proportion to the group's distinctiveness, elaborated in proportion to the intensity of its common tradition. The stylistic structures of literature are cognate with the organized features of personality and society. The ultimate source of the structure is in all cases the same: the intensive redundancy of social tradition— of culture. This redundancy can be traced to the peculiarly human ordering of individual relations through the endogamy and exogamy of family life.

The most intensive kind of redundancy that can be generated within the framework of human biology through specification of mating patterns would be that provided by preferential brother-sister mating. The most intensive kind actually known to occur ethnographically is preferential cross-cousin mating of the Australian type. Such a system results in the creation of a cultural tradition almost devoid of segmentation (that is, except for age and sex). Family tradition is coeval with the tradition of the residential, political, economic, and religious group—homogeneous and intense. Any long-term operation of a preferential marriage system should in theory lead to a quite unified cultural structure with a literature differentiated by age, sex, and residential group (band). In its simplest form, native Australian literature presents precisely these features.

As recorded, the most elaborated Australian lore is principally the property of old men, and in theory it is kept secret from women and uninitiated boys. Young men are initiated in these mysteries in seclusion at the time of puberty through formal schooling in the myths, with traditional songs, dancing, and ritual, while the women are "frightened off" with bull roarers. The women's lore is less well known, in part because of the prevalence of male ethnographers, but the mysteries of menstruation and childbirth are at least as awesome to Australian men as the bullroarer is supposed to be to their wives. The preferential marriage rule evidently discourages the development of a courtship literature, and, in fact, none is reported. The content of the lore of uninitiated Australian children is almost certainly different from that of the adult lores, but is not well reported.

Even in a primitive context, then, we may discern with some clarity the influence of social upon literary structure. And the source of this structure is equally clearly that of the precultural physical and biological matrix from which it springs (space and time, age and sex) transformed by that peculiar form of energy transmission, cultural communication. It is perhaps natural to begin a comprehensive survey of styles in primitive literature with those that bear on infancy, everywhere a specialized cultural or social situation.

INFANCY

The communication of infants is primarily with their mothers, and its literary characteristics are those of the lullaby, baby talk, pet names, simple games. The communication is notably one sided, but certainly the baby's responsiveness is a major factor in determining the communication's form and content, and there are some general similarities of infant lore around the world. It may be useful to distinguish the lore of infants from that of mothers, for although the former is dependent upon the latter and derives from it, it is much more restricted and necessarily more specific to the context. Much of this earliest kind of communication is gestural, and it is likely that the first metaphors that the child attempts to communicate are in that form. A fairly clear example might be peek-a-boo or other similar teasing play (mock feeding, "chase-me," and the like), games in which the child acts out with some awareness a primitive metaphor ("I am not here"; "I am not hungry"; "You can't catch me")—metaphoric precisely because of an infant understanding that it is an extended meaning. Such play as this is quite different from instrumental behavior, and in its fully elaborated form it is specifically human, though partially anticipated among some of the more playful animals.

CHILDHOOD

As the child learns language, he enters rapidly into the more complex lore of later childhood, echoing the literature of parents and playmates and eventually helping to shape the specific traditions of children. Children's lore is very highly structured. Its general repertoire includes names, sayings, riddles, jokes, and oaths in prose, an extensive poetry, some brief narrative, and a good deal of ritual play, thus generally paralleling adult lore, with which it is closely intertwined. Children have a good deal of contact with each other on planes not matched among their parents, and the result is a partial autonomy of their lore. There appears to be no warrant for assuming, as some authorities have, that adults have no part in the perpetuation of this lore, but much of it is sustained by transmission from child to child, and that is sufficient to give it a distinctive style.

The world of children, as reflected in their lore, has an institutional organization all its own. Age distinctions are extremely important, being generally associated with important differences in size and ability, and an enormous proportion of childish lore can be interpreted as essentially didactic and initiatory, introducing the younger child to the sophistications of the next age grade. One-upmanship, or having the last word, is a crucial feature, and there are long sequences of the type:

> What fer?
> Cat's fur to make kittens' breeches.

There are also didactic dicta (Funny "ha-ha" or funny "peculiar"?) and stock toppers ("Gosh, news! Now tell us the one about the three bears!"), and sophisticated traps for the unwary:

> *Child 1*: J'ai monté un escalier.
> *Child 2*: Comme moi.
> *Child 1*: Je suis entré dans la chambre.
> *Child 2*: Comme moi.
> (And so on, to:)
> *Child 1*: Il y avait une grosse bête.
> *Child 2*: Comme moi.

At later ages, children make constant use of riddles and pseudoriddles with the same pecking-order implications:

> Can the orange box? No, but the tomato can.

This kind of lore can be collected in quantity from any group of children, and is naturally age-graded in sophistication on a scale leading later to the shady Boy Scout ditty and the dirty limerick.

The differentiation of sex roles in children's lore is very markedly age-graded, early inculcating modesty:

> One o'clock at the waterworks. [Your pants are open.]

And:

> I see London. I see France.
> I see (somebody's) underpants. [Your skirt's up.]

Later on, the kiss and the pulling of hair become diffuse but important symbols of the battle of the sexes. Kissing is to be avoided at all costs by small boys, but later it becomes fashionable to have a "crush" on a girl and even to write notes stamped SWAK ("sealed with a kiss")—a primrose path lined with valentines that leads eventually to "Post Office" and fraternity parties. Kissing is powerful magic. If a little girl kisses her elbow, she will turn into a boy.

Children's sex lore is subject to extreme variation from culture to culture. In many cultures, for example, children play at copulation from very early ages, and even within Western culture there is far less sexual innocence among children than most folklore collections suggest. A truly comprehensive understanding of childish lore has tended to be lost in the subdivision of the subject among folklorists, psychologists, and anthropologists, and we have no really thorough summary for any culture.

If the coyness of many folklorists about sex (and particularly about infantile sexuality) has left us with a very partial documentation of that lore, no such inhibition exists in connection with family relations. Yet children's lore about kinship is quite remarkably scattered. A really intensive collection and analysis would be enormously valuable. Many of the examples of the genre are as sibylline as this Welsh poem:

> Taid a nain yn rhedeg râs
> I fyny'r ffordd fain ac at y plâs,
> Syrthiodd nain ar draws y stôl,
> "Ha! Ha!" ebe taid, "Mae nain ar ôl."

> (Grandfather and Grandmother running a race
> Up the narrow road and to the big house.
> Grandmother fell over a stool.
> "Ha! Ha!" cried Grandfather, "Grandmother is behind.")
> (Opie and Opie 1959:29)

The economics of childhood may involve quite elaborate arrangements for claiming possession ("dibs on . . .") or keeping it ("Indian giver!"), for underwriting or solemnizing bets or sealing bargains, and for swapping goods and presenting gifts. The laws of treasure trove are respected ("finders keepers"), loans are distinguished from gifts and purchases ("for keeps"), and bargaining may be precise and ruthless ("just see if I let you use my . . ."). Much of this lore is extensively documented among European children but is virtually unexplored elsewhere.

Childhood religion is equally complex, and is replete with charms, omens, and magic (as in wart curing). Secrets may be guaranteed by the most sacred oaths ("cross my heart and hope to die"), and luck, success, or courage may be ensured by spells ("knock on wood") or precautionary ritual ("needles and pins"). The rules of many games themselves may become ritualized, even to the point of being tied to the calendar. Quiche Indian children play a wax disk game something like tiddlywinks, but it is confined to Lent. Kite flying is similarly seasonal in the Orient, and Western children have a variety of calendrical rites from overturning privies on Hallowe'en to artful lying on April 1.

Sometimes the children's lore is closely linked to the adult religion. All Burmese children are familiar with an A-B-C rhyme for remembering the initial letters customarily used for personal names of people born under the eight constellations of the week—tiger, lion, dragon, rat, tusker, tuskless elephant, guinea pig, and griffin:

> Ka, kha, ga gha, nga, Taninla.
> Sa, hsa, za, zha, nya, Ainga.
> Ta, hta, da, dha, na, Sane.
> Pa, hpa, ba, bha, ma, Kyathabade.
> La, wa, Boddahu.
> Ya, ra, Yahu.
> Tha, ha, Thankkya.
> A, Taninganwe.
>
> (K, kh, g, gh, ng, Monday.
> S, hs, z, zh, ny, Tuesday.
> T, ht, d, dh, n, Saturday.
> P, hp, b, bh, m, Thursday.
> L and w, Wednesday morning.
> Y and r, Wednesday night.
> Th and h, Friday.
> A, Sunday.)
>   (Shway Yoe 1963:4–6)

The associations are important, because the constellations affect temperament, causing people to be, respectively, (1) jealous, (2) honest, (3) quarrelsome, (4) mild, (5) short-tempered, (6) very short-tempered, (7) talkative, or (8) parsimonious.

The politics of childhood is very complex, with highly polarized hero worship and axiomatic group rejection of formal adult authority (for example, of the teacher). This is accompanied by strong codes of peer-group loyalty and very strict rules of precedence and pecking order, both enforced by physical coercion as well as strong sentiment. Elaborate codes and ritual govern fighting, taunting, truce, and sanctuary ("King's X"). Parts of these traditions have become organized in proverbial sayings, nicknames, songs, and play, such as the insulting names for school meals, sanctioned truancy, or customarily licensed pranks.

Group organization of clubs and gangs among children may involve strongly focused partisanship (for example, fan clubs) and complex in-group traditions. An example of the result is the secret language, an invention known throughout the literate world and perhaps beyond, as the following examples of "pig Latin" (from my notes unless noted otherwise) illustrate.

> *Amharic*: 'Üvalalohu; ühedalohu. ("I am eating; I am going.")
> *Secret*: Hulolava'ü; hulodahe'ü.

> *Arabic*: Ana haruh a sinema. ("I am going to the movie.")
> *Bird Language*: Azanaza hazarazuh aza sinizema.

> *Bulgarian*: Dobre doshel! ("Welcome!")
> *Secret*: Pedopebre pedopeshel!

> *Chinese* (Szechuanese dialect) Wei shun moh ni bu lai? ("Why don't you come?")
> *Secret*: Lĕ wei lĕ shun lĕ moh li ni lu bu lĕ lai?

> *Danish*: Jeg ønsker at ga hjem med det samme. ("I want to go home at once.")
> *Secret*: Gejay rønskeay taay agay mhjeay demay teday esammay.

> *Dutch*: Wij hebben een aardig feestje. ("We are having a nice party.")
> *P-Taal*: Wepij hepebbepen epeen epaardepig fepestjepe.

> *English*: Do you understand?
> *Arague*: Daraguw yaraguw aragundagerstaragand? ("Egg" and "Thegegg" are dialects of "Arague"; all three are from England.)
> *Back Slang*: Od yuwoy dnatsrednu? (England and U.S.)
> *Double Talk*: Duduw yuyuw unundedersastatanandad? (U.S.)
> *Kemake*: Dikiokimeyk waykiokiukimeyk yukienkidikiikiarkieskiti-kieykienkidikimeyk? (U.S.)
> *Op*: Dopuw yopuw opundoperstopand? (U.S.)
> *"Pidgin"*: Dague yaguw agundagerstagand? (England)
> *Pig Latin*: Ude uye underye-andste? (England and U.S.)

Finnish: Mikä tämä on? ("What is this?")
Kontti: Koka-mintti koma-täntti kon-ontti?

French: Comment allez vous? ("How are you?")
Langage: Colimentli aliléli vouli?
Russe: Coskimentski askiléski vouski?

German: Wir stehen in der Küche. ("We are in the kitchen.")
Secret: Wirirlefir steehlefeh ininlefin dererlefer Küülefücheelefe.
Swiss German: Kannsch du d Flügesproch reden? ("Can you speak
  Fly Language?")
Fliegesprache: Kamça dumça flümçaspromça remça?

Greek: Éla stó spiti mou. ("Come to my house.")
Korakístika ("crow language"): Ékelaka stoko spikitiki moukou.

Gujerati: Toong avi sakse? ("Can you come?")
Secret: Toongsmoong asmavi sasmakse?

Hindi: Tu aa sake gi? ("Can you come?")
Cha Bhasya ("cha language"): Chatu chaaa chasachake chagi?

Icelandic: Aetlar thú út í kvöld? ("Are you going out tonight?")
Secret: Aessma thússma ússm í kvessma?

Italian: La donna è mobile. ("Woman is fickle.")
Cinese: Li dinni i mibili.
Lingua Segreta: Lander daizonnander eiz monderbaizilender.

Japanese: Watakushi wa ame ga hoshii. ("I want some candy.")
Sa no Kotoba ("sa language"): Wa no satakushi wa a no same ga
  ho no sashii.

Magyar: Akarsz moziba menni? ("Do you want to go to the movies?")
Secret: Avakavarsz movozivibava mevenivi?

Marquesan: Pehea oe? ("Where are you going?")
E'o Hu'i ("language turned over"): Peheiherea ooiroe?
Uhi Tua: Hepea oe? (Handy 1930:19)

Polish: Ja idę do lasu. ("I'm going to the woods.")
Secret: Janwa inwidęnwę donwo lanwasunwu.

Rumanian: Eu vorbese păsăreşte. ("I speak bird language.")
Păsăreşte ("bird language"): Eupu voporbepescupu păpăsăpărep-
  eştepe.

Spanish: ¿Cómo está usted, hijo? ("How are you, son?")
Aguara: ¿Coformófor escachustaguara uscachustescachú, izimir-
  jófor? (Venezuela)

Campana: ¿Campanacocampanamo campanestá campanusted, campanijo? (Venezuela)
Cifra: ¿Cofomofo efestafa ufustefed, ifijofi? (New Mexico)
Cuti: ¿Cocutimocuti ecutistacuti ucutistecuti, icutijocuti? (Venezuela)

Tagalog: Waláa na siyá ng kwaal ta. ("He has no more money.")
Baliktád ("upside down"): Laawa na yaasi ng taakwal. (Conklin 1956:138)

Telegu: Nivu vasthaava? ("Will you come?")
Ka Bhasha ("k language"): Kanikavu kavakasthaakava? (Similar forms in *ka-* were reported by the same Telegu-speaking informant to exist in Tamil and Kannada, but a Tamil-speaking informant did not recall the custom.)

Vietnamese: Tôi ăn bánh mì thịt heo. ("I eat bread with him.")
Tiêng Láng ("secret language"): Tăn ôi bí mành theo hit. (The ´ is a rising tone; ` is falling; . is low; the other syllables have even tone.)

The antiquity of "pig Latin" is unknown, but it may be relevant that a somewhat similar adult use of language is found in the *vakrokti* or "twisted language" of certain late Sanskrit epics.

ADOLESCENCE

The world of adults is variously set off from the world of children, and in most societies the transition is made by a more or less structured initiation. This may be gradual or abrupt, sudden and intensive, or continuous over many years. Often it is ritualized. The effect in any case is to introduce the child to the more esoteric lore of the adult in a manner consonant with his status and the pattern of his society. This initiatory lore is by no means restricted to adolescence. We have seen that much of the general lore of children is designed to school them in all manner of adult patterns, from ethics, morals, and etiquette to the names of Cabinet offices, sex roles, and the arts of competition. But the final stage is entered at puberty, and however it is treated, the adolescent experience will convert the boy into a man, the girl into a woman.

Because adolescence is not always institutionally set apart, its literature is not always distinctive. But in societies in which adolescents are differentiated, so is their literature. Our own is a good example, and presents a marked specificity of rhetoric (teenage slang), of songs (pop, neofolk, dance), of drama (elaborately organized sports, contests, club rituals, rallies, parades, panty raids, pranks), and of narrative (mostly jokes and short humorous pieces).

Formalization of the transition from childhood to adult status often leads to the formation of relatively stable associational groups. In primitive societies these may include the somewhat ephemeral "bush schools," long-range age grades, or various kinds of clubs, public and secret. The lore of these groups varies accordingly, attaining a maximally distinctive structure in groups that are formally exclusive and esoteric, usually sexually segregated organizations of some permanence and intensity of participation. Often there is considerable ritualization of the lore of initiation, and in sophisticated societies it may involve a great complexity of institutional settings and, consequently, of divergent styles. The schools of literate cultures are much more heterogeneous than the age grades of primitive ones and present a correspondingly heterogeneous literary face.

The object of initiation is everywhere partially a matter of introducing children to the more esoteric lores of adults. The stylistic diversification in even the simplest societies reflects the distinct organization of the sexes, and in more complex cases it may be subject to elaboration along numerous other lines as well. Not all societies "shelter" their children as we do, but initiation into adult status everywhere focuses upon the attainment of sexual maturity, and esoteric traditions universally include a phrasing of the mystique of sex. But the essence of becoming a full person is more global than sex. It comprises the whole problem of psychological identification, and both the organization and the literature of initiation reflect the full complexity of this sociopsychological transition. We know much less adequately how to read a Sioux vision quest story than, say, Joyce's *Portrait of the Artist as a Young Man*, but they are products of very similar dimensions of human experience, however different their contexts and styles.

Like many Indians of the American West, the Pimas paid little attention to male initiation, but a girl was felt to be a danger at the time of first menstruation, and she was initiated with four days of seclusion followed by songs, feasting, and dancing. The mood is captured in one of these ritual songs:

> Hurry and come forth,
>   Hurry and come forth.
> Already beginning to descend
>   Is the echoing night.
> Already beginning to descend
>   Is the echoing night. (*Repeat four times.*)
> Virgin woman,
>   Virgin woman,
> She is not sleepy,

She is indifferent there.
She is awake there,
    Awake and thoughtful in the night. (*Repeat.*)
            (Russell 1908:330)

Because of the circumstances of its composition, this song reflects the ideology of female initiation rather than the girl's feelings.

As our thoughtful Pima girl implies, there is much more to maturity than sex. But the leitmotif of the style that is specific to adolescence tends to be sexual, for everywhere at least some part of the primary meaning of maturity is sexual. In the nature of things, however, there can be no absolute disjunction between adult and adolescent sex lore, and in most societies there is more marked separation of the two sexes from one another than of teenagers from their parents. Patterns of sexual reticence and frequently strong taboos reinforce this tendency, but the result is a lore, not of age, but of sex.

SEX

The people of Ifaluk in the Caroline Islands have an extensive oral literature which includes oratory, long narrative cycles in prose and poetry, and various shorter genres of poetry: laments, invocations, and serenades. Each form is contextually specific. The myths are narrated and orations are given by chiefs; laments are performed at wakes; invocations of different forms are performed by men and women in relation to community ritual; serenades are sung to men by women. These genres are given different names in Ifaluk. Other forms may be isolated that are not singled out by the native terminology: men's work songs, storm spells and navigational songs, and perhaps others.

The love songs (*bwarux*) are a salient feature of this literature. They are composed by women to be sung (and danced to) for their lovers in private. Certain important aspects of these songs are more or less determined by this fact. The lives of men and women on Ifaluk are in many ways quite distinct. But it is no accident that the love songs do not attempt to communicate the structure of the women's world. Such obvious preoccupations as children, childbirth, gardening, and household work receive scarcely a mention. What does figure largely in the songs is the part of experience that men and women share—their love life, their common exposure to gossip, their fears of separation and joys of reunion. In a general way, they are like love songs anyplace.

Certain other themes in Ifaluk love songs require closer attention. The man's body is a frequent topic; the woman's body is rarely mentioned.

The man's fishing and sailing are often discussed, but women's occupations almost never. The man's costume—his tattooing, his loincloth, his comb and plumes—are extensively described. Women's clothing is rarely treated. Men's gatherings at the canoe house are figured, but women's gatherings in the cookhouse are not. The songs are markedly assymmetrical in this respect. It is not hard to see why tattooing, flowers, bathing, trysting places, perfume, and ghost fear should figure in a love poetry concerned with nighttime romances in deserted places on a coral atoll. But why the men's world should so dominate a poetry composed by women is a puzzle.

On closer inspection, we can see that it is a woman's view of the world of men that emerges. Technicalities of navigation, canoe building, or fishing are altogether lacking. Esoteric religious ideas are not mentioned. In short, truly masculine lore is not to be found in these songs any more than the delicate ladies of the troubadors represent the earthier realities of feminine life in the high Middle Ages. What does appear is a precise reflection of the part of experience common to men and women—ambiguous because the sharing is ambiguous.

When an Ifaluk woman tells her lover that he is like a man-of-war bird, the expression is more than flattery. The bird is to her a symbol of the man's seaward flights. To the man on the other hand, the bird signifies proximity to land, and hence return. The same bird may thus be a "sea bird" and a "land bird" at once, uniting in a single ambiguous metaphor two quite different perspectives at precisely the point where masculine and feminine experiences merge, the point of reunion. Many another metaphor has likely been dropped from Ifaluk poetry because it lacked this resonance.

In this perspective, the loading of Ifaluk love poetry with a preoccupation with the male would appear to imply a certain narcissistic egoism in Ifaluk men, but it also implies the acceptability of this to Ifaluk women. A detailed consideration of the poetic structure would no doubt give us a much more precise grasp of the roots of these attitudes, but we may guess that the basic process would be similar to that operating in the metaphor of the bird.

Ifaluk love poetry is highly structured, but it is certainly less so than many kinds of literature elsewhere, for there is diffuseness as well as structure to the context in which it is produced. If it were truly the case that these love poems were recited in secret by one woman to one man, we would certainly expect them to be much more individual in style. Actually, they circulate somewhat clandestinely among both men and women, and in some cases they have almost certainly come to Ifaluk from other islands. They have somewhat stylized poetic flourishes that certainly would never have been independently developed by each woman separately, and some of the otherwise puzzling features of their structure are almost surely because of their quite wide circulation in Ifaluk society. It follows that in addition to individual variation (no two love songs are supposed to be exactly alike) there is also a diffuse variability in structure and imagery caused by the diffuse pattern of communication of the songs.

All Ifaluk lovers have reason to be preoccupied with gossip; some have cause for concern with ghost fear; perhaps only an isolated couple shares the memory of a particular trysting place:

The *wut* tree grows off by itself (Burrows 1963:220).

In general, then, Ifaluk poetry reflects almost precisely the degree and kind of structure of the sociocultural context that produced it. And, of course, this context is as unique in culture as the poems are unique in literature. Here is one of them:

I wait in my house
Near the canoe house where my lover is.
At last we catch each other's eyes;
He signals with a finger.

I sit in my house.
I don't like the talk that's going round;
I won't heed what they say.
I am the blossom of the flowering tree;
That man looks at me
And dashes for me like a voracious fish.
He has such fine eyes!
We are like twin coconut trees.
I don't care for the others who come;
I love him, no matter what anyone says.

My love is reserved for him.
I won't take off my skirt for anyone else.
I don't give out my love; I keep it for him.
It belongs to that man like a soaring man-of-war bird,
That man like a far-ranging gannet.

He said to me,
"Let's go into the woods, quickly so no one will see!
Go to some open place by the shore,
Far from any house, where we can lie together."

I throw myself back and look up;
Out there you can see the sky.
He takes off my belt of beads,
And rolls up my skirt, striped black and red.

He says my thighs are white
Like a snowy tern.
He wants to lie with me.
We turn toward each other
And rub noses.
He strokes my thighs,
Says my legs are big and round,
And my buttocks, too;
He thinks them beautiful.
He likes the inside of my thighs,
And all about is white, he says,
As if it had been painted.
He thinks me a beautiful girl,
Whiter where my skirt covers me.
He forgets work, thinking of my body.
He loves me madly,
And I love him, too.

And then, one day,
He put paint on his face
And on his beard,
Drawing the lines straight.
His eyes and eyebrows are beautiful;
There is no one else like him.
When all men are together, he stands out among them
Like a great sea bird.
    (Burrows 1963:234)

Not all cultures have a developed literature of courtship, but love themes are represented in every literature. The expression of erotic ideas is everywhere subject to controls and taboos, and although they are very diversely regulated, they do find expression, albeit often in disguised and elliptical form. Even the explicitly taboo ideas are expressed under particularly furtive or licensed circumstances, and they are often developed into a quite elaborate lore that is not only sensuous or erotic but also explicitly pornographic.

PORNOGRAPHY

Pornographic lore, like children's lore, has been developed in a variety of genres—in speech (dirty words, euphemisms, curses, and slang), in narrative (dirty stories, fabliaux, dirty jokes, or lengthy erotic tales), in poetry (limericks, bawdy songs), and in drama (exhibitions, strip-tease, orgiastic rituals, and the like). Styles of pornography are often widely shared within a given language, but the pattern may also be very local. It is a commonplace of Latin American Spanish that the dirty slang of one country may be thoroughly innocent in the neighboring countries. Yet some items of pornography can be documented over extensive areas, such as the northern European titillation over whipping or the West African sensitivity to passing gas. A few may actually be universal, like the motif of the toothed vagina or of the man with the enormous penis.

Although the sources on the world's pornography are scattered, badly recorded, and difficult of access, it is clear that it bears everywhere a close relationship to the erotic in a broad and Freudian sense, as has already been implied. The degree of social control over such themes is culturally variable, and the emphasis on different aspects of erotic experience is very highly so, but there is everywhere a measure of limitation on the free expression of erotic themes. They are ritualized, institutionalized, suppressed, or repressed in a most striking fashion. A second feature of erotic lore closely related to this control is its strong emotional polarization. Love and hate are salient dimensions. Even in the unself-conscious lore of primitive peoples, pornography is permeated with a sense of power and danger.

Not only in Europe, but also elsewhere, the lore of pornography is predominantly male. The Indo-European peoples share the conviction that the male is and should be the aggressive partner, but even the Semitic peoples, who consider the female responsible for sex (an attitude which has had a profound influence upon Spain and Latin America), nonetheless, produce only male pornography. Women everywhere share in this lore, but largely in a derivative and attenuated way. The institutional history of pornography is the history of male institutions: the army, the fraternity, the Australian or African bush school, the locker room, the monastery, the smoking car, the saloon. In contrast, the pornographic content of the lore of the woman's club, the nunnery, or primitive women's societies is pretty thin. Even the bordello or the women's branches of the armed forces appear to serve more as a clearing house for men's lore than as a focus for a distinctively feminine pornography.

"Unnatural" or illicit sex acts constitute the bulk of what is considered lewd in all cultures. Although subject to widely varying definitions, incest, adultery, perversion, and immodesty are always so considered. The hierarchy of obscenity is also culturally variable, to the point that what is utterly unmentionable in one setting may be a public commonplace in another. Among the Urubú of South America, basic modesty requires a penis sheath, and a man is considered nude (and lewd) without one, but at the height of the ritual of human sacrifice, the hero who has captured an enemy removes his penis sheath and shows himself indifferent to sexual attack by the women, demonstrating ritually that he has become "sexless" like the god he personifies. Among the Maya there are a number of expressions for penis ("bird," "parrot," "middle," "bell clapper," "knowledge," "body," "spirit") and vagina ("love thing," "medicine," "monkey," "middle," "rat") with differential propriety values. None of them can be considered completely taboo words, but the idea of menstruation is obscene beyond mention. Everywhere the suggestion of mother-son incest is obscene, but in the Trobriand Islands it is less obscene than the suggestion of brother-sister incest. Slum dwelling Negroes in Brazil cannot afford to be squeamish about adultery, but may draw the line at exhibitionism. British prostitutes (*inter alias*) charge higher prices for perverse sex play than for simple intercourse. An Ashanti proverb declares that "the worst thing is to fart in the Coomassie market," and although the worst thing in any society is unlikely to be the subject of a proverb, the Ashanti really do think this is pretty bad. On the whole, the Anglo-American canons of public taste are among the most restrictive in the world about sex, but Europeans have registered a strong distaste for the American freedom in discussing body odor and kindred intimacies, a topic that is felt to be truly obscene in the otherwise broad-minded tradition of India.

Some distortion has been introduced into the comparative literature on obscenity through exaggerated claims about the earthy tolerance of primitive peoples. It does not seem excessive to say that this implication is completely false. The observer may accurately report an uninhibited candor in a foreign culture on matters considered delicate in his own, but the fact is that there are no cultures without strong sexual taboos. Many traditions characterized by a relative frankness about overt sexuality express their anxieties in the language of witchcraft, often with important sexual implications that are as unthinkable and unspeakable as any of our particular tribal foibles. Erikson relates an interesting encounter in this connection with a California Yurok Indian:

> When I asked a Yurok who loved to tell obscene stories about Irishmen to tell me a few genuine obscene Yurok jokes, he became abruptly serious and said almost anxiously that nobody would dare to "make up" stories about sex among the Yurok; he would only tell the old stories giving the historical foundation of how sex came to be (Erikson 1943:270).

Because some themes are taboo in each cultural tradition, and because these themes are everywhere generally erotic, the scientific study of obscene literature is of critical importance to our understanding of the whole of man. We cannot afford to disregard the part of human communication that takes place on relatively private and intimate planes, often through indirection and innuendo. Too many important connections between ideas and between events may be traceable to this level. The extensive and intensive attention paid to these problems since Freud does not, however, justify any radical claims for the unique importance of sex taboos to human literature. Erotic themes in literature, folk as well as sophisticate, demonstrate the continuity between "normal" and "pathological" ideas; they occur in virtually every genre, in most literary forms, and (with various modifications) in most sociocultural contexts, from the polymorphous perversity of the "dirty words" of very small children to the nuanced sadism of the academic limerick, the aggressive scatology of soldiers' curses, and the rich, full sexual neurosis of some modern novels.

Certain types of pornography are far more likely to be orally communicated than are most literary materials, but many of them can be demonstrated to have important ties to the fugitive but repetitive written literature on erotic themes, and social taboos have been powerless to control the circulation of such written materials. What is truly strategic about this lore, then, is not that it is immune to literary contagion but is that it tends to be restricted to particularly intimate and specialized contexts. The study of the erotic gives us an unique entrée to the more private channels of the cultural communications system. Sex happens to be one of the principal topics discussed on these circuits.

The significance of pornography in complex cultures is complicated by the existence of organized criminality and vice. In effect the underworld serves as a specialized purveyor of what is socially disapproved about as much in the field of ideas as in the field of actions. This is not to assert that it has a monopoly on either crime or obscenity, but that, by virtue of its position "beyond the law," it can maintain a relatively overt denial of public values, and it tends to do so. The underworld is an underprivileged culture. It is in no sense autonomous, and, *pace* certain folklorists, it is in no sense a "folk." There is a tradition in literature at least as old as folklore itself of using the demimonde, or the *germanía* (perhaps even the Roman Suburra) as a vehicle for expressing literary, social, or political protest. This mode, which is massively represented in modern American literature, has always had the effect of romanticizing the outcast, *épatant les bourgeois*, and corrupting the elite. In some literature of the modern United States we are invited to accept the pornography of criminality as an authentic expression of natural or real (as opposed to artificial or repressed) life. This is both silly and confused. We may perfectly well sympathize with people who are condemned by unfair and remediable social circumstances to unhappy, violent, or vicious lives, but we can hardly help them or ourselves by making their misery and marginality our general standard. It is only scientific to say that we need to be able to look on pornography and related problems with much more realism and equanimity, but we have no warrant, scientific or otherwise, to glorify it. In this connection, as in many others that recur in anthropology, it is imperative that we recognize the ethnocentrism imposed upon us by our own particular positions in the world, but it is arrogant folly to assume that such recognition liberates us from the values and prejudices that are part of these positions.

To identify with the overdrawn perversities of criminality is not an act of intellectual liberation; it is a self-deception that obscures the phenomenon we wish to study. Titillating though it is, we do not study pornography because it is nice. It is not. We study it because it exists.

Pornography, then, is not good, clean fun. Often, in fact, it is expressly ugly, and serves as a vehicle for the nastier human emotions. In such usage, it is intended to be offensive, insulting, or outrageous. Small children may say, "You're a pop (bop, poopoo, and so forth)," with perhaps only vague intimations of naughtiness or hostility. When they grow up they may learn to say, "Shithead!" The intention in either case is aggressive and antisocial. In many primitive societies this kind of feeling might be expressed by a murmured rumor that you have actually seen your enemy eating a corpse under ghastly circumstances.

Expressions of this sort may be permitted in patterns of strict contextual control. Ritual and humor are among the commoner contexts in which frankly erotic or pornographic themes can be allowed relatively direct enunciation. In myths, in clowning, and in jokes, therefore, such elements are frequent and blunt. In America, obscenity becomes acceptable if it is sufficiently witty, arty, or clinical. LaBarre (1939) has pointed out in detail the psychopathological themes that occur normally in the limerick: incest, necrophilia, sadism, masochism, homosexuality, bestiality, coprophilia, masturbation, satyriasis, nymphomania, adultery and fornication, sodomy and pederasty, and so on. A variety of other genres display the same range.

Private, submerged, or unconscious meanings are just as much a part of literature as those that are directly expressed. Style is often more a matter of what is eschewed than of what is stated. Hence, no general treatment of the structure of literature can avoid concern with what is disavowed. Precisely because of the controls to which eroticism is subject, however, literature is not our best scientific entrée to these problems. Marcus (1966), in his excellent literary study of the pornography of *The Other Victorians* has documented convincingly the strangely mechanical, repetitive, and unimaginative character of the pornographic novel. Clinical observations, psychological experiments, dream analysis, and psychiatric experience have provided us with far more information under conditions more conducive to precise analysis and interpretation.

On the basis of dream reports and free association, Freud identified the following metaphors as recurrent in the dreams of many individuals:

> breasts:sisters
> buttocks:brothers
> castrate:behead, lose hair or teeth (noncastration:lizard, multiple
>   penis)

child: small animal
childbirth: rescue (in women's dreams)
coitus: go up or down slope, ladder, stairs; be run over
emission: flying
exhibitionism: naked and embarrassed
feces: gold
female genitalia: landscape (vagina: container, cavity, vessel, room)
male genitalia: hat, three (penis: person, little person, child; elong-
    ated object; machine, weapon, tool; necktie; snake, fish, snail, cat,
    mouse, etc.)
masturbate: beat, play with a little child
mature: pass examination
men: smooth walls
parents: king and queen
self: prince, princess
sibling: small animal
submit: falling
urinate: fire
wish: event (*e.g.*, death of beloved person: wish for his death)
women: tables, boards, wood (Freud 1938: *passim*).

This is, of course, only a very introductory dictionary of dream symbols, but it has been the basis for an extensive rereading of literature and folklore in which we can now trace at least a part of the submerged analogic that often connects the diverse elements. A Freudian "reading" of myths and tales is not a substitute for other modes of interpretation and analysis, but it is an invaluable supplement. It is not more "real" but it is as "real," and cannot be overlooked.

Many attempts have been made to extend Freud's analysis to materials from other cultures, a necessary and obvious step for the purposes of comparative literature. Oddly, there has been no real effort to replicate Freud's work on dreams with the methodological rigor he himself used. We have several collections of primitive dreams, but in no case do we have the necessary double translation of the associated memories of the dreamers in relevant depth and quantity. In most contexts, of course, anthropologists or other foreign observers are hardly in a position to determine the degree of acceptability of a particular construal of the dream symbols to the person reporting the dream. In a study of Navaho dreams, Kluckhohn reports the following motifs. Those in italics were in some way confirmed by the subjects; the remainder are Kluckhohn's "best guesses":

aunt's hogan: mother's protection
bear almost bit me: I almost lost control and was punished
boy like brother: *brother*

brought me some candy:propositioned me
bullets:*phallus*
caught the bear and caged it:controlled impulses
girl just like mine:*my little girl*
hit the bear on the nose and it ran out:drove out sexual aggression
laid her hand on my head:*reassured me*
noise like an automobile in my head:warning noise
pulled the covers off everyone:incest
roses as high as that gas tank:phallus
something black and round sat on my chest:*ghost* (husband)
stretched out his neck a long way:erection of penis
teeth came out:was castrated
threw dirty water over me:scolded me (had intercourse with me)
wolf:sexually threatening male (Kluckhohn 1962:353 ff.)

It seems very likely that a more comprehensive study of Navaho dreams would reveal many of the same images Freud found in Vienna—as Kluckhohn supposes. Doubtless there are also some connotations that are distincly Navaho as well. There must be consequences to the fact that all men experience both sex and the control of sex, but there is abundant documentation for the fact that they do not experience them identically.

KINSHIP

Even very primitive societies may create a complex lore, structured by the institutional organization of age and sex groups. Each such group will impart a distinctive style to its lore. But the redundancy created by participation in these groupings is vastly less than that created by family life, and it is in kinship structure that we find the highest degree of organization of oral traditions. The isolation of the Australian marriage pool creates a corresponding autonomy and specificity of the literature of the "horde." As Strehlow (1947:1) remarks of the Aranda, "all legends—and hence all ceremonies, since the latter are always dramatizations of portions of the legends—are tied down to definite local centres in each group." The relative openness and generalization of marriage choice in other systems structures in their literatures a corresponding expansion.

The best example of the importance of kinship for cultural communication is unquestionably language itself. The positive and negative rules of marriage preference (endogamy and exogamy) that lie at the heart of kinship organization define the relationship between mating and descent that is unique to the human family, the social unit responsible for developing and transmitting language. And languages tend therefore to be overwhelmingly maintained within descent lines. Much of the rest of culture is carried along with them and tends towards a certain ethnic coherence and a certain quasigenetic transmission.

The general structure of kinship imposes upon literature much the same pattern that it imposes upon language. In primitive contexts the relationship is specific—folktales and other elements of traditional lore are passed on by the father or grandfather of a family (more rarely by the mother, grandmother, or other relatives). And the general similarity or dissimilarity of two literary traditions tends to be closely associated with divergence or relatedness in descent. It should follow, of course, that different kinds of marriage and descent systems should produce corresponding differences in literary pattern. This has not been proved, but seems very likely on the basis of the general evidence available.

Restrictive kinship systems like those of the aboriginal Australians certainly conduce to an extreme literary parochialism. More generalized systems create styles widely shared by very much larger populations. Segmentation of society into exogamous units such as clans divides it into subcultures, each with its own minor stylistic quirks, but it also guarantees a kind of marital circulation that precludes any really profound stylistic differentiation. Thus clan myths within a tribe differ mainly in detail, but commonly reflect very similar motif content, modes of expression, format, and so forth. Endogamous kinship segments, such as castes or paired lineages, on the other hand, may fracture the unity of the general society much more profoundly, with correspondingly divisive effects upon literary style. Kinship organization thus drastically affects literary heterogeneity or homogeneity within a society.

Kinship structure also places the individual in markedly diverse relationships to his fellows. His affiliations may be *inclusive,* as in lineage systems, *exclusive,* as in clan or caste, or *overlapping,* as in bilateral descent systems. Such differences might in specific cases have relatively little significance for the frequency of contact of different kinship persons, but might nonetheless have a very important bearing on the context in which such contacts would occur and thus on the content of what might be communicated in them. Status formalization is perhaps to be expected in segmentalized kinship systems, and indeed the oft-remarked tendency of many primitive literatures toward a formal and wooden characterization of personages may be contrasted suggestively with the greater interest in motives and individuality in a more atomized (for example, bilateral) social order.

The organization of family life may thus be expected to affect both general and specific aspects of literary form. It also structures content. The first and most obvious thing that family members have in common is their communal past, and much of family lore may be expected to deal with family history. Legends of the origins of the clan (family, lineage, caste) and of the deeds and events symbolizing its importance and distinctiveness are ubiquitous in primitive literature. Sometimes these are fairly straightforward annals. More often they are overlaid with somewhat obscure symbols, some of them ancient, conventionalizing, ritualizing, or mythologizing the mystique of family pride. The genre includes prose tales and myths, but it may also be cast in poetry (as in the clan praise poems or *kirāari* of the West African Hausa, or the long, quasihistorical *hud hud* of the Philippine Ifugao), or even in drama (as in totemistic or other commemorative family ritual). Family traditions may also include fables or somewhat ritual sermons of a strongly homiletic flavor. Moralistic fables are widespread in Old World literature; family sermons are equally common in New World literature.

Specific relationships within the family are likely to generate specific literary expressions. The Araucanian Indians of Chile, for example, have developed a type of flyting song in which husbands and wives chide each other over marital failings, which are then taken up for attention and "advice" by other members of the community. Stock jokes and clichés are common in relation to joking relatives, "kissing cousins," mothers-in-law and many other relatives. Standardized verses are part of the role of a traditional Russian groom and best man, as they are of courtship, marriage, and other life crises in many countries. We have no serious study of the relation between the form, content, and kinship context of these classes of literature, but we do have an extensive collection of samples of them from various parts of the world.

The depth implications of family organization for the psychology of literature have been better explored, for although much of familistic literature bears some obvious signs of its provenience, a great deal of literature in general appears to carry a more diffuse or more archaic stamp of sometime family involvement. The widely encountered kinship drama of Oedipus, often discoverable under considerable disguises of psychological and cultural makeup, can be readily matched by other themes representative of the basic recurrent roles of kinship. Sibling relations are particularly well documented, but there are others with isolable (if not totally isolated) meaning—stepmothers, grandfathers, half siblings, orphans and foundlings, and so on. It is clear that the most vital and persistent of these literary projections are those that form a part of the fundamental nuclear family experience of all men—parents, children, siblings, and spouses.

There are three important aspects to the primacy of the family in literary structure. It is the oldest of human institutions and therefore dominates the earliest literary expression in all cultures. It is a universal part of experience and therefore provides a common denominator for social communication within the group sharing a particular kinship system. And it is an early and intensive learning context for every individual, therefore providing him with his primary expectations concerning social relationships. The kinship themes in literature are correspondingly faceted, being compounded of archaic images preserved from early history, culturally arbitrary values precipitated from the often distinctive experience of particular ethnic groups, and deep-seated, sometimes repressed feelings acquired by socialization and incorporated into personality structure. These three dimensions are often mutually reinforcing, but they need not be so, and in a particular case they may be distinct in quite complex ways. Individual and social meanings, conscious and unconscious, ancient and modern, may all be part of a common structure, determinately combined by the history and context of the particular work.

No extant literary work expresses for us directly the simplest archetype of this structure. All societies today complicate the structure of kinship with other institutions that reinterpret and reorganize the underlying nuclear configuration, and all of them have had thousands of years in which to elaborate any truly primitive mythos along the lines of historically distinctive ethnic experience. It is thus only through psychologically and culturally comparative analysis that we can surmise the common substrate that appears to be general to human family life—a structure comprehending the mysteries of the incest taboo and fundamental family morality.

RELIGION

Religious organization has a marked influence on literature in all communities. A society with even part-time shamans tends to develop a specifically religious literature, related to the general body of tribal lore and derived from it but nonetheless elaborated along lines independent of age, sex, and kinship organization. This literature centers upon ritual, for the religious practitioner everywhere is concerned with the extremes of human anxiety that are controlled by ritualization.

The distance between simple religious lore and general familistic tradition is not great. The Ifugao of northern Luzon, for example, use the family designed myths and songs directly in ritual—the retelling of the myth takes place only as a part of a ceremony for a specific magical or religious purpose. No great amount of specialization is required, and the myths are relatively little changed by their incorporation into ritual. Many peoples who do not formally ritualize their myths nonetheless tell them only seasonally, observing various taboos. This vague degree of ceremonial treatment corresponds to semiprofessionalism: the myths are recounted, sometimes by family heads, sometimes by somewhat informally designated story tellers, occasionally by somewhat professional shamans. It is only when the shamans take over this function fairly consistently that a specifically religious lore is generated.

Full-time professionals are not required for this purpose, but specialization and contextual differentiation are. Elaboration of liturgy depends upon the transmission of religious lore from one ceremonial leader to another, and even though they may be part-time ceremonialists, their common preoccupation with ritual will in time stamp their lore with a distinctive style. The emergence of such a social arrangement and of its literary concomitants is gradual and partial, and many works are somewhat equivocally both familistic and religious without being consistently either. Among the Navaho, the characteristic ritual work is a *hatał* (chant), which is owned and performed by a *hatałi* (chanter). Navaho chants are lyrical and allusive, complex and esoteric. They are in these respects completely different from the Navaho tales (such as coyote stories) or traditional myths, none of which are the prerogatives of specialists. Eskimo ritual, on the other hand, is appreciably less specialized, and the style of the shaman's song is both individual and closely attuned to the individualized tenor of general Eskimo lore. There is, in fact, some variation among Eskimos on the point, those of western Canada and Alaska being somewhat more inclined to shamanistic specialization and correspondingly elaborate literary forms.

The South American Warao have a ceremonialism involving at least three types of medical practitioners. All of them are individualists rather than members of professional societies, and their lore is designed for the lay public rather than for esoterically self-conscious priesthoods. Even the *wisiratu* ("owner of pain"), who is the leader of the temple cult, is master of a lore little separated from that of the people at large. Here is one of his sermons on the coming of anger:

> Before there was no anger.
>> For a while they took each other's wives.
> When they did that there was no anger yet.
>> Now Anger came down from the sky.
> When he went around, he came to the house and came up
>> to the opening of it.
> When he came, he sat down on a rolled-up hammock.
> Having sat down, he looked around on all of us in the house.
>> When he looked on us we got angry.
> When we were angry, Anger spoke.
>> When he spoke one beat his wife.
> "My name is Anger.
>> My thoughts are bad."
> An Indian said,
>> "Anger looked on us.
> That's why I was angry.
>> Before we were all right.
> Now we have turned out bad.
>> Because of that we have one single thought.

My hand has come out bad.
I lose my temper.
Now there is anger.
This morning there was no anger.
When the day ended, anger came into being.
Now anger came into being for us."
That's all.

(Wilbert 1964:122)

The ritualistic organization of many societies is of extreme simplicity and rests upon individual religious (and artistic) inspiration. A somewhat informal novitiate system guarantees perpetuation of particular specializations, sometimes in partial relation to kinship or political leadership. Several types of medicine men may be recognized, each with a distinguishable literary style. Rain magic, for example, may be sharply separated from curing magic. Snake shamans may be quite apart from bear shamans. And when they are, they may develop literary distinctiveness.

Organization of shamanistic societies may further complicate the picture. The Algonkin Midé Society, the Pueblo Indian curing fraternities, and the Plains Indian dance societies are well-known American Indian examples. Such groupings act not only as centers of social and religious leadership but also as primitive literary societies, in which existing lore is remolded into more complex patterns. Shamanistic individualism yields ground to a communal product, best illustrated perhaps in the fully developed ritual drama (ceremonials, dances) that group professionalism tends to generate. The Algonkin Midé was a secret society. The accent on specialization and esoteric knowledge was such that a systematic effort was made to keep the lore of the society out of lay hands. Thus in the medicine ceremony of the Menomini the meaningful words of the medicine songs were swallowed up in a sea of meaningless repetitions unintelligible to the uninitiated:

Mitähe, he, he,
Mitähi, hi, hi,
Mitäho, ho, ho,
Mitäha, ha, ha, ha,
Mitäwi, hi, hi, hi,
Mitäwi, hi, hi, hi,
Mitähe, he, he,
Mitähi, hi, hi,
Mitäw'ikomîk hi,
Mitäw'ikomîk ha,
We ho, ho, ho, ho.
(Skinner 1920:20)

Only the italicized word (which means "medicine lodge") has any meaning in this text. The rest is poetic decoration, but only the members of the society can be sure of this, as the song rolls on endlessly to complete a single sentence.

Secret lore can come about in other ways, too. Sigi, the secret language of the West African Dogons, has a vocabulary of about 300 words, apparently derived from Mandingo. Presumably, some foreign contact was involved. Even the part-time specialists of Australia achieve a similar form on the basis of a secret kept from the women and children by the initiated men. Here is a segment of the chant of *Ulamba*, the sacred cave and mountain of the Aranda.

> His heart is filled with longing to return home.
> High in the heavens gleams the afternoon sun.

In normal Aranda prose this would go:

> Erarijarijaka albujika.
> Nkinzha ba iturala albujika.

The chant, however, rearranges the text to force it into a pattern of trisyllabic verse:

> (K)erare jarije kalbije . . .
> Kankinzha batuaree ualbijee . . .
> (Strehlow 1947:xx–xxi)

The change is sufficient to disguise the text completely for the uninitiated. It is also a notably sophisticated linguistic manipulation and a startling poetic form for so marginal a cultural region.

There is no absolute disjunction between such contexts and that of professional priesthoods. Indeed, even part-time practitioners may be sharply distinguished in particular societies in a variety of well-defined religious roles (diagnostician, diviner, prophet, curer, teacher, cult leader), and the distinction of practitioners dealing with individual needs (shamans, medicine men) from those ministering to society at large (priests) is very common. Priests occupy a position much more formally defined with respect to economic and political organization than is that of the shaman; hence the emergence of coordinated community ceremonials tends to be associated with them. The transition may be gradual, but eventually it produces a truly priestly literature. Previously disparate myths become fused into a more coherent set of beliefs; previously separate rites are programmed as parts of a ceremonial; previously varied styles are coordinated and traditionalized as the authentic mode of religious expression; previously heterogeneous teachings are fused and their contradictions rationalized or explained away in a more self-conscious, esoteric, and abstract system.

The formation of priesthoods brings with it the ranking of priestly offices, adding yet another complicating dimension to religious literature.

Coequal priests and shamans may enrich the religious thought of their people with an indefinitely extended pantheism untroubled by its contradictions. A ranked system inevitably establishes at least tacit canons of orthodoxy and provides relatively formal training to maintain them.

The Yucatecan Mayan priesthoods maintained a considerable control over all Mayan society in part through their monopoly over the authentic religious mysteries. They even tested the officials in knowledge of ritual riddles, a necessary proof of legitimate authority:

> These are the riddles
>> And enigmas
> Of the cycle which ends today,
>> And today is the time
> For questioning with riddles the Axe Men of the towns
>> To see if they know them
> So as to deserve power.
>> Whether they know them by inheritance,
> Whether they know
>> And understand them,
> The Axe Men
>> And Land Chiefs,
> As the chiefs they are.
>> If it is true that the Axe Men descend from lords,
> Lord princes,
>> Really from Land Chiefs, they must prove it.
> This is the first riddle put to them.
>> They are asked for food.
> "Bring me the sun," the Land Chief will say
>> To the Axe Men.
> "Bring me the sun, my sons,
>> That I may have it on my plate.
> It must have the lance of the high cross sunk into
>> the center of its heart
> Where Green Jaguar sits, drinking blood."
> This is the language of Zuyua.
>> This is what they are asked for:
> The Sun is a fried egg.
>> And the lance of the high cross sunk in its heart,
>> which is mentioned, is the benediction.
> And the Green Jaguar sitting on top drinking blood
>> Is green chile just beginning to turn red.
> Thus is the language of Zuyua.
>   (Barrera Vásquez 1948:204–205)

ECONOMICS

Primitive life tends to focus upon the hunting that is its principal means of livelihood. Hunting is also dangerous and prestigious, and its appearance in literature does not seem to correspond so much to its actual frequency (in comparison, for example, with root grubbing or berry picking) as to its strategic position in society. The Pygmies of the equatorial forest have an expectable preoccupation with the chase, and those of Gabon have an "Elephant Hunter's Song" expressing it in forceful poetry:

On the weeping forest, under the wing of the evening,
The night, all black, has gone to rest happy;
In the sky the stars have fled trembling;
Fireflies shine vaguely and put out their lights;
On high the moon is dark, its white light is put out.
The spirits are wandering.
Elephant hunter, take your bow!
Elephant hunter, take your bow!

In the frightened forest the tree sleeps, the leaves are dead,
The monkeys have closed their eyes, hanging from high branches.
The antelopes slip past with silent steps,
Eat the fresh grass, prick their ears attentively,
Lift their heads and listen frightened.
The cicada is silent and stops his grinding song.
Elephant hunter, take your bow!
Elephant hunter, take your bow!

In the forest lashed by the great rain,
Father elephant walks heavily, baou, baou,
Careless, without fear, sure of his strength.
Father elephant, whom no one can vanquish.
Among the trees which he breaks he stops and starts again.
He eats, roars, overturns trees and seeks his mate.
Father elephant, you have been heard from afar.
Elephant hunter, take your bow!
Elephant hunter, take your bow!

In the forest where no one passes but you,
Hunter, lift up your heart, leap, and walk.
Meat is in front of you, the huge piece of meat,
The meat which walks like a hill,
The meat which makes glad the heart,
The meat that will roast on the hearth,

The meat into which the teeth sink,
The fine red meat and the blood that is drunk smoking.
Elephant hunter, take your bow!
Elephant hunter, take your bow!
      (Trilles 1931:334–335)

Hunting elephants does not lend itself to song, nor is it done with a bow and arrow. It is clear that this song is not a specimen of the lore of the hunter; rather, it is a community product, celebrating the hunting life but not expressing it.

Solitary economic activities generate very little specific lore. The sharing of the experiences of hunting or fishing usually takes place in the wider community, as in this Pygmy example. The result may be evocative and individualistic boasting songs, as among some North American Indians; community ritual to ensure the food supply, as in totemism; or tall tales for the amusement or confusion of the laity, as among modern American fisherman. In any case, it is not a lore of specialists.

Group activities may be expected to generate a more specific and context-bound expression. Communal hunting, net fishing, and various kinds of team labor are simple examples. Commonly (and anciently) there are timing songs for coordinating effort. Work songs of this sort are known from ancient Egypt. Agricultural communities produce husking songs, harvest songs, and so on. But all such lore tends to feed back into the general cultural stock unless it is involved in an activity that is both group centered and segregated in some measure from the rest of life.

The more esoteric occupations develop a more esoteric lore—more slang, more traditions, more arbitrary customs and characteristic beliefs—as we have seen in connection with religious specialization. The specificity of mining and metallurgy in the ancient world led to a lore that likened the activities of the metal worker to those of the midwife, as has been documented extensively by Mircea Eliade (1956). The smiths of Africa are similarly set apart and similarly distinctive, often possessing a secret language of archaic character like the Sigi of the Dogons. Herding and sailing, when practiced by special groups within a larger society, exemplify the literary development of occupations that are both solidary and set apart.

The lore of cowboys is lonesome, violent, and self-pitying. The conditions of the job were similar in both the American and Argentine plains, providing little chance for family life, long periods of solitude, and periodic companionship on long drives. The result in each case was a highly developed professional slang, an exaggerated development of folk heroes, and a wistfully lyric poetry of unrequited love. The same is true of the *charro* tradition of northern Mexico. In the following verse, a Mexican cow-boy anticipates the same sentimentalized end familiar to us on the lone prairie or the streets of Laredo:

> Un domingo estando errando
> Se encontraron dos mancebos
> Metiendo mano a sus fierros
> Como queriendo pelear.
>
> Cuando se estaban peleando
> Pues llegó su padre de uno,
> "Hijo de mi corazón,
> Ya no pelees con ninguno."

> One Sunday just out a-wandering
> Two cowboys came on each other
> With both their guns at the ready
> And both a-spoiling for a fight.
>
> And so while they were still fighting,
> The father of one of 'em got there,
> "Now son, just listen to me—
> Don't you go fighting nobody."
>   (Traditional)

The song is a ballad (*corrido*) called "The Disobedient Son," and ends with death, burial, and a suitable moral.

Sailors have a somewhat similar life and a somewhat similar lore. "Tenderfeet" and "landlubbers" are equally out of it. The sea chanteys of the nineteenth century tell us little about sailing, but are very explicit about the feelings of the sailors: well-known (and well-dated) examples are "Reuben Ranzo," "Rio Grande," "Sally Brown," "Shenandoah," "Drunken Sailor," and "Haul on the Bowline" and "Whiskey, Johnny." But although we know the recent lore of the sea best, its antecedents are ancient. Stormalong and Davy Jones' locker belong to the days of frigates, but mermaids go back to Celtic and Hellenistic folklore. A recognizably maritime Latin chantey has survived with the refrain *Heia, viri, nostrum reboans echo sonet, heia!* ("Hey, men, now our echo bounces back resounding, hey there!") A similar chantey from Polynesia is also typical of the timing songs used for group effort:

> Toho, teka! Toho, teka!
> Toho te vaka ki Pukenga!
> Toho, lau! Toho lau!
> Toho te vaka ke au!

(Haul, roll! Haul, roll!
Haul the canoe to Pukenga!
Haul, sing! Haul, sing!
Haul the canoe, that it come away!)
(Burrows 1945:110)

Relatively few occupations provide the special circumstances that have given cowboys and sailors their distinctive places in literature, but even in the United States there are legends, songs, and traditions for railroading (Casey Jones), sign painting (Sloppy Hooper), steelworking (Joe Magarac), union organizing (Joe Hill), logging (Paul Bunyan), and others. Elsewhere the forms vary. In Latin Catholic cultures occupational traditions are often assimilated to religion through a patron saint, a reflection of the guild organization of many occupations in the late Middle Ages.

In ancient Middle America there were few occupations so specialized and set apart as that of the *pochteca*, the merchants who traveled from city to city under ritual guarantees of inviolability. A fragment of their lore that has survived is the "Exhortation of the Old Merchants" recorded by Sahagún:

Young man before me,
　Do not be a child.
You are already experienced with the roads
　And the labor of travelling,
And with the dangers there are in this office
　Of going from town to town trading.
You have already walked the roads;
　You have already been through the towns you
　　now wish to visit again.
We do not know what will happen.
　We do not know whether we shall see you again.
Perhaps your life
　Will be ended there
In one of those towns,
　Of those roads.
Remember then,
　Whatever happens to you,
The advice
　And tears
Of these your fathers
　Who love you as a son.

> May we be worthy of celebrating your return
>> And seeing you here
> In health
>> And prosperity.
> (Sahagún 1956:I:343)

The ritual, stoic tone, and the familistic imagery are expectable in a profession that was highly ritualized and commonly hereditary. Certainly we are a long way from the traveling salesman and the farmer's daughter!

POLITICS

The mythology of politics is in some respects its essence. All political systems rest on bodies of analogic thought reflecting some metaphorical extension of the fundamental feelings about solidarity and authority on which the regular exercise of power rests. The political solidarity of the clan is based on the metaphor that cousin:cousin::brother:brother. Hence the factionalism of clan systems is also based on this idea. In the Hopi villages there are two interpretations of the clan myths accounting for the origin of the clans and, incidentally, of the white man. Both assume that Hopi: white::brother:brother. But there is bitter disagreement about whether Americans are the true whites (*pahana*) mentioned in the myths. Progressive Hopis therefore address Americans as "brothers" and treat them more or less accordingly. Conservatives say "friend," with corresponding reservations, holding out for the validation promised in the myth—the true white man should produce the missing half of a particular broken ceremonial stone, and the Americans have not produced it.

The politics of bands and tribes remains fundamentally similar, although it involves increasingly intricate manipulation of the familistic metaphor of primitive democracy. Even the larger leagues and alliances of North American Indians continue to speak primarily in terms of brotherhood (ally:ally::brother:brother). But political acceptance of such metaphors is contingent on their congruence with other metaphors, often ritual or religious ones, as in the Hopi clan myths. The effective confederacies enforced brotherhood among disparate allies because they could invoke supernatural sanctions. In the political mythology of the highland Maya, for example, ally:ally::older brother:younger brother::the sun:the moon. Political morality was thus linked irrevocably to hierarchy and supported by the myths of how the world began. To justify one's own position or the political claims of one's lineage, it was necessary to relate oneself to this established axis of political life by reciting or devising a myth.

With the polarization of hierarchy and authority, a further metaphor may be added to political discourse—leader:follower::father:child. The thanes of ancient Britain, in common with the chiefs of many tribes around the world, understood and applied this principle. But again the operation of politics on this basis required ritualization, and the further postulate of divine kingship was added—king:subject::father:child::God:man. How explicitly this was felt is illustrated by the Assyrian proverb that "Man is but the shadow of a god; a slave is the shadow of a man; but the King is the [very] image of a god." And, indeed, the sanctity of the king's person in the ancient Near East, Sudanic Africa, or Polynesia was supported by the most ramifying ritualization and justification in just these terms. Perhaps the most elaborated political philosophy of this sort was that of Confucian China.

A further development of the idea of kingship is the dynastic idea, in which the principle of succession is further stabilized on the assumption that the king:the people::the king's descendants:posterity. A number of additional and supporting metaphors have been added by royalists, for example, as God:the orthodox, and as nobility:the peasants. The effect is a stable and conservative social order that moves simultaneously toward national integration and the sharp differentiation of social classes.

Under certain conditions, political differentiation may serve, very much as economic differentiation does, to create new social groups and consequent literary specialization. The best documented example is court literature, although the literature of other classes (slaves, serfs, commoners, bourgeoisie, bureaucracy, the army) can also be historically traced. European peasant literature is full of "Cinderella stories" and successful younger sons, fantasied social mobility in an age of fixed estates. The lore of the "poor but honest" drew apart from the "code of honor" and *noblesse oblige.*

But class solidarity was normally loose and the autonomy of the classes partial. Eventually the classes were all but swamped in the mythology of nationalism—of Jeanne d'Arc, Wilhelm Tell, George Washington's cherry tree, and the thin red line of Empire. That strange power sovereignty even passed out of the hands of sovereigns. The kings became increasingly human, but the People became divine. As nations stretched into empires, it even became possible for a time for the nation to usurp the parental role that formerly belonged to kings, taking up a "white man's burden" of paternalism toward races construed as children, and playing Great White Father to whole tribes of wards. Nor did it always stop there. While Latin American slavery in the Americas clung to the paternalistic metaphor, Anglo-Saxon slavery reduced slavery to a pure age metaphor, devoid of familistic responsibility—white:Negro::adult:child. The Latin slave-holder might be a bad father, but the Anglo-Saxon one was no father at all.

As the old "concert of Europe" gives way to a still vague "family of nations," the ancient and primitive metaphor that cousins are like brothers seems to have stretched about as far as it will go. But we can hardly return to preferential cross-cousin marriage. It seems clear that some part of the building of a world political structure rests on the development of comprehensible and acceptable metaphors on which to base it—in short, it awaits the further elaboration of a world literature. There can be no question that such a literature is already under construction.

SUMMARY

As we have seen, the descriptive classification of styles tends to be based upon locating particular stylistic phenomona in history, in society, and in personality. But useful as these classifications are, they do not in themselves explain the phenomenon of style. Their usefulness remains descriptive. What they do for us is to locate stylistic features in cultural space, which is an unavoidable preliminary to explaining them.

Descriptive accuracy is essential for analytic accuracy. One major problem of comparative literature in many areas has long been the inaccuracy of our information about it. In some cases, we must remain dependent upon poor data for our scanty comprehension of particular literatures for some time to come. On the other hand, our knowledge of the literary history of mankind is improving rapidly, and is better now than ever before. A "complete" description will forever elude us, but we already possess substantial information.

The central importance of style among the problems of literature derives from its completely global character. No dimension of literature is irrelevant to it. Content and context are as important to the definition of a style as the formal linguistic features of expression. The problem of style is nothing less than that of all literary structure, and a theory of style must constitute an explanation of this structure—its origin, stability, development, and change. I cannot agree with Saporta that "the aim of grammatical analysis is primarily predictive, the aim of stylistic analysis is primarily classificatory" (Sebeok 1960:93). I agree that grammar does not exhaust style, but I do not believe that the structure of style is any less subject to prediction than that of grammar. Only what is random can truly elude prediction, and it is clear that style is not random.

Any repetitive experience is likely to result in communication. Additional redundancy will cause formalization. The result may be a "saying" or other formalized pattern. Most commonly, of course, this order of redundancy is created by the structure of human physiology and its relation to its natural surroundings. Such a pattern may have instrumental or scientific significance, but it will not be connotative. It is in this mode that we talk about what things *are*. Connotative patterns require that we talk about what things are *like*. They require a greater degree of structure.

As an example, a man sitting down to dinner may comment, "I'm hungry." To a first approximation, such a remark is denotative. But when the man experiences hunger and its satisfaction in one context and also has the experience of hunting bears or starving on the march, he may say, "I'm hungry as a bear," or "I'm so hungry I could eat a horse." Such an equation of differentiated experiences is no longer reportage. It is proto-poetry, however crudely formed.

The minimal formula for this kind of pattern might be put $A:B::C:D$, in which A and B, C and D are differentiable elements experientially disso-ciated into two pairs, but pairs that have been brought together by the structure of culture and society. If a man sitting down to dinner shared his hunger with others but were unique in his experience of bears or horses, his cliché would stand no chance of being understood or repeated. It is in effect the congruence of two roles—eater and hunter (or soldier)—that provides the force of the metaphor. Analogy is the assimilation of experiential differences.

Even very primitive literature may involve multiple levels of super-imposed analogies of this sort. The scientific explanation of the style in such cases must rest upon an increasingly precise interpretation of the communicative history that underlies them. Style in this sense can be described in terms of the structure of the metaphors; it can be explained only by the structure of the sociocultural and psychological setting that produced them.

Chapter 8

The Great Tradition:
Chronological Outline of the World's Written Traditions

The invention of writing is the most sweeping revolution that has ever occurred in lore. As has often been remarked, writing has the effect of making all of literature contemporary. We do not have to wonder what Aristotle really said; we can read his own words. What man has committed to writing thus escapes significantly the ephemeral limitations of speech as a vehicle of communication; it becomes part of human lore in a special and relatively permanent sense, remaining available for consideration by any man capable of reading it. Written literature thus makes possible a more intensive continuity within each tradition of writing, while simultaneously facilitating the direct accessibility of what has been written for all of subsequent mankind. The result has been the gradual growth of a complex web of mutually related literatures, significantly different from each other but sufficiently interrelated to constitute parts of a single great tradition.

Traditions of literacy in particular languages have a considerable cultural autonomy. The system of meanings built into the language itself and the facility of intralinguistic communication conspire to give to each literature a distinctive pattern—an independent tone, stylistic history, and character. Nonetheless, it is apparent that from the dawn of writing there has been a very important interchange of ideas, including specifically literary ideas, between adjacent traditions. There is nothing unexpected in this, for we have seen that such influences were an essential part of "literary" history long before writing. What is distinctive to the diffusion of ideas in written form is the direct confrontation of ideas that are not contemporary.

In oral literature, a continual change in form and content is absolutely unavoidable. Some variation in degree is, of course, possible, depending on the care with which the traditions are perpetuated, but in no case can a complex work be passed along verbatim. In writing, however, a Hebrew story of the third century B.C. may be the direct inspiration of a French play of the fourteenth century A.D.; a Sanskrit text of the first century may be the exact source of a Chinese text of a thousand years later. There is no reason to suppose that the process of communication is any different from what takes place by verbal contact, but the historical manifestation of it is totally altered. A Sioux storyteller can have no inkling of the versions of his tale current a millennium before him. A modern novelist almost inevitably has some such awareness. In a diffuse, partial, and potential sense, writing does indeed make us contemporaries to all that has gone before us—provided only that it has been committed to writing and that we can read it.

It is in this sense demonstrable that writing greatly enriches literature. Literacy gives to a single individual a greatly expanded source of ideas. The extent to which this will be true and the directions of possible influences will be determined by technical questions more or less peculiar to literacy: the nature of the writing system, the existence of translations, the accessibility of translational dictionaries, the amassing of libraries, the reproduction of texts by scribes or presses, the organization of scholarship and instruction in schools, monasteries, or universities. The specialized features of literate traditions thus tend to create more complex patterns of literary communication within and between systems than is possible to purely oral literatures. This is, however, a matter of degree rather than of kind. Each individual works in either case with what is culturally transmitted to him, and he modifies or elaborates it in accordance with exactly the same psychocultural processes.

Because of the importance of time to written literature, following is a chronological outline of the world's written traditions. It attempts as complete a coverage of ancient and exotic literatures as possible up to about the twelfth century A.D., and enough sampling thereafter to provide a sketch of literary activity in more modern times. The numbers in parentheses with each heading indicate the century covered; a minus sign before the number indicates B.C. Although exceptions have been made in order to illustrate the development of the less-known literatures, the emphasis is on nonfragmentary works. English titles are used, and a somewhat abbreviated mode of reference is employed in order to include as much relevant material as intelligibly as possible. The fuller data needed for clearer identification will be found in the Appendix. Dating is to the nearest century, although many of the dates I have accepted are still disputed. In most cases they are as reliable as radiocarbon dates and may be read "plus or minus one century." The numerals are ordinal (sixth century A.D.) rather than cardinal (599–500 B.C.). Some works that cannot yet be dated to the nearest 300 years have been omitted, most notably in the Pali Buddhist canon.

The general structure of literary history may be conveniently divided into five broad traditions, and the surveys of each century are ordered in terms of them. They are: European, Semitic, Indic, Sinitic, and American. The earliest part of the story is, of course, "Semitic."

Gerzean (−35)*

The earliest fragments of literature may well be an Egyptian drama and a poem that were actually found among much later texts but that perhaps date to the Middle Predynastic period of Egyptian history, known archaeologically as the Gerzean period. The play is a fragmentary fertility ritual; the poem is a *Hymn* to Aton.

−35 Anon.: *Fertility, Hymn.*

Ghassulian (−33)

A fragmentary myth of *Ptah's Creation* also belongs to the earliest phase of ancient Semitic literature. It is referred to the Late Predynastic period, although it is known only from a much later text.

−33 Anon.: *Ptah's.*

First Dynasty (−30)

Egypt and Sumer were both literate by no later than the time of the first Egyptian dynasty. They did not, however, produce extant literature. The reign of Egypt's first pharaoh, Menes or Nar Mer, is commemorated in the "Narmer Palette," but it is a pictorial rather than a written record. Sumerian scribes were kept busy from a very early date, but it is estimated that over 95 percent of what they wrote was of the nature of bookkeeping rather than literature.

---

* In the citation lists for each century, works are alphabetized by the name of the author, if known. Anonymous works are listed by the first important word of the title. The full titles can be found in the "Authors" and "Works" sections of the Appendix.

Third Dynasty (−28)

By the time of the third dynasty in Egypt, both Sumerian and Egyptian were effectively literary languages. The *Essays* of Im Hotep, comprising useful information on practical affairs (politics, medicine, architecture, and agriculture), are assigned to this century. They are an interesting reflection of the knowledge and preoccupations of an Egyptian official, the first author in history: Im Hotep (whose name means "Im is content") was a vizier. The only body of Sumerian texts dating to before the Semitic conquests in Mesopotamia, the *Library of Tello*, is presumed to be of about this date, but probably includes earlier materials. It has not been chronologically analyzed and is only fragmentarily translated.

−28 Im, Anon.: *Library.*

Old Kingdom (−27)

The time of Snefru and Cheops of the fourth dynasty initiates the five-century history of the Old Kingdom in Egypt. The *Instructions* of Ptah Hotep from this period is the earliest example of a genre of didactic and moral discourse widely characteristic of ancient Near Eastern literature. The *Instructions for Kagemni* are another example from the same time.

−27 Ptah, Anon.: *Instructions.*

Sargonid (−26)

The following century was the time of the pharaoh Khafra (Chefren) and the building of the great Second Pyramid at Gizeh; Sargon I of Akkad conquered Mesopotamia and celebrated his victory in a proud poem, *King of Battle.* Sumerian continued to be the prestige language and a Sumerian poet, Dingir Addamu, also belongs to this century. The Sumerian myth of *Enlil and Ninhursag* probably does too, although our copy of it is many centuries later.

−26 Dingir, Sargon, Anon.: *Enlil.*

Harappan (−25)

The twenty-fifth century B.C. marks the appearance of urban civilization at Mohenjo Daro and Harappa in the Indus Valley, where certain seals contain pictures that may be protohieroglyphic, but where no literary remains were found. It also marks the first appearance of historical writing —the *War of the Seventeen Kings* by Naram Sin in Mesopotamia, and the *Egyptian Chronicle*, an annalistic king list. This is also the probable date of the Sumerian cycle of *Gilgamesh* myths as we now have them, although the texts date from eight centuries later and some parts of them may be from as much as six centuries earlier. Gilgamesh is the Sumerian prototype of the Greek Hercules, and the Sumerian texts constitute the earliest epic that has come down to us—an incomplete but poetic and sophisticated literary masterpiece subsequently much imitated. The same century also saw the earliest examples of two of the literary genres that were among the most characteristic forms of the ancient Near East: the dialogue and the lament. Both are Sumerian: the *Dialogues* of Gubarru and the *Lament* of Tabi Utul Enlil. There is also a Babylonian *Lament for Akkad* from this period. A quite different type of poetry is represented in the Egyptian *Work Songs*, also assigned to this date.

—25 Gubarru, Naram, Tabi, Anon.: *Egyptian, Gilgamesh, Lament, Work.*

Minoan (−24)

The following century was the time of the rise of Minoan Crete, but although we have Minoan texts, we have no translated remains from that development and none from contemporary Mesopotamia. The Greek texts from Crete are nine centuries later. The Egyptian *Song of the Troops of Uni* is from the twenty-fourth century B.C.

—24 Anon.: *Song.*

Gudean (−23)

The Old Kingdom (and the sixth Egyptian dynasty) came to an end with the ninety-year reign of Pepi II, the longest in history. That monarch's *Instructions to Harkhuf* is a trivial literary relic of the age. More important are the *Pyramid Texts* collected from the royal tombs, prayers and ritual formulas to guarantee the immortality of the dead god-kings of Egypt. Similar religious preoccupations appear in Mesopotamia in the Sumerian *Hymns to Ningursu* and the *Prayer to Bau* of King Gudea.

—23 Gudea, Pepi, Anon.: *Hymns, Pyramid.*

Middle Kingdom (−22)

After a time of troubles, the eleventh dynasty managed to stabilize Egypt, initiating the epoch there known as the Middle Kingdom. The anonymous *Peasant's Complaint* is an interesting reflection of the state of Egyptian society. The *Instructions for King Meri Kere* and the *Instructions* of Duauf continue the Egyptian tradition in that kind of didactic literature. A *Lament for Nippur* suggests that Mesopotamia, too, was unsettled, as in fact it was.

—22 Duauf, Anon.: *Instructions, Lament, Peasant's.*

Neo-Sumerian (−21)

The troubles ended in Mesopotamia with the Sumerian resurgence and the rise of the third dynasty of Ur, from which we possess several hymns— to Inanna, Enlil, and the Temples of Sumer. A *Hymn* of King Shulgi is also extant. The Sumerian myth of *Inanna and Tammuz* (the Isis and Osiris of Egypt) probably dates to no later than this time. We possess only the part dealing with *Inanna's Descent to the Nether World* in Sumerian, although a fuller text of the derivative Babylonian *Ishtar and Tammuz* has survived. We also have an Egyptian *Drama of the Gods*, treating similar materials in ritual dramatic form. A Babylonian *Hymn to Ishtar* parallels the Sumerian hymns already mentioned. In addition to the usual instructions (those of Sehete Pibre belong here), the Egyptians inaugurated a tradition of prophecy, beginning with the *Prophecies* of Nefer Rehu.

−21 Nefer, Sehete, Shulgi, Anon.: *Drama, Hymn, Inanna's, Ishtar.*

Hittite (−20)

Hittite made its literary debut with a military chronicle, Anittas' *Wars of the Six Cities.* The Egyptians continued to produce instructions (Ipu Wer and Amen Emhet), dialogues (*Quarrel of a Pessimist with His Soul*) and hymns (to *Min Horus* and *Osiris*), but additionally turned to narrative, including the tale of *Sinuhe* and the *Shipwrecked Sailor*, a distant ancestor of the story of Sinbad. Sumerian literature was also particularly rich, producing hymns, fables, proverbs, court records, myths, and instructions (*Instructions of a Peasant to His Son, The Training of a Scribe*). The traditional instructions and dialogues are usually called "wisdom literature" by Mesopotamian scholars. The Sumerian *Creation* cycle is assigned to this century, although much of it may be considerably earlier. It includes the earliest known version of much of the Hebrew creation story. Among the associated myths are the *Feats and Exploits of Ninurta, Lugalbanda and Enmerkar*, and the *Destruction of Kur* (a dragon probably cognate with the Biblical Leviathan). An Egyptian fragment on the *Founding of the Temple* by King Sen Usret I is among the public documents.

−20 Amen, Anittas, Ipu, Sen, Anon.: *Creation, Destruction, Fables, Feats, Hymn, Instructions, Lament, Lugalbanda, Me, Min, Osiris, Proverbs, Quarrel, Records, Shipwrecked, Sinuhe, Training.*

Babylonian (−19)

With the fall of Ur and the establishment of a Babylonian dynasty there, Sumerian literature came to an end. The language continued to be studied and written as a scholarly and scriptural tongue, and in fact the larger part of our extant collection of Sumerian texts actually dates from the eighteenth century B.C., when they were presumably copied from more antique originals by Babylonian scribes; but subsequent literature in Mesopotamia is mainly Akkado-Babylonian. The century after the Sumerian eclipse may have been a troubled one. In any case it produced no Mesopotamian literature. In Egypt the *Ebers* and *Kahun* papyri, the *Odes to Sen Usret III*, and the lament of Khekhe Perre Seneb are placed here.

—19 Kehkhe, Anon.: *Ebers, Kahun, Odes.*

Hammurabic (—18)

Hammurabi was king of Babylon and issued his famous code *When Anu the Exalted* in the eighteenth century B.C. The *Archives of Yamkhad*, a city in Syria which also wrote Babylonian, is of the same date, as is the Egyptian story of *King Antef*. The Hittites produced nothing that can be surely ascribed to the period.

—18 Hammurabi, Anon.: *Archives, King.*

Hyksos (—17)

The Hyksos "shepherd kings" invaded Egypt, whose literature of the period includes the *Surgical Papyrus* and the story of *King Cheops and the Magicians*. The Hittites are represented by the *Orations* of Hattusilis I and a book of *Anecdotes*, but the Babylonians are unaccountably silent.

—17 Hattusilis I, Anon.: *Anecdotes, King, Surgical.*

Vedic (—16)

The sixteenth century B.C. is presumed to be the date of the arrival of Indo-European peoples in northern India and of the composition of the *Rig Veda*, the first great work of Indic literature, and a subtle and sophisticated poetic achievement—a treasury of ancient Indic literature and mythology. Like other major literary works of the ancient world, the *Rig Veda* was certainly not an instantaneous composition, but reflects a long literary development of which the surviving version is the culmination and our only evidence. No actual texts from India can be dated earlier than the third century B.C., and the extant texts of the vedas are much later than that, so that the reconstruction of ancient Indic literature is more difficult and more involved in problems of oral transmission than is that of other traditions. Egyptian literature of the first century of the New Kingdom (the eighteenth dynasty) produced the *Adoration of the Nile*, *What Is in the Netherworld,* the hymn to *Ptah the Great,* and a memorial on *The Hyksos War.* Akkadian produced the epic *When Above,* a poetic story of the creation modeled after the Sumerian account.

−16 Anon.: *Adoration, Hyksos, Ptah, Rig, What, When.*

Shang (−15)

Chinese tradition and archaeological evidence agree in tracing the beginnings of the Bronze Age in China to the fifteenth century B.C., the Shang period, which may have been literate but was only protoliterary. Although Chinese scholars disagree, the earliest surviving Chinese literature is dated by Western scholarship to seven centuries later. The contemporary Egyptian literature includes hymns to *Thoth* and *Osiris* and historical memoranda on the *Victories of Thut Mose III* and the *Capture of Joppa.* The earliest Hittite myths are also dated here: *Gilgamesh, The Missing God,* and the song of *Ullikummi.* The Mesopotamian record is blank. The earliest translated Greek fragments are the *Votive Texts* of Minoan "Linear B" from this period. Their value is historical rather than literary.

−15 Anon.: *Capture, Gilgamesh, Missing, Osiris, Thoth, Ullikummi, Victories, Votive.*

Akhen Aton (−14)

Politically, the fourteenth century B.C. focused on the region of Palestine and Syria in which the influence of Egyptian, Hittite, and Babylonian culture met, conflicted, and blended. To about this date in Syrian belong the only surviving Phoenician works, the Canaanitic (Ugaritic) tablets of Rash Shamra, containing the stories of *Baal, Aqhat,* and *Keret.* The sole Babylonian remnant is provincial: Sharruwa's "Autobiography" of King Idri Mi, a minor monarch of northern Syria. An invaluable list of *The Kings of Egypt* belongs to this time, as do important Egyptian ritual texts, *The Saving of Mankind, Gates, Caverns, The Divine Cow,* and a hymn *To Amon* by Horus and Seth. Greater historical interest attaches to the strange figure of the heretic pharaoh Akhen Aton (Amen Hotep IV), whose monotheistic poetry (*Hymn to the Sun*) has been preserved together with much of his *Official Correspondence* (the "Tell el Amarna Letters"), covering Egypt's increasing involvements with the Babylonians and Hittites. The Hittites also contributed the historical *Annals* of Mursilis II and an epic on the siege of *Urshu.* Egyptian poetry is particularly abundant, including hymns, prayers, love songs, a *Banquet Song,* and an anthology (the *Thousand Songs*). But the most valuable compilation in all Egyptian literature is the collection of religious texts preserved for us in a recension from this period, the "book of the dead," more properly titled *Coming Forth by Day*. The title is a reference to resurrection, and the work is liturgical in character, constituting a full set of ritual texts suitable for copying on the walls of tombs or on papyri to be left with burials. The texts specify all the things the soul must know in order to overcome death, confront judgment, and purify and prepare itself for eternal life. Many of these texts are earlier in date. Some can be traced to the *Pyramid Texts* of 900 years before, but a thorough analysis of the compilation has not been made.

—14 Akhen, Horus, Mursilis, Sharruwa, Anon.: *Amon, Aqhat, Baal, Banquet, Caverns, Coming, Divine, Flowers, Gates, Good, Keret, Kings, Lovers', Maiden, Prayer, Saving, Sun, Thousand, Trees, Urshu.*

Mosaic (—13)

The time of Moses is also the century of the greatest extension of the Egyptian Empire under Ramses II, celebrated in *The Capture of Joppa* and *The Victory at Kadesh*, the *Hymn to Ramses*, and the *City of Ramses*. Of the numerous Hebrew texts attributed to Moses, it is likely that the only one that actually possesses such antiquity is the *Ten Commandments*. The time of Moses (whose name is Egyptian for "prince") was a flourishing period in Egyptian literature, which produced the *Letters* of Hori, hymns to Thoth, Re, and Amon, and several stories: *King Apophis and Sekenen Re, Anupu and Bitiu* (on a Damon and Pythias theme), and *The Bewitched Prince*. There are also *Exhortations to Schoolboys* and a textbook of *Model Letters*. One fragment of the period describes Astarte, although that goddess' homeland produced no recognized literature of this date. The *Autobiography* of Hattusilis represents the Hittites.

—13 Hattusilis, Hori, Moses, Anon.: *Amon, Anupu, Astarte, Bewitched, Capture, City, Exhortations, Hymn, King, Model, Re, Thoth, Victory.*

Trojan (—12)

The Trojan War was in progress on the western shore of Asia Minor when the Hittite kingdom reached its literary apogee in the twelfth century B.C., editing its legal code and writing poetic epics, at least five of which have survived. One of them, *The Slaying of the Dragon*, is the Hittite version of the old Babylonian and Sumerian story of the underground monster. Others are the *Tale of Appus*, the *Epic of the Tigris*, and the *Legend of Zalpa*. The period is a blank in Egypt and Mesopotamia. The Syrian *Library of Zapouna* of this date may contain additional Phoenician materials but is still untranslated. The Hebrew *Song of Deborah* is also assigned to this century.

—12 Anon.: *Code, Epic, Kessis, Legend, Library, Slaying, Song, Tale.*

Chou (−11)

In the twelfth century B.C., Shang China was conquered by the Chou, and in the following century the Duke of Chou stabilized the dynasty as regent for his nephew and became the first legendary "Confucian," five centuries before Confucius. Traditions concerning the period, however, come only from texts of many centuries later. In the Near East and in India we have virtually no literature from this time. Hittite civilization disappeared. Babylonia was silent. Egypt was wracked by disturbances that terminated the New Kingdom and established the brief twenty-first dynasty. India was still working upon the elaboration of Vedic traditions of ritual and theology, but textual criticism has as yet isolated nothing belonging to this century. Two fragments of the Old Testament traditions of the Hebrews are virtually the only literary remains: the *Red Sea Song* and the *Fable of Jotham*. An Egyptian journal, Un Amon's *Voyage to Byblos*, also describes the Palestine that produced them.

−11 Un, Anon.: *Fable, Red.*

Iron (−10)

Most of the Near East entered the Iron Age by about the tenth century B.C. Egypt continued to produce maxims and dialogues, and Babylonia was also still composing "wisdom literature," including a poetic dialogue

The Literate World in the Tenth Century B.C.

in acrostic form, the *Theodicy* of Saggil Kinam Ubbib. The Biblical biographies of Saul and David are contemporary, together with the sections of the Old Testament on the *Blessing of Moses*, the *Blessing of Jacob*, and the *Oracles of Balaam*.

—10 Saggil, Anon.: *Blessing, Dispute, King, Oracles, Prayers, Saul.*

Homeric (—9)

The century of Homer is something of a pivotal point in the history of ancient literature, for it witnessed not alone the fixing of the poetic canons of Greek and the emergence of Greek literature on the world scene in its first and in many ways finest ornaments, the *Iliad* and the *Odyssey*; it also marks the eclipse of the classic tradition of Egyptian literature with a final postscript, the *Maxims* of the scribe Ani, and the final fixing of Vedic tradition in India in the last of the canonical texts—on *Magic, Prayers*, and *Tunes*. For Hebrew, as for Greek, the century is one of beginning, for the older (*Jahveh*) text of Genesis was composed at this time. When we recall further the recently antecedent demise of Hittite literature and the imminent beginnings of Chinese literary tradition (in the following century) and Persian writing (another century later), the ninth century B.C. can be seen to represent a real change in pattern. The ancient literatures disappeared, and the younger traditions of Hebrew, Greek, Chinese, and Persian replaced them. Even Babylonian tradition was beginning to give way to Syrian tradition. The only continuity was provided by Sanskrit, which was to continue as the language of Brahmanic commentary until it ultimately rivaled the endurance of Egyptian itself.

—9 Amen, Ani, Homeros, Anon.: *Jahveh, Magic, Prayers, Tunes.*

Prophetic (—8)

The earliest of the Old Testament prophets, Amos, Hosea, Isaiah, and Micah, belong to the eighth century B.C. So does the *Elohim* text of Genesis. It is contemporary with the Chinese *Classic of History* and the beginning of the coverage of the later *Spring and Autumn Annals*, thus marking the beginning of effective literacy in China. A single Chinese poem on *The Sun*, referring to an eclipse, has been astronomically dated to this same period. In Babylonia the already ancient *Gilgamesh* story was rewritten in a new Assyro-Babylonian version, while Greek tradition was continued in the works of Hesiod and the *Homeric Hymns*. The earliest inscription in Syrian proper is Zakir's *Victory over Damascus*, from this date.

—8 Amos, Hesiodos, Hosea, Isaiah, Micah, Zakir, Anon.: *Classic, Elohim, Gilgamesh, Homeric, Sun.*

Assyrian (−7)

The earliest Persian literature is probably the *Gold Tablet* of Ariyar-amna in the seventh century B.C. Hebrew prophecy was continued by Habakkuk, Nahum, and Zephaniah; Hebrew law was reworked in *Second Giving of the Law* (*Deuteronomy*), and the book of *Joshua* was composed. Along with much of the rest of the Near East, Egypt was conquered and occupied at this time by the Assyrians, whose *Library of Nineveh* is the treasurehouse from which much of the rest of ancient Near Eastern litera-ture has been passed on to us, and who commemorated their conquests in a biography of the conqueror *Esarhaddon*. In India the Vedas continued being studied, and the *Commentaries of the Brahmans* belongs to this gen-eral period, some parts being earlier and some later than the seventh cen-tury. Among the undated examples are the *Cowpath Commentary* and the *True Path Commentary*. Aside from the annals, no Chinese texts of this date are known, although parts of the later classics are doubtless this old. Peisander's *Hercules* is the principal Greek work.

−7 Ariyaramna, Habakkuk, Nahum, Peisander, Zephaniah, Anon.: *Commentaries, Esarhaddon, Joshua, Library, Second;* Undated: *Cowpath, True.*

Buddhist (−6)

Old Master K'ung, Zarathustra, and Gautama Buddha set their marks on Asia in the sixth century B.C. K'ung Fu Tzu edited the Chinese chroni-cles known to the west as the *Spring and Autumn Annals* (a redundant translation, "spring" and "autumn" being the compound ideograph for "annals"), as well as the *Classic of Poetry*. His own teachings are recorded in the *Analects*. *The Art of War* by Sun Tzu reflects the realities of the age more bluntly. Among the innumerable texts of Buddhism, only the *Poem of the Way* is regarded as substantially the work of Gautama himself, whereas Zarathustra is similarly credited with the early Avestan *Hymns*. Kapila's *Aphorisms of Sankhya Philosophy* originated one of the most enduring of the Indian philosophic systems, whereas in Israel the Hebrew prophetic tradition flourished in the hands of Baruch, Haggai, Nehemiah, Obadiah, Samuel, Zechariah, and the anonymous authors of *Judges, Kings*, and the second *Isaiah*. The ballad of *Nabu Naid* and Nebuchadrezzar's *Speeches* have come down to us from the Assyria of this time, which is also the century of Sappho, Aesop, and Eugammon in Greece and of an early Syrian poem, the *Epitaph of Taba*. An Egyptian tribute to *King Darius* by Udjahorresne probably belongs to the closing years of the century.

−6 Aisopos, Baruch, Eugammon, Gautama, Haggai, Kapila, K'ung, Nebuchadrezzar, Nehemiah, Obadiah, Samuel, Sappho, Sun, Udjahorresne, Zarathustra, Zechariah, Anon.: *Epitaph, Isaiah, Judges, Kings, Nabu.*

Periclean (−5)

The era of Pericles is perhaps the nearest thing to a general golden age in ancient literature, with Chinese, Greek, Indic and Hebrew enjoying a simultaneous florescence. It marks the compilation of the *Five Books* of the Pentateuch and the *Priestly Story of Creation*, and the composition of *Joel* and *Malachi*. King Solomon himself has sometimes been credited with the *Song of Songs*, and Job composed his famous *Lamentations*. It was the era of classic Greek drama (Aeschylus, Euripides, Aristophanes, Sophocles) and the composition of poetic epics on *Thebes*, the *Persians*, and *Hercules*, of the odes of Pindar, the histories of Thucydides, Herodotus, and Xenophon, and the *Institutions of Athens*. India produced the *Surya, Paitamaha*, and *Vaisishtha Studies* and the *Śatapatha Lecture*. There is also a very large body of early Brahmanic commentary still undated, most of it among the "lectures" (*upaniṣads*): *The Asceticism of Rama, of the Cowherd, of the Lion Man*, the *Ashtottara Satam, Bahvricha Braahmana, Chandogya, Collection, Diet, Great Forest Book, Happiness, Maaṇḍuukya, Maitri, Naaraayana, Praśna, Siva, Relation* and *Śvetasvatara Lectures*. The very important *Etymological Commentary* of Yaska belongs to this century. So do the works of Saunaka (*Deities and Myths of the Vedas*). The building of the Confucian tradition continued in China in the works of Mo, Tso, Pien, Yang, and Yen and in one composition, the *Appendix of the Classic of Change*, which was later canonized as a classic. Syrian contributed the *Story of Ahiqar*, King Daraya (Darius I) of Persia left his *Autobiography*, and *The Three Prayers* of the later *Avesta* were composed.

−5 Aiskhylos, Antimakhos, Aristophanes, Bakkhylides, Daraya, Euripides, Herakleitos, Herodotos, Job, Khoerilos, Mo, Panyasis, Pien, Pindaros, Saunaka, Solomon, Sophokles, Thukydides, Tso, Xenophon, Yang, Yaska, Yen, Anon.: *Appendix, Ashtottara, Bahvricha, Chandogya, Five, Gopaala, Great, Institutions, Joel, Katha, Maaṇḍuukya, Maitri, Malachi, Naaraayana, Nrisimha, Paitamaha, Praśna,, Priestly, Raama, Rudra, Samhitaa, Śatapatha, Story, Suurya, Śvetasvatara, Three, Vaisishtha.*

Alexandrine (−4)

The figure of the young Iskandar, as Asia called Alexander of Macedon, bestrode the fourth century B.C. and captured the literary imagination as did that of no other conqueror before Genghis Khan. China alone among literate nations was uninfluenced by him, although even Mongolian literature eventually incorporated him. This was a time of continuing splendor in the classical languages. For Greece it was the age of Plato and Aristotle, Demosthenes, Euclid, and Hippocrates, of the *Idylls* of Theocritus and the *Historic Mysteries* of Euhemerus. The Ptolemaic Egyptian *Drama of Edfou* and Manetho's *History of Egypt* (in Greek) were late reminders of the glories of ancient Egypt, now well on the way to being Hellenized. Hebrew writing figured Ezekiel, Ezra (and the anonymous author of the book of *Ezra*), the *Book of the Levites* (Leviticus), *Proverbs*, and the authoritative but noncanonical *Analyses* (Midrashim). Persia is represented indirectly in the Hebrew story of *Tobit*, which is set in Persia, although the story derives from the Syrian *Story of Ahiqar*. In Persian the only remains of the time are probably the *Seven Chapters* section of the Avesta. In Syrian there is also *Lady Anat*, possibly the earliest ritual of a mystery cult. Panini's *Eight Sections* and Bhasa's *Dream of Vasava Datta* and *Life of Bala* are among India's contributions, as is the *Shwasamvedya Lecture*. The Aitareya and Kaushitaki schools of Brahmanic commentary were well established by this date, and the *Manual of Ceremony* of the former, by Asvala Ayana, is fourth century B.C. Each of the two schools composed a *Manual of Ceremony*, a *Forest Book*, a *Commentary*, and a *Lecture*. The *Kaushitaki Lecture* is by Mahi Dasa. These other works are at least of this general period. Also here we may place the early Prakrit texts of the *Jain Canon*. Chinese writers produced a *History*, an *Herbal*, the *Nei Ching Su Wen*, the *Elegies* of Ch'ü, and the *Book* of the Lord Shang. Two Confucian classics were also written: the *Great Learning* and the *Doctrine of the Mean*. The latter works have been attributed to Confucius' grandson, K'ung Chi.

−4 Aristoteles, Asvala, Bhasa, Ch'ü, Demosthenes, Euhemeros, Euklydes, Ezekiel, Ezra, Hippokrates, K'ung, Mahi, Manetho, Menander, Panini, Platon, Shang, Theokritos, Anon.: *Aitareya, Analyses, Book, Commentary, Drama, Ezra, Forest, Herbal, History, Jain, Kaushitaki, Lady, Manual, Nei, Proverbs, Seven, Shwasamvedya, Tobit.*

Taoist (−3)

In the third century B.C. the half legendary Chou dynasty gave way to that of Han, which was the culmination of ancient Chinese culture, the epoch of Taoism, Chuang Tzu, Han and Hsün, the *Documents of the Fighting States*, the *Bamboo Annals*, and *Formal Logic*. No less than four classics were added to the Confucian corpus: the works of Meng Tzu (Mencius), the *Ritual of the Chou*, the *Encyclopedic Dictionary*, and the *Classic of Change*. But the most influential single work of the period was not a classic —the *Way of Life* of Lao Tzu, the charter of the only Chinese philosophy to take on genuinely religious trappings.

India was politically unified in the empire of Asoka, but it had begun to be linguistically diverse. There is little agreement among Sanskritists about the classification of the resulting languages, which are loosely called Prakrits. Asoka's *Edicts* carved on stone are the earliest directly preserved literary remains from India and are vernacular rather than Sanskrit. Another vernacular, Pali, emerged as the primary language of Buddhist scripture with the compilation of the Three Baskets (*Tri Piṭaka*) of canonical Buddhist writings: the *Analytical Exercises, Rules of the Order,* and *Basket of the Law.* The Sanskrit literature of the same time included the *Vaisesika Verses* of Kanada and the *Supplementary Grammar* of Katsya Ayana.

The *Yasna, Vendidad,* and *All the Judges* sections of the Avesta are contemporary, as are the book of *Jonah* and the compilation of the *Law* (Torah) of the Hebrews. Greek literature of the time is extensive but unimpressive, the representative authors being Apollonios, Aratos, Eratosthenes, Kallimakhos, Megasthenes, Nikander, Rhianos, Theophrastos and Zenodotos. The *History* of Berosus in Greek provided much the same Hellenistic bridge for ancient Babylonian tradition as Manetho had for Egyptian tradition.

−3 Apollonios, Aratos, Asoka, Berosus, Chou, Chuang, Eratosthenes, Han, Hsün, Kallimakhos, Kanada, Katsya, Lao, Lü, Megasthenes, Meng, Nikander, Rhianos, Theophrastos, Wen, Zenodotos, Anon.: *All, Analytical, Bamboo, Basket, Documents, Encyclopedic, Formal, Jonah, Law, Rules, Vendidad, Yasna.*

Punic (−2)

Aside from fragments, the earliest surviving Latin literature belongs to the second century B.C., the epoch in which Republican Rome defeated Carthage in the third of the Punic Wars. The event is described in the *Punic War* of Naevius. The principal Latin writers were Ennius, Plautus, Terence, and Cato (whose *Agriculture* is interestingly paralleled by the contemporary Chinese work on the *Value of Agriculture* by Ch'ao Ts'o). Lykophron, Dionysios Thrax, and Polybius were the principal Greek writers, and Joshua and Daniel the principal Hebrew ones. The growing Hebrew Bible was also enriched by *Esther, Judith, Ruth, Susanna,* the *Psalms of David,* the *Wisdom of Jesus Ben Sirach* (Ecclesiasticus), and *The Preacher* (Ecclesiastes), as well as by the apocryphal book of *The Maccabees* and the noncanonical *Testament of Levi.* The Persian *Antidemonic Law* also dates here, and it was about this time that the great Indian epics took their present form: the *Epic of Rama* attributed to Valmiki, *The Great Bharatas,* and the *Song Celestial.* Patanjali's *Explanation, Great Commentary,* and *Mnemonic Rules* are of about the same date. So are the Pali *Thera* and *Therii Hymns* of Buddhist scripture. Two more classics were added to the Confucian library: *Etiquette and Ceremonial* and the *Commentary on the Spring and Autumn Annals* (Tso Chuan). The Chinese historical sense continued to express itself in the *Annals of Wu and Yüeh* and the histories of Szu Ma Ch'ien. Chinese poets were also active (Chia I, Tung Fang So, Liu Ch'ê, Liu Hêng), and one of them,

Mei Shêng, is credited with introducing the four-syllable line into Chinese verse.

—2 Cato, Ch'ao, Chia, Daniel, Ennius, Joshua, K'ung, Liu, Lykophron, Mei, Naevius, Patanjali, Plautus, Polybios, Szu Ma, Terentius, Thrax, Tung, Valmiki, Anon.: *Annals, Antidemonic, Commentary, Esther, Etiquette, Great, Judith, Maccabees, Preacher, Psalms, Ruth, Sibylline, Song, Susanna, Testament, Thera, Therii, Wisdom.*

Caesarian (—1)

Han China was interrupted in the time of Caesar by the revolutionary reign of Wang Mang, who ordered the destruction of the Classics and appears to have all but obliterated the literature of his own time. Among the surviving works are *Luxuriant Dew from the Spring and Autumn Annals* by Tung Chung Shu, the *Huai Nan Book*, the works of Yang Hsiung, an anonymous *Vocabulary*, and the *Songs of the South* of Liu Hsiang. The Indian *Code* of Manu belongs to about this time, together with many of the other Hindu codes that, however, are not dated (*Agni, Atri, Bharadvaja, Kanva, Narada, Sandilya, Vyasa, Yama,* and others); and the *Old Story of Vishnu* is also assigned here, other of the legends (*puraaṇas*) being perhaps much older but as yet undated (*Agni, Boar, Creation, Creator, Existence, Garuda, Linga, Lotus, Mandukya, Matsya, Nilamata, Siva, Theology, Vamana*). The earliest surviving Tamil writing, the *Tamil Grammar*, belongs to the first century B.C., as do our sole text in Etruscan—on *Etruscan Public Ceremonies*—and the Essene text called *The Coming Down* from among the Hebrew Dead Sea Scrolls of Qumran. A single Pali text, the *Kathaa Vatthu* of Tissa is known to have been added to the literature of Buddhism. A large body of Buddhist scriptures, remains undated but belongs to the period of growth of Indian Buddhism. It includes the Sanskrit *Diamond, Lankavatara,* and *Surangama Verses,* and the Pali *Anguttara Commentary,* the *Great Cycle of Being, The Great Speech, Mahaa Vyut Patti, Majjhima Nikaya, Samyatta Nikaya, Sigaloveda Suttanta, Song of a Monk in a Cauldron of Oil, Sutta Nipata,* and *Zenaka.* But for the *Lament for Bion,* Greek literature was in eclipse, and it is Latin that dominated the world scene in this its golden age—particularly in history (Diodorus, Livy, Sallust), poetry (Catullus, Horace, Lucretius, Vergil), military annals (*The African War, The Spanish War,* Caesar and Hirtius) and essays (Cicero, Vitruvius).

—1 Caesar, Catullus, Cicero, Diodorus, Grattius, Hirtius, Horatius, Liu, Livius, Lucretius, Manu, Sallustius, Tissa, Tung, Varius, Vergilius, Vitruvius, Yang, Anon.: *African, Coming, Etruscan, Huai, Lament, Old, Spanish, Tamil, Vocabulary;* Undated: *Agni, Anguttara, Atri, Bharadvaja, Bhavishya, Braahmaanda, Diamond, Kanva, Lakavatara, Legends, Mahaa, Mandukya, Matsya, Narada, Nilamata, Padma, Samyatta, Sandilya, Sigalovada, Song, Surangama, Sutta, Vaamana, Varaaha, Vyas, Yama, Zenaka.*

Christian (1)

The fragmentation of Jewish literature in the first century of the Christian era is illustrative of the intellectual turmoil of the time. Minimally we may distinguish the orthodox writers (Akiba, Ishmael, Yohai) from the Essene texts (*Blessings and Thanksgivings*, the *Formulary of Blessings*) in Hebrew and from the Christian writers (Levi, Lukas, Ioannis, Marcus) in Greek and pagan Jewish writers (Josephus) in Latin. Aramaic Syrian was also widely used in Judaism, although the considerable body of Syrian texts and the comparable texts of demotic Egyptian are not yet well explored. Among the classic Hebrew works that also remain undated but that belong to this approximate period are the *Book of Jubilees, Jashar, The Lost Apocrypha, The Mirror of Simple Souls, Sayings of the Jewish Fathers, Shabbath, The Treatise on Blessings* and various *Testaments* (Abraham, Asher, Benjamin, Enoch, Joseph, Judah, Naphtali, Reuben, and Zebulon).

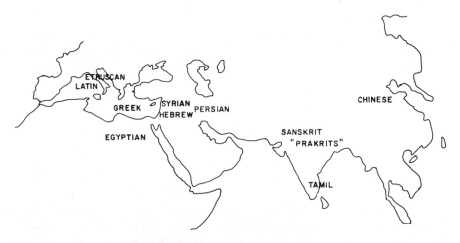

The Literate World in the First Century B.C.

Aside from the *Gospels*, the primary influence on the shaping of Christianity in this first century was the *Letters* of Saul (St. Paul). The other Greek compositions of the *New Testament* canon dated to this period are the *Acts of the Apostles* and the *Revelation of St. John the Divine*. Pagan Greek literature also enjoyed a revival in the first century, represented in the works of Dionysios (who also wrote in Latin), Strabo, and Dio.

For Latin the first century was a continuing florescence, the "silver age" of the early empire, which included such figures as Lucan, Tacitus, Suetonius, Seneca, Petronius, Ovid, Quintilian, and the older and the younger Pliny. Less well-known Latin authors were Germanicus, Silius, Statius, Valerius, Manilius, Calpurnius, Curtius, Mela, Scaurus, and Paterculus.

In India the building of Buddhist tradition continued with the works of Asva Ghosa (*Plays, Awakening of Faith in the Greater Vehicle, Life of Buddha*). One of the most remarkable texts is the confrontation of Buddhist mysticism and Greek skepticism in *The Questions of King Menander*. This was the crest of the Buddhist wave in India, and the Hindu literature of the period is trivial (for example, Manjusri, Kumara Lata). Buddhism is also reflected in the anonymous *Manimeekalai* in Tamil at about this time. This is also the first century of Buddhist influence in China, marked by the translation of the *Poem of Forty-Two Sections*. The Critical Essays of Wang Ch'ung are also a notable work of the time.

1 Akiba, Asva Ghosa, Calpurnius, Curtius, Dio, Dionysios, Germanicus, Ioannis, Ishmael, Josephus, Kumara, Levi, Lucanus, Lukas, Manilius, Manjusri, Marcus, Mela, Ovidius, Paterculus, Petronius, Plinius, Plinius Junior, Quintilianus, Saul, Scaurus, Seneca, Silius, Statius, Strabo, Suetonius, Tacitus, Tai, Valerius, Wang, Yohai, Anon.: *Acts, Blessings, Commentaries, Commentary, Epistle, Formulary, Mahaniddesa, Manimeekalai, Manual, Netti, New, Oration, Perfect, Periplus, Petako, Poem, Questions, Revelation, Sublime, War, Zadokite;* Undated: *Book, Jashar, Lost, Mirror, Sayings, Shabbath, Testaments, Treatise.*

Aurelian (2)

Han China, Imperial Rome, and the Alexandrian Greece continued the building of their respective classicisms in the second century, while the Persian *Avesta* and the Christian New Testament were becoming fixed in their present forms and the commentary of Judaism and Buddhism continued to grow. The *Meditations* of Marcus Aurelius were a characteristic product of this sophisticated age, which is the time of Martial, Juvenal, Lucian, Arrian, and Appian in Latin, and of Ptolemy, Plutarch, Galen and Pausanias in Greek. Of particularly literary interest are the *Banquet of the Learned* of Athenaeus, the *Attic Nights* of Gellius, and the anonymous *Dream of Venus*. Chariton's *Chaireas and Callirrhoe* is held by some to be the earliest anticipation of the modern novel. From China the works of Huai and Pan's history of *The Former Han* belong here, together with Hsü Shen's *Lexicon*, the commentaries of Ma Jung and Chêng Hsüan, and two commentaries later considered classics: the *Kung Yang* and *Ku Liang Commentaries* (the latter being of uncertain date). Mou's *Doubts Raised* is in the tradition of lively philosophical debate. *The Measure of the Mongol Horn* by Ts'ai Yen reports on her captivity among the Hsiung Nu.

The *Lotus of the Perfect Law* and Avalokite Svara's *Lotus Poem* were added to Buddhist literature, together with a *Life of Buddha*, the *Tales of Buddha's Former Births*, and *Tales of Buddha*, the works of Naga Arjuna (*The Conception of the Buddhist Nirvana, Poem of the Mean*). Sanskrit works included Charaka's *Encyclopedia of Medicine*, an anonymous *Medical Compendium*, Matri Cheta's *Hymns*, and the anonymous *Parables*, later poetically elaborated. South India was also productive—the *Lay of the Anklet* attributed to Prince Ilango Adigal and Tiruvallavar's *Songs of an Outcaste Priest* are dated here in Tamil.

In the Middle East this is the date of the earliest *Martyrdom* books in Syrian and of continuing apocryphal works in Hebrew: *Bel and the Dragon*, *Baruch*, *Esdras*, and the *Song the the Three Holy Children*. The Syrian *Baruch* and *Bereshith Rabba* are undated but may belong here. There is also a continuing literature in Coptic Egyptian through this period, but it is not well documented.

2 Aeolius, Appianus, Aristides, Arrianus, Athenaeus, Avalokite, Charaka, Chêng, Diogenes, Galen, Gellius, Hsü, Huai, Ignatius, Ilango, Ioannis, Justin, Juvenalis, Khariton, Lucianus, Ma, Marcus, Martialis, Matri, Mou, Naga, Nepos, Nikhomakhos, Pan, Pausanias, Plutarkhos, Ptolemaios, Tiruvallavar, Ts'ai, Varro, Anon.: *Apocalypse, Avesta, Baruch, Bel, Buddha's, Commentary, Dream, Esdras, Kung, Life, Lotus, Martyrdom, Medical, Parables, Second, Shepherd, Song, Tales;* Undated: *Baruch, Bereshith, Ku.*

Classic (3)

In a general sense the classic world may be said to have ended in the third century A.D. The Greek *Bible* (Septuagint) was completed. Buddhism began to recede in India. The body of Chinese classics stood complete with Liu Shao's *Classic of Filial Piety*, as the Han dynasty gave way to the period of the three kingdoms. The decline of Rome was well underway, with two dozen undistinguished emperors filling the third century between Septimus Severus and Diocletian.

Hebrew literature was represented by the *Repetitions* (Mishna) of Yehuda, and Syrian by the *Book of the Laws of the Countries* by Bar Daysan and the *Letter of Mara Bar Serapion*. The notable Latin authors were Lactantius and Apuleius, and the latter actually wrote as much in Greek as in Latin. His *Golden Ass* has been related to the contemporary Greek protonovels of Longus and Xenophon. Other Greek writers were Longinus, Plotinus, Dio Cassius, Herodian, and Rhodios. Several works of ancient Persian literature have been assigned to the same period: *Shayist ne Shayist, Opinions of the Spirit of Wisdom*, the narrative *Ard Viraf, Ground Giving*, and the *Index* of Mani, *The Tree of Babylon*, and the *History of Zarer*.

Indian works included the stories of Arya Deva, the *Pauline* and *Roman Studies*, and the *Code of Vishnu*, and probably the *Doctrine of Politics* of Kautilya (or possibly Chanakya). In the China of the Three Kingdoms, translation of Buddhist works continued (for example, Hsü Kan), and commentaries on the Confucian classics (Sun Shu Jan, Wang Pi) were matched by others on Chuang Tzu (Hsiang Hsiu) and a *Commentary on Mu T'ien*. There were active essayists (Huang Fu Mi, Hsün Hsü) and poets (Hsi K'ang, K'ung Jung, Ying Yang, Ts'ao Chih, Fu Mi) and a work on *Poetics* (by Wang Ts'an). The *Han Annals* were completed by Hsü Yueh, and the *Memoir of the Three Kingdoms* of Ch'en Shou describes the time. Liu Shao, who wrote the last of the Confucian classics, also composed a *Study of Human Abilities*. Like the anonymous *Classic of Mathematics*, it was not a "classic." Almost classical was the *Family Sayings of Confucius* by Wang Su.

3 Apuleius, Arya, Bar Daysan, Ch'en, Clement, Dio, Epiphanios, Fu, Herodianos, Hippolytus, Hsi, Hsiang, Hsü, Hsün, Huang, Irenaeus, K'ang, Kautilya, K'ung, Lactantius, Liu, Longinus, Longus, Mani, Origenos, Plotinus, Rhodios, Sun, Ts'ao, Wang, Xenophon, Yehuda, Ying, Anon.: *Ard, Books, Classic, Code, Ground, History, Letter, Mu, Opinions, Pauline, Pistis, Roman, Septuagint, Shayist, Tree.*

Byzantine (4)

Whereas the third century marked the completion of the Greek Bible, the fourth century made Christianity the state religion of the Roman Empire. The Coptic Egyptian *Bible* is of approximately this date, and Christian literature flowered in Latin (Ambrosius, Augustinus, the *Vulgate* of Jeronimus, Aetheria's *Journey to the Holy Places*), in Greek (Eusebios), and in Syrian (*Acts of the Persian Martyrs, Doctrine of Addai*, Marqa's *Commentary on the Pentateuch*, and additional *Martyrdom* books). Mesrob and Sahak produced an Armenian *Bible*, and the Syrian *Bible* (Peshitta) and a vulgar Aramaic (*targum*) version are also probably of this date.

Secular literature continued in the Latin histories of Ammianus, Spartianus, and Aurelius, and is represented in Greek by Quintus' *Sequel to the Iliad*, Soterichos' *Bassarica*, Erinna's *The Spindle*, Nonnus' *Dionysos*, and Heliodoros' *Tales of Ethiopia*. Ethiopia itself, otherwise shadowy before, the thirteenth century, left a fourth-century inscription on *The Wars of King 'Aizana*.

European vernacular literature may also be dated to this first postclassic century in Gothic, Georgian, and Armenian. The Gothic *Bible* of Ulfilas and the inscription on the *Golden Horn* by Holting were the earliest fragments of Germanic literature. Georgian was represented by the works of Bakur, and the *History* of Faustus initiated the long tradition of Armenian historiography.

Burzoe's *Society, Ethics and Religion* was the principal Persian contribution. Burzoe is also said to have translated an early version of the Sanskrit *Five Books*, but it has been lost. The Buddhist masterpieces were the *Poem of Buddha's Former Lives*, of Arya Sura, and Vasu Bandhu's *Buddhism, a Religion of Infinite Compassion*. In the main, however, this was in India a time of Hindu resurgence under the Gupta dynasty, producing the *Poem of Brahma* of Badara Ayana, the *Sankhya Philosophy* of Isvara, the *Elementary Grammar* of Sarva Varman, the *Puujaavaliya*, and the *Island Chronicle* (a history of Ceylon), and the *Laws of Love* of Vatsya Ayana. Furthermore, the poetry and plays of Kali Dasa (a subject of that King Sudraka who is himself remembered for *The Little Clay Cart*) lifted Hindu literature to one of its highest peaks. The tradition of medieval Indian poetic epics (*kaavya*) may be traced to Kali Dasa and his contemporaries, who drew their themes, as India continues to do, from the great classic epics of Rama and the Bharatas. The anthology of Asanga, the epic of Hari Sena, the *Seven Centuries* of Hala, and the works of Vimala, Susruta, Ghata, and Vatsa Bhatti are part of this Hindu renaissance, together with the anonymous *Ghaṭa Karpara, Sṛṅgaara Tilaka*, and *Sṛṅgaara Rasa Aṣṭaku*. The Tamil poems of Poygaiyar also date here.

This was a troubled period in China, which produced works on Taoism by Ko and Kuo Hsiang, the *Peach Blossom Fountain* of T'ao Ch'ien, the essays of Kuo P'o, and the works of Hsü Hsün, Wang Hsi Chi's *In the Orchard Pavilion*, the *Hua Hu Ching*, and the *Supernatural Researches* of Yü Pao.

4 Aetheria, Ambrosius, Ammianus, Arya, Asanga, Augustinus, Aurelius, Badara, Bakur, Burzoe, Erinna, Eusebios, Faustus, Ghata, Hala, Hari, Heliodoros, Holting, Hsü, Isvara, Jeronimus, Kali, Ko, Kuo, Marqa, Mesrob, Nonnus, Poygaiyar, Quintus, Sarva, Soterichos, Spartianus, Sudraka, Susruta, T'ao, Ulfilas, Vasu, Vatsa, Vatsya, Vimala, Wang, Yü, Anon.: *Acts, Bible, Doctrine, Duel, Ghaṭa, Hua, Island, Martyrdom, Puujaavaliya, Sṛṅgaara, Wars.*

Hunnic (5)

Attila raided Germany and was stopped by the Merovingian Franks on the Marne; the Goths and Vandals sacked Rome; and the Anglo-Saxons invaded Britain in the fifth century. These events were felt and noted even by the distant Syrians in Cyrillona's *Invasion of the Huns*. There was an expectable slump in Latin literature, the sole surviving work being Martianus' *Marriage of Philology and Mercury*. The more protected Byzantine Greeks continued to write of Troy (Priskos, Tryphiodoros, Koluthos). They also wrote history (Eunapios), romances (Tatius), religious biography (Marcus), and mathematics (Proklos, Hierokles). The Syrian literature of the time is mainly historical (Balai, Bar Sudhaili, Zenobius, and the aforementioned Cyrillona), although it included poetry as well (Bar Sauma). Its most influential work was Nestorius' *Bazaar of Heraclides*, the charter of Nestorian Christianity. The Armenian works were also principally histories (*The History of St. Gregory and Agathangelus*, the histories of Khoren, Lazar, Goriun, and Wardapet), and theology (Eznik). The works of Iver, *The Martyrdom of St. Shushanik*, and the Georgian *Bible* are the contemporary Georgian works. Hebrew literature still flourished, producing the *Sukka* and *Sanhedren*, the *Additions* (Tosefta), and the *Researches* (Talmud) of Babylon and Jerusalem.

Persia produced the tale of *Khusrau Kawadhan and His Page*. India remained active in both Sanskrit and Pali. The chief Pali works of this last productive century of Buddhist India were the *Chronicle* of Maha Naman and the works of Buddha Ghosa (*The Path of Purity* and *Footsteps of the Law*). Sanskrit produced an anonymous *Book of Studies*, the *Vasesika* and *Inquiry* commentaries of Prashasta Pada and Shabara Svamin respectively, the *Mudra Raksasa* of Visakha Datta, and the works of Guna Varman. The works of Tirumular represent Tamil. The continuing contact between India and China was recorded in the journal of Fa's visit to India, while Kumara Jiva, an Indian monk, was in China supervising the translation of some ninety-five Buddhist classics. Other Chinese works were Tsu's essay on the calendar, the works of Hui, Fan Yeh's *The Later Han*, the poems of T'ao and Pao Chao, and P'ei Sung Chih's commentary on the *Memoir of the Three Kingdoms*. The fragmentation of China had by this time become so thoroughgoing as to make a time of only three kingdoms seem imperial by comparison.

5 Balai, Bar Sauma, Bar Sudhaili, Buddha, Cyrillona, Eunapios, Eznik, Fa, Fan, Goriun, Guna, Hierokles, Hui, Iver, Khoren, Koluthos, Lazar, Maha, Marcus, Martianus, Nestorius, Pao, P'ei, Prasasta, Priskos, Proklos, Sabara, T'ao, Tatius, Tirumular, Tryphiodoros, Tsu, Visakha, Wardapet, Zenobius, Anon.: *Additions, Anuyogadvaara, Bible, History, Khusrau, Martyrdom, Researches, Sanhedren, Siddhaanta, Sukka.*

Gregorian (6)

The papacy had become the dominant institution in Italy; Justinian was codifying Roman law in Byzantium; Mohammed was a young man in Mecca; and Syria was the center of world literature as the sixth century ended. Perhaps the most written about figure of the time was John of Tella, a Syrian writer of theology and liturgy whose biography was written by John of Asia and again by Elias. The works of Paul and Ras'ain summarized the learning of the Hellenic world for transmission to the still dormant

Arabs, while the *Chronicle of Edessa* and the writings of Bar Aphtonya and Beth Arsham continue the Syrian interest in history and biography. More specifically literary pieces were the *Romance of Julian the Apostate*, the *Cave of Treasures*, and especially the *Kalila and Dimna* of Bodh, the Sanskrit original of which also dates to the sixth century in its present form, although deriving from the *Five Books* of the second century. The Georgian *St. Evstafy* and the first Arabic literature is from this last century before the Hegira. Shanfara's *Arabic Rhyme in L* and the *Ballad of Three Witches* exemplify the poetry and the anonymous *Suspended* the prose.

The Persians produced the *Deeds of Ardashire Babakan*. Sanskrit literature included Bharavi's *Duel of Siva and Arjuna*, the astrology of Varahamihira, Pravara Sena's *Setubandhu*, and a new *Life of Buddha*. The Tamil *Ethical Epigrams* were approximately contemporary, and Samgha wrote *Vasu Deva Hindii* in a Prakrit. Chinese works were the anthology and history of Hsiao T'ung, Shên Yo's works on the Ch'i, the Chin, and the Liu Sung, Wei's *Book*, and Lü Yüan Lang's *Defense of Confucianism*. The *Korean Historical Records* mark the beginning of literary history in that country.

The tradition of Greek romances was carried on by Musaios' *Hero and Leander*, that of Greek epic by Korippos' *Johannid*, and that of Greek history by Malalas, Prokopios, and Agathias. Latin literature included the *Book of Kells*, Lydus' essay on Roman administration, the edicts of Theodoric, the poetry of Fortunatus, the histories of Gregory of Tours, Gildas, and Jordanes, and the works of Cassiodorus, but the leading figures were the philosopher-moralist Boethius and the pope, St. Gregory I.

The nascent vernaculars of Europe were represented by the few Welsh poems that can be credibly attributed to Taliesin and by the earliest Irish works—the poems of Lanfili, the *Amra Choluim Chille* of MacForgaill, and the *Senchas Már*, a legal text, probably the first literary works of northwestern Europe.

6 Agathias, Amari, Arya, Asia, Bar Aphtonya, Beth Arsham, Bharavi, Bodh, Boethius, Cassiodorus, Elias, Fortunatus, Gildas, Gregorius, Hsiao, Jordanes, Justinianus, Korippos, Lanfili, Lü, Lydus, MacForgaill, Malalas, Musaios, Paul, Pravara, Prokopios, Ras'ain, Samgha, Shanfara, Shên, Taliesin, Tella, Theodoric, Tours, Varahamihira, Wei, Anon.: *Ballad, Book, Cave, Chronicle, Deeds, Ethical, Five, Korean, Life, Romance, St. Evstafy, Senchas, Suspended.*

T'ang (7)

The century of Mohammed's Hegira and *Koran* was an Asian century in literature. Writing in the West, now in the depths of the "dark ages," was confined to textbooks (Aldhelm and Sevillanus in Latin) and political history (Hispalis in Latin; Menander, Sebeos, and Simokatta in Greek; Djuansher, Kalantuatzi, and Ananiah in Armenian). In addition to the *History of Zacharias Rhetor*, the Syrians wrote biography (Rustam, Sahdona) and philosophy (Hedhayabh, Merv). The sole works of fiction produced west of Persia were the *Hexaemeron* of Jacob of Edessa in Syrian, Meskha's *Wisdom of Valovar* in Georgian, the *Adventures of Bran MacFebal*, in Irish, and Aneirin's *Gododdin* in Welsh. Arabic poetry was written by A'sha and Nabigha, Hebrew poetry by Ben Jose, and Persia produced the *Religious Acts* and *Book of Kings*.

In the east, on the other hand, the century was a splendid one. India produced traditional Sanskrit religious commentaries (Brahma Gupta, Santi Deva, Uddyotakara, Prabhakara, Mayura, Mati Chandra) and linguistic studies (Chandra Gomin, Jaya Ditya and Vamana, Bhartri Hari) and even medical works (Vagh Bata). But it added romances (Magha's *Slaying of Sisupala*, Kumara Dasa's *Rape of Siva*, Bhatti's *Slaying of Ravana*, Bhaumaka's *Ravana and Arjuna*, Subandhu's *Vaasava Datta*), annals (Kalhana's *Stream of Kings*), and poetry (Dandin's *Mirror of Poetry* and *Life of Dasa Kumara*). King Harsa himself contributed to the luster of the time with *Joy of the Snake World* and *Priyadarśikaa*, and his biography by Bana covers one of the most productive epochs in all the long history of India. Bana's other works (*Kaadambarii*, *Tale of Chandi*) were also important, and other items from the period are the *Maana Saara* and the works of Jinendra Buddhi. In Prakrit there are Jina Dasa's *Nandii Cuurṇi* and the *Commentary* of Jina Bhadra, and in Tamil the *Teevaaram* of Appar. The Tibetan *Book of the Dead*, together with the poetry of Ralopa and Ti Srong, initiated the literature of Tibet at about this time.

The T'ang dynasty of China was equally brilliant. United for the first time since the fall of the Hans four hundred years earlier (excepting 88 years under Chin and Sui), China experienced something like a renaissance —a resurgence of Confucianism that was in part a reassertion of the classical traditions, in part a reinterpretation of them in the light of Buddhist teachings, and in part a matter of new departures. It was a gay, bibulous, poetic, lively, and sophisticated age. Dynastic history was still maintained (by Yao Chien, Wei Chêng, Li Po Yao, Yen Shih Ku, Li Yen Shou, and the anonymous author of the *Book of Sui*), but a *Literary Encyclopedia* was prepared that was a new achievement. The first *Phonetic Dictionary* by Lu Fa Yen and Yen Chih T'ui was also a new development, which led to the earliest use of tone rhyme in Chinese poetry. Ch'en Tzu Ang is a notable poet of the seventh century, which also produced the *Classic of Mathematics* of Wang Hsiao T'ung, the *Book of the Original Term*, and the works of Seng. Continuing contact with and interest in India is reflected in the travel journals of Yuan Chwang, I Tsing, and Hsüan Tsang. And from this period on we have the preservation in China of the despised but popular nonclassical narratives, such as *The White Monkey*. Korean literature was represented by Koguryo's *Record of Remembrance*.

7 Aldhelm, Ananiah, Aneirin, Appar, A'sha, Bana, Ben Jose, Bhartri, Bhatti, Bhaumaka, Brahma, Chandra, Ch'en, Dandin, Djuansher, Edessa, Harsa, Hedhayabh, Hispalis, Hsüan, I, Jaya, Jina, Jinendra, Kalantuatzi, Kalhana, Koguryo, Kumara, Li, Lu, Magha, Mati, Mayura, Menander, Merv, Meskha, Mohammed, Nabigha, Prabhakara, Ralopa, Rustam, Sahdona, Santi, Sebeos, Seng, Sevillanus, Simokatta, Subandhu, Ti, Uddyotakara, Vagh, Vamana, Wang, Wei, Yao, Yen, Yuan, Anon.: *Adventures, Book, History, Literary, Maana, Religious, White.*

Islamic (8)

The flood of Islam rolled across Africa, Europe, and Asia in the eighth century. It was stopped at Tours by Charles Martel in 732. In England the saga of *Beowulf* was composed in Anglo-Saxon and the works of Bede in Latin. Adamnan and Boniface were also writing. Greek is scarcely better represented—by the *Fount of Knowledge* of John Damascene and the simplified code of the emperor Leo III. Hebrew commentary was continued by Ahai, Ashi, and Gaon, and Armenian Christian commentary by Catholicus and Asheruni. The *Great Treasure* and Isho'denah's *Book of Chastity* were the principal Syrian works, and Leoncius' *History of the First Caliphs* is an Armenian account of the astonishing Arab successes. Georgian produced the history of Djonanchiani and the *Treasury of St. Cyril*.

Like the preceding century, the eighth century was largely Asian. In Arabic it marks the beginning of the collection of the traditions (*hadiith*) of the Prophet, which later led to the editing of a definitive scriptural *Koran*. Awza'i and Zuhri were leading collectors. Ibn Ishaq wrote a *Life of the Prophet*. Ibn Munabbeh composed a description of *Africa*, our earliest written record of many regions of the continent, and Ibn Musa wrote on *Algebra* and *Asceticism*. Ibn Muqaffa produced an Arabic version of *Kalila and Dimna* and a *History of the Kings of Persia*. Among the more distinctive literary works were the *Suspended* of Rawiya, *The Levelled Path* of Ibn Anas, *Mufaddal's Book* by Ibn Ya'la, and the *Flytings* of Jarir and Farazdaq. *Religious Opinions* is a Persian work of the time.

Indian philosophy continued to flower, Sankhya and Vedanta teachings being summarized by Gauda Pada, and Yoga by Vyasa. The *Inquiry* of Kumarila and the *Pali Grammar* of Katsya Ayana are also of this era. The more strictly literary works are the heroic romances of Bhava Bhuti: *Malati and Madhava, The Life of the Great Hero*, and *The Later Life of Rama*. The collected epics of Bhamaha and the works of Damodara and Jina Sena may also be mentioned, and there were the Prakrit *Gaüdavaha* of Vak Pati Raja and the *Upadeśa Pada* of Hari Bhadra as well. Tiruman-gal was a leading Tamil poet. Tibet is not represented.

The brilliance of the T'ang period in China was maintained by two of the greatest Chinese poets, Li Po and Tu Fu, and the latter's *Autobiography* is one of the real masterpieces of Chinese literature. Other poets of the time were Mêng Hao Jan, Sung Chih Wên, Ts'ui Hao, and Chang Ch'ien. Improved phonetic dictionaries were compiled by Li Yang Ping and Sung Ch'i, and Tu Yu wrote a treatise on *Government*. Narrative was represented by the Chinese *Cinderella* of Tuan Ch'eng Shih and the anonymous story of *The Beautiful Li*. Other works of the period are the *Book of Chin*, Chen's *Chien Niang*, Chang Chih Ho's *Conservation of Vitality*, Wang Ping's *Commentary on the Nei Ching*, the *Itineraries of the Fifty-Six Monks*, and the *T'ang Kien Wen Tse*.

The equally brilliant dawn of Japanese literature also belongs to the century of *Beowulf*, the Nara period, from which a number of anonymous historical works have been preserved: *Japanese Notes, Topography, The Record of Ancient Matters, Chinese Poems*, and the *Book of Ten Thousand Leaves*. There appears to be no extant Korean literature from this century.

8 Adamnan, Ahai, Asheruni, Ashi, Awza'i, Bede, Bhamaha, Bhava, Bonifacius, Catho-licus, Chang, Chen, Damascene, Damodara, Djonanchiani, Gaon, Gauda, Hari, Ibn Anas, Ibn Ishaq, Ibn Munabbeh, Ibn Muqaffa, Ibn Musa, Ibn Ya'la, Isho'denah, Jarir, Jina, Katsya, Kumarila, Leo, Leoncius, Li, Mêng, Rawiya, Sung, Tirumangal, Ts'ui, Tu, Tuan, Vak, Vyasa, Wang, Zuhri, Anon.: *Beautiful, Beowulf, Book, Chinese, Great, Itineraries, Japanese, Record, Religious, T'ang, Topography, Treasury.*

Carolingian (9)

The Saxon kings ruled England, the Swedes Russia, and Charles the Great France and Germany. Literacy spread to half a dozen new European languages and now included: Saxon (*Heliand, Genesis*) and Anglo-Saxon (*Brunanburh*, Layamon's *Brut*, Cynewulf's *Poems*, and the translations of King Alfred), Old Low German (*Hildebrand*), Old High German (the Judgement Day poem of *Muspilli, Ludwig's Song* and the *Gospel History* of Otfrid), High Dutch (the *Wessobrunn Prayer*), French (the *Strassburg Oaths*), Irish (*The Sons of Usnech, The Cattle Raid of Cooley*), Welsh (*I Shall Not Talk, Songs of Llywarch Hen*), Russian (the translations of Cyril and Methodius), and Icelandic (Finsson's *Praise of Hakon*). The "Poetic Edda" of Iceland, formerly assigned to this century, almost certainly has parts that are as old as this, but as a compilation it is now assigned to the thirteenth century. Armenian literature remained religious, Moshtotz' *Armenian Rituals* and Zachariah's *Homilies* being the chief works of this time.

Philosophy and history continued in Latin—in this century represented by the *Universe* of Hrabanus, the textbooks of Amelarius and Alcuin, Erigena's *Division of Nature*, and the Frankish and Lombard histories of St. Gall, Ermoldus, Einhard, Nithard, and Paulus. A new Latin poetry appeared by Notker (*Sequences*), Sedulius (*Easter Hymn*), and Abbo. Walafrid Strabo's works were a highlight of the "Carolingian Renaissance" (*St. Blathmac, St. Faro, The Vision of Wettin, The Little Garden*). The Byzantine Greeks were trivially represented by the legal works of Leo VI and Basil I and a mime play of *Christ's Passion*, but more importantly by the bibliographic *Library* of Photios, one of our most important windows on the literature of the classic world. Hebrew works included the *Greater Laws* of Qayyara and the anonymous *Ten Tribes*, and Syria was represented by Taghrit's *Science of Rhetoric*, Romanus the Physician, and Timothy, the jurist.

In the century of Harun the Orthodox (Rashiid), the largest collections of the *Traditions* were made. Bukhari, Muslim, Abu Dawud, Ibn Maja, and Ibn Hanbal were the chief figures in this labor. Geography was enriched by Fazari's *Ghana* and Khurdadbih's *Road Book*, and history by the works of Hakam, Baladhuri, Dinawari, and Tabari. Mu'tazz wrote on *Poetics*, as did Ibn Qutayba, a prolific author on other subjects as well (*Poetry and Poets, Book of Classes, General Knowledge, Choice Histories, Accomplishments of the Secretary*). Abu Nuwas and Atahiya were leading poets, and Sukkari made a notable collection of old Arabic poetry. Essays include the *Gallantry* of Buhturi and of Abu Tammam, a type of work much imitated in later times, and the works of Jahiz (*Eloquence and Exposition, Animals*). *The Unique Necklace* by Rabbihi was a notable narrative. Other writers of the ninth century were Kindi, Shafi'i, Zahiri, Mubarrad, and Khayyat. Persian literature also began to flower again with the *Zadsparam* and the poetry of Rudagi, Bin Ba'ith, and Marv.

India continued its interest in Vedanta and Yoga philosophy in the works of Padma Pada and Vachas Pati Mitra and interest in the whole reach of traditional Hindu thought in the commentaries of perhaps the greatest of the medieval Indian scholars, Samkara (*Commentary on the Poem of Brahma, The Hammer of Folly, The Wave of Bliss*). The works of Visakha Datta, Mandana Misra, and Puspa Danta and an anonymous *Mahimnah Stotra* are also of this date. Romances were also composed: Siva Svamin's *Epic of Kashmir*, Rudrata's romances, the *Mythology* of Ratna Akara, and the works of Abhi Nanda, Udbhata, and Ananda Vardhana. In Prakrit there is the *Deeds of the Great Man* of Sila Acharya. From Dravidian India come the *Eastern Love Story* of Alagiyavanna, the works of Appar, the *Martyr of Truth* of Ari Chandra, and the *Tiruvasagan* of Manikka, all in Tamil. Kannada literature begins in this century with a

Treatise on Poetry by Nripatunga, Sinhalese with the *Edict* of Kassapa IV, and the medieval poetry of the *Baudhagan o Doha* marks the literary debut of proto-Bengali. Tibetan produced its national epic, the *Romance of Kesar.*

In the ninth century, T'ang China produced the works of Po Chü I, Han Yü's *Essay on Buddhism,* P'ei Hsiu's *Teachings of Hsi Yun,* Liu Tsung Yüan's *Catching Snakes,* and Chang Yen Yüan's *Eminent Painters of All Ages.* Among the poets of the period were Tu Ch'in Niang, Ch'ên T'ao, Hsü An Chên, Li Ho, Li Shê, Ma Tzu Jan, Ssu K'ung T'u, and Li Hua, whose poem *On an Old Battlefield* is particularly remembered. "Vulgar" stories continued to be written—by Li King Tso (*The Drunkard's Dream*) and Li Fu Yen (*The Man Who Became a Fish* and others). Korean literature reappeared at this time in the *Silla Folk Songs,* the drama of *The Palace Gate,* and the works of Ch'oe, while Japan was silent.

9 Abbo, Abhi, Abu Dawud, Abu Nuwas, Abu Tammam, Alagiyavanna, Alcuin, Alfred, Amelarius, Ananda, Appar, Ari, Atahiya, Baladhuri, Basil, Bin Ba'ith, Buddha, Buhturi, Bukhari, Chang, Ch'ên, Ch'oe, Cynewulf, Cyril, Dinawari, Einhard, Erigena, Ermoldus, Fazari, Finsson, Hakam, Han, Hrabanus, Hsü, Ibn Hanbal, Ibn Maja, Ibn Qutayba, Jahiz, Kassapa, Khayyat, Khurdadbih, Kindi, Layamon, Leo, Li, Liu, Ma, Mandana, Manikka, Marv, Moshtotz, Mubarrad, Muslim, Mu'tazz, Nithard, Notker, Nripatunga, Otfrid, Padma, Paulus, P'ei, Photios, Po, Puspa, Qayyara, Rabbihi, Ratna, Romanus, Rudagi, Rudrata, St. Gall, Sakya, Samkara, Sedulius, Shafi'i, Sila, Siva, Ssu, Sukkari, Tabari, Taghrit, Timothy, Tirmidhi, Tu, Udbhata, Vachas, Visakha, Walafrid, Zahiri, Zachariah, Anon.: *Baudhagan, Brunanburh, Cattle, Christ's, Genesis, Heliand, Hildebrand, I, Mahimnah, Muspilli, Palace, Romance, Silla, Songs, Sons, Strassburg, Ten, Wessobrunn, Zadsparam.*

Sung (10)

The T'ang dynasty ended and the Sung dynasty began in China. The Duke of Kiev and the King of Norway became Christians, and the Norse reached Greenland. The Capetian dynasty was established in France, and Ethelred the Unready was king of England. The Saxon line of the First German Reich under Otto I produced most of the Latin literature of the tenth century—by Richer, Ratpert, Ratherius, Ekkehard, Liutprand, Widukind, and Roswitha. The *Annales Cambriae* and *The Prisoner's Escape* by a monk of Toul and Ethelwold's *Concordance of Rules* also date here. Spain was almost entirely a Moorish province, but a Spaniard, Suarez, wrote *The Laws and God the Legislator* in Latin, and there were also a *History of Rheims* by Flodoard, a biography of *King Alfred* by Asser, and the *Chronicle of Kristian.*

Icelandic literature grew apace and produced the Ögmundarson love poems the *Raven Song* of Hornklofi, the *Son's Lament* of Skallagrimsson, and the *Praise of Eric Bloodaxe.* England was equally fertile, as evidenced by *Judith,* the *Blicking Homilies, Widsith, Deor's Lament,* and the

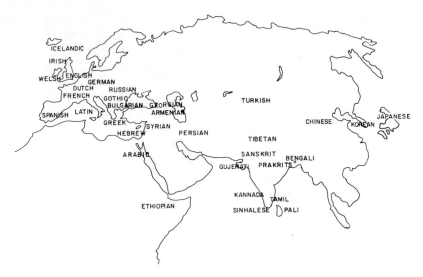

The Literate World in the Tenth Century A.D.

Lay of Maldon. The *Psalter of Quatrains, The Vision of Adamnan,* and the *Four Songs* represented Irish, and the *Prophecy of Britain* continued Welsh literature. French works of the time were the *Passion, St. Leger, St. Eulalia, Gormond and Isembart,* and the *Voyage of Charlemagne.* The first Spanish work is the anonymous *Princes of Lara.* Germany was apparently absorbed with Latin, but Russia produced a *St. Wenceslas,* and Bulgarian the *Shestodnev* and the *Book of Heaven* of Ioan.

The Hebrew literature of the tenth century was the work of Sherira, Donnolo, Ben Gorion, and Ben Joseph. It was not primarily literary, and had not yet entered its Islamic renaissance. The great Arabic anthology of the *Thousand and One Nights* was compiled at this time, and Islamic literature continued to explore the *Traditions* (Hasa'i), astronomy (Rahman), law (Qirqisani), history (Hamza, Eutychius), and geography (Ibn Hanqal, Istakhri, Husani, Hamdani). Other writers further emphasize the flowering of Islamic culture in comparison with European achievements of the same date: Wa'wa, Tanukhi, Farabi, Abu Talib (*Food of Hearts*), Ibn Durayd, Wahsiyya (*Nabatean Agriculture*), Mas'udi (*Golden Meadows, Admonitions and Recension*), Faraj (*Chronography, Book of Songs*), Abu Nasr, Mufaddal (*Proverbs*), Baghdadi (*Index*), Suli (*Literary History*), and the anonymous author of the *Tracts of the Brethren of Purity.* Persian participation in this development is signaled in Bal'ami's translation of the *Annals* of Tabari, the medical works of Bin 'Ali, the *Thousand Tales,* and an anonymous *Geography.*

On the borders of Islam, Syrian literature clung to its religiosity in the *Commentaries* of Bar Kepha. So did the Georgians in the *Collected Hymns* of Modrikili, and *St. Gregory of Khandtza*, and a version of *Barlaam and Joseph* by Iver, ultimately traceable to the life of Buddha, and the Armenians in the writings of Norek (*Meditations, Hymns*), Chosroes (*Commentary on the Rites*), and Asolik (*Commentary on Jeremiah*). The Armenian passion for history found its outlet in Mesrop, Artsruni, Asolik, and John VI. The Byzantine Greeks were represented by the *Digenis Akritas*, usually counted as the beginning of modern Greek literature, and by the works of Kephalas (*Anthology of Poetry*) and Konstantinos VII. Far away in Central Asia the *Orkhon Epic* of the Uighur Turks was carved for posterity, a shadowy portent of the eventual Turkish conquest of both Baghdad and Byzantium, still 3000 miles and 500 years away.

Writers of tenth-century India included Udayana, Siddharsi, Utpala Deva, Tri Vikrama Bhatta, Medhatithi, Sri Dhara, Kula Sekhara, and Kanaka Sena. Perhaps the leading figures were Raja Sekhara (*Poetic Inquiry, Series of Treasures, Karpura Digest, Biddhashala Bhanjika*), Dhana Pala (*Prakrit Lexicon, Tilaka Digest, Ṛṣabha Pañca Śikaa*), Jayanta (*Encyclopedia*), and the writers of epic romances: Hari Chandra, Hala Ayudha, and Bhaskara. Amita Gati produced a *Collection of Gems of Happy Sayings*, and there was a famous narrative anthology, the *Twenty Five Stories of the Vampire*. Tamil writers were Kamban (*Rama*), Nammalvar, Sri Andal, Vedanta Dasikar, and the anonymous author of the *Sigiri Poems*, and Kannada featured the anonymous *Voddaradhana*. Sinhalese is represented by the *Regulations* of Udaya III, and the poems of Dhan Pal are considered the first works in Gujerati, Tibet produced no literature surely datable to the tenth century.

The Chinese anthology of *T'ang Tales* was compiled by Li Fang as a kind of digest of the monumental *Sung Encyclopedia*. Tu Kwang T'ing's *Curly Beard* was among the late stories included. Another *Encyclopedia* was edited by Wu Shu. Yang I, Chang Pi, and Ch'en Tuan were leading poets, and the *Chiu T'ang Shu* is also tenth century, as was Liu Hsü's *History of the T'ang*. But it is clear that the Sung period did not approach the T'ang sparkle.

Japanese tales of the tenth century are also abundant: *Fourteen Miraculous Tales, Tales of a Stepchild, One Hundred Fifty Japanese Tales, The Human Fairy Tale*. This was a time of rich literary achievement in Japan—one of the greatest periods in that country's history. Japan produced an *Anthology of Prayers or Speeches*, and *Anthology of Poetry*, and the *Collection of Ancient and Modern Poetry* of Tsurayuki. There were also diaries (*Diary of a Woman*, the *Travel Diary* of Tsurayuki), and the deservedly famous *Pillow Sketches* of Lady Sei Shonagon. There were even novelistic tales (*Hamamatsu Chiunagon, The Hollow Tree*, and Ariwara's

Tales of Ise), as well as the *Oojooyooshuu* of Genshin and a legal compilation known as the *Supplementary Code*.

10 Abu Nasr, Abu Talib, Amita, Ariwara, Artsruni, Asolik, Asser, Baghdadi, Bal'ami, Bar Kepha, Ben Gorion, Ben Joseph, Bhaskara, Bin 'Ali, Chang, Ch'en, Chosroes, Dhan, Dhana, Donnolo, Ekkehard, Ethelwold, Eutychius, Farabi, Faraj, Flodoard, Genshin, Hala, Hamdani, Hamza, Hari, Hasa'i, Hornklofi, Husani, Ibn Durayd, Ibn Hanqal, Ioan, Istakhri, Iver, Jayanta, John, Kamban, Kanaka, Kephalas, Konstantinos, Kula, Li, Liu, Liutprand, Mas'udi, Medhatithi, Mesrop, Modrikili, Mufaddal, Muqaddasi, Nammalvar, Norek, Ögmundarson, Qali, Qirqisani, Rahman, Raja, Ratherius, Ratpert, Richer, Roswitha, Sei, Sherira, Siddharsi, Skallagrimsson, Sri Andal, Sri Dhara, Suarez, Suli, Tanukhi, Toul, Tri, Tsurayuki, Tu, Udaya, Udayana, Usaibi'a, Utpala, Vedanta, Wahsiyya, Wa'wa, Widukind, Wu, Yang, Anon.: *Annales, Anthology, Blickling, Chiu, Chronicle, Deor's, Diary, Digenis, Four, Fourteen, Geography, Gormand, Hamamatsu, Hollow, Human, Judith, Lay, One, Orkhon, Passion, Praise, Princes, Prophecy, Psalter, St. Eulalia, St. Gregory, St. Leger, St. Wenceslas, Sigiri, Sung, Supplementary, Tales, Thousand, Tracts, Twenty, Vision, Voddaradhana, Voyage, Widsith*.

A considerable number of literary works of the first millennium of our era remain unsatisfactorily dated. Among them are:

In Greek the works of Alexander (*Destiny*), Apameia (*Cynegetica*), Basil (*Ascetic Works*), Nicholas (*Learned Ignorance*), Oppianos (*Helieutika*), Palladios (*Dialogue on the Life of Chrysostom*), Porphyrios (*Abstention from Animal Food*) and Synesios (*Essays* and *Hymns*), and the anonymous *Apostolic Constitutions* and *Didakhe*.

In Latin the works of Aelius (*Commentary on Terence, Life of Vergil*), Anastasius (*Investigations*), Bernardus (*Rules of the Monks, Letters*), Comestor (*Scholastic History*), Fulgentius (*To Monimus*), Mamertus (*State of the Soul*), Nemesianus (*Cynegetica*), and Porretanus (*Six Principles*), and the anonymous *Dialectical Principles, Didascalia Apostolorum, Hypomnesticon*, and *Monsters*.

In Chinese the *Vaisesika Philosophy* of Ui.

In Japanese the *Kiuo Dowa, Konjaku Monogatari*, and *Blue Cliff Records*.

In Sanskrit a very large part of the surviving literature of the past is undated. Much of it cannot even be surely assigned to a particular millennium. Possibly relatively early are the works of Apastabama (*Srauta Suutra*), Bharata (*Naatya Śaastra*), Buddha Ghosa Acharya (*Consideration of Destruction*), Damodara (*Mirror of Music*), Guna Bhadra (*Collected Legends*), "Hanuman" (*Ten Incarnations of Vishnu*), Katsyaayana (*Notes on the Rig and Yajur Vedas*), Jaimini (*Inquiry of Demonstrations, Ancient Inquiry*), Narada (*Institutes*), Sabara (*Commentary*), Sada Ananda (*Account of Vedanta*), Sarvajna Mitra (*Sragdhara Stotra*), Vararuchi (*Prakrit Grammar, Treasury of Ethics*), Vasu Deva (*Nala, King of Nisadha*) and

Yajña Valka (*The Canon Law, The Vajasanaji Collection*) and the anonymous *Maanava Grihya Sutra, Eight Fortunes, Manual of Public Rites, Nala Victorious, Teachings of Kausika, Uttar Adhyayana Suutra, King Vikrama, Manava Canon Law, Vasistha Law, Eight Hymns to Devi, Five Hymns to Durga, Hymn to Chandi, Hymn to Sarasvati, Song of Siva, The Greatness of Siva, The War God, Story of Kalaka.*

Later but still undated Sanskrit works are those of Abhi Nava Gupta (*Commentary on the Doctrine of Tone*), Ananda (*Maadhava Anala Kathaa*), Ananta (*Life of the Hero, Romance of the Bharatas*), Chidambara (*Journey of Rama and Pandu*), Govar Dhana (*Seven Tales*), Hala Ayudha (*Death of the Elders*), Hara Datta Suri (*Rama and Nala*), Jaya Vallabha (*Vajjaallagga*), Kshemi Svara (*Chandra Kousika*), Kuntala (*Vakrokti Jiivita*), Lagadha (*Astronomy*), Muka (*Five Tales*), Odaya Deva (*Romance of Jivan Dhara*), Parama Ananda (*Śṛṅgaara Sapta Satika*), Pingala (*Treatise on Meter*), Rudra Bhatta (*Śṛṅgaara Tilaka*), Puru Sottama Deva (*Tri Kaaṇda Śesa, Rare Words*) Rupago Svamin (*Padya Avalii*), Sakalya (*Ṛk Praatiśaakhya*), Sankara (*Commentary on Bodily Inquiry*), Sara Svati (*Braahma Tattva Prakaśika, Light of Truth*), Vachas Pati Mitra (*Saaṁkha Tattva Kaumudii*), Venta Dhvarin (*Yaadava Raaghaviiya*), Vetala Bhatta (*Clarification of Ethics*), Vinayaka (*Introduction to the Ten Princes*), and the anonymous *Deeds of Dasopant, Narayana Bhatta, Nepaala Maaha Atmya, One-Syllable Words, Samyaktra Kaumudii, Śṛṅgaara Jñaana Nirṇaya, Śyaa Malaa Daṇḍaka, Technical Vocabulary, Thirty-Two Maidens on a Throne, Word Variants.*

Undated works of the last thousand years include the following:

In Persian the works of Kadiri (*Tales of a Parrot*) and the anonymous *Admonitions, Adventures of Hajji Baba,* and *Tale of Sinbad.*

In Russian the *Book of Enoch.*

In Vietnamese *The Precious Mirror of the Heart.*

In Chinese the works of Chin (*Inconstancy of Mme. Chuang*), Hsia Ping (*Wen Hsüan*), Lieh Tzu (*Book*), Sung (*Medical Jurisprudence*), Szen (*History*), and Yuan Chen (*Western Room*), and the anonymous *Common Tales to Rouse the World, The Counterfeit Seal, Dream of Sleeping Clouds, Ku Shin Shiao Shuo, Liu Chih Yüan, Chu Kung Tiao, Nan Chao Ye Che, P'ai An Chin Chi, Phonetic Dictionary, The Runaway Maid, Tuan Ch'eng Shih.*

In Arabic the works of Abu Abdallah (*Manual of Cosmography,*) Azraqi (*History of Mecca*), Baladhuri (*Arabic Conquests*), Ibn Bashkᵘwal (*Al Sila fii Akhbaari A'immati 'l Andalus*), Ibn Hasan (*Pearl Strings*), Ibn Muhammed (*Mujmil et Tarikh i Dnadirije*), 'Idhari (*Doctrines of the West*), Latif (*Description of Egypt*), "Mikhnaf" (*Death of Husayn*), Qazwini (*Aatharu 'l Bilaad*), Shebesteri (*Rose of Mystery*), Ya'qubi (*Works*),

Zaydan (*History of Islamic Civilization*), and the anonymous *Bani Hilal, Fawaatu 'l Wafayaat, Mother of Cities, The Schism, Shadharaatu 'l Dhahab, Story of Sayf Ibn Dhi Yazan.*

Norman (11)

The Normans took England, and the Tangut Mongols took Kansu. (The related Khitan had already seized Manchuria, and the Juchen would hold all of north China in the twelfth century.) Eastern and Western Christendom were finally divided by the schism that had threatened for 700 years. Islam was embattled by the Seljuk Turks and by the First Crusade, which occupied Jerusalem. Literary reflections of these events include the Persian *History* of Gardizi, the Armenian *History of the Seljuk Conquest* of Aristaces, the Byzantine *Book of Ceremonies* of Porphyrogenitus, the Latin *Assizes of Jerusalem*, the Syrian *Chronicles* of Bar Shinaya, and T'o's histories of the Juchen, the Khitan, and the Sung.

Latin literature was by this time overshadowed by the vernaculars, but produced the mystery of *The Magi*, the *Memento Mori*, Aelnoth's *St. Canute*, Honorius' *Jewels of the Soul*, Alphonsus' *Clerical Discipline*, the histories of Glaber, Bremen and Kosmas, and the *Gomorhianus* of St. Peter Damian. There are literary remains of the eleventh century in Icelandic (the *Settlement Book*, Sigvat's *Plain Speaker*, the *Lay of Biarki*, Skaldaspillar's *Praise of Hakon*), Irish (the poems of Caemain), Welsh (Meilyr's *Lament for Trahearn*), Frisian (*Law of the Magistrates*), German (*Earth*, Notker's translations, Williram's *Explanation of the Song of Solomon*), French (*St. Alexis, Legend of the Centuries, Floovent*), English (the *Homilies* of Wulfstan and Aelfric), Russian (Nikon's *Tale of Bygone Years*, the *Russian Code*, the works of Daniel the Palmer, the *Instructions* of Volodimir Monomakh, Zhidiata's *Instruction*), Provençal (*Holy Faith, Boèci, Alexander, Fors d'Oloron*), Catalan (*Usages*), Spanish (*The Cid*), Greek (*Stephanites and Ichnelates*), and Georgian (*Gospels* of Athos).

Hebrew, Arabic, and Persian literature were by this time closely linked. In addition to the Hebrew *Precepts* of Ben Jacob and the commentaries of Hai and Ben Judah, there was an *Introduction to the Talmud* by Ibn Nagdela and an Arabic *Lexicon* by Hai. Ibn Sina wrote in both Persian (*Poems*) and Arabic (*The Remedy, Manual of Philosophy, Canon of Medicine, Commentaries*). The schismatic Persians were already deep in Sufi mysticism, and the growing sectarianism occasioned Muhammad's *Doctrines of the Sects*. Among other works reflecting the Persian trend were Hujviri's *Revelation of Hidden Things*, Ansari's *Invocations to God*, and Sa'id's *Sufi Quatrains*. This was the golden age of Persian romances, producing the *Saam Naama, Johaangir Naama, Gushasp Naama, Faraamurz Naama*, the *Book of Kings* of Daqiqi, and the *Gershasp Naama* of Asadi, and crowned by the works of

Firdausi—*Joseph and Zuleika* and the *Epic of Kings* ("Sohrab and Rustam")—considered by Iranis as the culmination of their classical literature. The *Poems* of Tahir, the *Biographies* of Ansari, Asadi's *Glossary*, Nasiri's *Travels*, and the works of Baihaqi were additional elements in this Persian climax. The principal Turkish work was *The Science of the Governor* by Khass Hadjib.

Perhaps the most colorful Arabic author of the eleventh century was 'Ala, who wrote a *Parody of the Koran* and other works (*Spark of the Fire Stick, Epistle of Forgiveness, Luzuumiyyaat*). 'Ala, in common with Hariri and Hamadhani, also wrote *Assemblies*, a type of urbane essay peculiar to Arabic writing, and his *Letters* and those of Abu Bekr were among the best known works of this age. Other notable items were the *Book of Viziers* of Sabi, *The Dove's Necklace* of Ibn Hazm, *The Solitaire of the Time* of Tha'alibi, *The Statue of the Palace* of Bakharzi, and *The Fount of Life* of Ibn Gabirol. Ibn Rashiq wrote a work on poetics and A'lam compiled an anthology, *Lyrics of the Six Poets*. The very popular street drama of *Abu Zeyd* is probably from this period, and the works of Qushayri, Wahidi, Ibn Miskawayh, Ghazna, and Abu Zayd may also be mentioned. Sufism attracted the attention of Sulami (*Classes of the Sufis*), and politics attracted that of Mawardi (*Principles of Government*). The works of Isfahani were also notable (*Adornment of the Saints, Virgin Pearl of the Palace*).

If romances were popular in Europe and Islam by this time, they had all but swept the field in India. Examples are the *Epic* of Padma Gupta, Bilhana's *King Vikrama*, Bhoja's *The Neck Ornament of Sara Svati*, Murari's *Priceless Rama* and Soma Deva's *Ocean of Rivers*, but many other Sanskrit authors wrote in the same tradition: Soddhala, Sambhu, Lila Suka, Manikya, Lolimba Raja, and especially Ksemendra, who adapted both the *Great Bharatas* and the *Epic of Rama* and wrote several other epics. Similar influences were at work in the vernacular Indian literatures. Pampa, Ponna, and Ranna wrote Kannada epics, and Nannaya interpreted the *Great Bharatas* in Telegu. In Tamil Nambi wrote *The Works of the Three Saints*, and in Prakrit there is the *Suna Sundarii Cariya* of Dhane Svara. The earliest Oriya work is the *Chronicles of the Jagannath Temple at Puri*. The eleventh-century *Carya* songs are the earliest undisputed works in Bengali. Sinhalese is undocumented. In Tibet the great sage of the period was the poet Marpa, *guru* of the great poet saint Mila.

The Chinese appear to have been preoccupied at this time with history. In addition to the works of T'o, already mentioned, this century produced the *Old History of the Five Dynasties* (who ruled China in the confused tenth-century transition between T'ang and Sung), the *New History of the Five Dynasties* by Ou Yang Hsiu, and the *Mirror of History* of Szu Ma Kuang. Leading poets were Su Tung P'o, Ch'êng Hao, Huang T'ing Chien, and Shao Yung. Commentaries were written on the *Classic of Change* (by

Chou Tun I) and the *Way of Life* (by Su Chê), and a revised *Phonetic Dictionary* was compiled by Ch'en P'êng Nien. Other notable works were the *Journal* of Su Shih, *The Poets' Club* of Wang Chu, and *The Written Characters* by Wang An Shih. The *Ts'e Fu Yüan Kuei*, the *Hsin T'ang Shu*, and the works of Chu Fu and Lien Pu may also be mentioned.

Korean literature was represented by the *Kyunyŏ Chŏn*, the *Miscellaneous Stories* of Kim Tae Mun, and the *Parable of the Flower Kingdom* of Sol Ch'ong. Japanese works included *Torikaebaya*, *Sagoromo*, *Diary of Journeys by a Woman* and the *Diary* and *Tale of Genji* of Lady Murasaki. The latter work is generally considered a landmark in the world history of the novel.

11 Abu Bekr, Abu Zayd, Aelfric, Aelnoth, 'Ala, A'lam, Alphonsus, Ansari, Aristaces, Asadi, Athos, Baihaqi, Bakharzi, Bar Shinaya, Ben Jacob, Ben Judah, Bhoja, Bilhana, Bremen, Caemain, Ch'en, Ch'êng, Chou, Chu, Damian, Daniel, Daqiqi, Dhane, Firdausi, Gardizi, Ghazna, Glaber, Hai, Hamadhani, Hariri, Honorius, Huang, Hujviri, Ibn Gabirol, Ibn Hazm, Ibn Miskawayh, Ibn Nagdela, Ibn Rashiq, Ibn Sina, Isfahani, Kalabadhi, Khass, Kim, Kosmas, Ksemendra, Ksira, Lien, Lila, Lolimba, Manikya, Marpa, Mawardi, Meilyr, Muhammad, Murari, Murasaki, Nambi, Nannaya, Nasiri, Nikon, Notker, Ou, Padma, Pampa, Ponna, Porphyrogenitus, Qushayri, Ranna, Sabi', Sa'id, Sambhu, Shao, Sigvat, Simeon, Skaldaspillar, Soddhala, Sol, Soma, Su, Sulami, Szu Ma, Tahir, Tha'alibi, T'o, Volodimir, Wahidi, Wang, Williram, Wulfstan, Zhidiata, Anon.: *Abu, Alexander, Assizes, Boèci, Carya, Chronicles, Cid, Diary, Earth, Faraamurz, Floovent, Fors, Gushasp, Holy, Hsin, Johaangir, Kavi, Kyunyŏ, Law, Lay, Legend, Magi, Memento, Old, Russian, Saam, Sagoromo, St. Alexis, Settlement, Stephanites, Torikaebaya, Ts'e, Usages.*

Crusades (12)

The First Crusade took Jerusalem in 1099, and the Second Crusade lost it in 1146. The Crusaders never reached it again. Latin histories of the time cover Denmark (Aagesen), England (Monmouth, Glanvill), Wales (Giraldus), Poland (Gallus), Hungary (Petrus), and the Church (Salisbury). Pope Innocent III wrote an influential book *The Contempt of the World*, and Abelard was the foremost philosopher (*Yes and No, A History of Disasters, Ethics, Dialectics, Introduction to Theology*). John of Salisbury was scarcely less distinguished (*The Statesman, St. Anselm, St. Thomas, Metalogicon*). The anonymous *Great Etymology*, the *Dialogue of the Exchequer*, the works of Andreas and Odington, and *De Profectione Danorum in Terram Sanctam* should be mentioned. The narrative of the time is best exemplified in *The Wise Virgins and the Foolish Virgins* and in the animal allegory of *Ysengrimus*; and the drama included an anonymous *Daniel*, the *Daniel* by Hilarius, and the plays of Blois, *The Passion* and *The Anti-Christ*. In Greek, Anna Komnena's epic on the life of *Alexis* and the works of Theodorus Prodromos are the chief remains (*Dosicles and Rodanthe, The Twelve Months, Essays*).

In European literature of the twelfth century, English produced the *Anglo-Saxon Chronicle*. Ari's *Book of Iceland* appeared and Harpestreng wrote on medicine in Danish. German was active (*The Nibelungs, Reynard the Fox*, Konrad's *Roland*, Lamprecht's *Alexander*, Hartmann's *Iwein*, and a biography of *Anno, Bishop of Cologne*), as were Dutch (the *Aeneid* and *St. Servatius* of Veldeke), French (*Song of Roland, Romance of Reynard, The Game of Adam*, the *Parsifal* of Chrétien de Troyes, Benoit's *Romance of Troy*), Provençal (Carcassès' *Parrot*, Bochada's *Song of Antioch*, the poems of William IX, the works of Vidal, the *Fors de Morlaas*), Catalan (the poems of Palol), and Russian (the Kievan and Galician-Volynian chronicles, the *Lay of Igor's Campaign*, the works of Nestor). The *Black Book of Carmarthen* was composed in Welsh, and *The Vision of MacCon Glinne* in Irish.

The Jewish renaissance flowered in Spain and elsewhere. The chief works were Ben Maimon's *Guide for the Perplexed* and *Civil Laws*, Qimhi's *Book of the Covenant*, Ben David's *Book of Mystic Lore* and *Mighty Faith*, Bar Hiyya's *Philosophy*, Ha Levi's *The Kuzar Debate* and *Introduction to the Talmud*, Ben Yehiel's *Prepared*, and Ben Me'ir's *Book of the Righteous*, and the commentaries of Rashi and Hadassi. Islamic literature was similarly lively, in geography (Zouhri's *Ghana*, Edrisi's *Travels*, Ibn Jubair's *Journey to Mecca*), history (Ibn 'Asakir's *History of Damascus*, Ibn Ezra's *Literary History*), biography (Ibn Khallikan) and autobiography (Ibn Munqid), religion (Bhagawi, Zamakhshari, Shahrastani), poetry (Tughra'i, Himyari), drama (*Life of Antar*), philosophy (Ibn Ezra), and romance (Ibn Abbas' *Alive, Son of Awake*). But the leading figures of the Islamic world were Ibn Baja (*Republic*), Ghazali (*The Incoherence of the Philosophers, The Revival of the Religious Sciences, The Niche of Lights, the Deliverer from Error, The Alchemy of Happiness*), and Ibn Rushd (*The Incoherence of the Incoherence, Physics, Metaphysics*). These three authors were widely known also in Renaissance Europe (as Avempace, Algazel, and Averroës).

The Christian Near East produced the chronicles of Michael I in Syrian and of Ani, Gregory, and Edessa in Armenian, the commentaries and dogmatic works of Ignatius and Sargis, Tlay, and Lambron, and the letters, orations, and poetry of Nerses the Graceful. Georgian works were the *Abdul Messias* of Shavteli, Thruogveli's *Wis and Ramin*, Petritsi's *Origin of Man*, and Khoneli's *Amiran Darejniani*.

Persian writing was largely poetic (Minuchihri, Mu'izzi, Farrukhi, Shafarva, Sabir, 'Unsuri, Khaqani, Jamal ad Din). Rashid Vatvat wrote *Treatises on Poetry* as well as poems, and Omar Khayyam wrote his celebrated *Quatrains*. Equally celebrated in Iran are Anvari's *Tears of Khorasan* and *Odes*, Sana'i's *Garden of Truth*, and the romances of Nizami (*Khusrau and Shirin, Layla and Majnun, Alexander*). Persian chronicles from this period are also extant.

In Sanskrit, new versions of the stories from the *Five Books* were written by Chintaamani and Purna Bhadra. Commentaries on Kali Dasa's *Cloud Messenger* were written by Vallabha Deva, Daksina, and Malli Natha, and an imitation of it composed by Dhoi. It was a notable period in lexicography, marked by the dictionaries of Dhanam Jaya, Śri Harsa, Mahe Śvara, Hema Chandra, and Mankha, a dictionary of *Homonyms*, and a *Botanical Dictionary*. Related works on poetics were compiled by Vag Bhata and Hema Chandra, and especially by Mammata and Alata (*The Luster of Poetry*). Epics were written by Mankha (*Life of Śri Kantha*), Hema Chandra (*Life of Kumara Pala, Lives of Sixty-three Jains, Canto of the Early Jains*), Sandhya Akara Nandin (*Life of Rama Pala*), and Śri Harsa (*The King of Nisadha*), and one anonymous one exists on *The Victories of Prithvi Raja*. Other notable works of this period were those of Rama Nuja on philosophy, of Vandya Ghatiya Sarva Ananda (commentary), of Jaya Ratha, Krishna Miśra, and Dhanam Jaya (*Ten Kinds of Drama*). But the leading writer of the age, perhaps of medieval India, was Jaya Deva, whose *Song of the Divine Cowherd* is widely considered an inspired classic.

Prakrit writing included the *Supaasanaaha Cariya* and Asada's *Digest of Judgement*. The vernacular languages and "colonial India" are represented in this period by Marathi (initiated by Mukundaraj's *Viveká Sindhu*), Hindi (which begins with the *Bisaldeo Raso* of Narpati Nalh), Rajasthani (which came to life in the *Bardic Chronicles* of Chand Bardai), Tibetan (lighted by Tibet's greatest writer, Mila: *Cotton Clad Mila, A Hundred Thousand Songs*), Tamil (Sekkilar's *Book of Mysteries*), Kannada (Naga Chandra's *Legend of the Life of Rama Chandra*), and Burmese (which was inaugurated by the *Death Song* of Anantathuria). Sinhalese produced the anonymous *Parrot Message*. The oldest surviving Javanese work is the *Bharata Epic* of the twelfth century.

Neo-Confucian China's greatest interpreter of the classics was Chu Hsi, whose commentaries and explanations of the Confucian canon have been taken as definitive by most subsequent scholars. The leading poets were Chêng Ch'iao (who also wrote the best regarded *History of China*), Hung Chüeh Fan, Yeh Shih, and Kao Chü Nien. Other works were the *Method of Architecture, The Mirror of the Present, The Story Teller's Anthology, The Wolf of Chung Shan* (by Hsieh), *The Infernal Regions* (by Lin I Ching), and the writings of Fan Ch'eng Ta, and Lu Hsiang Shan. The *Remains of the Three Kingdoms* (Kim) from Korea and the *Tale of Yeigwa* and Tamenari's *Great Mirror* from Japan were the major works of this period in those countries.

12 Aagesen, Abelard, Anantathuria, Andreas, Ani, Anvari, Ari, Asada, Bar Hiyya, Ben David, Ben Maimon, Ben Me'ir, Ben Yehiel, Benoît, Bhagawi, Blois, Bochada, Carcassès, Chand, Chêng, Chintamani, Chu, Daksina, Dhanam, Dhoi, Edessa, Edrisi, Fan, Farrukhi, Gallus, Ghazali, Giraldus, Glanvill, Gregory, Ha Levi, Hadassi, Harpestreng, Hartmann, Hema, Hilarius, Himyari, Hsieh, Hung, Ibn Abbas, Ibn 'Asakir, Ibn Baja, Ibn Ezra, Ibn Jubair, Ibn Khallikan, Ibn Munqid, Ibn Rushd, Ibn Tufail, Ignatius, Innocentius III, Jamal, Jaya, Kao, Khaqani, Khayyam, Khoneli, Kim, Komnena, Konrad, Krishna, Lambron, Lamprecht, Lin, Lolimba, Lu, Mahe, Malli, Mammata, Mankha, Maydani, Michael I, Mila, Minuchihri, Monmouth, Mu'izzi, Mukundaraj, Naga, Narpati, Nerses, Nestor, Nizami, Odington, Palol, Petritsi, Petrus, Purna, Qimhi, Rama, Rashi, Rashid, Sabir, Salisbury, Sana'i, Sandhya, Sekkilar, Shafarva, Shahrastani, Shavteli, Śri, Tamenari, Theodoros, Thruogveli, Tlay, Troyes, Tughra'i, 'Unsuri, Vag, Vallabha, Vandya, Veldeke, Vidal, William IX, Yeh, Zamakhshari, Zouhri, Anon.: *Anno, Anti-Christ, Bhaaraataa, Black, Botanical, Chronicles, Daniel, Dialogue, Fors, Galician, Game, Great, Homonyms, Kievan, Lay, Life, Method, Mirror, Nibelungs, Parrot, Passion, Profectione, Reynard, Romance, Song, Story, Supaasanaaha, Tale, Victories, Vision, Wise, Ysengrimus.*

Mongol (13)

The Mongol conquests of the thirteenth century were without precedent. No previous historical event could have evoked the simultaneous response of Persia (Jurjani's *Mongol Invasion*), Italy (the *Travels* of Marco Polo), India (Juwaini's *The Mongols*), Russia (*The Downfall of Russia*), China (*The Secret History of the Mongols*) and Armenia (Malakia's *History of the Tatars*). The confrontation of Islam and Christendom in the West found comparable expression in Arabic ('Imad ad Din's *History of Saladin*), Persian (the *History of the Seljuks* of Ravandi), Latin (*Assizes of Romania*), and Provençal (Anelier's *War of Navarre*).

An astonishing Icelandic literature from this time has been preserved, including the prose *Edda* and *The Globe* of Sturluson, the anonymous poetic *Edda*, the *Laws* (Grágás), the *Sun Song*, and a large number of sagas: *Burnt Njal*, the *Volsung Saga*, and the *Old Volsung Lay*, the *Lay of Helgi*, *Helgi and Kara*, *Helgi and Swava*, *Egil's Saga*, *Fridthhjof's Saga*, *Grettis' Saga*, *The Confederates*, *Gísla Saga Sursonar*, *Hrafnkels Saga Freysgoda*, *Gunnlaug's Saga*, and the *Laxdaela Saga*. The earliest Norwegian literature was *The Dream Vision* and *The King's Mirror*, and the earliest Swedish literature was *Gutas Saga*. German produced the poems of Vogelweide, Zerklar's *The Italian Guest*, Strassburg's *Tristan and Isolde*, Eschenbach's *Titurel* and *Parsifal* and the anonymous *Gudrun*. England was preoccupied with the *Great Charter* of King John, the adventures of *Robin Hood* and the *Harrowing of Hell*, and the English folk ballad can be traced to this century. Dutch literature featured the poems of the nun Hadewych and Aernout's *Reynard the Fox*, and included *The Romance of*

Lancelot, William of Orange, the *Floris and Blanchefleur* of Assenede, *The Life of Our Lord,* the works of Maerlant (*The Holy Grail, St. Francis, Secret of Secrets, Flower of Nature, Bible Verses*), and especially the Flemish *Beatrice.* Celtic literature of this period gave us the poems of Cynddelw and the *Book of Taliesin* in Welsh and several Irish works: *The Sick Bed of Cuchulinn, The Colloquy of the Old Men, The Wandering of Uilix MacLeirtis, The Wooing of Ferb, The Feast of Bricriu,* and the *Book of Invasions.* Romance literatures were represented by *The Child of the Blind Man, Aucassin and Nicolette,* Lorris and Meung's *Romance of the Rose,* Adam's *Game of Leaves* and *Robin and Marion,* the works of Rutebeuf and Bodel and the *Quest for the Holy Grail* in French, Rouergue's song of *The Crusade* in Provençal, the *Chronicle* of James I, and the works of Lull in Catalan, the *Seven Sections* of Alfonso X, the anonymous *Bernard of Carpio,* and the works of Berceo in Spanish, and those of King Diniz in Portuguese and of Marco Polo in Italian. Alfonso X also wrote Galician poetry. Magyar inaugurated its vernacular literature with a *Funeral Discourse.* The earliest Czech fragments (*Lord Have Mercy on Us, St. Wenceslas*) are from this time; so is the Polish hymn *Mother of God;* and Russian produced the *Book of the Crypt Fathers, Prince Dovmont,* and other works.

The Latin literature of the thirteenth century was dominated by the philosophers: St. Thomas Aquinas, Albertus the Great, Roger Bacon, Anglicus, and Alexander of Hales, but it also featured histories—of Hungary (Kézai), Denmark (Grammaticus), and England (*Annals of the Monastery at Tewkesbury*)—and a famous papal bull *From Clergy to Laity* of Boniface VII. Other works were those of Beauvais, Hieronymus (on music), Cabham's *Penitential,* and Bracton's *Laws and Customs of England.* Narrative works were the *Trojan History* of Colonne and the *Golden Legend* of Voragine, and poetry included Rogerius' *Miserable Hymn.* Greek produced the *Aesop's Fables* of Planudes.

The *Brightness* (Zohar) and its *Outline* (Bahir) were the most influential Jewish works of the thirteenth century, but they were originally written in Syrian Aramaic. There were several notable Hebrew authors: Haziri (*Lyrics, Grammar and Medicine* and an imitation of Ibn Ezra—like the latter, Haziri also wrote in Arabic, namely, *The Ornament of Time*); Abraham Ben Moses (*Stories of Jerusalem,* and a *Theology* in Arabic), Isaac Ben Moses (*Light Is Sown, Stories of the Vestment*), Levita (*Tradition of the Tradition*), Ben Joseph (*Book of Excellence*), Israeli (*Foundation of the World*), Ben Jacob (*Precepts*), and Ben Hillel (*Mordekhai*).

Georgian literature reached a peak in *The Knight in the Tiger Skin* of Rustaveli, a verse romance influenced by Nizami. Syrian was represented by the *Book of the Bee* of Basrah, and Armenian by the histories of Vartan, Ganzak, and Sempat, the tale of *Farman and Asman,* and the legal work and *Fables* of Kosh.

The modern literature of Ethiopia, anticipated in fragmentary texts as early as the fourth century, may be dated to the thirteenth century with the Amharic *Bible*, the *Glory of Kings*, the *Qerlos*, the *Rules of Pachomius*, a *Bestiary* (Physiologus), and Abba Salama's *Acts of the Passion* and *Service for the Dead*.

Arabic continued to produce a varied literature in theology (Razi), history (Makin, Athir, 'Imad ad Din), linguistics (Ibn Malik, Ibn Qifti's *History of the Philologists*), geography (Feda's *Travels*, Yaqut's *Geographical Dictionary*), and poetry (especially the *Mantle Ode* of Busiri). Some of the particularly noteworthy works were Jawzi's *Mirror of Time*, Suhrawardi's *Bounties of Knowledge*, Athir's *Lions of the Jungle*, and Ibn 'Arabi's *Meccan Revelations* and *Be els of Philosophy*. Ibn 'Arabi is not to be confused with Ibn al 'Arabi (here listed as 'Arabi), whose works also belong to the thirteenth century.

In addition to the works of Jurjani and Ravandi already mentioned, the Persians produced the poems of Rumi and Isma'il, Kubra's *Rules of Conduct*, and two eminent writers: 'Attar (*The Speech of the Birds, The Book of Counsel, The Memorial of the Saints*) and Sa'adi (*The Orchard, The Rose, Lyrics*).

To this time belong the Sanskrit poetry anthologies of Śri Dhara Dasa and Jalhana, and the latter's *Life of Soma Pala* and *Wiles of Women*. There were also works on poetics by Vag Bhata and by Amara Chandra and Ari Sinha (*Advice to Poets*). Amara Chandra also wrote a *New Bharata*. Śaramga Deva's *Ocean of Music* and *Commentary on Panini* are perhaps the most highly regarded works of the period. Somesvara Datta wrote panegyrics on a minister at the court of Gujerat, and Jñanesvar wrote *Hymns*. Other writers of the time were Devanda (*The Whole Duty of a Brahman*), Hari Hara, Deva Prabha Suri, Kesava Svamin (*Lexicon*), Sara Datanaya (*Medicine*), and Soma Prabha.

A representative Prakrit work is Krishna Lila Suka's *Siricimdhakavvam*. Tamil is represented by the commentaries of Naccinarkkinyar, Bengali by Hari Datta's *Bihula and Lakhindar*, Hindi by poems and other works of Gorakh Nath, Oriya by the *Bhubaneswar Inscriptions* of King Nara Simha, and Kannada by Andayya's *Kabbigara*. Hema Sara Swati initiated Assamese literature with *Prahlad Charitra*. The *Sinhalese Grammar* and Gurulugomi's *Dharmmapradiipikaa* were among the surviving writings in Sinhalese, and there were *The Greater Vehicle Clarified* by Sitakantha in Kashmiri, Potana's *Song Celestial* in Telegu, and the poems of Jñanesvar in Marathi. *The Jewel Ornament of Liberation* of Gam Po Pa is one of the great works of Tibetan literature, and the earliest work in Thai is an inscription of this century on *The Life and Times of Ram Kamhaeng*. The surviving *Nestorian Texts* of Mongolian Christianity are from this period, too. The larger part of Burmese traditional literature is undated, much of it belonging to the period of the introduction of Buddhism after about the thirteenth century. It includes these works: *Bagawa, Book of Enfranchisement, Buddhist Beatitudes, Burmese Pali Grammar, Deikton, Dzanecka, The Five Hundred Ten Births of Buddha, Forms of Worship, Laws of Menu, Life of Gautama, Life of the Lord Buddha, Mahawthata, Nayidda, Pali Sermons, Proverbs, Sanda Gômma, Temi, Thingyo, Thuwunnashan, Vision of Hell, The Whole Duty of the Monk, Widuya.*

The Mongol period in China turned Chinese literature upside down. Classical scholarship was the minor mode, and the literary emphasis was on novels and plays: *Romance of the Three Kingdoms* (Lo), *Autumn in the Han Palace* (Ma Tuan Lin), *Rain under the Wutung* (Po Jen Fu), *History of the Western Pavilion* (Wang Shih Fu), *Orphan of the Chao* (Chi Chün Hsiang), *Tu Wo's Sorrow* and *Pavilion on the Stream* (Kuan Han K'ing). The plays of Kuan Han K'ing were particularly notable, though many others were included in later anthologies. Short stories were also numerous (for example, *Intrigues of a Maid, Slave of His Wealth,* and *The Mysterious Box*). The more classical literature included the encyclopedia and poetry of Wên T'ien Hsiang, the *Three-Character Classic* of Wang Ying Lin, and the *Six Scripts* of Tai Tung. Ma Tuan Lin wrote *Champa* and a *Treatise on Government,* and other works are Chou Ta Kuan's *Angkor Vat,* Sung's *Instructions to Coroners,* Chu Shi Chieh's and Ch'in's works on mathematics, the essays of Liu Yin and Chang Kuo Pin and the works of Li Kuan Chung. Chao Ju Kuo wrote a *Record of Foreign Peoples* in a rare burst of Chinese enthusiasm on that topic.

Korea was also conquered by the Mongols, but produced the *Remains of the Three Kingdoms* of Il Yŏn. Japan escaped through the destruction of the Mongol fleet by storm, and produced the Heiji, Gempei, and Hogen tales of Tokinaga, the *Tale of Heike,* verse anthologies (the *New Collection of Ancient and Modern Poetry,* Teika's *Single Verses by a Hundred People*), Chomei's *Record of Ten Feet Square,* the works of Shinran and Honen, and the *Woman's Travel Diary* of Abutsu.

13 Abba, Abutsu, Adam, Aernout, Albertus, Alfonso, Amara, Andayya, Anelier, Anglicus, Aquinas, 'Arabi, Ari, Assenede, Athir, 'Attar, Bacon, Basrah, Beauvais, Ben Hillel, Ben Jacob, Ben Joseph, A. Ben Moses, I. Ben Moses, Berceo, Bodel, Bonifacius, Bracton, Busiri, Cabham, Chang, Chao, Chi, Ch'in, Chomei, Chou, Chu, Colonne, Cynddelw, Deva, Devanda, Diniz, Eschenbach, Feda, Gam, Ganzak, Gorakh, Grammaticus, Gurulugomi, Hadewych, Hales, Hari, Haziri, Hema, Hieronymus, Honen, Ibn 'Arabi, Ibn Malik, Ibn Qifti, Il, 'Imad, Isma'il, Israeli, Jalhana, James, Jawzi, Jñanesvar, John, Jurjani, Juwaini, Keśava, Kézai, Kosh, Krishna, Kuan, Kubra, Levita, Li, Liu, Lo. Lorris, Lull, Ma, Maerlant, Makin, Malakia, Naccinarkkiniyar, Nara, Planudes, Po, Polo, Potana, Ravandi, Razi, Rogerius, Rouergue, Rumi, Rustaveli, Rutebeuf, Sa'adi, Sara, Saramga, Sempat, Shinran, Sitakantha, Soma, Somesvara, Śri, Strassburg, Sturluson, Suhrawardi, Sung, Tai, Teika, Tokinaga, Vag, Vahram, Vartan, Vogelweide, Voragine, Wang, Wên, Yaqut, Zerklar, Anon.: *Annals, Assizes, Aucassin, Beatrice, Bernardo, Bes-*

tiary, Bible, Book, Brightness, Burnt, Child, Colloquy, Conjederates, Downfall, Dream, Edda, Egil's, Farman, Feast, Fridthhjofs, Funeral, Gísla, Glory, Grettis, Gudrun, Gunnlaugs, Gutas, Harrowing, Helgi, Hrafnkels, Intrigues, King's, Laws, Laxdaela, Lay, Life, Lord, Mother, Mysterious, Nestorian, New, Old, Outline, Prince, Qerlos, Quest, Robin, Rules, St. Wenceslas, Secret, Sick, Sinhalese, Slave, Sun, Tale, Volsung, Wandering, Wooing.

Ming (14)

The Ming dynasty was established in China in the century of Chaucer and Dante, Ibn Khaldun, Hafiz, and Chikafusa. There was rapid extension of literature to new languages, some 48 of which were literarily active by this date. (Six centuries earlier two thirds of these had been preliterate; six centuries later there would be nearly two thirds more.) In the European vernaculars it was a lively time. Asgrímson (*The Lily*) and Gilsson represented Icelandic, and Birgitta's *Revelations* Swedish. German produced the *Strassburg Chronicle* of Closener and the *Great Rose Garden*. Dutch was represented by the works of Ruysbroek and the *Noble Play of Winter and Summer*. Danish and Norwegian were not notably active, but English produced the *Troilus and Cressida* and *Canterbury Tales* of Chaucer, Langland's *Vision of Piers Plowman, Gawain and the Green Knight*, and *Griseldis*. The *White Book of Rydderch* and the poems of Dyfadd ap Gwilym were Wales' contributions, and the poems of FitzGerald represented Irish. Vernacular French was used in Froissart's *Chronicles*; Italian in the works of Dante (*New Life, Divine Comedy*), Boccaccio (*Decameron*), and Petrarch (*Sonnets*), Spanish in those of Lopez de Ayala, Ruiz (*Book of Good Humor*), and Manuel; Galician in *Cancioneiros* and a *Trojan Chronicle*; and Portuguese in the works of Lobeira. Provençal works included *The Destruction of Jerusalem*, Molinier's *Laws of Love*, Perelhas' *St. Patrick's Journey to Purgatory*, Paternas' *Sufficiency and Necessity*, and Berenguer's *Mirall de Trobar*, and the *Chronicle* of Descoll was in Catalan. Sofony's *Beyond the Don* was perhaps Russia's most notable work. The *Psalter of Florjan* represented Poland, Evtymy's *Biographies of the Saints* Bulgaria, and the voluminous Czech literature included the *Pious Dialogues* and *Six Books* of Stitny, the *Chronicle* of Dalimil, *Tristram and Izalde*, and the clown play *Charlatan*. Magyar was represented by *Nyelvemléktár* and the *Legend of St. Margaret*.

Greek produced the *Chronicle of the Morea*, and Latin was used for Polish history (Czarnkow, Dlugosz), Walsingham's *Chronicles*, the works of Higden, Eckehardt, and Wiclif, and some of those of Boccaccio (*Genealogy of the Gods*) and Dante (*Monarchy, The Eloquence of Common Speech*), as well as for Padua's *Defender of the Peace*, Gower's *Confession of a Lover*, and the *Political Works* of William of Occam.

Hebrew writings of the fourteenth century included the *Garden of*

Eden, Commentaries, and *Philosophy* of Aaron; the *Discourses* and *Code* of Babya and Jacob Ben Asher, respectively; the *Ethics* of Ben Qalonymos; *The Pleasure of the World* of Bedersi; and *The Lighted Candelabra* of Aboab. The earliest Yiddish literary work is a romance on *Arthur's Court* from this same period.

In the Near East, Armenia continued to produce historians (Orbelian, Hethous, Airivanq) and religious commentators (Dathev, Orotu), and Turkey continued to produce poets (Kazu, Veled, 'Ashik). Also from this date are the *Dede Korkut Stories,* fragmentary remains of the lost national epic of the Turks. Ethiopian produced the *Chronicles of King 'Amda Şeyon,* and Georgian produced the *Acts of the Provinces* and the works of Russudanianu. Syrian continued its bent toward religious biography in the *Life of Catholicus Yabhalaha III.* Arabic letters were perhaps most notably distinguished by the works of Ibn Khaldun (*Book of Examples, Maqaddima*) and Ibn Battuta (*Marvels of India, Chain of Histories*). Other works included the *Proverbs* of Tiqtaqa, dictionaries (Safadi, Kashgari, Ibn Mukarram, Ibn Manzur), an encyclopedia (Nuwayri), and the writings of Ibn Fadlallah, Omari, Isnawi, and Sanhaji.

Persian literature was historical (Hamdullah, Rashid ad Din, Shiraz) and poetic (Amir Khusrau, Hasan, *The Tongue of the Invisible* of Hafiz). Among the more curious works of Persian literature was Zakan's indictment of *The Ethics of Aristocracy.* Other Persian works were those of Salman and the *Fables of Bidpai* of Husain Vaiz.

Sanskrit produced Madhava's *Summary of All the Demonstrations,* works on poetics by Vidya Dhara and Vidya Natha, and on poetics and drama by Visva Natha, the anthology of Sarnga Dhara and the legends about poets of the period written by Meru Tunga and Raja Sekhara. Romances were composed on the *Life of Jagadu* by Sarva Ananda and on other themes by Bhanu Datta. The *Dictionary* of Medinikara and the *Lexicon* of Irugapa may also be mentioned.

The *Praakṛta Pingala* of this century is an important source for the history of the Prakrits, and Vidya Pati also wrote *Kiirti Lataa* in Prakrit. Indic vernaculars literarily active were Kashmiri (the poems of Noor ud Din and Lal Ded), Sindhi (*Dodo Chanesar* and the *Mamui Prophecies*), Rajasthani (*Annals of Rajasthan*), Urdu (*Dah Majlis, Mi'raaj ul Aashiqiin, Hidaayat Naama, Ahkaam uṣ Ṣalavaat, Kalimaat ul Haqaaiq*), Hindi (the works of Jyotishwar), Marathi (the poems of Namdev, who also wrote Sanskrit hymns), Assamese (the *Ramayana* of Madhab Kandali), Malayalam (*Grammar and Linguistics*), Telegu (the *King Nala* of Śri Natha), Tamil (the commentaries of Uma Pati), Bengali (Badu's *Praise of Lord Krishna*), Oriya (*The Great Bharatas* of Sarala Das and the *Kalasha Chautisa* of Bachha Das), Gujerati (*Chronicles*), and Sinhalese (*Daḷadaasirita*). Outside India, Central and Southeast Asia were variously represented. The Mongolians translated the *Alexander* of Nizami. Tibet produced the *Life of Tsong Khapa*, a monk who edited a compilation called *The Secret Collection*. Putön's *Treasury of the Precious Scriptures* is an important historical source, but the most important works in Tibetan letters are probably the great Buddhist library of this period, *The Translated Commandments* (Kanjur) and *The Translated Explanations* (Tanjur), parts of which are often the sole surviving versions of notable Indian works. The earliest Malay works are the fourteenth-century *Epitaph of a Princess*, the *Chronicles of Pasai*, the *Tale of Panji*, and Kadli Hasan's *Tales of a Parrot*. From the same date are the last surviving works in the *kavi* alphabet of Old Javanese, the epics of *Rama* and *Arjuna*. Nothing can be dated to this century in Thai, but a number of Thai works remain undated, and some of them may be this early. These include *Cosmogony*, *The Dragon Princess*, *The Girl and the Elephant*, *Inthapat*, *The Life of Buddha*, *Maxims of Phra Ruang*, *Mynah Bird Lament*, *The Next to Last Life of Buddha*, *Rules for the Conduct of Kings*, *Wet Ya Sun Yin*, *Wo Ra Loongs*, *Phra Racha Kamnot*, *Phra Tamnon*, *Phra Tamra*, *The Princess and the Crocodile*, *The Princess and the Giant*, and *The Wars of King Mahasot*.

Chinese writers of the early Ming dynasty dutifully produced a *History of the Mongol Dynasty* and a *Penal Code*. The Mongol tradition of novels was continued in the *Tale of the Water Margins* attributed to Shi Nai An, and that of plays in the *Chalk Garden* of Huei. The *Essays* of Fang Hsia Ju and Liu Chi (and the latter's poems) represent the more classical tradition, as did Chang Yu Chin's *Astronomy and the Calendar*. Other works were K'iao's *Dream of Goldpieces*, the *Chien Teng Yü Hua* of Li Ch'ang Ch'i and the *Four-Element Precious Mirror*. The *Annals of Korea* of Chŏng also belong to the fourteenth century. Histories of Japan were produced by Kitabatake and Chikafusa, and a notable achievement in letters was a series of *noo* plays by Kiyotsugu. The *Taiheiki* of Kojuna may also be mentioned.

14 Aaron, Aboab, Airivanq, Asgrímsson, 'Ashik, Bachha, Badu, Bedersi, B. Ben Asher, J. Ben Asher, Ben Qalonymos, Berenguer, Bhanu, Birgitta, Boccaccio, Chang, Charles, Chaucer, Chikafusa, Chŏng, Closener, Czarnkow, Dante, Dathev, Descoll, Dlugosz, Eckehardt, Evtymy, Fang, FitzGerald, Froissart, Gilsson, Gower, Gwilym, Hafiz, Hamdullah, Hasan, Hethous, Higden, Huei, Husain, Ibn Battuta, Ibn Fadlallah, Ibn Khaldun, Ibn Manzur, Ibn Mukarram, Irugapa, Isnawi, Jyotishwar, Kadli, Kashgari, Kazu, Amir Khusrau, K'iao, Kitabatake, Kiyotsugu, Kojuna, Lal, Langland, Li, Liu, Lopez, Madhab, Madhava, Manuel, Medinikara, Meru, Molinier, Namdev, Noor, Nuwayri, Occam, Omari, Orbelian, Orotu, Padua, Paternas, Perelhas, Petrarca, Putön, Raja, Rashid, Ruiz, Russudanianu, Safadi, Salman, Sanhaji, Sarala, Sarnga, Sarva, Shi, Shiraz, Śri, Sofony, Stitny, Tiqtaqa, Tsong, Uma, Veled, Vidya, Visva, Walsingham, Wiclif, Zakan, Anon.: *Acts, Ahkaam, Alexander, Annals, Arjuna, Arthur's, Cancioneiro, Charlatan, Chronicle, Chronicles, Dah, Daladaasirita, Dede, Destruction, Dodo, Epitaph, Four, Gawain, Grammar, Great, Griseldis, Hidaayat, History, Kalimaat, Legend, Life, Mamui, Miftaah, Mi'raaj, Noble, Nyelvenléktár, Penal, Praakrta, Psalter, Rama, Tale, Translated, Tristram, Trojan, White.*

Columbian (15)

The century that ended in the discovery of America still retained the traditional pattern: Latin, Arabic, Sanskrit, and Chinese were still the major literary traditions, and there was as yet little sign of the massive development soon to overtake the vernaculars of Europe. The Persians and the Turks were more impressive than the English, the Germans, or the French. Among the modern European languages, in fact, Norwegian, Danish, and Swedish were literarily silent. Gutormsson wrote a *Key to Meters* in Icelandic. Notable German works were the *Fables* of Steinhöwel, the *Theuerdank* of Maximilian, and the *Ship of Fools* of Sebastian Brant. The *Frisian Rhymed Chronicle* continued the literature of that language. English works were Malory's *Morte d'Arthur* and the mystery play of *Everyman* (the later being perhaps a translation of Potter's Dutch original). Irish contributed O'Huiginn's poems, Welsh produced the poems of Edmund and the *Red Book of Hergest*, Breton produced the life of *St. Nonn*, and Cornish produced the *Passion of Our Lord, Mystery Plays,* and *Mount Calvary*. It was the time of Comines and François Villon in French, of da Vinci and Manuzio in Italian. Provençal produced *Joyas del Gay Saber* and Catalan *Tirant the White* and the *Love Songs* of March. Rojas' *Celestina* is probably the best-known Spanish work, Galician produced further *Cancioneiros*, and in Portuguese of the same time there are the *Chronicles* of Lopes and Gomes Eanes. Russian came up with a version of Tristan called *Peter and Fevronia of Murom* as well as *The Heroic Deeds of Mercurius of Smolensk* and Iskander's *Taking of Constantinople*. Parkosz gave Polish its modern alphabet and Czech nationalism found its voice in Hus and Chelčický. Hungarian works include Hunyady's *Oath*, Grigori's *Elegy upon John Both*, and the anonymous *Song of the Conquest of Pannonia*. The first fragment in Albanian was penned at this time by the Orthodox bishop of Durrës, and Serbian produced the poems of Menčetić.

Greek bowed under the Turkish triumph and produced nothing. Latin appeared in chronicles of Hungary (Thuróczi, *Chronicles*), Poland (Ostrorog), and England (Haldenstone), works of geometry (Regiomontanus) and *Perspective* (Witelo), poetry (Csezmiczei) and works of piety, both Catholic (Kempen's *Imitation of Christ*) and Protestant (Hus). Perhaps the most important Latin works were the tale anthology of the *Deeds of the Romans* and the popular *Jestbook* of Poggio.

Hebrew literature was by this time becoming Europeanized, but its major works were traditional: Melin's *Sacred Magic*, Duran's *Shield of the Fathers*, Albo's *Principles*, Crescas' *God's Light*, and Delmedigo's *Enjoyment of the Law*. Yiddish works included the *Epic of David* and the *Sacrifice of Isaac*. Medsoph produced a *History of Tamurlane* in Armenian. Georgian is represented by the *History of Georgia* of Vakhtung VI. Ethiopian works were the *Mystery of Heaven and Earth* of Ba Hailu Michael; the *Book of Light* and *Miracles of the Virgin Mary* of Zar'a Ya'kub; *The Lord Reigneth*; and the works of Na'od (*Sellase, Organ of Praises, Likeness of Mary*). Turkish literature reflected neatly the complex position of Turkish culture. The *History of Forty Viziers* of Zada was an anthology of tales cognate with the contemporary Greek one of Planudes. Yajiji Oghlu's *Mohammed* exemplified the Turkish allegiance to Islam. Persian influence was displayed in the *Khusrev and Shirin* of Kermiyan. The *Supplications* of Sinan and the poetry of Ahmed and Neva'i were other notable works of this time.

The fifteenth century was the last really florescent period in Arabic letters, for a hundred years later Arabic was overshadowed by both Persian and Turkish. Among the important works were Suyuti's *History of the Caliphs*, Sanusi's *Introduction to Theology*, Ibn 'Arabshah's *Marvels of Destiny* (a biography of Tamurlane), Abshihi's *Anecdotes*, Ibn Hajar's *Lives of the Companions of the Prophet*, and Maqrizi's *Description of Egypt*. The works of Jili, Qalqashandi, Nawaji and Mahasin may also be mentioned, together with the *Qaamus* of Fairuzabadi and an anonymous drama (*The History of the Warriors*).

Leading Persian works of the fifteenth century were the poems of Kabir and Bushaq, the history of Samarqandi, the geography of Abru, and Yazdi's *Book of Victories*. The earliest works in vernacular Pushtu in Afghanistan were the military annals of the conquest of Swat by Sheikh Mali and Kaju Khan, written at this time.

The Sanskrit literature was bulky but largely derivative. Śri Vara and Jona Raja wrote imitations of the *Stream of Kings* of Kalhana, and Śri Vara and Vallabha Deva each wrote an *Anthology of Poetry*. Traditional gnomic poetry was composed by Kusuma Deva and Dya Dviveda, traditional tales by Jina Kirti and Siva Dasa and the anonymous compiler of the *Continuation of the Five Books*, the latter two works dealing with King Vikrama. There were also a second-rate play by Vamana Bhatta Bana (*Paarvatii Parinaya*) and the commentaries of Raya Muku Tamani and Kulluka.

In Prakrit there is a *Rambhaa Mañjarii* by Naya Chandra. Among the Indic vernaculars, Rajasthani is undocumented but others were active: Kashmiri (the *Slaying of Bana Sura, Life of Zaina, Joy of Zaina*), Sindhi (the poems of Qazi Qazan), Hindi (*Sankhya Poems*), Bengali (Ojha's *Epic of Rama*), Urdu (the works of Daraz), Tamil (the commentaries of Adiyarkunallar), Gujerati (the poems of Mira Bai), Marathi (those of Ekanath), Sinhalese (*Kokila Sandesa*), Malayalam (the *Krishna Hymn* of Cherusseri), Assamese (the works of Sankar Deva and versions of the *Great Bharatas* and *Song Celestial*), Telegu (the *Life of Manu* of Peddana), Kannada (the works of Nijaguna Shivayogi, the *Great Bharatas* of Kumara

Vyasa, and the epic of Lakshmisha), and Tibetan (the *Teaching of Padma,* the *Blue Treasury of Records* by Gö, and Gelong's *Rosary of Gems,* a biography of Gedün). Mongolian and Burmese are not represented at this time but a number of Mongolian works are undated: *Gesser Khan, Jungariad, Persian Glossary,* and the poetic *Sea of Comparisons.* Thai works of the time are *Yuen Pai* and Trailok's *Magic Lotus.* A large number of pre-Islamic Malay works are dated to this century, including the *Malay Annals,* the *Romance of Lord Rama,* the *Bharata Epic,* the *Story of Bhauma,* the *Romance of King Vikrama, Malim Deeman, Ken Tambuhan, Cheekeel Waneng Pati,* and a number of other *hikayats* or romances. Jokya's *Play of Rama* and a *Ramayana* survive from fifteenth-century Javanese.

Chinese works were undistinguished, with the possible exception of the tale of *The Lute* by Kao Tsê Ch'êng. Chao Ts'ai Chi wrote poetry, and other works of the time were those of Yung Lo and Wang Yang Ming and the *P'ing Shan Lêng Yen, Lieh Kuo Chuan,* and *Yü Chiao Li.* The Koreans produced the *Songs of the Moon's Reflection on a Thousand Rivers,* the works of Nam, the *Complete Mirror of the Eastern Kingdom* of Sŏ and Chung, the adventure tales of Ka San (*Adventures of Hong Kil Dong*) and Ha Jong, and Yi Sang Ch'un's *Commentary to Dragons Flying to Heaven.* Japanese works were the anonymous *Abstraction,* Kenko's *Idle Thoughts,* the *Anthologies of Twenty-one Reigns* and the *Ninety-three Noo Plays* of Seami. Vietnamese produced the poems of Le Loi.

American Indian literature emerged from its hieroglyphic shadows at this time in the poetry of Netzahualcoyotl and others in Nahuatl and the still untranslated Yucatecan codices of *Astronomy and Divination.* No doubt other works of native literature will eventually be assigned to the pre-Conquest period, but only the barest beginning has been made on the necessary analysis and textual criticism.

15 Abru, Abshihi, Adiyarkunallar, Ahmed, Albo, Ba Hailu, Brant, Bushaq, Chao, Chelčický, Cherusseri, Columbus, Comines, Crescas, Csezmiczei, Daraz, Da Vinci, Delmedigo, Duran, Durrës, Dya, Edmund, Ekanath, Fairuzabadi, Gelong, Gö, Grigori, Gutormsson, Ha, Haldenstone, Hunyady, Hus, Ibn 'Arabshah, Ibn Hajar, Iskander, Jami, Jili, Jina, Jokya, Jona, Ka, Kabir, Kaju, Kao, Kempen, Kenko, Kermiyan, Kulluka, Kumara, Kusuma, Lakshmisha, Le, Mahasin, Malory, Maqrizi, March, Maximilian, Medsoph, Melin, Menčetić, Mira, Nam, Na'od, Nawaji, Naya, Netzahualcoyotl, Neva'i, Nijaguna, Ó Huiginn, Ojha, Ostrorog, Parkesz, Peddana, Pico, Poggio, Potter, Qalqashandi, Qazi, Raya, Regiomontanus, Rojas, Samarqandi, Sankar, Sanusi, Seami, Sheikh, Sinan, Šiva, Sŏ, Šri, Steinhöwel, Suyuti, Thuróczi, Trailok, Vakhtung, Vallabha, Vamana, Villon, Wang, Witele, Yajiji, Yazdi, Yi, Yung, Zada, Zar'a, Anon.: *Abraham's, Abstraction, Anthologies, Astronomy, Bana, Bhaaraataa, Bhagavata, Cancioneiro, Cheekeel, Chronicles, Continuation, Deeds, Epic, Everyman, Frisian, Great, Heroic, Hikayat, History, Joyas, Ken, Kokila, Lieh, Lord, Magic, Malay, Malim, Mount, Mystery, Pañca, Passion, Peter, P'ing, Ramayana, Red, Romance, Sacrifice, St. Nonn, Sankhya, Song, Songs, Story, Teaching, Tirant, Yü, Yuen, Zaina.*

Reformation (16)

Northern and central Europe seceded from the spiritual empire of Rome and produced vernacular *Bibles* in English (Tyndale and Coverdale), German (Luther), Danish (Pedersen), Swedish (Petri), Icelandic (Thorlaksson), Welsh and Czech (*Bible of Kralice*), and Belorussian. (The English "King James Version," the Dutch *Statenbijbel*, and the Finnish translation were completed in the following century.) While Europe was violently divided by the Reformation, it was unanimous in its rising nationalism, and the literary use of the vernacular languages burgeoned. The state of European literature may be suggested by a brief listing of representative works and authors: Icelandic (the Tristan story), Norwegian (Beyer's *Kingdom of Norway*), Danish (Plade's *Book of Visits*), Swedish (Petri's *Swedish Chronicle, Hymns, Homilies*), Finnish (Erici's *Sermons*), Estonian (Wanradt's *Catechism*), Dutch (the works of Castelein, the poems of Anna Bijns), German (*Tyl Eulenspiegel*, Tschudi's *Chronicle*, the poems of Zwingli and Sachs), Frisian (Bogerman's verses, Tsjessens' *Prophecy*), English (Shakespeare's *Julius Caesar*, Spenser's *Faerie Queen*, Marlowe's *Dr. Faustus*, Sidney's *Defense of Poesie*, Ascham's *Toxophilus*, Raleigh's *Discovery of Guiana*), Irish (O'Huiginn's poems), Welsh (those of Aled), Cornish (Hadton's *Life of Meriadec*), Scottish (*Book of the Dean of Lismore*), Breton (*The Great Mystery of Jesus, The Mystery of St. Barbara, The Mirror of Death*), French (Montaigne's *Essays*, La Boétie's *Discourse on Voluntary Servitude*, Ronsard's *Sonnets for Helen*, Charron's *Treatise on the Three Truths*, Rabelais' *Gargantua and Pantagruel*), Basque (the poems of Dechepare), Spanish (Ercilla's *Araucana*, Diaz' *True History of the Conquest of Mexico*, León's poems, Lope de Ruedas' *Pass of Olives*, Las Casas' *History of the Indies*, Garcilaso's *Royal Commentaries of Peru*), Provençal (*Petit Thalamus*, the poems of Galhard), Catalan (poems of García, Serafi), Portuguese (Camoës' *Lusiads*), Galician (*General Songbook*), Romansh (Travers' song of *The War of the Castle of Müs*), Rumanian (the *Gospels* of Coresi), Italian (Cellini's *Autobiography*, Tasso's *Jerusalem Delivered*, Ariosto's *Orlando Furioso*, Castiglione's *The Courtier*, Guicciardini's history, Aretino's satires), Magyar (Karádi's drama *Balassi Meynhért*, Székely's *Chronicle of the World*), Czech (Černý's *Treatise on the Plague*), Sorbian or Lusatian (Moller's *Hymnal*), Polish (Rej, Bielski's history), Russian (Macarius' *Saints' Calendar, Book of Classes*, Peresvetov's *Sultan Mehmed*), Ukrainian (*Bible*), Serbo-Croatian (Ranina's poems), Slovenian (Trubar), Lithuanian (Bretkun), Latvian (Grunau's *Lord's Prayer*), Armenian (Tulkourantzi's poems). Georgian is undocumented, but, over-all, in both quantity and quality the development of national literature in Europe was staggering.

Nor did this development take place entirely at the expense of Latin, for the Latin literature of Europe in the sixteenth century not only bears comparison with that of any previous century, but in one respect out-shines them all: the scientific literature has no parallel in any previous period anywhere. It not only touched upon most of the modern sciences; in many cases it created them: mathematics (Cataldi, Stifel), physics (Newton, Gilbert), zoology (Gessner), botany (Cesalpino), medicine (Par-acelsus, Vesalius), astronomy (Copernicus, Brahe), metallurgy (Agricola), and even anthropology (Hundt). In the central arena of the age, Luther's *Theses* and Calvin's *Institutes* confronted Loyola's *Spiritual Exercises*, More's *Utopia*, and Erasmus' *Praise of Folly*. Latin was everywhere, from Spain (Nuñez, Vitoria), France (Bodin), and Italy (Cardano, Bonfini) to Scotland (Boece), Germany (Fuchs), and Poland (Gornicki, Goslicki, Frycz, Orzechowski). It is notable that for all its liveliness, Latin was by this time lacking in poetry, drama, and oratory, and even narrative was only feebly represented. The muses of the arts had deserted it for the national languages.

Hebrew works of the sixteenth century included the histories of Zak-kuth and Gans, the *Apologetics* of Abravanel, and the *Prepared Table* (Shulhan 'Arukh) of Karo, *Faith Strengthened* and *Karaism* by Isaac and Solomon Troki, respectively, Ben Joshua's *Daily Words* and *Jewish Trou-bles*, Rossi's *From the Eyes' Light*, and Ibn Verga's *Tribe of Judah*. Yiddish literature was very active, producing the romance of *Brie and Zimre*, the *Story Book* anthology, the *Book of Conduct*, the *History of the Jews* (de-rived from Josephus), and the works of Levita (*Paris and Vienna*, *Bovo Bukh*). This is also the date of the earliest literary activity in Ladino or Judaeo-Spanish, resulting in a translation of the Old Testament.

The literature of the non-European world did not in most cases actually decline at this time (although something of the sort can be argued for Arabic and Sanskrit), but it did not participate in the European Renais-sance. It was not until the late nineteenth or early twentieth century, in fact, that the rest of world literature began to reflect the ideological revolu-tion that overtook Europe in the sixteenth century.

Turkish literature produced the *Imperial Book* of Chelebi, the *Joseph and Zuleika* and *Nigaaristan* of Kemal, and the *Spring* of Mesihi, but was principally represented by its poets (Lami'i, Yahya, Sa'd ud Din, Ruhi, Nev'i, Kemal, Fuzuli, Baki, Selim I). Arabic works were those of Zayyati, Sha'rani, and Ahmed Baba; the chronicles of Kati, Diyarbakri, and Sadi; and the *Kitaab al Manṣuuri* of Razi. Arabic influence was represented as far afield as Madagascar (*An Arabic-Malagasy Text*). Ethiopian literature produced the *Refuge of the Soul*, *Mazmura Chrestos*, *Barlaam and Joseph* (a much traveled tale that is traceable to the lives of Buddha), the *Book of Extreme Unction* and the *Confession of Faith* of the Emperor Claudius, Salik's *Encyclopedia of Nikon*, Bahrey's *History of the Gallas*.

Persian was the court language of India. Its principal achievements were the poems of Birbal, Faidi, and 'Urfi, the *Hart Iqliim* of Razi, Firishtah's *History of Hindustan*, Babur's *Memoirs*, Hatifi's biography of *Tamurlane*, and the history of Khond Amiir. Pushtu appeared in the *Fawayid es Sheriah* of Akhund Kazim. The notable Sanskrit works included Ballaala's *Legends of Bhoja*, Naga Raja's *Maxims of Bhava*, the *Love Poems* of Chandi Das, the undistinguished *Demon Romance* of Ravi Deva, and a curiosity, the *Rasika Rañjaña* of Rama Candra, which can be read forwards or backwards—as a eulogy of asceticism or as an erotic poem. Prajya Bhatta and Suka continued the court chronicle of Kashmir, Jayasi wrote *Padumavati*, and Gumani wrote verse maxims (*A Hundred Lessons*). Some of the vernaculars of Asia are undocumented in this century (Sindhi, Rajasthani, Sinhalese) and none of them was lively, but most were represented: Tamil (by the poems of Krishna Raya), Telegu (the works of Surana), Kashmiri (by those of Haba Khatun), Hindi (the *Krishna* of Sur Das), Malayalam (Ezhuttachan's *Epic of Rama* and *Great Bharatas*), Kannada (the epic of Ratnakaravarni), Oriya (*The Song Celestial* of Jagannath Das), Urdu (Gamdhani's *Jawaahiru 'l Asraar*), Marathi (Dasopant's *Gita Arnava*), Gujerati (the poems of Samala), Bengali (Chakravarty's *Chandi Mangal*), and Assamese (*Plays, Vaishnava Doctrine*). Tibet produced the *Life of Sönam Gyatso*, the third Dalai Lama, who was responsible for the conversion of the Mongols to Buddhism, and the Mongolian *Buddhist Tales* probably belong to this time. Thai produced the poems of Phra Narai, the poems, grammar, and *Yazawingyaw Chronicle* of Thilawuntha, the *Life of Anuruddha* and *Khong Kamruen* of Sri Praj, the *Jataka Verses* of Aggathamahdi, and Yaweshinhte's poem on *Fifty-five Coiffures*. Malay works include the ballads of *Bidasari* and *Lord Benian* and a colorful *Ballad of Senhor Costa* about a Portuguese who abducts the Burmese mistress of a Cantonese man. The *Romance of Alexander* and *Hikayat Shah i Mardan* also date here, and *Kalila and Dimna* was translated into Malay, Javanese, and Madurese.

Ming China produced an *Herbal* by Li Shih Chen, works of Tsung Ch'ên and Ch'en Tai Wei (*Mathematics*), the poems of Chao Li Hua, and various anonymous works (*King Hua Yüan, Hao K'in Chuan, Fêng Shên Yen I, Ch'ing P'ing Shan T'ang*). The most notable writing was narrative: *The White Serpent*, Wu Ch'êng Ên's *Western Journey*, *Ancient and Modern Marvellous Tales*, and Wang Shih Cheng's *Golden Lotus*. The *Rules for Wine Drinkers* of Yüan Hung Tao was also out of the ordinary. Korean literature is undocumented. Among the undated Korean works, some may go back to this time. They include the *Book of Interesting and Proper Things*, *The Female Physician's Remedy Book*, the *Five Rules of Conduct*, *Primary Literature*, and *The Three Principles of Conduct*.

Under the influence of the Spanish conquest, the protoliterate Indians of Central America burst briefly into a literary effort later to be swamped by Spanish. The Aztecs expressed themselves in the calendrical *Count of Days*, in chronicles (*Annals of Cuauhtitlán, Memorial of Tepetlaostoc, Toltec-Chichimec History*), and in the *Relation* of Sahagún. The Yucatecan Maya covered similar ground with the *Series of the Katuns* of Chilam Balam, the *Books of the Jaguar Priests* of Ixil, Kaua, Nah, and Tizimin, *Chronicles* of Calkini and Oxkutzcab, the *Notebook of Teabo*, and the *Language of Zuyua*. The Quiche Maya produced the *Lineage of the Lords of Totonicapan* of Reynoso, and the *Book of Counsel*; and the Cakchiquel king, 4 Imox, wrote the *Wars of the House of Zibak*.

16 Abravanel, Aggathamahdi, Agricola, Ahmed, Akhund, Aled, Aretino, Ariosto, Ascham, Babur, Bahrey, Baki, Ballaala, Ben Joshua, Beyer, Birbal, Bodin, Boece, Bogerman, Bonfini, Brahe, Bretkun, Bruno, Calepino, Calvin, Camoës, Cardano, Castiglione, Cataldi, Cellini, Černý, Cesalpino, Chakravarty, Chandi, Chao, Charron, Chelebi, Ch'en, Chilam, Claudius, Coresi, Dasopant, Dechepare, Diaz, Diyarbakri, Erasmus, Ercilla, Erici, Ezhuttachan, Faidi, Firishtah, Frycz, Fuchs, Fuzuli, Galhard, Gamdhani, Gans, García, Garcilaso, Gessner, Gilbert, Gornicki, Goslicki, Grunau, Guicciardini, Gumaani, Haba, Hadton, Hatifi, Hundt, Ibn Verga, 4 Imox, Jagannath, Jayasi, Juan, Karádi, Karo, Kati, Kemal, Khond, Kopernigk, Krishna, La Boétie, Lami'i, Las Casas, León, Levita, Li, Loyola, Luther, Macarius, Marlowe, Mesihi, Moller, Montaigne, More, Naga, Nev'i, Newton, Núñez, Ó Huiginn, Orzechowski, Paracelsus, Pederson, Peresvetov, Petri, Phra, Plade, Prajya, Rama, Razi, Rabelais, Raleigh, Ranina, Ratnakaravarni, Ravi, Rej, Reynoso, Ronsard, Rossi, Rueda, Ruhi, Sachs, Sa'd, Sadi, Sahagún, Salik, Samala, Selim I, Serafi, Shakespeare, Sha'rani, Sidney, Spenser, Śri, Stifel, Sur, Surana, Székely, Tasso, Thilawuntha, Thorlaksson, Travers, Troki, Trubar, Tschudi, Tsjessens, Tsung, Tulkourantzi, 'Urfi, Valdés, Vesalius, Vitoria, Wang, Wanradt, Wu, Yahya, Yaweshinhte, Yüan, Zakkuth, Zayyati, Zwingli, Anon.: *Ancient, Annals, Arabic, Ballad, Barlaam, Bible, Bidasari, Book, Brie, Buddhist, Ch'ing, Chronicle, Count, Fêng, General, Great, Hao, Hikayat, History, Kalila, King, Language, Life, Lord, Mazmura, Memorial, Mirror, Mystery, Notebook, Petit, Plays, Refuge, Romance, Story, Toltec, Tristams, Tyl, Vaishnava, White.*

Manchu (17)

The Manchus sat on the throne of China, and it was the century of gold in Spain. It was no less in France and England. It was the last really productive century for Latin, and there was continuing vitality in the traditions of Turkish, Persian, Sanskrit, Chinese, and Japanese. Other non-European literatures, including that of Arabic, were minor or decadent.

Spanish letters were crowned by the *Don Quijote* of Cervantes and the almost numberless plays of Quevedo (*Visions*), Tirso de Molina (*The Joker of Seville*), and Lope de Vega (*The Knight of Olmedo*) and were covered over with the baroque excesses of Góngora (*Solitudes*). Shakespeare (*Hamlet*), was still writing in England, to be joined or followed by Jonson

(*Volpone*), Beaumont (*The Knight of the Burning Pestle*), Milton (*Paradise Lost*), Donne (*Songs and Sonnets*), Dryden, Pepys (*Diary*), and Walton. Political and philosophic writers were Locke (*Essay*), Burke (*Speeches*), and Hobbes (*Leviathan*). Cotton Mather (*Wonders of the Invisible World*) in America also contributed to English letters. France was enthralled by the theater of Molière (*Tartuffe*), Racine (*Phaedra*), and Corneille (*The Cid*) and the philosophy of Pascal (*Thoughts*), Descartes (*Discourse on Method*), the stylistics of Boileau (*Poetic Art*), the *Fables* of La Fontaine, the works of Sales and Sévigné (*Letters*), the history of Bossuet (*Discourse on Universal History*).

The Germanic literatures were all active, producing the *Svipdag* and works of Jónsson and Magnússon in Icelandic, the works of Arrebo (*Hexaemeron*) and Dass (*The Trumpet of Nordland*) in Norwegian and of Syv in Danish, and those of Rudbeck and Stiernhielm in Swedish. It was the time of Gerhardt (*Hymns*) and Grimmelshausen (*Simplicissimus*) in German, of the *Frisian Poetry* of Japiks, and of the poems of Cats, Huygens, and Hooft and the plays of Bredero (*The Spaniard from Brabant*) and Vondel (*Lucifer*) in Dutch. Celtic works included the *Pursuit of Diarmaid and Gráinne* and Ó Gnímh's *Lament* in Irish, Llwyd's *Book of Three Birds* in Welsh, Macrae's *Fernaig Manuscript* in Scottish, Jordan's *Creation* and Lhuyd's *John of Chy an Hur* in Cornish. Breton remains undocumented. Except for the Latvian and Finnish *Bibles*, the Baltic litoral was silent.

Southern Europe was dominated by Spain and France, but other literatures were represented: Provençal by the sonnets of Larade; Catalan by Pujol's *Epic of Lepanto* and the *Summary* of Bosch, Portuguese by the works of Vieira, Melo, and Rodrigues Lobo, Galician by *Legal Texts*, Italian by Redi and Campanella, Basque by Ohienart, Maltese by Bonamico's sonnets. In the Balkans there was *Fishing and Fisherman's Talk* by Hektorović and the *Osman* of Gundulić in Serbo-Croatian, the *Catechism* of Petrabianca in Albanian, the *Chronicle of Moxa* in Rumanian, the *Erophile* of Khortatzes in Greek, and the poets Zrinyi and Gyongyossi in Magyar. Bulgarian was unrepresented.

In Eastern Europe the representative works were Avvakum's *Autobiography* and Palitsyn's *Stories* in Russian, Stránský's *Bohemian Republic* and Komenský's *Labyrinth* in Czech, Smotritsky's *Grammar* in Ukrainian, and the works of Kochowski in Polish. Armenian is represented by the poems of Kouchak, and Georgian produced the poems of Taymuraz I.

Latin literature continued to be predominantly philosophical (Bacon, Spinoza, Böhme), ecclesiastical (Innocent X, Baronius, Jansenius, Bellarmine, Crashaw, Komenský), and scientific (Galileo, Harvey, Kepler, Mercator, Wallis), although Latin could still be used for politics (Milton's *Defense of the Anglican People*).

Hebrew produced the *Hunted Stag* of Francis. Yiddish produced Ashkenazi's *Go Out and See*, the Hassidic hymn *Fine New Song about the Messiah*, and the moralistic *Elixir of Life* and *Good Heart*.

Turkish continued to produce poets (Nef'i, Nergisi), but also turned to biography (Ata Ullah, Tash, Veysi's *Mohammed*), history (Na'ima's *Chronicles*) and geography (the *Travels* of Evliya). A major achievement was the *Bibliographic and Encyclopedic Lexicon* of Hajji Khalifa, who also wrote in Arabic (*Khashfu 'l Zunuun*). In Arabic of this time there are also the works of Maqqari and Shirbini and Qadir's *Anthology of Spanish Arabic Verse*.

Ethiopian literature produced a *Life of King Lalibala* and *Ode to the Virgin* and the *Rules of Life* of Axum. The *History of the Imoro Tribes* was written in Malagasy.

Persian writing was mainly in and about India: Fazl's *Life of Akbar*, *Institutes of Akbar*, *Illuminator of Understanding*, Araqel's *History of the Persian Invasions*, Iskandar's *'Abbas the Great*, Nau'i's *Burning and Melting*, Mohsan's *School of Religious Doctrines*, and the dictionary of Baksh. Pushtu literature continued to develop in the *Afghan Chronicle* and the poems of Mirza Anzari, Kushal Khan Khatak, and Mollah Abdul Hamid. Sechen's *History of the Eastern Mongols* is a Mongolian classic from this century.

Probably the best-known Sanskrit work of the seventeenth century is the book of *Wholesome Counsel* (Hito Padeśa) of Nara Ayana, which includes many of the tales from the *Five Books*. So does the *Stream of Five Narratives* of Megha Vijaya from the same period. Nara Ayana also wrote a *Romance of Svaha and the Moon*. Other poetic works were the *Hymns* of Tukaram and the elegy of Jagan Natha (*Bhaaminii Vilaasa*), who also wrote on poetics (*Rasa Ganga Adhara*). Diksita wrote a *Compendium of Figures of Speech* and a *Revised Grammar of Panini*, and Vedanga Raya compiled a *Persian Dictionary*. The legal works of Mitra Misra and Kamala Akara and the writings of Jayasi and Maha Deva may also be mentioned. There is also the *Candralekha* of Rudra Dasa in Prakrit. The active vernacular literatures were Punjabi (the Sikh Bible—the *Origin Book*—and the *Sukhmani* of Arjun, the *Morning Prayer* and *Book of Victories* of the Guru Gobind Singh, the *Lives of the Gurus*, *Sassi Punnoo*, and *Sohnu Mahiwal*), Urdu (works of Tahsin ud Din, Gavvasi, Nusrati, and Rustami), Hindi (the *Seven Centuries* of Bihari Lal), Nepali (*Genealogical History of Nepal*), Marathi (the poems of Raghunath and Vaman, the epics of Mukteshwar), Gujerati (Premananda's *Tales*), Oriya (the *Bichitra Ramayana* of Biswanath Khuntia), Kashmiri (the poems of Nawshahri), Bengali (the *Lake of the Deeds of Rama* of Tulsi Das), and Assamese (*Chronicles of the Ahom Courts, Song of the Divine Cowherd*). All four of the Dravidian literatures are documented: Malayalam (*Kathakali*), Kannada (the satires of Sarvajna), Telegu (works of Venkatakavi, Teneli Ramakrishna, and Ramarajabhushana), and Tamil (the works of Nobili). Tibetan works include those of Ngawang (*Diary, Record of the Sayings*), Sanggye (*White Lapis Lazuli*), Palden (*Carriage of the Happy Ones*), and the worldly sixth Dalai Lama Tsangyang (*Poems*). Mongolian features Sechen's *History of the Eastern Mongols*. Seventeenth-century Malay works include translations of the *Book of the Thousand Questions* from Arabic and of the *Book of Morality* from Persian and several new translations of *Kalila and Dimna*, but Malay authors were also active: Shams al Din, Hamzah (*Poems*) and Raniri (*Sirat at Mustakim, The Garden of Kings*). Most of the Southeast Asian literature of this period has been lost or remains undated. Thai is known to be represented by *Si Prat*, the *Maxims* of Damrong, and an adaptation of an Indonesian story, the *Inao* of Chao Phya Dharmadhibes, drawn upon for the further *Inao Yai* and *Inao Lak* by two of the royal princesses.

The literature of Manchu China was fully as active as the leading European traditions. Its tenor was encyclopedic and eclectic. Not only were several encyclopedias compiled (two under K'ang Hsi, the *T'u Shu Chi Ch'êng* and the *Yüan Chien Lei Han*, and the *Encyclopedia of Agriculture* by Hsü Kuang Ch'i). There were also two concordances of literature (also under K'ang Hsi: the *P'ei Wên Yün Fu* and the *P'ien Tzǔ Lei P'ien*), anthologies of plays (the *Theatrical Miscellany* of Shen Te Fu, *Collected Mongol Plays, Ming and Manchu Plays*) and of tales (Feng's *Common Tales to Rouse the World*, P'u Sung Ling's *Strange Stories from a Chinese Studio*, the *Marvellous Tales Ancient and Modern*, and *Twice Flowering Plums*). Traditional scholarship was not lacking, being represented by the essays of Hsü Hsieh, the commentaries of Lin Hsi Chung and Ku Chiang, the works of Huang, Tai Chên, Yen Yüan, and Ku Wu Yen. Hsü Kuang Ch'i wrote on astronomy and mathematics, and K'ang Hsi is remembered also for his *Chinese Dictionary* and the *Sacred Edict*. Chu Yung Shun's *Family Maxims* were similarly influential. The anonymous *Government of the Manchus* is an important historical source. Fang Shu Shao was a leading poet, and Tung's *Reminiscences* were notable, but perhaps the most original figure was Li Yü (*Lampoon of Master K'ung, Mustard Seed Garden Drawing Book, Jou Pu Tuan*). Doubtless the most famous work of the age was Ts'ao's novel, *The Dream of the Red Chamber*. Other notable works were *Flower Shadows behind the Curtain* and the *Journal of a Townsman of Yangchow*.

Having reached the throne of China, Manchu became a literary language, producing the *Mirror of Successive Generations, Natural Philosophy in Chinese and Manchu, The Banners of the Khalkha Mongols*, and the *Address to the Magistrates on Moral Training* of the Emperor Shun. *The Cloud Dream of the Nine* by Kim Man Jung was a notable Korean work of this period. Japan produced the works of Karasumaru and Muro, and the poetry of Basho, the *Way of Yohei*, and *Kana Zooshi*. The notable story-tellers were Ihara (*The Man Who Spent His Life at Lovemaking, Treasury of Japan, The Japanese Family Storehouse*) and Chikamatsu (*Fair Ladies at a Game of Poem Cards, Battles of Coxinga*).

In America the native literatures were already in decline, but Nahuatl was represented by the *Annals* of Chimalpahin, Cakchiquel by the *Annals of the Cakchiquels* by the two Xahilas, father and son, and Chontal by the *Chronicles of Tixchel*.

17 Araqel, Arjun, Arrebo, Ashkenazi, Ata, Avvakum, Axum, Bacon, Baksh, Baronius, Basho, Beaumont, Bellarmine, Bihari, Biswanath, Böhme, Boileau, Bonamico, Bosch, Bossuet, Bunyan, Burke, Calderón, Campanella, Cats, Cervantes, Chao, Chikamatsu, Chimalpahin, Chu, Corneille, Crashaw, Damrong, Dass, Descartes, Diksita, Donne, Dryden, Evliya, Fang, Fazl, Feng, Francis, Galileo, Gavvasi, Gerhardt, Gobind, Góngora, Grimmelshausen, Grotius, Gundulić, Hajji, Hamzah, Harvey, Hektorović, Hobbes, Hooft, Hsü, Huang, Huygens, Ihara, Innocent X, Iskandar, Jagan, Jansenius, Japiks, Jayasi, Jonson, Jónsson, Jordan, Kamala, K'ang, Karasumaru, Kepler, Khortatzes, Kim, Kochowski, Komenský, Kouchak, Ku, Kushal, La Fontaine, Larade, Leibnitz, Lhuyd, Li, Lin, Llwyd, Locke, Lope, Macrae, Magnússon, Maha, Maqqari, Mather, Megha, Mercator, Milton, Mirza, Mitra, Mohsan, Molière, Mollah, Mukteshwar, Muro, Na'ima, Nara, Nau'i, Nawshahri, Nef'i, Nergisi, Ngawang, Nobili, Nusrati, Ó Gnímh, Ohienart, Palden, Palitsyn, Pascal, Pepys, Petrabianca, Premananda, P'u, Pujol, Qadir, Quevedo, Racine, Raghunath, Ramarajabhushana, Raniri, Redi, Rudbeck, Rudra, Ruiz, Rustami, Sales, Sanggye, Sarvajna, Sechen, Sévigné, Shams, Shirbini, Shun, Smotritsky, Spinoza, Stiernhielm, Stránský, Syv, Tahsin, Tai, Tash, Taymuraz I, Teneli, Tirso, Tsangyang, Ts'ao, Tukaram, Tulsi, Tung, Vaman, Vedanga, Venkatakavi, Veysi, Vondel, Wallis, Walton, Xahila, Yen, Anon.: *Afghan, Banners, Beautiful, Bible, Book, Chronicle, Chronicles, Collected, Elixir, Fine, Flower, Genealog-ical, Good, Government, History, Inao, Journal, Kalila, Kana, Kathakali, Legal, Life, Lives, Marvellous, Ming, Mirror, Natural, Ode, Pursuit, Sassi, Si, Sohnu, Song, Svipdag, Twice, Way.*

Enlightenment (18)

The century of the European Enlightenment was the age of the Found-ing Fathers in the United States, of the *Autobiography* of Benjamin Frank-lin, of the *Declaration of Independence*, and of the essays of Tom Paine (*Common Sense*). In England it was the century of Boswell's *Journals* and Johnson's *Dictionary*, Defoe's *Robinson Crusoe*, Chesterfield's *Letters*, and the voyage of Captain Bligh. Congreve (*Way of the World*), Pope (*Essay on Man*), Fielding (*Tom Jones*), Richardson (*Clarissa Harlowe*), Smollett (*Peregrine Pickle*), and Sterne are perhaps the most literary figures, to whom we may add Goldsmith, Sheridan, and Swift for Ireland and Odell for Canada.

In the Germanic literatures generally it was a great age—the century of Goethe (*Faust*), Lessing (*Nathan the Wise*), Schiller (*William Tell*), Klopstock (*Messiah*), and Kant (*Critique of Pure Reason*) in German; of Kellgren's *The New Creation* and Nordenflycht's *The Mourning Turtle Dove* in Swedish; of Baggesen's *Labyrinth* and *Comic Tales* in Danish; and of Holberg's comedies and *Niels Klim's Underground Journey* in Norwegian. (The last is of special interest as it is one of the last narratives in Latin, although it was published in Norwegian.) Icelandic contributed the *Journey through Iceland* of Ólafsson and the *Autobiography* of Steingrímsson. Finnish was relatively inactive, but the Estonian *Bible* dates here, with the works of Donalitius in Lithuanian and of Stender in Latvian. Dutch contributed the works of Effen, Poot, and Langendijk, and Frisian the comedies of Ploeg.

For France this was the great age of Voltaire (*Candide*) and the encyclopedists, of Condorcet, Saint-Simon, Buffon (*Natural History*), and Montesquieu (*Spirit of the Laws*). French Switzerland boasts Saussure and Rousseau (*Social Contract*). The leading figures in Italian literature were Maffei (*Merope*), Alfieri, Casanova, Metastasio, and Goldoni. The golden age was over in Spain, and the principal writers were Feijóo, Luzán, Moratín, and Jovellanos. Favre wrote *Mr. Sistre's Sermon* in Provençal, and Diniz wrote *Hissope* in Portuguese. Basque and Catalan are not documented, being suppressed as legal languages by the Bourbon kings of Spain. Sarmiento produced poems in Galician, and there is a *Catechism* in Maltese.

The Celtic languages were still literary, producing the *Song of Manannan Mac y Lheir* in Manx, MacDonald's poems in Scottish, Wynne's *Visions of the Sleeping Bard* in Welsh, Boson's *A Few Words about Cornish* in Cornish, and Comyn's *Lay of Oisín in the Land of Youth* and Merriman's *The Midnight Court* in Irish. Breton remains undocumented.

Russian features the satires of Kantemir, Trediakovsky's works on prosody, the poems of Derzhavin, and the various works of Lomonosov and Sumarokov. Ukrainian produced Skovoroda's *Friendly Conversation* and the *Aeneid* of Kotlyarevsky. Krasicki was perhaps the leading writer in Polish, the literary historian Dobrovský in Czech, and certainly Bajza (*Adventures and Experiences of Young René*) in Slovak. Serbian produced the *Mary Magdalene* of Georgjić and the *Pleasant Conversation* of Kačić-Miosić, and Slovenian the *Bible* of Japelj, the poems of Vodnik, and the plays of Linhart. Paisi wrote the *History of the Slavonic Bulgarians* in Bulgarian, Variboba produced a *Life of the Blessed Virgin* in Albanian, and Cantemir wrote the *Moldo-Wallachian Chronicle* in Rumanian. Magyar produced the poems of Faludi and Csokonai, and Greek those of Velestinlis and Dapontes.

Probably the leading Latin writers of the eighteenth century were Linnaeus (*System of Nature*), Celsius (*Flora of Uppsala*), Jussieu (*Genera of Plants*), and Swedenborg (*True Christian Religion*)—and, of course, the popes. By the nineteenth century the popes pretty well had Latin to themselves. Hebrew is represented by Luzzatto's *Glory to the Righteous* and *An Account of Karaism* by Solomon of Troki; and representative works in Yiddish were Amelander's *Remnant of Israel*, the *Parables* of Baal Shem Tov, and the *Memoirs of Glikl Haml*. Ladino writing included the *Zirḥe Zibur* and Ben Isaac Asa's *Shulḥan ha Meleḥ*.

The *Verse History of Georgia* of Archili III, Gabashvili's *Battle of Aspindzi*, and the *Wisdom and Lies* of Orbeliani were notable Georgian works, and Armenian produced the inevitable histories by Tchamitch and Abraham of Crete.

Islamic literature was by this time definitely in decline. Nabi was a leading Turkish poet. Arabic produced Murtada's *Commentary on the Qamus*, the *Memoirs* of 'Ali Hazin, and the *Life of Zahir*. Persian and Pushtu literature are undocumented, and Malagasy is also silent. The monkish poems of Gondar, especially those of Alaqa Tayya, were written in Ethiopian. Swahili produced the *Epic of Tambuka, Al Inkishafi* of Saiyid Abdallah, and *Al Hamziyah* of Saiyid Aidarus.

Sanskrit literature of this century dwindles to the hymns of Taumanavar and an epic by Sankara, and Indic literature in general was thin. There is an *Aananda Sundarii* by Ghana Syama in Prakrit. Nothing is documented for Rajasthani, Gujerati, or Singhalese. The active literatures included Nepali (the *Memoirs* of Prithvi Narayan Shah), Kashmiri (the *Ramavatara Charita* of Prakash Ram Kurigami, the poems of Arnimal), Oriya (the *Baidehisa Bilasa* of Upendra Bhanja), Sindhi (the *Kafis* of Sachal, the *Elegies* of Sabit Ali Shash, the *Risalo* of Abdul Latif, and the poems of Sami and Rohal), Punjabi (the *Kafis* of Bulhey Shah, the *Heer Ranjha* of Warris Shah), Hindi (the works of Sadasukh Lal and Insha Alla Khan), Urdu (the *Shah Nama i Islam* of Hafeez Jallundhari, the *Phuulban* of Nishati, and the *Bahraam o Gulandaam*), Marathi (the poems of Moropant), Malayalam (the works of Kunchan Nambiar), Tamil (the novels of the Italian priest Beschi), Telegu (a *Life of Christ*), Kannada (the epic of Chikadevaraya), Bengali (the *Vidyaasundar* of Ray), and Assamese (*The Creation* and Barkath's *Ocean of Elephant Lore*).

Southeast Asian languages were more lively, particularly Burmese, which produced the anonymous *Royal History of Kings, The Battle of Men and Monkeys, Aindarwuntha*, and Mywaddi's *Inao*. The Burmese *Rama Story* of Toe is cognate with the Thai *Rama Story* of Thonburi. Thai also produced the *Tales for Sam Sib* and the *Horatibodi*, a *Buddhist Cosmogony, Narint*, the *Annals of the Northern States*, and the *Annals of Ayuthia*. Cambodian is represented by *Prophecies*, the works of Uk (*The Conch and the Bow of Victory*), and those of Prah Bàt (*Women's Wisdom, Inao, The Princess and the Crocodile*). Tibetan produced the *Bouquet of Lotus*, the

Law of the Birds, the works of the Abbot of Sum (*Rhetoric and Drama, A General Account of the World,* and others), and Trinle's *Ocean Chariot of Real Attainment.* There were also a number of local religious histories, including one on Bhutan, *The Religious History of the South.* The Mongolian epic of *King Geser* is contemporary. Malay produced history (*Misa Melayu, Kedah Annals,* the *History of Johore*) and the works of Nipal Chand (*Gul Bakawali*).

The eighteenth-century Chinese were preoccupied with history, dynastic matters, and mathematics. They produced and then revised an anonymous *History of the Ming,* together with a *Draft History of the Manchu Dynasty* in 131 volumes, a history of *The Founding of the Manchu Empire* and a *Manchu Code,* an anonymous *Mathematics* and the *Equation Theory* of Li Chuan. Chao I, who wrote *The Wars of the Manchu Dynasty,* also wrote poetry, and an anthology of poetry was compiled by Ch'ien Lung. Another poet, Yüan Mei, was famous for his *Letters.* Ngu Ching Tsu wrote the satirical novel *Chu Lin Nguai Ch'i.* The leading classical scholar was Tai Chên, and Ch'ên Hung Mou also wrote a notable commentary. An anonymous *Sixteen Essays,* P'u Sung Ling's *Strange Stories,* the *Mirror of Flowers* of Ch'ên Hao Tzŭ, and the works of Yung, Yen Jo Chü, and Hsia Erh Ming may also be mentioned. Korean literature produced a *Korean Encyclopedia* and *The Frogs* of Yi Mun Jong. Notable Japanese writers were Norinaga and Kaibara (classical scholars), Arai (*History of the Daimyos*), and Santo (*Edifying Story Book*). Manchu is represented by an anonymous *Essay on the Origin of the Eight Banners,* and Vietnamese by the poetry of On Nhu Hau and Doan Thi Diem.

The colonial literature in American Indian languages continued with the Nahuatl play *Huehuence,* the Yucatecan *Ritual of the Batabs, Song of the Dance of the Bowman,* and Hoil's *Book of the Jaguar Priest of Chumayel,* the Quiche *Dance of the Conquest* and *The Count of Days and the Numbers of the Days,* and the Quechuan play *Ollantay.*

18 Abdul, Alaqa, Alfieri, 'Ali, Amelander, Arai, Archili, Arnimal, Baal, Baggesen, Bajza, Barkath, Ben Isaac, Beschi, Bligh, Boson, Boswell, Buffon, Bulhey, Casanova, Celsius, Chao, Ch'ên, Chesterfield, Ch'ien, Chikadevaraya, Clement XI, Clement XIV, Comyn, Condorcet, Congreve, Crete, Dapontes, Defoe, Derzhavin, Diniz, Doan, Dobrovský, Donalitius, Effen, Favre, Fielding, Franklin, Gabashvili, Georgjić, Ghana, Goethe, Goldoni, Goldsmith, Hafeez, Hoil, Holberg, Hsia, Insha, Japelj, Johnson, Jussieu, Kačić, Kaibara, Kant, Kantemir, Kellgren, Kleist, Klopstock, Kotlyarevsky, Krasicki, Kunchan, Langedijk, Lessing, Li, Linhart, Linnaeus, Lomonosov, MacDonald, Maffei, Merriman, Metastasio, Montesquieu, Moropant, Murtada, Myawaddi, Nabi, Nipal, Nishati, Nordenflycht, Norinaga, Odell, Ólafsson, On, Orbeliani, Paine, Paisi, Phra, Ploeg, Poot, Pope, Prah, Prakash, Prithvi, P'u, Ran, Ray, Richardson, Rohal, Rousseau, Sabit, Sachal, Sadasukh, Saint-Simon, Saiyid, Sami, Sankara, Santo, Sarmiento, Saussure, Schiller, Sheridan, Skovoroda, Smollett, Steele, Steingrímsson, Stender, Sum, Swedenborg, Swift,

Tai, Taumanavar, Tchanitch, Thonburi, Toe, Trediakovsky, Trinle, Troki, Uk, Upendra, Variboba, Velestinlis, Vodnik, Voltaire, Warris, Wynne, Yen, Yi, Yüan, Yung, Anon.: *Aindarwuntha, Annals, Bahraam, Battle, Bible, Bouquet, Buddhist, Catechism, Count, Creation, Dance, Declaration, Draft, Essay, Founding, History, Huehuence, Kedah, King, Korean, Law, Life, Manchu, Mathematics, Memoirs, Miracle, Misa, Narint, Ollantay, Prophecies, Religious, Revised, Ritual, Royal, Sixteen, Song, Tales, Zirhe.*

Victorian (19)

The nineteenth century created the British Empire and very nearly destroyed the American Union. For English letters it was a creative time, giving us in the United States the poems of Longfellow (*Hiawatha*), Poe (*The Raven*), and Whitman (*Leaves of Grass*); the essays of Emerson and Holmes (*Autocrat of the Breakfast Table*) and the autobiography of Thoreau (*Walden*); and the novels of Melville (*Moby Dick*) and Mark Twain (*Tom Sawyer*) and in England the novels of Dickens (*Bleak House*), Scott (*Ivanhoe*), Stevenson (*Treasure Island*), and Jane Austen (*Pride and Prejudice*) and the poems of Tennyson (*Idylls of the King*), Wordsworth (*Poems in Two Volumes*), Keats (*Endymion*), Shelley (*Prometheus Unbound*), and Browning (*The Ring and the Book*). The volume and variety of English literature were a fitting prelude to the flood of our own times and defy brief description. Perhaps the most influential English works were Darwin's *Origin of Species* and Harriet Beecher Stowe's *Uncle Tom's Cabin.* Ireland contributed the first works of the "Irish Renaissance," in which Russell (*Homeward*) was an early figure. The best-known Canadian writer was probably Seton (*Wild Animals I Have Known*).

German produced towering figures: Hegel (*Encyclopedia of the Philosophical Sciences*), Nietzsche (*Thus Spoke Zarathustra*), Burckhardt (*The Civilization of the Renaissance in Italy*), Mommsen (*History of Rome*), and Jakob and Wilhelm Grimm (*Fairy Tales*). The poetry of Heine (*Book of Songs*), the drama of Grillparzer (*The Dream Is Life*), Hauptmann (*Before Dawn*), and Sudermann (*Honor*) are among the more specifically literary achievements. But the most momentous book was certainly Karl Marx' *Capital.* The other Germanic literatures were also very lively, producing such works as Bjørnson's *The Bankrupt* or Ibsen's *Hedda Gabler* in Norwegian, Strindberg's *The Father* or Heidenstam's *The Charles Men* in Swedish, Gjellerup's *The Disciple of the Teutons* or Pontoppidan's *Lucky Peter* in Danish, the poems and plays of Jochumsson or Thomssen's *Battle of the Field of Death* in Icelandic, the novels of Bilderdijk or the poetry of Potgieter in Dutch, and *The Silver Rattle* of Dykstra in Frisian. Representative Baltic works include Stenvall's *Seven Brothers* and Päivärinta's *My Life* in Finnish, *Turi's Book of Lappland* in Lapp, Kreuzwald's *Son of*

Kalev in Estonian, and the works of Baranauskas in Lithuanian. Latvian produced Pumpurs' *Slayer of the Bear*.

The Celtic literatures were clearly in decline, but Breton reappeared in the *Breton Songs* of Villemarqué, and Owen's *Rhys Lewis* and the *Mabinogion* appeared in Welsh, Raftery's poems in Irish, Macintyre's poems in Scottish, and the *Maolchíardín* in Manx.

The nineteenth century was clearly a great if not indeed a golden age in French literature. The novelists alone are an imposing array: Flaubert (*Madame Bovary*), Zola (*Germinal*), Hugo (*The Hunchback of Notre Dame*), Dumas (*The Three Musketeers*), George Sand (*The Master Bell Ringer*), Stendhal (*The Red and the Black*), Verne (*Around the World in Eighty Days*), Balzac (*Eugenie Grandet*), Mérimée (*Carmen*). But the poetry of Gautier (*Ivories and Cameos*), Baudelaire (*Flowers of Evil*), Rimbaud (*A Season in Hell*), Verlaine (*Romances without Words*), Verhaeren (*Las Flamandes*), Lamartine (*Poetic Meditations*), and Mallarmé (*The Afternoon of a Faun*); the plays of Musset (*One Doesn't Joke with Love*); the stories of Maupassant (*The Necklace*) or Loti (*An Iceland Fisherman*) set a literary standard hard to parallel even in French history. Less flamboyantly the Romantic Movement produced in Italian the poetry of Leopardi (*Songs*) and the novels of Manzoni (*The Betrothed*) as realism gave rise to the novels of Verga (*Cavalleria Rusticana*). The works of Mazzini are of outstanding stylistic as well as political significance. Maltese figures in Azzopardi's *Susanna* and Vasallo's *The Turkish Galleon*. Spanish, too, enjoyed a notable revival, in which the leading figures were Zorrilla (*Don Juan Tenorio*), Rivas (*The Force of Destiny*), Espronceda (*The Student of Salamanca*), Larra (*The Page of Sir Henry the Sorrowful*), Bécquer (*Rhymes*), Pérez Gáldós (*Doña Perfecta*), Alarcón (*The Walls Have Ears*), Valera (*Pepita Jiménez*), Palacio Valdés (*Sister St. Sulpice*), and Pardo Bazán (*Mother Nature*). Portugal contributed the poetry of Quental (*Sonnets*), the plays of Almeida Garrett (*Brother Louis of Sousa*), and the novels of Castelo Branco (*The Mysteries of Lisbon*); and Brazil contributed the novels of Machado de Assis (*Dom Casmurro*). In Galician the poems of Rosalía de Castro are outstanding. Catalan produced the plays of Guimerà (*The Lowlands*) and the poetry of Verdaguer (*The Atlantid*), and Provençal produced the poems of Mistral (*Mirèio*) and Aubanel. Basque is represented by the poems of Moguel and Iztueta's *History of Guipuzcoa*, and in Romansh there are the works of Muoth.

The giants of Russian literature in this period lifted it to the plane of greatness, especially Pushkin (*Yevgeny Onegin*), Tolstoy (*War and Peace*), Dostoievsky (*Crime and Punishment*), Turgenev (*Fathers and Sons*), Gogol (*Dead Souls*), Chekhov (*The Cherry Orchard*), Krylov (*Fables*), Leskov (*Lady Macbeth of the Mtsensk District*), and Lermontov (*A Hero of Our Time).* Ukrainian reached comparable heights in the poetry of Shevchenko (*The Heretic*). Poland produced the poets Mickiewicz (*Pan Tadeusz*), Slowacki (*King Spirit*) and Krasinski (*The Psalms of the Future*) and the novelist Sienkiewiaz (*Quo Vadis?*); Slovak produced the *Death of Janoshik* by Botto; and Czech produced the poets Palacký and Kollar (*Daughter of Sláva*). Serbian produced *The Uskok* of Matavalj and *The Mother of the Jugovići* of Vojnović, and Slovenian produced the poems of Prešeren, Aškerc, Gregorčič, Jenko, and Stritar and the works of Levstik (*Martin Krpan*). Bulgarian features the poems of Botev, the works of Vazov, and the *Bay Ganyu* of Konstantinov. Lusatian (Sorbian or Wend) is represented by the poems of Čišinski-Bart. Magyar literature includes the poetry of Vorosmarty (*The Call*), Petofi (*Janos Vitez*), and Arany (*Toldi*), the drama of Charles Kisfaludy (*The Tatars in Hungary*), the poems of his brother Alexander (*The Loves of Himfy*), and the novels of Jókai (*A Hungarian Nabob*). Rumanian produced the poems of Eminescu and the plays of Caragiale, Albanian the *Skënderbeg* of Rada and *The Bektashis* of Frásheri, Greek *The Besieged Freemen* of Solomos, Psykhares' *My Journey*, and Palamas' poems, and Georgian Orbeliani's *Hope*.

Hebrew writing included *The Falashas* of Joseph Halevy and the works of Leon Gordon and Abramovich (*The Travels of Benjamin the Third*), although the latter also wrote in Yiddish. Yiddish works are the anonymous *Praises of the Besht*, the *Holiday Leaves* of Peretz, and *The Old Country* of Rabinovich ("Sholom Aleichem"). Ladino writing included *Yosef ha Zaddik* and Abulafia's *Shibbe ha Tanaím*. After five centuries of silence, Syrian flickered out with a final *Gospel*.

Turkish poets were numerous (Fazil, Fitnet, 'Izzet Molla, Kemal, Leyla, Neshet, Pertev, and Pertev Pasha, Wasif and 'Akif). Other Turkish works were *Beauty and Love* by Ghalib, a drama by Hamid, and the stories of Midhat. Turkish was already moving closer to Europe, as is illustrated by Shinasi's work on French poetry. Major Arabic works include Yaziji's *Assemblies*, the *Diary* and *History of Egypt* by Jabarti, and Muhammad Abduh's *Risaalatu 'l Tauḥiid*. Zenab's *King Theodore II* is a representative Ethiopian work, and Mazrui's *Ballad of Akida* a Swahili one. Callet's *History of the Hova Kings* was compiled in Malagasy. Persian literature revived in the *Pariishaan* of Qa'ani, the *Journey to Khorasan* of Sani', and the geographical dictionaries of Sani' and Shirvani. There is also an anonymous *History of India, 1600–1800,* and the *Book of Certitude* of Baha, the charter of Baha'i.

Nineteenth-century Sanskrit produced the *Rajangala Mahodyana* of Ramaswami Raju, the *Autobiography* of Korada, and the biography of *Pandit Bechana Rama* by Sarma, Vinayaka's *Coming of the English* and *Introduction to Ten Princes*, the *Nuutanodantotsa, Itahasa Dipikia*, and

Itahasa Tamomani. Two of the vernaculars remain undocumented (Rajasthani and Sinhalese) but others were active: Kashmiri (Gami's *Mystical Romances*, Maqbool Kralawari's poems, Wahab Pare's *History*), Nepali (Bhanubhakta's *Epic of Roma*), Sindhi (Pritamdas' *Ajib Bheta*, the poems of Gul Mahomed, Mirza Sahib, Dalpat, and Bedil), Punjabi (Vir Singh's *Life of the Guru Nanak* and other works), Hindi (the works of Bharatendu), Urdu (the *Parrot Tales* of Haidar Baksh, the *Aarish i Mahfil* of Sher 'Ali Afsos, Sarshar's *Exploits of Azad*, Rahab 'Ali Surur's *Fasaana e 'Ajaaib*, Nihal Chand Lahauri's *Mazhab i 'Ishq*, an anonymous *Śaakuntalaa*, the *Singhaasan Battiisii* of Kazim 'Ali Javan and Lalu Lal), Gujerati (the works of Govardhanram and Narmad), Marathi (the poems of Keshavsut, the works of Deval, Deshmukh, Kirloskar, Apte, Baba Pudmanji, and others), Malayalam (Kerala Varma's *Mayura Sandesam*), Bengali (the poems of Dutt and Chakravarti), Oriya (*The Great Journey* and poems of Radhanath, Madhusudan's poems, and Senapati's *Six Acres and Eight Decimals, Mother's Brother,* and *Expiation*), Assamese (*Khamba and Thoibi*), Tamil (Mudaliar's *Five Books*), Telegu (the works of Lakshminarasimhan, Vasuraya Kavi, and Viresalingam), and Kannada (the works of Krishna Raya, the *Mudra Manjusha* of Kempu Narayana, and Muddana's *Ramashwavedha*). In central Asia, religion remained central and Tibet continued to produce religious histories (*The Valley of Taste*, Jikme's *Religious History of Mongolia*) as well as general history (Sönam's *Clear Mirror of the Royal Line*). Among the Mongolian works is a divinatory treatise, *Various Uses of the Little Jade Chest Book.*

In Southeastern Asia literature continued to develop in new as well as established literary languages. Burmese contributed the *Legend of the Kyaukwaing Pagoda, Mahaa Yazawin, Wizaya Zat,* the *Romance of Zawta Gômma,* and the *Sawpé Sawmé,* the plays of U Pon Nya (*The Water Carrier, Waythandaya*), Saya Pwa's *Burmese Literary Art,* the works of Uggya Byan, Saya Thein's *History of Certain Burmese Characters,* Hamagyaw's *Tawla,* and the lyric poems of Letwethondra. Thai produced the *Entertainment of Nang Tantrai,* the *Book of the Birds,* the *Next to Last Life of Buddha,* Sunthorn Bhu's *Swasdi Raksa,* and the works of Rama III and Rama IV. Cambodian was particularly productive, the leading writers being the novelists Mohà Màs (*Tip Sanvàr, Advice to the King's Servants, Models of Artificial Verse*), Prêk Pranàk (*Prah Laksĕnavoṅ*), and Muk (*Prah Chinăṇàvon, Viman Chan, Cambodian Customs*). Kraisa Sórivoṅ was a leading poet; Kèp wrote *Advice on Hygiene* and *Ethics for Posterity,* Pan *Manual of the Household and Farm Economy,* Tien a *Legend of a Life of Buddha,* and Lôk Pŭtthèr an *Essay on Individual Ethics;* and there were an anonymous *Construction of Angkor Vat, Neath Outtami,* and *History of the Rabbit Judge.* The leading Malay writers were 'Ali Haji (*Malay Annals,*

Silsilah Melayu dan Bugis), Munshi 'Abdu'lla (*Autobiography, Voyage to Kelantan, Pilgrimage to Mecca, Kalila and Dimna*), and Alang Ahmad (*Aesop's Fables*). There was also an anonymous *Kalila and Dimna* and the *hikayats* of *Bestammam* and *Ganja Mara*. Balagtas' *Florante and Laura* in Tagalog completes the survey of "colonial India."

Nineteenth-century China produced the anonymous *Rewards and Punishments*, the works of Ku and Hsien and the *Diary* of Ssŭ Yŭ Têng. Perhaps the most distinguished scholar was Yüan Yüan, who wrote a *Topography of Kwantung* and edited the great *Sung Encyclopedia*. Other classicists were Wang Hsien Ch'ien (*Ch'ien Han Shu Pu Chu, Hsün Tzŭ Chi Chieh*) and Sun I Jang (*Mo Tzŭ Hsien Ku*). The leading poets were Huang Tsun Hsien and Chin Huo (*Song of the Autumn Cicada*). Other highly regarded works were Wen Kang's *Heroic Children*, Li Po Yuan's *Chinese Officialdom*, and Liu Tieh Yun's *Travels of Lao*. Also in Chinese was the *Summary of Korean History* by Chang Tong, and in fact Korean is otherwise undocumented. The Japanese also produced history, the *History of Great Japan* by Mitsu and the *General History of Japan* by Rai. Probably the best-known fictional works are Kyokutei's *The Moon Shining through Cloud Rifts on a Rainy Night*, Futabatei's *Drifting Cloud*, and Jippensha's *Hizakurige*. Vietnamese literature is represented by the *Phong Than Ba Ap Khao, Luc Van Tien, Tru'o'ng the Idiot*, the *Book of Three-Character Phrases*, Vuong Tan Than's *Commentary on Tam Tu Kinh*, and, most notably, Nguyen Du's *Kim Van Kieu*. Despite the fact that it was still the language of the court, Manchu does not appear to have produced literature.

In America the modest literary efforts of the American Indians all but came to an end with Bartolo Ziz' *Knight of Rabinal* in Quiche.

19 Abramovich, Abulafia, 'Aakif, Alang, Alarcón, 'Ali, Almeida, Apte, Arany, Aškerc, Aubanel, Austen, Azzopardi, Baba, Baha, Balagtas, Balzac, Baranauskas, Baudelaire, Bécquer, Bedil, Bhanubhakta, Bharatendu, Bilderdijk, Bjørnson, Botev, Botto, Browning, Burckhardt, Callet, Caragiale, Castelo, Castro, Chakravarti, Chang, Chekhov, Chin, Ćišinski, Dalpat, Darwin, Deshmukh, Deval, Dickens, Dostoievsky, Dumas, Dutt, Dykstra, Emerson, Eminescu, Espronceda, Fazil, Fitnet, Flaubert, Fràshëri, Futabatei, Gami, Gautier, Ghalib, Gjellerup, Gogol, Gordon, Govardhanram, Gregorčič, Grillparzer, Grimm, Guimerà, Gul, Haidar, Halevy, Hamagyaw, Hamid, Hauptmann, Hegel, Heidenstam, Heine, Holmes, Hsien, Huang, Hugo, Ibsen, Iztueta, 'Izzet, Jabarti, Jenko, Jikme, Jippensha, Jochumsson, Jókai, Kazim, Kemal, Kempu, Kèp, Kerala, Keshavsut, Kirloskar, Kisfaludy, Kollar, Konstantinov, Korada, Kraisa, Krasinski, Kreuzwald, Krishna, Krylov, Ku, Kyokutei, Lakshminarasimhan, Lamartine, Larra, Leopardi, Lermontov, Leskov, Letwethondra, Levstik, Leyla, Liu, Lôk, Longfellow, Loti, Machado, Macintyre, Madhusudan, Mallarmé, Manzoni, Maqbool, Marx, Matavalj, Maupassant, Mazrui, Mazzini, Melville, Mérimée, Mickiewicz, Midhat, Mirza, Mistral, Mitsu, Moguel, Mohà, Mommsen, Mudaliar, Muddana, Muhammad, Muk, Munshi,

Muoth, Musset, Narmad, Neshet, Nguyen, Nietzsche, Nihal, Orbeliani, Owen, Pavärinta, Palacio, Palacký, Palomas, Pan, Pardo, Peretz, Perez, Pertev, Poe, Pon, Pontoppidan, Potgieter, Prêk, Prešeren, Pritamdas, Psykhares, Pumpurs, Pushkin, Qa'ani, Quental, Rabinovich, Rada, Radhanath, Raftery, Rahab, Rai, Rama, Ramaswami, Rimbaud, Rivas, Russell, Sand, Sani', Sarma, Sarshar, Saya, Scott, Senapati, Seton, Shelley, Sher, Shevchenko, Shinasi, Shirvani, Sienkiewicz, Slowacki, Solomos, Sönam, Ssŭ, Stendhal, Stenvall, Stevenson, Stowe, Strindberg, Stritar, Sudermann, Sun, Sunthorn, Tennyson, Thomssen, Thoreau, Tien, Turgenev, Twain, Uggya, Valera, Vassallo, Vasuraya, Vazov, Verga, Verhaeren, Verlaine, Verne, Villemarqué, Vinayaka, Vir, Viresalingam, Vojnović, Vorosmarty, Vuong, Wahab, Wang, Wasif, Whitman, Wordsworth, Yaziji, Yüan, Zenab, Ziz, Zola, Zorrilla, Anon.: *Book, Construction, Entertainment, Gospel, Hikayat, History, Itahasa, Kalila, Kanjur, Khamba, Legend, Legends, Luc, Mabinogion, Mahaa, Maolchíaráin, Mulla, Neath, Next, Nuutanodantotsa, Phong, Praises, Rewards, Romance, Śaakuntalaa, Sawpé, Tanjur, Tru'o'ng, Turi's, Valley, Various, Wizaya, Yosef.*

Chapter 9

Modern Literature

CHRONOLOGICAL SUMMARY

Although the relationships among the world's literatures are extremely complex, it seems useful to describe their over-all structure in terms of five principal traditions: Semitic, Indic, European, Sinitic, and American. In the figures that follow, I have tried to provide a rough outline of these traditions, century by century and language by language. This will locate what we now know of the history of literature in broad temporal, spatial, and linguistic or cultural divisions. Some commentary is in order to supply additional qualifications not readily reducible to graphic form.

Semitic literature is centered on the Near East and its Semitic languages: Egyptian, Babylonian, Syrian, Hebrew, Arabic, and Ethiopian. For summary purposes, we may also include non-Semitic languages whose literature is closely related: Sumerian, Hittite, Turkish, Malagasy, and Swahili. The inclusion of Yiddish and Ladino is arbitrary, because they, together with modern Hebrew and perhaps Hittite and Turkish, are really European literatures. Babylonian is taken to include Akkadian and Assyrian.

A special problem is presented by the literature in "Syrian." A number of different dialects are here grouped together under this name. In the earliest period (the fourteenth century B.C.) these are Ugaritic, Canaanitic, and Phoenician. By the eighth century B.C. the speech of the area was standardized in literary Syrian, which was eclipsed in Hellenistic times by Greek but was later revived as a literary tongue about the second century A.D. By that time the common speech was Aramaic, and literary works in Syrian were often accompanied by a vernacular (*targum*) or Aramaic version. It seems simplest to refer to all these tongues as Syrian, which must be distinguished from Assyrian, a dialect descendant of Akkado-Babylonian and from modern Syrian Arabic. Syrian in this sense has one of the longest and least-known literary traditions in the Near East.

The ancient Semitic literatures were intimately interrelated, exchanging myths (for example, Osiris, Gilgamesh) and forms (for example, laments, dialogues, parallelistic couplets). Later influences were particularly associated with the great religious movements of Judaism, Christianity, and Islam, and tend to subdivide the tradition accordingly, Jewish tradition continuing in Hebrew, Yiddish, and Ladino, Islamic in Arabic, Turkish, Swahili, and Malagasy, and Christian in Syrian, Coptic Egyptian, and Ethiopian. But even these divisions did not prevent extensive sharing of literary forms (for example, dramas, rhymed and metered verse forms) and content (for example, Sinbad, bestiaries). Despite its diversity, the Semitic tradition has considerable coherence.

But although it is unitary in a degree, the Near East is not sharply bounded. Profound mutual influences link it at different times to the traditions of other areas, notably via Greek, Armenian, Spanish, Persian, Urdu, and Malay. The central location of the Semitic languages on the world stage has been a crucial feature of their history from the inception of literacy, and they have both given and received literary stimuli in copious quantities. Historically the Semitic literatures are not only the earliest but also the central components in the great tradition of writing. Their development is outlined in Figure 1.

The literary history of central and southern Asia is dominated by the cognate but somewhat disparate traditions of the Indo-Iranian languages. This is a huge and linguistically complex area, unified primarily by the great religious movements that have swept over it. The oldest and most influential of the Indic traditions are clearly those of Sanskrit, Persian, and the Prakrits, and they became the primary vehicles for this persistent three-way division of Indic religious and literary traditions. Sanskrit was the language of Vedic and Hindu, Persian of Zoroastrian and Islamic, and the Prakrits of Jain and Buddhist thought.

There is as yet no scholarly agreement on the classification of the Prakrit languages and dialects or on the way in which they relate to the modern vernacular languages and dialects, and they are here considered as a unit. The term *Prakrit* here covers all of the vernaculars of post-Vedic and medieval India. One of the Prakrits (Pali) became the scriptural language of Buddhism; others (Ardha-Magadhi, Maharastri, Savraseni) were used for Jain scriptures, and still others (Apabhramsa) for other works. Often they coexist with Sanskrit, as in the speech of some characters in the plays of Kali Dasa.

It is convenient to subdivide the Indic tradition therefore, according to the predominance of these three partly autonomous religious and literary developments. In addition to what we may call the Sanskrit, Persian, and

	LAD.	MAD.	SWA.
16	Bible	Arabic	
17		History	
18	Zirhe		Epic
19	Abulafia	Callet	Mazrui
20			Shaaban

	EGY.		BAB.		
−35	Fertility				
−34					
−33	Ptah's				
−32					
−31					
−30		SUM.			
−29					
−28	Im	Library	BAB.		
−27	Ptah				
−26		Enlil	Sargon		
−25	Work	Gubarru	Lament		
−24	Song				
−23	Pyramid	Gudea			
−22	Duauf	Lament		HIT.	
−21	Nefer	Shulgi	Ishtar		
−20	Quarrel	Creation		Anittas	
−19	Khekhe				
−18	K. Antef		Hammurabi		
−17	K. Cheops			Hattusilis	
−16	Hyksos		When		SYR.
−15	Capture	HEB.		Ullikummi	
−14	Coming		Sharruwa	Mursilis	Baal
−13	Anupu	Moses		Hattusilis	
−12		Song		Slaying	Library
−11	Un	Fable			
−10	Dispute	Oracles	Saggil		
−9	Ani	Jahveh			
−8		Amos	Gilgamesh	ARA.	Zakir
−7		Joshua	Esarhaddon		Bar Ga'yah
−6	Udjahorresne	Baruch	Nebuchadrezzar	Dedan	Epitaph
−5		Job	Epic		Story
−4	Drama	Analyses		Minaean	Lady
−3		Law			
−2		Maccabees			
−1		Coming			
1		Akiba			
2	Testament	Baruch	ETH.		Martyrdom
3	Elias	Yehuda			Bar Daysan
4	Bible	Ashi	Wars		Peshitta
5	St. Michael	Researches			Bar Sauma
6	Canons	Book		Shanfara	Bodh
7	Canons	Ben Jose		Mohammed	Edessa
8		Gaon		Ibn Anas	Isho'denah	TUR.
9		Qayyara		Ibn Qutayb	Taghrit
10		Ben Gorion		Thousand	Bar Kepha	Orkhon
11		Ibn Nagdela		Ibn Sina	Bar Shinaya	Khass
12	YID.	Ben Maimon		Ghazali	Michael
13		Haziri	Bible	Ibn 'Arabi	Brightness
14	Arthur's	Aaron	Chronicles	Ibn Khaldun	Life	Dede
15	Epic	Melin	Zar'a	Ibn 'Arabshah		Zada
16	Levita	Karo	Bahrey	Razi		Chelebi
17	Ashkenazi	Francis	Axum	Qadir		Hajji
18	Amelander	Troki	Alaqa	Murtada		Nabi
19	Rabinovich	Abramovich	Zenab	Yaziji	Gospel	Midhat
20	Singer	Mossensen	Walda	Gibran		Kudret

Figure 1   Semitic

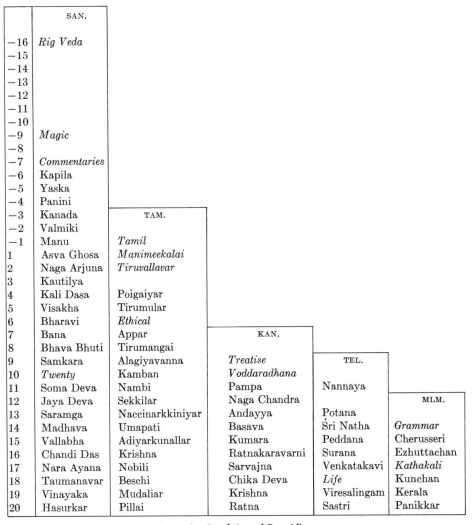

	SAN.	TAM.	KAN.	TEL.	MLM.
−16	Rig Veda				
−15					
−14					
−13					
−12					
−11					
−10					
−9	Magic				
−8					
−7	Commentaries				
−6	Kapila				
−5	Yaska				
−4	Panini				
−3	Kanada	TAM.			
−2	Valmiki				
−1	Manu	Tamil			
1	Asva Ghosa	Manimeekalai			
2	Naga Arjuna	Tiruvallavar			
3	Kautilya				
4	Kali Dasa	Poigaiyar			
5	Visakha	Tirumular			
6	Bharavi	Ethical			
7	Bana	Appar	KAN.		
8	Bhava Bhuti	Tirumangai			
9	Samkara	Alagiyavanna	Treatise		
10	Twenty	Kamban	Voddaradhana		
11	Soma Deva	Nambi	Pampa	Nannaya	
12	Jaya Deva	Sekkilar	Naga Chandra		MLM.
13	Saramga	Naccinarkkiniyar	Andayya	Potana	
14	Madhava	Umapati	Basava	Śri Natha	Grammar
15	Vallabha	Adiyarkunallar	Kumara	Peddana	Cherusseri
16	Chandi Das	Krishna	Ratnakaravarni	Surana	Ezhuttachan
17	Nara Ayana	Nobili	Sarvajna	Venkatakavi	Kathakali
18	Taumanavar	Beschi	Chika Deva	Life	Kunchan
19	Vinayaka	Mudaliar	Krishna	Viresalingam	Kerala
20	Hasurkar	Pillai	Ratna	Sastri	Panikkar

Figure 2   Sanskrit and Dravidian

Prakrit subtraditions, we may also usefully distinguish the Dravidian and Modern Indic literatures, both relating primarily to the tradition of Sanskritic Hinduism.

Dravidian India, south of the Deccan Plateau, produced the literate traditions of Tamil, Telegu, Kannada, and Malayalam. It has been politically autonomous during much of Indian history and is regarded by north India as the homeland of romance, much the way North Americans look at South America. It has an ancient literary history beginning before the birth of Christ and has been deeply influenced by all the major developments of northern Indian literature: Vedic, Brahmanic, Buddhist, Jain,

Epic, Romantic, and Modern. Like northern India it is predominantly Hindu in religion. Figure 2 outlines the Sanskritic and Dravidian traditions.

Hindu India proper centers on the great plain of northern India, and stretches east and west from Bombay to the Burmese border. Its literatures are those of Hindi in the center, Gujerati and Marathi in the west, and Oriya, Bengali, and Assamese in the east. Buddhism, which first arose in the central region (Uttar Pradesh), has been completely reabsorbed into Hinduism throughout north India; Jainism, which first began in the northeast and was later particularly influential in Gujerat, has been very nearly so absorbed. Literary traditions began in this section of India substantially with the time of Buddha and Jiina, the founders of these two religions, when Sanskrit moved into the valley of the Ganges from that of the Indus. But the modern vernaculars have been Hindu in religion and traditions from the beginnings of their literary use. Their development is outlined in Figure 3.

The themes of Hindu literature, modern and medieval, Dravidian and northern, are often traceable to origins in the early Sanskrit Vedas. They include not only a common mythology and religion but also the tales and romances codified in the epics of Rama and the Great Bharatas. There is a continuity of form as well—in dramas and dramatic dances, in the highly elaborated metric forms of Sanskrit verse, in the grammatically self-conscious anthologies of poetry and narrative, and in the polished and sometimes precious hymns and liturgical works, epics and romances, encyclopedias and dictionaries, and all-but-endless commentaries. Even into the twentieth century, minor episodes in the life of Rama continue to inspire epics, novels, and even movies.

To the northwest of Hindu India lies a zone of transition reflecting variously the impact of Islamic and Hindu tradition. Persian, Pushtu, Kashmiri, Sindhi, and Urdu are predominantly Moslem, and the other frontier languages—Rajasthani, Punjabi, and Nepali—while not actually Moslem in tradition, are not actually Hindu either, being dominated by the military ideals and habits of the soldier castes, Rajputs, Sikhs, and Gurkhas. Punjabi has formally seceded from Hinduism in favor of a religion of its own, Sikhism, with its own scriptures and distinctive customs and ritual.

Much of the content of these literatures is implied by this general characterization. The influence of Persian romance and Sufi mysticism is strong, stronger on the whole than Koranic tradition itself. (Only Persian, Pushtu, and Urdu in this group of languages write in the Arabic rather than the Indic alphabet.) Poetic forms that Persian shares with Arabic are found also in Kashmiri and elsewhere on this frontier. But Indian influences are also powerful, and Kashmir, for example, early produced classical Indian romances both in Kashmiri and in Sanskrit. The development of these Western Indic literatures is sketched in Figure 4.

	BEN.	GUJ.	ORI.	MAR.	HIN.	ASS.
9	*Baudhagan*					
10		Dhan Pal				
11	*Carya*					
12		Hema Chandra		Mukunda Raj	Nar Pati	
13	Hari Datta		*Chronicles*	Jhane Svar	Gorakh Nath	Hema Saraswati
14	Badu	*Chronicles*	Nara Sinha	Nam Dev	Jyoti Shwar	Madhab
15	Chakravarty	Mira Bai	Bachha Das	Eka Nath	*Sankhya*	Sankar
16	Ojha	Samala	Jagan Nath	Daso Pant	Sur Das	*Vaishnava*
17	Tulsi Das	Prem Anand	Biswa Nath	Mukte Shwar	Bihari	*Chronicles*
18	Ray	Dayaram	Upendra	Moro Pant	Sadasukh	*Creation*
19	Dutt	Nar Mad	Sena Pati	Deshmukh	Bharatendu	*Khamba*
20	Tagore	Gandhi	Gopa Bandhu	Madgulkar	Prem Chand	Chowdhuri

Figure 3   Central Indic

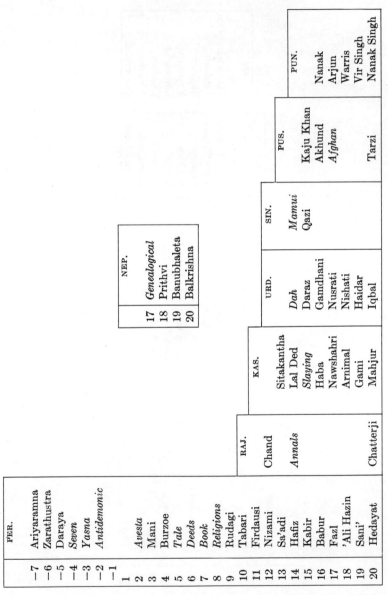

	PER.	RAJ.	KAS.	URD.	SIN.	PUS.	PUN.
−7	Ariyaramna						
−6	Zarathustra						
−5	Daraya						
−4	*Seven*						
−3	*Yasna*						
−2	*Antidemonic*						
−1							
1							
2	*Avesta*						
3	Mani						
4	Burzoe						
5	*Tale*						
6	*Deeds*						
7	*Book*						
8	*Religions*						
9	Rudagi						
10	Tabari						
11	Firdausi						
12	Nizami	Chand					
13	Sa'adi		Sitakantha				
14	Hafiz	*Annals*	Lal Ded	*Dah*	*Mamui*		
15	Kabir		*Slaying*	Daraz	Qazi	Kaju Khan	
16	Babur		Haba	Gamdhani		Akhund	Nanak
17	Fazl		Nawshahri	Nusrati		*Afghan*	Arjun
18	'Ali Hazin		Arnimal	Nishati			Warris
19	Sani'		Gami	Haidar			Vir Singh
20	Hedayat	Chatterji	Mahjur	Iqbal		Tarzi	Nanak Singh

	NEP.
17	*Genealogical*
18	Prithvi
19	Banubhaleta
20	Balkrishna

Figure 4 West Indic

Early Buddhist literature was written in both Sanskrit and the Prakrits, as well as other languages, but it was mainly in Pali that Buddhism was exported to the rest of central and eastern Asia. With the exception of Sinhalese, the literatures dominated by this movement were non-Indo-European: Tibetan and Mongolian in central Asia, Burmese, Thai, Arakanese, Cambodian, Laotian, and Karen to the southeast. Although it is not salient in the surviving literature, a general pre-Buddhist Hindu influence is traceable through most of Southeast Asia and in the Indies, particularly in Javanese, and the Indies remained outside the Buddhist sphere, succumbing rather to Islamic influences, often from Persian rather than Arabic. Javanese, Malay, Madurese, and Mindanao may be counted, in fact, as literarily akin to Western Indic rather than to the Hindu or Buddhist traditions. They are, however, summarized here together with the Buddhist literatures as a matter of geographical convenience. Ilocano and Tagalog are also added although linked to the rest of Indic tradition only in their early history.

The Buddhist literatures focus on themes drawn from the Pali scriptures and the tales of the lives of Buddha. These are treated dramatically in live and shadow dramas, in poetry, and in prose. A considerable autochthonous lore of giants and demons antedating Indian influence finds expression in these literatures as well. The poetic canons of Southeast Asia are quite different from those of India and Persia, both on the mainland and in the islands, possibly reflecting the different structure of the languages of the area. Figure 5 is an outline of these Buddhist and Malayan literatures.

The coherence of the broad tradition here called Indic may be described as a function of Indic mysticism, a pattern of thought shared by Vedic India and ancient Persia as well as by Hindu India and Moslem Persia. It finds expression in even the remotest literatures influenced by India, and its central tradition is that of Sanskrit. In Asia, in fact, Sanskrit occupies a commanding position not unlike that of Latin in Europe as the major scriptural language of the continent. Although it is a tradition apart, the Indic world has been no more isolated than the Semitic world. Not only has it contacted the West through Persian, Arabic, and Greek, but it has through Buddhism massively influenced the Far East as well, particularly through Chinese. More than a third of the world's extant literatures lie in the Indic area, many of them still virtually unknown in Europe.

It is convenient to divide the literature of Europe into four geographic zones. To a degree these correspond to religious and·cultural segments, a mainly Romance Catholic south, a predominantly Slavic Orthodox east, a preponderantly Germanic Protestant north, and a Celtic and more or less Pagan west. The unity of the whole centers on the Hellenistic and Christian

PRA.

-6	Gautama
-5	*Jain*
-4	Asoka
-3	*Thera*
-2	Tissa
-1	*Questions*
1	*Lotus*
2	Kunda Kunda
3	*Island*
4	Buddha Ghosa
5	Samgha Dasa
6	Jina Bhadra
7	Vak Pati
8	Sila Acharya
9	Raja Sekhara
10	Dhane Svara
11	Soma Prabha
12	Krishna
13	*Prakrita*
14	Naya Chandra
15	*Life*
16	Rudra Dasa
17	Ghana Syama

TIB.

- *Book*
- *Romance*
- Marpa
- Mila
- Gam
- *Translated*
- Gö
- *Life*
- Tsangyang
- Sum
- Jikme
- Denje

CEY.

9	Kassapa
10	Udaya
12	*Parrot*
13	*Sinhalese*
14	*Daladaasirita*
15	Kokila

MAL.

- Kadli
- *Malay*
- *Bidasari*
- Raniri
- Nipal
- Munshi
- Mihardja

CAM.

- Prah Bat
- Muk
- *Vorvong*

TAG.

- Balagtas
- Romulo

BUR.

- Anantathuria
- *Life* (?)
- Myawaddi
- Pon Nya
- Zawgyi

JAV.

- *Bhaaraataa*
- *Rama*
- Jokya
- *Kabila*
- Inao

THA.

- *Life*
- Trailok
- Thilawuntha
- Damrong
- *Annals*
- Sunthorn
- Luang

MON.

- *Nestorian*
- Alexander
- *Buddhist*
- Sechen
- *King*
- *Various*
- Damdinsuren

Figure 5 Buddhist and Malayan

	GRE.		POR.	ITA.	GAL.	BAS.	LAT.	ETR.		RSH.	MLT.	FRE.	SPA.	PRO.	CAT.
−15	*Votive*	13	Diniz	Polo	Alfonso										
−14		14	Lobeira	Dante	*Cancioneiro*										
−13		15	Lopes	Da Vinci	*Cancioneiro*										
−12		16	Camoës	Tasso	*General*	Dechepare									
−11		17	Vieira	Redi	*Legal*	Ohienart									
−10		18	Diniz	Maffei	Sarmiento	(Suppressed)									
−9	Homeros	19	Machado	Manzoni	Castro	Iztueta									
−8	Hesiodos	20	Amado	Lampedusa	Castelao	Monzon									
−7	Peisander														
−6	Sappho														
−5	Sophokles														
−4	Platon														
−3	Megasthenes														
−2	Polybios						Plautus		16	Travers					
−1	*Lament*						Vergil	*Etruscan*	17						
1	Strabo						Seneca		18		Bonamici				
2	Pausanias						Juvenalis		19	Muoth	*Catechism*				
3	*Septuagint*						Apuleius		20	Lansel	Azzopardi				
4	Eusebios						Augustinus				Dun Karm				
5	Tatius						Martianus								
6	Musaios						Boethius								
7	Menander						Sevillanus								
8	Damascene						Bede								
9	Photios						Alcuin					*Strassburg*			
10	*Digenis*						Roswitha					*Voyage*	*Infantes*		
11	*Stephanites*						Bremen					*Floovent*	*Cid*	*Alexander*	*Usages*
12	Komnena						Abélard					*Troyes*	*Bernardo*	William	Palol
13	Planudes						Aquinas					Lorris	Alfonso	Rouergue	Lull
14	*Chronicle*						Boccaccio					Froissart	Ruiz	Molinier	Descoll
15	(Tur. Conq.)						Kempen					Villon	Rojas	*Joyas*	*Tirant*
16							Luther					Rabelais	Ercilla	*Petit*	Garcia
17	Khortatzes						Newton					Molière	Cervantes	Larade	Pujol
18	Dapontes						Swedenborg					Voltaire	Moratín	Favre	(Suppressed)
19	Solomos						Pius IX					Hugo	Alarcón	Mistral	Guimerà
20	Kazantzakis						Lenard					Gide	Lorca	Chèze	Catalá

Figure 6   South European

traditions of Greek and Latin that underlay and shaped the forty national literatures of modern Europe, more than half of the literary languages now active.

The literatures of southern Europe are sketched in Figure 6. They include the Romance traditions of Latin, French, Spanish, Provencal, Catalan, Portuguese, Italian, Galician, and Romansh together with the geographically but not necessarily linguistically related Greek, Etruscan, Basque, and Maltese. Among the general features of these literatures are quantity meters in verse, a pronounced classicism involving highly explicit

	ARM.	GEO.	RUS.	BUL.	MAG.	CZE.
4	Faustus	Bakur				
5	Khoren	*Bible*				
6	(Per. Conq.)	*St. Evstafy*				
7	Djuansher	Meskha				
8	Leoncius	Djonanchiani				
9	Moshtotz		Cyril			
10	Norek	Modrikili	*St. Wenceslas*	*Shestodnev*		
11	Aristaces	Athos	Nikon	(Byz. Conq.)		
12	Nerses	Thruogveli	*Lay*			
13	Kosh	Rustaveli	*Book*		*Funeral*	*Lord*
14	Orbelian	Russudanianu	Sofony	Evtymy	*Legend*	Stítný
15	Medsoph	Vakhtung	Iskander	(Tur. Conq.)	Hunyady	Hus
16	Tulkourantzi		Macarius		Karadi	Černý
17	Kouchak	Taymuraz	Avvakum		Zrinyi	Stránský
18	Crete	Archili	Lomonosov	Paisi	Faludi	Dobrovský
19	Abovian	Orbeliani	Tolstoy	Konstantinov	Kisfaludy	Kollar
20	Aharonian	Abashvili	Gorky	Shishmanov	Molnar	Čapek

	POL.	ALB.	SER.	SLO.	RUM.	SOR.	UKR.
13	*Mother*						
14	*Psalter*						
15	Parkosz	Durrës					
16	Bielski		Ranina	Trubar	Coresi	Moller	*Bible*
17	Kochowski	Petrabianca	Gundulić		*Chronicle*		Smotritsky
18	Krasicki	Variboba	Georgjić	Japelj	Cantemir		Skovoroda
19	Mickiewicz	Rada	Vojnović	Levstik	Eminescu	Ćišinski	Shevchenko
20	Reymont	Konitza	Andrić	Kozak	Ionescu	Nowak	Vinnichenko

	LIT.	SLK.
16	Bretkun	
17		
18	Donalitius	Bajza
19	Baranauskas	Botto
20	Maculevičius	Hronsky

Figure 7   East European

standards of form in prose and drama as well as poetry, and a thorough-going assimilation of pagan Hellenism to Christianity. Theirs is an entirely Catholic Christian history, deeply steeped in Latin, and later influenced by Arabic and Hebrew with varying intensity in different places. It is perhaps a sufficient commentary on the grandeur that was Rome to note that more than 400 million people now speak one or another of the vernaculars derived from Latin and that nearly 600 million people are affiliated with the Roman Catholic Church.

Chronologically the second European region to develop literature was the Caucasus, where a continuous tradition exists in Armenian and Georgian from the fourth century A.D. Christian from their inception, these traditions nonetheless reflect a considerable Middle Eastern influence, especially from Persian and Syrian. They were also in contact with Byzantine Greek and later with Turkish, and are now incorporated literarily as well as politically within the Russian sphere of influence. More closely aligned with Greek was the early Slavonic literature, the exact relation of which to the modern Slavic languages is somewhat debated. It is here considered part of Russian tradition, with which it eventually merged. The complexity of the formation of east European cultures deserves special comment. Several groups (Russian, Belorussian, Bulgarian, Serbian) were Orthodox in religion and Greek influenced; some (Polish, Lithuanian, Slovak, Slovenian, Croatian, Rumanian) were Catholic in religion and Latin influenced. Some (Czech, Sorbian) became Protestant; one (Ukrainian), although Greek influenced remained Catholic; one (Magyar) set up a virtually autonomous national church; and one (Albanian) remained Moslem and Turkish oriented. The history of these traditions is sketched in Figure 7.

The earliest Germanic literature (Gothic) did not succeed in establishing a continuous tradition, and it is under the aegis of Latin and the Church that central and northwestern Europe inaugurated its vernacular literature. Eventually, however, the Germanic cultures unanimously turned Protestant, albeit with considerable struggle in England, the Low Countries, and southern Germany. Austria alone remained Catholic. The Baltic nations (Finland, Estonia, and Latvia) came to fall predominantly under Scandinavian and German influence and eventually became Protestant as well, although there remained a large Catholic minority in Latvia. Only the very earliest works of Germanic literature antedate Christian influence, and the predominant roots of all the northern cultures save Gothic are in Latin rather than Greek classicism. Aside from Gothic there are eleven north European literatures, eight of them Germanic: English, Dutch, German, Icelandic, Frisian, Danish, Norwegian, and Swedish, plus Finnish, Estonian and Latvian. Their history is outlined in Figure 8. Saxon is here considered a proto-Frisian language.

The Celtic fringe of western Europe has an old literary tradition beginning in the sixth century A.D. in Irish and Welsh. Breton, Cornish, Scottish, and Manx came later, beginning in the fifteenth century. Generally these languages yielded later and more partially to the influences of Latin and the Church, and they retain throughout, even with the Catholic Irish and Bretons, a distinctive autochthonous style and flavor all their own. Figure 9 gives a general outline of their development.

	GOT. / ENG.	DUT.	GER.	ICE.	FRI.	DAN.
4	Ulfilas					
5						
6	ENG.					
7						
8	*Beowulf*					
9	Cynewulf	*Wessobrunn*	Otfrid	Finsson	*Heliand*	
10	*Widsith*			Hornklofi		DAN.
11	Wulfstan		Notker	Sigvat	*Law*	
12	*Chronicles*	Valdeke	*Nibelungs*	Ari		Harpestreng
13	*Robin Hood*	*Beatrice*	Vogelweide	*Edda*		
14	Chaucer	Ruysbroek	Closener	Asgrimsson		
15	Malory	*Everyman*	Brant	Gutormsson	*Frisian*	
16	Shakespeare	Castelein	*Tyl*	*Tristan*	Bogerman	Plade
17	Milton	Bredero	Grimmelshausen	*Svipdag*	Japiks	Syv
18	Boswell	Effen	Goethe	Steingrimsson	Ploeg	Baggesen
19	Twain	Bilderdijk	Heine	Jochumsson	Dykstra	Gjellerup
20	Joyce	Dermout	Mann	Laxness	Troelstra	Jensen

	NOR.	SWE.	FIN.	EST.	LET.
13	*Dream*	*Gutas*			
14		Birgitta	FIN.	EST.	LET.
15					
16	Beyer	Petri	Erici	Wanradt	Grunau
17	Dass	Rudbeck	*Bible*		*Bible*
18	Holberg	Kellgren	*Kalevala*	*Bible*	Stender
19	Ibsen	Strindberg	Stenvall	Kreuzwald	Pumpurs
20	Undset	Lagerkvist	Sillanpää	Wilde	Steperman

Figure 8   North European

	WEL.	IRI.	BRE.	COR.	SCO.	MNX.
6	Taliesin	Lanfili				
7	Aneirin	*Bran*				
8						
9	*Llywarch*	*Cattle*				
10	*Prophecy*	*Vision*				
11	Meilyr	Cáemaín				
12	*Black*	*Vision*				
13	Cynddelw	*Sick*	BRE.	COR.		
14	Dyfadd	FitzGerald			SCO.	
15	*Red*	Ó'Huiginn	*St. Nonn*	*Passion*		
16	Aled	Ó'Huiginn	*Mirror*	Hadton	MacGregor	MNX.
17	Llwyd	Ó'Gnimh		Jordan	Macrae	
18	Wynne	Merriman		Boson	MacDonald	*Song*
19	Owen	Raftery	Villemarqué		Macintyre	*Maolchiaráin*
20	Gruffydd	Flower	Jaffrenou	Jenner		

Figure 9   West European

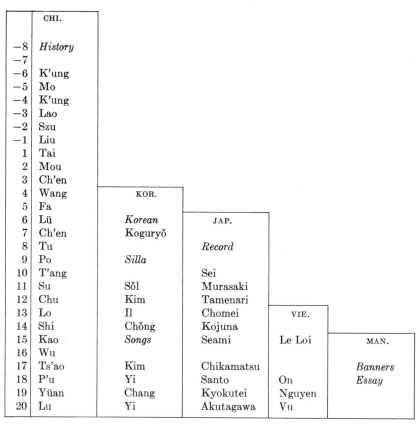

	CHI.	KOR.	JAP.	VIE.	MAN.
−8	*History*				
−7					
−6	K'ung				
−5	Mo				
−4	K'ung				
−3	Lao				
−2	Szu				
−1	Liu				
1	Tai				
2	Mou				
3	Ch'en				
4	Wang	KOR.			
5	Fa				
6	Lü	*Korean*	JAP.		
7	Ch'en	Koguryŏ			
8	Tu		*Record*		
9	Po	*Silla*			
10	T'ang		Sei		
11	Su	Sŏl	Murasaki		
12	Chu	Kim	Tamenari		
13	Lo	Il	Chomei	VIE.	
14	Shi	Chŏng	Kojuna		
15	Kao	*Songs*	Seami	Le Loi	MAN.
16	Wu				
17	Ts'ao	Kim	Chikamatsu		*Banners*
18	P'u	Yi	Santo	On	*Essay*
19	Yüan	Chang	Kyokutei	Nguyen	
20	Lu	Yi	Akutagawa	Vu	

Figure 10 Sinitic

	YUC.	NAH.	QUI.	CAK.	QUE.
15	*Astronomy*	Netzahualcoyotl			
16	*Books*	Sahagún	*Book*	4 Imox	
17		Chimalpahin	*Count*	Xahila	QUE.
18	Hoil	*Huehuence*	*Dance*		*Ollantay*
19			Ziz		
20			Burgess		*Kanata*

Figure 11 American Indian

	EUROPEAN	SEMITIC	INDIC	SINITIC	AMERICAN
−35	("Tardenoisian")	*Fertility*			
−34	("Azilian")				
−33		*Ptah's*			
−32					
−31	("Campignian")		("Neolithic")		
−30		Im Hotep		("Jomon")	
−29		Ptah Hotep			
−28		*Enlil*			
−27					
−26					
−25	("Danubian")	*Gilgamesh*		("Black")	("La Perra")
−24	("Minoan")	*Song*			
−23		*Pyramid*	("Harappa")		
−22		*Duauf*			
−21		*Inanna's*			
−20	Anittas	Amen Emhet		("Yang Shao")	("Arbolillo")
−19		Khekhe	("Mohenjo Daro")		
−18		Hammurabi			
−17	*Anecdotes*	*King*			
−16		*When*	*Rig*		
−15	*Ullikummi*	*Victories*		("Shang")	("Tlatilco")
−14	*Urshu*	Ikhn Aton			
−13	Hattusilis	Moses			
−12	*Kessis*	*Slaying*			
−11		*Red*			
−10		*Saggil*	*Magic*	("Chou")	("Ticoman")
−9	Homer	*Jahveh*			
−8	Hesiod	Isaiah		*Classic*	
−7	Peisander	*Esarhaddon*	Zarathustra		
−6	Aesop	Baruch	Kapila	K'ung	("Chalco")

−5	Sophocles	Job	Yaska	Mo	
−4	Aristotle	Ezra	Bhasa	K'ung	
−3	Megasthenes	Jonah	*Tripiṭaka*	Lao	
−2	Plautus	*Preacher*	Valmiki	*Etiquette*	
−1	Vergil	*Coming*	*Vishṇu*	Tung	("Miraflores")
1	Ovid	*Blessings*	Asva Ghosa	Tai	
2	M. Aurelius	*Martyrdom*	*Jatakas*	Pan	
3	Apuleius	Yehuda	Avalokite	Liu	
4	Ulfilas	*Doctrine*	Kali Dasa	Wang	
5	Iver	*Researches*	Buddha Ghosa	Fan	
6	Taliesin	Bodh	*Five Books*	*Korean*	("Toltec")
7	Aneirin	Edessa	Harsa	*Literary*	
8	*Beowulf*	Ibn Anas	Bhava Bhuti	Tu	
9	*Hildebrand*	Abu Tammam	Samkara	Ch'oe	
10	*Voyage*	*Thousand*	*Twenty-Five*	*T'ang*	
11	*Cid*	Ibn Sina	Soma Deva	Murasaki	("Aztec")
12	Troyes	Ibn Rushd	Jaya Deva	Chu	
13	Polo	*Brightness*	Saramga Deva	*Romance*	
14	Dante	Ibn Batuta	*Rajasthan*	Chikafusa	Netzahualcoyotl
15	Villon	Sanusi	Kabir	Seami	*Book*
16	Montaigne	Fazl	Tulsi Das	Wu	Xahila
17	Cervantes	Qadir	Arjun	Ts'ao	Hoil
18	Boswell	*Utendi*	*Battle*	Chikamatsu	Ziz
19	Dickens	Jabarti	Tagore	Chang	*Kanata*
20	Gide	Kudret	Gandhi	Akutagawa	

Figure 12 Outline of World Literature

Chinese literature is the most isolated of the four major Old World traditions and the last to develop (although there are Chinese scholars who reject the dating accepted in the West). Its principal defining feature was the "classics," its earliest and most revered works. The books that have been considered classics in China are

1. *The Classic of Change* of Wen and Chou (−3)
2. *The Classic of History* (−8)
3. *The Classic of Poetry* of K'ung Fu Tzu (−6)
4. *Notes on the Rites* by Tai and Tai (1)
5. *Etiquette and Ceremonial* (−2)
6. *Ritual of the Chou* by Chou (−3)
7. *Spring and Autumn Annals* of K'ung Fu Tzu (−6)
8. *Commentary on the Spring and Autumn Annals* (−2)
9. *Kung Yang Chuan* (2)
10. *Ku Liang Chuan* (2)
11. *Analects* of K'ung Fu Tzu (−6)
12. *Classic of Filial Piety* of Lü (3)
13. *Encyclopedic Dictionary* (−3)
14. *Works* of Meng (−3)
15. *The Great Learning* of K'ung Chi (−4)
16. *The Doctrine of the Mean* of K'ung Chi (−4).

This order is more or less traditional. The Chinese customarily refer to the "five classics" (Entries 1, 2, 3, 4 and/or 5, and 7—usually including 8) and the "four books" (Entries 11, 14, 15, and 16—the latter two of which are also chapters in Entry 4). In the second century A.D., six of these were considered to be classical enough to be carved on stone (Entries 1, 2, 3, 5, 7 and 9, and 11). By the twelfth century there were considered to be thirteen (Entries 8, 9, and 10 were somehow counted as two and Entries 15–16 were included under 4). This careful assessment of the core literature of Confucianism and the rigidity of the various lists are characteristically Chinese. And wherever Chinese influence (see Figure 10) reached—to Korean, Japanese, Vietnamese, or Manchurian literature—the classics were at the center of it.

Although the Maya were literate before the birth of Christ, the only pre-Conquest literature is a group of related hieroglyphic documents that remain undeciphered. The rest of American Indian literature was recorded in the European alphabet after the Conquest, and the languages that attained something like the functional literacy of Old World literary languages were mainly Mayan (Yucatec, Quiche, and Cakchiquel). Nahuatl and possibly Quechua among non-Mayan languages may be added.

The divinatory mysteries of the Middle American calendar constitute the "classicism" of American literary tradition. There are related annals, chronicles, prophecy, poetry, and drama, some of them dealing with the human sacrifice that so appalled the Spanish conquerors. Other works were more European influenced, like the Peruvian romance *Ollantay*. A sketch of these literatures is given in Figure 11.

Because of the complexity of the welter of languages and literatures that have been described, it may be useful to sum up the major literary traditions: European, Semitic, Indic, Sinitic, and American. This is done in Figure 12, illustrating each with a representative work or author for each century in which it has been literarily active. Because of its marginal position, Hittite is here considered a proto-European literature. Correspondences to some major archaeological cultures of prehistory are also indicated in parentheses, as ("Minoan").

GENRES AND INSTITUTIONS

It has been observed that the ancient literary traditions of Egypt and Mesopotamia produced nothing that can be called "great" literature. Relative to the sophistication of modern taste this is no doubt true. But the tedium of ancient (and often of primitive) literature is to be ascribed to a poverty in those stylistic and thematic complexities resulting from social diversity. Ancient societies were relatively simple. What, in fact, is to be expected of a literature produced by scribes? One may imagine the impoverishment of contemporary writing if it were entirely the prerogative of stenographers. The most ancient authors were bookkeepers with the souls of bookkeepers and they rarely lifted their thoughts from the tribute rolls long enough to record literature.

Perhaps, in fact, the most important structural feature of written literature in comparison with oral tradition is that it is always more partial, reflecting the perspectives of a literate class, institution, or aspect of society rather than the manifold interests of society at large. The earliest literature and by all odds the largest body of literature in most places throughout most of history is temple literature, and it is the preoccupations of priests that are reflected in the hymn and fragmentary ritual dated to the thirty-fifth century B.C. which probably constitute the oldest literary fragments still extant.

The literature of the temple may be distinguished from the literature of the court in early Egypt and Mesopotamia, but the distinction is not sharp. The kings were trained, advised, and dominated by the priests, and the institutions of church and state were never allowed to become sufficiently separate to come into conflict. Deviant ideas could be comfortably assimilated to the ample cult system of a convenient pantheism, which lent itself to an indefinite amount of contradiction without conflict. Literary diversity was thus possible. If writers chafed under the regnant orthodoxy,

they were able to innovate within broad limits both artistically and philosophically, and they did so freely. The panegyrics to the gods and kings
were balanced by laments and complaints. The optimism of the committed
courtier-priest was offset by the pessimism of the less committed, and from
the twenty-fifth century B.C. the dialogue of optimism and pessimism may
be considered an established genre in both Egyptian and Sumerian literature.

The cult organization of religion implies the formation of mythological
cycles. Myth motifs may presumably be borrowed from temple to temple,
but the principal elaboration of them will be within particular temples.
A somewhat disjointed mythology is the inevitable result. As the various
priestly communities become organized into a general system (for example, through ranking of the temples), the body of myths becomes more
coherent. Contradictions are smoothed out and a systematic cosmogony is
developed. One may trace the process in ancient Semitic literature as the
local gods become adjusted to each other's existence until the heterogeneous
divinities of first-dynasty Egypt are prepared to sit down to dinner together on Olympus. The pantheons of India and America never became
quite so chummy: the temples remained more autonomous.

Organized priesthood affects the form as well as the themes of temple
literature, elaborating and fixing the forms of liturgy. With literacy, the
tradition becomes "scripturalized"—it is not only written but it must be
written right, and the growing body of experts generates a formalism embodied in manuals of liturgy, doctrinal instructions, fixed poetic forms, and
textually specific myths and religious drama. The "word" becomes sacred
as written, and although it may be reinterpreted, it cannot be changed.
The complexities of the more primitive religious forms are maintained, but
they are articulated within a system. Although the surviving texts are
fragmentary, it is apparent that this process was far advanced in Egypt
and Sumer by the twenty-fifth century B.C.

It was not until the fourteenth century B.C. that the social structure
of ancient literature began to change in any fundamental way, confronting
perhaps the only really revolutionary challenge it could have generated—
the opposition of church and state—expressed in the only symbol it could
not blandly tolerate—monotheism. The immediate result was the failure of
the revolution. The heretic pharaoh Akhen Aton (Amen Hotep IV) was
overthrown by the priests, and his dangerous ideas (represented in his
surviving *Hymn to Aton*) were rebutted. An extant tract on the *Good
Fortune of the Dead* reasserts Egyptian orthodoxy. The event was no mere
palace revolution, but a symptom of underlying social changes, and this
century released the richest and most varied literature in Egyptian history,
representative of a wide variety of Egyptian institutions beyond the court
and the temple.

The threat to convert a new cult idea into a true sect—outside the system—remained unrealized in Mesopotamia and in Egypt, where court and temple were promptly reconciled, but it was achieved a century later among the Jews under Moses, and throughout Jewish history the court and the temple remained distinct. Our picture of the ancient Hebrew monarchy is decidedly less flattering than the monotonous roster of the ever-triumphant kings of Egypt or Babylon. The prophets did not like kings, and they said so in the most scathing terms. And the kings fought back, giving to Hebrew literature a diversity, a scope, and a liveliness quite removed from the global orthodoxy of former times. In social perspective, the idea of monotheism was perhaps of less intrinsic importance in this connection than the sectarianism it generated. And Palestine continued to grow sects.

Indic society, although certainly very different from Hebrew in many respects, early attained a generally similar structural division. Kings and priests, already differentiable in the early Vedic literature, become further separated in the period of Brahmanic commentary that fixed the classic Indian caste system. The result was the same: a rapid growth of sectarianism in which opposed "schools" of exegesis contested the correct interpretation of the Vedic traditions. This structuring of Indic literature is clearly visible as early as the seventh century B.C. and becomes dominant in the most dramatic form from the time of Gautama Buddha in the sixth century B.C. Like Palestine, India proved fertile ground for sects, and they have grown luxuriantly throughout the history of the country on a scale almost without parallel.

In China and in Greece, sectarianism is both late and imported. In both, the unity of the church and state remained intact—one might almost say unchallenged—but that protean institution was bifurcated in a quite different dimension by the growth of an independent literary tradition, that of the gentry-citizenry. This class, which remained intimately involved in both cult and government, nonetheless made Chinese and Greek literature an enterprise in a considerable degree separate from public affairs. It was consequently free from the inevitable involvements of orthodox responsibility implicit in priesthood and governmental authority, and in both countries the result was rapid development of secular philosophy and great diversity of literary form and thought.

Ultimately, the Greek and Chinese patterns diverged somewhat sharply, continuity in Greek letters being provided by a new and unique institution—the school. In China, the transmission of classical tradition was never entirely separated from the state. The Greeks might discuss philosopher-kings from the safely irresponsible vantage point of the academy. The Chinese sages, often with audible misgivings, took government jobs. But even in China the Mandarin scholars remained partly aloof and from the security of country seats deplored the shortcomings of emperors, generals, and ministers with a lofty detachment unmatched outside Greece.

The development of schools independent of both court and temple was possibly the most vital social invention of Hellenic society. It created a unique literature and for almost a millennium remained the heart of the literary and educational system of antiquity in both Greek and Latin. At the end of that time the secular school tradition was swallowed up by the church, and it is only in modern times that it has become distinct again. During antiquity, however, the variety, independence, and flexibility of literature in Greek and Latin can be largely attributed to the autonomy of its perpetuation through an institution separate from the obligations of orthodoxy or power. It is a literature that has deeply influenced our own both directly and indirectly in manifold ways, but it also seems modern to us because it was modern—institutionally so.

Sectarianism was introduced into Greece through Christianity and into China through Buddhism. The apparent triumphs of the conversion of the Roman and Chinese emperors, however, had the eventual social consequence of dividing the temple from the court, and from the first century of the Christian era we may trace separate temple and court literatures in both China and Europe, superimposed upon (and eventually displacing) the secular and gentlemanly writings of the educated class. China emerged first, and the reemergence of classical tradition was marked by the creative and innovative achievements of the T'ang Renaissance in the eight century. The European Renaissance was longer in coming but even more revolutionary.

In the Middle East in Babylonian, Persian, Phoenician, and Syrian, the Jewish type of sectarianism did not develop, and the priestly literature remained close to the more fragmentary relics of the kings. The impact of Hellenism and the rise of Christianity had a deep influence, particularly in Syria, but even before the rise of Islam the sectarian religious movements had overwhelmed the Greek academies. The Islamic literatures were heirs to these developments and involved separate traditions of court and temple, but like medieval Christianity they assimilated the Greek schools to the temple tradition.

After about the fourth century, then, in the literature of Europe, the Middle East, India, and China we may distinguish well-established and differentiated traditions of temple, court, and sect, and it was not until modern times that important changes began to restructure the social forms of literacy. It is in this medieval period that the epic, characteristic expression of the ancient courts, gave way to the romance. Secular poetry took on new forms as well as new themes (the Sanskrit *kaavya*, the Chinese *lü shih*, the Greek *political*, the Norse *dróttkvaet*, the Arabic *qaṣida*, the Japanese *tanka*). Court drama became distinct from religious ritual. Court oratory became separated from homiletics. To the institutional separation of politics from religion may thus be ascribed the great medieval court literatures. Linked as they were to the fortunes of the state, they flowered and decayed erratically, but virtually all the great dynasties patronized literature and in their moments of success fostered great writing: the Guptas, the T'angs, the Carolingians, and the Abbasids are notable examples among many.

The temple literature of the Middle Ages was, of course, less subject to political fluctuation, but it was also greatly influenced by its separation from the court, as well as by the organization of the various priesthoods that produced it. The traditional types of temple literature were continued (prayers, hymns, commentary, theology), but the schismatic and sectarian pluralism of the epoch placed more emphasis upon creeds and articles of faith and created a new and explicitly apologetic literature of religious controversy. Heresies were identified, named, refuted, and attacked, and orthodoxies became refined and explicit. The scriptures of the major literatures were collected, sifted, edited, and canonized. Ascetic and mystical works found their way into all the major religions, and mountains of exegesis and commentary served as bases to the great theological syntheses of medieval religion. The importance of belief to the increasingly sectarian societies of the time led to a great expansion in didactic literature, including inspirational tales and religious history and biography. Religious dramas cognate with the morality plays were popular from Ireland to Bali.

MODERN LITERATURE

The modern period of world literature comprises the last three centuries, a time of European ascendancy, of nationalism and secularization all over the world. It seems fair to say that it is but one more transitional phase in an already ancient process of the interchange and integration of literary ideas, but it is still too soon to guess its future shape. A time of unprecedented vitality in the European literatures, it has been overwhelmingly an epoch of colonial decadence elsewhere.

The social setting of modern literature is to be defined by the rapid and progressive extension of literacy to new nations, to new social classes, and to new institutions. The implied changes have brought into being a whole new range of literary forms and have resulted in the expression in writing of a whole new range of themes, some formerly found in oral traditions, others emergent from the novelties of modern life. Perhaps its most widely characteristic form is the modern novel. It is generally agreed that the novel developed out of the medieval romance, itself derivative from the epic. There is much less agreement about what a novel is. Indeed, it seems doubtful that any definition can satisfactorily deal with all the problems of the transitional and borderline cases. The "court novels" of Japan and China from as early as the eleventh century are unquestionably within this zone of ambiguity. But in both Europe and the Orient the real flowering of the novel was outside the bounds of court literature and inside the time span of the last three centuries. Like modern drama and poetry, novels are produced for and very largely by a new literary intelligentsia in considerable measure independent of both church and state and closely linked to the rise of a secular middle class.

Social and literary modernism were a gradual growth, attributable to an accelerating exchange of ideas among peoples traceable to the most ancient times. In recent centuries, however, first in western Europe and then elsewhere, the tempo of this interchange has risen sharply, and the quantitative change has become so dramatic as to create qualitatively new structures. Everywhere the result has been increased social complexity and new forms of segmentation of society, but the types of segmentation have been thoroughly diverse. The dynastic idea and religious orthodoxy have yielded ground as other institutions have come to enjoy a partly autonomous existence. Church and state confront the army, the bureaucracy, the university, the corporation, the party, the union on the most varied terms, and all of them produce literature.

One aspect of the secularization of literate society has been the development of literary elites, cliques of the intellectual leaders of a particular period and nation, who share a more or less intensive social life and may deeply influence each other's work. Highly structured and somewhat ephemeral and esoteric literary genres may result, with rapid and faddish changes in style. Salon literatures of this sort have developed their own stylistic mystiques, their elegant, rarefied, and difficult poetry, their in-bred *romans à clef*, their preciosities of theme and treatment, and local traditions of self-conscious literary theory and criticism. Such social groupings naturally overlap with other institutional groups within or between nations, and particular writers may be greatly or very little influenced by their participation in them.

Although there has been a marked tendency for modern writers to draw apart from any predominant identification with religious institutions, their relation to the state has been more complex. Explicit and implicit political pressures upon literature have steadily increased until much of modern writing has come to be importantly ideological and subject to various kinds of censorship and control. The result is a statist literature quite different from the court literature of former politics but similar in its emphasis upon loyalty and orthodoxy.

By the mid-twentieth century, some twenty-eight of the world's past literary languages had become primarily or exclusively written traditions. None of them is truly "extinct," for with the partial exception of Etruscan, they all continue to be read and studied. Some even have native speakers. But they all belong literarily to the past: Babylonian, Breton, Cakchiquel, Cherokee, Chontal, Cornish, Egyptian, Etruscan, Gothic, Hittite, Ilocano, Irish, Javanese, Ladino, Latin, Madurese, Manchu, Manx, Nahuatl, Pali and "Prakrit," Quechua, Quiche, Sanskrit, Saxon, Scottish, Sumerian, Syrian, Welsh, and Yucatec. There can be little question that the liveliest of these traditions in our own day is Sanskrit. Latin, which is perhaps the runner-up, has done little of note besides the papal encyclicals and Lenard's *Winnie Ille Pu*. (The latter work could well stand as a symbol of twentieth-century literature—an English children's story done into Latin by a Hungarian Brazilian.)

Welsh literature, for one, has enjoyed a considerable revival during the twentieth century, producing novels, plays, short stories, and poetry. Gruffydd, Gwynn-Jones, Roberts, and Lewis are among the leading figures in this development, which is centered at the University of Wales. A more modest revival of Cornish is represented by Henry Jenner's *An Dassergh-hyans Kernewek*, and Breton features Jaffrenou's *Harp of Steel*. There has been some effort to foster a modern literature also in Nahuatl and Yucatec, resulting in the publication of contemporary poetry and traditional stories, but the achievements have been modest and feeble.

Twentieth-century Sanskrit has produced quantities of historical works, including a history of World War I (the *Angla Jarmani Yuddha Vivarana* of Srinavasacharya); and biographies and autobiographies (a life of Jesus, *Yisu Charitam*, by Nilakantha Sastri, and of Buddha, *Buddha Charita Mrita*, by Alamelamma); even a traditional romance on the dialogue of Sita and Ravana (Rama Sastri's *Sita Ravana Samvada Jhari*). The historian Hasurkar is particularly outstanding. Essays cover the modern world from railroading to Western medicine and atomic energy, and there are numbers of specialized journals in Sanskrit, which thus remains after 36 centuries a significant, if minor, modern literature.

Aside from the literatures of the past, those of the present may be said to include approximately 78 different languages, so that we may place the number of literary languages of history at just over an even 100 (106). It has been estimated that there are 60 additional languages spoken at the present time by upwards of 1 million people each. It seems obvious that there may be additional literatures established, but it is likely that there will not be many more, and all 60 of these protoliterary languages confront major obstacles to modern literary achievement. Hausa, with about 13 million speakers, may stand as an example. A number of other languages appear to have been for some time on the borderline of functional literacy. They include Arakanese (the history of which includes a sixteenth-century poem and the eighteenth-century *Tiger Killing* or *Kya Khwetsa* of Ran Aung Myin Sayadaw), Ilocano (which produced the seventeenth-century epic *Lam Ang*), Champa (which is represented in the nineteenth century by *Prang Iyang* and the *Chronicle* of Po Nagar), Cherokee (which flowered briefly in Sequoyah's nineteenth-century newspaper, the *Cherokee Phoenix*), Laotian (which produced the nineteenth-century *Legends of Luang Prabang* and *Mulla Tantai*), Madurese (which produced a version of *Kalila and Dimna* in the sixteenth century), Mindanao (the nineteenth-century *Bantugan*), Karen (San Kan Too's *Thesaurus* and Saya Kieu Zan's *Sa Tu Waw* in the nineteenth century), Chontal (which produced the seventeenth-century *Chronicles of Acalan Tixchel*), and in the twentieth-century Khasi (*Ka Kitab Niam Khein Ki Khasi*). The only new literature to emerge with vigor in the twentieth century is probably that in Afrikaans.

For purposes of survey it is useful to distinguish major from minor literatures, and both from protoliteratures and from the preliteratures or oral traditions of smaller linguistic groups.

The scope of modern literature is only partly indicated by the figures in Table 1. The Library of Congress system now indexes around 18 million titles, and we may guess that the total extant world literature is at least twice that great and is increasing rapidly. For comparison, it has been estimated that the total extant corpus of Sumerian literature may run to around 250,000 tablets (roughly comparable to 1000 modern books), of which about 5 percent are truly literary, and none of the works is actually complete. Modern literature is of almost unimaginable bulk.

This point may be illustrated by the following table that chronicles in rough terms the growth (and decline) of the world's major libraries:

LANGUAGE	DATE	PLACE AND SIZE
Sumerian	(−20)	Ur (1000 vols.)
Egyptian	(−15)	Memphis (2000 vols.)
Babylonian	(−7)	Nineveh (5000 vols.)
Greek	(−3)	Alexandria (150,000 vols.)
Chinese	(1)	Loyang (11,000 vols.)
Latin	(4)	Rome (120,000 vols.)
Greek	(7)	Byzantium (100,000 vols.)
Arabic	(10)	Baghdad (75,000 vols.)
Latin	(12)	Canterbury (3,000 vols.)
Latin	(15)	Budapest (50,000 vols.)
German	(16)	Munich (20,000 vols.)
French	(17)	Paris (70,000 vols.)
German	(18)	Brunswick (60,000 vols.)
Italian	(19)	Vatican (400,000 vols.)
English	(20)	New York (14,000,000 vols.)

The major modern literatures are also of staggering diversity. A number of kinds of literature from the past continue to be produced—epic, comic, sacred, and secular; even epic poetry, tales, fables, anthologies of

TABLE 1   World Literary Traditions

	EUROPE	ASIA	AFRICA	AMERICA
Major	7	4	–	–
Minor	27	32	4	2
Protoliterary	14	21	23	2
Total	48	57	27	4

stories and jokes, essays, treatises, lectures, sermons, puns, proverbs and sayings, and plays and operas. In short, past traditions are maintained in the major modern literatures and continue to grow along many lines. But there are new components to modern literature as well. The advent of movies, television, and radio and improvements in publication and dissemination techniques have bound together larger masses of men within the scope of an expanded and still expanding literary universe. Storytelling has been elaborated in novels, short stories, formal jokes, cartoons, and cartoon books; poetry has come to include advertising doggerel, pop songs, political propaganda, folk and pseudofolk songs, as well as the traditional and experimental academic poetry of the little magazines and the established poets; drama is lively and active in legitimate and little theaters of new as well as traditional types, but it has moved also into the movies and television with skits, puppetry, cartoons, short plays, serials, ballet, opera, musical comedy, revues, and "happenings"; oratory has developed new uses too: the sales pitch, the fireside chat, the press conference, the seminar, the forum, the public lecture, and the after-dinner speech. In this welter of forms and styles, it is perhaps useful to single out certain items of genuinely salient interest. Newspapers, the short story, and (somewhat more narrowly) the novel have become characteristic of modernism in substantially all the world's literate languages. Plays are somewhat less widely produced, apparently requiring a more developed literary establishment. The production of movies and operas comes close to being a monopoly of the "major" literatures.

In singling out certain modern literatures as major a number of factors must thus be considered. A major language is one spoken by a large national community with a substantial tradition of literacy. It must be part of the modern world, which requires that it be the language of a major state or states, possess adequate presses, libraries, and schools, and produce modern types of literature—novels, plays, newspapers, and movies. Of the more than 100 languages that have produced literature, less than a dozen may be judged major modern languages by these criteria. Together they

TABLE 2 Modern Communications, 1960*

	SPEAKERS (millions)	READERS (millions)	NEWSPAPERS (daily)	MOVIES (yearly)	RADIO (stations)	TV (stations)	LIBRARIES (million vols.)
Chinese	505	145	494	384	184	7	2.0
(%)	(18)	(11)	(6)	(12)	(2)	(.3)	(1)
English	338	276	2312	478	4422	882	70.6
(%)	(12)	(22)	(30)	(15)	(47)	(42)	(56)
Spanish	173	82	726	198	1489	121	2.5
(%)	(6)	(7)	(9)	(6)	(16)	(6)	(2)
Russian	170	120	302	140	(291?)	291	16.0
(%)	(6)	(9)	(4)	(4)	(3)	(14)	(13)
Hindi	165	20	119	120	31	1	.4
(%)	(6)	(2)	(2)	(4)	(.3)	(—)	(—)
Japanese	98	70	162	535	287	237	1.5
(%)	(3)	(6)	(2)	(17)	(3)	(11)	(1)
Portuguese	78	28	291	31	910	34	1.0
(%)	(3)	(2)	(4)	(1)	(10)	(2)	(1)

German	86	69	659	137	464	115	9.0
(%)	(3)	(6)	(9)	(4)	(5)	(6)	(7)
Arabic	82	4	146	66	71	28	.2
(%)	(3)	(.3)	(2)	(2)	(1)	(1)	(—)
French	71	56	303	173	280	94	9.5
(%)	(3)	(5)	(4)	(5)	(3)	(4)	(8)
Italian	58	35	105	213	(132?)	(62?)	6.7
(%)	(2)	(3)	(1)	(7)	(1)	(3)	(5)
Other	1048	319	2042	767	940	249	5.6
(%)	(35)	(27)	(27)	(23)	(9)	(11)	(6)
Totals	2872	1244	7661	3232	9501	2121	125.0

* Estimates for this table are based upon Anon. 1964, 1965, 1966. The data are highly approximate. The table covers only speakers of the 76 literary languages of the present time, which omits an estimated 10 percent of the world's population. Insofar as possible "newspapers" means dailies; "movies" means full-length features; "radio" means broadcast band; "library" means number of volumes in the 45 libraries of over 1 million volumes located within countries speaking the language in question. I have arbitrarily included Russian radio stations in a number equaling the number of Russian television stations: it is impossible to equate the Russian radio system with those elsewhere. I have rejected the figures of 1325 radio and 627 television stations given for Italian in the *Encyclopedia Britannica World Atlas*. They appear to be off by a factor of 10. These would be, respectively, 12 and 23 percent of the world totals in these categories. I have prorated and guessed at the number of radio stations in countries that only report receiving sets.

are spoken by nearly two thirds of mankind and are read by more than three quarters of literate people. They produce nearly three quarters of the world's newspapers and almost four fifths of its movies. They command all the greatest libraries and most of the great universities. They are the languages of large and powerful states, and they perpetuate the great literary traditions of the past—European (English, Russian, Spanish, German, Portuguese, French, Italian), Semitic (Arabic), Indic (Hindi), and Sinitic (Chinese, Japanese). Table 2 summarizes data (largely estimated) on selected literary attributes of these languages.

Items are arranged in Table 2 in the approximate order of their invention, and hence should scale as a rough index of "modernism," from speaking to reading, newspapers, movies, radio, television, and modern research. It would appear that they do in fact scale in this fashion. Arabic, Hindi, and Chinese, in particular are weak at the "modern" end of the scale. The table also points up the specialization of particular traditions. Chinese registers more literacy than it would if there were not a considerable number of readers who do not speak it at all. The penchant of the Japanese and Italians for movies, the Germans and English for newspapers, and the Spanish and Portuguese for radios registers strikingly. The Russians, Japanese, and Germans have a similar focus on television.

The uses of literacy in the modern world are remarkably concentrated. Six major languages account for half (51 percent) of "civilized" people of the world (that is, those who are part of a literate tradition): Chinese, English, Spanish, Russian, Hindi, and Japanese. A different six (English, Chinese, Russian, Spanish, Japanese, and German) account for half (54 percent) of the world's literacy. Half the world's newspapers (54 percent) are printed in only four of them (English, Spanish, German, Chinese), and half the world's movies (51 percent) are produced in another four (Japanese, English, Chinese, Italian). Two thirds (67 percent) of the television stations broadcast in one of three languages (English, Russian, or Japanese), and nearly three fourths (73 percent) of the radio stations broadcast in English, Spanish, or Portuguese. The four scholarly languages (English, Russian, German, and French) have a virtual monopoly (84 percent) on the world's major library resources, English alone accounting for more than half (56 percent) in this concentration.

THE FARTHER TWENTIETH CENTURY

Because our own tradition is European, we manage to keep in fairly close touch with at least the major foreign literatures in European languages, albeit with some selectivity and distortion. It is otherwise with the non-European ones. Even books and university courses on "world literature" commonly make only the most cursory attempt to come to grips with the literature that is farther from us—even in the most important non-European traditions. The consequence is a continuing ethnocentrism bred of ignorance. We not only do not read the literature that is less accessible; we often remain unaware of its existence. The case may be illustrated with reference to China.

Modern Chinese literature is probably the most detached and independent of the major traditions of the modern world. It has been correspondingly forced to reexamine its autonomy from top to bottom, and the complexity of this issue is perhaps the dominating fact of Chinese writing in this century. The strangely anachronistic quality of the Chinese court at the beginning of the century is described autobiographically by a Westernized princess in Der Ling's *Two Years in the Forbidden City*. The program of republican modernization is set forth in Sun Yat Sen's *Three Principles of the People* and Chiang Kai Shek's *China's Destiny*. The direction of the Chinese Communist movement has been shaped by Mao Tse Tung, whose *Selected Works* have been published in four volumes in English.

But the modernization of China is not only a political question, nor have the reactions been all in one direction. Traditional history has been continued, for example, in the *Lives and Works of Manchu Scholars* (*Ch'ing Ju Hsueh An*), and Confucian scholarship has been maintained, notably by K'ang Yu Wei (*The Grand Commonwealth, Confucius Changes Institutions*) and Hu Shih (*History of Philosophy*). Yet even a traditionalist like Hu Shih could be (with the novelist Lu Hsün) a leading exponent of the vernacular (*pai hua*) rather than the classical language (*wen yen*) as a literary vehicle. Leading novelists of modern China include Ch'ien Chung Shu (*The Besieged City*), Shih T'o (*Marriage*), Pa Chin (*Destruction*), Mao Tun (*The Eclipse*), and Kuo Mo Jo, who has also written plays (for example, *Chu Yuan*). Lu Hsün, whose real name was Chou Shu Jen, is known for *The True Story of Ah Q* and has also written *A Brief History of Chinese Novels*. The leading novelist of Communist China is perhaps Lao Shê, whose *Rickshaw Boy* has been published in English. Probably the best-known Chinese writer to the West is the expatriate essayist and biographer Lin Yu Tang (*The Importance of Living, Essays, My Talks, The Gay Genius*, and other works). Perhaps the most distinguished Nationalist writers on Formosa are Eileen Chang (*The Rice-Sprout Song*) and Chiang Kuei (*The Whirlwind*). Other notable figures in modern Chinese literature are Shen Ts'ung Wen (*Autobiography*), Ku Chieh Kang, whose *Autobiography* has appeared in English, Tsang Keh Chia (*Poems*), Chen Shou Chu (*Spring Thunder*), Yao Hsueh Ying (*The Red Turnip*), Chang T'ien I (*The Strange Knight of Shanghai*), Wu Tsu Hsiang (*Mountain Torrent*), and Tsao Yu (*Lady in White*).

Although the Communist regime has made full use of newspapers,

TABLE 3

LANGUAGE	SPEAKERS (in millions)	READERS (in millions)	REPRESENTATIVE WORK
Chinese	505	100	Lu, *The True Story of Ah Q*
English	338	276	Joyce, *Ulysses*
Spanish	173	82	Paz, *El Laberinto de la Soledad*
Russian	170	120	Pasternak, *Dr. Zhivago*
Hindi	165	10	Prem Chand, *The Cow*
Malay	114	17	Mihardja, *The Atheist*
Japanese	98	70	Kawabata, *Thousand Cranes*
Bengali	86	11	Tagore, *Gitaañjali*
German	86	69	Grass, *The Tin Drum*
Arabic	82	4	'Anhuri, *The Unique Gem*
Portuguese	78	28	Amado, *Gabriela cravo e canela*
French	71	56	Genet, *A Thief's Journal*
Italian	58	35	Lampedusa, *Il Gattopardo*
Urdu	55	9	Iqbal, *Poems*
Ukrainian	41	28	Vinnichenko, *The Black Panther*
Tamil	37	6	Pillai, *Manoonmaniiyam*
Korean	36	10	Yi Kwang Su, *The Soil*
Telegu	36	6	Sastri, *Siva Bharatamu*
Marathi	34	9	Madgulkar, *The Village Had No Walls*
Polish	33	22	Reymont, *The Peasants*
Turkish	27	5	Kudret, *Classmates*
Vietnamese	26	2	Vu Dinh Long, *Cup of Poison*
Punjabi	26	5	Nanak Singh, *Chitta Lahoo*
Gujerati	22	8	Ghandi, *Autobiography*
Thai	21	14	Luang Vichitr, *Prao Chao Krung Dhon*
Persian	21	3	Hedayat, *The Blind Owl*
Kannada	20	2	Ratna, *Songs of Ratna*
Dutch	18	14	Dermout, *The Ten Thousand Things*
Rumanian	18	13	Gheorgiu, *The Twenty-Fifth Hour*
Rajasthani	17	1.4	Chatterji, *Raajasthaanii Bhaaṣaa*
Malayalam	17	4	Chandu Menon, *Indulekha*
Serbo-Croatian	17	4	Andrić, *The Bridge on the Drina*
Oriya	16	3	Gopabandhu Das, *Works*
Burmese	16	1.4	Zawgyi, *Works*
Magyar	13	10	Molnar, *The Paul Street Boys*
Tagalog	12	.8	Romulo, *Papers*
Pushtu	12	.6	Mahmud i Tarzi, *Sirajul Akhbar*
Swahili	11	.2	Shaaban Robert, *Works*
Belorussian	10	6	
Czech	10	8	Čapek, *An Ordinary Life*
Nepali	9	.1	Balkrishna, *Plays*
Swedish	9	6	Lagerkvist, *The Death of Ahasuerus*
Greek	9	3.5	Kazantzakis, *Zorba the Greek*
Ethiopian	8	.7	Walda-Selluse, *Wadaje Lebbe*
Sinhalese	8	2	

TABLE 3 *(continued)*

LANGUAGE	SPEAKERS (in millions)	READERS (in millions)	REPRESENTATIVE WORK
Bulgarian	8	5	Shishmanov, *Vision on the Acropolis*
Provençal	8	6	Chèze, *Una princessa dins la Tor*
Tibetan	7	.6	Denje, *Abridged Essence of Secular and Religious Histories*
Assamese	7	1	Kamalakanta, *Burning Thoughts*
Catalan	5	3	Catalá, *Solitude*
Sindhi	5	.4	
Malagasy	5	.4	
Danish	5	4	Jensen, *The Long Journey*
Afrikaans	4	1.4	Langenhoven, *Stories*
Slovak	4	3	Urban, *Living Whip*
Armenian	4	2	Aharonian, *Valley of Tears*
Norwegian	4	3	Undset, *Kristin Lavranstatter*
Finnish	4	3	Sillanpää, *Meek Heritage*
Cambodian	3	.2	Anona, *Vorvong and Saurivong*
Kashmiri	3	.2	Mahjur, *Poems*
Georgian	3	2	Abashvili, *Works*
Lithuanian	3	1	Maculevičius, *Works*
Latvian	3	1	Steperman, *Works*
Galician	3	1	Castelao, *Works*
Hebrew	2	1.2	Singer, *Satan in Goray*
Albanian	2	.5	Konitza, *Byzantine Symphony*
Mongolian	1	.1	Damdinsuren, *My Grey-Haired Mother*
Estonian	1	.7	Wilde, *Works*
Yiddish	1	.7	Asch, *Moses*
Basque			Monzon, *From Far Away*
Frisian			Troelstra, *Harvest*
Icelandic			Laxness, *Independent People*
Irish			Flower, *The Islandman*
Maltese			Dun Karm, *The Ego and Beyond*
Romansh			Lansel, *Works*
Slovenian			Župančić, *Poems*
Sorbian			Nowak, *Poems*
Khasi			*Ka Kitab Niani Khein Ki Khasi*

novels, poetry, and drama for purposes of political propaganda, it has also supported the traditional opera and certain forms of traditional writing. Despite its radically anti-Confucian commitment, the government decided to retain the established writing system, and the strongly nationalistic character of the Communist movement seems likely to result in a measure of real continuity in Chinese literature through all the turbulence of its twentieth-century development.

Even the most cursory survey of the twentieth-century literature of the 78 literary languages now active would require another book at least the size of this one. I have attempted, however, to draw together enough information to depict the reality of contemporary literature by compiling a table (Table 3) that includes at least a representative work for each language. The table also gives the number of speakers and the number of readers in each case, and is ordered by number of speakers.

A table can scarcely serve as an introduction to 78 different literatures, but this one may at least indicate the proper meaning of the abused expression "world literature." At the present time the international contacts among peoples, intensive as they are, have made only the merest start on breaking down the parochialism of literary tradition. It is safe to say that we confront a continuing and increasing development in this direction.

Even this broad panorama does not give us a complete view, for it omits the last tenth of the world's population, and its even more numerous and more diverse "literatures," not yet written. Many of these peoples have begun to move toward effective literacy. The African Fang have produced a novel (*Knanga Kön*). The Eskimos have a newspaper. The Navaho have radio broadcasts. The "little peoples of the north" have been given alphabets and textbooks by the Russians, and many other isolated people have been similarly initiated by missionaries. Acculturation is proceeding rapidly in almost all parts of the world in literature as in science.

The enormous range of literary diversity that has been sampled and sketched in this book provides us with a scientific opportunity of the greatest challenge and rewards. It is a laboratory in which we may test all manner of hypotheses about the subtle processes of communication, of human culture. The potentialities of literature as a laboratory have scarcely been touched, and I believe we may expect startling and important results as the momentum of studies in this area increases. It seems thoroughly likely that the broader sharing of awareness and understanding of the literature of the present and the past will in fact continue and grow, to the enormous enrichment of literature as well as science. The sciences of culture must participate in this growth not in a dialectic of opposition of literary and scientific comprehension but as a unitary effort, for culture is one.

Appendix

Appendix

Index of World Literature

Taken in conjunction with Chapter 8, the Appendix is designed to facilitate access to the less familiar literatures of the world by providing a reference list of titles, authors, languages, and dates. In addition to standard reference works, the compilation incorporates materials from a number of literary histories. The reader seeking further information on particular works is referred to Shipley 1946, Nicholson 1956, Lambert 1960, Erman 1927, Anon. 1959, Keith 1956, Garibay 1953, Gibb 1901, Hyvernat 1909, Bell 1931, and Keene 1955.

Dates are given in ordinal centuries, B.C. being indicated by (−). Languages are identified by abbreviations composed of the first three letters of their English names, except for ten irregular abbreviations to avoid duplication: *Ark.* for *Arakanese*; *Let.* for *Latvian*; *Mse.* for *Madurese*; *Mad.* for *Malagasy*; *Mlm.* for *Malayalam*; *Mlt.* for *Maltese*; *Mnx.* for *Manx*; *Rsh.* for *Romansh*; *Cey.* for *Sinhalese*, and *Slk.* for *Slovak*. A complete list of the languages represented is given below. Authors' names are as abbreviated as possible, preference being given to surnames, first element in compound names, place names in the case of persons customarily identified as "John of ...," and the first element following a definite article in the Arabic polynomials. Works of each author are cited in the native language when possible; they are translated in "Works," in which the primary listing (italicized) is in English where possible. Coverage attempts to be as complete as possible for centuries before the twelfth in all literatures and for non-European literatures thereafter. The twentieth century is omitted. No effort has been made to exclude "nonliterary" works (for example, mathematics, or any other science), but they have not been actively sought out. Citations are drawn from 111 languages and cover an estimated 4000 titles.

LIST OF LANGUAGES

Afrikaans	Greek	Phoenician (v. Syr.)
Albanian	Gujerati	Polish
Arabic	Hebrew	Portuguese
Arakanese (Ark.)	Hindi	Prakrit
Aramaic (v. Syr.)	Hittite	Provençal
Armenian	Icelandic	Punjabi
Assamese	Ilocano	Pushtu
Babylonian	Irish	Quechua
Basque	Italian	Quiche
Belorussian	Japanese	Rajasthani
Bengali	Javanese	Romansh (Rsh.)
Breton	Kannada	Rumanian
Bulgarian	Karen	Russian
Burmese	Kashmiri	Sanskrit
Cakchiquel	Khasi	Saxon (v. Fri.)
Cambodian	Khmer	Scottish
Canaanitic (v. Syr.)	Korean	Serbo-Croatian
Cantonese (v. Chi.)	Ladino	Sindhi
Catalan	Laotian	Sinhalese (Cey.)
Champa	Latin	Slovak (Slk.)
Cherokee	Latvian (Let.)	Slovenian
Chinese	Lithuanian	Sorbian
Chontal	Madurese (Mse.)	Spanish
Cornish	Magyar	Sumerian
Czech	Malagasy (Mad.)	Swahili
Danish	Malay	Swedish
Dutch	Malayalam (Mlm.)	Syrian
Egyptian	Maltese (Mlt.)	Tagalog
English	Manchu	Tamil
Estonian	Manx (Mnx.)	Telegu
Ethiopian	Marathi	Thai
Etruscan	Min (v. Chi.)	Tibetan
Finnish	Mindanao	Turkish
French	Mongolian	Ukrainian
Frisian	Nahuatl	Urdu
Galician	Nepali	Vietnamese
German	Norwegian	Welsh
Georgian	Oriya	Yiddish
Gothic	Pali (v. Pra.)	Yucatec
	Persian	

AUTHORS

Language and century are given in parentheses immediately following the author's name. Titles of the author's works follow that. When no date is given, the date is unknown. Anonymous works are to be found in "Works."

Aagesen (Lat. 12) *Compendiosa Historia Regum Daniae*

Aaron (Heb. 14) *'Ez Hayyim; Gan 'Eden; Kether Torah*

Abba Salama (Eth. 13) *Acts of the Passion; Service for the Dead*

Abbo (Lat. 9) *Poems*

Abdul Latif (Sin. 18) *Risalo*

Abélard (Lat. 12) *Dialetica; Ethica; Historia Calamitatum; Introductio ad Theologiam; Invectiva in Quemdam Igrarum Dialectices; Sic et Non*

Abhi Handa (San. 9) *Kaadambarii Kathaa Saara; Raama Carita*

Abhi Nava Gupta (San.) *Locana*

Aboab (Heb. 14) *Menorath ha Ma'or*

Abovian (Arm. 19) *Verk Hayastani*

Abramovich (Yid. 19) *Di Klyatche*

Abravanel (Heb. 16) *Yeshu'oth Meshiho*

Abru (Per.) *Geography*

Abshihi (Ara. 15) *Mustatraf*

Abu Abdalla (Ara.) *Nokhbet ed Dahr fi Adjaib il Birr wa 'l Bah'r*

Abu Bekr (Ara. 11) *Letters*

Abu Dawud (Ara. 9) *Sunan*

Abu Nasr (Ara. 10) *Kitaabu 'l Luma'*

Abu Nuwas (Ara. 9) *Diiwaan*

Abu Talib (Ara. 10) *Quutu 'l Quluub*

Abu Tammam (Ara. 9) *Al Hamaasa*

Abu Zayd (Ara. 11) *Jamharatu Ash'aari 'l 'Arab*

Abulafia (Lad. 19) *Shibbe ha Tanaïm*

Abutsu (Jap. 13) *Izayoi no Ki*

Adam (Fre. 13) *Jeu de la Feuillée; Jeu de Robin et Marion*

Adamnan (Lat. 8) *Vita Columbae*

Adiyarkunallar (Tam. 15) *Commentaries*

Aelfric (Eng. 11) *Homilies*

Aelius (Lat.) *Commentum Terenti; Vergilii Vita*

Aelnoth (Lat. 11) *Historia Ortus, Vitae et Passionis S. Canutis Regis Daniae*

Aeolius (Gre. 2) *Katholike Prosodia*

Aernout (Dut. 13) *Van den Vos Reinaerde*

Aetheria (Lat. 4) *Peregrinatio ad Loca Sancta*

Agathias (Gre. 6) *Contemporary History*

Aggathamahdi (Bur. 16) *Jataka Verses*

Agricola (Lat. 16) *De Re Metallica*

Ahai (Heb. 8) *She'iltoth*

Ahmed (Tur. 15) *Poems*

Ahmed Baba (Ara. 16) *Works*

Airivanq (Arm. 14) *Chronography*

Aiskhylos (Gre. −5) *Akharnoi; Basanisteriona; Oresteia; Promethios; Seven against Thebes*

Aisopos (Gre. −6) *Hoi Mythoi*

Akho (Guj. 17) *Poems*

Akhund Kazim (Pus. 16) *Fawayid es Sheriah*

Akiba (Heb. 1) *Sifreh*

'Akif (Tur. 19) *Poems*

'Ala (Ara. 11) *Al Fuṣuul wa 'l Ghaayaat; Letters; Luzuumiiyat; Maqaamaat; Risaalatu 'l Ghufraan; Saqṭu 'l Zand*

Alagiyavanna (Tam. 9) *Kusa Jatakaya*

A'lam (Ara. 11) *Diiwaans of the Six Poets*

Alang Ahmad (Mal. 19) *Hikayat Penerang Hati*

Alaqa Tayya (Eth. 18) *Gondar Poems*

Alaṭa (*see* Mammaṭa)

Albertus (Lat. 13) *De Caelo Mundoque; De Causis et Creatio Universi; De Cursibus et Virtutibus Planetorum Elementorum; De Meteoribus; Physica; De Spiritu*

Albo (Heb. 15) *'Iqqarim*

Alcuin (Lat. 9) *De Dialectica; Grammar; Rhetoric; Trivial Arts*

Aldhelm (Lat. 7) *De Laudibus Virginitatis; Aenigmata*

Aled (Wel. 16) *Poems*

Alexander (Gre.) *Destiny*

Alfonso X (Gal., Spa. 13) *Songs to the Virgin; Siete Partidas*

Alfred (Eng. 9) *Translations*

'Ali Haji (Mal. 19) *Sejarah Melayu; Silsilah Melayu dan Bugis*

'Ali Ḥazin (Ara. 18) *Memoirs*

Alphonsus (Lat. 11) *Disciplina Clericalis*

Amanat (Urd. 19) *Inder Sabha*

Amara Chandra (San. 13) *Baala Bhaarata; Kaavya Kalpalataa* (with Ari Sinha)

Amari Simha (San. 6) *Amara Kośa*

Ambrosius (Lat. 4) *The Duties of the Clergy; Hexaemeron*

Amelander (Yid. 18) *Sheyris Yisroel*

Ameliarus (Lat. 9) *De Ecclesiasticis Officiis*

Amen Emhet (Egy. −20) *Sbooyet*

Amen Emope (Egy. −9) *Sbooyet*

Amita Gati (San. 10) *Dharma Pariikṣaa; Subhaa Ṣita Ratna Saṁdoha*

Ammianus (Lat. 4) *Historia*

Amos (Heb. −8) *Prophecy*

Ananda (San.) *Maadhava Anala Kathaa*

Ananda Vardhana (San. 9) *Dhvanya Aloka; Devii Sataka*

Ananiah (Arm. 7) *The Calendar; Chronicon*

Ananta (San.) *Bhaarata Campuu; Viira Caritra*

Anantathuria (Bur. 12) *Death Song*

Anastasius (Lat.) *Quaestiones*

Andayya (Kan. 13) *Kabbigara*

Andreas (Lat. 12) *De Arte Honeste Amandi*

Aneirin (Wel. 7) *Gododdin*

Anelier (Pro. 13) *Histoire de la Guerre de Navarre*

Anglicus (Lat. 13) *The Properties of Things*

Ani (Egy. −9) *Maxims*

Ani (Arm. 12) *Chronicle*

Anittas (Hit. −20) *Wars of the Six Cities*

Ansari (Per. 11) *Munaajaat; Tabaqaat*

Antimakhos (Gre. −5) *Thebais*

Anvari (Per. 12) *Qasiida; The Tears of Khorasan*

Apameia (Gre.) *Cynegetica*

Apastabama (San.) *Srauta Suutra*

Apollonios (Gre. −3) *Argonautika*

Appar (Tam. 7) *Teevaaram*

Appianus (Gre. 2) *Studies in Roman History*

Apte (Mar. 19) *Pan Lakshyat Kon Gheto?; Madhli Stithi*

Apuleius (Lat. 3) *Metamorphoses; Discourse on Magic; The God of Socrates; Peri Hermeneias*

Aquinas (Lat. 13) *Being and Essence; The Governance of Rulers; Summa contra Gentiles; Summa Theologiae*

'Arabi (Ara. 13) *Works*

Arai (Jap. 18) *Hankampu*

Araqel (Per. 17) *History of the Persian Invasions, 1602–1661*

Aratos (Gre. −3) *Phainomena*

Archili III (Geo. 18) *Verse History of Georgia*

Ari (Ice. 12) *Islendingabók*

Ari Chandra (Tam. 9) *Martyr of Truth*

Ari Siṅha (*see also* Amara Chandra) (San. 13) *Sukṛta Saṁkiirtana*

Aristaces (Arm. 11) *History of the Seljuk Conquest*

Aristides (Gre. 2) *Apologia*

Aristophanes (Gre. −5) *Hoi Ptenoi; Hoi Batrakhoi; Hoi Akharnoi; Synnephona; Knights; Wasps; Ecclesiazusae; The Plutus; Thesmophoriazusae*

Aristoteles (Gre. −4) *Aesthetike; Ethike; Metaphysike; Organon; Physike; Poetike; Ta Politika; Rhetoric; The Soul*

Ariwara (Jap. 10) *Ise Monogatari*

Ariyaramna (Per. −7) *Gold Tablet*

Arjun (Pun. 17) *Adi Granth; Sukhmani*

Arnimal (Kas. 18) *Poems*

Arrebo (Nor. 17) *Hexaemeron*

Arrianus (Gre. 2) *The Anabasis of Alexander; Cynegeticus; Diatribai; Encheiridion; Indica; Periplus of the Euxine; Tactica*

Artsruni (Arm. 10) *History of the Clan*

Arya Bhata (San. 5) *Astronomical Verses*
Arya Deva (San. 3) *Catuḥ Śatikaa*
Arya Sura (San. 4) *Jaataka Maalaa*
Asadi (Per. 11) *Garshasp Naama; Lughat i Furs*
Asanga (San. 4) *Mahaayaana Suutra Alaṁkaara*
Asgrímsson (Ice. 14) *The Lily*
A'sha (Ara. 7) *Poems*
Asheruni (Arm. 8) *Commentary on the Jerusalem Lectionary*
Ashi (Heb. 4) *Gemara*
Ashi (Heb. 8) *She'iltoth*
'Ashik (Tur. 14) *Diiwan*
Ashkenazi (Yid. 17) *Tseno Ureno*
Asia (Syr. 6) *Life of John of Tella*
Aškerc (Slo. 19) *Ballads and Romances*
Asoka (San. −3) *Edicts*
Asolik (Arm. 10) *Commentary on Jeremiah; History of Armenia*
Assenede (Dut. 13) *Floris ende Blancefloer*
Asser (Lat. 10) *King Alfred*
Aśva Ghosa (San. 1) *Awakening of Faith in the Mahayana; Buddha Carita; Plays; Gaṇḍi Stotra Gaathaa; Saundara Ananda; Suutra Laṁkaara*
Asvala Ayana (San. −4) *Aaśvala Ayana Suutra*
Aṭa Ullah (Tur. 17) *Biographies*
Atahiya (Ara. 9) *Diiwaan*
Athenaeus (Lat., Gre. 2) *Deipnosophoi*
Athir (Ara. 13) *Kitaabu 'l Kaamil fi 'l Ta'riikh; Usdu 'l Ghaaba*
Athos (Geo. 11) *Gospels*
'Aṭṭar (Ara., Per. 13) *Mantiq uṭ Ṭair; Pand Naama; Tadkhiratu 'l Awliyaa*
Augustinus (Lat. 4) *Contra Adversarium Legis et Prophetarum; Contra Cresconium; De Diversis Quaestionibus; Enarcationes in Psalmos; Epistolae; De Fide et Symbolo; De Civitate Dei; Confessiones; De Magistro; Contra Faustum; De Natura Boni contra Manicheos; De Libero Arbitrio; De Genesi; Opus Imperfectum contra Julianum; De Ordine; Sermones; Soliloquorum; De Spiritu et Anima; De Trinitate*
Aurelius (Lat. 4) *Origin of the Roman Race; Illustrious Men; Caesars*
Avalokite Svara (San. 2) *The Lotus Sutra*
Avvakum (Rus. 17) *Autobiography*

Awbatha (Bur. 16) *Jataka Plays*
Awza'i (Ara. 8) *Hadiith*
Axum (Eth. 17) *Rules of Life*
Azraqi (Ara.) *History of Mecca*
Azzopardi (Mlt. 19) *Susanna*

Ba Hailu Michael (Eth. 15) *The Mystery of Heaven and Earth*
Baal Shem Tov (Yid. 18) *Parables*
Baba Pudmanji (Mar. 19) *Yamuna Paryatan*
Babur (Per. 16) *Babur Naama*
Bachha Das (Ori. 14) *Kalasha Chautisa*
Bacon (Lat. 17) *Novum Organum*
Badara Ayana (San. 4) *Braahma Suutra*
Baḍu (Ben. 14) *Śri Kṛṣṇa Kirttana*
Baggesen (Dan. 18) *Comic Tales; Labyrinthen*
Baghdadi (Ara. 10) *Fihrist*
Baha (Per. 19) *Kitabi Ikan*
Bahadur 'Ali Husaini (Urd. 19) *Nasr i Benaziir*
Bahrey (Eth. 16) *History of the Gallas*
Baihaqi (Per. 11) *Taariikh i Baihaqi*
Bajza (Slk. 18) *Adventures and Experiences of Young René*
Bakharzi (Ara. 11) *Dumyatu 'l Qaṣr*
Baki (Tur. 16) *Poems*
Bakkhylides (Gre. −5) *Poems*
Baksh (Per. 17) *Naama Maalaa*
Bakur (Geo. 4) *Works*
Baladhuri (Ara. 9) *The Arab Conquests; Kitaabu Ansaabi 'l Ashraaf; Kitaabu Futuuhi 'l Buldaan*
Balagtas (Tag. 19) *Florante at Laura*
Balai (Syr. 5) *History of Joseph*
Bal'ami (Per. 10) *The Annals of Ṭabarii*
Ballala Sena (San. 16) *Bhoja Prabandha*
Bana (San. 7) *Harṣa Carita; Kaadambarii; Caṇḍii Śataka*
Bar Aphtonya (Syr. 6) *Life of Severus*
Bar Daysan (Syr. 3) *Book of the Laws of the Countries*
Bar Ga'yah (Syr. −6) *Treaty with Mati'el*
Bar Hiyya (Heb. 12) *Philosophy*
Bar Kepha (Syr. 10) *Commentaries*
Bar Sauma (Syr. 5) *Poems*
Bar Shinaya (Syr. 11) *Chronicle*
Bar Sudhaili (Syr. 5) *Hierotheus*
Barkath (Ass. 18) *Hasti Vidyarnava*
Baronius (Lat. 17) *Annales Ecclesiastici*

Baruch (Heb. −6) *The Book of the Prophet Jeremiah; The Lamentations of Jeremiah*

Basava (Kan. 14) *Vacanas*

Basho (Jap. 17) *Poems*

Basil I (Gre. 9) *Procheiros Nomos; Epanogoge*

Basil (Gre.) *Ascetic Works*

Basrah (Syr. 13) *Book of the Bee*

Beauvais (Lat. 13) *The Greater Mirror*

Bede (Lat. 8) *De Arte Metrica; Historia Ecclesiastica Gentis Anglorum*

Bedersi (Heb. 14) *Behinath ha 'Olam*

Bedil (Sin. 19) *Poems*

Bellarmine (Lat. 17) *De Potestate Pontifici in Rebus Temporalibus*

Babya Ben Asher (Heb. 14) *Discourses; Kad ha Qemah*

Jacob Ben Asher (Heb. 14) *Tur*

Ben David (Heb. 12) *Enumah Ramah; Sepher ha Kabbalah*

Ben Ezra (*see* Ibn Ezra)

Ben Gorion (Heb. 10) *Josippon*

Ben Hillel (Heb. 13) *Mordekhai*

Ben Hophni (Heb. 11) *Law*

Ben Isaac Asa (Lad. 18) *Shulhan ha Meleh*

Moses Ben Jacob (Heb. 13) *Semag*

Nissim Ben Jacob (Heb. 11) *Ma'asiyyoth*

Ben Jose (Heb. 7) *Poems*

Aaron Ben Joseph (Heb. 13) *Sepher ha Mibhar*

Seadiah Ben Joseph (Heb. 10) *Works*

Ben Joshua (Heb. 16) *Dibhre ha Yamim; 'Emeq ha Bakhah*

Ben Judah (Heb. 11) *Commentaries*

Ben Maimon (Heb., Ara. 12) *Guide for the Perplexed; Mishneh Toreh*

Ben Me'ir (Heb. 12) *Sepher ha Yashor*

Abraham Ben Moses (Heb., Ara. 13) *Ma'aseh Yerushalmi; Kitaab al Kifayah*

Isaac Ben Moses (Heb. 13) *Ma'aseh Efod; Or Zarua'*

Ben Qalonymos (Heb. 14) *Eben Bohan*

Ben Yehiel (Heb. 12) *'Arukh*

Benedictus (Lat.) *Regula Monachorum*

Benoît (Fre. 12) *Roman de Troie*

Berenguer (Pro. 14) *Mirall de Trobar*

Bernardus (Lat.) *Epistolae*

Berosus (Gre. −3) *History of Babylon*

Beschi (Tam. 18) *Vaman Kathai; Paramartha Guru Kathai*

Beth Arsham (Syr. 6) *The Himyarites*

Beyer (Nor. 16) *The Kingdom of Norway*

Bhagawi (Ara. 12) *Masaabiihu 'l Sunna*

Bhallata (San.) *Sataka*

Bhamaha (San. 8) *Kaavya Alamkaara*

Bhanu Datta (San. 14) *Rasa Mañjarii; Rasa Taranginii*

Bhanubhakta (Nep. 18) *Raamaayana*

Bharata (San.) *Naatya Saastra*

Bharatendu (Hin. 19) *Works*

Bharavi (San. 6) *Kiraata Arjuniiya*

Bhartr Hari (San. 7) *Vaakya Padiiya; Niiti Sataka*

Bhasa (San. −4) *Baala Carita; Svapana Vaasava Dattaa*

Bhaskara (San. 10) *Bhaasya; Unmatta Raaghava*

Bhatta (San.) *Venii Samhaara*

Bhatti (San. 7) *Raavana Vadha*

Bhaumaka (San. 7) *Raavana Arjuniiya*

Bhava Bhuti (San. 8) *Mahaa Viira Carita; Malati Madhava; Uttara Raama Carita*

Bhava Misra (San. 16) *Bhaava Prakaasa*

Bhoja (San. 11) *Samaraangana Suutra Dhaara; Srngaara Prakaasa; Sarasvatii Kanthaa Bharana; Raamaayana Campuu* (with Laksmana Bhatta)

Bihari Lal (Hin. 17) *Sat' Saii*

Bilhana (San. 11) *Vikrama Anka Deva Carita; Karna Sundarii; Caurii Surata Pañcaa Sikaa*

Bin 'Ali (Per. 10) *Medicine*

Bin Ba'ith (Per. 9) *Poems*

Birbal (Per. 16) *Poems*

Birgitta (Swe. 14) *Revelations*

Biruni (Ara. 11) *Aathaar al Baaqiya; Ta'riikhu 'l Hind*

Biswanath Khuntia (Ori. 17) *Bichitra Ramayana*

Björnsen (Nor. 19) *Plays; Stories*

Blois (Lat. 12) *Geta; Querolus*

Boccaccio (Lat. 14) *De Genealogiis Deorum*

Bochada (Pro. 12) *Chanson d'Antioche*

Bodel (Fre. 13) *Le Jeu de St. Nicolas*

Bodh (Syr. 6) *Qualilag and Dimnag*

Bodin (Lat. 16) *Methodus ad Facilem Historiarum Cognitionem*

Boece (Lat. 16) *Scotorum Historiae*

Boethius (Lat. 6) *De Consolatione Philosophiae*

Bogerman (Fri. 16) *Verses*

Böhme (Lat. 17) *Signatura Rerum*
Bonamico (Mlt. 17) *Sonnets*
Bonfini (Lat. 16) *Works*
Bonifacius (Lat. 8) *Opera*
Bonifacius VIII (Lat. 13) *Clericis Laicos, Unam Sanctam*
Bosch (Cat. 17) *Summari*
Boson (Cor. 18) *Nebbaz Gerriau dro tho Cornack*
Botev (Bul. 19) *Poems*
Botto (Slk. 19) *Janošikova Smrt*
Bracton (Lat. 13) *De Legibus et Consuetudinibus Angliae*
Brahe (Lat. 16) *De Nova Stella*
Brahma Gupta (San. 7) *Braahma Siddhaanta*
Brant (Ger. 15) *Narrenschiff*
Bremen (Lat. 11) *Hamburg Church History*
Browne (Lat. 17) *Religio Medici*
Buddha Ghosa (Pal. 5) *Visuddhimagga; Dhamma Pada*
Buddha Ghosa Acharya (San.) *Padya Cuudaamani*
Buddha Svamin (San. 9) *Brhat Kathaa Sloka Samgraha*
Buhturi (Ara. 9) *Hamaasa*
Bukhari (Ara. 9) *Al Sahiih*
Bulhey Shah (Pun. 18) *Kafis*
Burzoe (Per. 4) *Society, Ethics and Religion*
Bushaq (Per. 15) *Poems on Food*
Buusiri (Ara. 13) *Burda*

Cabham (Lat. 13) *Penitential*
Cáemaín (Iri. 11) *Poems*
Caesar (Lat. −1) *Commentarii de Bello Civile; Commentarii de Bello Gallico*
Calepino (Lat. 16) *Cornucopiae*
Callet (Mad. 19) *Tantara ny Andriana*
Calpurnius (Lat. 1) *Eclogues*
Calvin (Lat. 16) *Christianae Religionis Institutio*
Caragiale (Rum. 19) *Plays*
Carcassès (Pro. 12) *Papagai*
Cardano (Lat. 16) *Ars Magna*
Cassiodorus (Lat. 6) *Institutiones; Variae*
Castro (Gal. 19) *Galician Songs; Poems*
Cataldi (Lat. 16) *Mathematica*
Catholicus (Arm. 8) *Against the Paulicians and Docetae; Liturgical Commentaries*

Cato (Lat. −2) *De Agri Cultura; Origines*
Catullus (Lat. −1) *Carmina*
Celsius (Lat. 18) *Hierobotanicon*
Černý (Cze. 16) *Treatise on the Plague*
Cesalpino (Lat. 16) *De Plantis; Ars Medica*
Chakravarty (Ben. 16) *Chandi Mangal*
Chanakya (San. 4) *Artha Śaastra (or see Kautilya)*
Chand Bardai (Raj. 12) *Prithi Raj Raso*
Chandi Das (San. 16) *Love Poems*
Chandra Gomin (San. 7) *Sanskrit Grammar; Śisyalekh Dharma Kaavya*
Chang Ch'ien (Chi. 8) *Poems*
Chang Chih Ho (Chi. 8) *Conservation of Vitality*
Chang Kuo Pin (Chi. 13) *Joining the Shirt*
Chang Pi (Chi. 10) *Poems*
Chang Tong (Kor. 19) *Tong Sa Kang Yo*
Chang Yen Yüan (Chi. 9) *Eminent Painters of All Ages*
Chang Yu Chin (Chi. 14) *Ko Hsia Hsin Shu*
Chao I (Chi. 18) *Wars of the Manchu Dynasty; Poems*
Chao Ju Kua (Chi. 13) *Chu Fan Chi*
Chao Li Hua (Chi. 16) *Poems*
Chao Phya Dharmadhibes (Tha. 17) *Inao*
Chao Ts'ai Chi (Chi. 15) *Poems*
Ch'ao Ts'o (Chi. −2) *The Value of Agriculture*
Charaka (San. 2) *Samhita*
Charitra Sundara Ganin (San.) *Mahii Paala Caritra*
Charles I (Lat. 14) *Maiestas Carolina*
Chelčický (Cze. 15) *The Thread of True Faith*
Chelebi (Tur. 16) *Humaayuun Naama*
Chen (Chi. 8) *Chien Niang*
Ch'ên Hao Tzŭ (Chi. 18) *Mirror of Flowers*
Ch'ên Hung Mou (Chi. 18) *Commentary*
Ch'en P'êng Nien (Chi. 11) *Kuang Yün*
Ch'en Shou (Chi. 3) *San Kuo Chih*
Ch'en Tai Wei (Chi. 16) *Su Hsia* (v. *Su Shu*)
Ch'ên T'ao (Chi. 9) *Poems*
Ch'en T'uan (Chi. 10) *Poems*
Ch'en Tzŭ Ang (Chi. 7) *Poems*
Ch'eng (Chi. 14) *Chien Niang*

Chêng Ch'iao (Chi. 12)   *Essays; History of China; Poems*

Ch'êng Hao (Chi. 11)   *Poems*

Chêng Hsüan (Chi. 2)   *Commentary*

Ch'êng I (Chi. 11)   *Commentary on I Ching; Poetics*

Cherusseri (Mlm. 15)   *Krishna Gatha*

Chi Chün Hsiang (Chi. 13)   *The Orphan of the Chao*

Chia I (Chi. −2)   *Poems*

Chidambara (San.)   *Raaghava Paandaviiya Yaadaviiya*

Ch'ien Lung (Chi. 18)   *Anthology of Poetry; Works*

Chikadevaraya (Kan. 18)   *Champu*

Chikafusa (Jap. 14)   *Jinkooshootooki*

Chikamatsu (Jap. 17)   *The Battles of Coxinga; Fair Ladies at a Game of Poem Cards*

"Chilam Balam" (Yuc. 16)   *The Series of the Katuns*

Chimalpahin (Nah. 17)   *Annals*

Ch'in (Chi. 13)   *Su Shu*

Chin Huo (Chi. 19)   *Song of the Autumn Cicada*

Chin Ku Chi (Chi.)   *The Inconstancy of Madame Chuang*

Chintamani Bhatta (San. 12)   *Śuka Saptati*

Ch'oe (Kor. 9)   *Works*

Chomei (Jap. 13)   *Hojiki*

Chǒng (Kor. 14)   *Koryŏ Sa*

Chosroes (Arm. 10)   *Commentary on the Rites*

Chou Kung (Chi. −3)   *Chou Li*

Chou Mi (Chi.)   *Kwei Hsin Tso Chih*

Chou Ta Kuan (Chi. 13)   *Angkor Vat*

Chou Tun I (Chi. 11)   *Commentary on I Ching*

Ch'ü (Chi. −4)   *Li Sao*

Chu Fu (Chi. 11)   *Ch'i Man Ts'ung Hsia*

Chu Hsi (Chi. 12)   *Chu Tzŭ Yü Lei— Ta Hsüeh; Ssŭ Shu Chu; T'ung Chien Kang Mu*

Chu Shi Chieh (Chi. 13)   *Suan Hsiao Chi Meng*

Chu Yu (Chi.)   *Chien Teng Hsin Hwa*

Chu Yung Shun (Chi. 17)   *Family Maxims*

Chuang (Chi. −3)   *Chuang Tzŭ*

Chung   (see Sǒ)

Cicero (Lat. −1)   *Epistolae; De Finibus; De Leges; De Natura Deorum; De Officiis; Orationes; De Re Publica; Tusculan Disputations*

Čišinski-Bart (Sor. 19)   *Poems*

Claudius (Eth. 16)   *Confession of Faith*

Clement (Gre. 3)   *Exhortation; The Tutor; The Teacher; Stromateis*

Clement XI (Lat. 18)   *Once Born*

Clement XIV (Lat. 18)   *Dominus ac Redemptor Noster*

Closener (Ger. 14)   *Strassburg Chronicle*

Colonne (Lat. 13)   *Historia Trojana*

Comestor (Lat.)   *Historia Scholastica*

Comyn (Iri. 18)   *Laoi Oisin i dT'ir na nÓg*

Coresi (Rum. 16)   *Gospels*

Crashaw (Lat. 17)   *Epigrammatum Sacrorum Liber*

Crescas (Heb. 15)   *Or Adonai*

Crete (Arm. 18)   *History*

Csezmiczei (Lat. 15)   *Poems*

Curtius (Lat. 1)   *Opera*

Cynddelw (Wel. 13)   *Poems*

Cyril and Methodius (Rus. 9)   *Works*

Cyrillona (Syr. 5)   *The Invasion of the Huns*

Czarnkow (Lat. 14)   *Chronica*

Daksina Varta Natha (San. 12)   *Commentary on Megha Duuta*

Dalpat (Sin. 19)   *Poems*

Damascene (Gre. 8)   *The Fount of Knowledge*

Damian (Lat. 11)   *Gomorhianus*

Damodara (San.)   *Hanumaan Naataka*

Damodara Gupta (San. 8)   *Kuttaniimata*

Damrong (Tha. 17)   *Klong Loka Niti*

Dandin (San. 7)   *Daśa Kumaara Carita; Kaavya Darśa*

Daniel (Heb. −2)   *Prophecy*

Daniel (Rus. 11)   *Works*

Dante (Lat., Ita. 14)   *De Vulgari Eloquentia; De Monarquia; Convivio*

Dapontes (Gre. 18)   *Poems*

Daqiqi (Per. 11)   *Khvaataay Naamak*

Daraya (Per. −5)   *Autobiography*

Daraz (Urd. 15)   *Works*

Dasopant (Mar. 16)   *Gita Arnava*

Dass (Nor. 17)   *Trumpet of the North Country*

Dathev (Arm. 14)   *Book of Questions*

Dayarama (Guj. 18)   *Garbis*

Dechepare (Bas. 16)   *Poems*

Delmedigo (Heb. 15) *Behinath ha Dath*
Demosthenes (Gre. −4) *The Crown; Olynthiac Orations; The False Legation*
Descoll (Cat. 14) *Chronicle*
Deshmukh (Mar. 19) *Works*
Deva Prabha Suri (San. 13) *Paandava Caritra; Mrqaavatii Caritra*
Devaanda (San. 13) *Smriti Chandrikaa*
Deval (Mar. 19) *Sharada*
Dhana Pala (San. 10) *Paaiyalacchii (Praakrta Laksmii) Naama Maalaa; Rsabha Pañca Sikaa; Tilaka Mañjarii*
Dhanam Jaya (San. 12) *Dasa Ruupaka; Raaghava Paandaviiya; Naama Maalaa*
Dhane Svara (Pra. 11) *Suna Sundarii Cariya*
Dhanpal (Guj. 10) *Poems*
Dhoi (San. 12) *Pavana Duuta*
Diksita (San. 17) *Siddhaanta Kaumudii; Kuvalayananda Kaarikaas*
Dinawari (Ara. 9) *Kitaabu 'l Akhbaar al Tiwaal*
Dingir Addamu (Sum. −26) *Poems*
Diniz (Por. 18) *Hissope*
Dio (Gre. 1) *The Hunters of Euboea; In Praise of Hair*
Dio Cassius (Gre. 3) *History of Rome*
Diodorus (Lat. −1) *Library of Universal History*
Diogenes (Gre. 2) *The Lives and Opinions of the Eminent Philosophers*
Dionysius (Lat., Gre. 1) *The Ancient History of Rome; Ancient Orators*
Diyarbakri (Ara. 16) *Ta'riikh al Khamiis*
Djonanchiani (Geo. 8) *History of Georgia*
Djonkadze (Geo. 19) *Sorami s Tsikhi*
Djuansher (Arm. 7) *History of the Iberians*
Dlugosz (Lat. 14) *Historia Poloniae*
Doan Thi Diem (Vie. 18) *Poems*
Dobrovský (Cze. 18) *History of Czech Language and Literature*
Donnolo (Heb. 10) *Commentary on the Sepher Yezirah*
Duauf (Egy. −22) *Sbooyet*
Duran (Heb. 15) *Magen Abhoth*
Durrës (Alb. 15) *Fragment*
Dya Dviveda (San. 15) *Niiti Mañjarii*
Dykstra (Fri. 19) *The Silver Rattle*

Eckehardt (Lat. 14) *Works*
Jacob of Edessa (Syr. 7) *Hexaemeron*

Matthew of Edessa (Arm. 12) *History of Armenia, 952–1136*
Edmund (Wel. 15) *Poems*
Edrisi (Ara. 12) *Travels*
Einhard (Lat. 9) *Vita Caroli*
Ekanath (Mar. 15) *Poems*
Ekkehard (Lat. 11) *Casus Sancti Galli*
Elias (Syr. 6) *Life of John of Tella*
Eminescu (Rum. 19) *Poems*
Ennius (Lat. −2) *Annalia*
Epiphanios (Gre. 3) *Heresies*
Erasmus (Lat. 16) *Colloquies; Modus Orandi Deum; In Praise of Folly; De Immensa Dei Misericordia; Opus Epistolarum*
Eratosthenes (Gre. −3) *Old Attic Comedy*
Erici (Fin. 16) *Sermons*
Erigena (Lat. 9) *De Divisione Naturae*
Erinna (Gre. 4) *The Spindle*
Ermoldus (Lat. 9) *De Gestis Ludovici Caesaris*
Eschenbach (Ger. 13) *Parzival; Titurel*
Ethelwold (Lat. 10) *Regularis Concordia*
Euhemeros (Gre. −4) *The Historic Mysteries*
Euklydes (Gre. −4) *Mathematics*
Eunapios (Gre. 5) *Continuation of the History of Dexippus*
Euripides (Gre. −5) *Alkestis; Hai Bakkhai; Elektra; Helen; Hippolytos; Hai Iliadai; Ion; Iphigenia eis Taurin; Medea*
Eusebios (Lat., Gre. 4) *Preparation for the Gospel; Demonstration of the Gospel; Church History; Life of Constantine*
Eutychius (Ara. 10) *Annals*
Evliya (Tur. 17) *Travels*
Evtymy (Bul. 14) *Biographies of the Saints*
Ezekiel (Heb. −4) *Prophecy*
Ezhuttachan (Mlm. 16) *Addhyatma Ramayanam; Maha Bharatam*
Eznik (Arm. 5) *Refutation of the Sects*
Ezra (Heb. −4) *Chronicles*

Fa (Chi. 5) *Journal in India*
Faidi (Per. 16) *Poems*
Fairuzabadi (Ara. 15) *Al Qaamuus*
Fan Ch'eng Ta (Chi. 12) *Kwei Hai Yu Heng*
Fan Yeh (Chi. 5) *Hou Han Shu*

Fang Hsiao Ju (Chi. 14) *Essays*
Fang Shu Shao (Chi. 17) *Poems*
Farabi (Ara. 10) *Works*
Faraj (Ara., Syr. 10) *Kitaabu 'l Agha-anii; Chronography*
Farazdaq (*see* Jarir)
Farid (Ara.) *Diiwaan*
Farrukhi (Per. 12) *Poems*
Faustus (Arm. 4) *History of Armenia, 344-392*
Favre (Pro. 18) *Lou Sermoun de Moussu Sistre*
Fazari (Ara. 9) *Ghana*
Fazil (Tur. 19) *Poems*
Fazl (Per. 17) *Khirad Afroz; Aaiin i Akhbarii; Akhbar Naama*
Feda (Ara. 13) *Travels*
Feng (Chi. 17) *Hsing Shih Heng Yen*
Finsson (Ice. 9) *Hákonarmál*
Firdausi (Per. 11) *Shah Naama; Yuusuf i Zulaykha*
Firishtah (Per. 16) *History of Hindustan*
Fitnet (Tur. 19) *Poems*
FitzGerald (Iri. 14) *Poems*
Flodoard (Lat. 10) *Historia Remensis*
Fortunatus (Lat. 6) *Poems*
Francis (Heb. 17) *Zevi Mudah*
Fráshëri (Alb. 19) *Fletore e Bektashinjet*
Frycz (Lat. 16) *On the Improvement of the Republic*
Fu Mi (Chi. 3) *Poems*
Fuchs (Lat. 16) *Historia Stirpium*
Fulgentius (Lat.) *Ad Monimum*
Futabatei (Jap. 19) *The Drifting Cloud*
Fuzuli (Tur. 16) *Poems*

Gabashvili (Geo. 18) *Battle of Aspindzi*
Galen (Gre. 2) *Medical Experience; The Natural Faculties; Tekhne Iatrike*
Galhard (Pro. 16) *Poems*
Galileo (Lat. 16) *Sidereus Mundi*
Gallus (Lat. 12) *Chronica Polonica*
Gam Po Pa (Tib. 13) *The Jewel Ornament of Liberation*
Gamdhani (Urd. 16) *Jawaahiru 'l Asraar*
Gami (Kas. 19) *Mystical Romances*
Gans (Heb. 16) *Zemah David*
Ganzak (Arm. 13) *History*
Gaon (Heb. 3) *Lesser Halakhoth*
Garcia (Lat. 16) *Poems*
Gardizi (Per. 11) *Zayn al Akhbaar*

Gauda Pada (San. 8) *Saaṁkhya Bhaaṣya; Maaṇḍukya Kaarikaa*
Gautama (Pal. −6) *Nyaaya Suutra*
Gavvasi (Urd. 17) *Saif ul Muluuk and Badii' ul Jamaal*
Gellius (Lat. 2) *Noctes Attica*
Gelong (Tib. 15) *Rosary of Gems*
Genshin (Jap. 10) *Oojooyooshuu*
Georgjić (Ser. 18) *Mary Magdalene*
Gerbert (Lat. 11) *Epistolae*
Germanicus (Lat. 1) *Phainomena*
Gessner (Lat. 16) *Historia Animalium*
Ghalib (Tur. 19) *Ḥusn u 'Ashk*
Ghana Śyama (Pra. 18) *Aananda Sundarii*
Ghaṭa Karpara (San. 4) *Niiti Saara*
Ghazali (Ara. 12) *Tahaafutu'l Falaasifa; Ihyaa'u 'Uluum al Din; The Niche of Lights; Munqidh mina 'l Ḍalaal; Kiimiyaa'u 'l Sa'aadat*
Ghazna (Ara. 11) *Kitaab al Yamiini*
Gilbert (Lat. 16) *De Magnete*
Gildas (Lat. 6) *De Excidio et Conquestu Britanniae*
Giraldus (Lat. 12) *Description of Wales*
Gjellerup (Dan. 19) *Book of My Love*
Glaber (Lat. 11) *Historiae*
Glanvill (Lat. 12) *Treatise on the Laws and Customs of the Kingdom of England*
Gö (Tib. 15) *Tep Ter Ngön Po*
Gobind Singh (Pun. 17) *Jup Sahib; Zafar Nama*
Gorakh Nath (Hin. 13) *Works; Poems*
Gorium (Arm. 5) *Life of Mesrop*
Gornicki (Lat. 16) *The Polish Courtier*
Goslicki (Lat. 16) *De Optimo Senatore*
Govar Dhana (San.) *Sapta Śatii*
Govardhanram (Guj. 19) *Works*
Gower (Lat. 14) *Confessio Amantis*
Grammaticus (Lat. 13) *Historia Danica*
Grattius (Lat. −1) *Cynegetica*
Gregorčič (Slo. 19) *Poems*
Gregorius (Lat. 6) *Dialogues; Moralia; Pastoral Rule*
Gregory (Arm. 12) *History of Armenia, 1136-1176*
Grigori (Mag. 15) *Siralomének Both János Veszedelmén*
Grimmelshausen (Ger. 17) *Simplicissimus*
Grotius (Lat. 17) *The Law of War and Peace*

Grunau (Let. 16) *Lord's Prayer*

Gubarru (Sum. −25) *Dialogues*

Gudea (Sum. −23) *Hymns to Ningursu; Prayer to Bau*

Guimerà (Cat. 19) *Terra Baixa*

Gul Mahomed (Sin. 19) *Diwan*

Gumani (San. 16) *Upadaśa Śataka*

Guṇa Bhadra (San.) *Uttara Puraaṇa*

Guṇa Varman (San. 5) *Works*

Gundulić (Ser. 17) *Osman*

Gurulugomi (Cey. 13) *Dharmapradiipikaa*

Gutormsson (Ice. 15) *Háttalykill*

Gwilym (Wel. 14) *Poems*

Ha Jong (Kor. 15) *Adventures of Kyong Op*

Ha Levi (Heb. 12) *Sepher ha Kuzari; Introduction to the Talmud*

Haba Khatun (Kas. 16) *Poems*

Habakkuk (Heb. −7) *The Vision*

Hadassi (Heb. 12) *Eshkol ha Kopher*

Hadewych (Dut. 13) *Poems*

Hadton (Cor. 16) *Beunans Meriasek*

Hafeez Jallundhari (Urd. 18) *Shah Nama i Islam*

Hafiz (Per. 14) *Lisaan al Ghaib; Poems*

Haggai (Heb. −6) *Prophecy*

Hai (Heb. 11) *Treatises on Law; Commentaries; Al Hawi*

Ḥaidar Bakhsh (Urd. 19) *Ṭoṭaa Kahaani*

Hajji Khalifa (Ara., Tur. 17) *Bibliographic and Encyclopedic Lexicon; Khashfu 'l Zunuun*

Ḥakam (Ara. 9) *Conquest of Egypt and the West*

Hala (Pra. 4) *Satta Saii*

Hala Ayudha (San. 10) *Abhi Dharma Ratna Maalaa; Kavi Rahasya*

Haldenstone (Lat. 15) *Copiale Prioratus Sanctiandree*

Hales (Lat. 13) *Summa Theologiae*

Hamadhani (Ara. 11) *Maqaamaat; Letters*

Hamagyaw (Bur. 16) *Tawla*

Hamdani (Ara. 10) *Al Ikliil; Ṣifatu Jaziirat al 'Arab*

Ḥamdullah (Per. 14) *Select History; Zafar Naama*

Hamid (Tur. 19) *A Drama*

Hammurabi (Bab. −18) *When Anu the Exalted*

Hamsun (Nor. 19) *Ny Jord*

Ḥamza (Ara. 10) *Annals*

Hamzah (Mal. 17) *Poems*

Han Fei Tzŭ (Chi. −3) *Han Shu*

Han Yü (Chi. 9) *Essay on Buddhism; Essays; Poems*

"Hanuman" (San.) *Khaṇḍa Praśasi*

Hara Datta Suri (San.) *Raaghava Naiṣadhiiya*

Hari Bhadra (Pra. 8) *Upadeśa Pada*

Hari Chandra (San. 10) *Dharma Śarma Abhyudaya; Jiivandhara Campuu*

Hari Datta (Ben. 13) *Bihulaa and Lakhindar*

Hari Hara (San. 13) *Saṅkha Paraabhava Vyaayoga*

Hari Sena (San. 4) *Kaavya; Prasaati*

Hariri (Ara. 11) *Maqaamaat; Durratu 'l Ghawwaaṣ*

Harpestreng (Dan. 12) *Medicine*

Harṣa (San. 7) *Priyadarśika; Naaga Ananda; Aṣṭa Mahaa Śrii Caitya Stotra; Supra Bhaata Stotra*

Hartmann (Ger. 12) *Iwein*

Harvey (Lat. 17) *The Motion of the Heart and Blood in Animals*

Hasa'i (Ara. 10) *Al Hadiitha*

Ḥasan (Per. 14) *Poems*

Hatifi (Per. 16) *Timur Naama*

Hattusilis (Hit. −13) *Autobiography*

Hattusilis I (Hit. −17) *Oration*

Ḥaziri (Ara., Heb. 13) *Sepher 'Anaq; Raphuath Geviyyah; Takhemoui; Zinaatu 'l Dahr*

Hedhaiyabh (Syr. 7) *Grammar; Philosophy*

Heidenstam (Swe. 19) *The Charles Men; Hans Alienus; Poems; Years of Pilgrimage and Vagabondage*

Hektorović (Ser. 17) *Ribanje; Ribarsko Prigovaranje*

Heliodorus (Gre. 4) *Tales of Ethiopia*

Hema Chandra (Pra., San. 12) *Abhi Dharma Cin Ṭaamaṇi; Deśii Naama Maalaa; Kaavya Anuśa Sana; Tri Ṣaṣṭi Śalaaka Apuruṣa Carita; Pariśiṣṭa Parvan; Yoga Śaastra; Kumaara Paala Carita; Chando 'nu Śaasana; Upadeśa Maala*

Hema Sara Swati (Ass. 13) *Prahlad Charitra*

Herakleitos (Gre. −5) *Epi ton Kosmon*

Herodianos (Gre. 3) *Katholike Prosodia; History of the Roman Empire after the Death of Marcus Aurelius*

Herodotos (Gre. −5) *Historiai*

Hesiodos (Gre. −8) *Theogonia; Works and Days*

Hethous (Arm. 14) *Chronography, 1076–1307; The Tatars*

Hierokles (Gre. 5) *The Golden Words of Pythagoras*

Hieronymus (Lat. 13) *Tractatus de Musica*

Higden (Lat. 14) *Works*

Hilarius (Lat. 12) *Daniel*

Hilarius (Lat.) *De Trinitate*

Ḥimyari (Ara. 12) *Al Qaṣiidatu 'l Ḥimyariyya*

Hippokrates (Gre. −4) *Air, Water and Locations; Aphorismi*

Hippolytus (Gre. 3) *Refutation of All Heresies*

Hirtius (Lat. −1) *Bellum Alexandrinum; Bellum Punicum*

Hispalis (Lat. 7) *Continuatio*

Hoil (Yuc. 18) *The Book of the Jaguar Priest of Chumayel*

Holberg (Lat., Nor. 18) *Comedies; Niels Klim's Underground Journey; Peder Paars*

Homeros (Gre. −9) *Iliados; Odysseia*

Honen (Jap. 13) *Works*

Honorius (Lat. 11) *Gemma Animae*

Horatius (Lat. −1) *De Arte Poetica*

Hori and Amen Emoope (Egy. −13) *Letters*

Hornklofi (Ice. 10) *The Raven Song*

Horus and Seth (Egy. −14) *To Amon*

Hosea (Heb. −8) *Prophecy*

Hrabanus (Lat. 9) *De Universo*

Hsi K'ang (Chi. 3) *Poems*

Hsia Ping (Chi.) *Wen Hsüan*

Hsia Erh Ming (Chi. 18) *Yeh Sao Pao Yen*

Hsiang Hsiu (Chi. 3) *Commentary on Chuang Tzŭ*

Hsiao T'ung (Chi. 6) *Wên Hsüan; Nanch'i Shu*

Hsiao Yen (Chi. 6) *Buddhist Ritual*

Hsieh (Chi. 12) *The Wolf of Chung Shan*

Hsü An Chên (Chi. 9) *Poems*

Hsü Hsieh (Chi. 17) *Essays*

Hsü Hsün (Chi. 4) *Works*

Hsü Kan (Chi. 3) *Pranyamuula Shaastra Tikaa*

Hsü Kuang Ch'i (Chi. 17) *Astronomy; Encyclopedia of Agriculture; Mathematics*

Hsü Shen (Chi. 2) *Shuo Wên Chieh Tzu*

Hsü Yueh (Chi. 3) *Han Chi; Su Shu Chi I*

Hsüan Tsang (Chi. 7) *Hsi Yü Chi*

Hsün (Chi. −3) *Hsün Shu*

Hsün Hsü (Chi. 3) *Essays*

Huai (Chi. 2) *Works*

Huang (Chi. 17) *Ming I Tai Fang Lu*

Huang Fu Mi (Chi. 3) *Essays*

Huang T'ing Chien (Chi. 11) *Poems*

Huang Tsun Hsien (Chi. 19) *Poems*

Huei (Chi. 14) *The Chalk Circle*

Hui (Chi. 5) *Works*

Hujviri (Per. 11) *Kashf al Mahjuub*

Hundt (Lat. 16) *Anthropologium de Hominis Dignitate*

Hung Chüeh Fan (Chi. 12) *Poems*

Hunyady (Mag. 15) *Oath*

Hus (Lat., Cze. 15) *De Sanguine Christi; Christi in Sacramento Altaris; De Arguendo Clero; The Simony of Postilla*

Husain Vaiz (Per. 14) *Anvaar i Suheylii*

Husani (Ara. 10) *Libya*

I Tsing (Chi. 7) *India*

Ibn Abbas (Ara. 12) *The Blessed Jew of Morocco*

Ibn Anas (Ara. 8) *Al Muwaṭṭa*

Ibn 'Arabi (Ara. 13) *Futuuhaat al Makkiyya; Fuṣuuṣuu 'l Ḥikam*

Ibn 'Arabshah (Ara. 15) *'Ajaa'ibu 'l Maqduur*

Ibn 'Asakir (Ara. 12) *History of Damascus*

Ibn Baja (Ara. 12) *The Republic*

Ibn Bashkuwal (Ara.) *Al Ṣila fii Akhbaari A'immati 'l Andalus*

Ibn Baṭṭuta (Ara. 14) *Chain of Histories; Marvels of India; Tuhfatu 'l Nuẓẓar*

Ibn Durayd (Ara. 10) *Al Jamhara fi 'l Lugha; Kitaabu 'l Ishtiqaaq; Maqṣuura*

Ibn Ezra (Ara. 12) *Falasafiiya; Kitaab al Mahadarah*

Ibn Faḍlallah (Ara. 14) *Masaalik al Abṣaar*

Ibn Gabirol (Ara. 11) *The Fount of Life*

Ibn Ḥajar (Ara. 15) *Iṣaaba fii Tamyiiz al Ṣahaaba*
Ibn Hanbal (Ara. 9) *Collection of Thirty Thousand Traditions*
Ibn Hanqal (Ara. 10) *Oriental Geography*
Ibn Ḥasan (Ara.) *The Pearl Strings*
Ibn Hawqal (*see* Istakhri)
Ibn Ḥazm (Ara. 11) *The Dove's Necklace; Kitaabu 'l Milal wa 'l Niḥal*
Ibn Ishaq (Ara. 8) *Siiratu Rasuuli 'llaah*
Ibn Jubair (Ara. 12) *Journey to Mecca*
Ibn Khaldun (Ara. 14) *Muqaddima; Kitaabu 'l Ibar*
Ibn Khallikan (Ara. 12) *Wafayaatu 'l A'yaan*
Ibn Khaqan (Ara. 9) *Qalaa'id al Iqyan*
Ibn Maja (Ara. 9) *Sunan*
Ibn Malik (Ara. 13) *Alfiyya; Summary of Grammar*
Ibn Manẓur (Ara. 14) *Lisaan al 'Arab*
Ibn Miskawayh (Ara. 11) *Works*
Ibn Muhammed (Per.) *Mujmil et Tarikh i Dnadirije*
Ibn Mukarram (Ara. 14) *Lisaanu 'l Arab*
Ibn Munabbeh (Ara. 8) *Africa*
Ibn Munqid (Ara. 12) *Autobiography*
Ibn Muqaffa (Ara. 8) *Kaliila wa Dimna; Siyaru Muluuki 'l 'Ajam*
Ibn Musa (Ara. 8) *Algebra; Kitaabu 'l Zuhd; Mughaazi*
Ibn Qifṭi (Ara. 13) *Ta'riikhu 'l Ḥukamaa*
Ibn Qutayba (Ara. 9) *Book of Classes; Adabu 'l Kaatib; Kitaabu 'l Ma'aarif; Kitaab al Shi'r wa 'l Shu'arra; 'Uyuunu 'l Akhbaar*
Ibn Rashiq (Ara. 11) *'Umda on the Art of Poetry*
Ibn Rushd (Ara. 12) *Tahaafut al Tahaafu; Metaphysics; Physics*
Ibn Sa'd (Ara. 9) *Kitaabu 'l Ṭabaqaat al Kabiir*
Ibn Said (Ara.) *Umm al Qura*
Ibn Sina (Ara., Per. 11) *Danish Naama i 'Alaa 'li; Commentaries; Poems; Qaanuun; Shifaa*
Ibn Ṭufail (Ara. 12) *Ḥayy Ibn Yaqẓaan*
Ibn Usaibi'a (Ara.) *Lives of the Physicians*
Ibn Verga (Heb. 16) *Shebet Yehudah*
Ibn Ya'la (Ara. 8) *Mufaddaliyyaat*

Ibsen (Nor. 19) *Plays*
'Idhadril (Ara.) *Al Bayaan al Mughrib*
Ignatius (Gre. 2) *Epistolai*
Ignatius and Sargis (Arm. 12) *Commentaries on Luke; The Catholic Epistles*
Ihara (Jap. 17) *The Man Who Spent His Life at Lovemaking; Treasury of Japan; Nippon Eitai Gura*
Ikhn Aton (Egy. −14) *Aton; Official Correspondence*
Il Yŏn (Kor. 13) *Sam Guk Yu Sa*
Ilango Adigal (Tam. 2) *Shilappadikaram*
Im Hotep (Egy. −28) *Essays*
'Imad ad Din (Ara. 13) *History of Saladin; History of the Seljuk Dynasty*
4 Imox (Cak. 16) *U Labal ri Zibaki Hay*
Innocent III (Lat. 12) *De Contemptu Mundi*
Innocent X (Lat. 17) *Cum Occasione Impressionis Libri*
Insha Alla Khan (Hin. 18) *Works*
Ioan (Bul. 10) *Book of Heaven; Shestodnev*
Ioannis (Gre. 2) *Epistolai; Evangelion*
Ipu Wer (Egy. −20) *Admonitions*
Irenaeus (Gre. 3) *Against Heresies*
Irugapa (San. 14) *Naana Artha Ratna Maalaa*
Isaiah (Heb. −8) *Prophecy*
Iṣfahani (Ara. 11) *Ḥilyatu 'l Awliyaa; Khariidatu 'l Qaṣr*
Ishmael (Heb. 1) *Mekilta; Sifreh*
Isho'denah (Syr. 8) *The Book of Chastity*
Iskandar (Per. 17) *'Aalomaaraa*
Iskander (Rus. 15) *Taking of Constantinople*
Isma'il (Per. 13) *Poems*
Isnawi (Ara. 14) *Shamsu 'l Diin al Dhanabii*
Israeli (Heb. 13) *Yesodh 'Olam*
Istakhri and Ibn Hawqal (Ara. 10) *Masaaliku 'l Mamaalik*
Isvara (San. 4) *Saaṁkhya Kaarikaa*
Iver (Geo. 5) *Works*
Iver (Geo. 10) *Barlaam and Josephat*
Iztueta (Bas. 19) *History of Guipuzcoa*
'Izzet Molla (Tur. 19) *Poems*

Jabarti (Ara. 19) *Diary; History of Egypt*
Jagan Natha (San. 17) *Rasa Ganga Adhara; Bhaaminii Vilaasa*
Jagannath Das (Ori. 16) *Bhagabata*

Jahiz (Ara. 9) *Kitaabu 'l Hayawaan; Kitaabu 'l Bayaan wa 'l Tabyiin*

Jaimini (San.) *Miimaamsaa Suutras; Puurva Miimaamsaa*

Jalhana (San. 13) *Soma Paala Vilaasa; Subhaa Sita Mukta Avalii; Mugdho Padesa*

Jamal ad Din (Per. 12) *Poems*

James I (Cat. 13) *Chronicle*

Jami (Ara., Per. 15) *Diiwani; Bahaaristaan; Nafahaat al Uns*

Jansenius (Lat. 17) *Augustinus*

Japelj (Slo. 18) *Bible*

Japiks (Fri. 17) *Frisian Poetry*

Jarir and Farazdaq (Ara. 8) *Naaqaa'id*

Jawzi (Ara. 13) *Mir'aatu 'l Zamaan*

Jaya Deva (San. 12) *Candra Aloka; Giitaa Govinda; Prasanna Raaghava*

Jaya Ditya (San. 7) *Kaasikaa Vrtti* (with Vaamana)

Jaya Ratha (San. 12) *Hara Carita Cin Taamani; Alamkaara Vimarsinii*

Jayaa Vallabha (Pra.) *Vajjaalagga*

Jayanta (San. 10) *Nyaaya Mañjarii*

Jayasi (San. 16) *Padumavati*

Jenko (Slo. 19) *Poems*

Jeronimus (Lat. 4) *Biblia*

Jikme (Tib. 19) *Hor Chö Jung*

Jili (Ara. 15) *Al Insaan al Kaamil*

Jina Bhadra (Pra. 7) *Bhaasya*

Jina Dasa (Pra. 7) *Nandii Cuurni*

Jina Kirti (San. 15) *Campakasresthi Kathaanaka; Paala Gopaala Kathaanaka*

Jina Sena (Pra. 8) *Paarsvanaatha*

Jinendra Buddhi (San. 7) *Nyaasa Kaara*

Jippensha (Jap. 19) *Hizakurige*

Jñanesvar (San., Mar. 13) *Hymns; Poems*

Job (Heb. −5) *Lamentations*

Jochumsson (Ice. 19) *Plays; Poems*

John (Lat. 13) *Magna Carta*

John VI (Arm. 10) *History of Armenia*

Jokya (Jav. 15) *Play of Rama*

Jona Raja (San. 15) *Raaja Taranginii*

Jónsson (Ice. 17) *Annals*

Jordan (Cor. 17) *Gwreans an Bys*

Jordanes (Lat. 6) *Romana et Gothica*

Josephus (Lat. 1) *The Ancient History of the Jews*

Joshua (Heb. −2) *Prophecy*

Jude (Gre. 2) *Letter*

Jussieu (Lat. 18) *Genera Plantarum*

Justin (Gre. 2) *Apologia*

Justin (Lat.) *Works*

Justinianus (Lat. 6) *Corpus Juris Civilis; Pandecta; Novellae*

Jurjani (Per. 11) *Fakhr ad Diin As'ad; Viis i Ramin*

Jurjani (Per. 13) *Minhaaj i Siraaj; The Mongol Invasion*

Juvenalis (Lat. 2) *Satires*

Juwaini (Per. 13) *Jahaan Gushaa*

Jyotishwar (Hin. 14) *Works*

Ka San (Kor. 15) *Adventures of Hong Kil Dong*

Kabir (Per. 15) *Poems*

Kali Dasa (San. 4) *Vikrama Urvasiiya; Maalavika Agnimitra; Megha Duuta; Saakuntalaa; Rtusamhaara; Kumaara Sambhava*

Kačić-Miosić (Ser. 18) *Razgovor Ugodni Naroda Slavinskoga*

Kadiri (Per.) *Tuti Naama*

Kadli Hasan (Mal. 14) *Hikayat Bayan Budiman*

Kaibara (Jap. 18) *Onna Daikaku*

Kaju Khan (Pus. 15) *Wars of Swat*

Kalabadhi (Ara. 11) *Works*

Kalankatuatzi (Arm. 7) *History of the Albanians of the Caucasus*

Kalhana (San. 7) *Raaja Taranginii*

Kallimakhos (Gre. −3) *Loutra Pallados*

Kamala Akara (San. 17) *Nirnaya Sindhu*

Kamban (Tam. 10) *Ramayana*

Kanada (San. −3) *Vaisesika Suutras*

Kanaka Sena Vaadi Raaja (San. 10) *Yasodhara Carita*

K'ang Hsi (Chi. 17) *K'ang Hsi Tzŭ Tien; P'ei Wên Yün Fu; P'ien Tzŭ Lei P'ien; Sacred Edict; T'u Shu Chi Ch'êng; Yüan Chien Lei Han*

K'ang T'ai (Chi. 3) *Fu Nan*

Kao Chü Nien (Chi. 12) *Poems*

Kao Tsê Ch'êng (Chi. 15) *P'i P'a Ki*

Kapila (San. −6) *Saamkhya Suutra; Tattva Samaasa*

Karádi (Mag. 16) *Balassi Meynhért*

Karasumaru (Jap. 17) *Chikusai Monogatari*

Karo (Heb. 16) *Beth Joseph; Shulhan Arukh*

Kashgari (Ara. 14) *Diiwan Lughat at Turk*

Kubra (Per. 13) *Ṣifat al Aadaab*

Kula Sekhara (San. 10) *Mukunda Maalaa*

Kulluka (San. 15) *Commentary on the Code of Manu*

Kumara Dasa (San. 7) *Janakiiharana*

Kumara Lata (San. 1) *Kalpanaa Maṇḍitikaa*

Kumāra Vyāsa (Kan. 15) *Mahaa Bhaarata*

Kumarila (San. 8) *Miimaaṁsaa; Śloka Vaarttika*

Kunchan Nambiar (Mlm. 18) *Works*

Kunda Kunda (Pra. 3) *Pravacana Sara; Pañca Astikaaya*

K'ung An Kuo (Chi. −2) *Works*

K'ung Chi (Chi. −4) *Chung Yung; Ta Hsüeh*

K'ung Fu Tzŭ (Chi. −6) *Lun Yü; Shih Ching; Ch'un Ch'iu*

K'ung Jung (Chi. 3) *Poems*

Kung Yang (Chi. −5) *Commentary on the Tso Chuan*

K'ung Ying Ta (Chi. 7) *Commentary on the Classic of Poetry*

Kuntala (San.) *Vakrokti Jiivita*

Kuo Hsiang (Chi. 4) *Lao Tzŭ and Chuang Tzŭ*

Kuo Po (Chi. 4) *Essays*

Kushal Khan Khatak (Pus. 17) *Poems*

Kusuma Deva (San. 15) *Dṛṣṭaanta Śataka*

Kutubi (Ara.) *Fawaatu 'l Wafayaat*

Kyin U (Bur. 19) *Plays*

Kyokutei (Jap. 19) *The Moon Shining through a Cloud Rift on a Rainy Night*

Lactantius (Lat. 3) *The Wrath of God; The Creation; The Divine Institutes; The Deaths of the Persecutors*

Lagadha (San.) *Jyotisha Vedaanga*

Lakshminari Simham (Tel. 19) *Works*

Lakshmisha (Kan. 15) *Epic*

Laksmaṇa Acharya (San. 15) *Caṇḍii Kuca Pañcaa Śikaa*

Laksmaṇa Bhaṭṭa (*see* Bhoja)

Lal Ded (Kas. 14) *Poems*

Lambron (Arm. 12) *Commentary on the Liturgy; Synodal Orations*

Lami'i (Tur. 16) *Poems*

Lamprecht (Ger. 12) *Alexander*

Lan Lu Chou (Chi. 18) *Works*

Lánfili (Iri. 6) *Poems*

Lao (Chi. −3) *Tao Tê Ching*

Larade (Pro. 17) *Sonnets*

Laskaris (Gre.) *Erotemata*

Latif (Ara.) *Description of Egypt*

Layamon (Eng. 9) *Brut*

Laz (Geo.) *Works*

Lazar (Arm. 5) *History of Armenia, 392-485*

Le Loi (Vie. 15) *Poems*

Leo III (Gre. 8) *Ekloga*

Leo VI (Gre. 9) *Basilika*

Leon (Heb. 14) *Sepher ha Zohar*

Leoncius (Arm. 8) *History of the First Caliphs*

Letwethondra (Bur. 19) *Ratus*

Levi (Gre. 1) *Evangelion*

Levita (Heb. 13) *Massoreth ha Massoreth*

Levita (Yid. 16) *Bovo Bukh; Paris un Viene*

Levstik (Slo. 19) *Fugitive King; Martin Krpan*

Leyla (Tur. 19) *Poems*

Lhuyd (Cor. 17) *John of Chy an Hur*

Li Ch'ang Ch'i (Chi. 14) *Chien Teng Yü Hua*

Li Chuan (Chi. 18) *K'ai Fang Shuo*

Li Fang (Chi. 10) *T'ai P'ing Kuang Chi*

Li Fu Yen (Chi. 9) *The Tiger; A Lodging for the Night; The Man Who Became a Fish; Matrimony Inn*

Li Ho (Chi. 9) *Poems*

Li Hua (Chi. 9) *On an Old Battlefield*

Li Kuan Chung (Chi. 13) *Works*

Li Kung Tso (Chi. 9) *The Drunkard's Dream*

Li Po (Chi. 8) *Poems; Works*

Li Po Yao (Chi. 7) *Pei Ch'i Shu*

Li Po Yuan (Chi. 19) *Chinese Officialdom*

Li Shê (Chi. 9) *Poems*

Li Shih Chen (Chi. 16) *Pên Ts'ao*

Li Yang Ping (Chi. 8) *Phonetic Dictionary*

Li Yeh (Chi. 13) *I Ku Yen Tuan; Ts'e Yüan Hai Ching*

Li Yen Shou (Chi. 7) *Nan Shih; Pei Shih*

Li Yü (Chi. 17) *Na Ho T'ien; Mustard Seed Garden Drawing Book; Jou Pu Tuan*

Lieh Tzŭ (Chi.) *Lieh Tzŭ Shu*

Lien Pu (Chi. 11) *Ch'ing Chun Lu*
Lila Śuka (San. 11) *Kṛṣṇa Karṇa Amṛta*
Lin Hsi Chung (Chi. 17) *Commentary*
Lin I Ching (Chi. 12) *Infernal Regions*
Linhart (Slo. 18) *Plays*
Linnaeus (Lat. 18) *Systema Naturae; Species Plantarum*
Lipit Ishtar (Sum. −19) *Hymn*
Liu Ch'ê (Chi. −2) *Poems*
Liu Chi (Chi. 14) *Essays; Poems*
Liu Hêng (Chi. −2) *Poems*
Liu Hsiang (Chi. −1) *Ch'u Tzŭ; Biographies of Eminent Women; Poems*
Liu Hsü (Chi. 10) *T'ang Shih*
Liu Shao (Chi. 3) *Hsia Ching; Jen Wu Chih*
Liu Tieh Shu (Chi. 19) *Travels of Lao*
Liu Tsung Yüan (Chi. 9) *Catching Snakes; Essays*
Liu Yin (Chi. 13) *Essays*
Liutprand (Lat. 10) *Legatio Constantinopolitana; Antapodosis*
Livius (Lat. −1) *Libri ab Urbe Condita*
Llwyd (Wel. 17) *Llyfr y Tri Aderyn*
Lo (Chi. 13) *San Kuo Chih Yen I*
Lôk Pŭtthèr (Cam. 19) *Chbăp Tunmãn Khluon*
Lolimba Raja (San. 11) *Hari Vilasa*
Longinus (Lat. 3) *Peri Hypsous*
Longus (Gre. 3) *Daphnis kai Khloe*
Lorris and Meung (Fre. 13) *Roman de la Rose*
Loyola (Lat. 16) *Exercitia*
Lu Fa Yen (with Yen Chih T'ui) (Chi. 7) *Ch'ieh Yun*
Lu Hsiang Shan (Chi. 12) *Hsiang Shan Hsien Shêng Ch'üan Chi*
Lü Pu Wei (Chi. −3) *Lü Shih Ch'un Ch'iu*
Lü Yüan Lang (Chi. 6) *Defense of Confucianism*
Lucanus (Lat. 1) *Pharsalia; De Bello Civile*
Lucianus (Lat. 2) *Charon; De Morte Peregrini; The Way to Write History; The True History; Alexander the Oracle Monger; The Sale of Lives; The Fisherman; Dialogues of the Gods; Dialogues of the Sea Gods; Dialogues of the Dead; Icaromanippus*
Lucretius (Lat. −1) *De Rerum Natura*
Lukas (Gre. 1) *Evangelion*

Lull (Cat. 13) *Libre de l'Amic e de l'Amat; Libre de Maravelles; Blanquerna*
Luther (Ger., Lat. 16) *Theses; Bible*
Lydus (Lat. 6) *De Magistratibus Populi Romani*
Lykophron (Gre. −2) *Alexandra*

Ma Jung (Chi. 2) *Commentary*
Ma Tuan Lin (Chi. 13) *Wên Hsien T'ung K'ao; Autumn in the Han Palace; Lin Yi*
Ma Tzŭ Jan (Chi. 9) *Poems*
Macarius (Rus. 16) *Chetyi Minéi; Stepénnaya Kniga*
MacDonald (Sco. 18) *Poems*
MacForgaill (Iri. 6) *Amra Choluim Chille*
Macintyre (Sco. 19) *Poems*
Macrae (Sco. 17) *Fernaig Manuscript*
Madhab Kandali (Ass. 14) *Ramayana*
Madhava (San. 14) *Sarva Darśana Saṅgraha*
Madhusudan (Ori. 19) *Songs*
Maerlant (Dut. 13) *Historie van den Grale; Rijmbijbel; Sinte Franciscus' Leven; Hemelychede der Hemelycheit; Der Naturen Bloeme*
Magha (San. 7) *Śiśupaala Vadha*
Magnússon (Ice. 17) *Pislarsaga*
Maha Deva (San. 17) *Abdhuta Darpaṇa*
Maha Naman (San. 5) *Mahaa Vaṁsa*
Maha Sena (Pal. 4) *Diipa Vaṁsa*
Mahasin (Ara. 15) *Al Nujuum al Zaahira*
Mahe Svara (San. 12) *Viśva Prakaaśa*
Mahi Dasa (San.) *Aitareya Upaniṣad*
Makin (Ara. 13) *Majmuu'al Mubaarak*
Malakia (Arm. 13) *History of the Tatars*
Malalas (Gre. 6) *Chronographia*
Malli Natha (San. 12) *Commentary on Megha Duuta*
Mamertus (Lat.) *De Statu Animae*
Mammata (with Alaṭa) (San. 12) *Kaavya Prakaaśa*
Mana Tunga (San. 9) *Bhakta Amara Stotra*
Mančetić (Ser. 15) *Poems*
Mandana Miśra (San. 9) *Vidhiviveka Nyaaya*
Manetho (Gre. −4) *History of Egypt*
Mani (Syr. 3) *Fihrist*
Manikka (Tam. 9) *Tiruvasagan*

Manikya Suri (San. 11) *Yaśodhara Carita*

Manilius (Lat. 1) *Astronomy*

Manjusri (San. 1) *Avatamsaka Suutra*

Maṅkha (San. 12) *Śrii Kaṇṭha Carita; Anekaartha Kośa*

Manu (San. −1) *Manu Smriti*

Maqbool Kralawari (Kas. 19) *Poems*

Maqqari (Ara. 17) *Nafḥu 'l Ṭiib Min Ghuṣni 'l Andalusi 'l Raṭiib wa Dhikri Waziirihaa Lisaani 'l Diin Ibni 'l Khaṭiib*

Maqrizi (Ara. 15) *Description of Egypt; Khiṭaṭ; Suluuk*

March (Cat. 15) *Cants d'Amor*

Marcus (Gre. 1) *Evangelion*

Marcus Aurelius (Gre. 2) *Syllogismoi*

Marpa (Tib. 11) *Poems*

Marqa (Syr. 4) *Memar*

Martialis (Lat. 2) *Epigrams*

Martianus (Lat. 5) *De Nuptiis Philologiae et Mercurii*

Marv (Per. 9) *Ma'muun*

Mas'udi (Ara. 10) *Maruuju 'l Dhahab; Kitaab al Awsaṭ; Akhbaaru 'l Zamaan; Kitaabu 'l Tanbiih wa 'l Ishraaf*

Matavulj (Ser. 19) *The Uskok*

Mati Chandra (San. 7) *Daśa Padaarthi*

Matṛcheṭa (San. 2) *Śata Pañca Satika Stotra*

Mawardi (Ara. 11) *Kitaabu 'l Aḥkaam al Sulṭaaniyya*

Maximilian (Ger. 15) *Theuerdank*

Maydani (Ara. 12) *Al Fakhrii*

Mayura (San. 7) *Suurya Śataka*

Mazrui (Swa. 19) *Utenzi wa Al Akida; Hadithi ya Barosisi; Hadithi ya Hasina*

Medhatithi (San. 10) *Nyaaya Śaastra*

Medinikara (San. 14) *Anekaartha Śabda Kośa*

Medsoph (Arm. 15) *History of Tamurlane*

Megasthenes (Gre. −3) *India*

Megha Vijaya (San. 17) *Pañca Akhyaanod Dhāra*

Mei Shêng (Chi. −2) *Poems*

Meilyr (Wel. 11) *Lament for Trahearn*

Mela (Lat. 1) *De Chorographia*

Melin (Heb. 15) *Sacred Magic*

Menander (Gre. −4) *Epitrepontes*

Menander (Gre. 7) *History of the Wars*

Menčetić (Ser. 15) *Poems*

Meng (Chi. −3) *Meng Tzŭ Shu*

Mêng Hao Jan (Chi. 8) *Poems*

Mercator (Lat. 17) *Logarithmotechnia*

Merriman (Iri. 18) *Cúirt An Mheadhán Oidhehe*

Meru Tuṅga (San. 14) *Prahandha Cinṭaamaṇi*

Merv (Syr. 7) *Catena Patrum on the Gospels; Commentaries*

Mesihi (Tur. 16) *Spring*

Meskha (Geo. 7) *The Wisdom of Valovar*

Mesrob and Sahak (Arm. 4) *Bible*

Mesrop (Arm. 10) *History of Nerses the Great*

Methodius (*see* Cyril)

Micah (Heb. −8) *Prophecy*

Michael I (Syr. 12) *Chronicle*

Midhat (Tur. 19) *Stories*

"Mikhnaf" (Ara.) *The Death of Ḥusayn*

Mila (Tib. 12) *Cotton Clad Mila; The Hundred Thousand Songs*

Milton (Lat. 17) *Defensio pro Populo Anglicano*

Minuchihri (Per. 12) *Diivaan*

Mir Amman (Urd. 19) *Baaq o Bahaar*

Mira Bai (Guj. 15) *Poems*

Mirza Anzari (Pus. 17) *Poems*

Mirza Sahib (Sin. 19) *Zeenat*

Mistral (Pro. 19) *Calendau; Mireio; Nerto; Lou Pouèmo dòu Rose*

Mitra Miśra (San. 17) *Viira Mitro Daya*

Mitsu (Jap. 19) *Dai Nihon Shi*

Mo (Chi. −5) *Mo Tzŭ*

Modrikili (Geo. 10) *Collected Hymns*

Moguel (Bas. 19) *Poems*

Mahà Mās (Cam. 19) *Ṭǐp Sanhvār; Bandàm Pāli; Bèp Kalabat*

Mohammed (Ara. 7) *Al Qur'aan*

Mohsan (Per. 17) *Dabistan ul Mazahab*

Molinier (Pro. 14) *Las Leys d'Amor*

Mollah Abdul Hamid (Pus. 17) *Poems*

Moller (Sor. 16) *Hymnal*

Monmouth (Lat. 12) *Historia Britonum*

More (Lat. 16) *Utopia*

Moropant (Mar. 18) *Poems*

Moses (Heb. −13) *The Ten Commandments*

Moshtotz (Arm. 9) *Armenian Rituals*

Mou (Chi. 2) *Mou Tzŭ*

Mubarrad (Ara. 9) *Kaamil*

Mudaliar (Tam. 19) *Panchatantram*

Muddana (Kan. 19) *Ramashwamedha*

Mufaḍḍal (Ara. 10) *Kitaabu 'l Faakhir*

Muḥammad (Per. 11) *Bayaan al Adyaan*

Muḥammad 'Abduh (Ara. 19)   *Risaalatu 'l Tauḥiid*
Mu'izzi (Per. 12)   *Poems*
Muk (Cam. 19)   *Praḥ Chinănhàvon; Vimān Chan; Cbăp Khmèr*
Muka (San.)   *Pañca Śatii*
Mukteshwar (Mar. 17)   *Epics*
Mukundaraaj (Mar. 12)   *Vivekásindhu*
Munshi 'Abdu'lla (Mal. 19)   *Autobiography; Kalila and Dimna; Pilgrimage to Mecca; Voyage to Kalantan*
Muoth (Rsh. 19)   *Works*
Muqaddasi (Ara. 10)   *Aḥsanu 'l Taqaasiim fii Ma'rifatu 'l Aqaaliim*
Murari (San. 11)   *Anargha Raaghava*
Murasaki (Jap. 11)   *Genji Monogatari; Shikibu Nikki*
Muro (Jap. 17)   *Works*
Mursilis II (Hit. −14)   *Annals*
Murtada (Ara. 18)   *Taj al 'Arus*
Musaios (Gre. 6)   *Hero kai Leander*
Muslim (Ara. 9)   *Al Ṣahiiḥ*
Mutanabbi (Ara. 10)   *Poems*
Mu'tazz (Ara. 9)   *Kitaabu 'l Badii'*
Myawaddi (Bur. 18)   *Eenaung*

Nabi (Tur. 18)   *Poems*
Nabigha (Ara. 7)   *Poems*
Naccinaarkkiniyar (Tam. 13)   *Commentaries*
Naga Arjuna (San. 2)   *Madhyamika Kaarikaa; Madhyamika Suutra; Suḥrllekha*
Naga Chandra (Kan. 12)   *Raama Candra Carita Puraana*
Naga Raja (San. 16)   *Bhaava Śataka*
Nahum (Heb. −7)   *Prophecy*
Na'ima (Tur. 17)   *Chronicles 1591–1695*
Nam (Kor. 15)   *Works*
Nambi (Tam. 11)   *Muuvar Aḍangan Mura*
Namdev (San., Mar. 14)   *Hymns; Poems*
Nammalvar (Tam. 10)   *Works*
Nanak (Pun. 16)   *Jup Sahib; Poems*
Nannaya (Tel. 11)   *Maha Bharata*
Na'od (Eth. 15)   *Sellase; Organ of Praises; Likeness of Mary*
Nara Ayaṇa (San. 17)   *Kito Padeśa; Svaahaasudhaakara Campuu*
Nara Simha (Ori. 13)   *Bhubaneswar Inscriptions*
Nara Simha (Guj. 15)   *Poems*

Narada (San.)   *Dharma Śaastra*
Naram Sin (Sum. −25)   *The War of the Seventeen Kings*
Narmad (Guj. 19)   *Works*
Narpati Nalh (Hin. 12)   *Bisaldeo Raso*
Naṣiri (Per. 11)   *Safar Naama*
Nau'i (Per. 17)   *Suz u Gadaz; Poems*
Nawaji (Ara. 15)   *Ḥalbatu 'l Kumayt*
Nawshahri (Kas. 17)   *Poems*
Naya Chandra (Pra. 15)   *Rambhaa Mañjarii*
Nebuchadrezzar (Bab. −6)   *Speeches*
Nefer Rehu (Egy. −21)   *Prophecy*
Nef'i (Tur. 17)   *Poems*
Nehemiah (Heb. −6)   *Prophecy*
Nemesianus (Lat.)   *Cynegetica*
Nepos (Lat. 2)   *Lives*
Nergisi (Tur. 17)   *Prose and Verse*
Nerses (Arm. 12)   *Elegy on the Capture of Edessa; Hymns; Pastoral Letters; Synodal Orations*
Neshet (Tur. 19)   *Poems*
Nestor (Rus. 12)   *St. Theodosius; Boris and Igor; Nachálnaya Létopis*
Nestorius (Syr. 5)   *Bazaar of Heraclides*
Netzahualcoyotl (Nah. 15)   *Poems*
Neva'i (Tur. 15)   *Poems*
Nev'i (Tur. 16)   *Poems*
Newton (Lat. 16)   *Principia Mathematica; Methodus Fluxionum*
Ngawang (Tib. 17)   *Diary; Record of the Sayings*
Nguyen Du (Vie. 19)   *Kim Van Kieu*
Nicholas (Gre.)   *Learned Ignorance*
Nihal Chand Lahauri (Urd. 19)   *Mazhab i 'Ishq*
Nijaguna Shivayogi (Kan. 15)   *Works*
Nikander (Gre. −3)   *Alexipharmaka; Theriaka*
Nikhomakhos (Gre. 2)   *Introduction to Arithmetic*
Nikon (Rus. 11)   *Nachálnaya Létopis*
Nipal Chand (Mal. 18)   *Gul Bakawali*
Nishati (Urd. 18)   *Phuulban*
Nithard (Lat. 9)   *History of the Wars of the Sons of Louis the Pious*
Nizami (Per. 12)   *Khusrau i Shiirin; Layla i Majnun; Iskandar Naama*
Nobili (Tam. 17)   *Atma Nirṇayam; Satya Veeda Lakshaṇam; Yeesunaadhar Charitram*
Nonnus (Gre. 4)   *Dionysos*
Noor ud Din (Kas. 14)   *Poems*

Nordenflycht (Swe. 18) *The Mourning Turtle Dove*
Norek (Arm. 10) *Meditations; Hymns*
Norinaga (Jap. 18) *Kojiki Den*
Notker (Lat. 9) *Sequentia*
Notker (Ger. 11) *Works*
Nṛpa Tuṅga (Kan. 9) *Kaviraajamaarga*
Núñez (Lat. 16) *Observations on the Obscure and Erroneous Passages in Pliny*
Nusrati (Urd. 17) *Gulshan i 'Ishq; Ali Nama*
Nuwayri (Ara. 14) *Encyclopedia; Nihaayatu 'l Arab*

Ó Gnímh (Iri. 17) *Lament*
Ó Huiginn (Iri. 15) *Poems*
O Huiginn (Iri. 16) *Poems*
Obadiah (Heb. −6) *Prophecy*
Ockham (Lat. 14) *Opera Politica*
Oḍaya Deva (San.) *Gadya Cintaamaṇi*
Odington (Lat. 12) *De Speculatione Musices*
Ögmundarson (Ice. 10) *Love Poems*
Ojha (Ben. 15) *Raamaayana*
Ólafsson (Ice. 18) *Búnadarbálkur; Reise igiennem Island*
Omari (Ara. 14) *Masalik al Absad; Africa without Egypt*
On Nhu Hau (Vie. 18) *Poems*
Oppian (Gre.) *Helieutika*
Orbelian (Arm. 14) *History of Siunik*
Orbeliani (Geo. 18) *Wisdom and Lies*
Orbeliani (Geo. 19) *Imedi*
Origenos (Gre. 3) *Philokalia; Bases*
Orm (Eng. 9) *Ormolum*
Orosius (Lat.) *Historiarum Adversum Paganos*
Orotu (Arm. 14) *Commentaries on the Gospel*
Orzechowski (Lat. 16) *Quincunx*
Ostrorog (Lat. 15) *Memoir on the Organization of the Republic*
Otfrid (Ger. 9) *Gospel History*
Ou Yang Hsiu (Chi. 11) *Hsin Wu Tai Shih; T'ang Shih*
Ovidius (Lat. 1) *Amores; Ars Amandi; Fasti; Heroides; Medea; Metamorphoses*
Owen (Wel. 19) *Rhys Lewis*

Padma Gupta (San. 11) *Navasaahasaan Carita*
Padma Pada (San. 9) *Pañca Paadika*

Padua (Lat. 14) *Defensor Pacis*
Paisi (Bul. 18) *History of the Slavonic Bulgarians*
Päivärinta (Fin. 19) *Elämäni*
Palacký (Cze. 19) *Poems*
Palamas (Gre. 14) *Poems*
Palden (Tib. 17) *The Carriage of the Happy Ones*
Palitsyn (Rus. 17) *Skazanie*
Palladios (Gre.) *Dialogue on the Life of Chrysostom*
Palol (Cat. 12) *Poems*
Pampa (Kan. 11) *Champu*
Pan (Cam. 19) *Bandàm Sèthĕ; Prah Rāch Ponhsàvadà*
Pan (Chi. 2) *Ch'ien Han Shu*
Panini (San. −4) *Aṣṭa Adhyaayii; Sikshaa*
Panyasis (Gre. −5) *Herakleia*
Pao Chao (Chi. 5) *Poems*
Parama Ananda (San.) *Sṛṅgaara Sapta Satikaa*
Parkosz (Pol. 15) *Works*
Patanjali (San. −2) *Maha Yoga Bhaaṣya; Tattva Vaicaradi*
Paterculus (Lat. 1) *Works*
Paternas (Pro. 14) *Lo Libre de Sufficència e de Necessitat*
Paul (Syr. 6) *Logic*
Paulus (Lat. 9) *Historia Lombardorum*
Pausanias (Gre. 2) *Description of Greece*
Peddana (Tel. 15) *Manu Charitra*
Pedersen (Dan. 16) *Bible*
P'ei Hsiu (Chi. 9) *The Teachings of Hsi Yun*
P'ei Sung Chih (Chi. 5) *Commentary on the Memoir of the Three Kingdoms*
Peisander (Gre. −7) *Herakleia*
Pepi II (Egy. −23) *Instructions to Harkhuf*
Peresvetov (Rus. 16) *Sultan Mehmed*
Peretz (Yid. 19) *Yom Tov Bletlekh*
Pertev (Tur. 19) *Poems*
Pertev Pasha (Tur. 19) *Poems*
Petrabianca (Alb. 17) *Catechism*
Petri (Swe. 16) *Bible; Homilies; Hymns; Svenska Krönika*
Petritsi (Geo. 12) *The Origin of Man*
Petronius (Lat. 1) *Satyricon; Trimalchio*
Petrus (Lat. 12) *Gesta Hungarorum*
Philo (Lat.) *Quod Omnis Probus Liber*
Photios (Gre. 9) *Myriobiblion*

Phra Horatibodi (Tha. 18) *Chindamani*
Phra Narai (Tha. 16) *Poems*
Pico (Lat. 15) *Oratio de Hominis Dignitate*
Pien (Chi. −5) *Nan Ching*
Pindaros (Gre. −5) *Odes*
Pingala (San.) *Treatise on Meter*
Plade (Dan. 16) *Visitatsbog*
Planudes (Gre. 15) *Aesop's Fables*
Platon (Gre. −4) *Ta Politeia; Ton Symposion; Protagoras; Phaido; Krito; Gorgias; Apologia; Meno; Lysis; Kratylos; Philebos; The Sophist; Thaetetos; Parmenides*
Plautus (Lat. −2) *The Captives; Menaechmi*
Plinius (Lat. 1) *Historia Naturalis*
Plinius Junior (Lat. 1) *Epistolae*
Ploeg (Fri. 18) *Comedies*
Plotinus (Gre. 3) *Enneadoi*
Plutarkhos (Gre. 2) *Bioi Paralleloi; Moralia*
Po Chü I (Chi. 9) *Poems; Works*
Po Jen Fu (Chi. 13) *Rain under the Wutung*
Po Nagar (Cha. 19) *Chronicle*
Poggio (Lat. 15) *Liber Facetiarum*
Polybios (Gre. −2) *Historiae*
Pompeius (Lat.) *Philippica*
Pon Nya (Bur. 19) *Wizaya Zat; Paduma; The Water Carrier; Waythandaya*
Ponna (Kan. 11) *Champu*
Pontoppidan (Dan. 19) *Soil*
Porphyrios (Gre.) *Abstention from Animal Food*
Porphyrogenitus (Gre. 11) *The Book of Ceremonies*
Porretanus (Lat.) *Commentaria in Boetii; De Sex Principiis*
Potana (Tel. 13) *Bhagavatam*
Potter (Dut. 15) *Elckerlyc*
Poýgaiyar (Tam. 4) *Poems*
Praajya Bhaṭṭa and Suka (San. 16) *Raaja Valipataakaa*
Prabhakara (San. 7) *Miimaaṁsaa*
Praḥ Bàt (Cam. 19) *Chbăp Srĕi; Enhàv; Chamhpà Thònh*
Prakash Ram Kurigami (Kas. 18) *Ramavatara Charita*
Prashasta Pada (San. 5) *Vaiśeṣika Bhaaṣya*
Pravara Sena (Pra. 6) *Setubandha*

Prêk Pranhàk (Cam. 19) *Praḥ Lakṣĕnavonh*
Prem Ananda (Guj. 17) *Poems; Akhyanas*
Preševeren (Slo. 19) *Poems*
Priskos (Gre. 5) *Modern History*
Pritam Das (Sin. 19) *Ajib Bheta*
Prithvi Narayan Shah (Nep. 18) *Memoirs*
Proklos (Gre. 5) *Commentary on Euclid*
Prokopios (Gre. 6) *Anecdota; Buildings; History of the Wars of Justinian*
Psykhares (Gre. 19) *Taxidi Mou*
Ptah Hotep (Egy. −27) *Sbooyet*
Ptolemaios (Gre. 2) *Almagesta*
P'u Sung Ling (Chi. 17) *Liao Chai Chih I*
Pujol (Cat. 17) *Epic of Lepanto*
Pumpurs (Let. 19) *Laačpleesis*
Puru Ṣottama Deva (San.) *Tri Kaaṇḍa Śeṣa; Hara Avalii*
Puṣpa Danta (Pra. 9) *Mahimnaḥ Stava; Mahaa Puraaṇu; Jasahara Cariü; Naaya Kumaara Cariü*
Putön (Tib. 14) *Treasury of the Precious Scriptures*
Puurṇa Bhadra (San. 12) *Pañca Akhyaanaka*

Qa'ani (Per. 19) *Pariishaan*
Qadir (Ara. 17) *Khizaanatu 'l Adab*
Qali (Ara. 10) *Kitaabu 'l Adab*
Qalqashandi (Ara. 15) *Subh al A'sha*
Qayyara (Heb. 9) *Greater Halakhoth*
Qazi Qazan (Sin. 15) *Verses*
Qazwini (Ara.) *Aatharu 'l Bilaad*
Qimhi (Heb. 12) *Sepher ha Berith*
Qirqisani (Ara. 10) *Kitaab al Anwai*
Quintilianus (Lat. 1) *Institutio Oratoria*
Quintus (Gre. 4) *The Sequel to the Iliad*
Qushayri (Ara. 11) *Risaalatu 'l Qushayriyya*

Rabbihi (Ara.) *Al 'Iqd al Fariid*
Rabinovitch (Yid. 19) *Menakhem Mendel*
Rada (Alb. 19) *Skënderbeg*
Radha Nath (Ori. 19) *Mahayatra; Poems*
Raffi (Arm. 19) *Khent*
Raftery (Iri. 19) *Poems*
Raghunath (Mar. 17) *Poems*
Rahman (Ara. 10) *The Fixed Stars*

Rai (Jap. 19) *Nihon Gwaishi*

Raja Sekhara (Pra. 10) *Karpura Mañjarii; Biddha Shala Bhanjika; Kaavya Miimaaṃsaa*

Raja Śekhara (San. 14) *Prabandha Kośa*

Ralopa (Tib. 7) *Poems*

Rama III (Tha. 19) *Mangalataka Dispani*

Rama VI (Tha. 19) *Koh Lok*

Rama Chandra (San. 16) *Rasikarañjana*

Rama Nuja (San. 12) *Śrii Bhaaṣya; Giitaa Bhaaṣya; Veda Artha Sanigraha; Vedaanta Saara*

Rama Raja Bhushana (Tel. 17) *Works*

Rama Swami Raju (San. 19) *Rajangala Mahodyana*

Ran Aung Myin Sayadaw (Ark. 18) *Kya Khwetsa*

Ranina (Ser. 16) *Poems*

Raniri (Mal. 17) *Bustan al Salatin; Sirat al Muskatim*

Ranna (Kan. 11) *Champu*

Ras'ain (Syr. 6) *Logic; The Causes of the Universe; Genus, Species and Individuality; The Action and Influence of the Moon*

Rashi (Heb. 12) *Commentaries*

Rashid ad Din (Per. 14) *Jaami' ut Tawaariikh*

Rashid Vatvat (Per. 12) *Qasiida; Treatises on Poetry*

Ratherius (Lat. 10) *Praeloquia; Phrenesis*

Ratnakara (San. 9) *Haravijaya; Vakrokti Pañca Śikaa*

Ratnakara Varni (Kan. 16) *Epic*

Ravandi (Per. 13) *Raahat aṣ Ṣuduur*

Ravi Deva (San. 16) *Rākṣasa Kaavya*

Rawiya (Ara. 8) *Al Mu'allaqaat*

Ray (Ben. 18) *Vidyaasundar*

Raya Muku Tamani (San. 15) *Commentary*

Razi (Ara. 13) *Comprehensive Book of Koranic Commentary*

Razi (Ara., Per. 16) *Haft Iqliim; Al Kitaab al Manṣuurii*

Regiomontanus (Lat. 15) *De Triangulis*

Reynoso (Qui. 16) *Otzoya*

Rhianos (Gre. −3) *The Messenians*

Rhodios (Gre. 3) *Argonautika*

Richer (Lat. 10) *Historiae*

Rogerius (Lat. 13) *Carmen Miserabile*

Rohal (Sin. 18) *Poems*

Romanus (Syr. 9) *Medicine*

Rossi (Heb. 16) *Me'or 'Enayim*

Roswitha (Lat. 10) *Carmen de Gestis Ottonis; Comedies*

Rouergue (Pro. 13) *Chanson de la Croisade*

Rudagi (Per. 9) *Poems; Kalila and Dimna*

Rudbeck (Swe. 17) *Atland*

Rudra Bhaṭṭa (San.) *Śṛṅgaara Tilaka*

Rudra Daasa (Pra. 17) *Candralekhaa*

Rudraṭa (San. 9) *Kaavya Alaṁkaara*

Ruhi (Tur. 16) *Poems*

Rumi (Per. 13) *Poems*

Rupago Svamin (San.) *Padya Avalii*

Russudianu (Geo. 14) *Works*

'Rustam (Syr. 7) *Lives*

Rustami (Urd. 17) *Khawor Nama*

Rustaveli (Geo. 13) *Vepkhis—T'qaosani*

Rutebeuf (Fre. 13) *Theophilus; Dit de l'herberie*

Ruysbroek (Dut. 14) *Die Chierheit der geesteliker Brulocht*

Ruyyaka (San. 12) *Alaṁkaara Sarvasva*

Sa'adi (Per. 13) *Buustaan; Gulistaan; Diiwan*

Śabara Svaamin (San. 5) *Miimaaṁsaa Bhaaṣya*

Sabi' (Ara. 11) *Book of Viziers*

Sabir (Per. 12) *Poems*

Sabit Ali Shah (Sin. 18) *Elegies*

Sachal (Sin. 18) *Kafis*

Sachs (Ger. 16) *Poems*

Sa'd ud Diin (Tur. 16) *Poems*

Sadashivendra (San.) *Brahma Tattva Prakaśika*

Sadasukh Lal (Hin. 18) *Works*

Sadi (Ara. 16) *Taariikh es Sudan*

Safadi (Ara. 14) *Dictionary; Waafii bi 'l Wafayaat*

Saggil Kinam Ubbib (Bab. −10) *Theodicy*

Sahdona (Syr. 7) *Life of Mar Jacob*

Sa'id (Per. 11) *Ṣuufii Quatrains*

St. Gall (Lat. 9) *De Carolo Magno*

Saiyid Abdallah (Swa. 18) *Al Inkishafi*

Saiyid Aidarus (Swa. 18) *Al Hamziyah*

Sakalya (San.) *Ṛk Pratiśaakhya*

Sakya Mitra (San. 9) *Pañca Krama*

Salik (Eth. 16) *Maṣhafa Ḥawi*

Salisbury (Lat. 12) *Metalogicon; Policraticus; Entheticus; Historia Pontifi-*

calis; *Vita Sancti Anselmi Archiepiscopi; Vita Sancti Thomae Cantaruensis Archiepiscopi et Martyris*

Sallustius (Lat. −1) *Bellum Jugurthinum; De Catalinae Coniuratione*

Salman (Per. 14) *To the Jalair Uvays*

Samala (Guj. 16) *Poems*

Samarqandi (Per. 15) *Matla' as Sa'dain*

Sambhu (San. 11) *Anyokti Muktaalataa Sataka; Raajendra Karna Puura*

Samgha Dasa (Pra. 6) *Vasu Deva Hindii*

Sami (Sin. 18) *Poems*

Samuel (Heb. −6) *Prophecy*

Sana'i (Per. 12) *Hadiiqat ul Haqiiqat*

Sandhya Akara Nandin (San. 12) *Raama Paala Carita*

Sanggye (Tib. 17) *Bai Durya Kar Po*

Sanghara Kkhita (San.) *Vuttodaya*

Sanhaji (Ara. 14) *Aajurruumiyya*

Sani' (Per. 19) *Mir'aat al Buldaan; Matla' ash Shams*

Sankar Deva (Ass. 15) *Works*

Sankara (San. 9) *Mohamudgara; Braahma Suutra Bhaasya; Aananda Laharii; Bhava Anyastaka; Sata Slokii; Dvaa Dasa Pañjarikaa Stotra*

Sankara (San. 18) *Sankara Ceto Vilaasa Campuu*

Santi Deva (San. 7) *Bodhi Carya Avatāra; Siksaa Samuccaya*

Santo (Jap. 18) *Edifying Story Book*

Sanusi (Ara. 15) *Introduction to Theology*

Sappho (Gre. −6) *Poems*

Sara Datanaya (San. 13) *Bhaava Prakaaśa*

Sara Svati (San.) *Satyarth Prakash; Brahma Tattva Prakaśika*

Sarala Das (Ori. 14) *Mahbharat*

Saramga Deva (San. 13) *Samgiitaa Ratnaakara; Durghatavrtti*

Sargis (*see* Ignatius)

Sargon I (Bab. −26) *King of Battle*

Sarma (San. 19) *Jitavrittanta*

Sarmiento (Gal. 18) *Poems*

Sarnga Dhara (San. 14) *Puddhati*

Sarshar (Urd. 19) *Fisana e Azad*

Sarva Ananda (San. 14) *Jagaduu Carita*

Sarva Varman (San. 4) *Kaa Tantra*

Sarvajna (Kan. 17) *Satires*

Sarvajña (San.) *Sragdhara Stotra*

Sasvata (San. 6) *Anekaartha Samuccaya*

Sau Kau Too (Kar. 19) *Thesaurus*

Saul (Gre. 1) *Epistolai*

Saunaka (San. −5) *Brihad Devata; Grihya Suutra; Deities and Myths of the Vedas*

Saya Kiaw Zan (Kar. 19) *Sa Tu Waw*

Saya Pwa (Bur. 19) *Burmese Literary Art*

Saya Thein (Bur. 19) *The History of Certain Burmese Characters*

Scaurus (Lat. 1) *Atreus*

Seami (Jap. 15) *Nakamitsu (Manju); Ninety-three Noo Plays*

Sebeos (Syr. 7) *Wars of Heraclius and the Arabs*

Sechen (Mon. 17) *Erdeni Yin Tobchi*

Sedulius (Lat. 9) *Carmen Paschale*

Seekkilar (Tam. 12) *Periya Puraanam*

Sei (Jap. 10) *Makura Zoshi*

Sehete Pibre (Egy. −19) *Sbooyet*

Selim I (Tur. 16) *Poems*

Sempat (Arm. 13) *Chronicle of Lesser Armenia*

Sen Usret I (Egy. −20) *Founding the Temple*

Sena Pati (Ori. 19) *Chhamana Athaguntha; Lachhama; Mamoo; Prayaschitta*

Seneca (Lat. 1) *Quaestiones Naturales; Medea; Consolatio ad Marciam; Consolatio ad Helvetiam; Consolatio ad Polybium; Essays on Stoicism*

Seng (Chi. 7) *Works*

Sequoyah (Che. 19) *Tsalagi Tsulehisanühi*

Serafi (Lat. 16) *Poems*

Sevillanus (Lat. 7) *Etymologiae sive Origines*

Shafarva (Per. 12) *Poems*

Shafi'i (Ara. 9) *Works*

Shahrastani (Ara. 12) *Kitaabu 'l Milal wa 'l Nihal*

Shams al Din (Mal. 17) *Works*

Shanfara (Ara. 6) *Laamiyatu 'l 'Arab*

Shang (Chi. −4) *Shang Chu Shu*

Shao Yung (Chi. 11) *Poems*

Sha'rani (Ara. 16) *Lataa'ifu 'l Intisaar; Yawaaqiit; Lawaaqihu 'l Anwaar*

Sharruwa (Bab. −14) *The Autobiography of Idri Mi*

Shavteli (Geo. 12) *Abdul Messia*

Shebisteri (Per.) *The Rose of Mystery*

Sheikh Mali (Pus. 15) *Conquest of Swat*

Shen Te Fu (Chi. 17) *Ku Ch'ü Tsa Yen*
Shên Yo (Chi. 6) *Sung Shu; The Ch'i; The Chin*
Sher 'Ali Afsos (Urd. 19) *Aaraaish i Mahfil*
Sherira (Heb. 10) *Letter*
Shi Nai An (Chi. 14) *Shui Hu Chuan*
Shinasi (Tur. 19) *French Poets*
Shinran (Jap. 13) *Works*
Shiraz (Per. 14) *Taariikh i Wassaf*
Shirbini (Ara. 17) *Hazzu 'l Quhuuf*
Shirvani (Per. 19) *Bustaan i Siyaahat*
Shulgi (Sum. −21) *Hymn*
Shun (Man. 17) *Han I Araha Ampasai Mutzilen Pe Dara Pure Bitkhe*
Siddharsi (San. 10) *Upamiti Bhava Prapañca Kathaa*
Sigvat (Ice. 11) *Bersöglis Viisur*
Śila Acharya (Pra. 9) *Mahaa Puruṣa Carita*
Silius (Lat. 1) *Punica*
Simokatta (Gre. 7) *Universal History; Dialogue between Philosophy and History*
Sinan (Tur. 15) *Tazarru'aat*
Sitakantha (Kas. 13) *Manayana Prakasa*
Śiva Svamin (San. 9) *Kapphiṇa Abhyudaya*
Śive Dasa (San. 15) *Vetaala Pañca Viṃśa Tikaa; Kathaarṇava; Śaalivaahana Kathaa; Bhikṣaaṭana Kaavya*
Skaldaspillar (Ice. 11) *Hákonarmál*
Skallagrímsson (Ice. 10) *Sonatorrek*
Skovoroda (Ukr. 18) *Ashkan; Friendly Conversation; Narcissus*
Smotritsky (Ukr. 17) *Grammar*
Sŏ and Chung (Kor. 15) *Tong Guk T'ong Gam*
Soddhala (San. 11) *Udaya Sundarii Kathaa*
Sofony (Rus. 14) *Zadonschina*
Sŏl Ch'ŏng (Kor. 11) *Hwa Wang Yu*
Solomos (Gre. 19) *Eleutheroi Poliorkemenoi*
Soma Deva (San. 11) *Kathaa Sarit Saagara; Yaśastilaka*
Soma Prabha (Pra. 13) *Kumarapāla Pratibodha; Śṛṅgaara Vaira Agya Taraṅginii*
Someśvara Datta (San. 13) *Kiirti Kaumudi; Surathotsava*
Sönam (Tib. 19) *Gyal Rap Sal Waï Me Long*

Sophokles (Gre. −5) *Antigone; Oidipous Basileus; Elektra; Philoktetes; Women of Trachis; Oedipus at Colonus*
Soterichos (Gre. 4) *Bassarica*
Spartianus (Lat. 4) *Historia Augusta*
Spinoza (Lat. 17) *De Intellectus Emendatione; Political Treatises*
Śri Andal (Tam. 10) *Works*
Sri Dhara (San. 10) *Nyaaya Kandalii*
Sri Dhara Daasa (San. 13) *Sadukti Karṇa Amṛta*
Śri Harṣa (San. 12) *Naiṣadhiiya; Khandanakhandakhaadya; Śleṣ Artha Pada Saṃgraha; Ṇavasaaha Saaṅka Carita*
Śri Natha (Tel. 14) *Naishadam*
Śri Praj (Tha. 16) *Anirud; Khlong Kamruen*
Śri Vara (San. 15) *Jaina Raaja Taraṅginii; Subhaa Ṣita Avalii*
Ssŭ K'ung T'u (Chi. 9) *Poems*
Ssŭ Yŭ Têng (Chi. 19) *Diary*
Statius (Lat. 1) *Thebais; Akhilleis; Silvae*
Steingrímsson (Ice. 18) *Autobiography*
Steinhöwel (Ger. 15) *Fables*
Stenvall (Fin. 19) *Parish Cobblers; Seitsemän Veljestä*
Stiernhielm (Swe. 17) *Hercules*
Stifel (Lat. 16) *Arithmetica Integra*
Stítný (Cze. 14) *Pious Dialogues; Six Books on the Common Christian Things*
Strabo (Gre. 1) *Geographia; Upomnemata Historika*
Stránský (Cze. 17) *The Bohemian Republic*
Strassburg (Ger. 13) *Tristan und Isolde*
Strindberg (Swe. 19) *Autobiography; Plays; I Havsbandet*
Stritar (Slo. 19) *Viennese Sonnets*
Sturluson (Ice. 13) *Edda; Heimskringla*
Su Chê (Chi. 11) *Commentary on Tao Tê Ching*
Su Shih (Chi. 11) *Journals*
Su Tung P'o (Chi. 11) *Essays; Poems*
Suárez (Lat. 10) *De Legibus ac Deo Legislatore*
Subandhu (San. 7) *Vaasava Dattaa*
Sudraka (San. 4) *Mṛcchaka Ṭikaa*
Suetonius (Lat. 1) *De Vita Caesarum*
Suhrawardi (Ara. 13) *'Awaarifu 'l Ma'aarif*
Śuka (San. 16) (*see* Praajya Bhaṭṭa)

Sukkari (Ara. 9) *Ash'aaru 'l Hudha-liyyiin; Old Arabic Poetry*
Sulami (Ara. 11) *Ṭabaqaatu 'l Ṣuufiyya*
Suli (Ara. 10) *Literary History*
Sum (Tib. 18) *Rhetoric and Drama; A General Account of the World*
Sun I Jang (Chi. 19) *Mo Tzŭ Hsien Ku*
Sun Shu Jan (Chi. 3) *Commentary*
Sun Tzŭ (Chi. −6) *Ping Fa*
Sung (Chi. 13) *Hsi Yüan Lu*
Sung Ch'i (Chi. 8) *Chi Yün*
Sung Chih Wên (Chi. 8) *Poems*
Sung Tzŭ (Chi.) *Medical Jurisprudence*
Sur Das (Hin. 16) *Krishna*
Surana (Tel. 16) *Kalapurnodayam; Prabhavati Pradyumnam*
Suśruta (San. 4) *Medicine*
Suyuṭi (Ara. 15) *Ḥusnu 'l Muhaadara; Itqaan; Muzhir; Tafsiiru 'l Khulafaa*
Swedenborg (Lat. 18) *Arcana Coelestia; Doctrina Vitae pro Novo Hierosolyma; Vera Christiana Religio*
Synesios (Gre.) *Essays and Hymns*
Syv (Dan. 17) *The Cimbric Language*
Székely (Mag. 16) *Cronica ez Világnac yeles Dolgairól*
Szu Ma Ch'ien (Chi. −2) *Shih Chi*
Szu Ma Kuang (Chi. 11) *Tzŭ Chih T'ung Chien*

Ṭabari (Ara. 10) *Tafsiir; Ta'riikhu 'l Rusul wa 'l Muluuk*
Tabi Utul Enlil (Sum. −25) *Lament*
Tacitus (Lat. 1) *Agricola; Annalia; Germania; De Oratoria*
Taghrit (Syr. 9) *The Science of Rhetoric*
Tagore (Ben. 19) *Giitaañjali*
Tahir (Per. 11) *Poems*
Tahsin ud Din (Urd. 17) *Qiṣṣa e Ruup o Kaalaa*
Tai Chên (Chi. 18) *Mêng Tzŭ Tzŭ I Su Chêng; Yüan Shan; Tai Tung Yüan*
Tai and Tai (Chi. 1) *Li Chi*
Tai Tung (Chi. 13) *Liu Shu Ku*
Taliesin (Wel. 6) *Poems*
Tamenari (Jap. 12) *O Kagami*
Tanukhi (Ara. 10) *Faraj Ba'd ash Shidda; Nishwaar al Muhaadara*
T'ao (Chi. 5) *Poems*
T'ao Ch'ien (Chi. 4) *Peach Blossom Fountain*
Ṭash (Tur. 17) *Biographies*

Tatius (Gre. 5) *Leukippe kai Kleitophon*
Taumanavar (San. 18) *Hymns*
Taymuraz I (Geo. 17) *Poems*
Tchamitch (Arm. 18) *History of Armenia*
Teika (Jap. 13) *Hyaku Nin Isshu*
Tella (Syr. 6) *Five Hundred Thirty-eight Canons; Answers to Sergius; Trisagion*
Teneli Rama Krishna (Tel. 17) *Works*
Terentius (Lat. −2) *Andria; The Eunuch; Heauton Timoroumenos; Phormio; Adelphi*
Tha'alibi (Ara. 11) *Yatiimatu 'l Dahr*
Theodolfus (Lat. 9) *Poems*
Theodoric (Lat. 6) *Edicts*
Theodoros (Gre. 12) *Dosicles and Rodanthe; Essays; The Twelve Months*
Theokritos (Gre. −4) *Idylls*
Theophrastos (Gre. −3) *Peri Semeion; Kharakteres*
Thilawuntha (Tha. 16) *Grammar; Poems; Yazawingyaw Chronicle*
Thomsen (Ice. 19) *Heljarslódarorusta*
Thonburi (Tha. 18) *Ramakien*
Thorláksson (Ice. 16) *Bible*
Thrax (Gre. −2) *Tekhne Grammatike*
Thruogveli (Geo. 12) *Visramiani*
Thukydides (Gre. −4) *History of the Peloponnesian War*
Thuróczi (Lat. 15) *Chronicon Rerum Hungaricum*
Ti Srong Dé Tsén (Tib. 7) *Poems*
Tien (Cam. 19) *Prah Chïnovonh*
Timothy (Syr. 9) *Epistles; Law*
Ṭiqtaqa (Ara. 14) *Al Fakhrii*
Tirmidhi (Ara. 9) *Jaami'*
Tirumangai (Tam. 8) *Poems*
Tirumular (Tam. 5) *Works*
Tiruvallavar (Tam. 2) *Kurral*
Tissa (Pal. −1) *Kathaa Vatthu*
Tlay (Arm. 12) *Dogma; Elegy on the Capture of Jerusalem*
T'o (Chi. 11) *Chin Shih; Liao Shih; Sung Shih*
Toe (Bur. 18) *Rama Yagan*
Tokinaga (Jap. 13) *Gempei Monogatari; Heiji Monogatari; Hogen Monogatari*
Tondaradipodi (San. 9) *Hymns*
Torres (Qui. 16) *Historia Quiché*
Toul (Lat. 10) *Ecbasis Captivi*
Tours (Lat. 6) *Historia Francorum*
Trailok (Tha. 15) *Phra Law*

Travers (Rsh. 16) *Chanzum de la guerra daig Chastè d'Müs*

Tri Vikrama Bhaṭṭa (San. 10) *Damayantii Kathaa; Madaalasaa Campuu*

Trinle (Tib. 18) *The Ocean Chariot of Real Attainment*

Isaac of Troki (Heb. 16) *Hizzuq Emunah*

Solomon of Troki (Heb. 18) *Appiryon*

Troyes (Fre. 12) *Perceval*

Trubar (Slo. 16) *Works*

Tryphiodoros (Gre. 5) *The Sack of Ilium*

Ts'ai Yen (Chi. 2) *Measure of the Mongol Horn*

Tsanyang (Tib. 17) *Poems*

Ts'ao (Chi. 17) *Hung Lou Meng*

Ts'ao Chih (Chi. 3) *Poems*

Tschudi (Ger. 16) *Chronicle*

Tsjessens (Fri. 16) *Prophecy*

Tso (Chi. −5) *Kuoh Yü*

Tsong Ka Pa (Tib. 14) (ed.) *The Secret Collection*

Tsu (Chi. 5) *Chui Shu*

Ts'ui Hao (Chi. 8) *Poems*

Tsung Ch'ên (Chi. 16) *Essays*

Tsurayuki (Jap. 10) *Kokinshu; Tosa Nikki*

Tu Ch'in Niang (Chi. 9) *Poems*

Tu Fu (Chi. 8) *Autobiography; Poems*

Tu Kwang T'ing (Chi. 10) *Curly Beard*

Tu Yu (Chi. 8) *T'ung T'ien*

Tuan Ch'eng Shih (Chi. 8) *Cinderella*

Ṭughra'i (Ara. 12) *Laamiyyatu 'l 'Ajam*

Tukaram (San. 17) *Hymns*

Tulkourantzi (Arm. 16) *Poems*

Tulsi Das (Ben. 17) *Raama Carita Manasa*

Tung (Chi. 17) *Reminiscences*

Tung Chung Shu (Chi. −1) *Luxuriant Dew from the Spring and Autumn Annals*

Tung Fang So (Chi. −2) *Poems*

Udaya III (Cey. 10) *Regulations*

Udayana (San. 10) *Kiri Naavalii; Lakṣa Naavalii; Taatparya Ṭiika Pariśuuddhi; Kusa Maañjalii*

Udbhata (San. 9) *Kaavya Alamkaara Sara Samgraha; Alamkaara Samgraha*

Uddyotakara (San. 7) *Nyaaya Vaarttika*

Udjahorresne (Egy. −6) *King Darius*

Uggya Byan (Bur. 19) *Tase Hna Ra Thi Ratu*

Ui (Chi.) *The Vaiśeṣika Philosophy according to the Dasa Padartha Śaastra*

Uk (Cam. 19) *Sành Sĕl Chei*

Ulfilas (Got. 4) *Bible*

Umapati (Tam. 14) *Commentaries*

Un Ammon (Egy. −11) *Voyage to Byblos*

'Unsuri (Per. 12) *Poems*

Upendra Bhanja (Ori. 18) *Baidehisa Bilasa*

'Urfi (Per. 16) *Poems*

Usaibi'a (Ara. 10) *Ṭabaqaatu 'l Aṭibbaa; 'Uyunnu 'l Anbaa*

Utpala Deva (San. 10) *Stotra Avalii*

Vachas Pati Mitra (San. 9) *Bhaamati; Nyaaya Vaarttika Taatpara Ṭiikaa; Saamkha Tattva Kaumudii; Tattva Vaiśa Araadii*

Vag Bhaṭa (San. 13) *Kaavya Anuśa Asana*

Vag Bhaṭa (San. 12) *Nemi Nirvaaṇa; Alamkaara*

Vagh Bata (San. 7) *Medical Compendium*

Vahram (Arm. 13) *Chronicle of the Kings of Lesser Armenia*

Vak Pati Raja (Pra. 8) *Gaüdavaha*

Vakhtung VI (Geo. 15) *History of Georgia*

Valerius (Lat. 1) *Argonautica; Factorum et Dictorum Memorabilium*

Vallabha Deva (San. 12) *Commentary on Megha Duuta*

Vallabha Deva (San. 15) *Subhaa Ṣita Avalii*

Valmiki (San. −2) *Raamaayana*

Vaman (Mar. 17) *Poems*

Vamana (see Jaya Ditya)

Vamana Bhatta Bana (San. 15) *Paarvatii Pariṇaya*

Vandya Ghaṭiya Sarva Ananda (San. 12) *Commentary*

Varahamihira (San. 6) *Pañca Siddhaantika*

Vararuchi (San.) *Praakṛta Prakaaśa; Niiti Saara*

Variboba (Alb. 18) *Life of the Blessed Virgin*

Varius (Lat. −1) *Thyestes*

Varro (Lat. 2) *De Lingua Latina*

Vartan (Arm. 13) *World History*

Vasallo (Mlt. 19) *Il Gifen Tork*

Vasu Bandhu (San. 4) *Abhi Dharma Kosa Suutra*

Vasu Deva (San.) *Nalodaya*

Vasu Raya Kavi (Tel. 19) *Works*

Vatsa Bhaṭṭi (San. 4) *Puurvaa*

Vatsya Ayana (San. 4) *Kaama Suutra*

Vazov (Bul. 19) *Works*

Vedanga Raaya (San. 17) *Paardsii Prakaaśa*

Vedanta Dasikar (Tam. 10) *Rahasya Traya Sara*

Veldeke (Dut. 12) *Eneit; St. Servatius*

Veled (Tur. 14) *Poems*

Velestinlis (Gre. 18) *Poems*

Venkatakavi (Tel. 17) *Vijayavilasamu; Sarangodhara Charitramu*

Ventadhvarin (San.) *Yaadava Raaghaviiya*

Vergilius (Lat. −1) *Aeneis; Georgica; Bucolica*

Vesalius (Lat. 16) *Theatrum Orbis Terrarum*

Vetala Bhaṭṭa (San.) *Niiti Pradiipa*

Veysi (Tur. 17) *Mohammed*

Vidal (Pro. 12) *Abrils Issia; Castia Gelos; Judici d'Amor; Las Razons de Trobar*

Vidya Dhara (San. 14) *Eka Avalii*

Vidya Natha (San. 14) *Prata Apurudraya Śobhuuṣana*

Vidya Pati (Pra. 14) *Puruṣa Pariikṣaa Klirtilataa*

Villemarqué (Bre. 19) *Barzaz Breiz*

Vimala Suuri (Pra. 4) *Paumacariya*

Vinayaka (San. 19) *Angreja Chandrika*

Vinayaka (San.) *Daśa Kumaara Puurva Piiṭhikaa*

Vir Singh (Pun. 19) *Baba Naudh Singh; Guru Nanak Chamatkar; Kalgidhar Chamatkar; Merey Saiyan Jio; Rama Surat Singh; Satwant Kauri; Sundari; Vijay Singh*

Viresalingam (Tel. 19) *Works*

Viśakha Datta (San. 5) *Mudra Raksasa*

Viśakha Datta (San. 9) *Works*

Viśva Natha (San. 14) *Saahitya Darpaṇa*

Vitoria (Lat. 16) *The Indians, and Reflections on the Art of War*

Vitruvius (Lat. −1) *De Architectura*

Vodnik (Slo. 18) *Poems*

Vogelweide (Ger. 13) *Poems*

Vojnović (Ser. 19) *The Mother of the Jugovići*

Volodimir Monomakh (Rus. 11) *Instructions*

Voragine (Lat. 13) *Legenda Aurea*

Vuong Tan Thang (Vie. 19) *Commentary on the Tam Tu Kinh*

Vyasa (San. 8) *Yoga Bhaaṣya*

Wahab Pare (Kas. 19) *History*

Waḥidi (Ara. 11) *Commentary on Mutanabbii*

Wahsiyya (Ara. 10) *Kitaabu 'l Falaaḥat al Nabaṭiyya*

Walafrid (Lat. 9) *Hortulus; Vision of Wettin; St. Faro; St. Blathmac*

Walid II (Ara.) *Poems*

Wallis (Lat. 17) *Arithmetica Infinitorum*

Walsingham (Lat. 14) *Chronicles*

Wang An Shih (Chi. 11) *The Written Characters*

Wang Chien (Chi. 8) *Poems*

Wang Chu (Chi. 11) *The Poets' Club*

Wang Ch'ung (Chi. 1) *Lun Hêng*

Wang Hsi Chi (Chi. 4) *In the Orchard Pavilion*

Wang Hsiao T'ung (Chi. 7) *Ch'i Ku*

Wang Hsien Ch'ien (Chi. 19) *Ch'ien Han Shu Pu Chu; Hsün Tzŭ Chi Chieh*

Wang Pi (Chi. 3) *Commentaries on I Ching and Tao Tê Ching*

Wang Ping (Chi. 8) *Commentary on Nei Ching*

Wang Po (Chi. 7) *Poems*

Wang Shih Fu (Chi. 13) *Hsi Hsiang Ki*

Wang Shih Cheng (Chi. 16) *Chin P'ing Mei*

Wang Su (Chi. 3) *Chia Yü*

Wang Tao (Chi. 8) *Treatise on Medicine*

Wang Tao K'un (Chi. 16) *Works*

Wang Ts'an (Chi. 3) *Poetics*

Wang Wei (Chi. 8) *Poems*

Wang Yang Ming (Chi. 15) *Wang Wên Ch'êng Kung Ch'üan Shu*

Wang Ying Lin (Chi. 13) *San Tzŭ Ching*

Wanradt (Est. 16) *Catechism*

Waqidi (Ara. 9) *Kitaabu 'l Maghaazii; Conquest of Syria*

Wardapet (Arm. 5) *History of Wardan*

Warris Shah (Pun. 18) *Heer Ranjha*

Wasif (Tur. 19) *Poems*

Wa'wa (Ara. 10)   *Works*
Wei (Chi. 6)   *Wei Shu*
Wei Chêng (Chi. 7)   *History*
Wen (Chi. −3)   *I Ching*
Wen Kang (Chi. 19)   *Er Nu Ying Hsiung Chuan*
Wên T'ien Hsiang (Chi. 13)   *Encyclopedia; Poems*
Wiclif (Lat. 14)   *Civil Dominion*
Widukind (Lat. 10)   *History of the Saxons*
William IX (Pro. 12)   *Poems*
Williram (Ger. 11)   *Explanation of the Song of Solomon*
Witelo (Lat. 15)   *De Perspectiva*
Wu Ch'êng Ên (Chi. 16)   *Hsi Yü Chi*
Wu Shu (Chi. 10)   *Shih Lei Fu*
Wulfstan (Eng. 11)   *Homilies*
Wynne (Wel. 18)   *Gweledigaetheu y Bardd Cwsc*

Xahila and Xahila (Cak. 17)   *Annals of the Cakchiquels*
Xenophon (Gre. −5)   *Anabasis; Hellenika*
Xenophon (Gre. 3)   *An Ephesian Tale*

Yahya (Tur. 16)   *Poems*
Yajiji Oghlu (Tur. 15)   *Mohammed*
Yajña Valka (San.)   *Dharma Śaastra*
Yang (Chi. −5) *Works*
Yang Hsiung (Chi. −1)   *T'ai Hsüan Ching; Fa Yen*
Yang I (Chi. 10)   *Poems*
Yao Chien (Chi. 7)   *Liang Shu; Ch'ên Shu*
Ya'qubi (Ara.)   *Works*
Yaqut (Ara. 13)   *Mu'jamu 'l Udabaa; Mu'jamu 'l Buldaan; Mushtarik*
Yaska (San. −5)   *Nirukta*
Yaweshinhtwe (Bur. 16)   *Fifty-five Coiffures*
Yazdi (Per. 15)   *Zafar Naama*
Yazid I (Ara.)   *Poems*
Yaziji (Ara. 19)   *Muqaamaat*
Yeh Shih (Chi. 12)   *Poems*
Yehuda (Heb. 3)   *Mishna*
Yen Chih T'ui (*see* Lu Fa Yen)

Yen Jo Chü (Chi. 18)   *Shang Shu Ku Wen Shu Cheng*
Yen Shih Ku (Chi. 7)   *History of the Han Dynasty*
Yen Ying (Chi. −5)   *Yen Tze Ch'un Ch'iu*
Yen Yüan (Chi. 17)   *Yen Li Ts'ung Shu—Ts'ung Hsing*
Yi Mun Jong (Kor. 18)   *The Frogs*
Yi Sang Ch'un (Kor. 15)   *Chu Hai Yong Bi Ŏ Ch'ŏng Ga*
Ying Yan (Chi. 3)   *Poems*
Yohai (Heb. 1)   *Mekilta*
Yü Pao (Chi. 4)   *Supernatural Researches*
Yuan Chen (Chi.)   *The Western Room*
Yuan Chwang (Chi. 7)   *Hsi Yü Chi*
Yüan Hung Tao (Chi. 16)   *Shang Chêng*
Yüan Mei (Chi. 18)   *Poems; Hsi Ts'ang Shan Fang Ch'ih Tu*
Yüan Yüan (Chi. 19)   *Topography of Kwantung; T'ai P'ing Yü Lan*
Yung (Chi. 18) *Encyclopedia*
Yung Lo (Chi. 15)   *Yung Lo Ta Tien*

Zachariah (Arm. 9)   *Homilies*
Zada (Tur. 15)   *History of Forty Viziers*
Zahiri (Ara. 9)   *Works*
Zakan (Per. 14)   *Akhlaaq al Ashraaf*
Zakir (Syr. −8)   *Victory over Damascus*
Zakkuth (Heb. 16)   *Sepher Yuhasin*
Zamakhshari (Ara. 12)   *Kashshaaf*
Zar'a Ya'kub (Eth. 15)   *Mashafa Berhan; Miracles of the Virgin Mary*
Zarathustra (Per. −6)   *Gathas*
Zaydan (Ara.)   *Ta'riikhu 'l Tamaddun al Islaami*
Zayyati (Ara. 16)   *Works*
Zechariah (Heb. −6)   *Prophecy*
Zenab (Eth. 19)   *King Theodore II*
Zenobius (Syr. 5)   *History of Taron*
Zenodotos (Gre. −3) *Homeric Glossary*
Zephaniah (Heb. −7)   *Prophecy*
Zerklar (Ger. 13)   *The Italian Guest*
Zhidiata (Rus. 11)   *Instruction*
Ziz (Qui. 19)   *Rabinal Achi*
Zouhri (Ara. 12)   *Ghana*
Zuhri (Ara. 8)   *Traditions*
Zwingli (Ger. 16)   *Poems*

WORKS

In parentheses are foreign titles, followed by a colon and their English translations. Full information may be found under the English titles. Language and century are there given in parentheses immediately following a title. The author's name immediately follows that. When no date is given, the date is unknown. Original titles of anonymous works are given in parentheses after the English listings. Original titles of other works are listed in "Authors."

(Aaiin i Akbarii: The Institutes of Akbar)
Aajurruumiyya (Ara. 14) Ṣanhaajii
('Aalomaaraa: 'Abbaas the Great)
(Aananda Laharii: The Wave of Bliss)
Aananda Sundarii (Pra. 18) Ghana Syaama
Aaraish i Mahfil (Urd. 19) Sher 'Alii Afsos
(Aaśvala Ayana Suutra: Manual of Ceremonial of the Aitareya)
(Aathaar al Baaqiya: Surviving Monuments)
Aatharu 'l Bilaad (Ara.) Qazwiinii
'Abbaas the Great (Per. 17) Iskandar
Abdul Messia (Geo. 12) Shavteli
(Abel Spel vande Winter ende Somer: Noble Play of Winter and Summer)
(Abhi Dharma Cin Taamaṇi: Synonyms)
(Abhi Dharma Piṭaka: Analytical Exercises)
(Abhi Dharma Kosa Suutra: Buddhism, a Religion of Infinite Compassion)
(Abhi Dharma Ratna Maalaa: Short Dictionary)
(Abhijnan Shakuntalam: Śaakuntalaa)
Above (San. 4) Vatsa Bhaṭṭi
Abraham's Sacrifice (Gre. 15) (Thysia tou Avraam)
Abrils Issia (Pro. 12) Vidal
Abstention from Animal Food (Gre.) Porphyrios
Abstraction (Jap. 15)

Abuu Zeyd (Ara. 11) (Siiratu Abuu Zeyd)
(Acallam na Senórech: The Colloquy of the Old Men)
Accomplishments of the Secretary (Ara. 9) Ibn Qutayba
An Account of Karaism (Heb. 18) Solomon of Troki
The Acharnians (Gre. −5) Aiskhylos
The Acharnians (Gre. −5) Aristophanes
(Achilleis: The Epic of Achilles)
The Action and Influence of the Moon (Syr. 6) Ras'ain
The Acts of the Apostles (Gre. 1) (Bible)
The Acts of the Passion (Eth. 13) Abba Salama
The Acts of the Persian Martyrs (Syr. 4)
Acts of the Provinces (Geo. 14) (Dzeglo Eristhava)
(Adabu 'l Kaatib: Accomplishments of the Secretary)
Adbhuta Darpaṇa (San. 17) Mahaa Deva
Addhyatma Ramayanam (Mlm. 16) Ezhuttachan
Additions (Heb. 5) (Tosefta)
Address to the Magistrates on Moral Training (Man. 17) Shun
(Adelphi: Brothers)
(Adi Granth: Origin Book)
The Administration of the Empire (Gre. 10) Konstantinos VII

Admonitions (Per.) (Andarz Naamak)

Admonitions (Egy. −20) Ipu Wer

Admonitions and Recension (Ara. 10) Mas'uudi

Adoration of the Nile (Egy. −16)

Adornment of the Saints (Ara. 11) Isfahaanii

Adventures of Bran MacFebal (Iri. 7) (Echtrae Brain Maic Febail)

Adventures and Experiences of Young René (Slo. 18) Bajza

Adventures of Hong Kil Dong (Kor. 15) Ka San

(The Adventures of Hsi Men and His Six Wives: The Golden Lotus)

Adventures of Kyong Op (Kor. 15) Ha Jong

Advice on Hygiene (Cam. 19) Kèp

Advice to the King's Servants (Cam. 19) Mohà Màs

Advice to Poets (San. 13) Amara Candra and Ari Sinha

Aeneid (Ukr. 18) Kotlyarevsky

Aeneid (Dut. 12) Veldeke

(Aeneis: The Epic of Aeneas)

(Aenigmata: Riddles)

Aesop's Fables (Mal. 19) Alang Ahmad

Aesop's Fables (Gre. 13) Planudes

Aesthetics (Gre. −4) Aristoteles

Afghan Chronicle (Pus. 17) (Tarikh i Murassah)

Africa (Ara. 8) Ibn Munabbeh

Africa without Egypt (Ara. 14) Omari

The African War (Lat. −1) (Bellum Africanum)

Against Cresconius (Lat. 4) Augustinus

Against the Foes of the Law and the Prophets (Lat. 4) Augustinus

Against Faustus (Lat. 4) Augustinus

Against Heresies (Gre. 3) Irenaeus

Against the Paulicians and Docetae (Arm. 8) Catholicus

Agni Puraana (San.)

(Agni Smriti: The Code of Agni)

(De Agri Cultura: Agriculture)

Agricola (Lat. 1) Tacitus

Agriculture (Lat. −2) Cato

Ahkaam uṣ Ṣalavaat (Urd. 14)

Ahsanu 'l Taqaasiim fii Ma'rifati 'l Aqaaliim (Ara. 10) Muqaddasii

Aindarwuntha (Bur. 18)

Air, Water and Locations (Gre. −4) Hippokrates

(Aitareya Aaranyaka: The Forest Book of the Aitareya)

(Aitareya Braahmana: The Commentary of the Aitareya Brahmans)

Aitareya Upaniṣad (San.) Mahi Daasa

('Ajaa'ibu 'l Maqduur: Marvels of Destiny)

Ajax (Gre. −5) Sophokles

Ajib Bheta (Sin. 19) Pritamdas

(Akeydas Yitskhok: Sacrifice of Isaac)

Akhbaaru 'l Zamaan (Ara. 10) Mas'uudi

(Akhbar Naama: Life of Akbar)

(Akhlaaq al Ashraaf: The Ethics of Aristocracy)

(Akhyanas: Tales)

(Alamkaara: Verses on Poetics)

(Alamkaara Samgraha: Poetic Expressions)

(Alamkaara Sarvasva: Pictorial Poetry)

(Alamkaara Vimarśinii: Poetics)

Alcestis (Gre. −5) Euripides

Alchemy of Happiness (Ara. 12) Ghazaalii

Alexander (Pro. 11)

Alexander (Ger. 12) Lamprecht

Alexander (Per. 13) Niẓaamii

Alexander (Mon. 14)

Alexander the Oracle Monger (Lat. 2) Lucianus

Alexandra (Gre. −2) Lykophron

The Alexandrine War (Lat. −1) Hirtius

(Alexiados: The Epic of Alexis)

(Alexipharmaka: Antidotes)

(Alf Layla wa Layla: Thousand and One Nights)

Alfiyya (Ara. 13) Ibn Maalik

Algebra (Ara. 8) Ibn Mūsā

Ali Nama (Urd. 17) Nuṣratii

Alive, Son of Awake (Ara. 12) Ibn Ṭufayl

All the Judges (Per. −3) (Vispered)

(All Men Are Brothers: Tale of the Water Margins)

Almagest (Gre. 2) Ptolemaios

(Altan Tobchi: Mongol Chronicle)

(Am Duat: What Is in the Netherworld)

(Amara Kośa: The Immortal Treasury)

(Amba Aṣṭaka: Eight Hymns to Devii)

Amiran Darejaniani (Geo. 12) Khoneli

To Amon (Egy. −14) Horus and Seth

To Amon (Egy. −13)

(Amores: Loves)

Amphitheatrum Universitatis Rerum (Lat. 17) Komenský

Amracholuim Chille (Iri. 6) MacForgaill (Anabasis: Cyrus' March into the Interior)

The Anabasis of Alexander (Gre. 2) Arrianus

Analects (Chi. −6) K'ung Fu Tzŭ

Analyses (Heb. −4) (Midrashim)

Analytical Exercises (Pal. −3) (Abhi Dhamma Piṭaka)

Anargha Raaghava (San. 11) Muraari

The Ancient History of Rome (Lat. −1) Dionysius

The Ancient History of the Jews (Lat. 1) Josephus

Ancient Inquiry (San.) Jaimini

Ancient and Modern Marvelous Tales (Chi. 16) (Kin Ku K'i Kuan)

Ancient Orators (Lat. 1) Dionysius (Andarz Naamak: Admonitions)

Andria (Lat. −2) Terentius (Anecdota: Secret History)

Anecdotes (Chi. 19) (Hsiao Lin Kuang Chi)

Anecdotes (Hit. −17)

Anecdotes (Ara. 15) Abshiihii (Anekaartha Kośa: Dictionary) (Anekaartha Śabda Kośa: Dictionary) (Anekaartha Samgraha: Homonyms) (Anekaartha Samuccaya: Dictionary)

Angkor Vat (Chi. 13) Chou Ta Kuan

Anglo-Saxon Chronicle (Eng. 11) (Angreja Chandrika: The Coming of the English)

The Anguttara Commentary (Pal.)

Animals (Ara. 9) Jaahiz (Anirud: Life of Anuruddha) (Ankiya Nats: Plays)

Annales Cambriae (Lat. 10) (Annales Ecclesiastici: Church Annals) (Annalia: Annals)

Annals (Nah. 17) Chimalpahin

Annals (Lat. −2) Ennius

Annals (Ara. 10) Eutychius

Annals (Ice. 17) Jónsson

Annals (Ara. 10) Hamza

Annals (Hit. −14) Mursilis II

Annals (Lat. 1) Tacitus

Annals of the Apostles and the Kings (Ara. 9) Ṭabarii

Annals of Ayuthia (Tha. 18) (Ponsawadan Krung Kao)

Annals of the Cakchiquels (Cak. 17) Xahila

Annals of Cuauhtitlan (Nah. 16)

Annals of Korea (Kor. 14) Chŏng

Annals of Lü (Chi. −3) Lü Pu Wei

Annals of the Monastery of Tewkesbury (Lat. 13)

Annals of the Northern States (Tha. 18) (Ponsawadan Tshonok)

Annals of Rajasthan (Raj. 14)

Annals of Ṭabarii (Per. 10) Bal'amii (Annals of Wei: Bamboo Annals)

Annals of Wu and Yüeh (Chi. −2) (Wu Yüeh Ch'un Ch'iu)

Anno, Bishop of Cologne (Ger. 12)

Answers to Sergius (Syr. 6) Tella (Antapodosis: Retribution)

Anthologies of Twenty-one Reigns (Jap. 15) (Ni Juu Ichi Dai Shuu)

Anthology (Jap. 10) (Gosenshiu)

Anthology (Chi. 19) (Huang Ch'ing Ching Chieh)

Anthology (Chi. 6) Hsiao T'ung

Anthology (San. 14) Śaarnga Dhara

Anthology of Poetry (Chi. 18) Ch'ien Lung

Anthology of Poetry (Gre. 10) Kephalas

Anthology of Poetry (Per. 18) Vaalih

Anthology of Prayers or Speeches (Jap. 10) (Yengi Shiki)

Anthology of Spanish-Arabic Verse (Ara. 17) Qaadir

An Anthropological Inquiry into the Position of Man (Lat. 16) Hundt

The Anti-Christ (Lat. 12)

Antidemonic Law (Per. −2) (Videvdat)

Antidotes (Gre. −3) Nikander

Antigone (Gre. −5) Sophokles (Anukramaṇiis: Notes on the Rig and Yajur Vedas)

Anupu and Bitiu (Egy. −13) (Anuyogadvaara: Preliminary Ritual) (Anvaar i Suheylii: Fables of Bidpai) (Anyokti Muktaalataa Śataka: Gnomic Poem)

Aphorisms (Gre. −4) Hippokrates

Aphorisms of Sankhya Philosophy (San. −6) Kapila

Apocalypse of St. John (Gre. 2)

Apologetics (Heb. 16) Abravanel (Apologia: Socrates on Trial)

Apology (Gre. 2) Aristides

Apology (Gre. 2) Justin

The Apostolic Constitutions (Gre.)

Appendix of the Classic of Change (Chi. −5) (Hi Tse)

(Appiryon: An Account of Karaism)

Aqhat (Syr. −14)

The Arab Conquests (Ara.) Balaadhurii

Arabic Dictionary (Ara. 14) Ibn Man-ẓuur

Arabic Dictionary (Ara. 14) Ibn Mukar-ram

An Arabic-Malagasy Text (Mad. 16)

Arabic Rhyme in L (Ara. 6) Shanfaraa

The Aramaic Bible (Syr. 4) (Targum)

(Arban Jüg ün Ejen Geser Qaghan u Tughuji Orosiba: King Geser)

Arbitration (Gre. −4) Menander

Architecture (Lat. −1) Vitruvius

The Archives of Yamkhad (Bab. −18)

Ard Viraf (Per. 3)

The Argonauts (Gre. −3) Apollonios

The Argonauts (Gre. 3) Rhodios

The Argonauts (Lat. 1) Valerius

De Arguendo Clero (Lat. 15) Hus

The Arithmetic of Infinites (Lat. 17) Wallis

(Arithmetica Integra: Integral Arithmetic)

Arjunaa Wiwaahaa (Jav. 14)

Armenian Rituals (Arm. 9) Moshtotz

(Armes Prydein: Prophecy of Britain)

(Ars Amatoria: The Art of Love)

(Ars Magna: Great Art)

(Ars Medica: The Medical Art)

The Art of Honest Lovemaking (Lat. 12) Andreas

The Art of Love (Lat. 1) Ovidius

The Art of Poetry (Lat. −1) Horatius

The Art of War (Chi. −6) Sun Tzŭ

(De Arte Honeste Amandi: The Art of Honest Lovemaking)

(De Arte Poetica: The Art of Poetry)

(Artha Śaastra: Doctrine of Politics)

Arthur's Court (Yid. 14) (Artus Hof)

(Artus Hof: Arthur's Court)

('Arukh: Prepared)

Ascetic Works (Gre.) Basil

Asceticism (Ara. 8) Ibn Muusaa

(Ash'aaru 'l Hudhaliyyiin: Poems of the Hudhaylites)

Ashkan (Ukr. 18) Skovoroda

Ashtottara Satam Upaniṣad (San.)

Assemblies (Ara. 11) 'Alaa

Assemblies (Ara. 11) Hamadhaanii

Assemblies (Ara. 11) Ḥariirii

Assemblies (Ara. 19) Yaazijii

The Assizes of Jerusalem (Lat. 11)

The Assizes of Romania (Lat. 13)

(Asta Adhyaayii: Eight Sections)

Aṣṭa Mahaa Śrii Caitya Stotra (San. 7) Harṣa

Astarte (Egy. −13)

Astronomical Verses (San. 5) Arya Bhata

Astronomy (Chi. 17) Hsü Kuang Ch'i

Astronomy (San.) Lagadha

Astronomy (Lat. 1) Manilius

Astronomy and the Calendar (Chi. 14) Chang Yu Chin

Astronomy and Divination (Yuc. 15) (The Dresden Codex)

(Atharva Veda: Magic)

Atland (Swe. 17) Rudbeck

Atma Nirṇayam (Tam. 17) Nobili

Atreus (Lat. 1) Scaurus

(Atri Smriti: The Code of Atri)

Attaining to Buddha (San. 7) Śaanti Deva

Attic Nights (Lat. 2) Gellius

Aucassin and Nicolette (Fre. 13)

Aucitya Vicaara (San. 11) Ksemendra

Augustan History (Lat. 4) Spartianus et al

Augustinus (Lat. 17) Jansenius

Autobiography (Rus. 17) Avvakum

Autobiography (Per. −5) Daraya

Autobiography (Hit. −13) Hattusilis

Autobiography (Ara. 12) Ibn Munqid

Autobiography (San. 19) Korada

Autobiography (Mal. 19) Munshi 'Abdu'lla

Autobiography (Ara. 16) Sha'raanii

Autobiography (Ice. 18) Steingrímsson

Autobiography (Swe. 19) Strindberg

Autobiography (Chi. 8) Tu Fu

The Autobiography of Idri Mi (Bab. −14) Sharruwa

Autumn in the Han Palace (Chi. 13) Ma Tuan Lin

(Avadaana Śataka: Parables)

Avatamsaka Suutra (San. 1) Manjusri

Avesta (Per. 2)

('Awaarifu 'l Ma'aarif: Bounties of Knowledge)

Awakening of Faith in the Mahayana (San. 1) Aśva Ghoṣa

Baal (Syr. −14)
(Baala Bhaarata: The New Bharata)
Baaq o Bahaar (Urd. 19) Miir Amman
Baba Naudh Singh (Pun. 19) Vir Singh
(Babur Naama: Memoirs)
The Bacchae (Gre. −5) Euripides
Bagawa (Bur.)
Bahaar i Daanish (Urd. 19)
(Bahaaristaan: Spring Garden)
(Bahir: Outline of the Zohar)
Bahraam o Gulandaam (Urd. 18)
Bahvricha Braahmaṇa Upaniṣad (San.)
(Bai Durya Kar Po: White Lapis Lazuli)
Baidehisa Bilasa (Ori. 18) Upendra
Bhanja
(Bala Carita: Life of Bala)
Balassi Meynhért (Mag. 16) Karádi
Ballad of Akida (Swa. 19) Mazrui
Ballad of Senhor Costa (Mal. 16) (Sha'eer
Sinyor Kosta)
Ballad of the Three Witches (Ara. 6)
Ballads and Romances (Slo. 19) Aškerc
Bamboo Annals (Chi. −3) (Chu Shu
Chi Nien)
Banasura Vadha (Kas. 15)
(Bandàm Pāli: Advice to the King's
Servants)
(Bandàm Sèthĕi: Manual of Household
and Farm Economy)
(Bandamanna Saga: The Confederates)
The Bani Hilal (Ara.)
The Banners of the Khalkha Mongols
(Man. 17) (Kalka Dulimbi Chugun
Gosa)
The Banquet (Lat. 14) Dante
The Banquet of the Learned (Gre. 2)
Athenaeus
Banquet Song (Egy. −14)
Bantugan (Min. 19)
Bardic Chronicles (Raj. 12) Chaṇḍ Bar-
dai
Barlaam and Joseph (Eth. 16)
Barlaam and Josephat (Geo. 10) Iver
(Bargits: Hymns)
Baruch (Syr.)
Baruch (Heb. 2) (Bible)
(Barzaz Breiz: Breton Songs)
Bases (Gre. 3) Origenos
(Basilika: Compilation of Decrees)
Basket of Doctrine (Pal. −3) (Sutta
Piṭaka)
Bassarica (Gre. 4) Soterichos

The Bath of Pallas (Gre. −3) Kalli-
makhos
The Battle of Aspindzi (Geo. 18) Gabash-
vili
The Battle of the Field of Death (Ice. 19)
Thomsen
The Battle of Men and Monkeys (Bur. 18)
(Ramazat)
The Battles of Coxinga (Jap. 17) Chika-
matsu
Baudhagan o Doha (Ben. 9)
Bay Ganyu (Bul. 19) Konstantinov
(Bayaan al Adyaan: Doctrines of the
Sects)
(Al Bayaan al Mughrib: Doctrines of the
West)
Bazaar of Heraclides (Syr. 5) Nestorius
Beatrice (Dut. 13) (Beatrijs)
The Beautiful Li (Chi. 8)
The Beautiful Shepherdess (Gre. 17) (He
Bospopoula he Omorfe)
Beauty and Love (Tur. 19) Ghaalib
(Behinath ha Dath: Enjoyment of the
Law)
(Behinath ha 'Olam: Pleasure of the
World)
Being and Essence (Lat. 13) Aquinas
The Bektashis (Alb. 19) Frásheri
Bel and the Dragon (Heb. 2) (Bible)
(De Bello Civili: The Civil War)
(Bellum Africanum: The African War)
(Bellum Alexandrinum: The Alexandrine
War)
(Bellum Hispaniense: The Spanish War)
(Bellum Iugurthinum: The History of the
Jugurthine War)
(Bellum Punicum: The Punic War)
The Beloved Vision (San. 7) Harsa
Bengal Anthology of Poetry (San. 13) Srii
Dhara Daasa
Beowulf (Eng. 8)
(Bèp Kala Bat: Models of Fantasy Verse)
(Bèp Kamhnhăp: Verse Models)
(Berachoth: A Treatise on Blessings)
(Berachoth ve Hodayoth: Blessings and
Thanksgivings)
Bereshith Rabba (Syr.)
Bernardo del Carpio (Spa. 13)
(Bersöglis Viisur: Plain Speaker)
The Besieged Freemen (Gre. 19) Solomos
The Best Senator (Lat. 16) Goslicki
Bestiary (Eth. 13)

(Beth Joseph: The House of Joseph)
(Beunans Meriased: Life of Meriadec)
The Bewitched Prince (Egy. −13)
Beyond the Don (Rus. 14) Sofony
Bezels of Philosophy (Ara. 13) Ibn 'Arabii
(Bhaamatii: Vedantism)
Bhaaminii Vilaasa (San. 17) Jagan Naatha
(Bhaaraataa Yuddha: The Great Bharatas)
(Bhaarata Campuu: Romance of the Bharatas)
(Bhaarata Mañjarii: Digest of the Bharatas)
(Bhaasya: Commentary)
(Bhaava Prakaaśa: Dramaturgy)
(Bhaava Prakaaśa: Medicine)
(Bhaava Śataka: Maxims of Bhaava)
(Bhagabata: The Song Celestial)
(Bhagavad Giitaa: The Song Celestial)
(Bhagavata Puraana: Legends of the Song Celestial)
(Bhagavatam: The Song Celestial)
Bhakt Maalaa (San.)
(Bhakta Amara Stotra: St. Risabha)
(Bharadvaaja Smriti: The Code of Bharadvaaja)
(Bharataka Dvaa Trin Śikaa: Thirty-two Bharata Tales)
(Bhatti Kaavya: The Slaying of Raavana)
(Bhava Anya Astaka: Hymns to Devii)
Bhavishya Puraana (San.)
(Bheda Samhitaa: Medical Compendium)
(Bhiksaatana Kaavya: Epic of Śiva Begging)
(Bhoja Prabandha: Legends of Bhoja)
Bhubaneswar Inscriptions (Ori. 13) Nara Simha
(Biarkamál in Fornu: Lay of Biarki)
Bible (Bel. 16)
Bible (Egy. 4)
Bible (Est. 18)
Bible (Eth. 13)
Bible (Fin. 17)
Bible (Geo. 5)
Bible (Lad. 16)
Bible (Let. 17)
Bible (Ukr. 16)
Bible (Wel. 16)
Bible (Slo. 18) Japelj
Bible (Ger. 16) Luther

Bible (Arm. 4) Mesrob and Sahak
Bible (Dan. 16) Pedersen
Bible (Swe. 16) Petri
Bible (Ice. 16) Thorláksson
Bible (Got. 4) Ulfilas
Bible of Kralice (Cze. 16)
Bible Verses (Dut. 13) Maerlant
Biblical Antiquities (Gre.) Philo
Bichitra Ramayana (Ori. 17) Biswanath Khuntia
Bidasari (Mal. 16) (Sha'eer Bidasari)
Biddhashala Bhanjika (San. 10) Raaja Śekhara
Bihulaa and Lakhindar (Ben. 13) Hari Datta
The Binding of the Braid (San. 9) Bhatta
Biographical Dictionary (Ara. 12) Ibn Khallikan
Biographical Dictionary of Mathematics (Chi. 19) (Ch'ou Jen Chuan)
Biographies (Per. 11) Ansaari
Biographies (Tur. 17) 'Ataa Ullaah
Biographies (Tur. 17) Tash
Biographies of Eminent Women (Chi. −1) Liu Hsiang
Biographies of the Saints (Bul. 14) Evtymy
(Bioi Paralleloi: Parallel Lives)
The Birds (Gre. −5) Aristophanes
The Birth of the War God (San. 4) Kaali Daasa
Bisaldeo Raso (Hin. 12) Narpati Nalh
(Bitaghat Thôn Bôn: Burmese Tripitaka)
The Bites of Beasts (Gre. −3) Nikander
The Black Book of Carmarthen (Wel. 12)
(The Black Moor Turned White: The Blessed Jew of Morocco)
Blanquerna (Cat. 13) Lull
The Blessed Jew of Morocco (Ara. 12) Ibn Abbas
The Blessing of Jacob (Heb. −10) (Genesis 27–28)
The Blessing of Moses (Heb. −10) (Deuteronomy 33)
Blessings and Thanksgivings (Heb. 1) (Berakhôth we Hodayôth)
Blickling Homilies (Eng. 10)
The Blood of Christ (Lat. 15) Hus
Blue Cliff Records (Jap.) (Hekigan Roku)
Blue Treasury of Records (Tib. 15) Gö

(Bodhi Carya Avataara: Attaining to Buddha)
Boèci (Pro. 11)
(Bogurodzica: Mother of God)
The Bohemian Republic (Cze. 17)   Stránský
(Book of Adam: The Great Treasure)
(Book of the Basket: Tripiṭaka)
Book of the Bee (Syr. 13)   Basrah
Book of the Birds (Tha. 19)   (Paksi Pakaranam)
Book of Ceremonies (Gre. 11)   Porphyrogenitus
Book of Certitude (Per. 19)   Baha
Book of Ch'ên (Chi. 7)   Yao Chien
Book of Chin (Chi. 8)   (Chin Shu)
Book of Chronicles (Lat. 13)   Kézai
Book of Conduct (Yid. 16)   (Seyfer Mides)
Book of Counsel (Qui. 16)   (Popol Vuh)
Book of Counsel (Per. 13)   'Aṭṭaar
Book of the Covenant (Heb. 12)   Qimhi
Book of Creations (Heb. 6)   (Sepher Yezirah)
Book of the Crypt Fathers (Rus. 13)   (Pechérsky Paterík)
(Book of the Dead: Coming Forth By Day)
Book of the Dead (Tib. 7)   (Jetsun Kahbum)
Book of the Dean of Lismore (Sco. 16)
Book of Degrees (Rus. 16)   Macarius
Book of Enfranchisement (Bur.)
Book of Enoch (Rus.)
Book of Examples (Ara. 14)   Ibn Khalduun
Book of Excellence (Heb. 13)   Aaron Ben Joseph
Book of Extreme Unction (Eth. 16)   (Mashafa Kandil)
Book of Fables (Arm. 13)   Kosh
Book of Heaven (Bul. 10)   Ioan
Book of Iceland (Ice. 12)   Ari
Book of Interesting and Proper Things (Kor.)   (Kam Öng P'yŭn)
Book of Invasions (Iri. 13)   (Lebor Gabála)
Book of the Jaguar Priest of Chumayel (Yuc. 18)   Hoil
Book of the Jaguar Priest of Ixil (Yuc. 16)
Book of the Jaguar Priest of Káua (Yuc. 16)

Book of the Jaguar Priest of Nah (Yuc. 16)
Book of the Jaguar Priest of Tizimin (Yuc. 16)
(Book of the Jaguar Priest of Tusik: The Language of Zuyua)
Book of Jubilees (Heb.)
Book of Kells (Lat. 6)
Book of Kings (Per. 7)   (Khvaataay Naamak)
Book of the Laws of the Countries (Syr. 3)   Bar Daysan
Book of the Levites (Heb. −4)   (Leviticus)
Book of Liang (Chi. 7)   Yao Chien
Book of Light (Eth. 15)   Zar'a Ya'kub
Book of the Lord Shang (Chi. −4)   Shang
Book of Morality (Mal. 17)
Book of My Love (Dan. 19)   Gjellerup
Book of Mysteries (Tam. 12)   Seekkilar
Book of Mystic Lore (Heb. 12)   Ben David
(Book of Odes: Classic of Poetry)
The Book of the Original Term (Chi. 7)   (Pen Tsi King)
The Book of Questions (Arm. 14)   Dathev
The Book of the Righteous (Heb. 12)   Ben Me'ir
The Book of Songs (Ara. 10)   Faraj
The Book of Sui (Chi. 7)   (Sui Shu)
The Book of Taliesin (Wel. 13)
The Book of Ten Thousand Leaves (Jap. 8)   (Man'yooshuu)
Book of the Thousand Questions (Ara. 10)   (Kitaab sa Ribu Masa'alah)
The Book of the Three Birds (Wel. 17)   Llwyd
The Book of Three-Character Phrases (Vie. 19)   (Tam Tu Kinh)
The Book of Victories (Pun. 17)   Gobind Singh
The Book of Victories (Per. 14)   Ḥamdullaah
The Book of Victories (Per. 15)   Yazdi
The Book of Visits (Dan. 16)   Plade
The Book of the Viziers (Ara. 11)   Ṣaabi'
The Book of Wei (Chi. 6)   Wei
The Book of Wonders (Pro. 13)   Lull
Books of Jeû (Gre. 3)
Boris and Gleb (Rus. 12)   Nestor
(He Bospopoula he Omorfe: The Beautiful Shepherdess)
Botanical Dictionary (San. 12)   (Nighantu Śesa)

Bounties of Knowledge (Ara. 13) Suhrawardii

Bouquet of Lotus (Tib. 18)

Bovo Bukh (Yid. 16) Levita

(Braahma Puraana: Legend of Brahma)

(Braahma Siddhaanta: Brahma Studies)

(Braahma Suutra: Poem of Brahma)

(Braahma Suutra Bhaasya: Commentary on the Brahma Sutras)

Braahma Tatva Prakashika (San.) Sara Svati

Braahma Vaivarta Puraana (San.)

Brahma Studies (San. 7) Brahma Gupta

(Brahmaana: Commentaries of the Brahmans)

Brahmaanda Puraana (San.)

Breton Songs (Bre. 19) Villemarqué

(Brhat Kathaa Mañjarii: Digest of the Brihat Romance)

(Brhat Kathaa Śloka Samgraha: Collected Verses of the Brihat Romance)

Brie and Zimre (Yid. 16) (Maase Brie Vezimre)

Brief Code (Gre. 9) Basil I

Brief Commentary (Lat. 16) Kopernigk

Brightness (Syr. 13) (Zohar)

(Brihad Aaranyaka Upanisad: The Great Forest Book Upanishad)

Brihad Devata (San. −5) Śaunaka

Brothers (Lat. −2) Terentius

Brunanburh (Eng. 9)

Brut (Eng. 9) Layamon

(Bucolica: Pastoral Poems)

(Buddha Carita: Life of Buddha)

Buddha's Former Births (Pal. 2) (Jatakas)

Buddhism, a Religion of Infinite Compassion (San. 4) Vasu Bandhu

Buddhist Beatitudes (Bur.) (Mingala Thut)

Buddhist Cosmogony (Tha. 18) (Trai Bhume Katha)

Buddhist Ritual (Chi. 6) Hsiao Yen

Buddhist Tales (Mon. 13) (Siddi Kuur)

(Budiyat: Life of Buddha)

Buildings (Gre. 6) Prokopios

Búnadarbálkur (Ice. 18) Olafsson

(Bundahishn: Ground Giving)

(Buranjis: Chronicles of the Ahom Courts)

(Burda: Mantle Ode)

Burmese Literary Art (Bur. 19) Saya Pwa

Burmese Pali Grammar (Bur.) (Thadda)

Burning and Melting (Per. 17) Nau'i

Burnt Njal (Ice. 13) (Njáls Saga)

(Bustaan: The Orchard)

(Bustaan i Siyaahat: Geographical Dictionary)

(Bustan al Salatin: Garden of Kings)

(Byrhtnoth: The Lay of Maldon)

(Caaru Caryaa Śataka: One Hundred Verse Maxims)

Caataka Astaka (San.)

Cabalistic Philosophy (Heb. 14) Leon

Caesars (Lat. 4) Aurelius

The Calendar (Arm. 7) Ananiah

Cambodia (Chi. 3) K'ang T'ai

Cambodian Customs (Cam. 19) Muk

Camels (Ara. 9) Asma'ii

Campakaśresthi Kathaanaka (San. 15) Jina Kirti

Cancioneiro de Ajuda (Gal. 14)

Cancioneiro de Baena (Gal. 15)

Cancioneiro de Colocci-Brancutti (Gal. 15)

Cancioneiro de Vaticana (Gal. 14)

(Cancioneiro Geral: General Songbook)

(Candii Kuca Pañcaa Sikaa: Fifty Stanzas on the Breasts of Candii)

(Candii Śataka: Praise of Candii)

(Candikaa Stotra: Hymn to Candii)

(Candra Aloka: Figures of Speech)

Candralekha (Pra. 17) Rudra Daasa

The Canon Law (San.) Yaajña Valka

The Canon of History (Chi. −2) K'ung An Kuo

The Canon of Medicine (Ara. 11) Ibn Siina

Canto of the Early Jains (San. 12) Hema Candra

(Cants d'Amor: Love Songs)

(Canu Llywarch Hen: Songs of Llywarch Hen)

The Captives (Lat. −2) Plautus

The Capture of Joppa (Egy. −15)

(The Capua Tile: Etruscan Public Ceremonies)

(Carmen de Gestis Ottonis: Hymn to the Deeds of Otto)

(Carmen Miserabile: Miserable Hymn)

(Carmen Paschale: Easter Hymn)

(Carmen Saeculare: Secular Hymn)

(Carmina: Poems)

Carpets (Gre. 3) Clement

The Carriage of the Happy Ones (Tib. 17) Palden

Carthage (Lat. 1) Silius

Carya (Ben. 11)

The Case against the Gentiles (Lat. 13) Aquinas

De Casibus Monasterii Sancti Galli (Lat. 10) Ratpert

Casus Sancti Galli (Lat. 11) Ekkehard

Castia Gelos (Pro. 12) Vidal

(De Catalinae Coniuratione: The Conspiracy of Catiline)

Catching Snakes (Chi. 9) Liu Tsung Yüan

Catechism (Mlt. 18)

Catechism (Alb. 17) Petrabianca

Catechism (Est. 16) Wanradt

Catena Patrum on the Gospels (Syr. 7) Merv

The Catholic Epistles (Arm. 12) Tlay

The Cattle Raid of Cooley (Iri. 9) (Táin Bó Cúailnge)

Catuḥ S̓atikaa (San. 3) Aarya Deva

(Catur Varga Saṁgraha: Four Ends of Life)

(Caurii Surata Pañcaa S̓ikaa: Fifty Stanzas on a Secret Love)

Causes and Creation of the Universe (Lat. 13) Albertus

The Cave of Treasures (Syr. 6) (Me'arrath Gazze)

Caverns (Egy. −14)

Ceremonies for the Twelve Months (Tha.) (Pitti Sibsong Deun)

Chaereas and Callirhoe (Gre. 2) Khariton

The Chain of Histories (Ara. 14) Ibn Baṭṭuuṭa

(Chalawan: The Princess and the Crocodile)

The Chalk Circle (Chi. 14) Huei

(Chamhpà Thònh: The Princess and the Crocodile)

Champa (Chi. 13) Ma Tuan Lin

(Champu: Epic)

(Chan Kuo Ts'ê: Documents of the Fighting States)

Chanda Kousika (San.) Kshemi Svara

Chandi Mangal (Ben. 16) Chakravarty

Chandogya Upaniṣad (San.)

(Chando'nu S̓aasana: Poetic Meters)

(Chanson d'Antioche: Song of Antioch)

(Chanson de la Croisade: The Crusade)

(Chanson de Sainte-Foi: The Holy Faith)

(Chanzum de la Guerra daig Chastè d'Müs: The War at the Castle of Müs)

(Chap Jŏn: Miscellaneous Stories)

Characters (Gre. −3) Theophrastos

(Charaka Saṃhitaa: Encyclopedia of Medicine)

Charlatan (Cze. 14) (Mastičkář)

The Charles Men (Swe. 19) Heidenstam

Charles the Great (Lat. 9) St. Gall

Chastity (Syr. 8) Isho'denah

(Chbăp Khmèr: Cambodian Customs)

(Chbăp Srëi: Women's Wisdom)

(Chbăp Tunmān Khluon: Essay on Individual Ethics)

Cheekeel Waneng Pati (Mal. 15)

(Ch'ên Shu: The Book of Ch'ên)

Cherokee Phoenix (Che. 19) Sequoyah

(Chetyí Minéi: Saints' Calendar)

(Chhamana Athaguntha: Six Acres and Eight Decimals)

(Chhandaḥ Suutra: Treatise on Meter)

The Ch'i (Chi. 4) Shên Yo

(Ch'i Ku: Mathematical Classic)

Ch'i Man Ts'ung Hsia (Chi. 12) Chu Fu

(Chi Yün: Phonetic Dictionary)

(Chia Yü: Family Sayings of Confucius)

(Ch'ieh Yun: Phonetic Dictionary)

(Ch'ien Han Shu: The Former Han)

Ch'ien Han Shu Pu Chu (Chi. 19) Wang Hsien Ch'ien

Chien Niang (Chi. 8) Chen

Chien Niang (Chi. 14) Cheng

Chien Teng Hsin Hua (Chi. 17) Chü Yu

Chien Teng Yü Hua (Chi. 14) Li Ch'ang Ch'i

Die Chierheit der geesteliker Brulocht (Dut. 14) Ruysbroek

Chikusai Monogatari (Jap. 17) Karasumaru

The Child and the Blind Man (Fre. 13) (L'Enfant et l'Aveugle)

The Chin (Chi. 4) Shên Yo

(Chin Kang Chin: The Diamond Sutra)

(Chin Ku Ch'i Kuan: Marvelous Tales Ancient and Modern)

(Chin P'ing Mei: The Golden Lotus)

(Chin Shih: History of the Juchên)

(Chin Shu: The Book of Chin)

(Chindamani: Primer)

Chinese Dictionary (Chi. 17) K'ang Hsi

Chinese Officialdom (Chi. 19) Li Po Yuan

Chinese Poems (Jap. 8) (Kaifusoo)
Ch'ing Chun Lu (Chi. 12) Lien Pu
(Ch'ing Ju Hsueh An: The Lives and
Works of Manchu Scholars)
(Ching Pen T'ung Shu Shiao Shu: Story-
tellers' Anthology)
Ch'ing P'ing Shan T'ang (Chi. 16)
(Ch'ing Shih Kao: Draft History of the
Manchu Dynasty)
(Ching Shih T'ung Yen: Anthology of
Stories)
Chiu T'ang Shu (Chi. 10)
(Chiu Wu Tai Shih: Old History of the
Five Dynasties)
Choice Histories (Ara. 9) Ibn Qutayba
(Chol Q'ih, Ahilabal Q'ih: The Count of
Days and the Numbers of the Days)
(De Chorographia: Geography of the
World)
(Ch'ou Jen Chuan: Biographical Diction-
ary of Mathematics)
(Chou Li: Ritual of the Chou)
(Chou Pei: Classic of Mathematics)
Christ in the Sacrament of the Altar (Lat.
15) Hus
Christ's Passion (Lat. 9) (Khristos
Paskhoon)
(Christianae Religionis Institutio: The
Institution of the Christian Religion)
Chronicle (Syr. 11) Bar Shinaya
Chronicle (Lat. 14) Czarnkow
Chronicle (Cat. 14) Descoll
Chronicle (Cat. 13) James I
Chronicle (San. 5) Maha Naaman
Chronicle (Cha. 19) Po Nagar
Chronicle (Syr. 12) Michael I
Chronicle (Arm. 12) Samuel
Chronicle (Ger. 16) Tschudi
Chronicle (Lat. 14) Walsingham
Chronicle of Calkini (Yuc. 16)
Chronicle of Dalimil (Cze. 14)
Chronicle of Edessa (Syr. 6)
Chronicle of the Kings of Lesser Armenia
(Arm. 13) Vahram
Chronicle of Kristian (Lat. 10)
Chronicle of Lesser Armenia (Arm. 13)
Sempat
Chronicle of Moxa (Rum. 17)
Chronicle of Oxkutzcab (Yuc. 16)
Chronicle of the Morea (Gre. 14)
Chronicle of the World (Mag. 16) Székely
Chronicles (Heb. −4) Ezra (Bible)

Chronicles (Per. 12) (Mujmal ut Ta-
waariikh)
Chronicles (Eng. 12)
Chronicles (Guj. 14)
Chronicles, 1591–1695 (Tur. 17) Na'iimaa
Chronicles of the Ahom Courts (Ass. 17)
(Buranjis)
Chronicles of the Bohemians (Lat. 11)
Kosmas
Chronicles of the Hungarians (Lat. 15)
Chronicles of the Jagannath Temple at Puri
(Ori. 11) (Madala Panji)
Chronicles of Pasai (Mal. 14)
Chronicles of Tixchel (Cho. 17)
*Chronicles of the Wars of King 'Amda
Ṣeyon* (Eth. 14)
Chronicon (Arm. 7) Ananiah
Chronicon of Hungarian Affairs (Lat. 15)
Thuróczi
Chronography (Gre. 6) Malalas
Chronography (Arm. 14) Airivanq
Chronography (Syr. 13) Faraj
(Chu Fan Chi: Record of Foreign Peoples)
(Chu Hae Yong Bi Ŏ Ch'ŏn Ga: Com-
mentary to Dragons Flying to Heaven)
Chu Mai Than (Vie. 19)
(Chu Shu Chi Nien: Bamboo Annals)
(Ch'u Tzŭ: Songs of the South)
Chu Tzŭ Yü Lei—Ta Hsüeh (Chi. 12)
Chu Hsi
Chuang Tzŭ (Chi. −3) Chuang
(Chui Shu: Theory of the Calendar)
(Ch'un Ch'iu: Spring and Autumn Annals)
(Chung Yung: Doctrine of the Mean)
Church Annals (Lat. 17) Baronius
Church History (Gre. 3) Eusebios
The Cid (Spa. 11)
The Cimbric Language (Dan. 17) Syv
Cinderella (Chi. 8) Tuan Ch'eng Shih
Circle Measurement Sea Mirror (Chi. 13)
Li Yeh
The Citadel of Sourami (Geo. 19) Djon-
kadze
The City of God (Lat. 4) Augustinus
The City of Ramses (Egy. −13)
Civil Dominion (Lat. 14) Wiclif
The Civil War (Lat. 1) Lucanus
Clarification of Ethics (San.) Vetala
Bhatta
Classes of the Sufis (Ara. 11) Sulamii
Classic of Change (Chi. −3) Wen and
Chou

Classic of Filial Piety (Chi. 3) Liu Shao
Classic of History (Chi. −8) (Shu Ching)
Classic of Mathematics (Chi. 3) (Chou Pei)
Classic of Poetry (Chi. −6) K'ung Fu Tzŭ
Clear Mirror of the Royal Line (Tib. 19) Sönam
Clerical Discipline (Lat. 11) Alphonsus
Clericis Laicos (Lat. 13) Bonifacius VIII
The Cloud Dream of the Nine (Kor. 17) Kim Man Jung
The Cloud Messenger (San. 4) Kaali Daasa
Clouds (Gre. −5) Aristophanes
Code (Hit. −12)
Code of Agni (San.) (Agni Smriti)
Code of Atri (San.) (Atri Smriti)
Code of Bharadvaaja (San.) (Bharadvaaja Smriti)
(Code of Hammurabi: When Anu the Exalted)
Code of Kaanva (San.) (Kaanva Smriti)
Code of Manu (San. −1) Manu
Code of the Prepared Table (Heb. 14) Jacob Ben Asher
Code of Śaandilya (San.) (Śaandilya Smriti)
Code of Vishnu (San. 3) (Visnu Smriti)
Code of Vyaasa (San.) (Vyaasa Smriti)
Code of Yama (San.) (Yama Smriti)
Collected Hymns (Geo. 10) Modrikili
Collected Letters (Lat. 16) Erasmus
Collected Mongol Plays (Chi. 17) (Yüan Ch'ü Hsüan Tsa Chi)
Collected Verses of the Brihat Romance (San. 9) Buddha Svaamin
Collection of Ancient and Modern Poetry (Jap. 10) Tsurayuki
Collection of Gems of Happy Sayings (San. 10) Amita Gati
Collection of Poetry (San. 15) Śrii Vara
Collection of Poetry (San. 15) Vallabha Deva
Collection of Poetry and Poets (San. 13) Jalhana
Collection of Thirty Thousand Traditions (Ara. 9) Ibn Hanbal
Colloquies (Lat. 16) Erasmus
The Colloquy of the Old Men (Iri. 13) (Acallam na Senórech)
Columba (Lat. 8) Adamnan

Comedies (Nor. 18) Holberg
Comedies (Fri. 18) Ploeg
Comedies (Lat. 10) Roswitha
Comic Tales (Dan. 18) Baggesen
The Coming Down (Heb. −1)
Coming Forth by Day (Egy. −14) (Pert em Hru)
The Coming of the English (San. 19) Vinayaka
Commentaries (Heb. 1)
Commentaries (Tam. 15) Adiyaarkunallar
Commentaries (Syr. 10) Bar Kepha
Commentaries (Heb. 12) Hadassi
Commentaries (Heb. 11) Hai
Commentaries (Ara. 11) Ibn Siina
Commentaries (Syr. 7) Merv
Commentaries (Tam. 13) Naccinaarkkiniyar
Commentaries (Tam. 14) Umaapati
Commentaries on Boethius (Lat.) Porretanus
Commentaries of the Brahmans (San. −7) (Brahmanas)
Commentaries on the Civil War (Lat. −1) Caesar
Commentaries on the Classic of Change and the Way of Life (Chi. 3) Wang Pi
Commentaries on the Gallic War (Lat. −1) Caesar
Commentaries on the Gospel (Arm. 14) Orotu
Commentaries on Luke (Arm. 12) Ignatius and Sargis
(Commentarii de Bello Civili: Commentaries on the Civil War)
(Commentarii de Bello Gallico: Commentaries on the Gallic War)
(Commentariolus: Brief Commentary)
Commentary (Heb. 14) Aaron
Commentary (Ara. 13) Baydaawii
Commentary (Chi. 18) Ch'ên Hung Mou
Commentary (Chi. 2) Chêng Hsüan
Commentary (Pra. 7) Jina Bhadra
Commentary (San. 11) Ksiira Svaamin
Commentary (Chi. 17) Ku Chiang
Commentary (Chi. 17) Lin Hsi Chung
Commentary (Chi. 2) Ma Jung
Commentary (San. 15) Raaya Muku Tamani
Commentary (San.) Śabara
Commentary (Chi. 3) San Shu Jan

Daniel (Lat. 12)
Daniel (Lat. 12)   Hilarius
Danish History (Lat. 13)   Grammaticus
(Danish Naama i 'Alaa'ii: Manual of Philosophy)
Daphnis and Chloe (Gre. 3)   Longus
(Darpadalana: Folly of Pride)
(Dasa Avaatara Carita: The Ten Incarnations)
(Dasa Kumaara Carita: Ten Princes)
(Dasa Kumaara Puurvapiithikaa: Introduction to the Ten Princes)
Dasa Padaarthi (San. 7)   Mati Candra
(Dasa Ruupaka: Ten Kinds of Drama)
Dasopant Charitra (San.)
Daughter of Sláva (Cze. 19)   Kollar
Death of Husayn (Ara.)   "Mikhnaf"
Death of Peregrinus (Lat. 2)   Lucianus
Death Song (Bur. 12)   Anantathuria
Deaths of the Persecutors (Lat. 3)   Lactantius
Dedan Inscriptions (Ara. −6)
Dede Korkut Stories (Tur. 14)   (Kitab i Dede Korkut)
Deeds of Ardashiire Baabakaan (Per. 6)   (Kaarnaamake Artakhshatre Paapakaan)
Deeds of the Hungarians (Lat. 12)   Petrus
Deeds of Louis the Pious (Lat. 9)   Ermoldus
Deeds of the Romans (Lat. 15)   (Gesta Romanorum)
Defender of the Peace (Lat. 14)   Padua
Defense of the Anglican Population (Lat. 17)   Milton
Defense of Confucianism (Chi. 6)   Lü Yüan Lang
Deikton (Bur.)
(Deipnosophoi: Banquet of the Learned)
Deities and Myths of the Vedas (San. −5)   Saunaka
Deliverer from Error (Ara. 12)   Ghazaalii
Demon Romance (San. 16)   Ravi Deva
Demonstration of the Gospel (Gre. 3)   Eusebios
Deor's Lament (Eng. 10)
Description of Greece (Gre. 2)   Pausanias
Description of Egypt (Ara.)   Latiif
Description of Egypt (Ara. 15)   Maqriizii
Description of Wales (Lat. 12)   Giraldus
(Desii Naama Maalaa: Non-Sanskritic Prakrit Vocabulary)

Destiny (Gre.)   Alexander
The Destruction of Jerusalem (Pro. 14)
The Destruction of Kur. (Sum. −20)
(Deuteronomy: The Second Giving of the Law)
(Devii Sataka: Hymn to Devii)
(Dhamma Pada: Footsteps of the Law)
(Dharma Pariiksaa: Examination of the Law)
(Dharma Saastra: Canon Law)
(Dharma Sarma Abhyudaya: Life of Dharma Naatha)
(Dharma Suutra: Code of Vishnu)
Dharmmapradiipikaa (Cey. 13)   Gurulugomi
(Dhvanya Aloka: Doctrine of Tone)
Dialectical Principles (Lat.)
Dialectics (Lat. 9)   Alcuin
Dialectics (Lat. 12)   Abélard
Dialogue of the Exchequer (Lat. 12)
Dialogue on the Life of Chrysostom (Gre.)   Palladios
Dialogue on Orators (Lat. 1)   Tacitus
Dialogues (Sum. −25)   Gubarru
Dialogues (Lat. 6)   Gregorius
Dialogues of the Dead (Lat. 2)   Lucianus
Dialogues of the Gods (Lat. 2)   Lucianus
Dialogues of the Sea Gods (Lat. 2)   Lucianus
The Diamond Sutra (San.)   (Prajna Paramita)
Diary (Ara. 19)   Jabartii
Diary (Jap. 11)   Murasaki
Diary (Tib. 17)   Ngawang
Diary (Chi. 19)   Ssŭ Yŭ Têng
Diary of Journeys by a Woman (Jap. 11)   (Sarashina Nikki)
(Diatribai: Dissertations)
(Dibhre ha Yamim: Daily Words)
Dictionary (Per. 17)   Baksh
Dictionary (Lat. 16)   Calepino
Dictionary (San. 12)   Dhanam Jaya
Dictionary (San. 14)   Irugapa
Dictionary (San. 12)   Mahe Svara
Dictionary (San. 12)   Mankha
Dictionary (San. 14)   Mediniikara
Dictionary (San. 6)   Saasvata
Dictionary (Ara. 14)   Safadii
Dictionary of Men of Letters (Ara. 13)   Yaaquut
Didakhe (Gre.)
Didascalia Apostolorum (Lat.)

Digenis Akritas (Gre. 10)

Digest (Gre. 6) Justinianus

Digest of the Bharatas (San. 11) Kṣe-mendra

Digest of the Brihat Romance (San. 11) Ksemendra

Digest of the Epic of Rama (San. 11) Kṣemendra

Digest of Ethics (San. 15) Dya Dviveda

(Diipa Vaṃsa: Island Chronicle)

(Diiwaan: Lyrics)

(Dinkard: Religious Acts)

The Dinner Party (Gre. −4) Platon

Dionysius (Gre. 4) Nonnus

(Disciplina Clericalis: Clerical Discipline)

Discourse on Magic (Lat. 3) Apuleius

Discourses (Heb. 14) Babya Ben Asher

Dispute of the Body and the Head (Egy. −10)

Dissertations (Gre. 2) Arrianus

Dit de L'Herberie (Fre. 13) Rutebeuf

(Divan: Lyrics)

(De Diversis Quaestionibus: Various Questions)

The Divine Cow (Egy. −14)

The Divine Institutes (Lat. 3) Lactantius

The Division of Nature (Lat. 9) Erigena

(Divya Avadaana: Tales of Buddha)

(Diwan: Lyrics)

(Diwan Lughat at Turk: Encyclopedia of Turkish)

Doctrine of Addai (Syr. 4)

Doctrine of Life for the New Jerusalem (Lat. 18) Swedenborg

Doctrine of the Mean (Chi. −4) K'ung Chi

Doctrine of Politics (San. 4) Caṇakya or Kauṭilya

Doctrine of the Sects (Per. 11) Muhammad

Doctrine of Tone (San. 9) Aananda Vardhana

Doctrines of the West (Ara.) 'Idhaarii

Documents of the Fighting States (Chi. −3) (Chan Kuo Ts'ê)

Dodo Chanesar (Sin. 14)

Dogma (Arm. 12) Tlay

(Dominus ac Redemptor Noster: Our Lord and Redeemer)

Dosicles and Rodanthe (Gre. 12) Theodoros

Doubts Raised (Chi. 2) Mou

The Dove's Necklace (Ara. 11) Ibn Hazm

The Downfall of Russia (Rus. 13)

Draft History of the Manchu Dynasty (Chi. 18) (Ch'ing Shih Kao)

The Dragon Princess (Tha.) (Nang u Thay)

A Drama (Tur. 19) Haamid

Drama of Edfou (Egy. −4)

Drama of the Gods (Egy. −21)

Dramaturgy (San. 13) Śaara Daatanaya

(Draumkvaedet: Dream Vision)

Dream of the Goldpieces (Chi. 14) K'iao

Dream of the Red Chamber (Chi. 17) Ts'ao

Dream of Sweeping Clouds (Chi.)

Dream of Vaasava Dattaa (San. −4) Bhaasa

Dream of Venus (Lat. 2) (Pervigilium Veneris)

Dream Vision (Nor. 13) (Draumkvaedet)

(Dresden Codex: Astronomy and Divination)

The Drifting Cloud (Jap. 19) Futabatei

(Dṛṣṭaanta Śataka: Illustrated Maxims)

The Drunkard's Dream (Chi. 9) Li Fu Yen

The Duel of Siva and Arjuna (San. 6) Bhaaravi

(Dumyatu 'l Qaṣr: Statue of the Palace)

(Durghatavṛtti: Commentary on Paanini)

(Durratu 'l Ghawwaaṣ: The Pearl of the Diver)

The Duties of the Clergy (Lat. 4) Ambrosius

The Duties of the Clergy (Lat. 9) Ameliarus

Dvaa Daśa Pañjarikaa Stotra (San. 9) Śaṃkara

(Dvi Ruupa Kośa: Word Variants)

(Dvyaaśvaya Kaavya: Life of Kumaara Paala)

The Dynasty of Raghu (San. 4) Kaali Daasa

Dzanecka (Bur.)

(Dzeglo Eristhava: Acts of the Provinces)

The Earth (Ger. 11) (Merigarto)

Easter Hymn (Lat. 9) Sedulius

(Enuma Elish: When Above)
(Epanogoge: Customary Law)
Epic (Kan. 18)   Chikadevaraya
Epic (San. 4)   Hari Sena
Epic (Kan. 15)   Lakshmisha
Epic (Kan. 11)   Pampa
Epic (Kan. 11)   Ponna
Epic (Kan. 11)   Ranna
Epic (Kan. 16)   Ratnakaravarni
Epic of Achilles (Lat. 1)   Statius
Epic of Aeneas (Lat. −1)   Vergilius
Epic of Alexis (Gre. 12)   Komnena
Epic of David (Yid. 15)   (Shmuel Bukh)
Epic of Irra (Bab.)
Epic of Kashmir (Kas. 9)   Śiva Svamin
Epic of Kings (Per. 11)   Firdausi
Epic of Krishna (Hin. 16)   Sur Das
Epic of Lepanto (Cat. 17)   Pujol
Epic of Odysseus (Gre. −9)   Homeros
Epic of Rama (Jav. 14)   (Raamaayana)
Epic of Rama (Nep. 19)   Bhanubhakta
Epic of Rama (Tam. 10)   Kamban
Epic of Rama (Ass. 14)   Madhab Kandali
Epic of Rama (Ben. 15)   Ojhaa
Epic of Rama (Tha. 18)   Thonburi
Epic of Rama (San. −2)   Vaalmiiki
Epic of Siva Begging (San. 15)   Śiva Daasa
Epic of Tambuka (Swa. 18)   (Utendi wa Tambuka)
Epic of the Tigris (Hit. −12)   (Gurparanzakhus)
Epic of Thebes (Lat. 1)   Statius
Epic of Troy (Gre. −9)   Homeros
Epics (Mar. 17)   Mukteshwar
(Epigrammatum Sacrorum Liber: Sacred Epigrams)
Epigrams (Lat. 2)   Martialis
Epistle of Clement (Gre. 1)
Epistle of Forgiveness (Ara. 11)   'Alaa
(Epistolae: Letters)
Epitaph of a Princess (Mal. 14)
Epitaph of Taba (Syr. −6)
(Epitrepontes: Arbitration)
Epodes (Lat. −1)   Horatius
Equation Theory (Chi. 19)   Li Chuan
(Er Nu Ying Hsiung Chuan: Heroic Children)
(Erdeni Yin Tobchi: History of the Eastern Mongols)
(Erh Tou Mei: Twice Flowering Plums)
(Ĕrh Ya: Encyclopedic Dictionary)

Erophile (Gre. 17)   Khortatzes
(Erotemata: Grammar)
Esarhaddon (Bab. −7)
Esdras (Gre. 2)   (Bible)
(Eshkol ha Kopher: Commentary on the Decalogue)
Essay on Individual Ethics (Cam. 19)   Lôk Pŭtthèr
Essay on the Origin of the Eight Banners (Man. 18)   (Jagôn Gosai Tung Tzi Sutchung Ga Weileghe Bitkhe)
Essays (Chi. 12)   Chêng Ch'iao
Essays (Chi. 14)   Fang Hsiao Ju
Essays (Chi. 9)   Han Yü
Essays (Chi. 17)   Hsü Hsieh
Essays (Chi. 3)   Hsün Hsü
Essays (Chi. 3)   Huang Fu Mi
Essays (Egy. −28)   Im Hotep
Essays (Ara. 9)   Jaahiz
Essays (Chi. 4)   Kuo P'o
Essays (Chi. 14)   Liu Chi
Essays (Chi. 13)   Liu Yin
Essays (Chi. 11)   Su Tung P'o
Essays (Gre. 12)   Theodoros
Essays (Chi. 16)   Tsung Ch'ên
Essays and Hymns (Gre.)   Synesios
Essays on Stoicism (Lat. 1)   Seneca
Esther (Heb. −2)   (Bible)
Ethical Epigrams (Tam. 6)
Ethics (Chi. −5)   Mo
Ethics (Gre. 2)   Plutarkhos
Ethics (Lat. 6)   Gregorius
Ethics (Lat. 12)   Abélard
Ethics for Posterity (Cam. 19)   Kèp
The Ethics of Aristocracy (Per. 14)   Zaakaan
Etiquette and Ceremonial (Chi. −2)   (I Li)
Etruscan Public Ceremonies (Etr. −1)   (The Capua Tile and the Zagreb Mummy Wrapping)
Etymological Commentary (San. −5)   Yaaska
(Etymologicum Magnum: The Great Etymology)
Etymologies or Origins (Lat. 7)   Sevillanus
Eulogy of Vastu Paala (San. 13)   Somesvara Datta
The Eunuch (Lat. −2)   Terentius
(Evangelion: The Gospel)
The Everlasting Wrong (Chi. 9)   Po Chü I

Flower of Nature (Dut. 13)   Maerlant
Flower Shadows behind the Curtain (Chi. 17)   (Ko Lien Hua Ying)
The Flowers in the Garden (Egy. −14)
Flytings (Ara. 8)   Jarir and Farazdaq
Folly of Pride (San. 11)   Ksmendra
Food of Hearts (Ara. 10)   Abuu Taalib
Footsteps of the Law (Pal. 5)   Buddha Ghosa
The Forest Book of the Aitareya (San.)   (Aitareya Aaranyaka)
The Forest Book of the Kaushiitaka (San.)   (Kaushiitaki Aaranyaka)
The Forests (Lat. 1)   Statius
Formal Logic (Chi. −3)   (Siao Ts'iu P'ien)
The Former Han (Chi. 2)   Pan
Forms of Worship (Bur.)   (Paya Shikho)
A Formulary of Blessings (Heb. 1)
Fors de Morlaas (Pro. 12)
Fors d'Oloron (Pro. 11)
Foundations of the World (Heb. 13)   Israeli
The Founding of the Manchu Empire (Chi. 18)   (Huang Ts'ing K'ai Kuo Fang Lüeh)
The Founding of the Temple (Egy. −20)   Sen Usret I
The Fount of Knowledge (Gre. 8)   Damascene
The Fount of Life (Ara. 11)   Ibn Gabirol
Four Decades of Hungarian Affairs (Lat. 16)   Bonfini and Sambucus
Four-Element Precious Mirror (Chi. 14)
Four Ends of Life (San. 11)   Ksmendra
The Four Lectures of Śaunaka (San.)   (Śaunakiiyaa Chatura Adhyaayikaa)
Four Songs (Iri. 10)
Fourteen Miraculous Tales (Jap. 10)   (Utsubo Monogatari)
Fragment (Alb. 15)   Durrës
Free Will (Lat. 4)   Augustinus
French Poets (Tur. 19)   Shinaasii
(Thet Freske Riim: Frisian Rhymed Chronicle)
Fridthhjofs Saga (Ice. 13)
Friendly Conversation (Ukr. 18)   Skovoroda
Frisian Poetry (Fri. 17)   Japiks
Frisian Rhymed Chronicle (Fri. 15)   (Thet Freske Riim)
The Frogs (Gre. −5)   Aristophanes

The Frogs (Kor. 18)   Yi Mun Jong   (Fu Nan: Cambodia)
Fugitive King (Slo. 19)   Levstik
A Full History of the Danish Kings (Lat. 12)   Aagesen
Funeral Discourse (Mag. 13)   (Halotti Beszéd)
(Al Fusuul wa 'l Ghaayaat: Parody of the Koran)
(Fusuusuu 'l Hikam: Bezels of Philosophy)
(Futuuhaat al Makkiyya: Meccan Revelations)

(Gadya Cintaamani: Romance of Jiivan Dhara)
Galician Songs (Gal. 19)   Castro
Galician-Volynian Chronicle (Rus. 12)
Gallantry (Ara. 9)   Abuu Tammaam
Gallantry (Ara. 9)   Buhturii
The Game of Adam (Fre. 12)   (Le Jeu d'Adam)
The Game of Leaves (Fre. 13)   Adam   (Gan 'Eden: The Garden of Eden)
Gandii Stotra Gaathaa (San. 1)   Aśva Ghosa
The Garden of Eden (Heb. 14)   Aaron
The Garden of Kings (Mal. 17)   Raniri
The Garden of Pleasure (Chi. −5)   Yang
The Garden of Truth (Per. 12)   Sanaa'ii
Garshaasp Naama (Per. 11)   Asadii
(Garuda Puraana: Legend of Garuda)
Gates (Egy. −14)
(Gathas: Hymns)
Gaüdavaha (Pra. 8)   Vaakpati Raja
Gawain and the Green Knight (Eng. 14)
(Gemara: Learning)
(Gemma Animae: Jewels of the Soul)
(Gempei Monogatari: The Tale of Gempei)
Genealogical History of Nepal (Nep. 17)
Genealogies of the Gods (Lat. 14)   Boccaccio
Genealogy of the Gods (Gre. −8)   Hesiodos
Genera of Plants (Lat. 18)   Jussieu
A General Account of the World (Tib. 18)   Sum
The General Epistle of James (Gre. 1)   Iakobos
General History of Japan (Jap. 19)   Rai
General Knowledge (Ara. 9)   Ibn Qutayba

General Songbook (Gal. 16) (Cancioneiro Geral)

Genesis (Sax. 9)

On Genesis (Lat. 4) Augustinus

(Genji Monogatari: The Tale of Genji)

The Genuine (Ara. 9) Bukhaarii

The Genuine (Ara. 9) Muslim

Genus, Species and Individuality (Syr. 6) Ras'ain

Geographical Dictionary (Per. 19) Shiirvaanii

Geographical Dictionary (Ara. 13) Yaaquut

Geography (Per. 10) (Huduud al 'Aalam)

Geography (Per. 15) Abru

Geography (Gre. 1) Strabo

Geography of Arabia (Ara. 10) Hamdaanii

Geography of the World (Lat. 1) Mela

Georgics (Lat. −1) Vergilius

Germany (Lat. 1) Tacitus

Gesser Khan (Mon.)

(Gesta Hungarorum: Deeds of the Hungarians)

(Gesta Romanorum: Deeds of the Romans)

Geta (Lat. 12) Blois

Ghana (Ara. 9) Fazari

Ghana (Ara. 12) Zouhri

Ghaṭakarpara (San. 4)

(Il Gifen Tork: The Turkish Galleon)

Giitaa Bhaaṣya (San. 12) Raama Nuja

(Giitaa Govinda: Song of the Divine Cowherd)

Giitaañjali (Ben. 19) Tagore

Gilgamesh (Sum. −25) (Cambridge Ancient History)

Gilgamesh (Hit. −15)

Gilgamesh (Bab. −8)

(Ginza Rabba: The Great Treasure)

(Giraa Sardesaya: The Parrot Message)

The Girl and the Elephant (Tha.) (Phum Hon)

Gísla Saga Súrssonar (Ice. 13)

Gita Arnava (Mar. 16) Daasopant

The Globe (Ice. 13) Sturluson

The Glory of Kings (Eth. 13) (Kebra Nagaset)

Gloss on Vyasa's Yoga Commentary (San. 9) Vaacaspati Mitra

Glossary (Per. 11) Asadii

Gnomic Poem (San. 11) Śambhu

Go Out and See (Yid. 17) Ashkenazi

The God of Socrates (Lat. 3) Apuleius

Gododdin (Wel. 7) Aneirin

God's Light (Heb. 15) Crescas

Gold Tablet (Per. −7) Ariyaramna

(Gold, Vase and Plumes: The Golden Lotus)

The Golden Ass (Lat. 3) Apuleius

The Golden Legend (Lat. 13) Voragine

The Golden Lotus (Chi. 16) Hsü Wei

Golden Meadows (Ara. 10) Mas'uudi

The Golden Words of Pythagoras (Gre. 5) Hierokles

Gomorhianus (Lat. 11) Damian

Gondar Poems (Eth. 18) Alaqa Tayya

The Good Fortune of the Dead (Egy. −14)

Good Heart (Yid. 17) (Lev Tov)

Gopaala Taapaniiya Upanishad (San.)

Gopatha Braahmaṇa (San.)

Gorgias (Gre. −4) Platon

Gormond and Isembart (Fre. 10)

(Gosenshiu: Anthology of Poetry)

The Gospel (Syr. 19)

The Gospel (Gre. 1) Ioannis (Bible: John)

The Gospel (Gre. 1) Levi (Bible: Matthew)

The Gospel (Gre. 1) Lucas (Bible: Luke)

The Gospel (Gre. 1) Marcus (Bible: Mark)

Gospel History (Ger. 9) Otfrid

Gospels (Geo. 11) Athos

Gospels (Rum. 16) Coresi

Gothic History (Lat. 6) Jordanes

The Governance of Rulers (Lat. 13) Aquinas

Government (Chi. 8) Tu Yu

The Government of the Manchus (Chi. 17) (Ta Ch'ing Hui Tien)

(Grágás: Laws)

Grammar (Lat. 9) Alcuin

Grammar (Syr. 7) Hedhaiyabh

Grammar (Gre.) Laskaris

Grammar (San. −4) Paanini

Grammar (Ukr. 17) Smotritsky

Grammar (Bur. 16) Thilawuntha

Grammar and Linguistics (Mlm. 14)

Grammar and Medicine (Heb. 13) Haziri

Grammarians and Speakers (Lat. 1) Suetonius

(Granth: Adi Granth)

Great Art (Lat. 16) Cardano

The Great Bharatas (Ass. 15)
The Great Bharatas (Jav. 12)
The Great Bharatas (San. −2) (Mahaa Bhaarata)
The Great Bharatas (Mlm. 16) Ezhuttachan
The Great Bharatas (Mal. 15) (Hikayat Perang Pandawa Jaya)
The Great Bharatas (Kan. 15) Kumaara Vyaasa
The Great Bharatas (Tel. 11) Nannaya
The Great Bharatas (Ori. 14) Sarala Das
The Great Book of the Classes (Ara. 9) Ibn Sa'd
The Great Charter (Lat. 13) John
The Great Commentary (San. −2) Patañjali
The Great Etymology (Lat. 12) (Etymologicum Magnum)
The Great Forest Book Lecture (San.) (Brihad Aaranyaka Upaniṣad)
The Great Journey (Ori. 19) Radhanath
The Great Learning (Chi. −4) K'ung Chi
The Great Learning for Women (Jap. 18) Kaibara
The Great Legend (Pra. 9) Puṣpa Danta
The Great Liberation (Tib.)
The Great Mirror (Jap. 12) Tamenari
The Great Mystery of Jesus (Bre. 16)
The Great Rose Garden (Ger. 14)
The Great Treasure (Syr. 8) (Ginza Rabba)
Greater Ethics (Gre. −4) Aristoteles
The Greater Laws (Heb. 9) Qayyara
The Greater Mirror (Lat. 13) Beauvais
The Greatness of Siva (San.) (Puṣpa Danta)
Grettis Saga (Ice. 13)
Grihya Suutra (San. −5) Śaunaka
Ground Giving (Per. 3) (Bundahishn)
Gudrun (Ger. 13)
Guide for the Perplexed (Heb. 12) Ben Maimon
(Guirrimears: Mystery Plays)
Gul Bakawali (Mal. 18) Nipal Chand
(Gulistaan: The Rose)
Gulshan i 'Ishq (Urd. 17) Nuṣratii
Gunnlaugs Saga (Ice. 13)
(Gurparanzakhus: Epic of the Tigris)
(Guru Nanak Chamatkar: Life of the Guru Nanak)

Gushaasp Naama (Per. 11)
Gutas Saga (Swe. 13)
(Gweledigaetheu y Bardd Cwsc: The Visions of the Sleeping Bard)
(Gwreans an Bys: The Creation)
(Gyal Rap Sal Waï Me Long: Clear Mirror of the Royal Line)

(Haara Avalii: Rare Words)
Habib as Siyar (Per. 16) Khond Amiir
(Hadiiqat ul Haqiiqat: The Garden of Truth)
(Al Hadiitha: Traditions)
Hadithi ya Barasisi (Swa. 19) Mazrui
Hadithi ya Hasina (Swa. 19) Mazrui
Haft Iqliim (Per. 16) Raazii
(Hákonarmál: Praise of Hakon)
Ḥalbatu 'l Kumayt (Ara. 15) Nawaajii
(Halotti Beszéd: Funeral Discourse)
(Al Ḥamaasa: Gallantry)
Hamamatsu Chiunagon (Jap. 10)
Hamburg Church History Lat. 11) Bremen
The Hammer of Folly (San. 9) Śankara
Al Hamziyah (Swa. 18) Saiyid Aidarus
Han Annals (Chi. 3) Hsü Yüeh
(Han Chi: Han Annals)
(Han I Araha Ampasai Mutzilen Pe Dara Pure Bitkhe: Address to the Magistrates on Moral Training)
(Hankampu: History of the Daimyos)
Hans Alienus (Swe. 19) Heidenstam
(Hanumaan Naaṭaka: The Story of Rama)
Hao K'in Chuan (Chi. 16)
(Haptanghati: Seven Chapters)
Hara Carita Cinṭaamaṇi (San. 12) Jayaa Ratha
(Hara Vijaya: Mythology)
Hari Vilaasa (San. 11) Lolimba Raaja
The Harmonies of the World (Lat. 17) Kepler
The Harrowing of Hell (Eng. 13)
(Harṣa Carita: Life of Harsha)
(Hasti Vidyarnava: An Ocean of Elephant Lore)
(Háttalykill: Key to Meters)
(I Havsbandet: At the Edge of the Sea)
(Al Hawi: Lexicon)
(Ḥayy Ibn Yakẓaan: Alive, Son of Awake)
(Hazaar Afsaana: Thousand Tales)

Hazzu 'l Quḥuuf (Ara. 17) Shirbiinii
(Heauton Timoroumenos: The Masochist)
Heaven and Earth (Lat. 13) Albertus
The Heavenly Arcana (Lat. 18) Sweden-
borg
Heer Ranjha (Pun. 18) Warris Shah
(Heiji Monogatari: Tale of Heiji)
(Heike Monogatari: Tale of Heike)
(Heimskringla: The Globe)
(Hekigan Roku: Blue Cliff Records)
Helen (Gre. −5) Euripides
Helgi and Kara (Ice. 13)
Helgi and Svava (Ice. 13)
Heliand (Sax. 9)
Helieutika (Gre.) Oppianos
(Heljarslódarorusta: Battle of the Field of
Death)
(Hellenica: History of Hellenic Affairs)
(Hemelychede der Hemelycheit: Secret of
Secrets)
Heraclides (Syr. 5) Nestorius
(Herakleia: Hercules)
The Herbal (Chi. −4) (Pên Ts'ao)
The Herbal (Chi. 16) Li Shih Chen
Hercules (Gre. −5) Panyasis
Hercules (Gre. −7) Peisander
Hercules (Swe. 17) Stiernhielm
Heresies (Gre. 3) Epiphanios
(Peri Hermeneias: Interpretation)
Hero and Leander (Gre. 6) Musaios
Heroic Children (Chi. 19) Wen Kang
Heroic Deeds of Mercurius of Smolensk
(Rus. 15)
Heroics (Lat. 1) Ovidius
(Heroides: Heroics)
Hexaemeron (Lat. 4) Ambrosius
Hexaemeron (Nor. 17) Arrebo
Hexaemeron (Syr. 7) Jacob of Edessa
(Hexateuch: Genesis through Joshua)
(Hi Ts'e: Appendix of the Classic of
Change)
Hidaayat Naama (Urd. 14)
(Hierobotanicon: The Plants of Uppsala)
Hierotheus (Syr. 5) Bar Sudhaili
Hikayat Awang Sulong (Mal. 15)
(Hikayat Bayan Budiman: Tales of a
Parrot)
Hikayat Bestammam (Mal. 19)
(Hikayat Galuh Di Gantong: Tale of
Panji)
Hikayat Ganja Mara (Mal. 19)
(Hikayat Golam: Kalila and Dimna)

Hikayat Hang Tuah (Mal. 15)
Hikayat Indra Bangsawan (Mal. 15)
Hikayat Indraputra (Mal. 15)
(Hikayat Iskandar: Romance of Alex-
ander)
(Hikayat Kalila dan Damina: Kalila and
Dimna)
(Hikayat Maharaja Bikrama Sakti: Ro-
mance of King Vikrama)
(Hikayat Merang Mahawangsa: Kedah
Annals)
Hikayat Nakhoda Muda (Mal. 15)
Hikayat Pelandok Jinaka (Mal. 15)
(Hikayat Penerang Hati: Aesop's Fables)
(Hikayat Perang Pandawa Jaya: The
Great Bharatas)
(Hikayat Puspa Wiraja: Kalila and
Dimna)
(Hikayat Raja Raja Pasai: Chronicles of
Pasai)
(Hikayat Sang Boma: Story of Bhauma)
Hikayat Shah i Mardan (Mal. 16)
(Hikayat Śri Rama: Romance of the Lord
Rama)
Hildebrand (Ger. 9)
(Hilyatu 'l Awliyaa: Adornment of the
Saints)
The Himyarite Ode (Ara. 12) Himyarii
The Himyarites (Syr. 6) Beth Arsham
Hippolytus (Gre. −5) Euripides
Hissope (Por. 18) Diniz
(Histoire de la Guerre de Navarre: The
War of Navarre)
(Historia Danica: Danish History)
(Historia Ecclesiastica Gentis Anglorum:
Ecclesiastical History of the English)
(Historia Naturalis: Natural History)
(Historia Ortus, Vitae et Passionis S.
Canutis Regis Daniae: St. Canute)
(Historia Pontificalis: Pontifical History)
(Historia Romana: Roman History)
(Historia Trojana: The Trojan Story)
(Historiai: Histories)
The Historic Mysteries (Gre. −4) Eu-
hemeros
Historical Memoranda (Gre. −1) Strabo
Historical Records (Chi. −2) Szu Ma
Ch'ien
Historico-Geographical Dictionary (Per.
19) Sanii'
(Historie van den Grale: The Holy Grail)
Histories (Lat. 11) Gleber

Histories (Gre. −2) Polybios
Histories (Lat. 10) Richer
Histories (Lat. 1) Tacitus
Histories of the Scots (Lat. 16) Boece
History (Chi. −4) (Kuo Yü)
History (Lat. 4) Ammianus
History (Arm. 18) Crete
History (Heb. 16) Gans
History (Arm. 13) Ganzak
History (Per. 11) Gardizi
History (Per. 16) Khond Amiir
History (Heb. 16) Rossi
History (Per. 15) Samarqandi
History (Chi.) Szen
History (Kas. 19) Wahab Pare
History (Chi. 7) Wei Chêng
History (Heb. 16) Zakkuth
History, 952–1136 (Arm. 12) Matthew of Edessa
History, 1136–1176 (Arm. 12) Gregory the Priest
History and Philosophy (Chi. 12) Chu Hsi, ed.
History, Biography, Chronology, Geography (Tur. 17) Ḥajji Khaliifa
History of the Albanians of the Caucasus (Arm. 7) Kalankatuatzi
History of Animals (Lat. 16) Gessner
History of Armenia (Arm. 10) Asolik
History of Armenia (Arm. 10) John VI
History of Armenia (Arm. 18) Tchamitch
History of Armenia, 344–392 (Arm. 4) Faustus
History of Armenia, 392–485 (Arm. 5) Lazar
History of Armenia to 450 (Arm. 5) Khoren
History of Babylon (Gre. −3) Berosus
History of the Britons (Lat. 12) Monmouth
History of the Caliphs (Ara. 15) Suyuuṭii
History of Certain Burmese Characters (Bur. 19) Saya Thein
History of China (Chi. 12) Chêng Ch'iao
History of the Clan (Arm. 10) Artsruni
History of Czech Language and Literature (Cze. 18) Dobrovský
History of the Daimyos (Jap. 18) Arai
History of Damascus (Ara. 12) Ibn 'Asaakir

History of East and West (Gre. −5) Herodotos
History of the Eastern Mongols (Mon. 17) Sechen
History of Egypt (Ara. 19) Jabartii
History of Egypt (Gre. −4) Manetho
History of the First Caliphs (Arm. 8) Leoncius
History of the Forty Viziers (Tur. 15) Zaada
History of the Franks (Lat. 6) Tours
History of the Gallas (Eth. 16) Bahrey
History of Georgia (Geo. 8) Djonanchiani
History of Georgia (Geo. 15) Vakhtung VI
History of Great Japan (Jap. 19) Mitsu
History of Guipuzcoa (Bas. 19) Iztueta
History of the Han Dynasty (Chi. 7) Yen Shih Ku
History of Hellenic Affairs (Gre. −5) Xenophon
History of Hindustan (Per. 16) Firishtah
History of the Hova Kings (Mad. 19) Callet
History of the Iberians (Arm. 7) Djuansher
History of the Imoro Tribes (Mad. 17)
History of India, 1600–1800 (Per. 19) (Jaarj Naama)
History of Islamic Civilization (Ara.) Zaydaan
History of Japan (Jap. 14) Chikafusa
History of Japan (Jap. 14) Kitabatake
History of the Jews (Heb. 10) Ben Gorion
History of the Jews (Yid. 16) (Yosifen)
History of Johore (Mal. 18)
History of Joseph (Syr. 5) Balai
History of the Juchen (Chi. 11) T'o
History of the Jugurthine War (Lat. −1) Sallustius
History of the Khitan (Chi. 11) T'o
History of the Kings of Persia (Ara. 8) Ibn Muqaffa
History of the Lombards (Lat. 9) Paulus
History of Mecca (Ara.) Azraqii
History of the Ming (Chi. 18) (Ming Shih)
History of the Mongol Dynasty (Chi. 14) (Yüan Shih)
History of Otto (Lat. 10) Liutprand

History of the Peloponnesian War (Gre. −4)   Thukydides

History of the Persian Invasions, 1602–1661 (Arm. 17)   Araquel

History of the Philologists (Ara. 13)   Ibn Qiftii

History of the Physicians (Ara. 13)   'Usaybi'a

History of the Plants (Gre. −3)   Theophrastos

History of Poland (Lat. 14)   Dlugosz

History of the Rabbit Judge (Cam. 19)

History of Rheims (Lat. 10)   Flodoard

History of the Roman Empire after the Death of Marcus Aurelius (Gre. 3)   Herodianos

History of Rome (Gre. 3)   Dio Cassius

History of Rome (Lat. −1)   Dionysius

History of Rome (Lat. −1)   Livius

History of St. Gregory and Agathangelus (Arm. 5)

History of Saladin (Ara. 13)   'Imad ad Din

History of the Saxons (Lat. 10)   Widukind

History of the Seljuk Dynasty (Ara. 13)   'Imad ad Din

History of the Seljuks (Per. 13)   Raavandi

History of Siunik (Arm. 14)   Orbelian

History of the Slavonic Bulgarians (Bul. 18)   Paisi

History of the Sung (Chi. 11)   T'o

History of the T'ang (Chi. 10)   Liu Hsü

History of the T'ang (Chi. 11)   Ou Yang Hsiu

History of Taron (Syr. 5)   Zenobius

History of the Tatars (Arm. 13)   Malakia

History of the Three Kingdoms (Kor. 12)   Kim

History of the Tribes (Lat. 16)   Fuchs

History of Wardan (Arm. 5)   Wardapet

History of the Warriors (Ara. 15)   (Siiriit el Mugaahidiin)

History of the Wars (Gre. 7)   Menander

History of the Wars of the Sons of Louis the Pious (Lat. 9)   Nithard

History of the Western Pavilion (Chi. 13)   Wang Shi Fu

History of Zacharias Rhetor (Syr. 7)

History of Zarer (Per. 3)

(Hito Padesa: Wholesome Counsel)

Hizakurige (Jap. 19)   Jippensha

(Hogen Monogatari: Tale of Hogen)

(Hojiki: Record of Ten Feet Square)

Holiday Leaves (Yid. 19)   Peretz

The Hollow Tree (Jap. 10)

The Holy Faith (Pro. 11)   (Chanson de Sainte-Foi)

The Holy Grail (Dut. 13)   Maerlant

Homeric Glossary (Gre. −3)   Zenodotos

Homeric Hymns (Gre. −8)

Homilies (Eng. 11)   Aelfric

Homilies (Swe. 16)   Petri

Homilies (Eng. 11)   Wulfstan

Homilies (Arm. 9)   Zachariah

Homonyms (San. 12)   (Anekaartha Samgraha)

Hope (Geo. 19)   Orbeliani

(Hor Chö Jung: Religious History of Mongolia)

Horses (Ara. 9)   Asma'ii

(Hortulus: The Little Garden)

(Hospodin Pomiluj Ny: Lord Have Mercy on Us)

(Hou Han Shu: The Later Han)

The House of Joseph (Heb. 16)   Karo

How to Pray to God (Lat. 16)   Erasmus

Hrafnkels Sàga Freysgoda (Ice. 13)

Hrdaya Darpana (San.)   Bhatta Naayaka

(Hsi Hsiang Ki: History of the Western Pavilion)

(Hsi Yü Chi: Western Journey)

(Hsi Yüan Lu: Instructions to Coroners)

(Hsia Ching: Classic of Filial Piety)

(Hsia Lin Kuang Chi: Anecdotes)

(Hsia Ts'ang Shan Fang Ch'ih Tu: Letters)

Hsiang Shan Hsien Shêng Ch'üan Chi (Chi. 12)   Lu Hsiang Shan

Hsin T'ang Shu (Chi. 11)

(Hsin Wu Tai Shih: New History of the Five Dynasties)

(Hsing Shih Heng Yen: Common Tales to Rouse the World)

Hsün Tzŭ Chi Chieh (Chi. 19)   Wang Hsien Ch'ien

Hua Hu Ching (Chi. 4)

Huai Nan Tzŭ (Chi. −1)

(Huang Ch'ing Ching Chieh: Anthology)

(Huang Ts'ing K'ai Kuo Fang Lüeh: Founding of the Manchu Empire)

(Huduud al 'Aalam: Geography)

(Humaayuun Naama: Imperial Book)

Human Fairy Tale (Jap. 10)   (Taketori Monogatari)

The Indians and Reflections on the Laws of War (Lat. 16) Vitoria

(Los Infantes de Lara: The Princes of Lara)

Infernal Regions (Chi. 12) Lin I Ch'ing

Al Inkishafi (Swa. 18) Saiyid Abdallah

Inquiry (San. 8) Kumaarila

Inquiry (San. 7) Prabhaakara

Inquiry into the Religion of the Sufis (Ara. 11) Kalaabaadhii

The Inquiry of Demonstrations (San.) Jaimini

Al Insaan al Kaamil (Ara. 15) Jiilii

Institutes (Gre. 6) Justinianus

Institutes (San.) Narada

The Institutes of Akbar (Per. 17) Fazl

The Institutes of Oratory (Lat. 1) Quintilianus

The Institution of the Christian Religion (Lat. 16) Calvin

Institutions (Lat. 6) Cassiodorus

The Institutions of Athens (Gre. −5)

Instruction (Rus. 11) Zhidiata

Instruction on the Basket (Pal. 11) (Petakopadesa)

Instructions (Egy. −20) Amen Emhet I

Instructions (Egy. −22) Duauf

Instructions (Egy. −27) Ptah Hotep

Instructions (Egy. −19) Sehete Pibree

Instructions (Rus. 11) Volodimir Monomakh

Instructions for Kagemni (Egy. −27)

Instructions for King Meri Kere (Egy. −22)

Instructions of a Peasant to His Son (Sum. −20)

Instructions to Coroners (Chi. 13) Sung

Instructions to Harkhuf (Egy. −23) Pepi II

Integral Arithmetic (Lat. 16) Stifel

(De Intellectus Emendatione: The Improvement of the Mind)

Interpretation (Lat. 3) Apuleius

Interpretation (Gre. −4) Aristoteles

Inthapat (Tha.)

Intrigues of a Maid (Chi. 13)

Introduction to Arithmetic (Gre. 2) Nikhomakhos

Introduction to the Study of Mathematics (Chi. 13) Chu Shi Chieh

Introduction to the Talmud (Heb. 11) Ibn Nagdela

Introduction to the Ten Princes (San.) Vinaayaka

Introduction to Theology (Lat. 12) Abélard

Introduction to Theology (Ara. 15) Sanusi

The Invasion of the Huns (Syr. 5) Cyrillona

Invective on Those Ignorant of Dialectics (Lat. 12) Abélard

Investigations (Lat.) Anastasius

Invocations to God (Per. 11) Ansaari

Ion (Gre. −5) Euripides

Iphigenia in Tauris (Gre. −5) Euripides

(Al 'Iqd al Fariid: The Unique Necklace) ('Iqqarim: Principles)

(Isaaba fii Tamyiiz al Sahaaba: Lives of the Companions of the Prophet)

(Isaavaasya Upanishad: The Upanishad of the Vaajasaneya Collection)

Isaiah (Heb. −6) (Isaiah 40–66)

(Ise Monogatari: Tales of Ise)

Ishtar and Tammuz (Bab. −21)

(Iskandar Naama: Alexander)

Island Chronicle (Pal. 4) Mahaa Sena

(Islendingabók: Book of Iceland)

Itahasa Dipikia (San. 19)

The Italian Guest (Ger. 13) Zerklar

Itihasa Tamomani (San. 19)

Itineraries of the Fifty-six Monks (Chi. 8)

Itqaan (Ara. 15) Suyuuti

Iwein (Ger. 13) Hartmann

(Izayoi no Ki: A Woman's Travel Diary)

(Izumo Fudoki: Topography)

Jaami' (Ara. 9) Tirmidhi

(Jaami' ut Tawaariikh: World History)

(Jaarj Naama: History of India)

(Jaataka Atthakathaa: Buddha's Former Births)

(Jaataka Maalaa: Poem of Buddha's Former Lives)

(Jaatakas: Buddha's Former Births)

(Jagaduu Carita: Life of Jagaduu)

(Jagôn Gosai Tung Tzi Sutchung Ga Weileghe Bitkhe: Essay on the Origin of the Eight Banners)

Jahveh (Heb. −9) (Hexateuch passim)

Jaiminiiya Nyaaya Maalaa Vistara (San. 14) Maadhava

Jain Canon (Pra. −4) (Jaina Aagama)

(Jaina Aagama: Jain Canon)

Jaina Raaja Taranginii (San. 15) Śrii Vara

To the Jalair Uvays (Per. 14) Salmaan (Jalan Jalan I Hafu Puleku: Mirror of Successive Generations)

Al Jamhara fi 'l Lugha (Ara. 10) Ibn Durayd

Jamharatu Ash'aari 'l 'Arab (Ara. 11) Abu Zayd

(Janakiiharana: The Rape of Siva)

(Janam Sakhis: The Lives of the Gurus)

(Janošíkova Smrt: Death of Janoshik)

The Japanese Family Storehouse (Jap. 17) Ihara

Japanese Notes (Jap. 8) (Nihongi)

Jasahara Cariü (Pra. 9) Puṣpa Danta

Jashar (Heb.)

Jataka Plays (Bur. 16) Awbatha

Jataka Verses (Bur. 16) Aggathamahdi

Jawaahiru 'l Asraar (Urd. 16) Gaamdhanii

(Jen Wu Chih: Study of Human Abilities)

Jeremiah (Heb. −7) Baruch (Bible)

Jestbook (Lat. 15) Poggio

(Jetsun Kahbum: Book of the Dead)

(Le Jeu d'Adam: The Game of Adam)

(Le Jeu de la Feuillée: The Game of Leaves)

(Le Jeu de Robin et Marion: Robin and Marion)

(Le Jeu de St. Nicolas: St. Nicholas)

The Jewel Ornament of Liberation (Tib. 13) Gam Po Pa

Jewels of the Soul (Lat. 11) Honorius

(Jewish Roots: Sacrifice of Isaac)

Jewish Troubles (Heb. 16) Joseph Ben Joshua

The Jewish War (Lat. 1) Josephus

(Jih Chih Lu: Commentary)

(Jiivan Dhara Campuu: Romance of Jiivan Dhara)

(Jinkooshootooki: History of Japan)

(Jitavrittanta: Pandit Bechana Rama)

(In Joannis Evangelium Tractatus: Treatise on John's Gospel)

Joel (Heb. −5) (Bible)

Johaangiir Naama (Per. 11)

The Johannid (Gre. 6) Korippos

John of Chy an Hur (Cor. 17) Lhuyd

John of Tella (Syr. 6) Asia

John of Tella (Syr. 6) Elias

Joining the Shirt (Chi. 13) Chang Kuo Pin

Jonah (Heb. −3) (Bible)

Joseph and Zuleika (Per. 11) Firdausi

Joseph and Zuleika (Tur. 16) Kemaal

Joshua (Heb. −7) (Bible)

(Josippon: History of the Jews)

Jou Pu Tuan (Chi. 17) Li Yü

Journal in India (Chi. 5) Fa

Journal of a Townsman of Yangchow (Chi. 17)

Journals (Chi. 11) Su Tung Po

Journey of Rama and Pandu (San.) Chidambara

Journey through Iceland (Ice. 18) Ólafsson

Journey to the Holy Places (Lat. 4) Aetheria

Joy of the Snake World (San. 7) Harsa

Joyas del Gay Saber (Pro. 15)

Judges (Heb. −6) (Bible)

Judici d'Amor (Pro. 12) Vidal

Judith (Heb. −2) (Bible)

Judith (Eng. 10)

Jungariad (Mon.)

(Jup Sahib: Morning Prayer)

(Jyotisha Vedaanga: Astronomy)

(Kaa Tantra: Elementary Grammar)

Kaadambarii (San. 7) Baaṇa

Kaadambarii Kathaa Saara (San. 9) Abhi Nanda

(Kaama Suutra: The Laws of Love)

Kaamil (Ara. 9) Mubarrad

(Kaaṇva Smriti: Code of Kaaṇva)

(Kaarnaamake Artakhshatre Paapakaan: Deeds of Ardashire Babakan)

(Kaaśikaa Vṛtti: Commentary on Paanini)

(Kaavya: Epic)

(Kaavya Alaṁkaara: Metaphorical Romance)

Kaavya Alamkaara Sara Samgraha (San.) Udbhata

(Kaavya Anuśa Asana: Poetics)

(Kaavya Darśa: The Mirror of Poetry)

(Kaavya Kalpalataa: Advice to Poets)

(Kaavya Miimaamsaa: Poetic Inquiry)

(Kaavya Prakaaśa: The Luster of Poetry)

Kabbigara (Kan. 13) Aaṇḍayya

Kad ha Qemah (Heb. 14) Babya Ben Asher

Kafis (Pun. 18)   Bulhey Shah
Kafis (Sin. 18)   Sachal
(Kagero Nikki: Diary of a Woman)
Kahun Papyrus (Egy. −19)
(K'ai Fang Shuo: Equation Theory)
(Kaifusoo: Chinese Poems)
Kalaa Vilaasa (San. 11)   Ksemendra
(Kalaka Charya: Story of Kalaka)
Kalapurnodayam (Tel. 16)   Surana
Kalasha Chautisa (Ori. 14)   Bachha Das
(Kalevipoeg: The Son of Kalev)
(Kalgidhar Chamatkar: Life of the Guru
   Gobind Singh)
(Kaliila wa Dimna: Kalila and Dimna)
Kalila and Dimna (Mad. 16)
Kalila and Dimna (Mal. 19)
Kalila and Dimna (Mal. 16)
Kalila and Dimna (Jav. 16)
Kalila and Dimna (Mal. 17)   (Hikayat
   Golam)
Kalila and Dimna (Mal. 17)   (Hikayat
   Puspa Wirajal)
Kalila and Dimna (Mal. 18)   (Hikayat
   Kalila dan Damina)
Kalila and Dimna (Syr. 6)   Bodh
Kalila and Dimna (Ara. 8)   Ibn Muqaffa
Kalila and Dimna (Mal. 19)   Munshi
   'Abdu'lla
Kalila and Dimna (Per. 10)   Ruudagi
Kalila and Dimna (Gre. 11)   Simeon
(Kalila dan Damina: Kalila and Dimna)
Kalimaat ul Haqaaiq (Urd. 14)
(Kalkai Dulimbi Chugun Gosa: The
   Banners of the Khalkha Mongols)
Kalpanaa Manditikaa (San. 1)   Kumaara
   Lata
(Kam Öng P'yŭn: Book of Interesting and
   Proper Things)
(Kammawaasaa: Life of Gautama)
(Kan Ying P'ien: Rewards and Punish-
   ments)
Kana Zooshi (Jap. 17)
(K'ang Hsi Tzŭ Tien: Chinese Dic-
   tionary)
(Kanjur: The Translated Command-
   ments)
(Kapphina Abhyudaya: Epic of Kashmir)
Karna Sundarii (San. 11)   Bilhana
Karpura Mañjarii (Pra. 10)   Raaja
   Sekhara
(Kashf al Mahjub: The Revelation of
   Hidden Things)

Kashshaaf (Ara. 12)   Zamakhsharii
Katha Upanishad (San.)
(Kathaa Kośa: Treasury of Tales)
(Kathaa Sarit Saagara: The Ocean of
   Rivers)
Kathaa Vatthu (Pal. −1)   Tissa
Kathaarnova (San. 15)   Siva Daasa
Kathakali (Mlm. 17)
(Katholike Prosodia: Universal Prosody)
(Kaushiitaki Aaranyaka: The Forest
   Book of the Kaushiitaka)
Kaushiitaki Upanishad (San.)
(Kauśika Suutra: The Teachings of
   Kauśika)
Kavi Indra Vacana Samuccaya (San. 11)
Kavi Kanthaa Bharana (San. 11)   Kse-
   mendra
(Kaviraajamaarga: Treatise on Poetry)
Kavirahasya (San. 10)   Hala Ayudha
(Kebra Nagaset: The Glory of Kings)
Kedah Annals (Mal. 18)   (Hikayat Me-
   rang Mahawangsa)
Ken Tambuhan (Mal. 15)
Keret (Syr. −14)
Kessis the Hunter (Hit. −12)
(Kether Torah: Commentary)
Key to Meters (Ice. 15)   Gutormsson
Khamba and Thoibi (Ass. 19)
(Khanda Praśasti: The Ten Incarnations
   of Vishnu)
Khandanakhandakhaadya (San. 12)   Śrii
   Harsa
(Kharakteres: Characters)
(Khariidatu 'l Qasr: Virgin Pearl of the
   Palace)
Khashfu 'l Zunuun (Ara. 17)   Hajji
   Khaliifa
Khawor Nama (Urd. 17)   Rustami
Khent (Arm. 19)   Raffi
(Khirad Afroz: The Illuminator of
   Understanding)
Khitat (Ara. 15)   Maqriizii
(Khizaanatu 'l Adab: Anthology of
   Spanish-Arabic Verse)
Khlong Kamruen (Tha. 16)   Sri Praj
(Khristos Paskhoon: Christ's Passion)
Khusrau and Shirin (Per. 13)   Nizaami
Khusrau and Shirin (Tur. 15)   Kermi-
   yaan
Khusraue Kawaadhan and His Page
   (Per. 5)
(Khvaataay Naamak: The Book of Kings)

Kievan Chronicle (Rus. 12)
(Kiimiyaa'u 'l Sa'aadat: Alchemy of Happiness)
(Kiirti Kaumudi: Eulogy of Vastu Paala)
Kiirti Lataa (Pra. 14) Vidyaa Pati
Kim Van Kieu (Vie. 19) Nguyen Du
(Kin Ku K'i Kuan: Ancient and Modern Marvellous Tales)
King Alfred (Lat. 10) Asser
King Antef (Egy. −18)
King Apophis and Sekenen Re (Egy. −13)
King Cheops and the Magicians (Egy. −17)
King Darius (Egy. −6) Udjahorresne
King David (Heb. −10) (II Samuel)
King Geser (Mon. 18) (Arban Jüg ün Ejen Geser Qaghan u Tughuji Orosiba)
King Hua Yüan (Chi. 16)
King Oedipus (Gre. −5) Sophokles
King of Battle (Bab. −26) Sargon I
The King of Nishadha (San. 12) Śrii Harsa
King Theodore II (Eth. 19) Zenab
King Vikrama Ditya (San. 11) Bilhana
The Kingdom of Norway (Nor. 16) Beyer
Kings (Heb. −6) (Bible)
The King's Mirror (Nor. 13) (Konungsskuggsjá)
The Kings of Egypt (Egy. −14) (The Turin Papyrus)
(The Kingship of the Gods: Ullikummi)
(Kiraata Arjuniiya: The Duel of Siva and Arjuna)
Kiri Naavalii (San. 10) Udayana
(Kitaab al Anwai: Law)
Kitaab al Awsat (Ara. 10) Mas'uudi
(Kitaab al Kifayah: Theology)
(Kitaab al Mahadarah: Literary History)
Al Kitaab al Mansuuri (Ara. 10) Raazii
(Kitaab al Shi'r wa 'l Shu'arra: Poetry and Poets)
Kitaab al Yamiinii (Ara. 11) Ghazna
(Kitaab sa Ribu Masa'alah: Book of the Thousand Questions)
(Kitaabu Ansaabi 'l Ashraaf: Lineages of the Nobles)
Kitaabu Futuuhi 'l Buldaan (Ara. 9) Balaadhurii
Kitaabu 'l Adab (Ara. 10) Qaalii
(Kitaabu 'l Aghaanii: Book of Songs)

(Kitaabu 'l Ahkaam al Sultaaniyya: Principles of Government)
(Kitaabu 'l Akhbaar al Tiwaal: Long Histories)
Kitaabu 'l Amaalii (Ara. 10) Qaalii
(Kitaabu 'l Badii': Poetics)
(Kitaabu 'l Bayaan wa 'l Tabyiin: Eloquence and Exposition)
(Kitaabu 'l Faakhir: Proverbs)
(Kitaabu 'l Falaahat al Nabatiyya: Nabatean Agriculture)
(Kitaabu 'l Hayawaan: Animals)
(Kitaabu 'l 'Ibar: Book of Examples)
(Kitaabu 'l Ibil: Camels)
Kitaabu 'l Intisaar (Ara. 9) Khayyaat
Kitaabu 'l Ishtiqaaq (Ara. 10) Ibn Durayd
(Kitaabu 'l Kaamil fi 'l Ta'riikhi: Perfect Book of Chronicles)
Kitaabu 'l Khalqi 'l Insaan (Ara. 9) Asma'ii
(Kitaabu 'l Khayl: Horses)
Kitaabu 'l Luma' (Ara. 10) Abuu Nasr
(Kitaabu 'l Ma'arif: General Knowledge)
(Kitaabu 'l Maghaazii: The Wars)
(Kitaabu 'l Masaalik wa 'l Mamaalik: Roads and Countries)
(Kitaabu 'l Milal wa 'l Nihal: Religions and Sects)
(Kitaabu 'l Ta'arruf li Mahhabi ahli 'l Tasawwuf: Inquiry on the Religion of the Sufis)
(Kitaabu 'l Tabaqaat al Kabiir: Great Book of the Classes)
(Kitaabu 'l Tanbiih wa 'l Ishraaf: Admonitions and Recension)
(Kitaabu 'l Zuhd: Asceticism)
(Kitab i Dede Korkut: Dede Korkut Stories)
(Kitabi Ikan: Book of Certitude)
Kiuo Dowa (Jap.)
(Klong Loka Niti: Maxims)
(Di Klyatche: The Mare)
The Knight in the Tiger Skin (Geo. 13) Rustaveli
The Knight of Rabinal (Qui. 19) Ziz
Knights (Gre. −5) Aristophanes
(Ko Hsiao Hsin Shu: Astronomy and the Calendar)
(Ko Lien Hua Ying: Flower Shadows behind the Curtain)
Koh Lok (Tha. 19) Rama VI

(Koheleth: The Preacher)
(Kojiki: Record of Ancient Matters)
(Kojiki Den: Commentary on the Record of Ancient Matters)
Kokila Sandesa (Cey. 15)
(Kokinshuu: Collection of Ancient and Modern Poetry)
(Kón Chau: Ethics for Posterity)
Konjaku Monogatari (Jap.)
(Konungsskuggsjá: The King's Mirror)
Koran (Ara. 7)   Mohammed
Korean Encyclopedia (Kor. 18)   (Ton Guk Mun Hŏn Pi Go)
Korean Historical Records (Kor. 6)
(Koryŏ Sa: Annals of Korea)
Krishna (Hin. 16)   Sur Das
Krishna Gatha (Mlm. 15)   Cherusseri
(Krito: Socrates in Prison)
Krsna Karna Amrta (San. 11)   Liila Suka
Ku Chin Shiao Shuo (Chi.)
(Ku Ch'ü Tsa Yen: Theatrical Miscellany)
(Ku Liang Chuan: Commentary on the Tso Chuan)
(Kuang Yün: Phonetic Dictionary)
Kuda Sumirang Sri Panji Pandai Rupa (Mal. 15)
(Kudatku Bilik: The Science of the Governor)
(Kumaara Paala Carita: Life of Kumaara Paala)
Kumaarapaala Pratibodha (Pra. 13) Soma Prabha
(Kumaara Sambhava: The Birth of the War God)
Kumaara Vyasa Bharata (Kan.)
(Kumarbi: Ullikummi)
(Kung Yang Chuan: Commentary on the Tso Chuan)
(Kuo Yü: History)
(Kuoh Yü: Conversations)
(Kurral: Songs of a Pariah Priest)
(Kusa Jatakaya: Eastern Love Story)
Kusa Maanjalii (San. 10)   Udayana
(Kuttaniimata: Lessons of a Matchmaker)
(Kuun Mong: The Cloud Dream of the Nine)
(Kuurma Puraana—Iisvara Giitaa: The Song of Siva)
(Kuvalayananda Kaarikaas: Compendium of Figures of Speech)

The Kuzar Debate (Ara. 12)   Ha Levi
Kwei Hai Yu Heng (Chi. 12)   Fan Ch'eng Ta
Kwei Hsin Tso Chih (Chi.)   Chou Mi
(Kwŏlhŭi: The Palace Gate)
(Kya Khwetsa: Tiger Killing)
Kyunyŏ Chŏn (Kor. 11)

(Laačpleesis: Slayer of the Bear)
(Laamiyatu 'l 'Ajam: Non-Arabic Rhyme in L)
(Laamiyatu 'l 'Arab: Arabic Rhyme in L)
(U Labal ri Zibaki Hay: The Wars of the House of Zibak)
Labyrinth of the World and the Paradise of the Heart (Cze. 17)   Komenský
Labyrinths (Dan. 18)   Baggesen
Lachhama (Ori. 19)   Senapati
Lady Anat (Syr. −4)
Lake of Ethics (San. 4)   Ghata Karpara
The Lake of the Deeds of Rama (Ben. 17) Tulsi Das
Laksa Naavalii (San. 10)   Udayana
Laksana Phra Thamasat (Tha.)
(Lalita Vistara: Life of Buddha)
Lam Ang (Ilo. 17)
Lament (Iri. 17)   Ó Gnímh
Lament (Sum. −25)   Tabi Utul Enlil
Lament for Akkad (Bab. −25)
Lament for Bion (Gre. −1)
Lament for Nippur (Sum. −22)
Lament for Sumer (Sum. −20)
Lament for Trahearn (Wel. 11)   Meilyr
Lament for Ur (Sum. −20)
Lamentations (Heb. −7)   Job (Bible)
The Lamentations of Jeremiah (Heb. −6) Baruch (Bible)
Lampoon of Master Kung (Chi. 17)   Li Yü
(Landnámabók: Settlement Book)
The Language of Zuyua (Yuc. 16)   (Zuyua Than Yetel Naat)
The Lankavatara Sutra (San.)
Lao Tzŭ and Chuang Tzŭ (Chi. 4)   Kuo Hsiang
(Laoi Oisín i dTír na n Óg: Lay of Oisín in the Land of Youth)
The Last Conversation (Gre. −4)   Platon
Lataa'ifu 'l Intisaar (Ara. 16)   Sha'raani
(Lataa'ifu 'l Minan: Autobiography)
The Later Han (Chi. 5)   Fan Yeh
The Later Life of Rama (San. 8)   Bhava Bhuuti

The Latin Language (Lat. 2) Varro

De Laudibus Virginitatis (Lat. 7) Aldhelm

Law (Syr. 9) Timothy

Law (Heb. 10) Qirqisani

The Law (Heb. −3) (Torah)

Law of the Birds (Tib. 18)

Law of the Magistrates (Fri. 11)

The Law of War and Peace (Lat. 17) Grotius

Lawaaqihu 'l Anwaar (Ara. 11) Sha'raanii

Laws (Lat. −1) Cicero

Laws (Ice. 13) (Grágás)

The Laws and Customs of England (Lat. 13) Bracton

The Laws and God the Legislator (Lat. 16) Suárez

The Laws of Love (Pro. 14) Molinier

The Laws of Love (San. 4) Vaatsya Ayana

The Laws of Menu (Bur.)

Laxdaela Saga (Ice. 13)

The Lay of the Anklet (Tam. 2) Ilango Adigal

The Lay of Biarki (Ice. 11) (Biarkamál in Fornu)

The Lay of Helgi (Ice. 13)

The Lay of Igor's Campaign (Rus. 12) (Slóvo o Pŭlku Igorevĕ)

The Lay of Maldon (Eng. 10) (Byrhtnoth)

The Lay of Oisin in the Land of Youth (Iri. 18) Comyn

Layla and Majnun (Per. 12) Niẓaamii

Learned Ignorance (Gre.) Nicholas

Learning (Heb. 4) Ashi

(Lebor Gabála: Book of Invasions)

Lecture of the Collection (San.) (Saṃhitaa Upaniṣad)

Lecture of Siva (San.) (Rudra Upaniṣad)

Legal Texts (Gal. 17)

(Legatio Constantinopolitana: The Constantinople Legation)

Legend of Brahma (San.) (Braahma Puraaṇa)

Legend of the Centuries (Fre. 11) (La Légende des Siècles)

Legend of Garuda (San.) (Garuḍa Puraaṇa)

Legend of the Kyaukwaing Pagoda (Bur. 19)

Legend of a Life of Buddha (Cam. 19) Tien

Legend of St. Margaret (Mag. 14) (Margit Legenda)

Legend of Zalpa (Hit. −12)

Legends of Bhoja (San. 16) Ballaala Sena

Legends of Luang Prabang (Lao. 19)

Legends of the Song Celestial (Ass. 15)

Legends of the Song Celestial (San.) (Bhagavata Puraaṇa)

(De Leges: Laws)

(De Legibus ac Deo Legislatore: The Laws and God the Legislator)

(De Legibus et Consuetudinibus Angliae: The Laws and Customs of England)

Lessons of a Matchmaker (San. 8) Daamo Dara Gupta

Letter (Gre. 2) Jude (Bible)

Letter (Heb. 10) Sherira

Letter of Mara Bar Serapion (Syr. 3)

Letter of Paul the Apostle to the Hebrews (Gre. 1) (Bible)

Letter to Pompeius (Lat. 1) Dionysius

Letters (Ara. 11) Abuu Bakr

Letters (Ara. 11) 'Alaa

Letters (Lat. 4) Augustinus

Letters (Lat.) Bernardus

Letters (Lat. −1) Cicero

Letters (Lat. 11) Gerbert

Letters (Ara. 11) Hamadhaanii

Letters (Egy. −13) Hori and Amen Emope

Letters (Gre. 2) Ignatius

Letters (Gre. 2) Ioannis

Letters (Lat. 1) Plinius Junior

Letters (Lat. 12) Salisbury

Letters (Gre. 1) Saul (Bible)

Letters (Syr. 9) Timothy

Letters (Chi. 18) Yüan Mei

Letters from Pontus (Lat. −1) Ovidius

Letters to Ammaeus (Lat. 1) Dionysius

Leucippe and Cleitophon (Gre. 5) Tatius

(Lev Tov: Good Heart)

The Leveled Path (Ara. 8) Ibn Anas

(Levens ons Heren: Life of Our Lord)

(Leviticus: Book of the Levites)

Lexicon (Heb. 11) Hai

Lexicon (Chi. 2) Hsü Shen

Lexicon (San. 13) Keśava Svaamin

(Las Leys d'Amor: The Laws of Love)

(Li Chi: Notes on the Rites)

(Li Sao: Elegies)

(Liang Shu: Book of Liang)
(Liao Chai Chih I: Strange Stories from a Chinese Studio)
(Liao Shih: History of the Khitan)
(Liber Chronicorum: Book of Chronicles)
(Liber Facetiarum: Jestbook)
(Liber Monstrorum: Monsters)
(De Libero Arbitrio: Free Will)
Library (Gre. 9)   Photios
Library of Nineveh (Bab. −7)
Library of Tello (Sum. −28)
Library of Universal History (Lat. −1) Diodorus
Library of Zapouna (Syr. −12)
Libre de l'Amic e de l'Amat (Pro. 13) Lull
(Libre de Maravelles: Book of Wonders)
(Lo Libre de Sufficència e de Necessitat: Sufficiency and Necessity)
(Libri ab Urbe Condita: History of Rome)
Libya (Ara. 10)   Husani
Lieh Kuo Chuan (Chi. 15)
Lieh Tzŭ Shu (Chi.)   Lieh Tzŭ
Life and Times of Ram Kamhaeng (Tha. 13)
Life of Akbar (Per. 17)   Fazl
Life of 'Antar (Ara. 12)   (Siiratu 'Antar)
Life of Anuruddha (Tha. 16)   Sri Praj
Life of Bala (San. −4)   Bhasa
Life of the Blessed Virgin (Alb. 18) Variboba
Life of Buddha (San. 1)   Asva Ghosa
Life of Buddha (Bur.)   (Budiyat)
Life of Buddha (San. 2)   (Lalita Vistara)
Life of Buddha (San. 6)   (Parinirvana Sutta)
Life of Buddha (Tha.)   (Pattama Sompothiyan)
Life of Catholicus Yabhalaha III (Syr. 14)
Life of Charles (Lat. 9)   Einhard
Life of Christ (Tel. 18)
Life of Constantine (Gre. 3)   Eusebios
Life of Dharma Naatha (San. 10)   Hari Candra
Life of Gautama (Bur.)   (Kammawaasaa)
Life of the Great Hero (San. 8)   Bhava Bhuuti
Life of the Guru Gobind Singh (Pun. 19) Vir Singh
Life of the Guru Nanak (Pun. 19)   Vir Singh

Life of Harṣa (San. 7)   Baana
Life of Jagadu (San. 14)   Sarva Ananda
Life of King Lalibala (Eth. 17)
Life of Kumaara Paala (San. 12)   Hema Chandra
Life of the Lord Buddha (Bur.)   (Malla Lingaya Wuttu)
Life of Mar Jacob (Syr. 7)   Sahdona
Life of Meriadec (Cor. 16)   Hadton
Life of Mesrop (Arm. 5)   Goriun
Life of Mohammed (Tur. 15)   Yaziji Oghlu
Life of Na'akueto la Ab (Eth. 15)
Life of Our Lord (Dut. 13)   (Levens ons Heren)
Life of the Prophet (Ara. 8)   Ibn Ishaaq
Life of the Prophet (Tur. 17)   Veysii
Life of Rama (San. 9)   Abhi Nanda
Life of Severus (Syr. 6)   Bar Aphtonya
Life of Soma Paala (San. 13)   Jalhana
Life of Sönam Gyatso (Tib. 16)
Life of Tekla Haymanot (Eth. 15)
Life of Tsong Khapa (Tib. 14)
Life of Vergil (Lat.)   Aelius
Life of Yared (Eth. 15)
Life of Zahir (Ara. 18)   (Siiriit ez Zahir)
Light in Shadows (Lat. 17)   Komenský
The Light Is Sown (Heb. 13)   Isaac Ben Moses
The Light of Truth (San.)   Sara Svati
The Lighted Candelabra (Heb. 14)   Aboab
(The Lights of Canopus: Fables of Bidpai)
(Lilathilakam: Grammar and Linguistics)
The Lily (Ice. 14)   Asgrímsson
(Lin Yi: Champa)
The Lineage of the Lords of Totonicapan (Qui. 16)   Reynoso
The Lineages of the Nobles (Ara. 9) Balaadhurii
Linga Puraana (San.)
(De Lingua Latina: The Latin Language)
Lions of the Jungle (Ara. 13)   Athiir
(Lisaanu 'l 'Arab: Arabic Dictionary)
(Lisaanu 'l Ghaib: The Tongue of the Invisible)
Literary Encyclopedia (Chi. 7)
Literary History (Ara. 12)   Ibn Ezra
Literary History (Ara. 10)   Ṣuulii
The Little Clay Cart (San. 4)   Śuudraka
The Little Garden (Lat. 9)   Walafrid

Liturgical Commentaries (Arm. 8) Catholicus

Liu Chih Yüan Chu Kung Tiao (Chi.)
(Liu Shu Ku: Six Scripts)

The Liu Sung (Chi. 6) Shên Yo

Lives (Lat. 2) Nepos

Lives (Syr. 7) 'Rustam

Lives and Opinions of the Eminent Philosophers (Gre. 2) Diogenes

Lives of the Companions of the Prophet (Ara. 15) Ibn Hajar

Lives of the Gurus (Pun. 17)

Lives of the Physicians (Ara. 10) Usaibi'a

Lives of Sixty-three Jains (San. 12) Hema Candra

Lives of the Twelve Caesars (Lat. 2) Suetonius

(Llyfr y Tri Aderyn: Book of the Three Birds)

(Locana: Commentary on the Doctrine of Tone)

A Lodging for the Night (Chi. 9) Li Fu Yen

Logarithmic Method (Lat. 17) Mercator (Logarithmotechnia: Logarithmic Method)

Logic (Gre. −4) Aristoteles

Logic (Syr. 6) Ras'ain

Long Histories (Ara. 9) Diinawarii

The Long North Wall (Kor. 12) Kim Pu Sik

(Longes Mac n Usnig: The Sons of Usnech)

Lord Benian (Mal. 16) (Śri Benian)

Lord Have Mercy on Us (Cze. 13) (Hospodin Pomiluj Ny)

The Lord Reigneth (Eth. 15) (Eqzi'abher Nagsa)

Lord's Prayer (Let. 16) Grunau

The Lost Apocrypha (Heb.) (James)

The Lotus Legend (San.) (Padma Puraana)

The Lotus of the Perfect Law (San. 2)

The Lotus Sutra (San. 2) Avalokite Svara

(Loutra Pallados: The Bath of Pallas)

Love (Lat. 1) Ovidius

Love Poems (San. 16) Chandi Das

Love Poems (Ice. 10) Ögmundarson

Love Songs (Cat. 15) March

Lovers' Discourse (Egy. −14)

The Lowlands (Cat. 19) Guimerà

(Lü Shih Ch'un Ch'iu: Annals of Lü)

Luc Van Tien (Vie. 19)

Ludwig's Song (Ger. 9) (Ludwigslied)

Lugalbanda and Enmerkar (Sum. −20)

(Lughat i Furs: Glossary)

(Lun Yü: Analects)

The Luster of Poetry (San. 12) Mammata and Alata

The Lute (Chi. 15) Kao Tsê Ch'êng

(Lux in Tenebris: Light in Shadows)

Luxuriant Dew from the Spring and Autumn Annals (Chi. −1) Tung Chung Shu

Luzuumiiyyaat (Ara. 11) 'Alaa

Lyric Poems (Bur. 19) Letwethondra

Lyrics (Ara. 9) Abuu Nuwaas

Lyrics (Tur. 14) 'Ashik

Lyrics (Ara. 9) Ataahiya

Lyrics (Ara.) Faarid

Lyrics (Sin. 19) Gul Mohammed

Lyrics (Heb. 13) Haziri

Lyrics (Tur. 14) Kazu

Lyrics (Per. 13) Sa'adii

Lyrics of the Six Poets (Ara. 11) A'lam

Lysis (Gre. −4) Platon

Maadhava Anala Kathaa (San.) Aananda

Maadhava and Maalatii (San. 8) Bhava Bhuuti

(Maagha Kaavya: The Slaying of Śiśupaala)

(Maalatii Maadhava: Maadhava and Maalatii)

Maalavikaa and Agnimitra (San. 4) Kaali Daasa

Maana Saara (San. 7)

The Maanava Canon Law (San.) (Maanava Dharma Śaastra)

(Maanava Dharma Śaastra: The Maanava Canon Law)

Maanava Grihya Suutra (San.)

(Maanduukya Kaarikaa: Vedanta Philosophy)

Maanduukya Upanisad (San.)

Maarkandeya Puraana (San.)

(Maase Brie Vezimre: Brie and Zimre)

(Maase Bukh: Story Book)

(Ma'aseh Efod: Stories of the Vestment)

(Ma'aseh Yerushalmi: Stories of Jerusalem)

(Ma'asiyyoth: Edifying Stories)

Mabinogion (Wel. 19)

The Maccabees (Heb. −2) (Bible)
Madaalasaa Campuu (San. 10) Tri Vikrama Bhaṭṭa
(Madala Panji: Chronicles of the Jagannath Temple at Puri)
(Madhyamika Kaarikaa: The Conception of the Buddhist Nirvana)
Madhli Stithi (Mar. 19) Apte
Madhyamika Suutra (Pal. 2) Naaga Arjuna
(Magen Abhoth: Shield of the Fathers)
Maghaazii (Ara. 8) Muusaa
The Magi (Lat. 11)
Magic (San. −9) (Atharva Veda)
The Magic Lotus (Tha. 15) Trailok
(De Magistratibus Populi Romani: Roman Officials)
(De Magistro: The Teacher)
(Magna Carta: The Great Charter)
(Maha Bharatam: The Great Bharatas)
(Mahaa Bhaarata: The Great Bharatas)
(Mahaa Bhaaṣya: The Great Commentary)
Mahaa Parinirbana Suttanta (Pal.)
(Mahaa Puraaṇu: The Great Legend)
Mahaa Puruṣa Carita (Pra. 9) Śiila Acaarya
Mahaa Vagga (Pal.)
(Mahaa Vamsa: Chronicle)
(Mahaa Viira Carita: The Life of the Great Hero)
Mahaa Yazawin (Bur. 19)
(Mahaa Yoga Bhaaṣya: The Great Commentary)
Mahaavyut Patti (San.)
Mahaayana Suutra Alaṁkaara (San. 4) Asanga
(Mahachat Kham Thet: The Next to Last Life of Buddha)
Mahaniddesa (Pal. 1)
(Mahasot: Wars of King Mahasot)
(Mahatra: The Great Journey)
Mahawthata (Bur.)
Mahayana Prakasa (Kas. 13) Sitakantha
(Mahbharat: The Great Bharatas)
Mahii Paala Caritra (San.) Caritra Sundara Gaṇin
Mahimnaḥ Stava (Pra. 9) Puṣpa Danta
Mahimnaḥ Stotra (San. 9)
The Maiden in the Meadow (Egy. −14)

(Maiestas Carolina: The Majesty of Charles)
Maitri Upaniṣad (San.)
The Majesty of Charles (Lat. 14) Charles I
Majjhima Nikaya (Pal.)
(Majmuu' al Mubaarak: Universal Chronicles)
Major Work (Lat. 13) Roger Bacon
Maker of the Way (San. 7) Jinendra Buddhi
(Makura no Zooshi: Pillow Sketches)
Malachi (Heb. −5) (Bible)
Malay Annals (Mal. 15) (Sejarah Melayu)
Malay Annals (Mal. 19) 'Ali Haji
Malim Deeman (Mal. 15)
(Mamoo: Maternal Uncle)
Mamui Prophecies (Sin. 14)
(Ma'muun: Ode to the Prince)
The Man Who Became a Fish (Chi. 9) Li Fu Yen
The Man Who Spent His Life at Lovemaking (Jap. 17) Ihara
The Manchu Code (Chi. 18) (Ta Ch'ing Lü Li)
Mangala Aṣṭaka (San.)
Mangalataka Dispani (Tha. 19) Rama III
Maṇimeekhalai (Tam. 1)
(Manju Nikan Ghergen Kamtsiha Sing Li Bitkhe: Natural Philosophy in Manchu and Chinese)
(Mantiq uṭ Ṭair: The Speech of the Birds)
Mantle Ode (Ara. 13) Buuṣiirii
Manu Charitra (Tel. 15) Peddana
(Manu Smriti: Code of Manu)
Manual of Ceremonial of the Aitareya (San. −4) Aśvala Ayana
Manual of Ceremonial of the Kaushiitaka (San.)
Manual of Cosmography (Ara.) Abu Abdallah
Manual of Discipline (Heb. 1)
Manual of Discipline for the Future Congregation of Israel (Heb. 1)
Manual of Household and Farm Economy (Cam. 19) Pan
Manual of Philosophy (Per. 11) Ibn Sina
Manual of Public Rites (San.) (Vaitaana Suutra)

(Man'yooshuu: The Book of Ten Thousand Leaves)
Maolchiaráin (Mnx. 19)
(Maqaamaat: Assemblies)
Maqṣuura (Ara. 10)   Ibn Durayd
The Mare (Yid. 10)   Abramovitch
(Margit Legenda: Legend of St. Margaret)
The Marriage of Mercury and Philology (Lat. 5)   Martianus
Martin Krpan (Slo. 19)   Levstik
The Martyr of Truth (Tam. 9)   Ari Chandra
The Martyrdom of Bar Samya (Syr. 2)
The Martyrdom of Deacon Habbibh (Syr. 4)
The Martyrdom of Gurya (Syr. 4)
The Martyrdom of St. Shushanik (Geo. 5)
The Martyrdom of Shamona (Syr. 4)
The Martyrdom of Sharbel (Syr. 2)
(Maruuju 'l Dhahab: Golden Meadows)
Marvelous Tales Ancient and Modern (Chi. 17)   (Chin Ku Ch'i Kuan)
Marvels of Destiny (Ara. 15)   Ibn 'Arabshaah
Marvels of India (Ara. 14)   Ibn Baṭṭūṭa
Mary Magdalene (Ser. 18)   Georgjić
Maṣaabiihu 'l Sunna (Ara. 12)   Baghawi
Masaalik al Abṣaar (Ara. 14)   Ibn Faḍlallah
(Masaaliku 'l Mamaalik: Routes of the Provinces)
(Mashafa Berhan: Book of Light)
(Mashafa Hawi: Encyclopedia of Nikon)
(Mashafa Kandil: Book of Extreme Unction)
The Masochist (Lat. −2)   Terentius
(Massoreth ha Massoreth: Tradition of the Tradition)
(Mastičkář: Charlatan)
Maternal Uncle (Ori. 19)   Senapati
Mathematical Classic (Chi. 7)   Wang Hsiao T'ung
Mathematical Principles of Natural Philosophy (Lat. 17)   Newton
Mathematics (Lat. 16)   Cataldi
Mathematics (Chi. 16)   Ch'en Tai Wei
Mathematics (Chi. 13)   Ch'in
Mathematics (Gre. −4)   Euklydes
Mathematics (Chi. 17)   Hsü Kuang Ch'i
Mathematics (Chi. 18)   (Su Li Ching Yün)
(Matla' as Sa'dain: History)

(Matla' ash Shams: Journey to Khorasan)
Matrimony Inn (Chi. 9)   Li Fu Yen
Matsya Puraaṇa (San.)
Maxims (Egy. −9)   Ani
Maxims (San.)   Bhallaṭa
Maxims (Tha. 17)   Damrong
Maxims of Bhaava (San. 16)   Naga Raja
Maxims of Phra Ruang (Tha.)
Mayura Sandesam (Mlm. 19)   Kerala Varma
Mazhab i 'Ishq (Urd. 19)   Nihal Cand Lahauri
Mazmura Chrestos (Eth. 16)
Me the Foe Hath Ravished (Bab. −20)
(Me'arrath Gazze: The Cave of Treasures)
Measure of the Mongol Horn (Chi. 2)   Ts'ai Yen
Meccan Revelations (Ara. 13)   Ibn 'Arabi
Medea (Gre. −5)   Euripides
Medea (Lat. 1)   Ovidius
Medea (Lat. 1)   Seneca
The Medical Art (Lat. 16)   Cesalpino
Medical Compendium (San. 2)   (Bheḍa Samhitaa)
Medical Compendium (San. 7)   Vagh Bhata
Medical Experience (Gre. 2)   Galen
Medical Jurisprudence (Chi.)   Sung Tz'ŭ
Medicine (San. 16)   Bhava Miśra
Medicine (Per. 10)   Bin 'Ali
Medicine (Dan. 12)   Harpestreng
Medicine (Heb. 13)   Haziri
Medicine (Syr. 9)   Romanus
Medicine (San. 4)   Suśruta
Meditations (Gre. 2)   Marcus Aurelius
Meditations (Arm. 10)   Norek
(Megha Duuta: The Cloud Messenger)
(Mekilta: Commentary on Exodus)
(Mellezour am Maru: Mirror of Death)
(Memar: Commentary on the Pentateuch)
Memento Mori (Lat. 11)
Memoir of the Three Kingdoms (Chi. 3)   Ch'en Shou
Memoirs (Ara. 18)   'Ali Ḥazin
Memoirs (Per. 16)   Babur
Memoirs (Nep. 18)   Prithvi Narayan Shah
Memoirs of Glikl Haml (Yid. 18)
Memoirs of the Saints (Per. 13)   'Aṭṭar
(Memorial of Solola: Annals of the Cakchiquels)

The Mongol Chronicle (Mon. 17) (Altan Tobchi)

The Mongol Invasion (Per. 13) Jurjani

To Monimus (Lat.) Fulgentius (Monkey: Western Journey)

Monsters (Lat.) (Liber Monstrorum)

The Moon Shining through a Cloud Rift on a Rainy Night (Jap. 19) Kyokutei

The Moonrise of Intelligence (San. 12) Krishna Miśra

The Moral Discourses of Epictetus (Gre. 2) Arrianus (Moralia: Ethics)

Mordekhai (Heb. 13) Ben Hillel

Morning Prayer (Pun. 17) Gobind Singh

Morning Prayer (Pun. 16) Nanak (De Morte Peregrini: The Death of Peregrinus)

Mother of Cities (Ara.) Ibn Said

Mother of Convention (San. 11) Kṣemendra

Mother of God (Pol. 13) (Bogurodzica)

The Mother of the Jugovići (Ser. 19) Vojnović

The Motion of the Heart and Blood in Animals (Lat. 17) Harvey (Mou Tzŭ: Doubts Raised)

Mount Calvary (Cor. 15)

The Mourning Turtle Dove (Swe. 18) Nordenflycht (Mrcchakatikaa: The Little Clay Cart)

Mrita Sanjiivanii (San.) Hala Ayudha

Mrqaavatii Caritra (San. 13) Deva Prabha Suri

Mu T'ien Tzŭ Chuan (Chi. 3) (Al Mu'allaqaat: Suspended)

Mudra Manjusha (Kan. 19) Kempu Narayana

Mudra Raksasa (San. 5) Viśakha Datta

Mufaddal's Book (Ara. 8) Ibn Ya'la (Mufaddaliiyaat: Mufaddal's Book) (Mugdho Padeśa: The Wiles of Women)

Mughaazi (Ara. 8) Ibn Muusaa (Muhammediya: Life of Mohammed) (Mu'jamu 'l Buldaan: Geographical Dictionary)

Mu'jamu 'l Udabaa (Ara. 13) Yaaquut (Mujmal at Tawaariikh: Chronicles)

Mujmil et Tarikh i Dnadirije (Ara.) Ibn Mohammed

Mukunda Maalaa (San. 10) Kula Śekhara

Mulla Tantai (Lao. 19) (Munaajaat: Invocations to God)

Mundaka Upanishad (San.) (Munqidh mina 'l Dalaal: Deliverer from Error)

Muqaddima (Ara. 14) Ibn Khaldun

Mushtarik (Ara. 13) Yaqut

Muspilli (Ger. 9)

The Mustard Seed Garden Drawing Book (Chi. 17) Li Yü (Mustatraf: Anecdotes) (Al Mu'tazilah: The Schism) (Muuvar Adangan Mura: Works of the Three Saints) (Al Muwatta: The Leveled Path)

Muzhir (Ara. 15) Suyuti

My Journey (Gre. 19) Psykhares

My Life (Fin. 19) Päivärinta

The Mynah Bird Lament (Tha.) (Rong Lam Nok Khun Thong) (Myriobiblion: Library)

The Mysterious Box (Chi. 13)

The Mystery of Heaven and Earth (Eth. 15) Ba Hailu Michael

The Mystery of St. Barbara (Bre. 16)

Mystery Plays (Cor. 15) (Guirrimears)

Mystical Romances (Kas. 19) Gami

Mythology (San. 9) Ratnakara

(Na Ho T'ien: Lampoon of Master K'ung) (Naaga Ananda: The Joy of the Snake World) (Naama Lingaanu Śaasana: Amara Kośa) (Naama Maalaa: Dictionary) (Naana Artha Arnava Samkṣepa: Lexicon) (Naana Artha Ratna Maalaa: Dictionary)

Naaraayana Upaniṣad (San.)

The Naarada Code (San.) (Naarada Smriti: The Naarada Code) (Naaradiiya Dharma Śastra: The Naarada Code)

Naatya Śaastra (San.) Bharata

Naaya Kumaara Cariü (Pra. 9) Puṣpa Danta

Nabatean Agriculture (Ara. 10) Wahsiyya

Nabu Naid (Bab. −6) (Nachálnaya Létopis: Tale of Bygone Years)

Nafahaat al Uns (Per. 15) Jami

Nafhu 'l Tiib Min Ghusni 'l Andalusi 'l Ratiib wa Dikhri Waziirihaa Lisaani 'l Diin Ibni 'l Khatiib (Ara. 17) Maqqari

(Naisadha Carita: The King of Nisadha)

(Naisadhiiya: The King of Nisadha)

Naishadham (Tel. 14) Śri Natha

Nakamitsu (Jap. 15) Seami

(Nala Campuu: Romance of Nala)

Nala Damayantii (San.)

Nala, King of Nisadha (San.) Vasu Deva

(Nalodaya: Nala, King of Nisadha)

Nan Chao Ye Che (Chi.)

(Nan Ch'i Shu: The Southern Ch'i)

Nan Ching (Chi. −5) Pien

Nandii Cuurni (Pra. 7) Jina Daasa

(Nang u Thay: The Dragon Princess)

(Naqaa'id: Flytings)

Narayana Bhatta (San.)

Narcissus (Ukr. 18) Skovoroda

Narint (Tha. 18)

Narratives in the Psalms (Lat. 4) Augustinus

(Narrenschiff: Ship of Fools)

The Narrow Road of Oku (Jap. 17) Basho

Nasr i Benaziir (Urd. 19) Bahadur 'Ali Husaini

The Natural Faculties (Gre. 2) Galen

Natural History (Lat. 1) Plinius

Natural Philosophy in Chinese and Manchu (Man. 17) (Manju Nikan Ghergen Kamtsiha Sing Li Bitkhe)

The Nature of the Gods (Lat. −1) Cicero

The Nature of the Good (Lat. 4) Augustinus

The Nature of Things (Lat. −1) Lucretius

(Der Naturen Bloeme: Flower of Nature)

Navasaaha Saan Carita (San. 11) Padma Gupta

Navasaaha Saanka Carita (San. 12) Śrii Harsa

Nayidda (Bur.)

Neath Outtami (Cam. 19)

(Nebbaz Gerriau dro tho Cornack: A Few Words about Cornish)

The Neck Ornament of Sara Svatii (San. 11) Bhoja

Nei Ching Su Wen (Chi. −4)

Nemi Nirvaana (San. 12) Vag Bhata

(Nemi Zat: Vision of Hell)

Nepaala Maaha Atmya (San.)

Nerses the Great (Arm. 10) Mesrop

Nerto (Pro. 19) Mistral

Nestorian Texts (Mon. 13)

Netti Pakarana (Pal. 1)

The New Bharata (San. 13) Amara Chandra

A New Collection of Ancient and Modern Poetry (Jap. 13) (Shin Kokinshu)

The New Covenant (Heb. 1)

The New Creation (Swe. 18) Kellgren

A New History of the Five Dynasties (Chi. 11) Ou

A New Instrument (Lat. 17) Francis Bacon

New Laws (Gre. 6) Justinianus

The New Star (Lat. 16) Brahe

The Next to Last Life of Buddha (Tha.) (Mahachat Kham Thet)

(Ni Juu Ichi Dai Shuu: Anthologies of Twenty-one Reigns)

The Nibelungs (Ger. 12) (Nibelungenlied)

(Nibhatkin: Miracle Plays)

The Niche of Lights (Ara. 12) Ghazali

Nichomachean Ethics (Gre. −4) Aristoteles

Nidaana Suutra (San.)

Niels Klim's Underground Journey (Lat. 18) Holberg

Nigaaristaan (Tur. 16) Kemal

(Nighantu Śesa: Botanical Dictionary)

(Niguorcosam: I Shall Not Talk)

Nihaayatu 'l 'Arab (Ara. 14) Nuwayri

(Nihon Gwaishi: General History of Japan)

(Nihongi: Japanese Notes)

(Nihonshoki: Japanese Notes)

Niilamata Puraana (San.)

(Niiti Mañjarii: Digest of Ethics)

(Niiti Pradiipa: Clarification of Ethics)

(Niiti Ratna: Treasury of Ethics)

(Niiti Saara: Lake of Ethics)

Niiti Śataka (San. 7) Bhartr Hari

Ninety-three Noo Plays (Jap. 15) Seami

(Nippon Eitai Gura: The Japanese Family Storehouse)

Nirnaya Sindhu (San. 17) Kamala Akara

(Nirukta: Etymological Commentary)

Nishwaar al Muhaadara (Ara. 10) Tanuukhii

(Njáls Saga: Burnt Njal)
Noble Play of Winter and Summer (Dut. 14) (Abel Spel vande Winter ende Somer)
(Noctes Attica: Attic Nights)
(Nok Khum: Cosmogony)
(Nokhbet ed Dahr fi Adjaib Il Birr Wa 'l Bah'r: Manual of the Cosmology of the Middle Ages)
Non-Arabic Rhyme in L (Ara. 12) Tughra'i
Non-Sanskritic Prakrit Vocabulary (San. 12) Hema Candra
The Northern Ch'i (Chi. 7) Li Po Yao
Northern History (Chi. 7) Li Yen Shou
The Notebook of Teabo (Yuc. 16)
Notes on the Rig and Yajur Vedas (San.) Kaatsya Ayana
Notes on the Rites (Chi. 1) Tai and Tai
(De Nova Stella: The New Star)
(Novellae: New Laws)
(Novum Organum: A New Instrument)
Nrisimha Taapaniiya Upanisad (San.)
Nrpaavali (San. 11) Ksemendra
Al Nujuum al Zaahira (Ara. 15) Mahassin
(De Nuptiis Philologiae et Mercurii: The Marriage of Mercury and Philology)
Nuutanodantotsa (San. 19)
(Ny Jord: Shallow Soil)
(Nyaaya Bhaasa: Explanation of the Way)
(Nyaasa Kaara: Maker of the Way)
(Nyaaya Kandaali: Section on the Way)
(Nyaaya Mañjarii: Encyclopedia)
(Nyaaya Saastra: Teaching of the Way)
(Nyaaya Suutra: Poem of the Way)
(Nyaaya Vaarttika: Treasury of the Way)
Nyaaya Vaarttika Taatparyatiikaa (San. 9) Vachaspati Mitra
(Nyang Chö Jung: The Valley of Taste)
Nyelvemléktár (Mag. 14)

(O Kagami: The Great Mirror)
(O Ryun Hŭng Sil: Five Rules of Conduct)
Oath (Mag. 15) Hunyady
Observations on the Obscure and Erroneous Passages in Pliny (Lat. 16) Núñez
The Ocean Chariot of Real Attainment (Tib. 18) Trinle

The Ocean of Music (San. 13) Saramga Deva
The Ocean of Rivers (San. 11) Soma Deva
(Ochikubo Monogatari: Tales of a Stepchild)
Ode to the Prince (Per. 9) Marv
Ode to the Virgin (Eth. 17) (Weddase Maryam)
Odes (Lat. −1) Horatius
Odes (Gre. −5) Pindaros
Odes of Solomon (Heb.)
Odes to Sen Usret III (Egy. −19)
(Odysseia: The Epic of Odysseus)
Oedipus at Colonus (Gre. −5) Sophokles
The Office of a Christian Prince (Lat. 17) Bellarmine
Offices (Lat. −1) Cicero
Official Correspondence (Egy. −14) Ikhn Aton
Old Arabic Poetry (Ara. 9) Sukkari
Old Attic Comedy (Gre. −3) Eratosthenes
Old History of the Five Dynasties (Chi. 11) (Chiu Wu Tai Shih)
The Old Story of Siva (San.) (Siivaa Puraana)
The Old Story of Vishnu (San. −1) (Visnu Puraana)
The Old Volsung Lay (Ice. 13)
Ollantay (Que. 18)
Olynthiac Orations (Gre. −4) Demosthenes
On an Old Battlefield (Chi. 9) Li Hua
Once Born (Lat. 18) Clement XI
One Holy (Lat. 13) Boniface VIII
One Hundred Fifty Japanese Tales (Jap. 10) (Yamato Monogatari)
One Hundred Hymns to the Sun (San. 7) Mayura
One Hundred Verse Maxims (San. 11) Ksemendra
One Hundred Verses (San. 9) Sankara
One-syllable Words (San.) (Eka Aksara Kosa)
(Onna Daikaku: The Great Learning for Women)
Oojooyooshuu (Jap. 10) Genshin
Opinions of the Spirit of Wisdom (Per. 3) (Menogi Khrad)
(De Optimo Senatore: The Best Senator)

(Opus Epistolarum: Collected Letters)
(Or Adonai: God's Light)
(Or Zarua': The Light Is Sown)
The Oracles of Balaam (Heb. −10)
(Numbers 22–24)
Oration (Hit. −17) Hattusilis I
The Oration of Moses (Heb. 1)
Oration on the Dignity of Man (Lat. 15) Pico
Orations (Lat. −1) Cicero
The Orchard (Per. 13) Sa'adi
In the Orchard Pavilion (Chi. 4) Wang Hsi Chi
Order (Lat. 4) Augustinus
(Oresteia: The Saga of Orestes)
Organ of Praises (Eth. 15) Na'od
(Organon: Logic)
Oriental Geography (Ara. 10) Ibn Hanqal
Origin Book (Pun. 17) Arjun
The Origin of Man (Geo. 12) Petritsi
The Origin of the Roman Race (Lat. 4) Aurelius
Origins (Lat. −2) Cato
The Orkhon Epic (Tur. 10)
Ormolum (Eng. 9) Orm
Ornament of Time (Ara. 12) Haziri
The Orphan of the Chao (Chi. 13) Chi Chün Hsiang
To Osiris (Egy. −15)
To Osiris (Egy. −10)
Osman (Ser. 17) Gandulić
(Otzoya: Lineage of the Lords of Totonicapan)
Our Lord and Redeemer (Lat. 18) Clement XIV
Outline of the Zohar (Heb. 13) (Bahir)
Outlines and Trends of Sacred Scripture (Lat. 8) Bede

(Paaiyalacchi — Praakrta Laksmii — Naama Maalaa: Prakrit Lexicon)
Paala Gopaala Kathaanaka (San. 15) Jina Kiirti
Paandava Caritra (San. 13) Deva Prabha Suuri
(Paarasii Prakaaśa: Persian Dictionary)
Paarśvanaatha (Pra. 8) Jina Sena
Paarvatii Parinaya (San. 15) Vaamana Bhatta Baana
(Paddhati: Anthology)
(Padma Puraana: Lotus Legend)
Paduma (Bur. 19) Pon Nya

Padumavati (San. 17) Jayasi
Padya Avalii (San.) Ruupago Svamin
Padya Cuudaamani (San.) Buddha Ghosa Acarya
Padya Kaadambarii (San. 11) Ksemendra
P'ai An Chin Ch'i (Chi.)
Paitaamaha Siddhaanta (San. −5)
(Paksi Pakaranam: Book of the Birds)
The Palace Gate (Kor. 9) (Kwŏlhŭi)
Palatine Anthology (Gre. 10) Kephalas
Pali Grammar (Pal. 8) Katsya Ayaana
Pali Sermons (Bur.) (Payeit Gyi)
Pan Lakshyat Kon Gheto? (Mar. 19) Apte
(Pañca Akhyaanaka: Five Tales)
Pañca Akhyaanod Dhaara (San. 17) Megha Vijaya
(Pañca Krama: The Five Methods)
(Pañca Paadika: Vedanta Thought)
Pañca Śatii (San.) Muuka
(Pañca Siddhaantika: Complete System of Natural Astrology)
(Pañca Stavii: Five Hymns to Durgaa)
(Pañca Tantra: The Five Books)
(Pañca Tantra Cchatra Prabandha: Continuation of the Five Books)
(Panchatantram: The Five Books)
(Pand Naama: Book of Counsel)
(Pandecta: Digest)
Pandit Bechana Rama (San. 19) Sarma
Panegyric (San. 4) Hari Sena
Panegyric (Lat. 1) Plinius Junior
(Pao Pu Tse: Taoism)
Papagai (Pro. 12) Carcassès
Parable of the Flower Kingdom (Kor. 11) Sŏl Ch'ŏng
Parables (San. 2) (Avadaana Śataka)
Parables (Yid. 18) Baal Shem Tov
Parallel Lives (Gre. 2) Plutarkhos
Paramartha Guru Kathai (Tam. 18) Beschi
Pariishaan (Per. 19) Qa'ani
(Parinirvana Sutta: The Life of Buddha)
Paris and Vienna (Yid. 16) Levita
The Parish Cobblers (Fin. 19) Stenvall
(Parisista Parvan: Canto of the Early Jains)
Parmenides (Gre. −4) Platon
Parody of the Koran (Ara. 11) 'Ala
The Parrot Message (Cey. 12) (Gisaa Sandesaya)

Parrot Tales (Urd. 19) Haidar Bakhsh
Parsifal (Ger. 13) Eschenbach
Parsifal (Gre. 12) Troyes
(Pascon Agan Arluth: The Passion of Our Lord)
(Passion: The Western Room)
The Passion (Lat. 12)
The Passion (Fre. 10)
The Passion of Our Lord (Cor. 15) (Pascon Agan Arluth)
Pastoral Poems (Lat. −1) Vergilius
Pastoral Rules (Lat. 6) Gregorius
The Path of Purity (Pal. 5) Buddha Ghosa
(Pattama Sompothiyan: Life of Buddha)
Pauline Studies (San. 3) (Paulisa Siddhaanta)
(Paulisa Siddhaanta: Pauline Studies)
Paumacariya (Pra. 4) Vimala Suri
(Pavana Duuta: Messenger of Purification)
The Pavilion on the Stream (Chi. 13) Kuan Han K'ing
(Paya Shikho: Forms of Worship)
(Payeit Gyi: Pali Sermons)
Peach Blossom Fountain (Chi. 4) T'ao Ch'ien
The Pearl Necklace (San. 7) Bana
The Pearl of the Diver (Ara. 11) Hariri
The Pearl Strings (Ara.) Ibn Hasan
A Peasant's Complaints (Egy. −22)
(Pechérsky Paterík: Book of the Crypt Fathers)
Pedar Paars (Nor. 18) Holberg
*Pei Ch'i Shu: The Northern Ch'i)
Pei Hu Lu (Chi. 8) Tuan
(Pei Shih: Northern History)
(P'ei Wên Yün Fu: Concordance of Literature)
(Pên Ts'ao: The Herbal)
(Pen Tsi King: Book of the Original Term)
Penal Code (Chi. 14)
Penitential (Lat. 13) Cabham
(Pentateuch: The Law)
(Peregrinatio ad Loca Sancta: Journey to the Holy Places)
The Perfect Book of Chronicles (Ara. 13) Athir
Perfect Wisdom (San. 1)
Periplus of the Erythraean Sea (Gre. 1)
Periplus of the Euxine (Gre. 2) Arrianus

(Periya Puraanam: Book of Mysteries)
Persian Dictionary (San. 17) Vedaanga Raaya
A Persian-Mongolian Glossary and Grammar (Mon.)
The Persian Wars (Gre. −5) Khoerilos
The Persians (Gre. −5) Aiskhylos
Perspective (Lat. 15) Witelo
(Pert em Hru: Coming Forth by Day)
(Pervigilium Veneris: The Dream of Venus
(Peshitta: The Syriac Bible)
(Petakopadesa: Instruction on the Basket)
Peter and Fevronia of Murom (Rus. 15)
Petit Thalamus (Pro. 16)
(Phaido: The Last Conversation)
Pharsalis (Lat. 1) Lucanus
Phenomena (Gre. −3) Aratos
Phenomena (Lat. 1) Germanicus
Philebus (Gre. −4) Platon
Philippic Orations (Gre. −4) Demosthenes
Philippics (Lat. 1) Pompeius
Philoctetes (Gre. −5) Sophokles
Philokalia (Gre. 3) Origenos
(The Philosopher Self-taught: Alive, Son of Awake)
Philosophy (Syr. 7) Hedhaiyabh
Philosophy (Heb. 12) Bar Hiyya
Philosophy (Heb. 14) Aaron
Philosophy (Ara. 12) Ibn Ezra
The Philosophy of Language (San. 7) Bhartr Hari
Phonetic Dictionary (Chi.) (Kuang Yün)
Phonetic Dictionary (Chi. 11) Ch'en P'êng Nien
Phonetic Dictionary (Chi. 8) Li Yang Ping
Phonetic Dictionary (Chi. 7) Lu Fa Yen and Yen Chi T'ui
Phonetic Dictionary (Chi. 8) Sung Ch'i
Phonetics (San. −4) Paanini
Phong Than Ba Ap Khao (Vie. 19)
Phormio (Lat. −2) Terentius
(Phra Law: The Magic Lotus)
Phra Racha Kamnot (Tha.)
Phra Tamnon (Tha.)
Phra Tamra (Tha.)
Phrenesis (Lat. 10) Ratherius
(Phum Hon: The Girl and the Elephant)
Phuulban (Urd. 18) Nishati
Physics (Lat. 13) Albertus

Physics (Gre. −4)   Aristoteles
Physics (Ara. 12)   Ibn Rushd
(Physiologus: Bestiary)
(Peri Phyton Aition: The Causes of Plants)
(Peri Phyton Historias: The History of the Plants)
(P'i P'a Ki: The Lute)
Pictorial Poetry (San. 12)   Ruyyaka
(P'ien Tzŭ Lei P'ien: Concordance of Literature)
Pilgrimage to Mecca (Mal. 19)   Munshi 'Abdu'lla
Pillow Sketches (Jap. 10)   Sei
(Ping Fa: The Art of War)
P'ing Shan Lêng Yen (Chi. 15)
Pious Dialogues (Cze. 14)   Stítný
(Píslarsaga: Story of Torments)
Pistis Sophia (Gre. 3)
(Pitti Sibsong Deun: Ceremonies for the Twelve Months)
Plain Speaker (Ice. 11)   Sigvat
Plants (Lat. 16)   Cesalpino
The Plants of Uppsala (Lat. 18)   Celsius
The Play of Rama (Jav. 15)   Jokya
Plays (Ass. 16)   (Ankiya Nats)
Plays (San. 1)   Aśva Ghoṣa
Plays (Nor. 19)   Björnson
Plays (Rum. 19)   Caragiale
Plays (Nor. 19)   Ibsen
Plays (Ice. 19)   Jochumsson
Plays (Chi. 13)   Kuan Han K'ing
Plays (Slo. 18)   Linhart
Pleasant Conversation of the Slav People (Ser. 18)   Kačić-Miosić
Pleasure of the World (Heb. 14)   Bedersi
The Plutus (Gre. −5)   Aristophanes
Poem of Brahma (San. 4)   Badara Ayana
Poem of Buddha's Former Lives (San. 4)   Arya Sura
Poem of the Way (Pal. −6)   Gautama
Poems (Lat. 9)   Abbo
Poems (Tur. 15)   Ahmed
Poems (Guj. 17)   Akho
Poems (Tur. 19)   'Akif
Poems (Wel. 16)   Aled
Poems (Kas. 18)   Arnimal
Poems (Ara. 7)   A'sha
Poems (Tur. 16)   Baḳi
Poems (Gre. −5)   Bakkhylides
Poems (Syr. 5)   Bar Sauma
Poems (Jap. 17)   Basho

Poems (Sin. 19)   Bedil
Poems (Heb. 7)   Ben Jose
Poems (Per. 9)   Bin Ba'ith
Poems (Per. 16)   Birbal
Poems (Bul. 19)   Botev
Poems (Iri. 11)   Cáemaín
Poems (Gal. 19)   Castro
Poems (Lat. −1)   Catullus
Poems (Chi. 8)   Chang Ch'ien
Poems (Chi. 9)   Chang Pi
Poems (Chi. 18)   Chao I
Poems (Chi. 16)   Chao Ts'ai Chi
Poems (Chi. 9)   Ch'ên T'ao
Poems (Chi. 10)   Ch'en T'uan
Poems (Chi. 7)   Ch'en Tzŭ Ang
Poems (Chi. 12)   Chêng Ch'iao
Poems (Chi. 11)   Ch'êng Hao
Poems (Chi. −2)   Chia I
Poems (Sor. 19)   Ćišinski-Bart
Poems (Lat. 15)   Csezmiczei
Poems (Wel. 13)   Cynddelw
Poems (Eng. 9)   Cynewulf
Poems (Sin. 19)   Dalpat
Poems (Gre. 18)   Dapontes
Poems (Bas. 16)   Dechepare
Poems (Guj. 10)   Dhanpal
Poems (Sum. −26)   Dingir Addamu
Poems (Vie. 18)   Doan Thi Diem
Poems (Wel. 15)   Edmund
Poems (Mar. 15)   Ekanath
Poems (Rum. 19)   Eminescu
Poems (Per. 16)   Faiḍi
Poems (Per. 12)   Farrukhi
Poems (Tur. 19)   Fazil
Poems (Tur. 19)   Fitnet
Poems (Iri. 14)   FitzGerald
Poems (Lat. 6)   Fortunatus
Poems (Chi. 3)   Fu Mi
Poems (Tur. 16)   Fuzuli
Poems (Pro. 16)   Galhard
Poems (Cat. 16)   Garcia
Poems (Hin. 13)   Goralch Nath
Poems (Slo. 19)   Gregorčič
Poems (Wel. 14)   Gwilym
Poems (Kas. 16)   Haba Khatun
Poems (Dut. 13)   Hadewych
Poems (Per. 14)   Hafiz
Poems (Mal. 17)   Hamzah
Poems (Chi. 9)   Han Yü
Poems (Per. 14)   Hasan
Poems (Swe. 19)   Heidenstam
Poems (Chi. 3)   Hsi K'ang

Poems (Geo. 17)   Taymuraz I
Poems (Lat. 9)   Theodolfus
Poems (Bur. 16)   Thilawuntha
Poems (Tib. 7)   Ti Srong Dé Tsén
Poems (Tam. 8)   Tirumangai
Poems (Tib. 17)   Tsangyang
Poems (Chi. 3)   Ts'ao Chih
Poems (Chi. 8)   Ts'ui Hao
Poems (Chi. 9)   Tu Ch'in Niang
Poems (Chi. 8)   Tu Fu
Poems (Arm. 16)   Tulkourantzi
Poems (Chi. −2)   Tung Fang So
Poems (Per. 12)   Unsuri
Poems (Per. 16)   'Urfi
Poems (Mar. 17)   Vaman
Poems (Tur. 14)   Veled
Poems (Gre. 18)   Velestinlis
Poems (Slo. 18)   Vodnik
Poems (Ger. 13)   Vogelweide
Poems (Tur. 19)   Wasif
Poems (Chi. 8)   Wang Chien
Poems (Chi. 7)   Wang Po
Poems (Chi. 8)   Wang Wei
Poems (Chi. 13)   Wên T'ien Hsiang
Poems (Pro. 12)   William IX
Poems (Tur. 17)   Yahya
Poems (Chi. 10)   Yang I
Poems (Chi. 12)   Yeh Shih
Poems (Chi. 3)   Ying Yang
Poems (Chi. 18)   Yüan Mei
Poems (Ger. 16)   Zwingli
Poems of the Hudhaylites (Ara. 9)   Sukkari
Poetic Expressions (San. 9)   Udbhata
Poetic Inquiry (San. 10)   Raja Sekhara
Poetic Meters (San. 12)   Hema Chandra
Poetics (Gre. −4)   Aristoteles
Poetics (Chi. 11)   Ch'êng I
Poetics (San. 12)   Hema Chandra
Poetics (San. 12)   Jaya Ratha
Poetics (Ara. 9)   Mu'tazz
Poetics (San. 13)   Vag Bhaata
Poetics (San. 14)   Vidyā Dhara
Poetics (Chi. 3)   Wang Ts'an
Poetry and Poets (Ara. 9)   Ibn Qutayba
The Poets' Club (Chi. 11)   Wang Chu
(Poh Shi K'i Chuan: The White Serpent)
(Policraticus: The Statesman)
Polish Chronicle (Lat. 12)   Gallus
Political Treatises (Lat. 17)   Spinoza
Political Works (Lat. 14)   Occam
Politics (Gre. −4)   Aristoteles

Polychronicon (Lat. 14)   Higden
(Ponsawadan Krung Kao: Annals of Ayuthia)
(Ponsawadan Tshonok: Annals of the Northern States)
Pontifical History (Lat. 12)   Salisbury
(Popol Vuh: Book of Counsel)
Lou Pouèmou dòu Rose (Pro. 19)   Mistral
The Power of the Supreme Pontiff in Temporal Affairs (Lat. 17)   Bellarmine
(Pra Law: The Magic Lotus)
Praakṛta Pingala (Pra. 14)
(Praakṛta Prakāśa: Prakrit Grammar)
Prabandha Cintaamaṇi (San. 14)   Meru Tuṅga
Prabandha Kośa (San. 14)   Raja Śekhara
Prabhavati Pradyumnam (Tel. 16)   Surana
(Prabodha Chandrodaya: The Moonrise of Intelligence)
Praeloquia (Lat. 10)   Ratherius
Prah Chinănàvon (Cam. 19)   Muk
(Prah Chïnovonh: Legend of a Life of Buddha)
Prah Laksĕnavonh (Cam. 19)   Prêk Pranhàk
(Prah Rāch Ponhsàvadà: Royal Annals)
Prahlad Charitra (Ass. 13)   Hema Sara Swati
Praise of Candii (San. 7)   Baaṇa
Praise of Eric Bloodaxe (Ice. 10)   (Eiriksmál)
Praise of Hakon (Ice. 9)   Finsson
Praise of Hakon (Ice. 11)   Skaldaspillar
In Praise of Folly (Lat. 16)   Spinoza
In Praise of Hair (Gre. 1)   Dio
Praises of the Besht (Yid. 19)   (Shivkhey Besht)
(Prajna Paramitra: The Diamond Sutra)
Prakrit Grammar (San.)   Vararuchi
Prakrit Lexicon (San. 10)   Dhana Pala
Prang Iyang (Cha. 19)
(Prang Tong: The Princess and the Giant)
Pranyamuula Shaastra Tikaa (Chi. 3)   Hsü Kan
(Prasaati: Panegyric)
Prasanna Raaghava (San. 12)   Jaya Deva
Praśna Upaniṣad (San.)
Prata Apurudraya Śobhuuṣaṇa (San. 14)   Vidyaa Naatha
Pravacana Sara (Pra. 3)   Kunda Kunda Acharya

(Prayaschitta: Expiation)
Prayer (Gre. 2) Manasses (Bible)
Prayer for the King (Egy. −14)
Prayer to Bau (Sum. −23) Gudea
Prayers (San. −9) (Yajur Veda)
Prayers of One Unjustly Persecuted (Egy. −10)
The Preacher (Heb. −2) (Koheleth) (Ecclesiastes)
Precepts (Egy. −20) Amen Emhet
Precepts (Heb. 13) Moses Ben Jacob
Precious Mirror of the Heart (Vie.)
Preliminary Ritual (Pal. 5) (Anuyogadvaara)
Preparation for the Gospel (Gre. 3) Eusebios
Prepared (Heb. 12) Ben Yehiel
The Prepared Table (Heb. 16) Karo
The Priestly Story of Creation (Heb. −5) (Hexateuch *passim*)
Primary Literature (Kor.) (So Hak)
Primer (Tha. 18) Phra Horatibodi
Prince Alexander Nevsky (Rus. 13)
Prince Dovmont (Rus. 13)
The Princes of Lara (Spa. 10) (Los Infantes de Lara)
The Princess and the Crocodile (Cam. 19) Prah Bàt
The Princess and the Crocodile (Tha.) (Chalawan)
The Princess and the Giant (Tha.) (Prang Tong)
(Principia Dialecticae: Dialectical Principles)
Principles (Heb. 15) Albo
The Principles of Government (Ara. 11) Maawardii
The Prisoner's Escape (Lat. 10) Toul
(Prithi Raj Raso: The Bardic Chronicles)
(Priyadarśikaa: The Beloved Vision)
(Procheiros Nomos: Brief Code)
De Profectione Danorum in Terram Sanctam (Lat. 12)
Prometheus Bound (Gre. −5) Aiskhylos
The Properties of Things (Lat. 13) Anglicus
Prophecies (Cam. 18)
Prophecy (Heb. −8) Amos (Bible)
Prophecy (Heb. −2) Daniel (Bible)
Prophecy (Heb. −6) Ezekiel (Bible)
Prophecy (Heb. −6) Haggai (Bible)
Prophecy (Heb. −8) Hosea (Bible)

Prophecy (Heb. −8) Isaiah (Isaiah 1–39)
Prophecy (Heb. −2) Joshua (Bible)
Prophecy (Heb. −8) Micah (Bible)
Prophecy (Heb. −7) Nahum (Bible)
Prophecy (Egy. −21) Nefer Rehu
Prophecy (Heb. −5) Nehemiah (Bible)
Prophecy (Heb. −6) Obadiah (Bible)
Prophecy (Heb. −6) Samuel (Bible)
Prophecy (Fri. 16) Tsjessens
Prophecy (Heb. −6) Zechariah (Bible)
Prophecy (Heb. −7) Zephaniah (Bible)
Prophecy of Britain (Wel. 10) (Armes Prydein)
Prose and Verse (Tur. 17) Nergisii
Proverbs (Chi. 19) (Ming Hsien Chi)
Proverbs (Sum. −20)
Proverbs (Bur.) (Lawkanidi)
Proverbs (Heb. −4) (Bible)
Proverbs (Bas. 17) Ohienart
Proverbs (Ara. 14) Taqiaqaa
Proverbs (Ara. 12) Maydaanii
Proverbs (Ara. 10) Mufaddal
(Prthvii Raaja Vijaya: Victories of Prithvii Raaja)
The Psalms of David (Heb. −2) (Bible)
The Psalter of Florjan (Pol. 14)
The Psalter of Quatrains (Iri. 10) (Saltair na Rann)
Ptah the Great (Egy. −16)
Ptah's Creation (Egy. −33)
The Punic War (Lat. −2) Naevius (Punica: Carthage)
Pursuit of Diarmaid and Gráinne (Iri. 17)
Purusa Pariiksaa (San. 14) Vidyaa Pati
(Puspa Danta: The Greatness of Siva)
Puujaavaliya (San. 4)
(Puurva: Above)
(Puurva Miimaamsaa: Ancient Inquiry)
Pyramid Texts (Egy. −23)

Al Qaamuus (Ara. 15) Fairuzaabaadii
(Al Qaanuun: Canon of Medicine)
Qalaa'id al Iqyaan (Ara. 12) Ibn Khaaqaan
(Qasiida: Poems)
(Al Qasiidatu 'l Himyariyaa: The Himyarite Ode)
Qerlos (Eth. 13)
Qissa e Ruup o Kaalaa (Urd. 17) Tahsin ud Diin

(Qaestiones Naturales: Researches on Nature)

Qualilag and Dimnag (Syr. 6) Bodh

Quarrel of a Pessimist with His Soul (Egy. −20)

Quatrains (Per. 12) Khayyam

Querolus (Lat. 12) Blois

The Quest for the Holy Grail (Fre. 13) (La Queste del Saint Graal)

Questions (Heb. 8) Ashi

The Questions of King Menander (Pal. 1) (Milinda Pañha)

Quiche History (Qui. 16) Torres

(Quincunx: The Example of the Polish Crown)

Quod Omnis Probus Liber (Lat.) Philo (Al Qur'aan: Koran)

Qushayrite Tract (Ara. 11) Qushayri

(Quutu 'l Quluub: Food of Hearts)

(Raaghava Naiṣadhiiya: Rama and Nala)

(Raaghava Paandaviiya: Rama and Pandu)

(Raaghava Paandaviiya Yaadaviiya: Journey of Rama and Pandu)

(Raahat as Suduur: History of the Seljuks)

(Raaja Taranginii: The Stream of Kings)

Raaja Valipataakaa (San. 16) Praajya Bhatta and Suka

Raajendra Karna Puura (San. 11) Sambhu

(Raakṣasa Kaavya: Demon Romance)

Raama Candra Carita Puraana (Kan. 12) Naaga Candra

(Raama Carita: Life of Rama)

(Raama Carita Manasa: The Lake of the Deeds of Rama)

Raama Paala Carita (San. 12) Sandhya Akara Nandin

Raama Taapaniiya Upaniṣad (San.)

(Raamaayana: The Epic of Rama)

(Raamaayana Mañjarii: Digest of the Epic of Rama)

(Raavana Arjuniiya: Ravana and Arjuna)

(Raavana Vadha: The Slaying of Ravana)

(Rabinal Achi: The Knight of Rabinal)

(Raghu Vaṁśa: The Dynasty of Raghu)

Rahasya Traya Sara (Tam. 10) Vedanta Desikar

Rain under the Wutung (Chi. 13) Po Jen Fu

Rajangala Mahodyana (San. 19) Ramaswami Raju

Rama and Nala (San.) Hara Datta Suri

Rama and Pandu (San. 12) Dhanam Jaya

Rama and Pandu (San. 12) Kavi Raja

Rama Surat Singh (Pun. 19) Vir Singh

Rama Yagan (Bur. 18) Toe

(Ramakien: Epic of Rama)

Ramashwamedha (Kan. 19) Muddana

Ramavatara Charita (Kas. 18) Prakash Ram Kurigami

(Ramayana: Epic of Rama)

(Ramazat: The Battle of Men and Monkeys)

Rambhaa Mañjarii (Pra. 15) Naya Candra

The Rape of Helen (Gre. 5) Koluthos

The Rape of Siva (San. 7) Kumaara Daasa

(Raphuath Geviyyah: Grammar and Medicine)

Rare Words (San.) Puru Ṣottama Deva

Rasa Ganga Adhara (San. 17) Jagan Naatha

Rasa Mañjarii (San. 14) Bhaanu Datta

Rasa Taranginii (San. 14) Bhaanu Datta

(Rasaa'ilu Ikhwaan al Safaa: Tracts of the Brethren of Purity)

Rasikarañjana (San. 16) Raama Candra

(Ratnaavalii: The Pearl Necklace)

(Ratus: Lyric Poems)

Ravana and Arjuna (San. 7) Bhaumaka

The Raven Song (Ice. 10) Hornklofi

(Razgovor Ugodni Naroda Slovinskoga: Pleasant Conversation of the Slav People)

Las Razons de Trobar (Pro. 12) Vidal

To Re (Egy. −13)

(De Re Metallica: Metallurgy)

(De Re Publica: The Republic)

(De Re Rustica: Rural Life)

Record of Ancient Matters (Jap. 8) (Kojiki)

Record of Foreign Peoples (Chi. 13) Chao

Record of Remembrance (Kor. 7) Koguryŏ

Record of the Sayings (Tib. 17) Ngawang

Romance of Jiivan Dhara (San. 10) Hari Candra

Romance of Jiivan Dhara (San.) Odaya Deva

Romance of Julian the Apostate (Syr. 6)

Romance of King Vikrama (Mal. 15) (Hikayat Maharaja Bikrama Sakti)

Romance of Launcelot (Dut. 13) (Roman van Lancelot)

Romance of the Lord Rama (Mal. 17) (Hikayat Śri Rama)

Romance of Nala (San. 10) Tri Vikrama Bhaṭṭa

Romance of Reynard (Fre. 12) (Roman de Renard)

Romance of the Rose (Fre. 13) Lorris and Meung

Romance of Svaha and the Moon (San. 17) Naara Ayaṇa

Romance of the Three Kingdoms (Chi. 13) Lo Kuan Chung

Romance of Troy (Fre. 12) Benoît

Romance of Zawta Gômma (Bur. 19) (Zawta Gômma Pyazat)

Romanum Decet Pontificem (Lat. 16) Innocent XII

(Rong Lam Nok Khun Thong: The Mynah Bird Lament)

Rosary of Gems (Tib. 15) Gelong

The Rose (Per. 13) Sa'adii

The Rose of Mystery (Ara.) Shebisteri

The Rotations of the Heavenly Bodies (Lat. 16) Kopernigk

Royal Annals (Cam. 19) Pan

Royal History of Kings (Bur. 18)

Rṣabha Pañca Śikaa (San. 10) Dhana Paala

(Rubáiyat: Quatrains)

(Rudra Upaniṣad: Lecture of Siva)

Rules for the Conduct of Kings (Tha.)

The Rules of Ceremonial (Jap. 18) (Reigi Ruiten)

The Rules of Conduct (Per. 13) Kubraa

Rules of Life (Eth. 17) Axum

The Rules of Love (San. 8) Vaatsya Ayana

Rules of the Monks (Lat.) Benedictus

The Rules of the Order (Pal. −3) (Vinaya)

The Rules of Pachomius (Eth. 13)

The Runaway Maid (Can.)

Rural Life (Lat. 1) Columella

Rural Matters (Lat. −1) Varro

Russian Code (Rus. 11) (Russka Pravda)

Ruth (Heb. −2) (Bible)

(Ṛtusaṁhaara: The Seasons)

Sa Tu Waw (Kar. 19) Saya Kiaw Zan

Saahitya Darpaṇa (San. 14) Viśva Naatha

Śaakuntalaa (San. 4) Kaali Daasa

Śaakuntalaa (Urd. 19)

Śaalivaahana Kathaa (San. 15) Śiva Daasa

Saam Naama (Per. 11)

(Saama Veda: Tunes)

Saaṁkha Tattva Kaumudii (San.) Vaacaspati Mitra

(Saaṅkhaayana Braahmaṇa: The Commentary of the Kaushiitaka Brahmans)

(Saaṅkhaayana Suutra: Manual of Ceremonies of the Kaushiitaka)

(Saaṅkhya Bhaaṣya: Sankhya Commentary)

(Saaṅkhya Kaarikaa: Sankhya Philosophy)

(Saaṅkhya Pravachana: Aphorisms of Sankhya Philosophy)

(Saaṅkhya Suutra: Aphorisms of Sankhya Philosophy: Sankhya Poems)

Śaariiraka Miimaaṁsaa Bhaaṣya (San.) Sankara

The Sack of Troy (Gre. 5) Tryphiodoros

Sacred Edict (Chi. 17) K'ang Hsi

Sacred Epigrams (Lat. 17) Crashaw

Sacred Magic (Heb. 15) Melin

The Sacrifice of Isaac (Yid. 15) (Akeydas Yitskhok)

(Sadukti Karna Amrta: Bengal Anthology of Poetry)

(Safar Naama: Travels)

The Saga of Orestes (Gre. −5) Aiskhylos

Sagoromo (Jap. 11)

(Al Ṣaḥiih: The Genuine)

Saif ul Muluuk and Badii' ul Jamaal (Urd. 17) Gavvaasii

St. Alexis (Fre. 11)

St. Anselm (Lat. 12) Salisbury

St. Blathmac (Lat. 9) Walafrid

St. Canute (Lat. 11) Aelnoth

St. Eulalia (Fre. 10)

St. Evstafy of Mtsket (Geo. 6)

St. Faro (Lat. 9) Walafrid

St. Francis (Dut. 13) Maerlant

St. Gregory of Khandtza (Geo. 10)
St. Léger (Fre. 10)
St. Nicholas (Fre. 13)   Bodel
St. Nonn (Bre. 15)
St. Patrick's Journey to Purgatory (Pro. 14)   Perelhas
St. Riṣabha (San. 9)   Maana Tunga
St. Servatius (Dut. 12)   Veldeke
St. Theodosius (Rus. 12)   Nestor
St. Thomas (Lat. 12)   Salisbury
St. Wenceslas (Sla. 10)
St. Wenceslas (Cze. 13)
Saints' Calendar (Rus. 16)   Macarius
The Sale of Lives (Lat. 2)   Lucianus
(Saltair na Rann: The Psalter of Quatrains)
(Sam Gang Hăng Sil: Three Principles of Conduct)
(Sam Guk Yu Sa: Remains of the Three Kingdoms)
(Sam Khayim: Elixir of Life)
Samaraangaṇa Suutra Dhaara (San. 11)   Bhoja
(Samaya Matṛkaa: Mother by Convention)
(Saṃgiita Darpaṇa: The Mirror of Music)
(Saṃgiita Ratnaakara: The Ocean of Music)
(Saṃhitaa Upaniṣad: Lecture of the Collection)
Samyaktra Kaumudii (San.)
Samyatta Nikaya (Pal.)
(San Kuo Chih: Memoir of the Three Kingdoms)
(San Kuo Chih Yen I: Romance of the Three Kingdoms)
(San Tzŭ Ching: Three-character Classic)
Sanda Gômma (Bur.)
(Sandilya Smriti: The Code of Śandilya)
(De Sanguine Christi: The Blood of Christ)
(Sành Sĕl Chei: The Conch and the Bow of Victory)
Sanhedren (Heb. 5)
Śaṅkara Ceto Vilaasa Campuu (San. 18)   Saṅkara
Śaṅkha Paraabhava Vyaayoga (San. 13)   Hari Hara
(Sankhya Commentary (San. 8)   Gauda Pada
Sankhya Philosophy (San. 4)   Iiśvara

Sankhya Poems (Hin. 15)   (Saaṅkhya Suutra)
Sanskrit Grammar (San. 7)   Candra Gomin
Sapta Śatii (San.)   Govar Dhana
(Saqṭu 'l Zand: Spark of the Fire Stick)
Sarangodhara Charitramu (Tel. 17)   Venkatakavi
(Sarashina Nikki: Diary of Journeys by a Woman)
(Sarasvatii Kanṭhaa Bharaṇa: The Neck Ornament of Śarasvatii)
(Sarasvatii Stotra: Hymn to Sarasvatii)
Sartorial Poems (Per. 15)   Yazdi
(Sarva Darśana Saṅgraha: Summary of All the Demonstrations)
Sassi Punnoo (Pun. 17)
(Sat' Saii: Seven Centuries)
Sata Pañca Satika Stotra (San. 2)   Marṭ̣ceta
(Śata Ślokii: One Hundred Verses)
(Śataka: Maxims)
Satapatha Braahmaṇa (San.)
Satapatha Upaniṣad (San. −5)
Satires (Lat. 2)   Juvenalis
Satires (Kan. 17)   Sarvajna
(Satra Keng Kantray, Mea Joeung: The Construction of Angkor Vat)
(Satta Saii: Seven Centuries)
Satwant Kaur (Pun. 19)   Vir Singh
Satya Veeda Lakshaṇam (Tam. 17)   Nobili
(Satyarth Prakash: The Light of Truth)
Satyricon (Lat. 1)   Petronius
Saubhadra (Mar. 19)   Kirloskar
Saul (Heb. −10)   (Bible)
(Śaunakiiyaa Chatura Adhyaayikaa: The Four Lectures of Śaunaka)
(Saundara Nanda: The Conversion of Nanda)
(Saundarya Lahari: The Wave of Bliss)
The Saving of Mankind (Egy. −14)
Sawpé Sawmé (Bur. 19)
Saxon Deeds (Lat. 10)   Widukind
The Sayings of the Jewish Fathers (Heb.)
(Sbooyet: Instructions)
(De Schematibus et Tropis Sacrae Scripturae: Outlines and Trends of Sacred Scripture)
The Schism (Ara.)   (Al Mu'tazilah)
Scholastic History (Lat.)   Comestor

The School of Religious Doctrines (Per. 17)
Mohsan
The Science of the Governor (Tur. 11)
Khass Hadjib
The Science of Rhetoric (Syr. 9) Taghrit
(Scotorum Historiae: Histories of the
Scots)
Sea of Comparisons (Mon.) (Uuliger
uun Dalai)
The Seasons (San. 4) Kaali Daasa
The Second Epistle of Clement (Gre. 2)
The Second Giving of the Law (Heb. −7)
(Deuteronomy)
The Secret Collection (Tib. 14) Tsong Ka
Pa (ed.)
Secret History (Gre. 6) Prokopios
The Secret History of the Mongols (Chi. 13)
(Yüan Cho Pi Shi)
Secret of Secrets (Dut. 13) Maerlant
Secret Teachings (San. −6) (Upanisads)
Section on the Way (San. 10) Sri Dhara
Secular Hymn (Lat. −1) Horatius
(Seitsemän Veljestä: Seven Brothers)
(Sejarah Melayu: Malay Annals)
Select History (Per. 14) Hamdullaah
The Seljuk Conquest (Ara. 11) Aristaces
Sellase (Eth. 15) Na'od
(Semag: Precepts)
(Peri Semeion: Signs)
Senchas Már (Iri. 6)
(Sepher 'Anaq: Imitation of Moses Ben
Ezra)
(Sepher ha Berith: Book of the Covenant)
(Sepher ha Kabbalah: Book of Mystic
Lore)
(Sepher ha Kuzari: The Kuzar Debate)
(Sepher ha Mibhar: Book of Excellence)
(Sepher ha Yashor: Book of the Right-
eous)
(Sepher ha Zohar: Cabalistic Philosophy)
(Sepher Yezirah: Book of Creations)
(Sepher Yuhasin: History)
Septuagint (Gre. 3) (Bible)
The Sequel to the Iliad (Gre. 4) Quintus
Sequences (Lat. 9) Notker
The Series of the Katuns (Yuc. 16)
"Chilam Balam"
Sermons (Lat. 4) Augustinus
Sermons (Fin. 16) Erici
(Lou Sermou de Moussu Sistre: Mr.
Sistre's Sermon)
The Serpent Hedammu (Hit. −12)

Service for the Dead (Eth. 13) Abba
Salama
Settlement Book (Ice. 11) (Landnáma-
bók)
Setubandha (Pra. 6) Pravara Sena
Seven against Thebes (Gre. −5) Aiskhy-
los
The Seven Beauties (Per. 13) Nizaamii
Seven Brothers (Fin. 19) Stenvall
Seven Centuries (Hin. 17) Bihaari Laal
Seven Centuries (Pra. 4) Haala
Seven Chapters (Per. −4) (Haptanghati)
Seventy Stories of the Parrot (San. 12)
Cintaamani Bhatta
(Sevyasevako Padesa: Advice to Servants
and Masters)
Seyf Zu 'l Yezen (Ara. 15)
(Seyfer Mides: Book of Conduct)
(Shaah Naama: Epic of Kings)
Shabbath, Mishna (Heb.)
Shadharaatu 'l Dhahab (Ara.)
(Sha'eer Bidasari: Bidasari)
(Sha'eer Si Lindong Delima: Lord Benian)
(Sha'eer Silambari: Ballad of Senhor
Costa)
(Sha'eer Sinyor Kosta: Ballad of Senhor
Costa)
Shah Nama i Islam (Urd. 18) Hafeez
Jallundhari
Shallow Soil (Nor. 19) Hamsun
Shamsu 'l Diin al Dhanabii (Ara. 14)
Isnawii
(Shang Chêng: Rules for Wine Drinkers)
(Shang Chu Shu: Book of the Lord Shang)
Shang Shu Ku Wen Shu Cheng (Chi. 18)
Yen Jo Chü
Sharada (Mar. 19) Deval
Shayist ne Shayist (Per. 3)
(Shebet Yehudah: The Tribe of Judah)
(She'iltoth: Questions)
Shepherd of Hermas (Gre. 2)
Shestodnev (Bul. 10) Ioan
(Ayn Sheyn Nay Lid fun Meshiakh: Fine
New Song about the Messiah)
(Sheyris Yisroel: The Remnant of Israel)
Shibbe ha Tanaïm (Lad. 19) Abulafia
Shield of the Fathers (Heb. 15) Duran
(Shifaa: Remedy)
(Shih Chi: Historical Records)
(Shih Ching: Classic of Poetry)
(Shih Lei Fu: Encyclopedia)
(Shih Li: Etiquette and Ceremonial)

(Shikibu Nikki: Diary)
(Shilappadikaram: Lay of the Anklet)
(Shin Kokinshuu: New Collection of Ancient and Modern Poetry)
Ship of Fools (Ger. 15) Brant
The Shipwrecked Sailor (Egy. −20)
(Shivkhey Besht: Praises of the Besht)
(Shmuel Bukh: Epic of David)
Short Dictionary (San. 10) Hala Ayudha
(Shu: Works)
(Shu Ching: Classic of History)
(Shui Hu Chuan: Tale of the Water Margins)
(Shulhan 'Arukh: The Prepared Table)
Shulḥan ha Meleḥ (Lad. 18) Ben Isaac Asa
(Shuo Wên Chieh Tzu: Lexicon)
Shvetasvatara Upaniṣad (San.)
Shwasamvedya Upaniṣad (San. −4)
Si Prat (Tha. 17)
(Siao Ts'iu P'ien: Formal Logic)
Sibylline Oracles (Gre. −2)
(Sic et Non: Yes and No)
The Sick Bed of Chuchulinn (Iri. 13)
(Sidat Saṅgarǎ: Sinhalese Grammar)
Siddhaanta (San. 5)
(Siddhaanta Kaumudii: Revised Grammar of Paaṇini)
(Siddhaanta Śiromaṇi: Commentary on the Vedanta Suutras)
(Siddi Kuur: Buddhist Tales)
(Sidereus Mundi: Star of the World)
(Sifat al Aadaab: Rules of Conduct)
(Ṣifatu Jaziirat al 'Arab: Geography of Arabia)
(Sifra: Commentary on Leviticus)
(Sifreh: Commentary on Deuteronomy)
(Sifreh: Commentary on Numbers)
Sigalovada Suttanta (Pal.)
Sigiri Poems (Tam. 10)
The Signature of All Things (Lat. 17) Böhme
Signs (Gre. −3) Theophrastos
(Siiratu Abuu Zeyd: Abuu Zeyd)
(Siiratu 'Antar: Life of 'Antar)
(Siiratu el Mugaahidiin: History of the Warriors)
(Siiratu eẓ Ẕahir: Life of Ẕahir)
(Siiratu Rasuuli 'llaah: Life of the Prophet)
(Śiivaa Puraaṇa: Old Story of Siva)
(Sikṣaa: Phonetics)

Śikṣaa Samuccaya (San. 7) Śaanti Deva
Al Ṣila fii Akhbaari A'immati 'l Andalus (Ara.) Ibn Bashkuwaal
Silla Folk Songs (Kor. 9)
Silsilah Melayu dan Bugis (Mal. 19) 'Ali Haji
(Silvae: The Forests)
The Silver Rattle (Fri. 19) Dykstra
The Simony of Postilla (Cze. 15) Hus
Simplicissimus (Ger. 17) Grimmelshausen
Simplified Code (Gre. 8) Leo III
(Sindbaad Naama: Tale of Sinbad)
Siṅghaasan Battiisii (Urd. 19) Kaazim 'Alii Javaan and Lalluu Laal
Single Verses by a Hundred People (Jap. 13) Teika
(Siṅha Asana Dva Trin Śikaa: Thirty-two Maidens on a Throne)
Sinhalese Grammar (Cey. 13) (Sidat Saṅgarǎ)
(Sinte Franciscus' Leven: St. Francis)
(Siralomének Both János Veszedelmén: Elegy upon John Both)
Sirat al Mustakim (Mal. 17) Raniri
Siricimdhakavvam (Pra. 13) Krishna Lila Suka
(Śiśupaala Vadha: The Slaying of Śiśupaala)
Śiṣyalekha Dharma Kaavya (San. 7) Candra Gomin
(Sitaabu 'l Falaahat al Nabaṭiyya: Nabatean Agriculture)
Six Acres and Eight Decimals (Ori. 19) Senapati
Six Books on the Common Christian Things (Cze. 14) Stítný
Six Principles (Lat.) Porretanus
Six Scripts (Chi. 13) Tai Tung
Sixteen Essays (Chi. 18)
(Siyaru Muluuki 'l 'Ajam: History of the Kings of Persia)
(Skandi Puraaṇa: The War God)
(Skazánie: Stories)
(Skeltana Riucht: Law of the Magistrates)
Skënderbeg (Alb. 19) Rada
The Slave of His Wealth (Chi. 13)
The Slayer of the Bear (Let. 19) Pumpurs
Slaying a Son at the Yamên Gate (Chi. 13)
The Slaying of the Dragon (Hit. −12)
The Slaying of Raavaṇa (San. 7) Bhaṭṭi

The Slaying of Siśupaala (San. 9)   Maa-gha
(Śleṣ Artha Pada Saṁgraha: Thesaurus of Double Meanings)
Śloka Vaarttika (San. 8)   Kumaarila
(Slóvo o Pŭlku Igorevĕ: Lay of Igor's Campaign)
(Smith Papyrus: Surgical Case Book)
(Smriti Chandrikaa: The Whole Duty of a Brahman)
(So Hak: Primary Literature)
Society, Ethics and Religion (Per. 6)   Burzoe
Socrates in Prison (Gre. −4)   Platon
Socrates on Trial (Gre. −4)   Platon
Sohnu Mahiwal (Pun. 17)
Soil (Dan. 19)   Pontoppidan
(Sólarljód: Sun Song)
Soliloquies (Lat. 4)   Augustinus
Solitaire of the Time (Ara. 11)   Tha'aali-bii
(Soma Paala Vilaasa: Life of Soma Paala)
The Son of Kalev (Est. 19)   Kreuzwald
(Sonatorrek: Son's Lament)
The Song of Antioch (Pro. 12)   Bochada
Song of the Autumn Cicada (Chi. 19)   Chin Huo
The Song Celestial (San. −2)   (Bhagavad Giitaa)
The Song Celestial (Ori. 16)   Jagannath Das
The Song Celestial (Tel. 13)   Potana
The Song of the Conquest of Pannonia (Mag. 15)   (Enek Pannónia Megvé-teleröl)
The Song of the Dance of the Bowman (Yuc. 18)   (X 'Okoot Kay H Ppum t Huul)
The Song of Deborah (Heb. −12)   (Judges 5)
The Song of the Divine Cowherd (Ass. 17)
The Song of the Divine Cowherd (San. 12)   Jaya Deva
The Song of Manannan Mac y Lheir (Mnx. 18)
The Song of a Monk in the Cauldron of Oil (Pal.)   (Telekaṭaahaa Gaathaa)
The Song of Roland (Fre. 12)   (Chanson de Roland)
The Song of Siva (San.)   (Kurma Pur-aana—Iiśvara Giitaa)
The Song of Songs (Heb. −4)   (Bible)
The Song of the Three Holy Children (Gre. 2)   (Bible)

Song of the Troops of Uni (Egy. −24)
Songs (Ori. 19)   Madhusudan
Songs of a Pariah Priest (Tam. 2)   Tiru-vallavar
Songs of Llywarch Hen (Wel. 9)   (Canu Llywarch Hen)
Songs of the Moon's Reflection on a Thou-sand Rivers (Kor. 15)   (Wŏ Rin Ch'ŏn Gang Chi Gok)
Songs of the South (Chi. −1)   Liu Hsiang
Songs to the Virgin (Gal. 13)   Alfonso X
Sonnets (Mlt. 17)   Bonamico
Sonnets (Pro. 17)   Larade
Son's Lament (Ice. 10)   Skallagrímsson
The Sons of Usnech (Iri. 9)   (Longes Mac n Usnig)
The Sophist (Gre. −4)   Platon
(Sorami s Tsikhi: The Citadel of Sourami)
The Soul (Lat. 13)   Albertus
The Soul (Gre. −4)   Aristoteles
The Southern Ch'i (Chi. 6)   Hsiao T'ung
Southern History (Chi. 7)   Li Yen Shou
(Sŏvotiraksà: Advice on Hygiene)
The Spanish War (Lat. −1)   (Bellum Hispaniense)
Spark of the Fire Stick (Ara. 11)   'Alaa
Species of Plants (Lat. 18)   Linnaeus
De Speculatione Musices (Lat. 13)   Odington
(Speculum Maius: The Greater Mirror)
The Speech of the Birds (Per. 13)   'Aṭṭaar
Speeches (Bab. −6)   Nebuchadrezzar II
The Spindle (Gre. −4)   Erinna
Spirit and Soul (Lat. 4)   Augustinus
Spiritual Couplets (Per. 13)   Ruumii
Spiritual Exercises (Lat. 16)   Loyola
Spring (Tur. 16)   Mesiihii
Spring and Autumn Annals (Chi. −6)   K'ung Fu Tzŭ
Spring Garden (Per. 15)   Jaamii
Sragdhara Stotra (San.)   Sarvajña Mitra
Srauta Suutra (San.)   Apastabama
(Sri Benian: Lord Benian)
Sri Kṛṣṇa Kirttana (Ben. 14)   Baḍu
Śrii Bhaaṣya (San. 12)   Raama Nuja
Śrii Kaṇṭha Carita (San. 12)   Maṅkha
Śṛngaara Jñaana Nirnaya (San.)
Śṛngaara Prakaaśa (San. 11)   Bhoja
Śṛngaara Rasa Aṣṭaku (San. 4)
Śṛngaara Sapta Satikaa (San.)   Parama Ananda
Śṛngaara Tilaka (San. 4)
Sṛngaara Tilaka (San.)   Rudra Bhaṭṭa

Surgical Case Book (Egy. −17) (Smith Papyrus)
Survey of India (Ara. 11) Biiruunii
Survey of Theology (Lat. 13) Aquinas
Survey of Theology (Lat. 13) Hales
Surviving Monuments (Ara. 11) Biiruunii
Susanna (Mlt. 19) Azzopardi
Susanna and the Elders (Heb. −2) (Bible)
Suspended (Ara. 6) (Al Mu'allaqaat)
Suspended (Ara. 8) Rawiya
(Suśruta Saṃhitaa: Encyclopedia of Medicine)
Sutta Nipata (Pal.)
(Sutta Piṭaka: Basket of Doctrine)
Ṣuufii Quatrains (Per. 11) Sa'iid
(Suukt Karṇa Amṛta: Sadukti Karṇa Amṛta)
(Suurya Śataka: One Hundred Hymns to the Sun)
Suurya Siddhaanta (San. −5)
Suutra Alaṁkara (San. 1) Aśva Ghoṣa
Suutra Commentary (San. 5) Shabara Svamin
Suutra of Forty Two Sections (Chi. 1)
(Suz u Gadaz: Burning and Melting)
(Svaahaasudhaakara Campuu: Romance of Svaha and the Moon)
(Svapana Vaasava Dattaa: The Dream of Vaasava Dattaa)
(Svenska Krönika: Swedish Chronicle)
Svipdag (Ice. 17)
(Svodaya Kaavya: Autobiography)
Swasdi Raksa (Tha. 19) Sunthorn Bhu
Swedish Chronicle (Swe. 16) Petri
Śyaa Malaa Daṇḍaka (San.)
(Symposion: The Dinner Party)
Synodal Orations (Arm. 12) Lambron
Synodal Orations (Arm. 12) Nerses
Synonyms (San. 12) Hema Candra
The Syriac Bible (Syr. 4) (Peshitta)
The System of Nature (Lat. 18) Linnaeus

(Ta Ch'ing Hui Tien: The Government of the Manchus)
(Ta Ch'ing Lü Li: The Manchu Code)
(Ta Hsüeh: The Great Learning)
(Ta Tai Li Chi: Notes on the Rites)
(Taaj al 'Aruus: Commentary on the Qaamuus)
Taariikh el Fettach (Ara. 16) Kati

Taariikh es Sudan (Ara. 16) Sadi
Taariikh i Baihaqi (Per. 11) Baihaqi
(Taariikh i Hind: Survey of India)
(Taariikh i Waṣṣaf: History)
Taatparya Ṭikaa Pariśuuddhi (San. 10) Udayana
(Tabaaqaat: Biographies)
(Tabaaqaat i Naaṣiri: The Mongol Invasion)
(Ṭabaqaatu 'l Aṭibbaa: Lives of the Physicians)
(Ṭabaqaatu 'l Ṣuufiyya: Classes of the Sufis)
Tactics (Lat. 2) Arrianus
(Tadhkiratu 'l Awliyaa: Memoirs of the Saints)
(Tafsiir: Commentary)
(Tafsiiru 'l Jalaalayn: Commentary of the Jalaals)
(Tahaafut al Falaasifa: The Incoherence of the Philosophers)
(Tahaafut al Tahaafu: The Incoherence of the Incoherence)
T'ai Hsüan Ching (Chi. −1) Yang Hsiung
(T'ai P'ing Kuang Chi: T'ang Tales)
(T'ai P'ing Yü Lan: Sung Encyclopedia)
Tai Tung Yüan (Chi. 17) Tai Chên
Taiheiki (Jap. 14) Kojuna
(Táin Bó Cúailnge: The Cattle Raid of Cooley)
(Taj ut Tewaariikh: Crown of Chronicles)
Tajal 'Arus (Ara. 18) Murtada
(Tajal Salatin: Book of Morality)
(Taketori Monogatari: Human Fairy Tale)
(Takhemoui: Lyrics)
The Taking of Constantinople (Rus. 15) Iskander
Tale of Appus (Hit. −12)
Tale of Bygone Years (Rus. 12) Nestor
Tale of Bygone Years (Rus. 11) Nikon
Tale of Gempei (Jap. 13) Tokinaga
Tale of Genji (Jap. 11) Murasaki
Tale of Heiji (Jap. 13) Tokinaga
Tale of Heiki (Jap. 13) (Heike Monogatari)
Tale of Hogen (Jap. 13) Tokinaga
Tale of Panji (Mal. 14) (Hikayat Galuh Di Gantong)
Tale of Sinbad (Per.) (Sindbaad Naama)
Tale of Sinuhe (Egy. −20)

(Tale of Two Brothers: Anupu and Bitiu)

Tale of Urvashi Won by Valor (San. 4) Kaali Daasa

Tale of the Water Margins (Chi. 14) Shi Nai An

Tale of Yeigwa (Jap. 12) (Yeigwa Monogatari)

Tales (Guj. 17) Premananda

Tales for Sam Sib (Tha. 18)

Tales of Buddha (San. 2) (Divyaavadaana)

Tales of Ethiopia (Gre. 4) Heliodoros

Tales of Ise (Jap. 10) Ariwara

Tales of a Parrot (Per.) Kadiri

Tales of a Parrot (Mal. 14) Kadli Hasan

Tales of a Stepchild (Jap. 10) (Ochikubo Monogatari)

(Talmud: The Research of Babylon; The Research of Jerusalem)

(Tam Tu Kinh: Book of Three-character Phrases)

Tamil Grammar (Tam. −1) (Tolkappiyam)

Tamurlane (Per. 16) Hatifi

Tamurlane (Ara. 15) Medsoph

T'ang Kien Wen Tse (Chi. 8)

(T'ang Shih: History of the T'ang)

T'ang Tales (Chi. 10) Li Fang

(Tanjur: The Translated Explanations)

(Tantara ny Andriana: History of the Hova Kings)

Tantra Vaarttika (San. 8) Kumaarila

(Tao Tê Ching: The Way of Life)

Taoism (Chi. 4) Ko

(Targum: The Aramaic Bible)

Ta'riikh al Khaamiis (Ara. 16) Diyaarbakrii

(Ta'riikhu 'l Ḥukamaa: History of the Philologists)

(Ta'riikhu 'l Khulafaa: History of the Caliphs)

(Ta'riikhu 'l Rusul wa 'l Muluuk: Annals of the Apostles and the Kings)

(Ta'riikhu 'l Tammaddun al Islaami: History of Islamic Civilization)

(Tarikh i Murassah: Afghan Chronicle)

Tase Hna Ra Thi Ratu (Bur. 19) Uggya Byan

The Tatars (Arm. 14) Hethoum

Tattva Samaasa (San. −6) Kapila

(Tattva Vaicaradi: The Explanation)

(Tattva Vaiśaaraadii: Gloss on Vyasa's Yoga Commentary)

Tawla (Bur. 16) Hamagyaw

(Taxidi Mou: My Journey)

(Tazarru'aat: Supplications)

The Teacher (Lat. 4) Augustinus

The Teaching of Padma (Tib. 15)

The Teaching of the Way (San. 10) Medhatithi

The Teachings (Egy. −9) Amen Emoope

The Teachings of Hsi Yun (Chi. 9) P'ei Hsiu

The Teachings of Kauśika (San.) (Kauśika Suutra)

The Tears of Khorasan (Per. 12) Anvari

Technical Vocabulary (San.) (Tri Ruupa Kośa)

Teevaaram (Tam. 7) Appar

(Tekhne Grammatike: A Method of Grammar)

(Telakaṭaahaa Gaathaa: Song of a Monk in the Cauldron of Oil)

Telegonia (Gre. −6) Eugammon

(Telipinu: The Missing God)

(Tell el Amarna Letters: Official Correspondence)

Temi (Bur.)

The Ten Commandments (Heb. −13) Moses (Exodus 20–23)

The Ten Courts of Purgatory (Chi. 19) (Yü Li Ch'ao Chuan)

The Ten Incarnations (San. 11) Ksemendra

The Ten Incarnations of Vishnu (San.) "Hanumaan"

Ten Kinds of Drama (San. 12) Dhanam Jaya

Ten Princes (San. 7) Dandin

The Ten Tribes (Heb. 9) (Eldad ha Dani)

(Tep Ter Ngön Po: Blue Treasury of Records)

(Terra Baixa: Low Land)

The Testament of Abraham (Heb.)

The Testament of Asher (Heb.)

The Testament of Benjamin (Heb.)

The Testament of Enoch (Heb.)

The Testament of Joseph (Heb.)

The Testament of Judah (Heb.)

The Testament of Levi (Heb. −2)

The Testament of Naphtali (Heb.)

The Testament of Reuben (Heb.)

The Testament of Zebulun (Heb.)
Texts and Commentary of the Yogachara School (San. 7)   Hsüan
(Thadda: The Burmese Pali Grammar)
Thaetetus (Gre. −4)   Platon
The Theater of the Lands of the Globe (Lat. 16)   Vesalius
Theatrical Miscellany (Chi. 17)   Shen Te Fu
(Thebais: Epic of Thebes)
Themes (Gre. 10)   Konstantinos VII
Theodicy (Bab. −10)   Saggil Kiinam Ubbib
(Theogonia: Genealogy of the Gods)
Theology (Ara. 13)   Abraham Ben Moses
Theophilus (Fre. 13)   Rutebeuf
The Theory of the Calendar (Chi. 5)   Tsu
Thera Gaathaa (Pal. −2)
(Theriaka: The Bites of Beasts)
Therii Gaathaa (Pal. −2)
Thesaurus (Kar. 19)   Sau Kau Too
Thesaurus of Double Meanings (San. 12)   Srii Harsa
Theses (Lat. 16)   Luther
Thesmophoriazusae (Gre. −5)   Aristophanes
Theuerdank (Ger. 15)   Maximilian
Things to Be Done (Lat. 1)   Ovidius
Thingyo (Bur.)
Third Work (Lat. 13)   Roger Bacon
Thirty-two Bharata Tales (San. 16)   (Bharataka Dvaa Trin Śikaa)
Thirty-two Maidens on a Throne (San.)   (Sinha Asana Dvaa Trin Śikaa)
To Thoth (Egy. −15)
To Thoth (Egy. −13)
The Thousand and One Nights (Ara. 10)   (Alf Layla wa Layla)
The Thousand Songs (Egy. −14)
Thousand Tales (Per. 10)   (Hazaar Afsaana)
The Thread of True Faith (Cze. 15)   Chelicicky
Three-Character Classic (Chi. 13)   Wang Ying Lin
The Three Prayers (Per. −5)
Three Principles of Conduct (Kor.)   (Sam Gang Hăng Sil)
Thuwunnashan (Bur.)
Thyestes (Lat. −1)   Varius
(Thysia tou Avraam: Abraham's Sacrifice)
The Tiger (Chi. 9)   Li Fu Yen
Tilaka Mañjarii (San. 10)   Dhana Paala

(Timur Naama: Life of Tamurlane)
T'ing Lin Hsien Shêng I Shu Hui Chi— Wen Chi (Chi. 17)   Ku Yen Wu
Tip Sanhvăr (Cam. 19)   Mohà Măs
Tirumurai (San. 11)
Tiruvasagan (Tam. 9)   Manikka
Titurel (Ger. 13)   Eschenbach
Tobit (Heb. −4)   (Bible)
(Tochmarc Ferbe: The Wooing of Ferb)
(Tolkappiyam: Tamil Grammar)
Toltec-Chichimec History (Nah. 16)
(Tonalpohualli: The Count of Days)
(Tong Guk Mun Hŏn Pi Go: Korean Encyclopedia)
(Tong Guk T'ong Gam: The Complete Mirror of the Eastern Kingdom)
(Tong Sa Kang Yo: Summary of Korean History)
The Tongue of the Invisible (Per. 14)   Haafiz
Topography (Jap. 8)   (Izumo Fudoki)
Topography of Kuangtung (Chi. 19)   Yüan Yüan
(Torah: The Law)
Torikaebaya (Jap. 11)
(Tosa Nikki: Travel Diary)
(Tosefta: Additions)
(Totaa Kahaanii: Parrot Tales)
Tracts of the Brethren of Purity (Ara. 10)
Tradition of the Tradition (Heb. 13)   Levita
Traditions (Ara. 8)   Awza'i
Traditions (Ara. 10)   Hasaa'i
Traditions (Ara. 8)   Zuhri
(Trai Bhume Katha: Buddhist Cosmogony)
The Training of a Scribe (Sum. −20)
Transformations (Lat. 1)   Ovidius
The Translated Commandments (Tib. 14)   (Kanjur)
The Translated Explanations (Tib. 14)   (Tanjur)
Translations (Eng. 9)   Alfred
Travel Diary (Jap. 10)   Tsurayuki
Travels (Ara. 12)   Edrisi
Travels (Tur. 17)   Evliyaa
Travels (Ara. 13)   Feda
Travels (Per. 11)   Khusrau
Travels of Lao (Chi. 19)   Liu Tieh Yun
Treasury of Ethics (San.)   Vararuchi
A Treasury of Japan (Jap. 17)   Ihara
Treasury of the Precious Scriptures (Tib. 14)   Putön

The Treasury of St. Cyril (Geo. 8)
Treasury of Tales (San.) (Kathaa Kośa)
Treasury of the Way (San. 7) Uddyotakara
A Treatise on Blessings (Heb.) (Berakhoth)
Treatise on Government (Chi. 13) Ma Tuan Lin
Treatise on John's Gospel (Lat. 4) Augustinus
Treatise on the Laws and Customs of the Kingdom of England (Lat. 12) Glanvill
Treatise on Medicine (Chi. 8) Wang Tao
Treatise on Meter (San.) Pingala
Treatise on Music (Lat. 13) Hieronymus
Treatise on the Plague (Cze. 16) Černý
Treatise on Poetry (Kan. 9) Nṛpatuṅga
Treatise on Poetry (Per. 12) Rashiid Vaṭvaat
Treaty with Mati'el (Syr. −6) Bar Ga'yah
The Tree of Babylon (Per. 3)
The Trees in the Garden (Egy. −14)
Tri Kaaṇḍa Śesa (San.) Puru Ṣottama Deva
(Tri Pitaka: Rules of the Order; Basket of Doctrines; Analytical Exercises)
(Tri Ruupa Kośa: Technical Vocabulary)
(Tri Saṣṭi Śalaakaa Puruṣa Carita: Lives of Sixty-three Jains)
Triangles (Lat. 15) Regiomontanus
The Tribe of Judah (Heb. 16) Ibn Verga
Trimalchio (Lat. 1) Petronius
The Trinity (Lat. 4) Augustinus
The Trinity (Lat.) Hilarius
Trisagion (Syr. 6) Tella
Tristams Kvaedi (Ice. 16)
Tristan and Isolde (Ger. 13) Strassburg
Tristia (Lat. −1) Ovidius
Tristram and Izalde (Cze. 14)
Trivial Arts (Lat. 9) Alcuin
Trojan Chronicle (Gal. 14) (Crónica Troyana)
Trojan Women (Gre. −5) Euripides
The Trojan Story (Lat. 13) Colonne
The True Christian Religion (Lat. 18) Swedenborg
The True History (Lat. 2) Lucianus
Trumpet of the North Country (Nor. 17) Dass
Tru'o'ng the Idiot (Vie. 19)
(Tsalagi Tsulehisanũhi: Cherokee Phoenix)

Ts'e Fu Yüan Kuei (Chi. 11)
(Ts'e Yüan Hai Ching: Circle Measurement Sea Mirror)
(Tseno Ureno: Go Out and See)
(Tso Chuan: Commentary on the Spring and Autumn Annals)
(Tsuredzure: Idle Thoughts)
(T'u Shu Chi Ch'êng: Encyclopedia)
Tu Wo's Sorrow (Chi. 13) Kuan Han K'ing
Tuan Ch'eng Shih (Chi.)
Tuḥfatu 'l Nuẓẓar (Ara. 14) Ibn Baṭṭuuṭa
Tunes (San. −9) (Sama Veda)
(T'ung Ch'ien: The Mirror of History)
(T'ung Chien Kang Mu: History and Philosophy)
(T'ung Chien Kang Mu San Pien: Revised History of the Ming Dynasty)
(T'ung T'ien: Government)
(Tur: Code of the Prepared Table)
(Turin Papyrus: The Kings of Egypt)
The Turkish Galleon (Mlt. 19) Vasallo
Tusculan Disputations (Lat. −1) Cicero
(Tuṭi Naama: Tales of a Parrot)
The Tutor (Gre. 3) Clement
The Twelve Months (Gre. 12) Theodoros
The Twenty-five Stories of the Vampire (San. 15) Śiva Daasa
Twice Flowering Plums (Chi. 17) (Erh Tou Mei)
(The Two-Column Fragment: Manual of Discipline for the Future Congregation of Israel)
Tyll Eulenspiegel (Ger. 16)
(Tzu Chih T'ung Chien: Mirror of History)

Udaya Sundarii Kathaa (San. 11) Soddhala
Ullikummi (Hit. −15) (Kumarbi)
'Umda on the Art of Poetry (Ara. 11) Ibn Rashiiq
(Umm al Qara: Mother of Cities)
(Unam Sanctam: One Holy)
(Unigenitus: Once Born)
The Unique Necklace (Ara. 9) Rabbihi
Universal Chronicle (Ara. 13) Makin
Universal History; Dialogue between Philosophy and History (Gre. 7) Simokatta
Universal Prosody (Gre. 2) Aeolius
The Universe (Gre. −5) Herakleitos
The Universe (Lat. 9) Hrabanus

Unmatta Raghava (San. 10) Bhaaskara
Upadaśa Śataka (San. 16) Gumaani
Upadeśa Maala (Pra. 12) Hema Candra
Upadeśa Pada (Pra. 8) Hari Bhadra
Upamiti Bhava Prapañca Kathaa (San. 10) Siddharsi
(Upaniṣad: Secret Teachings)
(Upomnemata Historika: Historical Memoranda)
Urshu (Hit. −14)
Usages (Cat. 11) (Usatges)
(Usdu 'l Ghaaba: Lions of the Jungle)
The Uskok (Ser. 19) Matavulj
(Utendi wa Tambuka: Epic of Tambuka)
(Utendi wa Al Akida: Ballad of Akida)
Utopia (Lat. 16) More
(Utsubo Monogatari: Fourteen Miraculous Tales)
Uttar Adhyayana Suutra (San.)
Uttara Puraaṇa (San.) Guṇa Bhadra
(Uttara Raama Carita: The Later Life of Rama)
(Uuliger Uun Dalai: Sea of Comparisons)
('Uyuunu 'l Akhbar: Choice Histories)
('Uyuunu 'l Anbaa: History of the Physicians)

The Vaajasaneya Collection (San.) Yaajña Valkya
(Vaajasaneyi Samhitaa: The Vaajasaneya Collection)
(Vaakya Padiiya: The Philosophy of Language)
Vaamana Puraaṇa (San.)
(Vaarttika: Supplementary Grammar)
Vaasava Dattaa (San. 7) Subandhu
Vaasishṭha Dharma Śaastra (San.)
Vassishṭha Siddhaanta (San. −5)
Vacanas (Kan. 14) Basava
Vaiśeṣika Bhaaṣya (San. 5) Prashasta Pada
Vaiśeṣika Philosophy (Chi.) Ui
Vaiśeṣika Suutras (San. −3) Kaṇaada
Vaishnava Doctrine (Ass. 16)
(Vaitaana Suutra: Manual of Public Rites)
Vajjaalagga (San.) Jaya Vallabha
Vakrokti Jiivita (San.) Kuntala
(Vakrokti Pañca Śikaa: Five Pun Tales)
The Valley of Taste (Tib. 19) (Nyang Chö Jung)
The Value of Agriculture (Chi. −2) Ch'ao Ts'o

Vaman Kathai (Tam. 18) Beschi
(Vamśa Avalii: Genealogical History of Nepal)
Varaaha Puraaṇa (San.)
(Variae: Miscellaneous Correspondence)
Various Questions (Lat. 4) Augustinus
Various Uses of the Little Jade Chest Book (Mon. 19) (Eldeb Keregtü Qas Qaghurchay Neretü Bichig Orusibai)
(Vasantasena: The Little Clay Cart)
(Västgötalagen: West Götland Laws)
Vasu Deva Hiṇdii (Pra. 6) Saṁgha Daasa
Veda Artha Samgraha (San. 12) Raama Nuja
Vedaanta Saara (San. 12) Raama Nuja
Vedaanta Saara (San.) Sada Ananda
Vedanta Philosophy (San. 8) Gauda Pada
Vedanta Thought (San. 9) Padma Paada
Vedantism (San. 9) Vaacaspati Mitra
Vendidad (Per. −3)
(Veṇiisamhaara: The Binding of the Braid)
(Vepkhis—T'qaosani: The Knight in the Tiger Skin)
(Verk Hayastani: The Wounds of Armenia)
Verse History of Georgia (Geo. 18) Archili III
Verse Models (Cam. 19) Kraisa Sórivonh
Verses (Fri. 16) Bogerman
Verses (Sin. 15) Qazi Qazan
Verses on Poetics (San. 12) Vaag Bhaṭa
(Vetaala Pañca Vimśa Tikaa: The Twenty-five Stories of the Vampire)
(Vibhasa: Commentary on the Analytical Exercises)
Victories of Prithvii Raaja (San. 12) (Pṛthvii Raaja Vijaya)
Victories of Thut Mose III (Egy. −15)
The Victory at Kadesh (Egy. −13)
The Victory of Merne Ptah (Egy. −13)
The Victory over Damascus (Syr. −8) Zakir
(Videvdat: Antidemonic Law)
Vidhiviveka Nyaaya (San. 9) Mandana Miśra
Vidyaasundar (Ben. 18) Raay
Viennese Sonnets (Slo. 19) Stritar
Viira Caritra (San.) Ananta
Viira Mitro Daya (San. 17) Mitra Miśra

(Viis u Raamin: Wis and Ramin)
Vijay Singh (Pun. 19) Vir Singh
Vijayavilasamu (Tel. 17) Venkatakavi
(Vijnapti Matrata Siddhi: Texts and Commentary of the Yogachara School)
(Vikramaanka Deva Charita: King Vikramaa Ditya)
Vikramodaya (San.)
(Vikramorvaśiiya: Tale of Urvashi Won by Valor)
Vimān Chan (Cam. 19) Muk
(Vinaya: Rules of the Order)
Virgin Pearl of the Palace (Ara. 12) Isfahaanii
The Vision (Heb. −7) Habakkuk (Bible)
The Vision of Adamnán (Iri. 10)
The Vision of Hell (Bur.) (Nemi Zat)
The Vision of Mac Con Glinne (Iri. 12)
The Vision of the Prophet Habakkuk in Kartasa (Eth. 17)
The Vision of Wellin (Lat. 9) Walafrid
The Visions of the Sleeping Bard (Wel. 18) Wynne
(Visitatsbog: Book of Visits)
(Visnu Puraana: The Old Story of Vishnu)
(Visnu Smriti: Code of Vishnu)
(Vispered: All the Judges)
(Visramiani: Wis and Ramin)
(Visudhimagga: The Path of Purity)
(Visva Prakaaśa: Dictionary)
(De Vita Caesarum: Lives of the Twelve Caesars)
(Vita Sancti Anselmi: St. Anselm)
(Vita Sancti Thomae: St. Thomas)
Viveka Mañjari (Pra. 12) Aasada
Viveká Sindhu (Mar. 12) Mukundaraaj
Vocabulary (Chi. −1) (Fang Yen)
Voddaradhana (Kan. 10)
The Volsung Saga (Ice. 13) (Völsunga Saga)
(Van den Vos Reinaerde: Reynard the Fox)
Votive Texts (Gre. −15)
(Voyage au Purgatoire de Saint Patrice: St. Patrick's Journey to Purgatory)
Voyage of Charlemagne (Fre. 10)
Voyage to Byblos (Egy. −11) Un Amon
Voyage to Kelantan (Mal. 19) Munshi 'Abdu'lla
(De Vulgari Eloquentia: The Eloquence of Common Speech)
Vulgate (Lat. 4) Jeronimus

(Vuttodaya: Exposition of Meter)
(Vyaakarana: Grammar)
(Vyaasa Smriti: Code of Vyaasa)

Waafi bi 'l Wafaayat (Ara. 14) Safadii
(Wafayaatu 'l A'yaan: Biographical Dictionary)
Waltherius (Lat. 10) Ekkekard
Wandering of Uilix MacLeirtis (Iri. 13) (Meregud Uilix MeicLeirtis)
Wang Wên Ch'êng Kung Ch'üan Shu (Chi. 15) Wang Yang Ming
The War at the Castle of Müs (Rsh. 16) Travers
The War God (San.) (Skandi Puraana)
The War of Navarre (Pro. 13) Anelier
The War of the Seventeen Kings (Sum. −25) Naram Sin
The War of the Sons of Light and Darkness (Heb. 1)
The Wars (Ara. 9) Waaqidii
The Wars of Heraclius and the Arabs (Syr. 7) Sebeos
The Wars of the House of Zibak (Cak. 16) 4 Imox
The Wars of King 'Aizana (Eth. 4)
The Wars of King Mahasot (Tha.) (Mahasot)
The Wars of the Manchu Dynasty (Chi. 18) Chao I
The Wars of the Six Cities (Hit. −20) Anittas
The Wars of Swat (Pus. 15) Kaju Khan
Wasps (Gre. −5) Aristophanes
The Water Carrier (Bur. 19) Pon Nya
The Wave of Bliss (San. 9) Sankara
The Way of Life (Chi. −3) Lao Tzŭ
The Way of Yohei (Jap. 17)
The Way to Write History (Lat. 2) Lucianus
Waythandaya (Bur. 19) Pon Nya
(Weddase Maryam: Ode to the Virgin)
(Wei Shu: Book of Wei)
(Wên Hsien T'ung K'ao: Treatise on Government)
Wen Hsüan (Chi.) Hsia Ping
The Wessobrunn Prayer (Dut. 9)
West Götland Laws (Swe. 13)
Western Journey (Chi. 7) Hsüan Tsang
Western Journey (Chi. 16) Wu Ch'êng Ên
Western Journey (Chi. 7) Yuan Chwang
The Western Room (Chi.) Yuan Chen

Wet Ya Sun Yin (Tha.)

What Is in the Netherworld (Egy. −16) (Am Duat)

When Above (Bab. −16)   (Enuma Elish)

When Anu the Exalted (Bab. −18) Hammurabi

White Book of Rydderch (Wel. 14)

White Lapis Lazuli (Tib. 17)   Sanggye

The White Monkey (Chi. 7)

The White Serpent (Chi. 16)   (Poh Shi K'i Chuan)

The Whole Duty of a Brahman (San. 13) Devaanda

The Whole Duty of the Monk (Bur.) (Wini)

Wholesome Counsel (San. 17)   Naara-Ayana

Widsith (Eng. 10)

Widuya (Bur.)

The Wiles of Women (San. 13)   Jalhana

William of Orange (Dut. 13)   (Willem van Oringen)

(Wini: The Whole Duty of the Monk)

Wis and Ramin (Per. 11) Jurjani

Wis and Ramin (Geo. 12)   Thruogveli

Wisdom and Lies (Geo. 18)   Orbeliani

The Wisdom of Jesus Ben Sirach (Heb. −2)   (Ecclesiasticus)

The Wisdom of Solomon (Heb. 1)

The Wisdom of Valovar (Geo. 7)   Meskha

The Wise Virgins and the Foolish Virgins (Lat. 12)

With the Occasion of the Printing of a Book (Lat. 17)   Innocentius X

Wizaya Zat (Bur. 19)   Pon Nya

Wo Ra Loongs (Tha.)

(Wŏ Rin Ch'ŏn Gang Chi Gok: Songs of the Moon's Reflection on a Thousand Rivers)

The Wolf of Chungshan (Chi. 12)   Hsieh

A Woman's Travel Diary (Jap. 13) Abutsu

Women of Trachis (Gre. −5)   Sophokles

Women's Wisdom (Cam. 19)   Prah Bàt

The Wooing of Ferb (Iri. 13)   (Tochmarc Ferbe)

Word Variants (San.)   (Dvi Ruupa Kośa)

Work Songs (Egy. −25)

Works (Ara. 16)   Ahmed Baba

Works (Ara. 13)   'Arabii

Works (Geo. 4)   Bakur

Works (Heb. 10)   Seadiah Ben Joseph

Works (Hin. 19)   Bharatendu

Works (Lat. 16) Bonfini

Works (Lat. 8)   Bonifacius

Works (Chi. 18)   Ch'ien Lung

Works (Kor. 9)   Ch'oe

Works (Lat. 1)   Curtius

Works (Rus. 9)   Cyril and Methodius

Works (Rus. 11)   Daniel

Works (Urd. 15)   Daraaz

Works (Mar. 19)   Deshmukh

Works (Gre.)   Dionysios

Works (Lat. 14)   Eckehardt

Works (Ara. 10)   Faaraabi

Works (Hin. 13)   Gorakh Nath

Works (Guj. 19)   Govardhanram

Works (San. 5)   Guna Varman

Works (Chi. −3)   Han

Works (Lat. 14)   Higden

Works (Jap. 13)   Honen

Works (Chi. 4)   Hsü Hsün

Works (Chi. −3)   Hsün

Works (Chi. 2)   Huai

Works (Chi. 5)   Hui

Works (Hin. 18)   Insha Alla Khan

Works (Geo. 5)   Iver

Works (Lat.)   Justin

Works (Hin. 14)   Jyotishwar

Works (Ara. 11)   Kalaabaadhii

Works (Ara. 9)   Kindi

Works (San. 12) Krishna Misra

Works (Kan. 19)   Krishna Raya

Works (Mlm. 18)   Kunchan Nambiar

Works (Chi. −2) K'ung An Kuo

Works (Tel. 19)   Lakshminarisimham

Works (Chi. 18)   Lan Lu Chou

Works (Geo.)   Laz

Works (Chi. 13) Li Kuan Chung

Works (Chi. 8)   Li Po

Works (Chi. −3)   Meng

Works (Rsh. 19)   Muoth

Works (Jap. 17)   Muro

Works (Kor. 15)   Nam

Works (Tam. 10)   Nammalvar

Works (Guj. 19)   Narmad

Works (Kan. 15)   Nijaguna Shivayogi

Works (Ger. 11)   Notker

Works (Pol. 15)   Parkosz

Works (Lat. 1) Paterculus

Works (Chi. 9)   Po Chü I

Works (Tel. 17)   Ramarajabhushana

Works (Geo. 14)   Russudanianu

Works (Hin. 18)   Sadasukh Lal
Works (Ass. 15)   Sankardeva
Works (Chi. 7)   Seng
Works (Ara. 9)   Shafi'i
Works (Mal. 17)   Shams al Din
Works (Tam. 10)   Sri Andal
Works (Tel. 17)   Tenali Ramakrishna
Works (Tam. 5)   Tirumular
Works (Slo. 16)   Trubar
Works (Tel. 19)   Vasuraya Kavi
Works (Bul. 19)   Vazov
Works (Tel. 19)   Viresalingam
Works (San. 9) Visakha Datta
Works (Chi. 16)   Wang Tao K'un
Works (Ara. 10)   Wa'waa
Works (Chi. −5) Yang
Works (Ara.)   Ya'quubii
Works (Ara. 9)   Zaahiri
Works (Ara. 16)   Zayyati
Works and Days (Gre. −8)   Hesiodos
Works of the Three Saints (Tam. 11)
    Nambi
World History (Gre. −3)   Polybios
World History (Per. 14)   Rashiid ad Diin
World History (Arm. 13)   Vartan
The Wounds of Armenia (Arm. 19)
    Abovian
The Wrath of God (Lat. 3)   Lactantius
The Written Characters (Chi. 11)   Wang
    An Shih
(Wu Yüeh Ch'un Ch'iu: Annals of Wu
    and Yüeh)

(X 'Okoot Kay H 'Ppum t Huul: Song
    of the Dance of the Bowman)

Yaadava   Raaghaviiya   (San.)   Ven-
    tadhvarin
(Yad Hahazaqoh: Strong Hand)
(Yajur Veda: Prayers)
(Yama Smriti: Code of Yama)
(Yamato Monogatari: One Hundred Fifty
    Japanese Tales)
Yamuna   Paryatan   (Mar.   19)   Baba
    Pudmanji
Yaśas Tilaka (San. 11)   Soma Deva
Yasna (Per. −3)
Yaśodhara   Carita   (San.   10)   Kanaka
    Sena Vaadi Raaja
Yaśodhara   Carita   (San.   11)   Maanikya
    Suuri
(Yatiimatu 'l Dahr: Solitaire of the Time)

Yawaaqiit (Ara. 16)   Sha'raanii
Yazawingyaw Chronicle (Bur. 16)   Thila-
    wuntha
Years of Pilgrimage and Vagabondage
    (Swe. 19)   Heidenstam
Yeesunaadhar Chritram (Tam. 17)   Nobili
Yeh Sao Pao Yen (Chi. 18)   Hsia Erh
    Ming
(Yeigwa Monogatari: Tale of Yeigwa)
Yen Li Ts'ung Shu—Ts'ung Hsing (Chi.
    17)   Yen Yüan
Yen Tze Ch'un Ch'iu (Chi. −5)   Yen
    Ying
(Yengi Shiki: Anthology of Prayers or
    Speeches)
(Yeshu'oth Meshiho: Apologetics)
(Yesodh   'Olam: Foundations   of   the
    World)
(Yidisher Shtam: Sacrifice of Isaac)
(Yŏ Eui Chŏng Jŭng: Female Physician
    Remedy Book)
(Yoga Bhaasya: Yoga Commentary)
Yoga Commentary (San. 8)   Vyasa
Yoga Śaastra (San. 12)   Hema Candra
(Yoga Suutras: Mnemonic Rules)
(Yom Tov Bletlekh: Holiday Leaves)
Yosef ha Zaddik (Lad. 19)
(Yosifen: History of the Jews)
Ysengrimus (Lat. 12)
Yü Chiao Li (Chi. 15)
(Yü Li Ch'ao Chuan: Ten Courts of
    Purgatory)
(Yüan Ch'ao Pi Shih: Secret History of
    the Mongols)
(Yüan Chien Lei Han: Encyclopedia)
(Yüan Ch'ü Hsüan Tsa Chi: Collected
    Mongol Plays)
Yüan Shan (Chi. 17)   Tai Chên
(Yüan   Shih: History   of   the   Mongol
    Dynasty)
Yuen Pai (Tha. 15)
(Yung Lo Ta Tien: Encyclopedia)
(Yuusuf u Zulaikhaa: Joseph and Zuleika)
(The Yuzgat Tablet: The Missing God)

The Zadokite Document (Heb. 1)
(Zadonschina: Beyond the Don)
Zadsparam (Per. 9)
(Zafar Naama: Book of Victories)
(The Zagreb Mummy Wrapping: Etruscan
    Public Ceremonies)
Zaina Charita (Kas. 15)

Zaina Vilasa (Kas. 15)
(Zaqi Q'axol: Dance of the Conquest)
(Zats: The Five Hundred Births of Buddha)
(Zawta Gômma Pyazat: The Romance of Zawta Gômma)
(Zayn al Akhbaar: History)
Zeenat (Sin. 19)   Mirza Sahib
(Zemah David: History)

Zenaka (Pal.)
(Zevi Mudah: Hunted Stag)
(Zinātu 'l Dahr: Ornament of Time)
Zirhe Zibur (Lad. 18)
(The Zirni Manuscript: Persian-Mongolian Glossary and Grammar)
(Zohar: Brightness)
(Zuyua Than Yetel Naat: The Language of Zuyua)

Bibliography

Bibliography

Abrahams, Roger D., 1962, Playing the Dozens. *Journal of American Folklore,* 75: 209–220.

Adam, Jerôme, 1941, Nouvel extrait du folklore du Haut-Ogooué. *Anthropos,* 35–36: 131–152.

Aesop, n.d., *Fables.* London: Routledge.

Anonymous, n.d., *The Holy Bible.* London: Oxford.

———, 1726, *Zaqiq'oxol or Dance of the Conquest of Mexico.* Unpublished manuscript, Latin American Library, Tulane University, New Orleans.

———, 1948, *Everyman and Other Interludes.* New York: Dutton.

———, 1955, *Popol Wuj.* (Ed. and trans. by D. M. Burgess and Patricio Xec.) Quezaltenango: El Noticiero Evangélico.

———, 1959, *Contemporary Indian Literature.* New Delhi: Sāhitya Academy.

———, 1964, *World Communications.* New York: UNESCO.

———, 1965, *World Almanac.* New York: World Telegram.

———, 1966, *Encyclopedia Britannica World Atlas.* Chicago: Encyclopedia Britannica.

Arguedas, José María, 1949, *Canciones y cuentos del pueblo quechua.* Lima: Editorial Huascarán.

Astrov, Margot, ed., 1946, *The Winged Serpent.* New York: John Day.

Aung, Maung Htin, 1956, *Burmese Drama.* Calcutta: Oxford.

Austerlitz, Robert, 1958, *Ob-Ugric Metrics.* Helsinki: Academia.

Barrera Vásquez, A., 1948, *El Libro de los libros de Chilam Balam.* Mexico City: Fondo de Cultura Económica.

Bastide, Roger, 1967, *Les Amériques noires.* Paris: Payot.

Beckwith, M. W., 1951, *The Kumulipo: A Hawaiian Creation Chant.* Chicago: University of Chicago Press.

Bell, Charles A., 1931, *The Religion of Tibet.* Oxford: Clarendon Press.

Bellows, Henry Adams, 1936, *The Poetic Edda.* Princeton, N.J.: Princeton University Press.

Berndt, R. M., 1953, *Djanggauwul*. New York: Philosophical Library.

Bird, Junius, 1946, The Alacaluf. In Julian Steward, ed., *Handbook of South American Indians*, 1: 54–79, Washington, D.C.: Government Printing Office.

Black, Glenn A., *et al.*, 1954, *Walam Olum or Red Score*. Indianapolis: Indiana Historical Society.

Bouquet, A. C., 1954, *Sacred Books of the World*. Harmondsworth: Penguin.

Brasseur de Bourbourg, Charles Etienne, 1862, *Grammaire de la langue quiche*. Paris: Arhus Bertrand.

Budge, E. A. Wallis, 1956, *The Book of the Dead*. London: Routledge.

Burrows, Edwin Grant, 1945, Songs of Uvea and Futuna. *Bernice P. Bishop Museum Bulletin* (Honolulu), 183.

———, 1963, *Flower in My Ear: Arts and Ethos of Ifaluk Atoll*. Seattle: University of Washington Press.

Caillois, Roger, and Jean-Clarence Lambert, eds., 1958, *Trésor de la poésie universelle*. Paris: Gallimard.

Carvalho Neto, Paulo de, 1956, *Folklore y psicoanalisis*. Buenos Aires: Editorial Psique.

Chao, Yuen Ren, 1956, Tone, Intonation, Singsong, Chanting, Recitative, Tonal Composition and Atonal Composition in Chinese. In Morris Halle *et al.*, eds., *For Roman Jacobson*, The Hague: Mouton, pp. 52–59.

———, 1957, *Mandarin Primer*. Cambridge, Mass.: Harvard University Press.

Child, Francis James, 1857–1859, *English and Scottish Ballads*. 8 vols., Boston: Little Brown.

———, 1882–1898, *The English and Scottish Popular Ballads*. 5 vols. Boston: Houghton Mifflin.

Clarke, Humphrey, 1958, *The Message of Milarepa*. Wisdom of the East Series. London: Murray.

Collocott, E. E. V., 1928, Tales and Poems of Tonga. *Bernice P. Bishop Museum Bulletin* (Honolulu), 46.

Condominas, Georges, 1957, *Nous avons mangé la forêt*. Paris: Mercure de France.

Conklin, Harold C., 1956, Tagalog Speech Disguise. *Language*, 32: 136–139.

Conze, Edward, 1959, *Buddhist Scriptures*. Harmondsworth: Penguin.

Coolidge, Dane, and Mary R., 1930, *The Navajo Indians*. Boston: Houghton Mifflin.

Cox, Marian E. R., 1893, *Cinderella*. London: Folk-Lore Society.

Creel, H. G., 1953, *Chinese Thought from Confucius to Mao Tse-tung*. Chicago: University of Chicago Press.

Czaplicka, M. A., 1914, *Aboriginal Siberia: A Study in Social Anthropology*. Oxford: Oxford.

Daenecke, Eric, 1960, *Tales of Mullah Nasir-ud-Din*. New York: Exposition Press.

Dante Alighieri, 1924, *Purgatorio*. London: Dent.

Densmore, F., 1939, Nootka and Quileute Music. *Bureau of American Ethnology Bulletin* (Washington, D.C.), 124.

Driberg, J. H., 1923, *The Lango: A Nilotic Tribe of Uganda*. London: Fisher & Unwin.

Dundes, Alan, 1965, *The Study of Folklore*. Englewood Cliffs, N. J.: Prentice-Hall.

Eberle, Oskar, 1955, *Cenalora: Leben, Glaube, Tanz und Theater der Urvölker*. Olten und Freiburg im Breisgau: Walter Verlag.

Edgerton, Franklin, 1952, *The Bhagavad Gītā: Part 1: Text and Translation.* Cambridge, Mass.: Harvard University Press.

Edmonson, Munro S., 1970, *The Book of Counsel: The Popol Vuh of the Quiche Maya of Guatemala.* New Orleans: Middle American Research Institute Publications.

Eliade, Mircea, 1956, *Forgerons et alchimistes.* Paris: Flammarion.

Eliot, T. S., 1958, *The Waste Land and Other Poems.* New York: Harcourt.

Erikson, Erik Homburger, 1943, Observations on the Yurok: Childhood and World Image. *University of California Publications in American Archaeology and Ethnology* (Berkeley), 35(10).

Erman, Adolf, 1927, *The Literature of the Ancient Egyptians.* London: Methuen.

Faublée, Jacques, 1947, Récits Bara. *Travaux et Mémoires de l'Institut d'Ethnologie* (Paris), 48.

Fastenberg, R., 1945, *Everybody's Russian Reader.* New York: Language Student Press.

Fischer, John L., 1959, Meter in Eastern Carolinian Oral Literature. *Journal of American Folklore,* 72: 47–52.

Fitts, Dudley, 1956, Eight Poems by Martial. *New World Writing* (New York), 9: 131–133.

Foster, George E., 1885, *Se-quo-yah.* Philadelphia: Indian Rights Association.

Fowler, H. W., 1965, *Dictionary of Modern English Usage.* 2d ed., revised by Sir Ernest Gowers. Oxford: Clarendon Press.

Fremantle, Anne, ed., 1956, *The Papal Encyclicals in Their Historical Context.* New York: Mentor.

Freud, Sigmund, 1938, *Basic Writings.* New York: Random House.

Garibay K., Angel María, 1940, *Llave del náhuatl.* Mexico City: Imprenta Mayli.

———, 1953, *Historia de la literatura náhuatl.* Mexico City: Porrua.

Gibb, E. J. W., 1901, *Ottoman Literature.* Washington: Dunne.

Goins, John F., 1954, *Huayculi: The Quichua of the Cochabamba Valley, Bolivia.* Unpublished doctoral dissertation, University of California, Berkeley.

Graham, David Crockett, 1954, Songs and Stories of the Ch'uan Miao. *Smithsonian Miscellaneous Collections* (Washington, D.C.), 123(1).

Graham-Lujan, James, and Richard L. O'Connell, 1941, *Three Tragedies.* New York: Scribner.

Gummere, Francis B., 1959, *The Popular Ballad.* New York: Dover.

Gurney, O. R., 1952, *The Hittites.* Harmondsworth: Penguin.

Hale, Horatio, 1883, *The Iroquois Book of Rites.* Philadelphia: D. G. Brinton.

Hammond, Peter B., 1964, Mossi Joking. *Ethnology,* 3: 259–267.

Handy, E. S. C., 1930, Marquesan Legends. *Bernice P. Bishop Museum Bulletin* (Honolulu), 69.

Hart, Donn V., 1964, *Riddles in Filipino Folklore: An Anthropological Analysis.* Syracuse, N.Y.: Syracuse University Press.

Hawkes, Jacquetta, and Leonard Woolley, 1963, *Prehistory and the Beginnings of Civilization.* UNESCO "History of Mankind." London: G. Allen.

Hawthorne, Julian, *et al.,* eds., 1903, *The Masterpieces and the History of Literature.* New York: Dumont.

Henderson, Harold G., 1958, *An Introduction to Haiku.* New York: Doubleday.

Herskovits, Melville J., 1938, *Dahomey.* New York: Augustin.

Hinawy, Mbarak Ali, 1950, *Al-Akida and Fort Jesus, Mombasa.* London: Macmillan.

Homer, 1848, *Iliad.* Boston: James Munroe & Co.

Hooykaas, C., 1958, *The Lay of Jaya Prana: The Balinese Uriah.* London: Luzac.

Howard, James H., 1960, Butterfly's Mandan Winter Count: 1833–1876. *Ethnohistory,* 7: 28–43.

Hunningher, Benjamin, 1961, *The Origin of the Theater.* New York: Hill & Wang.

Hyman, S. E., 1962, *The Tangled Bank.* New York: Athenaeum Press.

Hymes, Dell, ed., 1964, *Language in Culture and Society.* New York: Harper & Row.

Hyvernat, Henri, 1909, History of Coptic Literature. *Catholic Encyclopedia,* 5: 356–363.

Jacobson, Roman, and Marc Szeftel, 1949, The Vseslav Epos. In R. Jacobson and E. J. Simmons, eds., Russian Epic Studies. *Memoirs of the American Folklore Society* (Philadelphia), 42: 13–86.

Keene, Donald, 1955, *Japanese Literature: An Introduction for Western Readers.* New York: Grove.

Keith, A. Berriedale, 1956, *A History of Sanskrit Literature.* London: Oxford.

Ker, W. P., 1958, *The Dark Ages.* New York: Mentor.

Kilpatrick, J. F. and A. G., 1965, *Walk in Your Soul: Love Incantations of the Oklahoma Cherokees.* Dallas: Southern Methodist University Press.

Kirby, William F., tr., 1907, *Kalevala.* New York: Dutton.

Kluckhohn, Clyde, 1962, *Culture and Behavior.* New York: Free Press.

Kotewall, Robert, and Norman L. Smith, 1962, *The Penguin Book of Chinese Verse.* Harmondsworth: Penguin.

Kramer, S. N., 1962, Cultural Anthropology and the Cuneiform Documents. *Ethnology,* 1: 299–314.

Kuo Mo Jo, 1953, *Chu Yuan.* Peking: Foreign Language Press.

La Barre, Weston, 1939, The Psychology of Drinking Songs: A Study of the Content of the Normal Unconscious. *Psychiatry,* 2: 203–212.

Lambert, W. G., 1960, *Babylonian Wisdom Literature.* Oxford: Oxford.

Lane, E. W., 1944, *The Manners and Customs of the Modern Egyptians.* New York: Dutton.

Lang, Andrew, Walter Leaf, and Ernest Myers, n.d., *The Complete Works of Homer.* New York: Modern Library.

Lasebikan, E. L., 1956, The Tonal Structure of Yoruba Poetry. *Présence Africaine* (Paris), 8–10: 43–50.

Laski, Vera, 1959, Seeking Life. *Memoirs of the American Folklore Society* (Philadelphia), 50.

Leach, Maria, ed., 1949–1950, *Standard Dictionary of Folklore, Mythology and Legend.* New York: Funk & Wagnalls.

Lentz, Rodolfo, 1895–1897, *Estudios araucanos.* Santiago: Imprenta Cervantes.

Leonard, W. E., 1934, *Gilgamesh, Epic of Old Babylonia.* New York: Viking.

Leslau, Wolf, 1950, Ethiopic Documents: Gurage. *Viking Fund Publications in Anthropology* (New York), 14.

Lestrade, G. P., 1938, Traditional Literature. In I. Schapera, ed., *The Bantu Tribes of South Africa.* London: Routledge, pp. 291–308.

Lévi-Strauss, C., 1964, *Le Cru et le cuit*. Paris: Plon.

Levin, M. G., and L. P. Potpov, eds., 1964, *The Peoples of Siberia*. Chicago: University of Chicago Press.

Levine, Donald N., 1965, *Wax and Gold: Tradition and Innovation in Ethiopian Culture*. Chicago: University of Chicago Press.

Lowes, J. L., 1927, *The Road to Xanadu*. Boston: Houghton Mifflin.

Lowie, Robert H., 1945, The Crow Language. *University of California Publications in American Archaeology and Ethnology* (Berkeley), 39 (1).

Mace, Carroll, 1954, *Charamiyex or the Flute Dance of Rabinal*. Unpublished manuscript, Latin American Library, Tulane University, New Orleans.

Maingard, L. F., 1962, *Korana Folktales*. Johannesburg: Witwatersrand University Press.

Marcus, Steven, 1966, *The Other Victorians*. New York: Basic Books.

Marshall, Lorna, 1962, !Kung Bushman Religious Beliefs. *Africa*, 32: 221–252.

Martí, Samuel, 1961, *Canto, danza y música precortesianos*. Mexico City: Fondo de Cultura Económica.

Métraux, Alfred, 1946, Myths of the Toba and Pilagá Indians of the Gran Chaco. *American Folklore Society Memoirs*, 40.

Meyerowitz, Eva L. R., 1951, *The Sacred State of the Akan*. London: Faber.

———, 1958, *The Akan of Ghana: Their Ancient Beliefs*. London: Faber.

Monmouth, Geoffrey of, 1958, *History of the Kings of Britain*. New York: Dutton.

Nash, Ogden, 1944, *The Ogden Nash Pocket Book*. New York: Pocket Books.

Neihardt, John G., 1961, *Black Elk Speaks*. Lincoln, Neb.: University of Nebraska Press.

Nettl, Bruno, 1956, *Music in Primitive Culture*. Cambridge, Mass.: Harvard University Press.

Nicholson, Reynold A., 1956, *A Literary History of the Arabs*. Cambridge: Cambridge University Press.

Nygard, Holger Olaf, 1958, *The Ballad of Heer Halewijn*. Knoxville, Tenn.: University of Tennessee Press.

Olmsted, A. T., 1948, *History of the Persian Empire*. Chicago: University of Chicago Press.

Opie, Iona and Peter, 1959, *The Lore and Language of Schoolchildren*. Oxford: Oxford.

Perry, Janet H., n.d., *The Heath Anthology of Spanish Poetry*. Boston: Heath.

Poppe, Nikolaus, 1955, *Mongolische Volksdichtung*. Wiesbaden: Franz Steiner Verlag.

Propp, Vladimir, 1958, Morphology of the Folktale. *Indiana University Research Center in Anthropology, Folklore, and Linguistics, Publication 10*. Bloomington.

Pushkin, A. S., 1924, Zimnyaya Doroga. In M. Baring, ed., *The Oxford Book of Russian Verse*. Oxford: Clarendon Press.

Quain, Buell H., 1942, *The Flight of the Chiefs*. New York: Augustin.

Rasmussen, K., 1929, *The Intellectual Culture of the Iglulik Eskimos*. Report of the Fifth Thule Expedition, 1921–1924, Vol. 7, Part 2. Copenhagen:

Rassers, Willem Hulbert, 1959, *Panji, The Culture Hero*. The Hague: Nijhoff.

Ristaino, Richard E., 1964, Two *Sijo* Translated from the Korean. *East-West Center Review* (Honolulu), 1: 36.

Russell, Frank, 1908, The Pima Indians. *Bureau of American Ethnology Annual Report* (Washington, D.C.), 26.

Ryder, Arthur W., tr., 1949, *The Panchatantra*. Bombay and Calcutta: Jaico.

Ryder, Frank G., 1962, *The Song of the Nibelungs*. Detroit: Wayne State University Press.

Sahagún, Bernardino de, 1956, *Historia general de las cosas de Nueva España*. Mexico City: Porrua.

Sandars, K. N., 1962, *The Epic of Gilgamesh*. Harmondsworth: Penguin.

Schebesta, P., 1957, *Die Negrito Asiens*. Vienna-Mödling: St. Gabriel Verlag.

Scott, Charles T., 1963, New Evidence of American Indian Riddles. *Journal of American Folklore*, 76: 236–244.

Sebeok, Thomas A., ed., 1960, *Style in Language*. New York: M.I.T. Press and Wiley.

Sein, Maung Than, and Alan Dundes, 1964, Twenty-three Riddles from Central Burma. *Journal of American Folklore*, 77: 69–75.

Shannon, Claude E., 1949, *The Mathematical Theory of Communications*. Urbana, Ill.: University of Illinois Press.

Shimkin, Dmitri, 1947, Wind River Shoshone Literary Forms. *Journal of the Washington Academy of Sciences*, 37: 329–352.

Shipley, Joseph T., 1946, *Encyclopedia of Literature*. New York: Philosophical Library.

Shway Yoe, 1963, *The Burman: His Life and Notions*. New York: Norton.

Simenov, Konstantin, 1945, Zhdi Menya. In R. Fastenberg, ed., *Everybody's Russian Reader*. New York: Language Student Press, pp. 124.

Skeat, Walter William, 1967, *Malay Magic*. New York: Dover.

Skendi, Stavro, 1954, Albanian and South Slavic Oral Epic Poetry. *Memoirs of the American Folklore Society* (Philadelphia), 44.

Skinner, Alanson B., 1920, Medicine Ceremony of the Menominee, Iowa and Wahpeton. *Indian Notes and Monographs* (New York), 4.

Snow, C. P., 1960, *The Two Cultures and the Scientific Revolution*. Cambridge, Mass.: Cambridge University Press.

Soury-Lavergne and De la Devèze, S. J., 1913, La Fête nationale du fandroana en Imerina (Madagascar). *Anthropos*, 8: 306–324.

Strehlow, T. G. H., 1947, *Aranda Traditions*. Melbourne: Melbourne University Press.

Ström, Hilmer, 1939, Old English Personal Names in Bede's History. *Lund Studies in English*, 8, Lund, Sweden: University of Lund.

Taggart, Barbara Ann, 1957, *Flores de Anáhuac: Literatura Náhuatl prehispánica*. Mexico City: the author.

Tauxier, L., 1932, *Religion, moeurs et coûtumes des agnis de la Côte-d'Ivoire*. Paris: Librairie Orientaliste Paul Geuthner.

Temple, G., 1955, Style and Subject in the Literature of Mathematics. In *Literature and Science*. Proceedings of the Sixth Triennial Congress of the International Federation for Modern Languages and Literatures, 1954. Oxford: Blackwell, pp. 11–16.

Thompson, Stith, 1929, *Tales of the North American Indians*. Cambridge, Mass.: Harvard University Press.

————, 1946, *The Folktale.* New York: Dryden Press.

————, 1955, *Motif-Index of Folk-Literature.* 6 vols., Bloomington, Ind.: Indiana University Press.

Thompson, Eben F., 1907, *Fitzgerald's Omar Khayyām with Persian Text.* Worcester: Commonwealth.

Townsend, G. F., n.d., *Aesop's fables.* London: Routledge.

Trilles, R. P., 1931, *Les Pygmées de la forêt equatoriale.* Paris: Bloud & Gay.

Underhill, Ruth, 1936, The Autobiography of a Papago Woman. *Memoirs of the American Anthropological Association* (Menasha), 46.

Valency, Maurice, 1958, Introduction to Jean Giraudoux *Four Plays.* New York: Hill & Wang.

Vernadsky, George, and Dzambulat Dzanty, 1956, The Ossetian Tale of Iry Dada. *Journal of American Folklore,* 69: 216–235.

Villacorta Calderón, José Antonio, 1934, *Memorial de Tecpán Atitlán.* Guatemala City: Tipografía Nacional.

Virgil, 1862, *Opera.* New York: Sheldon & Co.

Waley, Arthur, n.d., *The Nō Plays of Japan.* New York: Grove.

Ware, James R., tr., 1963, *The Sayings of Chuang Chou.* New York: Mentor.

Warner, W. Lloyd, 1958, *A Black Civilization.* New York: Harper & Row.

Wassén, Henry, 1949, Contributions to Cuna Ethnography. *Etnologiska Studier,* 16: 3–139.

Wilbert, Johannes, 1964, *Warao Oral Literature.* Caracas: Editorial Sucre.

Williams, Ifor, 1944, *Lectures on Early Welsh Poetry.* Dublin: Dublin Institute for Advanced Studies.

Winner, Thomas G., 1958, *The Oral Art and Literature of the Kazakhs of Russian Central Asia.* Durham, N.C.: Duke University Press.

Winstedt, Richard, 1950, *The Malays: A Cultural History.* London: Routledge.

Wun, Min Thu, 1947, *Thabyenyo and Other Poems.* Rangoon.

Zall, P. M., ed., 1963, *A Hundred Merry Tales.* Lincoln, Neb.: University of Nebraska Press.

Index

Index

Index

Poetic passages quoted in the text are indexed by first lines; all materials quoted are indexed by title and author where possible. Such materials are also listed by language and language family and cross-referenced by genre. For cross-indexing of the authors and works of written literature, the reader is referred to the "Authors" and "Works" sections of the Appendix, and to Chapter 8.

Parallelism, 83–84, 96–98, 104–105, 119–120
Paressí, 152
Parody, 133, 187–189
Parrot and Duck, 139
Patronymic, 69, 75
Paul Bunyan, 61, 150, 231
Pedro de Urdemales, 150
Peek-a-boo, 203
Penelope, 61
Penutian (*see* Maidu, Yurok)
Percy, Thomas, 32
Periphrasis, 94
Perrault, Charles, 32
Persian, 5, 8, 70, 122–123, 151–152, 162, 247 *ff*, 301, 304, 306–307, 311, 320, 330
Personification, 54–56, 74, 84, 92, 169
Pert em Hru, 31, 148, 174
Philology, 35–36
Phoenician (*see* Syrian)
Pig Latin (*see* Secret language)
Pillar of Heaven, 171–172
Pima, 72, 210–211
Piropo, 168
Play,
  modern, 325–328
  morality (*see* Morality play)
  mystery, 10–11, 183–184, 280
  shadow, 180
  word (*see* Word play)
  See also Drama, *Noo*, *Kabuki*, Puppetry, Tableau
The Plover Who Fought the Ocean, 143–144
Pochteca, 231
Poem (*see* *Arofo*, *Coplas*, *Corrido*, Epic, *Kiráari*, Limerick, *Pantun*, *Piropo*, Praise, Sonnet, *Yunca*)
Poet, 133–134

Poetic license (*see* License, poetic)
Poetry, 90, 133–134
  secular, 320
Polish, 19, 164, 208, 274 *ff*, 310–311, 330
Political meter, 320
Political Testament, 82
Polynesian, 141–142, 159, 230–231
Polynomial, 76, 98, 114
Ponapean, 111–112
Popol Vuh, 98, 286
Pornography, 214–220
Portuguese, 19, 130, 151, 274 *ff*, 309, 326, 330
Possession, 171–172, 174–175
Praise poem, 108–109, 222, 239
Praise song, 107–108
Prakrit, 152–153, 249 *ff*, 301, 303, 307–308, 323
Prayer, 91
Precept, 77
Priamel, 79
Pronoun, 55, 64–65
Prophecy, 147–150
Propp, Vladimir Iakovlevich, 47, 144–145
Provençal, 268 *ff*, 309, 331
Proverb, 32, 77, 139–140, 207, 233, 249
Proverbial phrase, 78
Psalm, 250
Psychology, 39–42
Pueblo Indian, 175–178, 194, 225
Pun, 80, 88–90, 148, 167–168, 198
Punch and Judy, 180
Punjabi, 69, 122, 151, 288 *ff*, 304, 306, 330
Puppetry, 180, 190
Pushkin, Aleksandr Sergeevich, 131–132
Pushtu, 72, 285 *ff*, 304, 306, 330
Pygmalion, 61